D0891615

The Problems of Success

A HISTORY OF THE
CHURCH MISSIONARY SOCIETY
1910-1942

GORDON HEWITT

The Problems of Success

A HISTORY OF THE
CHURCH MISSIONARY SOCIETY
1910–1942

Volume One
In Tropical Africa · The Middle East
At Home

Published for the Church Missionary Society by
SCM PRESS LTD

334 00252 4

First published 1971
by SCM Press Ltd
56 Bloomsbury Street London WC1

© SCM Press Ltd 1971

Printed in Great Britain by
Western Printing Services Ltd Bristol

TO MY WIFE

CONTENTS

ACKNOWLEDGMENTS

The author owes thanks to many people who have helped generously in the preparation of this book, particularly to the Executive Committee of the Church Missionary Society which entrusted him with its preparation; to successive general secretaries of the CMS, Canon M. A. C. Warren and Canon J. V. Taylor, their fellow secretaries and personal assistants; to the Society's archivist, Miss Rosemary Keen; librarian, Miss Jean Woods; and publicity officer, Bernard Nicholls; to three historians who served on an *ad hoc* advisory committee, H. B. Thomas, OBE, Canon G. C. B. Davies and Canon Michael Hennell. To Miss Ella Jennings who typed all the earlier drafts, and to Miss D. White who made skilful summaries of many of the CMS Précis Books which were a main source of material; to many serving missionaries of the CMS who helped to make brief visits to East Africa (1965), the Middle East (1968) and Sierra Leone (1969) as pleasant as they were fruitful, especially Dr Louise Pirouet (Uganda), Jesse Hillman (Kenya), Canon Arthur Howden (Iran), Miss Ida Barlow (Egypt) and the Rev. Eric Clark (Sierra Leone).

Special thanks must be recorded to the Leverhulme Research Awards Committee for a generous grant which made possible the visit to West Africa in 1969.

April, 1970   GORDON HEWITT

KEY TO ABBREVIATIONS

AIM	Africa Inland Mission
AOH	All Other Heads (i.e. miscellaneous expenses of a CMS overseas mission)
AR(MS)	Bound typescript annual reports based on the annual letters of CMS missionaries
BCMS	Bible Churchmen's Missionary Society
BELRA	British Empire Leprosy Relief Association
BERLIN I, III	(see pp. 179, 196)
BFBS	British and Foreign Bible Society
CEZMS	Church of England Zenana Missionary Society
CMJ	Church Missions to Jews
CMO	*Church Missionary Outlook*
CMR	*Church Missionary Review*
CMTA	Church Missionary Trust Association
CSM	Church of Scotland Mission
CUMP	Cambridge University Missionary Party
EVS(S)	Elementary Vernacular School(s)
FES	Female Education Society
GMS	Gospel Missionary Society
Groups I, II, III	(see p. 439)
IMC	International Missionary Council
LGB	Local Governing Body (i.e. of a CMS mission)
LJS	London Jews' Society
MMA	Medical Mission Auxiliary
MSL	Missionary Service League
NAC	Native Anglican Church
PC	Parent Committee (i.e. Group Committee for mission area)
PNCC	Palestine Native Church Council
RTS	Religious Tract Society
SAWMMS	South African Wesleyan Methodist Missionary Society
SCM	Student Christian Movement
SIM	Sudan Interior Mission
SPCK	Society for Promoting Christian Knowledge
SPG	Society for the Propagation of the Gospel
SUM	Sudan United Mission
UMCA	Universities, Mission to Central Africa
UNA	United Native African Church
WAE	West African Episcopal Church
WMMS	Wesleyan Methodist Missionary Society

General Introduction

A history of the Church Missionary Society was planned on comprehensive lines in 1891 in preparation for the Society's centenary in 1899. The Rev. Charles Hole, Lecturer on Ecclesiastical History at King's College, London, was invited to write a 'library history' in four or five substantial volumes. Unfortunately 'the thoroughness with which he executed the earlier part of his work became an insuperable obstacle to the accomplishment of this scheme'.[1] Mr Hole in fact completed one volume only, taking the story to 1814. It was published separately as *The Early History of the Church Missionary Society*. When the manuscript of this volume was ready for the press, the time available before the centenary was almost half gone; and in view of Hole's other commitments it was decided to continue the plan of several volumes, but on a smaller scale and in other hands. The CMS committee invited Dr W. P. Mears, formerly of the Society's South China mission, to undertake it. He started on it, but ill-health compelled him to abandon it. The committee now wisely turned to Mr Eugene Stock, the Society's Editorial Secretary since 1875. He was asked to take over the project, and was relieved of his ordinary editorial duties in order to give time to it. The centenary was now so close that he could not attempt to write anything on the vast scale that Hole's one volume suggested. He decided to start again from scratch and wrote his first three volumes in two years. They were published in 1899, by the Society, under the title *The History of the Church Missionary Society, Its Environment, Its Men and Its Work*. He told an editorial colleague later that in all the vast manuscript, making up close on two thousand pages in print, he only wrote out a single page a second time. The rest went to the printer as it stood.[2]

Stock wrote a fourth supplementary volume covering the years from 1899 up to the time when he was writing it. It was published in 1916 in a format uniform with the earlier three volumes but with a shorter title. By that time Stock was eighty years old, and his pen, not unnaturally, a little tired. There is no lapse from his high standards of accuracy and the basis of the supplementary volume is one of those 'fifteen year periods' which he handled in such masterly fashion in earlier volumes; but his preface shows that he was not entirely satisfied with it, and the fact that he was writing up to and into the year of publication gives the chapters on the different missions the air of interim reports. Here, if at all, is the justification for the decision, which might otherwise be seen as an impertinence, to plan further volumes of the Society's history from 1910 rather than from Dr Stock's final date in 1916. His great achievement as a historian of Christian missions stands on his first three volumes, particularly on the third volume with eight hundred pages of text, and covering a period (1872–99) throughout which he was no mere observer but himself an actor of consequence in the history he records (e.g. of Uganda). Of Stock's history as a whole Archbishop Randall Davidson wrote: 'In the field it covers I can think of few, if any, books which equal it as a quarry not merely of facts and figures, but of wise and fruitful thought.'[3] A more recent historian of missions, Professor Roland Oliver, paid this tribute:

> His viewpoint was essentially metropolitan; but within this limitation the few chapters in which he traced the growth of the East African Missions of the CMS leave little to be desired, while his general chapters on the development of the Society's policy with regard to the 'edification' of indigenous churches are of the first importance to any student of missionary history.[4]

Stock entered the CMS editorial department in 1873 and he ceased to be Editorial Secretary in 1902, continuing as secretary without portfolio until 1906, when he retired; but until the mid-1920s his contact with the day-to-day affairs of the Society remained close. He died in September 1928 at the age of ninety-two.

The 'scope and design' of Stock's History of CMS is expressed in the carefully chosen words of the second half of its title *Its Environment, Its Men and Its Work*.

> I have deliberately set myself [he wrote] to try and describe the Society's *environment* at home and abroad; and a very large part of the book is devoted to that attempt. . . . the history of the Society is quite a different thing from the history of the Society's Missions. Accepting this fact as a guiding principle, I have devoted probably one third of the whole work to the affairs of the Church and Society at home.[5]

These statements in the Author's Preface are tantalizing. Why is it 'natural', for instance, that collateral matter, as Stock calls it, should be so extensive, and should be 'most conspicuous' in the chapters on India? Was this broad canvas the instinctive choice of a man of large humanity, a student of affairs, for whom the three-decker biography of the Victorian age was favourite reading? Or was it controlled by a philosophy of history which saw all history as under God's hand and therefore nothing that happens among men is merely collateral or environmental? It looks as though Stock had come to accept, by the end of his great task, the kind of 'adventist' or eschatalogical view of history which was so prominent in the missionary apologetics of Dr John R. Mott.

No one will dare to say that the present is *not* 'the hour of setting sun'. Our clear duty, then, and our only course of safety, is to assume that it is so, and 'the work that centuries might have done' it is for us to 'crowd' into that hour.[6]

It was his conviction that the advent of Christ, the supreme event of history, depends 'in part at least' on the church's obedience to her Lord's command to proclaim the gospel to all mankind. The story he had told of the work done in obedience to that commission, and of its triumphant achievements in every continent, clearly fortified his conviction that the end of the present dispensation was at hand. But it is interesting to note that his instinct as a historian was not to accept this end as final.

If this is indeed the hour of setting sun, that sunset will not be the end of all things. There are ages and ages to follow, and it may well be that when the sun has risen upon a new dispensation, some individual now amongst us unnoticed, some casual incident of our day now thought of no consequence, may then be recognized as among the chiefest men and the most conspicuous events of the twentieth century.[7]

Here Eugene Stock declares his interest, so to speak, as a historian of mission. He is content to leave the paradoxes of Scripture side by side: 'We need not try to find a formula that will reconcile them.'[8] The proof for him of God's hand upon human affairs is the way in which the weak go forth as the mighty; the growth of great movements from inconspicuous beginnings; the providential timing by which the right man is in the right place at the right moment; and the way in which setbacks and disappointments, accepted in faith, lead to a new and more fruitful obedience, until the end comes. It was his delight to trace such things in the history of one missionary society, and to do this in a century during which Britain's commitment overseas in commerce and over-rule was always growing, and for the most part growing alongside and in close relation to the missionary expansion. He needed a large frame in order to trace God's purpose through 'the unnoticed individual, the casual incident' as well as through the great movements and the conspicuous leaders and policy-makers.

Any successor of Stock, who tries to apply his method of presentation to a later period, will find himself in considerable difficulty. In the first world war (in fact before it, in the Russo-Japanese War of 1905–6) the framework of a comparatively settled, European-dominated world order began to disintegrate. The 'deglorification of the West' and the upsurge of Asian self-consciousness was veiled for most of the inter-war period by the emergence of the United States of America as a major world-power; and Tropical Africa remained apparently acquiescent under new colonial policies governed by the doctrine of trusteeship; but European self-confidence was badly shaken.

This loss of confidence had a profound and progressive effect on Christian missions in Asia and Africa.

Imperialism in general and missions in particular fell sharply in the esteem of a public opinion which no longer felt that western civilization had incalculable benefits to confer upon inferior races. . . . This unpopularity was inevitably reflected in the financial support of missions in the sending countries and in the recruitment of workers.[9]

In the missions themselves, as in their environment, the process of change was to some extent veiled in the inter-war period. Although the rapid expansion in the number of missionaries in the 1890s was not maintained, the number of Protestant missionaries at work all over the world increased by 43 per cent between 1911 and 1925 and only slightly declined between 1925 and 1938.[10] But the maintenance of the number of serving missionaries, despite the declining budgets of the home boards of the missions, was due largely to two new developments: government grants for mission-sponsored education in the colonial territories of tropical Africa, and the greatly increased participation of North America in missionary work especially in China. This can be illustrated by a comparison of the figures for CMS missionaries for the years 1910 and 1942. In 1910 there were 1,360 CMS missionaries, 253 in Africa; 479 in India and Ceylon; 302 in China. In 1942 there were 1,088 missionaries, 450 in Africa; 259 in India and Ceylon, and 158 in China. It will be noticed that Africa and India virtually exchanged their numerical role, Africa gaining almost 200 missionaries, and India and Ceylon losing 220. In China the number of CMS missionaries is about halved in these thirty-three years. In the statistical survey in the CMS *Annual Report* for 1942 a significant footnote is added against the total number of missionaries: 'Of this total a considerable number of missionaries are wholly or partly supported otherwise than by the Parent Committee, e.g. by local funds, government grant, or as honorary missionaries, etc.' (1942 was of course a 'war' year, but the general swing from Asia to Africa was almost as obvious in the 1939 statistical survey, and the qualifying footnote had been used in all annual reports since 1933.)

There is one further weighty reason for questioning the validity of Stock's plan of writing as applied to the period after 1910. Since his time, and especially since the second world war, the history of Christian missions has engaged the interest of professional historians. The local records and the archives of missionary headquarters are being examined and re-assessed from a standpoint outside the missionary bodies themselves. This is a healthy and welcome development; but it was not even in sight when Stock laid down his pen. There is thus a task in missionary apologetics laid upon his successors which did not concern him, writing when he did. Had it done so, he would have enjoyed it; and he would have carried it through superbly. This new historiography at least raises the question whether the type of mission history which is primarily 'a record of achievement' of the missionaries and of the home boards of missions is viable any longer. To take one example: the doubling of the CMS missionary strength in the decade 1890–1900 (1889–90: 630; 1899–1900: 1238) was for Stock a glorious achievement in missionary obedience. For the contemporary historian whose concern is primarily with the development of African churches as a social phenomenon, this flood of missionaries was nothing short of a disaster. (See, for example, J. B. Webster, *The African Churches among the Yoruba, 1888–1922*, Oxford, 1964). It may be that the apologetic task can best be carried through in specialized studies such as Dr M. A. C. Warren's two books *The Missionary Movement from Britain in Modern History*, and *Social History and Christian Mission* (SCM Press, 1965 and 1967) and Dr J. V. Taylor's *The Growth of the Church in Buganda* (SCM Press, 1958). Even so, the chronicler of missions cannot be indifferent to this task. He has to concern himself with the question of missionary motivation which is now seen to be immensely more complicated than appeared to be the case to anyone of Stock's generation; and at the least it requires a more cautious approach in recording achievements.

For these three reasons – the change in the environment, the falling away in missionary response, and the equivocal nature of that response – some modification of Dr Stock's plan of writing appears to be required in any further volumes of CMS History. What is attempted here might perhaps best be described as a *constitutional history* of the Church Missionary Society from 1910 to 1942. It was a period of rapid social change in Tropical Africa and in the Middle East, and consequently of change in the character of the missionary opportunity in those regions. Seven areas of special concern for the historian may be identified as follows.

1. How did a society, traditionally equipped for pioneer missionary enterprise and perennially concerned with the proclamation of the gospel in 'the regions beyond' the settled church, adapt its thinking and tactics to a changed situation?

2. How did the large missionary institutions, the major schools and hospitals, with their voracious appetite for missionary recruits with specialized qualifications, adapt themselves to a period of recession when the total supply of recruits was becoming static or diminishing?

3. How did these major missionary institutions relate themselves to the growingly self-conscious indigenous churches and to the still powerful local governing bodies of the CMS?

4. How did the transition from mission to church, commonly expressed in a policy of 'diocesanization', affect the role of the individual missionary – in his relationship to the parent committee in London and to the local governing body of the mission (normally the executive committee or the standing committee of the missionaries' annual conference)?

5. How was the missionary opportunity affected by, on the one hand, the increasing involvement of the territorial governments in education and medicine, and, on the other hand, by the fluctuating financial commitment of the home support of the Society whether in Britain or in the Dominions? (The greatly

increased commitment of Australia and New Zealand, within the fellowship of the CMS, was a notable feature of this period.)

6. How did the Society, as an evangelical association within the Church of England and the Anglican Communion, come to terms with the variety in evangelical insights represented among its missionaries and home supporters during a period in which these insights were more sharply diversified by biblical and liturgical controversy within the wider church?

7. How was episcopal government, still normally exercised by 'European' bishops, related to the dual structure of the mission and the indigenous church with its own small, but steadily growing, group of clergy?

The dominance of themes such as these in the period 1910–42 suggested the possibility of a radical change in the presentation of the Society's history – by 'subject-studies' rather than by a chronicle of the constituent missions. The decision, however, went against such a radical change, and in favour of a presentation sufficiently close to Stock's to allow the reader to take up the story of a mission – in Iran, or Sierra Leone, or Uganda – near to the point where Stock left it, and to carry it forward to the middle of the second world war.

Some of the risks involved in this decision were recognized and accepted. For example, it has proved almost impossible to avoid some repetition or quasi-repetition in moving from one mission to another in the same period. The reaction to 'a round-robin' from the parent committee to all local missions of the CMS asking each to comment on the likely effect of complete withdrawal from their territory is predictably, even monotonously, the same – 'Impossible!' But the response to a similar circular asking for reactions to a five per cent cut in personal allowances, or twenty per cent in the general budget of the mission, may demonstrate considerable variety. It may even be taken cautiously as a barometer of the general health of that mission. The responses shown by local governing bodies to the initiatives, or restrictions, communicated from the parent committee as it mediates the wishes of the home constituency, are one resource for building up the portrait of a local mission during this period.

A more serious risk is that the decision to concentrate on the network of relationships with one missionary society may be taken to imply an indifference to, or an under-valuing of, the achievements of other missionary bodies working in the same region. Within the limits of space available, everything possible has been done to avoid any such impression or hint of superiority. In several areas with which this volume is concerned the CMS mission was a quite minor Anglican contribution alongside much larger and more effective contributions of Lutheran, Presbyterian, interdenominational or Roman Catholic missions. The concentration upon CMS implies nothing more than a conviction that it is still possible and worthwhile to trace the progress of one member of a large family of missionary societies, and to do so at a time when all such bodies were under similar pressures.

A similar point needs to be made in relation to the growth of indigenous churches. A concentration upon 'the mission' rather than 'the church' in no way implies that what the missionaries were busily doing between 1910 and 1942 was *more important* for the reign of Christ than the things the local clergy or catechists or congregations were doing in the same period. In some cases it will be suggested that some of the things the missionaries were doing ought not to have been done by them at all at that time and in that place. But it is still possible, and perhaps important, to write of these things from within the missionary fellowship when so many are writing about them from outside it. It would be inept to write of the local missions of CMS in the 1960s as though they were entities separable from the local church: but in the 1920s and 1930s they can be studied in this way. The separateness of the mission from the church – whether it was viewed as still desirable, or as a regrettable necessity for a little longer, or as something shameful to be faced and dealt with – remained a feature of the Christian presence in Africa and the Middle East during the two world wars and the inter-war period. There was, of course, a movement away from such separateness towards integration; and the difficulties encountered in this process, and the different ways in which these difficulties were faced and overcome, is part of the story that follows here. It can, and ought to be, told from the standpoint of the indigenous church as well. But that is a separable task and is not attempted here.

One further question must be asked. Did the range of new problems and opportunities which CMS was facing in the period from 1910 to 1942 lead to any discernible shift in the theology of mission? A short confident answer to such a question is almost certain to be a wrong answer. The kind of 'adventism' which Stock's generation learned from John R. Mott was a powerful missionary dynamic, and it continued to be such for many missionaries of a later generation. 'Act as though it is the last hour' will always remain a missionary incentive for a bible-reading Christian who prays for the fullness of Christ's reign. But it was only one source of output for missionary energy. Commitment to Christ, obedience to the promptings of the Spirit, rarely depended on a predictable end of this dispensation, even among those who looked in longing for the signs that the end was near. After the second world war Christian missionary work proved an attractive field for the professional theologian as well as for the professional historian: but the theology of mission was not apparently a subject of great interest in the period under review. The indexes of the eighteen annual volumes of *The Church Missionary Review* from 1910 to 1927 (when it ceased publication) are noticeably thin on this subject. The kind of formulation put forward in Dr Harry R. Boer's interesting study, *Pentecost and Missions* (Lutterworth Press, 1961) appears alien to the way missionaries reflected upon their call to service overseas in this period. The 'great commission' of Matt. 28.19f. was certainly one ingredient of the working theology of most missionaries; but the experience and expectation of a fresh outpouring of the Holy Spirit was appealed to with at least equal force and frequency. They read their bibles, and said their prayers, and found a strong support in the fellowship of like-minded Christians. An integrated theology of mission was not felt to be a necessary part of the equipment of most missionaries. Having themselves turned to Christ and offered him their obedience, they could think of no better way of spending their lives than 'feeding' Christ to others: and those who supported them with their gifts and their prayers felt the same way about it.

If this impressionistic picture is at all true it means that for the great majority of missionaries there was little discernible shift or change in the theology of mission in this period. On the other hand, among the new generation of missionaries there were not a few who were beginning to discover new elements in their working theology in which 'wholeness in this world' was tending to replace the adventist hope. These men and women were no less concerned than their predecessors to introduce men and women, boys and girls, to Christ whom they saw as 'the Lord of all life'. They believed that they were building for a long future, and felt no disloyalty in planning for generations yet unborn. Among them were some, mostly teachers in the larger missionary schools, who found their bible-study stimulated by contemporary works of 'higher criticism' such as S. R. Driver's commentary on Genesis. Some of their fellow-missionaries looked askance at them. They felt they were drinking from poisoned wells and that loss of faith and of missionary zeal was bound to follow. Thus a lack of trust developed among missionaries overseas and among evangelical clergy in home supporting parishes. It led to the 'crisis' in 1922, which caused pain and bewilderment to a great many people, and also led to the formation of the Bible Churchmen's Missionary Society. The crisis was slow in developing and had a long aftermath.[11] The more one reflects upon this crisis, the more it seems that what was at stake was not the inspiration of the Bible or standards of liturgy and churchmanship (though the argument centred upon these issues) but the theology of mission, and particularly the Christology from which it derived. For some the utter trustworthiness of Christ's utterances were the bedrock on which everything else was built – the certainty of their call, the promise of spiritual power to fulfil it, their technique of evangelism. For others Christ's lordship of the world, which was central in their missionary calling, did not depend on the authenticity of all his recorded sayings. A good deal of the pain might have been eased, and mutual trust more quickly restored, if the underlying issue had been brought to the surface: namely the complex character of the missionary dynamic. The issue still remains veiled, but there are welcome signs of a new openness: and the trust engendered by fellowship in the missionary calling has shown itself strong enough to unite a considerable diversity of conviction.

A Note About Sources

1. *Main Sources* A glance at the footnote references at the end of each chapter will quickly reveal the main manuscript source used for the period 1910–34, though the general reader may well need some explanation of it. After several years spent floundering among the mass of material available in the CMS archives and library it became clear that the best foundation for a volume of general history was the series of *Précis Books* compiled for each CMS mission (indicated by the normally shortened reference beginning with 'P'). These volumes give full summaries of all incoming letters from the mission to the parent committee; summaries of the minutes of the missionaries' conference and of its executive or standing committees; and the text, in full or summarized, of local memoranda – all this on left-hand pages; and they show on right-hand pages, numbered in Roman rather than Arabic, the action taken by the group committee in London. For the larger missions two or more Précis Books were required to cover the period 1910–1934 (e.g. Uganda: G3 A7/P2/1909–15; G3 A7/P3/1915–27; G3 A7/P4/1927–34); for the smaller missions the period is covered in one volume. These Précis Books ceased to be compiled after 1934. For the last eight years of the period, 1935–42, the *General Secretary's Files* have been used as a main source (indicated by a reference beginning with 'G').

The chief printed source from 1910 to 1927 (when it ceased publication) is *The Church Missionary Review*, bound in annual volumes, with page numbers running through the year. The *CMR* articles were written at a level which seems very close to the present author's intention and aspiration – they deal for the most part with broad themes in a reflective and questioning manner, unlike the Society's popular magazines such as *The Church Missionary Gleaner* and its successor *The Church Missionary Outlook* which are frankly and properly propagandist in tone.

The volumes entitled *CMS Annual Report* (typescript), compiled largely from missionaries' 'annual letters' and much fuller than the printed annual reports, are often quoted with the reference AR (MS).

2. *Specialized Sources* A few collections of personal papers in the CMS archives were consulted, notably those of A. B. Fisher (Uganda), W. E. Owen (Kenya), R. Banks (Tanganyika), A. Shaw (Southern Sudan). A visit to Uganda and Kenya in 1964 provided an opportunity to consult the Archbishop's archives at Namirembe, the CMS papers in Makerere University College Library, and a selection of the papers then housed in the CMS office, Nairobi, since removed to the Kenya National Archives. A visit to Egypt and Iran in 1968 gave similar, though less extensive, opportunities in Cairo, Tehran, and Isfahan, Yezd and Shiraz. A visit to Sierra Leone in 1969 included a week's work in the excellent library of Fourah Bay College.

In the course of preparing this volume a number of former CMS missionaries were consulted, some of whom were kind enough to loan material in manuscript or print, notably Bishop W. J. Thompson (Iran), Archdeacon F. E. Wilcock (Niger), the Rev. Donald Blackburn (Palestine and Egypt), Mrs R. Banks (Tanganyika). A few manuscript theses, mission histories, or biographies were lent by their authors to whom grateful acknowledgement is made in footnotes.

For the 'Home' end of the Society's work during this period the *CMS Home Gazette* was a useful source from 1910 until 1934 when its publication ceased. A manuscript compiled by Miss R. E. Doggett, when Editorial Secretary of the Society – 'CMS at Home, 1915–45' and intended for publication at that time, proved most valuable. In connection with the 'controversy of 1922', the specialized source most used was H/HI/AX 1, 2 in the CMS archives. Mr H. H. Busfield, formerly Administrative and Financial Secretary of CMS, prepared the display of the finances of the Society for the years 1910 to 1942 which is indispensable as background to the history of the period.

For the Society's medical work during this period Dr Harold Anderson's manuscript 'History of CMS Medical Missions 1799–1944' was most helpful. The Society's medical periodicals – *Mercy and Truth* (to 1921) and its successor *Mission Hospital* (from 1922) were also consulted, though on particular points rather than *seriatim*.

The published material relevant to CMS missions in Africa and the Middle East during these thirty-three years is extensive and grows steadily each year. Since some selection was necessary the choice has gone in favour of (*a*) books published by CMS within the period and mainly concerned with it; (*b*) standard works such as Lord Hailey's *African Survey* and the *Tambaram Madras Series*, published within the period; (*c*) more recent works which by reason of their relevance or intrinsic authority (or on both counts) have acquired the character of text-books. Professor Roland Oliver's *The Missionary Factor in East Africa* is outstanding in this category; and the lack of anything comparable for West Africa or the Middle East has been felt as a deprivation.

NOTES

1. Eugene Stock, *The History of the Church Missionary Society*, CMS, 1899, Vol. I, p. vii.

2. Georgina A. Gollock, *Eugene Stock: A Biographical Study, 1836 to 1928*, CMS, 1929, p. 128.

3. Letter to *The Times*, 28th February, 1929.

4. Roland Oliver, *The Missionary Factor in East Africa*, Longmans, 1952, p. viii.

5. Stock, op. cit., Vol I, pp. viii, ix.

6. op. cit., Vol. IV, 1916, p. 567.

7. ibid., pp. 568–9.

8. ibid., p. 570.

9. Oliver, op. cit., pp. 232, 233.

10. ibid., p. 232.

11. See Part IV, 'A Decade of Controversy, 1912–1922'.

PART ONE

West Africa

West Africa: Introduction

From the beginning of the twentieth century until the late 1950s atlases showed
the whole of West Africa except Liberia as ruled by, or under the protection of,
European powers. The area under French rule was enormous, not far short of
two million square miles. Germany, until the first world war, came next with
Togoland and the Cameroons. The British area of colonies and dependencies
covered 480,000 square miles, in four comparatively small segments – Gambia,
Sierra Leone, the Gold Coast (Ghana), and Nigeria – separated from each other
by French territory. Between 1920 and 1925 the last three received constitutions
which provided for the election of Africans to a legislative council, but it was
not until 1945 in Nigeria and 1948 in Sierra Leone that a majority of unofficial
over official members was established in these councils.

The power and influence of the colonial powers in West Africa was nothing
like as pervasive as the maps of the period tend to suggest, and there were
considerable differences in the way European rule was exercised. In the French
territories traditional African organization was regarded for the most part as
irrelevant; but in the British territories it was taken a good deal more seriously.
'In British West Africa we find the political officer almost more than the chief
acting as an agent for conserving traditional society.'[1] The classic example of
'Indirect Rule' was northern Nigeria (see below, pp. 71–72). Following this
policy, British colonial rule was comparatively light-handed. Chiefs received reinforcement of their authority in most directions. This partly explains the lack
of anti-British disturbances in Sierra Leone and northern Nigeria in the
first world war, in spite of pan-Islamic propaganda and Turkey's entry into
the war on Germany's side.

Both the British and French colonial administrations were *laissez-faire* in
their attitude to African agriculture and they stood firm against occasional
commercial pressures to alienate land to Europeans. In 1926, for example, Lord
Leverhulme, campaigning for some relaxation of this policy in the interests of
his Niger Company, was rebuffed by the British House of Commons.[2] The

world depression of 1929–32 affected West African trade severely and, as the colonial governments relied on export and import duties for the greater part of their revenue, they were hard put to it to keep their administrative establishments going; but by cuts in public works and reduction of staff almost to danger point they kept going. The depression persuaded the British and colonial governments to take a more direct interest in basic agriculture in West African dependencies and from 1940 the Colonial Development Fund helped with substantial grants.

Education along European lines was left almost entirely in the hands of missionaries until near the end of the period 1910–42. The colonial governments, with minuscule budgets for educational purposes, were content for the most part to supervise the education which the missionaries provided, although the expanding responsibilities of mission schools and colleges could not have been met without the government grants-in-aid made available from the 1920s onwards.[3] Much the same was true of medical services. Until the later 1930s mission hospitals were still setting the pace in medical care and leprosy treatment, with the help of government grants.

The colonial governments introduced railways in the early decades of the twentieth century, but the 'railway age' in West Africa was short-lived. Already by the 1920s metalled roads and lorry transport were superseding the single-line, narrow-gauge railways as the chief means of moving goods between the coast and the hinterland, although river-traffic retained its importance in the Niger delta and on the Niger and Benue rivers far inland. The many rivers of Sierra Leone were not much use for such traffic because of rapids.

African criticism of the colonial governments in the British territories was not so strident in West Africa as in East Africa, where the political activities of the settlers exacerbated every issue; but in 1920, a year before Harry Thuku founded the Young Kikuyu Association in Kenya, a body calling itself the National Congress of British West Africa held a delegates' conference in Accra. The great majority of the fifty-two delegates were from the Gold Coast, but there were six from Nigeria, three from Sierra Leone and one from Gambia. The Congress demanded that half the seats in the legislative councils should be kept for elected African members and that municipal councils, with four-fifths elected membership, should be set up in all the large towns. They also asked for reforms in the educational and medical services in order to give more scope to Africans of ability and education. The members of the Congress had no great backing in their constituent territories. At first they were virtually self-selected, representing the educated *élite* of the large towns. They were not aiming at immediate self-government, still less independence, which did not have a central place in the Congress programme until after the second world war. The Congress was chiefly concerned to draw attention to the claims of the educated townsmen to political leadership, over against the traditional African rulers who had been courted by the colonial officials. In Sierra Leone the NC BWA was more active than elsewhere and transformed itself into a political party with elected members, some of whom supported a railway strike in 1926. In the 1930s a younger generation, radical rather than reformist, began to bid for African political leadership. Many members of the Nigerian Youth Movement (1934) and the West African Youth League (1938) in Sierra Leone had been students in Britain, and their aim was a complete transformation of the colonial system. But it was the thousands of young West Africans who fought in Burma, Abyssinia and elsewhere during the second world war who took complete independence as their political platform, and after the war the pace of decolonization was rapid.[4] Ghana became an independent sovereign state in 1957; Nigeria (and thirteen former French territories) in 1960; Sierra Leone in 1961; and Gambia in 1965.

In the colonial period traditional religion in West Africa was eroded by the advances of Islam, Christianity and secularism; but it remained a strong binding force in the community and no study of Christian missionary work during the period 1910–42 can ignore evidence of the persistence of some elements of this traditional religion among many of those who accepted Christian baptism. Professor Geoffrey Parrinder in a comprehensive survey of West African religion distinguishes four main categories of traditional belief: (1) a supreme God or creator, such as Olorun among the Yoruba and Chuku among the Ibo, usually as the dominant figure in a pantheon; (2) chief divinities, generally conceived as non-human spirits, frequently associated with natural forces; (3) the cult of the human, but divinized, ancestors of the clan; (4) the use of charms and amulets.[5] As Parrinder makes clear, these categories tend to merge (Shango in Yoruba religion is both a storm-god and the fourth king of Oyo); and the first category is far less important in day-to-day religion than the other three. He finds no evidence for a common monotheism which later degenerated into pantheism. In so far as traditional religion has persisted it is the magical element which continues to be attractive even to apparently sophisticated town-dwellers. The continued use of charms and amulets, and the consultation of oracles, and the offering of road-side sacrifices and traditional burial rites among apparently sincere converts caused as much distress and heart-searching for many European missionaries as did the continuing advance of Islam.

The progress of Islam in West Africa during the fifty years of European colonial rule was noted anxiously by successive generations of missionaries, and they were not slow to accuse the British administration of favouritism towards Islam. This charge will be examined in greater detail in the chapters which follow, especially in the chapter on northern Nigeria (pp. 71–88). It was certainly true that the application of the doctrine of 'indirect rule' sometimes provided excellent opportunities for the advance of Islam; but the rapidity of its penetration towards the coast, in western Nigeria for example, cannot be attributed to government policy. Islam had certain inherent advantages over Christianity as it was represented in tropical Africa. For example, it could fairly claim to be indigenous to Africa with a thousand years' continuous history in at least parts of the continent; it did not suffer the disadvantage of being identified as the religion of the white man. It was more readily adaptable than Christianity to the traditional customs and conventions of African society; for example, Islam did not attack polygamy and was for the most part permissive about magic. Its initial demands were less exacting than those made by the Christian missions. It required neither the putting away of all but one wife nor a basic standard of literacy from those who sought membership. The spread of Islam was largely due to believers themselves, in the course of trade or seasonal migration of labour, and through marriage of Muslims to non-Muslims. Christianity, of course, spread by similar means, and contemporary historians of Christian missions in West Africa are properly concerned to correct the record on this matter, and to give more credit to the evangelistic achievements of Africans. All the same, the ministerial structure of the Christian churches left Islam with a definite cultic advantage.

> The real difference between Islam and Christianity in this respect [wrote Professor Spencer Trimingham] is that an untrained Islamic cleric can perform any clerical function, whereas the Christian lay catechist cannot celebrate the central rite of the Church, which in consequence is almost unknown to the average villager. . . . A mosque can be provided with the minimum of effort. In the villages it consists simply of a square defined by sticks, or stones, or a low mud wall.[6]

Further, as Trimingham points out, the mosque is not as crucial for Muslim worship as the church building is for Christians. Islamic family festivals take place in the home, not in the mosque.

On the other hand, Christianity as it was planted in West Africa, had certain cultural advantages which Islam lacked. The newness of the Christian gospel, its unlikeness to the known and familiar forms of religion, its revolutionary social ethic, its stress on individual choice and responsibility, and above all its provision of an education which offered prospects of personal achievement made a strong appeal to Africans who were becoming dissatisfied with their old tribal *mores*. These discontents, and dreams of a bright future, prepared the ground for response to Christian preaching and teaching, first in the towns but increasingly among the village people. The remarkably rapid growth of the Christian church in the 'middle belt' and eastern region of Nigeria in the inter-war years belied any assumption that Christianity must remain, for West Africa, predominantly an urban religion.

NOTES

1. Michael Crowder, *West Africa under Colonial Rule*, Hutchinson, 1968, p. 233.
2. op. cit., p. 319.

3. See F. H. Hilliard, *A Short History of Education in British West Africa*, Nelson, 1957, pp. 167ff.

4. Crowder, op. cit., pp. 433–81.

5. Geoffrey Parrinder, *West African Religion*, Epworth Press (1949), 2nd edition, 1961.

6. J. Spencer Trimingham, *The Christian Church and Islam in West Africa*, SCM Press, 1955, p. 31.

Sierra Leone

The Country

The name was given by fifteenth-century Portuguese seamen to the twenty-five mile long mountainous peninsula which juts northward to make the fine natural harbour on which Freetown now stands. These rounded, thickly-wooded heights crouching like a lion above the Atlantic coast, must have been a welcome sight after hundreds of miles of Saharan coast and hundreds more of swamp and muddy inlets backed by rain forest. The name was later applied not only to the peninsula but to its hinterland, bounded on the north and east by (French) Guinea and on the south-east by Liberia.

Sierra Leone owes its origin as a separate state to the abolition of slavery in Britain and its dependencies between 1772 and 1807 and to the enforcement by British naval patrols in the next five decades of international agreements against slave-trading. Between 1787 and 1800 three groups of black settlers from London, Nova Scotia and Jamaica were landed on the Sierra Leone peninsula to form what Granville Sharp called 'the Province of Freedom'.[1] The settlement was declared a British Crown Colony in 1808 and in the next half-century there were added to the original freed slave community some 60,000 to 70,000 'recaptives', i.e. Africans liberated from slave ships by the British naval patrols and brought to Freetown, sometimes from a distance of over a thousand miles on voyages taking many weeks. These liberated Africans included representatives of almost every people and state in West Africa from Senegal to the north and Angola to the south, but from about 1830 it was Yorubas from the west of the future Nigeria, and to a lesser extent Ibos from the east of it who made the greatest contribution to the development of the Creole culture which made Freetown famous as 'the Athens of West Africa'.

It was not until almost the end of the nineteenth century that British colonial administration was extended to the hinterland of Sierra Leone. In 1896 an area about the size of Scotland was declared a British protectorate. The African rulers of this region, in which the Temne to the north and the Mende to the east of Freetown formed the largest ethnic groups, were not consulted about this take-over; but the colonial administration was light-handed, and a policy of 'indirect rule' was applied in a somewhat casual fashion. An ill-advised and ill-prepared attempt by Governor Cardew in 1898 to impose a hut tax led to armed resistance by large sections of the Temne and Mende peoples which resulted in the killing of a small number of Europeans and several hundred Creoles. The Bai Bureh War, so-called after the Temne chief who first refused to pay the tax, had long-lasting results. It strengthened the determination of the colonial government to keep the protectorate separate, culturally and administratively, from the colony which by then comprised the whole Freetown peninsula. The population of the colony (75,000 in 1910, rising to 96,000 in 1931) was negligible compared with that of the protectorate (1,313,000 in 1910, rising to 1,672,000 in 1931); but it was the colony, with its able, and resilient, Creole community, which earned for Sierra Leone the title of 'the Mother of British West Africa'. After the Bai Bureh War the Creoles, who had suffered from it most, were blamed for encouraging the rebellion, and were deprived of the administrative responsibilities and opportunities for which their education had equipped them. In 1892 fifty per cent of the senior administrative posts had been held by Creoles, but by 1917 only ten per cent. Further, the entry of Syrian and Lebanese traders undermined the commercial prosperity of the Creoles and led to riots in Freetown in 1919. It is not surprising that many of them began to feel bitter, defensive and insecure. 'The British began to talk of their imperial mission, shunned social mixing with the Creoles and were placed above the law by being exempted from trial by Creole juries.'[2] The up-country peoples despised them as foreigners, which they were; and as 'black Englishmen', which they were not. As Professor Peterson and others have shown, Creole culture was too complex to deserve such denigration.[3] But there is no doubt that it was the difficulties encountered in attempting a genuine partner-ship of Africans and Europeans, as well as healthier conditions for Europeans after the control of malaria, which led the British administration between 1898 and 1950 to dismantle the partnership; but it did little to encourage African political leadership in the protectorate.

Fortunately Dr Milton Margai, leader of the Sierra Leone Peoples' Party which achieved political ascendancy in 1951 commanded respect both in Free-town and up-country; and he led Sierra Leone peacefully into independence in 1961. The productive soil in the humid climate of most of the country, the discovery in 1932 of considerable deposits of alluvial diamonds, iron-ore and other valuable exports, and, more significantly, the recovery of Creole self-confidence assured this small country of a place among the independent states of West Africa not unworthy of its pre-eminence in the nineteenth century. In the period 1910–42, however, the Creoles were under economic and psy-chological pressure, and the undertakings and decisions of the CMS in Sierra Leone during this period cannot be understood apart from this.

The CMS Mission in Retrospect, 1804–1910

It is no accident that Sierra Leone heads the list of CMS missions. There was a shared purpose as well as a common membership among those who led the anti-slavery movement in Britain, who founded the Sierra Leone Company in 1791 and the CMS in 1799. The Society's 'Instructions' to its first two missionaries in 1804 give painful and penitent expression to this:

> Though Western Africa may justly charge her sufferings from this trade upon all Europe, directly or remotely, yet the British nation is now, and has long been, most deeply criminal. We desire therefore, while we pray and labour for the removal of this evil, to make Western Africa the best remuneration in our power for its manifold wrongs.[4]

In 1799 Zachary Macaulay, after five years as governor of the freed slave colony, returned to England with twenty-nine boys and four girls. He started a school for them at Clapham, and it was from boys of the Susu tribe at this school that the first CMS missionaries, Peter Hartwig and Melchior Renner, learned the rudiments of the Susu language. They arrived in Freetown in April 1804, and after a few months Hartwig settled in the town of Basia, among the Susu, a hundred miles or so north of Freetown. Renner followed him somewhat reluctantly in 1806, but from 1804 onwards there was always a CMS missionary in Freetown or one of its neighbouring villages. The Susu mission was closed down in 1816 on the advice of the Rev. Edward Bickersteth who had been sent out by the Society on a commission of inquiry. He saw a growing missionary opportunity in the peninsula, where liberated Africans were arriving in large numbers each year. Of the first eighteen CMS missionaries in Sierra Leone all were German except Gustav Nylander (1806–24) who was a Pole. The first English missionaries were four Wesleyan Methodists in 1811. The loss of life in the early years of both missions was appalling. Fifty-three of the seventy-nine CMS missionaries between 1804 and 1824 died at their posts. But as chaplains and schoolmasters in Freetown and as superintendents of the newly-formed villages they taught and evangelized, and baptized only those who gave evidence of 'a heart that had been pricked'.[5] What followed has been described by Mr Christopher Fyfe as

> one of the outstanding triumphs of concentrated missionary work. Missionaries of the Church Missionary Society and the Methodist Missionary Society preached to these people and, cut off as they were from the religions of their homelands all over West Africa, most of them became Christians.[6]

Not only so, but many of the second and third generations of liberated Africans, as well as some of the first, took Christianity with them as they returned to their homelands or moved elsewhere along the coast. In the early years of the twentieth century Sierra Leonean clergy were playing a major part in the evangelization of the more remote areas of Yorubaland, and for much of the period 1910–42 the Niger Delta Pastorate Church was under the leadership of Sierra Leoneans (see below, p. 90).

The 'unsurmountable problem of sickness and death' among Europeans, as well as the proven effectiveness of Creole missionaries in Nigeria, encouraged the great CMS secretary, Henry Venn, to make Sierra Leone the experimental field for applying his doctrine of the 'euthanasia of a mission'. In 1853 'articles of arrangement' were drawn up between the CMS and the first Anglican Bishop of Sierra Leone, Owen Emeric Vidal. Their purpose was to bring into being a self-governing African church, and eight years later the Sierra Leone Native Pastorate Church was formed. Nine parishes in the colony were handed over by the CMS to the Sierra Leone church in 1861-2, and self-support for pastors, churches and schools was gradually introduced. The system of 'class pence' adapted from Methodism, payable at weekly bible classes, was still a major source of income for the Freetown churches in the 1920s.

A self-supporting and self-governing African church in the colony was one thing: the 'self-extension' of this church into the tribal areas of the protectorate was quite another; but in 1908 the CMS handed over its remaining missionary commitments in the hinterland to the Sierra Leone Native Pastorate Church with an annually diminishing grant which came to an end in 1928. The result of this policy was that no CMS missionaries were stationed in the Sierra Leone pastorate between 1907 and 1926, and nearly all the thirty-two missionaries who served in the Sierra Leone mission between 1910 and 1942 were engaged in whole-time educational work at the three Freetown institutions founded by the Society in the first half of the nineteenth century – Fourah Bay College (1827), the boys' grammar school (1845), and the Annie Walsh Memorial School for girls (1849).

This policy of withdrawal from direct missionary commitment up-country was often criticized by CMS missionaries during the inter-war years and has been the subject of adverse comment more recently.[7] Some of this criticism shows an inadequate appreciation of the pressures under which the 1908 decision was made. The Society was passing through one of the most difficult financial crises in its history, and the running down of Fourah Bay College to an anticipated closure in 1910 was part of the same policy decision which reduced the Society's missionary commitment in the protectorate. The criticism has also tended to underestimate the solid achievements of the Sierra Leone church missions under the leadership of Archdeacon E. T. Cole. Few of the missionaries, it is true, learned Temne and Mende, and the more distant missions among the Yalunka and Limba were abandoned fairly quickly, but the missionaries worked faithfully as pastors and evangelists among their own people in what to them was a foreign land, and they were supported in doing so by the churches and schools in the colony. 'The organization,' writes P. E. H. Hair, 'was torn between two separate and not entirely reconcilable duties – to be a mission to the tribal heathen and to be a chaplaincy to the Creole Christians.'[8] If for the most part they chose the latter, there were historical and cultural pressures upon them to do so (see above, p. 9), and any judgment of the relative failure of the Sierra Leone church missions in the protectorate must be balanced by an appreciation of the faithfulness and effectiveness of the Creole missionaries elsewhere, especially in Nigeria.[9]

Other Missions and Churches

CMS was not first in the field in Sierra Leone. In 1795 the Baptist Missionary Society sent two missionaries there but their effort was short-lived and was not followed up. In 1797 the Scottish, Glasgow and London Missionary Societies made a concerted effort to reach the Fulas in the Susu area to the north-east of Freetown. One of the Scottish missionaries, Peter Greig, was murdered, and it was partly to continue his work that the earliest CMS missionaries were located to work among the Susu in 1804. In 1811, as already recorded, the first missionaries of the Wesleyan Methodist Missionary Society reached Freetown from Britain. These two societies were still in amicable partnership during the period from 1910 to 1942. They co-operated at Fourah Bay College from 1918 and at Union College, Bunumbu, from its formation in 1933. Other Protestant missions and denominations represented in Sierra Leone during the period were: the Evangelical United Brethren (1882), the most successful mission among the peoples of the protectorate; Lady Huntingdon's Connection, introduced by settlers from Nova Scotia; the African Methodist Episcopal Church (from 1891); the United Brethren in Christ (from 1855); the Wesleyan Methodist Church of America; the General Council of the Assemblies of God; and the Seventh Day Adventists. Roman Catholic missions were represented by the Society of African Missionaries (Lyons) for a time from 1859 and then by the Congregation of the Holy Ghost assisted by nuns of the Order of St Joseph of Cluny. The Christian communities associated with these missions were none of them large. A survey in 1931 gave the following figures: CMS (Sierra Leone Pastorate Church) 14,858; WMMS 12,544; United Brethren in Christ 2,600 (communicants); Roman Catholics (total community) 5-6,000.[10]

The churches of Freetown developed a family likeness through interdenominational borrowing. For example, the dominant building style was the colonial gothic of the Church of Ireland. Most non-Anglican churches used parts of the Book of Common Prayer, and all the non-Roman Catholic churches adopted the Methodist class-system, which gave their membership a sense of personal involvement in church affairs. Christianity was embedded in Creole culture from the beginning, but it was marked by free adaptation to local needs rather than any slavish following of any one denominational tradition or missionary ethos. This is no doubt the main reason why indigenous secessionist churches were almost unknown in Sierra Leone. A further reason was the early development of voluntary associations of various kinds within the local churches rather than in opposition to them. Church 'compins' (companies) were formed in many of the villages in the early days for the relief of sick or needy members, and this tradition was still alive in the period 1910–42. For example, the Martha Davies Confidential Benevolent Association was founded in Freetown in 1910 by Mrs Davies and nine other women. The members met three times a week for worship, and they distributed alms in the villages. The Association had its own building from 1922, but it was in no sense a breakaway church.[11]

In Sierra Leone, as in most other West African countries during this period, Islam was still advancing at the expense of traditional African religion and offering an attractive alternative to Christianity. It is an over-simplification to think of the peoples of the protectorate as mainly Muslim and the Creoles of the colony as almost exclusively Christian. Mandinka and Fula traders from up-country had introduced Islam into the peninsula before the arrival of the first freed slaves in 1787, and a significant number of Hausa and Yoruba, who came later, were Muslims. Between 1921 and 1931 the number of Muslims in the colony increased by fifty per cent (16,611 to 25,349) and by the 1960s Muslims were to outnumber Christians in Freetown itself. Most Muslims in Sierra Leone are 'orthodox', but after the first world war the Ahmadiyya reforming sect made considerable impact in Mendeland with Bo, the provincial capital, as a main centre of influence.

Although the spread of Islam was often regarded as the main obstacle to Christian missions in the hinterland, it remained a minority religion in Sierra Leone, and traditional African beliefs continued to be a chief integrating factor in the lives of the up-country people into the 1960s. 'The presuppositions of animism pervade the whole life of the people even after they have become Muslim or Christian.'[12]

Bishops and the Diocese, 1910–42

Following the death of Bishop E. H. Elwin in November 1909, the Archbishop of Canterbury appointed as his successor Canon John Walmsley, a former vice-principal of Wycliffe Hall, Oxford, and vicar for the previous five years of St Ann's, Nottingham. He was remembered at this time as 'a tall slim figure, leaning slightly forward, with a curious little twist of the neck, clear grey eyes, unusually far apart'. He was consecrated bishop in Westminster Abbey on St John the Baptist's Day, 1910, and he reached Freetown in October. He gave his first impressions in an article in *The Church Missionary Review* in May 1912. Half the forty thousand inhabitants of Freetown were, he thought, Muslims or pagans, and many of them immigrants from up-country who had come seeking work. He regretted the 'arrested development' which prevented many boys and girls from the primary schools going forward to secondary education. He noted sadly that many church workers in the protectorate preferred to minister to their own Freetown people 'rather than to learn a tribal language'. He hoped to develop both educational and medical work in the protectorate, but apart from a small boys' boarding school at Port Loko, these hopes were not realized.

Bishop Walmsley was remembered in Freetown as a scholar who was largely responsible for nursing Fourah Bay College through a critical period which lasted much of his episcopate (see below, p. 19); and as a great walker who disdained the use of a rickshaw. He was a bachelor, and apart from two years, 1912–14, when his sister kept house for him at Bishopscourt, he was happiest on his frequent journeys up-country, sometimes with his bicycle but mostly on foot. The enervating climate did not seem to worry him. His energy made other Europeans feel guilty. The Rev. H. A. Lewis, his chaplain in 1919–20, recalled him 'perpetually dashing round Freetown or out to one of the neighbouring villages. He would bolt his food in a shocking manner, sit waiting as patiently as he could while we struggled to finish ours, and then rush off at his usual swinging gait.' In 1921, after a severe attack of blackwater fever, he was invalided home to England and was warned of the risk involved in returning to the tropics; but he was determined to get the diocesan constitution accepted and in working order. In February 1922 he was back in Freetown, filling the day with engagements and crossing the garden each evening to take prayers in the wards of the Princess Christian Hospital which his predecessor Bishop Ingham had built in the Bishopscourt grounds in 1892. In October of that year he made a thousand-mile tour of the churches in the protectorate and in French Guinea. He died of a second attack of blackwater fever on 9th December, 1922.[13]

The later years of Bishop Walmsley's episcopate were clouded by the probability that CMS would withdraw altogether from Sierra Leone. In November 1919 a review committee was appointed in London to consider the Society's strategy in face of an accumulated deficit of £80,000; and it was inevitable that Sierra Leone should come high on the list of possible withdrawals. It was a very small mission, almost entirely institutionalized, and operating in a diocese with a long-established indigenous church and clergy. On 11th February, 1920 James Denton, the mission secretary, after consulting the bishop and the Rev. H. Dallimore, wrote to the parent committee strongly opposing the suggestion of withdrawal. The continuing presence of the mission, they argued, was necessary to maintain standards in the Freetown schools and in Fourah Bay College, and to support the Native Pastorate Church in its mission to the peoples of the protectorate. Withdrawal would be a setback to co-operative projects with the WMMS, especially to the scheme started two years earlier in 1918 for shared responsibility at Fourah Bay College. The financial saving achieved by withdrawal would not, in their view, be substantial – approximately £500 a year on 1919 figures.[14] The parent committee, however, remained firm in its intention to hand over all its responsibilities to the Sierra Leone Pastorate Church. The prospect was not unwelcome to the church. The bishop thought an immediate hand-over was not practicable, but in 1922, as already noted, he revived a committee set up by his predecessor to prepare a new diocesan constitution which would provide for such development. Denton, in an interview with the CMS Group III secretary in London in April 1922, appeared ready to accept a phased withdrawal from at least some of the Society's responsibilities. Once a diocesan synod had been set up with a properly constituted educational board, he thought the grammar school could be handed over to it.[15] By this time the Society's financial crisis which had given urgency to the proposal of withdrawal had passed, and the parent committee was ready to accept a continuing responsibility in Sierra Leone for a further period of some years at least.

Bishop Walmsley was succeeded, after an interval of nearly a year, by George William Wright, vicar of Boulton, Derby, who was consecrated tenth Bishop of Sierra Leone on All Saints Day, 1923. He arrived at Freetown on the 30th November. Bishop Wright had served for fifteen years as a CMS missionary in Kenya, mostly in Mombasa in a climate not dissimilar from Freetown. He is remembered as the first Bishop of Sierra Leone who did not wear gaiters as his day-to-day garb. He continued his predecessor's interest in providing a proper constitution for the diocese, and after the necessary consultations and revisions, the constitution was promulgated in 1930. It incorporated provision for the cathedral chapter, with the bishop as dean, and for the lease of property to the parochial and missionary clergy. It also provided, as the constitution of 1900 had done, for various diocesan boards responsible to the synod, but with somewhat strengthened powers and membership. Bishop Wright soon came to share his predecessor's opinion that a complete handover from mission to diocese must not be hurried.

> The Church of Sierra Leone [he wrote in 1929] has a history differing from that of many mission fields. Speaking quite frankly, self-support and self-government have been forced upon it, owing chiefly to the death of the missionary in large numbers. . . . Spiritually, therefore, the young child-church has not arrived even today at the stage when it is capable of developing intensively and extensively.[16]

This point of view was fully shared by the Rev. Cecil Horstead, Principal of Fourah Bay College and mission secretary from 1926. In an interview with the CMS Africa and general secretaries in May 1933, Canon Horstead said that the Sierra Leone church seemed to have been spiritually unable to cope with the missionary situation, particularly in the protectorate. 'It looks as though the diocese,' he wrote in a memorandum at this time, 'is only held together by the rather unique combination of gifts in the present Bishop.' Horstead had himself been appointed Canon Missioner in the hope that he could improve the situation evangelistically, but his other commitments prevented him from doing what he and the bishop believed to be needed. He asked the parent committee of CMS to locate a missionary to Sierra Leone whose specific task would be to train and help the Sierra Leone Pastorate Church in evangelism.[17]

These doubts about the capacity of the indigenous church to manage without the European missionaries may account for the reluctance of Bishop Wright to transfer responsibility for the two Freetown CMS secondary schools. In 1922 the executive committee of the mission agreed to hand over the grammar school and the Annie Walsh Memorial School to the diocesan synod, when formed; and Fourah Bay College to a West African provincial synod, when formed. An 'address', signed by representative clergy and laity of the church, was presented to the CMS African secretary, the Rev. H. D. Hooper, when he visited Sierra Leone in 1930. It asked that the 1922 undertaking should now be honoured. But the schools remained under the Society's control, though representatives of the church were appointed to the schools' visiting committees.

A complicating factor in revising the diocesan constitution in the 1920s was the enormous extent of the diocese of Sierra Leone. The Gold Coast and Lagos had been separated from it in 1898 but, on paper at least, its territories extended up to the West Coast to Morocco and included Madeira and the Canaries. Outside the colony and the protectorate the number of Anglican congregations was very small, but they included the adherents of the Rio Pongas mission, a small number of congregations in the Gambia, and converts and missionaries connected with a BCMS mission recently established in Morocco. The distances involved meant that the Bishop of Sierra Leone had to spend a good deal of time in travel. Visiting CMS headquarters in October 1930 Bishop Wright asked the Society's support for a plan for dividing the diocese. He suggested a three-fold division – one diocese for the colony and protectorate of Sierra Leone: another for Gambia and the French territories of the West Coast; and a third for North Africa and the islands. This plan was carried through. Gambia and the Rio Pongas were constituted first as a separate diocese and a Yorkshire vicar, John Daly, was consecrated as its first bishop on 1st May, 1935. Bishop Wright's plea for a separate diocese for North Africa had found strong support from the Rev. Daniel Bartlett, secretary of the BCMS. That society was prepared to underwrite the stipend of a bishop, and eventually Bishop Wright was himself invited to move to North Africa. He had for some time been thinking of retiring from Sierra Leone, after a total of twenty-nine years of missionary service, and had notified CMS of his intention to do so not later than 1936.[18] But the lighter duties of the proposed new diocese, and the challenge presented by it, appealed to him; and with the approval of the Archbishop of Canterbury and the CMS, he was translated from Sierra Leone to become Bishop in North Africa in May 1936.

In a letter to the CMS parent committee in April 1935 Bishop Wright had discussed the possibility of an African bishop as his successor in the truncated diocese of Sierra Leone. He thought such an appointment would be feasible, with Canon Horstead remaining in support as Principal of Fourah Bay College; and he suggested for consideration the name of Bishop A. W. Howells, who had been an assistant bishop in Nigeria since 1920. The CMS secretariat, however, decided to nominate Horstead himself for the Archbishop's consideration, and he was consecrated bishop on 24th June, 1936. The diocese thereafter consisted of the colony and protectorate only, with approximately twenty parishes in the former, and twenty mission centres in the latter. On St Barnabas Day, 1937 Archdeacon T. S. Johnson, a Sierra Leonean, was consecrated assistant bishop. He had varied experience behind him, most recently as principal of the grammar school in Freetown. Looking back on the episcopal ministry which he shared with Horstead, Johnson wrote of him:

> He took a keen interest in the work of preparing candidates for the ministry, arranging refresher courses for deacons and others, and did much to maintain the high standard already attained by the clergy.[19]

The finances of the diocese in the later 1930s were causing some anxiety. In 1938 Bishop Horstead reported a debt of £1,000 on the fund for paying church workers. The upkeep of the large parish churches, many of them elaborate stone structures, was proving a great burden. Although opportunities of missionary work in the protectorate were far greater than they had been in 1908 'not a single worker in our [i.e. the Sierra Leone Church] mission staff can be considered fully trained, and many have no training whatever'.[20]

A co-operative effort between several missionary societies had been started at Bunumbu in the protectorate in 1933 for training teacher-catechists for the villages; but there was much leeway to make up. A representative inter-mission conference held in Freetown in January 1937 regretted that there was no common system for grading workers or their allowances, and no common policy in education in the protectorate. In 1942 Bishop Horstead reported that the executive board of the Sierra Leone church had agreed in principle to the resumption of CMS work in the mission areas of the protectorate.[21]

Partnership in Education, 1910–42

The Sierra Leone government had been active in the supervision of education for a long time before 1910. In 1867 a 'director of public instruction' was appointed by the government, and three years later grants-in-aid for schools were introduced. In the 1880s the government set up a board of education and instituted an examination for a teachers' certificate; and teacher-training was introduced at Fourah Bay College with grants from SPCK and, for a time, from the government. But secondary education in the colony had been left to the missions, and it was a matter of corporate concern for them when, in October 1910, it was rumoured that the government intended to start a 'higher grade' school and a teacher-training scheme of its own. Denton, the CMS mission secretary, saw such proposals as in direct competition with the grammar school, and he was not mollified by the government's assurance that its new model school would be purely 'primary'. He felt there were already too many primary schools in the colony. There were in fact ninety-six, thirty-nine of them Anglican, and twenty-two Wesleyan Methodist. Bishop Walmsley and the WMMS superintendent made a joint approach to the governor, Sir Leslie Probyn, to restore teacher-training at Fourah Bay College, which had lapsed for some years.[22]

The first world war slowed down the government plans for teacher-training and for its own secondary school, but in May 1919 a public meeting at Government House, Freetown, supported the proposal for a government secondary school as well as the model school for teacher-training, and in September the governor met CMS and WMMS secretaries in London to explain the policy of his administration. They were not willing, he said, to leave all secondary education in Sierra Leone to the missionary societies. To do so was unfair to the Muslim community; and a high school such as was proposed would give competitive freedom of selection to parents. It would also set the government free from the embarrassment of having to regulate religious teaching. He was proposing, however, to raise the *per capita* grant available to mission secondary schools from £3 to £5.[23] This was a mollifier which, at that time and in those circumstances, CMS was not prepared to accept; and it was another decade before either of its secondary schools received government grants.

The missions in the end had to accept the situation. The demand for secondary education was growing and their schools did not suffer to the extent that they had feared when the Prince of Wales School was opened in 1926. In 1925 teacher-training was re-introduced at Fourah Bay College on the initiative of Mr H. S. Keigwin, government Director of Education. The Rev. T. S. Johnson (later to become assistant bishop) was appointed as one of two 'normal' masters, the other being a European. In 1926 Mr R. R. Young and Miss E. D. Laycock (CMS missionary recruits who were already engaged and who were married in September of that year) were appointed as supervising teachers for mission schools in the protectorate, the government underwriting the whole cost of their work under a co-operative scheme with other missions. In 1928 the government undertook to pay one hundred per cent of the salaries of teachers in primary schools and to provide equipment, the churches and missions continuing to provide and maintain their school buildings. A United Christian Council was formed, to represent the non-Roman Catholic denominations as an advisory body in educational matters. It soon proved the value of its watching brief. In May 1930 an Education Ordinance gave much wider powers to the Director of Education. The Council protested that the powers were too wide, and the Ordinance was modified.

In the same year, 1930, the United Christian Council approved plans for a college at Bunumbu, over two hundred miles to the east of Freetown. Its aim was to train teacher-catechists for pastoral and missionary work in the protectorate, developing the training already started at Bunumbu by the WMMS. The initial cost of the scheme (£1,000) was to be shared according to the number of students sent from each mission. The parent committee of CMS promised £100 to £200 for buildings, and made provision for a married recruit on its 1932 quota of new missionaries.[24] The WMMS and the United Brethren synods also approved the Bunumbu scheme, and the Union College was opened in June 1933 with the Rev. R. H. Crosby (WMMS) as principal. CMS contributed a staff member, R. R. Young, and the United Brethren Church provided an African as assistant tutor. In 1936 Young reported that the college was fully established with twenty students. Its aim was to send out resourceful and versatile men who would take a lead in village life. The curriculum was practical as well as literary, and emphasized agricultural training. The students were encouraged to make experiments in native music, and training in evangelism was paramount in the early years.[25] Later, government educational plans required greater emphasis on the training of teachers.

Fourah Bay College

In 1910 the college could look back with pride over more than eighty years of history to a time when, in 1827, the 'Christian Institution' (founded in 1816) moved to the estate of a former governor at Fourah Bay, overlooking Freetown harbour, and began training Africans as schoolmasters, catechists and clergy. Samuel Adjai Crowther, first Bishop on the Niger, was among the first six students to be enrolled; and from that time, and particularly after its affiliation to Durham University in 1876, the college provided training for most of the educated *élite* of West Africa. The list of celebrated *alumni* includes James Johnson, Assistant Bishop on the Niger from 1900 (his visit to England in 1873 was largely responsible for the Durham University affiliation); three brothers also named Johnson – Henry (Archdeacon of the Niger); Nathaniel (Archdeacon of Lagos) and Obadiah, (a well-known doctor in Lagos); A. W. Howells and Isaac Oluwole, both assistant bishops in Nigeria; Dr A. W. Easmon, a gold medallist of Edinburgh University; G. M. C. Thompson, a leading barrister; and Henry Carr, Director of Education and Assistant Colonial Secretary at Lagos, and for many years Chancellor of the dioceses of Western Equatorial Africa and, later, of Lagos.[26]

In spite of, partly indeed because of, the character of this fine achievement in higher education, Fourah Bay College in 1910 was without a principal and under threat of closure. The CMS was passing through a period of financial strain, and the college had diverged, certainly, from its original purpose of supplying clergy and teachers. The Society did not feel justified in spending money entrusted to it for evangelism on a liberal education for Africans entering secular professions as lawyers and doctors. The number of CMS scholarships was reduced and, on the initiative of the parent committee, it had been decided that no further students were to be matriculated.[27] A public meeting in Freetown took up with enthusiasm the idea of raising a £10,000 endowment fund for the college principal but subscribers were so few that their money was returned to them. The college was saved, humanly speaking, by three things: (1) by Bishop Walmsley's readiness to earmark for the college the whole of the interest on the £3,000 allocation to Sierra Leone from the Pan-Anglican Thank-offering Fund raised by the Anglican Congress of 1908; (2) by Denton's readiness to accept the post of acting-principal and then of principal of the college, to which he gave himself with devotion from 1911 to 1921, and again in 1925–6; (3) by the vision and self-denial of the Rev. T. S. Johnson, seconded from the Cathedral School. Like Denton, he served for several years without salary, confident that the college could be saved.

In 1917–18 plans for co-operation between CMS and WMMS in running the college took definite shape. A college council was formed with the Bishop of Sierra Leone as chairman, the superintendent of WMMS as vice-chairman, and seven representatives from each of the two missions, including at least three laymen from each; the principal was to be a European, appointed by CMS; and the vice-principal also a European, appointed by WMMS. WMMS agreed to support five students and to maintain a contribution at this level if the number fell short of five. These new arrangements were accepted by Durham University on the understanding that the principal and vice-principal would be qualified Europeans of British nationality and graduates of universities within the British Empire; and that nine terms' minimum residence were kept before graduation. In the early 1920s a science department was developed at the college, greatly helped by the bequest of £5,000 from Dr O. Johnson; and by the offer of another Sierra Leonean, Dr Randle, to underwrite the salary of a science teacher. The outstanding teaching ability of Mr Eric Downing, the CMS missionary appointed to the post in the 1930s, gave to science an assured place in the college curriculum.

The Rev. F. B. Heiser succeeded Denton as principal in 1921 but he was forced to resign on health grounds in 1923. He was remembered as one who took a keen interest in the students and 'loved them as an elder brother'. Back in England, he served for many years as Principal of St Aidan's College, Birkenhead.

In 1925 James Denton, near the age of retirement, accepted the principalship again. He did so with some reluctance, but no-one was better fitted to lead the college at its centenary and jubilee (i.e. of the Durham affiliation) celebrations in 1926. The guests of honour were Dr Dawson Walker, Professor of Divinity at Durham University and Dr J. E. Aggrey, Vice-Principal of Achimota College in the Gold Coast. Denton received the honorary degree of DCL of Durham University, and was awarded an MBE for his services to education in Sierra Leone.[28] He was succeeded as principal by the Rev. J. C. L. Horstead, a graduate and Lightfoot Scholar of Durham University, who served for ten years before his consecration as Bishop of Sierra Leone in 1936. In his early years at the college he came in for some outspoken criticism in the Freetown press for his efforts to restore the college to its original purpose in training catechists and schoolmasters. The rumour went round that he intended to abolish the arts course, but the CMS Africa secretary, the Rev. H. D. Hooper, on his visit in 1930, helped to quieten the misgivings that had been aroused.[29] The college was strengthened under Horstead's leadership and the training of teachers was put on a firmer footing with more students working for the Diploma in Education of Durham University. The last principal of the period, the Rev. E. A. H. Roberts (1937–46), guided the college through a time of great difficulty including war-time evacuation from Freetown and depletion of staff.

In 1938 the Secretary of State for the Colonies appointed a commission, under the chairmanship of Dr A. W. Pickard-Cambridge, to examine the viability of the college in the development of university education in Sierra Leone and in other British dependencies in West Africa. The commission found the thirty-two students 'well-mannered, earnest, thoughtful, but very friendly'. It commented on the excellence of the science teaching and the promising start that had been made with a pre-medical course. But other items in its report did not encourage the hope of an early development towards independent university status. The commission found that co-operation with the WMMS had virtually ceased. The college council rarely met and the principal tended to work directly under the guidance of the local CMS executive committee, consulting on more important matters only with the CMS parent committee in London. There was no regular consultation with Durham University, nor with the Department of Education in Sierra Leone about the appointment of staff. The commission noticed that the CMS missionaries on the staff received a lower salary than their qualifications would command elsewhere. It found that the teaching in the arts course was below university standard, and thought the college could not develop as the nucleus of a West African university unless this teaching was considerably improved. It saw little likelihood of Nigerian students coming to Fourah Bay College in future years in view of the development of theological teaching at Yaba College, Lagos.

The Pickard-Cambridge Commission's report throws some light on a problem which at this period the CMS was having to face in other countries. The Society had been a pioneer of secondary education in Africa at a time when the colonial governments were unable or unwilling to take any share in it. By the late 1930s these governments were beginning to think seriously of the development of African universities and in terms of staffing, building and equipment their thinking was a long way beyond anything a missionary society could contemplate. The point can be made succinctly. In May 1950 the legislative council of Sierra Leone passed a bill for the maintenance and development of Fourah Bay College as a government institution. Six months later the Colonial Welfare and Development Fund granted to the Sierra Leone government for the development of the college the sum of £450,000; only once in the period

1910–42 had the *total* annual income of the CMS available for general purposes approached this figure, and in most years it was not more than half of it. The college under CMS oversight had always been small, seldom more than forty students, and there had been times when it had limped along because of lack of adequate finance and uncertainty of aim, but the tribute of Bishop T. S. Johnson was typical of the gratitude felt by the Creole community for the Society's steadfastness in keeping it open in the lean years. 'One cannot find words adequate to express the great debt which the country owes to the CMS for having shouldered, almost unaided over a century, the work at Fourah Bay College.'[30]

The Grammar School

In a historical sketch, published for the school's ninetieth birthday in 1935, Mr A. E. Toboku-Metzger gives an attractive picture of its origins and development.[31] It had been started in 1845 to provide 'an intermediate stage between elementary school and college, and to give a sound religious and general education for boys'. By 1935 the grammar school had long held a place of honour in the community life and with many of its old boys holding posts of responsibility in church and state, education and commerce it was confidently looking forward to expansion on a new site and in new buildings. The minutes and correspondence of the CMS local governing body, however, give a somewhat different impression. The oversight of the grammar school was on more than one occasion cause for anxiety and a focus-point of that discrepancy in aims and expectations which has been already noted. The missionaries tended to use criteria of effectiveness which remained alien to Creole ways of thought. Tension was thus unavoidable.

The principal of the grammar school in 1910 was a CMS missionary, the Rev. G. G. Garrett. His immediate predecessors had both been African, and successively they had guided the school for over fifty years. There had been protests at the time of Garrett's appointment in 1905 but he gained the confidence of the people of Freetown and his introduction of the typical features of the English public school – houses, prefects, a troop of boy scouts (1909) and good playing-fields – was readily accepted. When Garrett left in 1912 for further missionary service in India, there was a confident expectation in Freetown that the CMS would once more appoint an African head. However the Sierra Leone Department of Education was pressing for higher standards in the secondary schools, all still under missionary control, and the local CMS executive committee advised the appointment of a European, with assurance of its 'ultimate intention' to appoint an African. It proved difficult to find a suitable candidate in England and early in 1913 the parent committee agreed to appoint an African if no European had been found by its July meeting.[32] After some further delay a missionary recruit, the Rev. Henry Dallimore, accepted the appointment, and he arrived in Freetown in December 1914.

Dallimore was soon in difficulty with some of the senior boys. In May 1915, to quote Toboku-Metzger's account 'some trouble arose when he introduced an alteration in the rules of the boarding-house. Boys resented the alteration and this led to five of them being expelled.' Their parents sued Dallimore for damages, and in a case heard in the Supreme Court of the Colony 'judgment was given against the Principal as acting *ultra vires* and the boys had to be taken back'. Dallimore wrote to CMS in London saying that in view of the judge's 'animadversions' at the trial he would have to resign. The parent committee did not accept his resignation, but approved of his returning to England for a time. In August Denton wrote to London saying that African opinion was 'still hostile'; and that the Europeans in Freetown were 'condoning' the judgment of the Supreme Court and were urging stronger action by the Society either to settle the school or to abandon it.[33]

The situation created by the court-case was one in which outside help was clearly needed, and the parent committee asked T. E. Alvarez to go to Freetown to consult and advise about the school's future. Alvarez, who had been a CMS missionary in Sierra Leone before going to Northern Nigeria, spent a few weeks in Freetown in 1916, and he recommended closing the school for a time. Some old boys started raising funds for a new school but Denton took charge for a time, and things settled down. Dallimore returned in 1917 with the Rev. T. C. John, an African member of the Fourah Bay College staff, as his vice-principal. In 1919 the amalgamation of the CMS grammar school with the WMMS high school was considered. They were only a mile apart, but there was not much local enthusiasm for the idea, and Bishop Walmsley was also against it. He wrote to CMS headquarters saying that he would prefer the appointment of another European to succeed Dallimore who was on the point of leaving: but rather than amalgamation with the high school he would support the appointment of T. C. John.[34] Dallimore left for Nigeria where he gave twenty-five years of valuable service in the Lagos diocese, most of them as an archdeacon. He kept in touch with many of the old boys of the grammar school, including some who had opposed him in his early days. He was remembered as a good teacher 'especially of geography', and for the school expeditions which he led into the protectorate.

T. C. John, Dallimore's successor as principal from 1920 to 1933, was an old boy of the school, a native of the village of Hastings. The school prospered under his leadership: numbers increased to 250 (nearly 50 of them boarders) with a staff of thirteen African masters. John was at pains to keep before the school the vocation to missionary work and he restored the Junior Missionary Association. One of the many changes he introduced was the division of the school into senior, middle and junior departments. In 1933 he was consecrated as assistant bishop for service in the Niger diocese and was succeeded by another African, the Rev. T. S. Johnson. After only four years he too was made an assistant bishop, in Sierra Leone diocese in 1937. The next principal, the

Rev. P. H. Willson, had been an assistant master at the school before becoming a tutor at Fourah Bay College. He was described by a former pupil as 'a particularly sensitive headmaster' who saw the need to widen the curriculum and to improve the teaching of science. Dallimore was the last European to serve on the staff during the period 1910–42, but the school remained a CMS institution until the end of it, and the local governing body received regular reports from the principal. Government grants-in-aid were received from the late 1930s onwards. Most of the leaders of the Sierra Leone Anglican Church in the 1960s were proud to be counted among its old boys.

The Annie Walsh Memorial School

Unlike the grammar school, all the principals of the Annie Walsh girls' school until the 1960s were CMS missionaries. The first of them, Miss Sass, was a woman of great vision and will-power. Before she retired, after twenty years' service in 1869, she had supervised much of the building of the main block which was still in use a century later, standing in five acres of ground among the busy streets of Freetown. This building was made possible by the gift of £2,500 from the Rev. James and Mrs Walsh of Warminster in England in memory of their daughter, Annie, who had hoped to serve as a missionary in Africa but who died at the age of twenty-two. From 1865 the school, previously known as the Female Institution, took her name.

The school aimed at 'discipline, health and moral culture', and personal discipleship to Jesus Christ.[35] In its early days discipline was prominent and took forms, such as periods of solitary confinement, which a later generation would come to regard as reprehensible; but the school gradually won its way as one of the major girls' schools on the West Coast of Africa, and pupils came from Nigeria, Ghana and other countries.

The principal serving in 1910 was Miss H. H. Bissett (1894–1916). In a report in June of that year she described the daily routine. The boarders (22 of the 115 pupils) rose at 5.30 a.m. Lessons were from 8.0 a.m. to 11.0 a.m., and from 1.0 p.m. to 3.0 p.m. Dinner was at 3.30 p.m. and there was a further spell of school from 6.15 p.m. to 7.45 p.m. The curriculum was comprehensive – 'Scripture, English, Geography, History, Arithmetic, Composition, French, Domestic Economy, English Literature, Dressmaking, Elementary Science, Plain and Fancy Needlework'. Daughters of CMS agents received tuition free except for music, and there was a reduction of fees for the children of clergy of the Native Pastorate Church.[36]

The next principal, Miss C. H. Pidsley (1917–26), had been an assistant mistress for twenty years. She added typing and shorthand to the curriculum, and the first company of Girl Guides in Freetown was started at the school in 1924. Her successor, Miss W. B. Hamblett (1926–30), introduced the distinctive green uniform, and built new class-rooms, and it was in her time that the

CMS mission committee agreed to a capitation grant from the Sierra Leone government, at the rate of £250 a year.

Miss D. F. Pole (1930–54) developed the school further along the lines of an English public school with a house-system and house and school prefects. The efficiency of the school had been hampered by the wide age-range and it was Miss Pole's policy gradually to eliminate the junior forms so as to become fully a secondary school, though the kindergarten department was kept in being. From the early 1930s old girls of the school were among the first women entrants of Fourah Bay College. The first woman graduate of the college became also the first African principal of the Annie Walsh School.

Although the records of the CMS mission in Sierra Leone from 1910 to 1942 indicate a degree of restiveness, almost a sense of shame, at the lack of 'real' missionary work, and at restriction to the oversight of two secondary schools and Fourah Bay College, the outcome of this faithfulness was that, a quarter of a century later, these three institutions, no longer under CMS control but still under Christian leadership, were still serving the educational needs of an independent Sierra Leone.

NOTES

1. John Peterson, *Province of Freedom: A History of Sierra Leone 1787–1870*, Faber, 1969, p. 13.

2. J. B. Webster and A. A. Boahen, *The Revolutionary Years: West Africa since 1800*, Longmans, 1967, p. 151.

3. Christopher Fyfe and Eldred Jones (ed.), *Freetown: A Symposium*, Sierra Leone University Press, 1968; Harry Sawyerr, 'Sacrificial Rituals in Sierra Leone', *S.L. Bulletin of Religion*, June 1959, June 1960.

4. Stock, 1, p. 95.

5. Peterson, op. cit., p. 127.

6. In *The Listener*, 27th April 1961, p. 725.

7. Gilbert W. Olson, *Church Growth in Sierra Leone*, Eerdmans, Michigan, 1969; R. S. Foster, *The Sierra Leone Church*, SPCK, 1961: See also the Bishop of Sierra Leone, 'Towards an Indigenous Church in Sierra Leone', *East and West Review*, April 1946, pp. 41–46.

8. P. E. H. Hair, 'Creole Endeavour and Self-Criticism in the Sierra Leone Church Missions, 1900–1920', *S.L. Bulletin of Religion*, June 1966, p. 13; see also T. S. Johnson, *The Story of a Mission*, SPCK, 1953.

9. M. A. C. Warren, 'Continuing Growth in Nigeria', *East and West Review*, October 1958, p. 126.

10. J. J. Cooksey and A. McLeish, *Religion and Civilization in West Africa*, World Dominion Press, 1931, pp. 95–122.

11. Fyfe and Jones, op. cit., pp. 128ff.; Peterson, op. cit., pp. 259ff.; 'The Martha Davies Confidential Benevolent Association', *S.L. Bulletin of Religion*, December 1961, pp. 64–67.

12. Olson, op. cit., p. 42. Recent studies of African traditional religion in S.L. include W. T. Harris and Harry Sawyerr, *The Springs of Mende Belief and Conduct*, S.L.

University Press, Freetown, 1968, and Harry Sawyerr, *Creative Evangelism*, Lutterworth Press, 1968.

13. E. G. Walmsley (ed.), *John Walmsley: Ninth Bishop of Sierra Leone*, SPCK, 1923.

14. G3/A1/P4, 1920/7 (reference abbreviated below).

15. P4, 1922/iii.

16. *AR* (MS), 1929–30, pp. 7, 8.

17. G/Y/A1/2, memo by Cash, 29th May, 1933.

18. ibid., letter of 20th August, 1935.

19. Johnson, op. cit., p. 78.

20. G/Y/A1/2, Survey of diocese, June 1938.

21. ibid., memo for Africa Committee, 24th November, 1942.

22. P4, 1910/95, 100.

23. P4, 1919/42.

24. P5, 1930/38, 44, xi.

25. *AR* (MS) 1936–37, pp. 3, 4; 1938–39, pp. 4–6.

26. F. B. Heiser, 'Fourah Bay College', *CMR*, March 1926, pp. 60–72.

27. Johnson, op. cit., pp. 102–3.

28. T. J. Thompson, *The Jubilee and Centenary Volume of Fourah Bay College, 1827–1927*, Freetown, 1930, pp. 111–14.

29. ibid., pp. 167–73.

30. Johnson, op. cit., p. 107.

31. A. E. Toboku-Metzger, *A Historical Sketch of the S.L. Grammar School, 1845–1935*, Freetown, 1935.

32. P4, 1913/xviii.

33. P4, 1915/9, 15, 25, 31, 41.

34. P4, 1919/48, xiv.

35. Effie M. Colbeck, 'The Annie Walsh School', *East and West Review*, October 1956, pp. 116–22.

36. Oredola Palmer, 'The Annie Walsh Memorial School and the part it played in the emancipation of women on the West Coast of Africa', MS thesis 1965 (Fourah Bay College Archives).

Nigeria: A General Survey

The Country

'A vast square on the Bights of Benin and Biafra, a square with the south-eastern corner pushed in' – so Sir Rex Niven describes Nigeria.[1] With an area not much short of 350,000 square miles, it is the fourth largest country in the British Commonwealth. It is considerably larger than France and East and West Germany put together, stretching some 700 miles from Dahomey in the west to the Cameroon Republic in the east, and 650 miles from the coast to its northern border with the Republic of Niger. Its heraldic emblem is a black shield with a wavy silver 'Y', representing the two great rivers that give it a geographical unity – the Niger itself, 2,500 miles long, rising behind Sierra Leone, curving round to the east and then dropping southwards into the vast swamps and creeks of its delta; and the Benue, 800 miles long, rising in the Cameroun mountains and joining the Niger at Lokoja in the centre of the country.

Nigeria has four more or less clearly defined belts of vegetation from south to north – mangrove swamps along most of its 500 miles of coast; a belt of tropical rain forest 50 to 100 miles wide; a wide area of savannah grasslands in the middle belt; and near-desert in the far north. North of the Benue the land rises steadily to the Bauchi plateau at 3,000 to 4,000 feet around Jos. The northern towns of Kaduna and Zaria are lower, but still around 2,000 feet above sea-level. On the north-east boundary is Lake Chad, 15,000 square miles of water. As might be expected, the rainfall is heaviest in the Niger Delta area (130″ at Port Harcourt); still heavy on the western coast (75″ at Lagos); and light in the north (20″ near Lake Chad). June, July, and August are the wettest months, and near the coast there is only a short dry season, when the *harmattan*, the dry desert wind, brings welcome relief.

The population (estimated as 19,000,000 in 1926; 55,500,000 in 1961) is most dense in the south; Owerri Province (200–300 per square mile) and

Onitsha Province (300–400 per square mile) gave some of the highest density figures for Tropical Africa in the 1930s. The proportion of town-dwellers is in general higher than in East Africa. Ibadan, with a population approaching half a million in the 1960s, has long been the largest purely African city in the continent. Lagos (pop. 600,000 in 1967), largely built on a sandbank at the mouth of the Ogun river, was a centre of the slave-trade before it developed as a major West African port in the mid-nineteenth century. Although by no means central, being in fact close to the western coastal extremity of Nigeria, Lagos succeeded Calabar fairly early in the colonial period as the capital city and centre of government, and remained so after independence. Other towns with which our story will be concerned are Abeokuta, sixty miles north, and Ibadan, some hundred miles north-east of Lagos; Oyo, thirty miles north of Ibadan; Benin City, one hundred and sixty miles east of Lagos, and Owo sixty miles or so north of Benin. Further to the east on the Niger is Onitsha, one hundred and fifty miles inland; Enugu fifty and Awka twenty-five miles to the north-east, and Owerri sixty miles to the south of Onitsha; Port Harcourt, growing rapidly to become a major port in the 1920s, in the Niger delta, and Calabar, east of the delta, on a hill surrounded by swamps and creeks; Lokoja, at the junction of the Niger and Benue rivers, and Bida one hundred miles north-west of Lokoja. Further north are the walled Muslim cities of the Fulani-Hausa states – Zaria, about five hundred miles north from Port Harcourt; Kano one hundred miles further on to the north-east; Katsina about one hundred and fifty miles north of Zaria; and Sokoto in the far north-west.

Nigeria remained an unhealthy country for Europeans long after the disastrous loss of life in the 1841 Niger expedition earned for West Africa the title of 'the white man's grave'. Five out of six CMS missionaries died within a few weeks of landing at Lagos in 1894 and the sixth only survived for another year. A Baptist missionary, S. G. Pinnock, gave his own health record for five years (1888–93) as follows:

> *First year* – general health, good. Four fevers in the second half of the year. *Second year* – general health, good. One fever only in the course of the year. *Third year* – general health, good. One fever only. *Fourth year* – general health, excellent, and no fever. *Fifth year* – general health, poor. No fever; but a prolonged attack of dysentery, recovery being followed by a relapse, necessitating a change of climate.[2]

But it was not only Europeans who suffered. 'Disease,' wrote a colonial administrator in 1945, 'is the scourge enemy in Nigeria.' Malaria, venereal disease, the intestinal worms, leprosy and other skin troubles, yellow fever, smallpox, and oddly enough measles (in Nigeria a deadly disease), were the things that were holding back the country more than deficient education, communications, and wealth.[3]

For all that, the land of Nigeria was generously productive, yielding a wide range of cereals and fruit, and its exportable products soon came to be valued all over the rest of the world as the slave-trade declined – cocoa, chiefly from the west; ground-nuts and cotton from the north; palm-oil and kernels from the south. Coal was discovered at Enugu in 1904 and coal-mining developed in that area, though chiefly for home consumption. Exports reached a total value of £16,800,000 by 1920, exceptionally high among British colonial territories in Africa at that time.

Railways were built extensively in the early years of the present century. A railway line from the mainland opposite Lagos reached Abeokuta in 1899 and Jebba on the Upper Niger, 300 miles from Lagos, in 1909. A northern line from Kano to Jebba was completed by 1911 and the final link made by the building of a bridge over the Niger in 1916. In the same year, on the eastern line, the first coal-trains from Enugu reached Port Harcourt. This line was later extended northwards from Enugu to join the Kano line at Minna in 1924. By the early 1940s Nigeria had over 2,000 miles of railway, and trains setting out on alternate days from Lagos, Kano and Port Harcourt met at Kaduna junction. Thus a journey which in 1900 took Bishop Tugwell and his mission party three months from Lagos had become a comfortable forty-eight hours by train.

At the beginning of the period 1910–42 the only roads were feeders to the railway, and as the tsetse fly ruled out the use of horses, travellers going north-ward from the coast mostly went on foot. 'Conditions were very harsh: much time was spent in so-called rest-houses; someone once said of them that they were seldom houses and never afforded rest.'[4] By 1938 there were nearly 4,000 miles of roads maintained by the Public Works Department and a further 20,000 miles maintained by native administrations. Lorries for commercial transport were by then beginning to compete with the railways especially on the Lagos-Ibadan road, and air travel was just beginning.[5]

The People

A tribal map shows these main groupings: Yoruba filling most of the area between the Niger and the western border of Nigeria: Hausa and Fulani covering all the western and central areas north of the Niger and Benue; Kanuri in the north-east corner adjoining Lake Chad; Ibo over a comparatively small but heavily populated area east of the lower Niger, with Ibibio to the south-east towards Calabar; Nupe across the upper Niger as it curves west below Bida; and Tiv across, but mostly to the south of the Benue. Population figures for these groups at the end of our period (1942) were, in broad figures: Hausa, 3½ million; Ibo and Yoruba, just over 3 million; Fulani, over 2 million; Kanuri, 1 million; Ibibio, ¾ million; Tiv, ½ million. Smaller groups included several hundred thousand Ijaw in the Niger delta and coastal areas to the west of it and Efik on the Cameroon border. The word 'tribe', implying a language-race identity, is out of favour nowadays among ethnologists and its use in relation to Nigeria could be particularly misleading. 'The great human groups, such as the Yoruba, the Ibo, or the Hausa are linguistic and cultural rather than racial, and indeed each may contain a variety of racial strains.'[6] The Ibo and Ibibio of the south-east have little in common except their languages. The Yoruba form 'a linguistic group with much cultural but no political unity, divided into some twenty-five kingdoms with populations varying from twenty-five thousand to nearly half a million'. The 'Hausa states' of the north, dating from the (European) medieval era, have been ruled since the beginning of the nineteenth century by Fulani emirs, following the Muslim revival and subsequent conquests inspired by Usuman Dan Fodio (died 1817). Again there are great differences between the placid 'Cow-Fulani' and the Fulani of the towns who tended to develop the kind of Muslim fanaticism exhibited by Dan Fodio.

The linguistic-cultural unity of the Yoruba is no less historically conditioned than that of the Hausa states, though myth plays a larger part in it. There was once a vast Yoruba empire between the Gold Coast and the Niger which looked to Ile Ife as its centre. By the eighteenth century, in a much-contracted area, the Alafin of Oyo had become the holder of political power among the Yoruba. Thus although their kinship-lineage structure is immensely complicated, 'all the millions of the Yoruba could regard Ife as the sacred house of their first founder, Oduduwa, and a million or more could look to the Alafin as the lineal descendent of his son Oranyah'.[7] The history of the Ibo and other groups in the south-east remains extremely obscure and, before the colonial period, they had no cities comparable to the northern Muslims or the Yoruba.

> The only really functioning social unit was the group of kindred families, containing up to a few hundred persons and called in official language, not very accurately, a village. Above this could be discerned a number of such kindreds, officially called a village-group, or, far less appropriately, a town.

Such larger groups 'might claim a common ancestor and might share a common market place and combine for defence, but that was usually . . . all they had of unity. Indeed, they were not seldom at war with each other and the only really certain mark of their community was that they would not eat each other'. And yet it was the 'apparently backward Ibo, spurred on by poverty and over-crowding [who] made an immense contribution to the material development of Nigeria, not only in their own Region, but elsewhere, and especially in the north'.[8] And in response to Christian proclamation it was 'the relatively unorganized Ibo and Ibibio of the South-East and the pagans of the Middle Belt' who proved 'more receptive than the closely-knit and more traditionalist society of the Yoruba'.[9]

From Exploration to Colonial Rule

'The European exploration of inner Africa was in large measure yet another manifestation of the humanitarian movement which was attacking the slave trade and seeking to put Christianity and legitimate commerce in its place.'[10] As the colonial fever among European powers rose to its height in Africa, George Taubman, (Sir George Goldie from 1901) found political support for his United Africa Company (1879) and its successor the Royal Niger Company (1886) which kept the Niger open for British trade. By an international treaty (the Berlin Act, 1885) the European powers agreed that the Niger with all its connected waterways should be open to all nations: but it also recognized Britain's suzerainty over the whole coastal area of the present Nigeria. All of it apart from the small Lagos colony was at first called the Oil Rivers Protectorate, and then from 1893 the Niger Coast Protectorate. Sir Gilbert Carter, as Governor of Lagos, made treaties with the rulers of Abeokuta and Ibadan and, by 1896, the whole of Yoruba territory east of a boundary defined by agreement with the French came under the care of the Lagos Colonial Government. In 1900 the Niger Coast Protectorate was renamed the Protectorate of Southern Nigeria and was transferred from the Foreign Office to the Colonial Office with Sir Ralph Moor as high commissioner. In the same year the Royal Niger Company's charter was withdrawn and Northern Nigeria was declared a protectorate with Col. Frederick Lugard (KCMG in 1901) as the first high commissioner. Six years later the southern protectorate was united with the colony of Lagos. In 1912 Lugard returned to Nigeria after six years as Governor of Hong Kong, and in 1914 the northern and southern Nigerian governments were united, though not strictly speaking amalgamated, under Lugard as governor-general (1914–18). The title was peculiar to Lugard himself and not accorded to the governors who succeeded him.[11]

Lugard was one of the greatest of British colonial administrators, and his best years were given in service to Nigeria. For the story of those years and the scope of his achievement the reader is referred to Dr Margery Perham's *Lugard: the Years of Authority* (Collins, 1960). 'His physique allowed him to do two men's work in a climate and in conditions which halved the capacities of most men.' He is remembered, perhaps too well remembered, as the architect of the 'indirect rule' of the Hausa states, which in its outworking virtually barred the door to missionaries in the 'true' north of Nigeria for many years; but Lugard was above all a sensitive administrator and the northern policy, which missionaries deplored and sought to circumvent, was, as Dr Perham's book makes clear, to a large extent a romantically insensitive application of Lugard's ideas, worked out by a Lieutenant Governor, C. F. Temple, and backed by the Colonial Office against the more mature and more flexible judgment of Lugard himself, and much to his annoyance. Given the huge extent of territory which in 1900 he was called upon to govern, and the meagreness of the resources in money and personnel with which he was expected to do so, there was really no alternative to his plan 'to retain the native authority and to work through and by the native emirs', yet with the hope of bringing them 'gradually into approximation with our ideas of justice and humanity'.

He called his chief civil officers Residents, intending to imply thereby 'one who carries on diplomatic relations', but in areas less well organized than the Hausa states he expected Residents to be a good deal more than diplomats.[12] It is a common criticism of Lugard, and one to which Dr Perham allows some justice, that in seeking as governor-general to apply the principles of indirect rule to the Yoruba states and the extremely complex and confused social structures of the south-east of Nigeria, he underestimated the difference between south and north. But he never flagged in his attempt to find the true leaders among the eastern peoples of Nigeria; and his reluctance to give opportunities of political advancement to the educated Yoruba is at least understandable in the light of his love for the north and his conviction that 'it would be unjust to place under their control the interior tribes, who themselves have a right to a measure of self-rule'.[13]

For the same reason, and because he thought the governor-general should be free of day to day routine, Lugard rejected proposals for several large provinces, and retained the broad division between north and south with a lieutenant governor responsible for each. He kept the small, wholly official executive council common to British colonial administrations of this period; but he reduced the legislative council (extended in 1906 to represent the whole of southern Nigeria) to its former status as the legislature of Lagos colony. Instead he established a Nigerian council composed of the chief officials with six nominated Africans, three from the north and three from the south.[14] His successor as governor, Sir Hugh Clifford (1919–25), restored the wider scope of the legislative council in 1922, with nineteen 'unofficials', including ten Africans, in a total membership of forty. The 1922 constitution lasted for twenty-five years, though the number of 'unofficials' in the legislative council was slightly increased. The main public services, which had hitherto been separately organized for northern and southern Nigeria, were mostly assimilated during the governorship of Sir Donald Cameron (1931–5). It was not until 1942, at the end of our period, that the first Nigerian took his seat in the executive council, but the process of 'Africanization' was rapid after the second world war. Nigeria received independence on 1st October, 1960, and in 1963 became a republic within the British Commonwealth.

The Christian Missions in Retrospect, 1841–1910

The story of the first phase of modern missionary enterprise in Nigeria has been told with great insight and a wealth of detail by Professor J. F. A. Ajayi in *Christian Missions in Nigeria 1841–1891*. Taking as his starting point the Niger expedition of 1841 and ending with the death of Bishop Adjai Crowther, he describes this 'seedling' time as one in which the missions had a greater measure of initiative than under British colonial rule later. 'Their work had its own decisive influence. Things had not "fallen apart".'[15]

The first five societies to enter the country were (giving their commonly accepted entry dates and first locations) the Wesleyan Methodist Missionary Society (Badagry, 1842); the Church Missionary Society (Badagry, 1845); the Foreign Missionary Committee of the United Free Church of Scotland (Calabar, 1846); the Foreign Missionary Committee of the Southern Baptist Convention, USA (Ijaye, 1853) and the Roman Catholic Society of African Missionaries (Lagos, 1867). All of them could claim that they were invited to come by Africans – the Baptists and Presbyterians indirectly by Africans in the West Indies or on the American mainland whose homeland it was; the Methodists and Anglicans by direct invitation from liberated slaves who had recently returned to their Yoruba homes from Sierra Leone; and the Roman Catholics to minister to African emigrants from Brazil and Cuba who had settled in and around Lagos. All the missions, except the Presbyterians, were already at work in other parts of West Africa before entering Nigeria and the dominant position achieved by CMS in the early stages of missionary occupation in Nigeria can in part be explained by this. For the other societies their existing commitments elsewhere in the West Coast were still paramount, but in the outworking of Henry Venn's policy CMS administrative control in Sierra Leone was already passing in the 1850s to the Sierra Leone Native Pastorate Church. The Society was thus more free to concentrate in its new areas of mission in Yorubaland, on the Niger, and in the Niger delta. Another factor in the comparatively rapid advance of the CMS was the crippling effect of the American Civil War on the Southern Baptist mission and of the Franco-Prussian War on the Lyons-based Society of African Missionaries, and although the Wesleyan Methodists shared with CMS the advantage of Africans on their staff and existing immigrant congregations in close touch with their base in Sierra Leone, the heavy commitment of the WMMS in the Gold Coast meant that they were less well placed to build upon it.

In the west the Yoruba wars of the 1860s halted missionary expansion for a time, and the annexation of Lagos by the British government in 1861 made missionaries less welcome inland through fear of further annexations. When Henry Townsend, the CMS pioneer in Abeokuta, started putting up the walls of the first stone building there, the African authorities were persuaded only with difficulty that he was not building a fort; and in 1867 all missionaries were ejected from Abeokuta, and were unable to return there for nearly two decades.

In the last fifteen years or so of the nineteenth century British colonial rule was established over the whole of southern Nigeria. It provided the conditions for a rapid expansion of the established missions though with some deflection from their original purpose, if Professor Ajayi's thesis is to be accepted. New missionary groups also entered the country – notably the Qua Iboe mission west of Calabar and the Primitive Methodist mission among the Efik-speaking people on the Akwayafe River.

Although the concentration of missionary effort had so far been in the south, 'it was the Niger-Benue waterway that first attracted them to the country, and the North remained their lodestar'.[16] It was the challenge of the Muslim north that led to the founding of two interdenominational societies – the Sudan Interior Mission (1893) and the Sudan United Mission (1902–4). One of the three Canadian pioneers of the SIM, Walter Gowans, almost reached Zaria but he died at Girku, thirty miles to the south of it, in 1894. In 1902 H. K. W. Kimm (SUM) opened a mission station on the Bauchi plateau. The CMS had been looking northwards for some years. Crowther's intention in accompanying the 1857 Niger expedition had been to travel overland from the upper reaches of the Niger to Sokoto; but the wreck of the steamer *Dayspring* near Jebba postponed expansion northwards. In 1890 Graham Wilmot Brooke (leader of the CMS Upper Niger mission) and J. A. Robinson intended to work north-wards from a base at Lokoja, but their unhappy involvement in questions of discipline within the Niger mission delayed their plans. Robinson died in 1891, and Brooke in 1892. In 1900 a CMS party led by Herbert Tugwell left Lagos with the intention of settling missionaries in the northern Hausa states. The project had been prepared with great care in view of previous disappointments. Three members of the party had spent a year in Tripoli studying the Hausa language. On their first visit they were well received by the Emir of Zaria, but the im-mediate hostility shown by the Emir of Kano affected him also. Settlement in either town was ruled out and after a year at Girku, the remaining members of the party were compelled to return to Lokoja. One of their company, J. C. Dudley Ryder, died at Girku and another, Dr Walter Miller, became desperately ill. Miller was, however, allowed to return to Girku in 1902 and in 1905 to Zaria itself. By that time the government policy of excluding missionaries from the Muslim areas of the northern protectorate had developed, but there were still vast areas of the north which Islam had scarcely penetrated, and where missionaries were not discouraged. The Cambridge University Missionary Party, soon affiliated to the CMS, began work at Panyam (1907) and Kabwir (1910) in the Bauchi highlands, among the Sura and Angas peoples.

In Nigeria, as in Uganda, the expansion of the church owed much to African initiative, both lay and clerical. The most notable example of this was the founding of churches in the Niger delta under Bishop Crowther's leadership; but the Methodist centre at Shagamu, forty-five miles north-east of Lagos, was the fruit of lay evangelism. The mission to Ijebu-Ode, some fifteen miles further on, was organized by the Anglican Lagos Pastorate under the leadership of Sierra Leone clergy, and resulted in a Christian community which soon out-grew that of Lagos itself. Charles Phillips, later to become Assistant Bishop on the Niger, was the pioneer around Ondo of what became a thriving Anglican church.[17] For Crowther, education and evangelism were inseparable; he opened mission schools at Abeokuta in the early days there and later at Bonny and Brass in the Delta in the 1860s.

Abeokuta was the first main centre of mission for both Anglicans and Methodists but by the later 1850s it was yielding place to Lagos, in spite of Henry Townsend's vigorous championship. Lagos grammar school was started by T. B. Macaulay, a 'Sierra Leonean', in 1859: the CMS girls' school (at first known as 'the Female Institution') in 1872; and the Methodist boys' high school in 1879. In the early 1880s two more schools were started in Lagos – the Roman Catholic St Gregory's College and the Baptist Academy. None of them in their early years was strictly a secondary school. Professor Ajayi describes them as 'no more than senior primary schools'; but they were foundations on which a secondary education could be built.[18]

Missionaries in Nigeria were known at first as the 'book people' and translation of the Bible and other Christian literature had an important place in their strategy of evangelism. Africans and Europeans of the different missions worked at it together. Thomas Jefferson Bowen, the Baptist missionary, produced a Yoruba grammar and dictionary that were widely used. S. A. Crowther and Thomas King were the chief translators of the Bible and Prayer Book into Yoruba, and Crowther was given an Oxford Doctorate of Divinity in the year of his consecration as bishop for his translation work. David Hinderer, the first CMS missionary in Ibadan, produced a Yoruba translation of *Pilgrim's Progress*. F. J. Schön, who accompanied Crowther on the 1841 expedition, was an accomplished linguist. He produced a grammar of the Hausa language in 1862. J. C. Taylor, a 'Sierra Leonean' Ibo and pioneer missionary of the CMS in Onitsha from 1857, took over from Crowther the task of translating the New Testament into Ibo, completing it in 1866. Translators are not always tolerant of each other's work, and Schön's criticism of Taylor's effort so upset him that he returned to Sierra Leone soon afterwards. The outstanding achievements of W. R. S. Miller and T. J. Dennis in the field of translation will be noted later.

A Change of Temper

It is now widely accepted that there was a change in missionary attitudes in the 1880s and 1890s. It led, among other things, to a denigration of African leadership and the assumption, or resumption, of European control in the churches. It was quite foreign to the spirit and temper of the pioneer days. This thesis has been stated most forcefully by Dr J. B. Webster in his book *African Churches among the Yoruba, 1882–1922*.

The purge of the Niger Mission [he writes] undertaken by G. W. Brooke and J. A. Robinson in 1890, which resulted in discrediting the Sierra Leonean clergy, was more than simply directed against the African agency. Brooke and Robinson were convinced that the whole missionary approach to the heathen was wrong. They sought to change the traditional West Coast missionary method.[19]

In a more general context, but referring to the same period, Dr Ajayi notes that European missionaries 'were beginning to see themselves as rulers, and the word "native" was acquiring a new and sinister meaning'.[20] He sees this attitude as something new at the end of the century, quite different from the earlier protests made by Townsend at the proposed ordination of two 'Sierra Leonean' catechists in 1854, and by Townsend and other missionaries at Venn's announced intention to seek Crowther's consecration as bishop in 1864.

Acceptance, however qualified, of the fact of some change of attitude among European missionaries to their African colleagues seems unavoidable. It was not confined to Nigeria or to the West African coast. The causes of it are complex. A comprehensive list of them is likely to include: (1) The dissemination in the missionary 'home-bases' of Europe and America of the views of anthropologists at that time about the intrinsic inferiority of Africans. (2) The sense of commanding superiority engendered by Britain's industrial and imperial achievements, and by the no less striking achievement of the North Americans within their own vast territories. (3) The effect of missionary propaganda which, without any such conscious intention, prepared the minds of readers of missionary magazines for the African's 'failure' by its pictures of the utter degradation of his life in the unconverted state. (4) The deep-rooted fear of 'nakedness' evident in the clothes and furnishings and architecture of late Victorian England. (5) The disappointment experienced by the first generation of missionaries in having failed to convert the existing *élite* of West Africa, the kings and chiefs. (6) The recoil of a new, confident generation of Europeans – traders and administrators as well as missionaries – from the Africanization policy of their predecessors. (The change of attitude in CMS central leadership after Venn's thirty-one years as Secretary of the Society may be seen as an example of this.) (7) The increasing recruitment of missionaries from the English upper-middle class, trained in the new public schools and the reformed universities of Oxford and Cambridge. (8) The shaping of their spirituality by the 'second evangelical awakening' in the latter half of the nineteenth century. (9) The fight-back by Africans – rulers, traders, clergy and mission agents – against European assumptions of superiority which in turn provoked a desire in Europeans to 'put them in their place' and prove their limitations as leaders.

Discussion no doubt will continue about the items to be included in any list of causes for this change of temper, and about the precise timing of it; but the evidence for it, at least in terms of a new wariness and distrust between Europeans and Africans, is unhappily very widespread. The crisis in the CMS Niger mission, culminating in Archdeacon Crowther's repudiation, after his father's death, of any CMS authority over the Niger Delta Pastorate Church, was not an isolated event in one mission, explicable in terms of the tensions and misunderstanding which prepared it. Actual secessions, going far beyond anything that happened on the Niger, gravely weakened the Yoruba church associated with the CMS mission, and its counterparts in the Baptist and

Methodist mission churches. By 1921 the African Church Movement had become the second largest denomination in western Nigeria. Repudiation of European leadership on so wide a front requires the kind of explanation Webster has attributed to the African churches themselves. They maintain, he writes,

> that they are the fulfilment of missionary policies pursued in the middle nineteenth century. They were brought into being as a revolt against new policies and practices introduced by the missions to meet the situation created by the penetration, partition, and subjugation of Africa by imperial European forces.[21]

Since this movement reached its peak in the early 1920s, during the period with which we are particularly concerned, a brief account of it is appropriate here.

The African Church Movement

Although dividing lines should not be drawn too sharply, two main types of African-led churches or Christian groups emerged in Nigeria between 1888 and 1925. Groups in which the main motive was to become free of European dominance were: The Native Baptist Church, 1888; The United Native African Church (UNA), 1891, sometimes known as the 'minor secession'; The African Church (AC), 1901, the 'major secession'; The West African Episcopal Church (WAE), 1903; and the United African Methodist (Elijah) Church, 1917. All five were based on Lagos, and all broke away from major denominational churches in which European missionary leadership had re-asserted itself at the expense of African leadership. For example, the appointment of European bishops (J. S. Hill in 1893, and Herbert Tugwell in 1894) to succeed the African Bishop Crowther was much resented, the more so as they were given a wider jurisdiction, as Bishops of Western Equatorial Africa, than Crowther was ever allowed to exercise. The appointment of an African, James Johnson, as an *assistant* bishop on the Niger in 1900 added to a resentment in which Johnson openly shared. He refused the appointment three times and finally accepted only on the condition that he could initiate a West African Bishopric Endowment Fund, at the time of his consecration, to prepare for the appointment of an African *diocesan* bishop. In the same way, in the Methodist and Baptist churches, Africans were replaced in senior positions by Europeans, from the 1880s onwards. The Baptist group in 1914 re-entered the Yoruba Baptist Association. The other four remained separate though, from about the same time (1914–22), there was a school of thought in their leadership which favoured a gradual return to the position of the missionary societies on polygamy. There was, however, another school of thought, vigorously led by J. K. Coker, which 'yearned to embed Christianity in a polygamous society'. The 'African Communion' which Coker initiated in 1913 brought some degree of unity to the secessionist churches, though this unity remained precarious. Apart from the toleration of polygamy, these groups remained basically orthodox and deeply attached to the traditions and practices learned from the missionaries in their parent denominations; and, as J. B. Webster has shown, their attitude to polygamy varied, according to the social background of the group, from a mere toleration in UNA to strong advocacy in WAE, which forbade 'foreign marriage'.[22] The issue of polygamy led to a further split among Baptist churches in 1938, although after two decades of separation the majority of the defecting churches returned to fellowship in the Baptist Convention in 1961.

The African churches were by no means all static splinter-groups. The African Church (1901) came nearest to being so. It was composed largely of second-generation Egba Christians, and half its clergy in 1920 had been ordained in the mission from which they had separated. J. K. Coker called them, unkindly, 'old parrots of the Anglican Church'.[23] But UNA had a considerable proportion of direct converts among its members by 1920, and WAE claimed at that time that out of its 4,000 members less than two hundred were formerly members of other churches. 'Our policy,' said one of its leaders, 'is to go among the heathen and find our own members.' Thus the African churches grew by direct evangelism as well as by a continuing drift away from the 'missionary' churches.

In 1921 their total membership in Southern Nigeria was recorded as 100,000 out of a Christian community of 500,000. Their claim to be continuing the Christian mission in African terms deserved to be taken seriously.

The second main type of African church, usually known as a 'prophet' church, was more exotic and more heterodox than those so far named. The chief bodies in this group, founded between 1915 and 1925, were: The Garrick Braid Church and The Christ Army Church (1916); The Christ Apostolic Church (1918); The Cherubim and Seraphim Society (1925); and The Church of the Lord (1925). The founder of the first two was Garrick Sokari Braid, a pastor of the Niger Delta (Anglican) Church. He claimed to be the second Elijah, and said things about an imminent end of the power of the white man which, combined with other actions and attitudes, earned him a prison sentence. Braid's movement was in part a protest against the continued dominance in the Niger Delta Church of 'foreign' Sierra Leonean clergy. Bishop Johnson was at first impressed by his zeal against idolatry, his emphasis on prayer, and his gift as a healer, and saw the movement with its 'mixture of good and evil' as calling for 'a thorough overhauling of our work in every one of its departments'.[24] In 1916 some of the clergy of the Niger Delta Church were disciplined by the church board for association with Braid, and he founded the Christ Army Church. He died in 1918, and some of his following continued to use his name. In the 1921 census the total membership of the Garrick Braid groups was given as 43,000, mostly in Owerri and Calabar provinces.

The Christ Apostolic Church was founded by Joseph B. Shadare, a member of the synod of the Anglican diocese of Lagos. During the devastating influenza epidemic of 1918, Shadare started a prayer-group which developed a little later into the Precious Stone Society. It stressed healing through prayer as a pentecostal gift and it rejected infant baptism. After being censured by the Bishop of Lagos at the 1922 diocesan synod, Shadare detached his followers from the Anglican Church and sought affiliation with the Faith Tabernacle, Philadelphia, USA. Other leaders associated with the *aladura* ('prayer-people') were Isaac B. Akinyele from Ibadan, also a prominent Anglican, who started a prayer-group in his house in 1925: and Joseph Babalola, who began preaching in and around Ibadan in 1929. Under his leadership the *aladura* movement spread rapidly in Yorubaland in the early 1930s. The founder of the Church of the Lord, Josiah Olunowo Oshitelu, was a first generation Christian, who had psychic experiences from his childhood onwards. He became an Anglican catechist and in 1925, when he was about twenty-three, he had visions which directed him to preach judgment on idolatry and native medicines; and to practise faith-healing and baptism by the Holy Spirit. He was suspended by the Anglican synod in 1926 and for a time joined the other *aladura* leaders in Ibadan. The first centre of the Church of the Lord (July 1930) was at Ogere, thirty miles or so east of Abeokuta. It spread widely in the next two decades as far north as Kano and along the coast to Ghana, Liberia and Sierra Leone. In the 1960s Oshitelu, as 'Primate and Founder', was still vigorously leading it.[25]

The Cherubim and Seraphim Society was founded by Moses Orimolade Tunolashe and a girl-medium, Christiana Abiodun Akinsowan. It split in 1929, and by the 1960s there were over two hundred separate groups.

The general features of the prophet group of African churches have been summarized as follows: (1) local autonomy; (2) biblical preaching of a funda-mentalist character; (3) a tendency to syncretism with Islam and traditional West African religion; (4) integration of religion with everyday life and stress on the ministry of healing.[26] Like the 'church-order' secessionist churches mentioned earlier, the 'prophet churches' caused a good deal of anxiety and heart-searching among the European missionary leaders. Bishop Melville Jones of Lagos, in his diocesan synod in May 1931, spoke thus of them:

> Such movements are generally begun by some earnest spirit with little education and a not very balanced grasp of the truth. At first they did not attempt to draw people away from our churches, but later on they have endeavoured to get sites for building their own churches, and even to take our churches from us.

It is unfair, perhaps, to take one statement out of context but comments on the 'prophet movement' in missionary letters tend to run on the same lines – the threat to the church, its congregations, and its buildings, with little understanding of the roots of the African protest that found expression in such movements. Similar things were said about the separatist movements in East Africa in the 1920s by leading missionaries, but Nigeria seems to have lacked an interpreter of the calibre of Archdeacon W. E. Owen.

Comity and the Search for Unity

Some writers about Nigeria give the impression that the various missionary bodies were at loggerheads with each other, but CMS records for the period 1910 to 1942 do not support this picture. Of course in Nigeria, as elsewhere at the time, there was a great gulf between the evangelical and the Roman Catholic missions, and the possibility of any sort of fellowship with the African Church Movement does not appear to have been contemplated; but among themselves the Anglican, Methodist, Presbyterian and Baptist missionaries behaved for the most part towards each other with brotherly affection, as those who shared in a common, God-given task. Michael Marioghae and John Ferguson give a number of illustrations of this co-operative spirit from the early days of the missions:

When Henry Townsend of CMS arrived in 1842, Freeman, a Methodist, was there to welcome him, to guide him, to give him practical help. Hope Waddell consulted with the Baptists at Fernando Po before establishing the Presbyterian Mission at Calabar in 1846. Later Samuel Bill stayed with the Presbyterians at Calabar before launching out into Qua Iboe territory. The pioneers of SIM and SUM took careful note of the experiences of CMS, and pushed out themselves into areas where no Christian work was being done at all. What is more, as early as 1905 . . . leaders of the Church of Scotland, the Niger Delta Pastorate and CMS met in Calabar. . . . From that meeting can be dated the real beginning of the movement towards Church unity in Nigeria.[27]

The informal conversations of 1905 were followed by a series of further conferences at two-yearly intervals in which Primitive Methodist and Qua Iboe representatives also joined. At the 1911 conference discussion covered such matters as education, conditions of church membership, and the attitude of the missions to African customs. One of the Calabar hosts of the conference, A. W. Wilkie, spoke prophetically of their common task:

We are not here primarily to establish in Africa Presbyterianism or Methodism or any other -ism, but to *Preach Christ*, and to take a lowly place, under the guidance of the Spirit of God, in laying the foundations of a church which shall not be foreign to the African.[28]

At another Calabar inter-mission conference in 1919 Dr J. T. Dean pointed forward to the goal of a united church in Nigeria. In 1923 an Evangelical Union was formed in the Eastern Region. The four missions were all reaching northwards towards the River Benue and the annual meetings of the union helped to ensure that they did so in partnership rather than as competitors. In the west, as early as 1911, the CMS and WMMS agreed to form a 'federal council' to prevent overlapping and to regulate baptisms, and they invited the Baptist mission to join them. Four years later the Anglican and Baptist missions consulted about new sites in and around Ilorin.[29]

In 1930 the Christian Council of Nigeria was formed to determine the policy of churches and missions (excluding matters of doctrine and denominational church order); to foster unity with the world church and the International Missionary Council; and to speak and act together on all matters affecting Christianity in Nigeria. Regional committees of the council were formed for the eastern, western and northern regions. The council brought into fellowship, with the bodies that had already become accustomed to meeting in the Calabar conferences, the Wesleyan Methodists and American Baptists whose work was largely confined to western Nigeria. The Salvation Army and the Sudan United Mission also joined later in the 1930s.

The impetus towards church unity owed much to a series of conferences of a group called 'Senior African Agents' who were African delegates of the eastern regional committee of the council. At their 1931 conference this group pleaded for more prayer and instruction about Christian unity; for an agreed statement on Christian doctrine; for a central church in each town; for a common name and catechism; and for inter-church visitation and exchange of pulpits. Two years later the eastern regional committee formed a church union committee under the leadership of the Rev. S. H. Childs, principal of the CMS training college at Awka, and with the enthusiastic support of the Rev. A. C. Onyeabo, who later became Assistant Bishop in the Niger diocese. The South India scheme of church union was taken as a model, and the committee issued a draft basis of union in 1937. The Methodists and Presbyterians of the eastern region were ready to go ahead with a united church for that region alone, but the Anglican delegates of the Niger diocese made it clear that they could not separate themselves in a union scheme from their fellow-Anglicans of the diocese of Lagos. The second world war delayed progress in negotiations and it was not until 1947 that an all-Nigeria conference on church unity could be held, at Onitsha. As in East Africa, not all the churches that shared in the fellowship of the Christian council found it possible to contract together for organic union; but the Anglicans, Methodists and Presbyterians worked together through the various stages of revision and the necessary approvals of their parent churches to the point of naming a date for the inauguration of a united church of Nigeria – 11th December 1965. Unfortunately last minute difficulties prevented union at that time.

The Growth of the Church

During the period 1910–42 a number of missions entered Nigeria for the first time. They included the Dutch Reformed Church mission in 1911 among the Tiv people around the River Benue; the Danish (Lutheran) Society in 1913 among the Bachuma; the Salvation Army (1920) in Lagos, and many other towns subsequently; the Church of the Brethren in Bornu Province from 1922; and the Lutheran Synod Conference of North America from 1936.

The period of most rapid expansion for the well-established missions was in the period immediately before and during the first world war. In an article in *The Church Missionary Review*, January 1918, significantly entitled 'The Mass Movement in Nigeria', the Rev G. T. Basden gave comparative figures for church growth in southern Nigeria, for the CMS Yoruba and Niger missions, the Niger Delta Pastorate, the United Free Church of Scotland, Qua Iboe, Wesleyan Methodist, and Primitive Methodist missions. They showed a baptized church membership in 1916 of almost 79,000 compared with under 26,000 in 1906. Statistics based on baptized membership are distorted during this period by the drift away to the 'African churches'; and the figures Basden gives for those 'under definite instruction' are also distorted by the monogamy rule in the mission churches. Many listed under this head would still be lifelong catechumens who never went forward to baptism. For all that, the figures indicate a rapid advance in all the main churches of eastern Nigeria – Anglican, Presbyterian, Primitive Methodist and Qua Iboe. In the west the church associated with the CMS Yoruba mission remained by far the largest in the country, more than doubling its baptized membership in these ten years (1906–16), from 21,709 to 51,826.[30]

In their valuable study, *Church Growth in Central and Southern Nigeria*, John B. Grimley and Gordon E. Robinson fill in the details for the inter-war years. The most rapid advance in the 1920s and 1930s was in the 'central belt' of the country. This belt was included, administratively, in the northern region but most of the ethnic groups living in it were neither Hausa-speaking nor Muslim. The missions most active in this region were the Sudan United Mission, the Sudan Interior Mission, and the Church of the Brethren, but most of the denominations were reaching northwards into this area, from the eastern and western regions. Robinson's figures for southern Nigeria, given in terms of communicants or of full church membership, show an actual decline among the Wesleyan Methodists from 1925; a slower growth-rate for churches associated with CMS missions: and a continuing and rapid advance for the American Baptists, the Primitive Methodists and Presbyterians. The most rapid growth was in the Qua Iboe Church – from 245 communicants in 1911 to 41,738 in 1938.[31]

Social Problems

1. Polygamy

A CMS missionary writing in 1923 described polygamy as 'universal throughout pagan and Mohammedan Nigeria';[32] and, as we have seen, the right to continue this traditional form of African marriage was by that time claimed by 100,000 members of the 'African Church' movement. Though hard-pressed, the 'missionary churches' stood firm against polygamy. In 1857 Henry Venn, persuaded by intensive Bible study on the question that the practice was unscriptural, issued a memorandum of guidance for CMS missions. He was clear that polygamists should not be accepted into the membership of the church. The Lambeth Conference of Anglican Bishops in 1888 confirmed Venn's ruling in its opinion 'that persons living in polygamy be not admitted to baptism', but with two qualifications: first that polygamists could be accepted as candidates for baptism and kept under Christian instruction 'until such time as they shall be in a position to accept the law of Christ'; and second, that wives of polygamists 'may be admitted in some cases to baptism', but that it must be left to the local authorities of the church to decide under what circumstances they may be baptized.[33] The Methodist, Baptist, and Presbyterian missions followed the same course, excluding polygamists from church membership. One lonely voice, that of S. G. Pinnock, was raised in defence of Bishop Colenso's view that exclusion or inclusion was a local pastoral decision and that polygamists might, in certain circumstances, be baptized. After thirty years of effective service as a Baptist missionary in southern Nigeria, Pinnock was asked to resign unless he was prepared to make a definite stand on the exclusion of polygamists. He was not, and he resigned.

The use of excommunication as a disciplinary measure in the case of Christians who took more than one wife after being baptized was deplored by some missionaries. Walter Miller, the CMS pioneer in Zaria, wrote after his retirement: 'If the sacrament of Holy Communion is the highest expression of the love of Christ and His members, expulsion from it should surely never be used as a means of discipline.'[34] The ruling about the implications of monogamy was usually left to local decision in the spirit of the Lambeth resolutions of 1888, but it produced some agonizingly difficult problems. In 1910 the CMS Niger mission executive committee debated whether a polygamist on becoming a Christian might renounce all his wives and take a fresh one. It was decided, with one dissentient, that he might choose any one of his former wives but must not renounce them all in order to marry a new one. The dissentient, Archdeacon T. J. Dennis, was 'of the opinion that in the present state of affairs it is impossible to legislate on such points'.[35]

As the number of infant baptisms increased, the monogamous rule, cutting so deeply into traditional African social and economic structures, caused an almost intolerable strain on church life. In some congregations, where church order allowed some form of associate membership for polygamists, the number of those eligible to receive Holy Communion shrank to a minute proportion of the whole fellowship, in one case only twenty or thirty couples out of a congregation of a thousand members. A report published by the Christian Council of Nigeria in the 1960s quoted a report from one denomination that 'probably there is not a single Nigerian in a position of leadership in the denomination who has not been disciplined at some time for marital irregularities.'[36] As educated Africans became aware, by travel abroad or observation at home, of the extent of marital breakdowns and promiscuity in the monogamous societies of Europe and North America, some of the arguments commonly used against polygamy appeared to them to be tainted with hypocrisy – the argument, for example, that acceptance of polygamy led to a general lowering of moral standards. Increasing prosperity among church members, who formed the bulk of the emerging African middle-class in Nigeria, made the monogamy rule increasingly hard to maintain. A CMS missionary noted in 1923 that many of the most well-to-do Christians had become polygamists; the traders regarded wives as an investment and as a status-symbol.[37]

On the other hand there were many converts to Christianity who accepted monogamy, with its heavy personal demands, as part of the cost of discipleship. Archdeacon F. E. Wilcock preserved a typescript statement of one church member giving the story of his struggles and adversities in the search for acceptance as a full church member. It is worth quoting at length. In 1919 this young African was appointed a junior clerk to the Onitsha Native Court. On transfer to another court in 1920, feeling confident of his future career, he married two wives.

> Stopped from receiving Holy Communion [he wrote later] I used to be afraid of going near the Christians, for many had known me to be a zealous churchman. Not being a full member of the church created unhappiness in my soul. I started looking for somewhere else, to join myself to some other body; for I knew what would happen if I dared to go near the CMS people under that condition.

He approached a Roman Catholic priest who agreed to baptize his first (twin) children, 'but not any others, as I was a polygamist'. After a time in which he decided 'to go deep into worldly pleasure' and became an expert dancer, he was transferred to Nsukka as a court interpreter.

> Christ was clearly revealed to me there. . . . I decided to get back to my position as a full church member. I called my two faithful wives and told them of my intention to become a monogamist, whereby I can joyfully serve my God. I told them I had no intention to drive them away; that all we should do is jointly to call upon the Lord to work our ways so that we all might come into his fold at the same time. We all then started praying and singing every night, praising God for the new light.

When one of his twin daughters became ill, both his wives went to live with his mother for a time; and he was left alone for seven months. He told the missionary superintendent that he would like to remain unmarried but was told that 'these two wives of mine at home would still be counted as mine, even if they were to be sent to their parents; and that nobody would agree to marry them'. The daughter who had been taken ill died, and he took one of his wives to the Enugu-Inyi Training Home and the other to the Enugu-Ngwo Training Home

> to learn more about Christ and to be separate. I told the superintendent that I had given up my wives. I was then restored to a full member. Though I was

glad for having my name put in the Class Register once again, yet I was still carrying a burden because the two women still had no better position.

In the end he decided to take back as his one wife 'the one that had not been thoroughly converted', and he wrote to the other telling her that the fault was entirely his: that her acceptance of the situation would 'secure a good place for us all in heaven and would be the means of turning some misled people to God'. The Christian marriage to the chosen wife took place in 1929, and in 1930 the rejected one married someone else. 'After her marriage peace, which I had never experienced in my life, was brought to my heart.'[38]

A conviction supported by such experiences as this in all the monogamous churches, led the Nigerian Scheme of Church Union to declare: 'The Church of Nigeria holds that marriage is by Divine institution an indissoluble, exclusive, and lifelong union and partnership between one man and one woman.'

2. The Liquor Traffic

By the end of the nineteenth century the importation of 'trade spirits', especially gin, into Nigeria and the Gold Coast had increased alarmingly. The value of gin imports through Lagos, for example, had risen from £7,164 in 1874 to £47,629 in 1890.[39] The greater part of it went up-country and was consumed by the non-Muslim African population. Appalled by the demoralizing effects of spirit-drinking among Red Indians and Pacific islanders, the leading European colonial powers took concerted action to control the liquor trade in tropical Africa. The Brussels General Act of 1890 recommended the gradual prohibition of the import of trade spirits between 20° North Latitude and 22° South Latitude. This period was one in which concern for drunkenness in Britain found expression in 'temperance societies' of various kinds. These had a large membership in common with the supporters of missionary societies; for evangelical Christians there was a close link between overseas missions and 'temperance', and propaganda for the suppression of the liquor traffic in West Africa found a ready response. Bishop Tugwell was prominent among the missionary leaders who kept this issue before the British public, and he found an unexpected ally in Sir Frederick Lugard. In 1898, before his appointment as High Commissioner for the Northern Nigeria Protectorate, Lugard extracted a promise from Joseph Chamberlain that the prohibition of the liquor traffic in the north should be retained. In the south control was more difficult. It became, through a high import duty, a major source of revenue and commercial interests were strongly entrenched in its defence. A government *Inquiry into the Liquor Trade in Southern Nigeria* (Cd. 4906, 1909) found no evidence of demoralization resulting from imported spirits, but an editorial in the *Missionary Record* of the United Free Church of Scotland noted the 'disproportionate prominence' given in the report 'to what is favourable to the maintenance of the liquor traffic, and disproportionate pains taken to discredit points in the evidence led against it'.[40]

Lugard was far away governing Hong Kong at the time when the report was published, but when he returned to Nigeria in 1912 he took further steps to control the liquor trade. He raised the duty on trade spirits from 5s 6d a gallon in 1913 to 10s in 1918 while at the same time reducing the spirit content of imported gin. In 1917 he introduced a comprehensive Liquor Ordinance which strengthened the enforcement of the existing prohibitions in the northern and part of the southern provinces. The ordinance also imposed a licensing system and made local distillation illegal. Lugard's strong action as governor-general combined with the restriction on shipping during the first world war reduced the import of spirits drastically – from 4,500,000 gallons in 1913 to 269,000 in 1917. It was a courageous action for a colonial governor to take since it meant a huge loss of revenue (£700,000 in 1909 rising to nearly £1,000,000 in 1913); but he regarded it as a disgrace to an administration 'that the bulk of its Customs, and nearly half its revenue, should be derived from such a source. It was a sterile import, upon which the native wasted one and a half million sterling annually without securing any improvement in his standard of comfort or increasing his productive output'.[41] The test came after the war when shipping facilities were restored, but once Lugard had decided upon the rightness of a course of action he was not easily shaken; and he could count on the continuing support of missionaries and churches in Nigeria and the philanthropic lobby in Britain. Bishop Tugwell continued to use letters to *The Times* as a means of keeping the question before the British public. In a letter published on 19th April, 1919 the bishop described a meeting at Ijebu Ode some months previously at which 1,500 people had resolved that 'the declining liquor traffic be not re-established after the war . . . but that good and useful articles be introduced to take its place'.[42] Similar resolutions had been passed at meetings all over the southern provinces of Nigeria. The prohibitionists rejoiced when in 1919, by the Convention of St Germain-en-Laye, France and Britain prohibited the importation and sale of spirits in the African territories which were in their control. But the trade continued in a much reduced volume in Nigeria. In February 1929 a united conference of Protestant missionary societies, meeting at Port Harcourt, set up a commission on the liquor trade and in the same month the CMS Niger mission executive committee decreed that no baptized church member may sell foreign intoxicants. Churchmen who held liquor licences must allow them to lapse. In March 1930 the Christian Council of Nigeria expressed its concern about the granting of licences and the need for greater publicity to be given to application for licences.

3. House-rule and Domestic Slavery

It was one thing to end the export of slaves. As the consuls of the early days of British interest in Nigeria came to realize, it was quite another thing to end internal slave-raiding and slave-dealing in areas where the British navy could not operate. It meant in fact that a number of local wars of conquest had to be fought before the African rulers of southern Nigeria realized that British interest in this matter was not confined to slave-export. And when these wars were over, and the British administration was firmly though thinly established, the problem of slave-status remained to be solved.

As with the control of the liquor traffic, so with domestic slavery, the northern administration moved forward ahead of the southern. In 1900 Lugard named a date for the abolition of the legal status of domestic slavery in the northern protectorate. From the 1st April, 1901 no new slave could be made, no baby could be born into slavery, and no owner could recapture a slave who appealed to the courts. In the same year in the southern protectorate slave-trading was made a criminal offence, but a Native House-Rule Ordinance legalized domestic slavery within the limits of the house-system, including a recognition of the right of a chief to recapture slaves who were members of his house.

In their out-working the northern and southern policies were not so far apart. Slavery was deeply embedded in the Hausa social system, and Lugard was clear that any attempt to abolish it at one stroke would provoke rebellions on a scale far beyond the capacity of his administration to deal with. Residents in the northern provinces were instructed to discourage chiefs and emirs from rapid and wholesale emancipation. Lugard saw clearly that the transfer to wage-labour must be made gradually in co-operation with the emirs if forced labour was to be avoided; and he was determined that it should be avoided. But on the basis of his proclamation of 1900 he was able 'to stiffen up his legislation and its execution, and also to suppress almost entirely slave-raiding and slave-dealing – two evils which admitted of no compromise'.[43]

In southern Nigeria the 'House' system was a complicated social organism and its immediate abolition was judged by the southern administration as too difficult to attempt with the forces at its disposal. During centuries of trading with Europeans at first with slaves and later with palm-oil, the coast chiefs had collected around them 'hundreds and in some places, thousands, of supporters and slaves who worked to produce food, manned the canoes, and went inland to collect the trade goods, human or vegetable, for shipment at the coast'.[44] Dr K. O. Dike, an Ibo historian, described the House as 'at once a co-operative trading unit and a local government institution'.[45] But the House Rule Ordinance of 1901 was regarded by many missionaries as a shameful confession of weakness on the part of the protectorate government; and they could count on powerful support, in any case of house slavery which they referred home to England, from the Anti-Slavery Society and the Aborigines Protection Society.

In September 1911 a CMS missionary at Patani, the Rev. H. Proctor, wrote to the parent committee about two men from Brass who were preparing for ordination as deacons but who were held back by an ownership claim under the House system. His letter was forwarded by the Society to the committee of the Aborigines Protection Society, and Bishop Tugwell got in touch with the Archbishop of Canterbury, who in turn approached the Secretary of State for the Colonies.[46] In April 1913 Bishop Tugwell wrote from Bonny saying that he had heard rumours that some British residents, in conjunction with African chiefs, were seeking 'to provide cheap or forced labour under the shelter of House Rule Ordinance'. Two women church members had been put under a native court summons for £150 by a chief who claimed to be their owner. The bishop had written, he said, to the district commissioner but had received no reply. He had then approached the Colonial Secretary at Lagos. The secretary, Mr C. G. Boyle, took strong action. The claim made by the chief was dismissed; application for the summons and its issue by the clerk was repudiated; and the chief was reminded in open court that slavery had been abolished and that the use of the term 'slave' might incur legal action. The executive committee of the CMS Niger mission decided to send copies of the Colonial Secretary's letter reporting these actions to each superintendent missionary 'for the information of agents'.[47] In 1914 when Lugard became governor-general the House Rule Ordinance of 1901 was repealed, and legal support was withdrawn from the House system.

In southern Nigeria relations between missionaries and government officials were good for the most part but while slavery persisted in any form they could scarcely be cordial, at least from the missionary side. One CMS missionary wrote to the parent committee in 1910:

> There is a growing feeling that it is possible for Missionaries to be too passive about government affairs and that there are some occasions when action ought to be taken for righteousness' sake. It is felt to be much safer not to be on visiting terms with the officials generally, although there are exceptions.[48]

The repeal of the House Rule Ordinance in 1914 removed one of the severest points of tension. Missionaries and officials continued to work side by side, a little aloof from each other but respectful of each other's duties and hardships, and with a shared conviction that in bringing to West Africa the faith and the values most dear to themselves, they were spending their lives profitably.

The Diocese of Western Equatorial Africa, 1893–1921

Venn intended that S. A. Crowther's jurisdiction as bishop should cover the CMS Yoruba mission churches as well as those of the Niger mission but the outspoken opposition of Henry Townsend, and other senior CMS missionaries in the Yoruba mission, held up any arrangements for transfer during Crowther's episcopate.[49] After Bishop Crowther's death the CMS parent committee in 1892, for reasons of 'the present distress' (i.e. the repudiation by Archdeacon Crowther of the Society's authority over the Niger Delta Pastorate), recommended the appointment of an English bishop, and asked the Archbishop of Canterbury to include the Yoruba country in his jurisdiction. The committee at the same time minuted its desire to see African bishops, 'assistant or independent', in West Africa as early as possible. Archbishop Benson approved the Society's suggestion of Joseph Sidney Hill for nomination as bishop of a diocese now to be called 'Western Equatorial Africa', in which the Yoruba mission would be included. He appointed Hill as his commissary with a special commission to go to West Africa and to report in particular on the position of the new Delta Pastorate. Hill spent five months visiting mission stations in 1892–3. He returned to England with two African clergy, Charles Phillips and Isaac Oluwole, and presented them to the Archbishop for consecration, along with himself, as his assistant bishops. All three bishops were consecrated at St Paul's Cathedral on St Peter's Day, 1893. Following Bishop Hill's death on the 6th January, 1894, Herbert Tugwell was recalled from Nigeria by telegram and consecrated as Hill's successor on 4th March, 1894.[50]

Years later, in 1919, when plans for a division of the diocese were maturing, Bishop Oluwole recalled that Bishop Hill intended that he should have some measure of separate jurisdiction as an assistant bishop – a sphere in which the diocesan would not exercise episcopal functions directly and in which the assistant would give both Letters of Orders and Licences to the clergy and also ordain them. Bishop Hill, however, kept the issue of licences in his own hands, and Bishop Tugwell followed his policy without change. Tugwell, according to Melville Jones, did give Bishop Oluwole some special territorial responsibility 'for certain districts near Lagos in which the church life was more developed than in the districts further up country', and this was continued.

A third assistant bishop, James Johnson, was consecrated in 1900. His reluctance to accept this office has been noted earlier and his final acceptance on condition that a West African Native Bishopric Fund was opened to provide the stipend for a *diocesan* bishop of African race, 'the diocese to be one in which the Delta of the Niger or the major part thereof' was situated. The target for this endowment fund, £10,000, was reached in 1928. In 1933 the Charity Commissioners in London accepted a change of trust which allowed the interest to be used for the stipend of 'a Bishop Suffragan, Assistant Bishop, or Coadjutor Bishop of African descent . . . to a yearly sum of £300, or such larger sum as the Metropolitan . . . of West Africa (i.e., when a Province was formed) . . . or the Archbishop of Canterbury shall approve'.[51] The Archbishop of Canterbury received protests from Sierra Leone and Nigeria about this use of the trust money and asked CMS for further information. On the Society's assurance that the bishops concerned had agreed to a change of trust, the Archbishop said he would write to West Africa to say that he thought this was the best use of the money.[52]

The changed climate of opinion, described earlier in this chapter, is unhappily sufficient to account for the continuing reluctance of the Archbishop and his advisers to appoint another African diocesan bishop at least until a province was formed; and the extremely dependent role accorded to suffragan bishops in England goes far in accounting for the withdrawal of the promised jurisdiction of which Bishop Oluwole complained; but he served nevertheless with great faithfulness in the role assigned to him, resigning from his assistant bishopric only a few weeks before his death in July 1932. Bishop Phillips died much earlier, in 1906; Bishop Johnson died in 1917. The last-named was a fine preacher and a vigorous disciplinarian, and he provided for many years the sort of leadership in the Anglican Church on the Niger which Bishop Tugwell, based on Lagos, was quick to appreciate. When Johnson died, Tugwell consulted the Niger Delta Board about a successor, but the Board seemed happy to trust 'the wisdom and good judgment of those responsible for filling the vacancy'. Tugwell would have liked to nominate Archdeacon Dandeson Crowther but felt that he was not justified in doing so because of the Archdeacon's 'age and of his increasing infirmities'. Instead he suggested the Rev. A. W. Howells, an Abeokutan who since 1901 had been vicar of St John's, Aroloya, Lagos and for over ten years secretary of the diocesan synod.[53] He served from 1921 to 1932 as Assistant Bishop on the Niger, and then at the invitation of Bishop Melville Jones, he returned to his Yoruba homeland to succeed Bishop Oluwole as Assistant Bishop of Lagos.

Bishop Tugwell resigned from 30th September, 1920, but continued to serve in eastern Nigeria for some months longer. He had been secretary of the CMS Yoruba mission from 1890 until his consecration in 1894. His episcopate of twenty-seven years was the longest of any European bishop in West Africa up to that time. He had led the Anglican Church in Nigeria forward from being a small body with a total membership of three or four thousand, confined to a dozen or so centres in Yorubaland and on the Niger, to one with many hundreds of congregations in the towns and villages of the southern provinces of Nigeria. At the time of his consecration there were only twenty-three African clergy in the diocese. When he resigned there were over a hundred. The constitution of the diocese which he drew up, and which was adopted in 1906, became a model for similar constitutions in other West African dioceses. He was remembered for the 'love and sweetness of his disposition' and, as well, for the moral courage which led him to give much time and energy for the suppression of the liquor traffic.

During the closing years of his episcopate plans were made for dividing the overlarge diocese of Western Equatorial Africa. Bishop Tugwell wanted a threefold division, with a diocese for the north as well as eastern and western dioceses in the south. He felt the north had suffered from lack of a man to travel, and to open up new districts. He thought a diocesan bishop would be able to move more freely in the Hausa states than a CMS mission secretary because, in any conflict with the administration, the latter's action would involve the Society. 'I should be prepared to do things which Mr Alvarez would not be prepared to do, and I could do them. If the Government forbade him, I should challenge them to stop me.'[54] The executive committee of the CMS northern Nigeria mission supported Bishop Tugwell's plea for a threefold division, but several members of the new dioceses planning committee, both African and

European, were not persuaded that three dioceses were necessary, and on the 1st May, 1919 the CMS general committee gave their opinion as follows: (1) immediate division was called for and the Society would be responsible for the stipend and allowances of a second European bishop; (2) they did not favour a threefold division at present but they looked forward with hope 'to such development of the work in the Northern Provinces as may render this desirable at some future time'; (3) in order to leave the way open for such further division they advocated that the new diocese should be bounded as follows:

on the *south* by the sea coast: on the *west* by Longitude 6° from the sea northward to the point where the line is intersected by the line of Latitude 6° 30' which is to be followed till it touches the Niger, and then by the river Niger northwards to Lokoja; on the *north* by the River Benue; and on the *east*, by the boundary of the Protectorate so understood as to include any portion of the Camerouns which shall come under British protection or influence. The other Diocese to consist of the remaining portions of the existing Diocese.[55]

This meant that northern Nigeria remained part of the western diocese, for which three titles were discussed at the last synod of the undivided diocese in 1919. The laity voted by a large majority for 'Yorubaland'; the clergy voted by a large majority for 'Western Nigeria'. The objection was made to 'Lagos' as a title on the ground that it was the Portuguese name for a town Africans knew as Eko. But in view of the way the voting divided, Bishop Tugwell reported to the Archbishop that the title proposed for the western diocese was *Lagos*, as suggested by the Rev. G. K. A. Bell.[56]

Alternative titles for the eastern diocese were also discussed. One was 'Bishop of the Niger Territory' but this was objected to by the (British) Foreign Office on the grounds that there is no country known by this name; and in June 1921 the decision was made by the Archbishop in consultation with the Foreign Office that it should be 'Bishop on the Niger'.[57] The boundaries suggested by the resolution of the CMS general committee in 1919 were also accepted. The new diocese consisted in terms of church membership of the Niger Delta Pastorate, still organized as a separate district, with 16,000 adherents and fourteen African clergy, eleven of whom were still 'Sierra Leoneans'; and the CMS mission area centred upon Onitsha with 31,000 adherents, and nine African clergy, two of them West Indians and the rest Ibos.

NOTES

1. Rex Niven, *Nigeria*, Ernest Benn, 1967, p. 13.
2. S. G. Pinnock, *The Romance of Missions in Nigeria*, Southern Baptist Convention, Richmond, Virginia 1918, p. 122.
3. Rex Niven, *Nigeria: Outline of a Colony*, Nelson, 1946, pp. 110ff.

4. Niven, *Nigeria*, 1967, p. 75.

5. Lord Hailey, *An Africa Survey*, OUP, 1938, pp. 1558–1559.

6. K. M. Buchman and J. C. Pugh, *Land and People in Nigeria*, University of London Press, 1961, p. 82.

7. Margery Perham, *Lugard: The Years of Authority 1898–1945*, Collins, 1960, p. 440.

8. ibid., pp. 460, 468.

9. Walter Schwarz, *Nigeria*, Pall Mall Press, 1968, p. 74.

10. Roland Oliver and J. D. Fage, *A Short History of Africa*, Penguin, 1962, p. 141.

11. Perham, op. cit., ch. xx.

12. ibid., pp. 140, 142.

13. ibid., p. 605.

14. ibid., p. 416.

15. J. F. A. Ajayi, *Christian Missions in Nigeria, 1841–1891*, Longmans, 1965, p. xiii.

16. ibid., p. xv.

17. T. S. Garrett and R. M. C. Jeffrey, *Unity in Nigeria*, Edinburgh House Press, 1965, p. 23.

18. Ajayi, op. cit., pp. 152ff.

19. J. B. Webster, *African Churches among the Yoruba 1888–1922*, Clarendon Press, 1964, p. 8.

20. Ajayi, op. cit., p. 260.

21. Webster, op. cit., p. xvi.

22. C. G. Baeta (ed.), *Christianity in Tropical Africa*, J. B. Webster, 'Attitudes and Policies of the Yoruba African Churches towards Polygamy', OUP, 1968, pp. 224ff.

23. ibid., p. 230n.

24. *CMR*, James Johnson, 'Elijah II', August 1916, pp. 455–62.

25. H. W. Turner, *History of an African Independent Church: The Church of the Lord (Aladura)*, Vol. I, Clarendon Press, 1967.

26. John B. Grimley and Gordon E. Robinson, *Church Growth in Central and Southern Nigeria*, Eerdmans, Michigan 1966, pp. 314, 315.

27. Michael Marioghae and John Ferguson, *Nigeria under the Cross*, Highway Press, 1965, p. 43.

28. C. P. Groves, *The Planting of Christianity in Africa*, Vol. III, Lutterworth Press, 1955, p. 292.

29. G3/A2/P5, 1911/33; 1915/61. (See also Jeffery and Garrett, op. cit., p. 27.)

30. *CMR*. G. T. Basden, 'The Mass Movement in Nigeria'. January 1918, pp. 30–1. (Niger Delta Pastorate figures for 1906 were not quoted.)

31. Grimley and Robinson, op. cit., pp. 317–51.

32. *CMR*, January 1923, E. T. Pakenham, 'Polygamy: a Problem in Nigeria', pp. 15–21.

33. *The Lambeth Conferences 1867–1948*, SPCK, 1948, p. 294.

34. W. R. S. Miller, *Reflections of a Pioneer*, CMS 1936, p. 166.

35. A3/P5, 1910/83.

36. Christian Council of Nigeria report, *Christian Responsibility in an Independent Nigeria*, 1962, p. 76.

37. *CMR*, January 1923, pp. 17, 18.

38. Typescript, 'My Second Conversion', 5th August 1933, T. O. Iloabachie.

39. Ellen Thorp, *Ladder of Bones*, Cape, 1956, p. 88.

40. *CMR*, G. Furness Smith, 'The Liquor Trade in Southern Nigeria', January 1910, pp. 16–29.

41. Perham, op. cit., pp. 559–61.

42. *CMR*, June 1919, p. 107, A. J. Macdonald, 'A new development in the West Africa Liquor Traffic'.

43. Perham, op. cit., p. 172.

44. ibid., p. 457.

45. ibid., quoting Dike, *Trade and Politics in the Niger Delta, 1830–1885*, 1956, pp. 34–6.

46. A3/P5, 1911/67.

47. P5, 1913/42, 43, 76.

48. P5, 1910/116.

49. Ajayi, op. cit., pp. 183–96.

50. Stock, III, pp. 397–401.

51. G/Y/Aw 2 'West African Native Bishoprics Fund' memorandum of 14th July, 1930: Charity Commissioners' Scheme, March 1933.

52. T. S. Johnson, *The Story of a Mission*, pp. 122–4, and Archbishop Fisher's Foreword.

53. G/Y/A2/2, Letter of Bishop Tugwell, 24th May, 1918.

54. ibid., report of Conference on the Proposed Division of the Diocese of Western Equatorial Africa, 28th February, 11th March, 1919 at CMS headquarters, London.

55. G/C1/83. p. 281.

56. G/Y/A2/2 Letter of Bishop Tugwell to the Archbishop of Canterbury, 15th September, 1919.

57. G/Y/A2/2 (1937–39), letter from Lee, Bolton and Lee, 9th January, 1922.

Western Nigeria

The CMS Yoruba Mission, 1910–19

In 1910, the Anglican Church in western Nigeria was still expanding rapidly, particularly to the east and north of the long-established church centres of Lagos, Ibadan, and Abeokuta. Comparative figures show that the number of communicants doubled in the decade 1910–19 (from 7,519 to 15,697) and the total church membership increased almost threefold (from 27,398 to 76,113). The areas of most rapid expansion were among the Ijebu to the east of Lagos and the Ekiti to the north-east. The CMS annual report for 1910 tells of 'something akin to a mass movement' in the Ekiti country. In the years 1914–17 some 2,000 adults were baptized in this region, and twenty new churches opened. The 1915 annual report records similar progress in the Ijebu area, where there were over 13,000 Christians, and 'almost every village has its church'. Dr E. A. Ayandele suggests differing reasons for the response of these two Yoruba groups to Christian teaching. In the case of the Ijebu he traces it back to the 1892 military expedition and conquest. The people were curious to know the secret of the white man's power, which could overthrow their divine king. With the Ekiti, however, the basic reason was gratitude, felt by the people towards the missionaries and the Lagos administration, for bringing peace and independence to their country for the first time in a hundred years.[1] The initial evangelization in both cases was largely the achievement of former slaves. In Ekiti it was ex-captives of the Yoruba wars who led the advance; and it was liberated slaves of an earlier generation who were chiefly responsible for the adoption of the Ijebu area as a mission-field of the Lagos District Church Council.

The European missionaries were fully aware of the mixed motives that lay behind the insistent requests for more teachers and the readiness to receive Christian baptism. 'The desire for education and self-respect is uppermost,' one of them wrote from Oshogbo (Ekiti) in 1911. Another in 1919 reported that there were 110 congregations in the Oyo district, to the west of Oshogbo, but added regretfully: 'It is fashionable to be a Christian, and the Christianity of the converts is often only nominal.' This awareness led to stricter requirements in preparation for baptism towards the end of the first world war, with disquieting results. For example, in the Ode Ondo district the number of candidates for baptism was reduced from 443 in 1918 to only 42 in 1919.

Further east, in the Owo district some sixty miles north of Benin City, this stricter baptismal policy proved difficult to explain.

Some think it a very grievous thing [wrote the Rev. E. T. Pakenham] to be postponed for six months to give them a chance of gaining a more intelligent grasp of Christian truth, and they come prostrating themselves and begging forgiveness, feeling that the real reason is that the missionary has found out some fault.

The demand for baptism had outrun the capacity of either the CMS Yoruba mission or the district church councils to supply trained teachers for these outlying areas. In July 1916 the Rev. F. Hedger found a congregation of 400 to 500 at Oka, north of Owo. They were prepared to accept the guidance of any teacher, Wesleyan, Roman Catholic, or Anglican who would stay and help them.[2]

In The Church Missionary Review, January 1919, Archdeacon Melville Jones gave a progress report on 'The Mass Movement in the Yoruba Country'. He described the attempts of some Ekiti chiefs to suppress the new religion by force when they felt both their authority and revenues were at stake; but he thought that converts were often not free from blame.

In resisting any attempt on the part of the chief to coerce them into idolatrous practices, they sometimes go too far and disobey his authority in things lawful. . . . The result is the chiefs become angry, and perhaps set fire to the church, or drive the Christians out of their town.

No doubt he had in mind the troubles at Ushi in 1912.[3] He had maintained at the time that the inaction of a political officer was to blame, though Lugard attributed the troubles to lack of qualified teachers among the Christian faction. Melville Jones thought of such outbreaks as a passing phase. The real struggle in the Yoruba country, as he saw it, was not between Christianity and tribal religion, but between Christianity and Islam. Its outcome would depend largely on the timely supply of Christian teachers, and more effective work among women. 'The mass movement is essentially a young man's movement. The women are much more conservative than the men . . . and one great problem before the Church is where the male converts are to find Christian wives.' The task of primary evangelism was already being cared for by a self-propagating African church. 'Just as the Moslem trader carries his religion with him as he goes about, so does the Christian.' But more European missionaries were needed – men 'to staff our institutions adequately and superintend our huge missionary districts'; and more women missionaries to organize the work among women and girls in the interior districts which the Yoruba mission had previously neglected. A few months after writing this article Melville Jones became Bishop

of Lagos. His episcopate both in its strength and limitations is foreshadowed
in this assessment.

In 1918 a large tract of country, about a hundred miles from north to south
and eighty miles from east to west, was added to the Yoruba mission area. This
was the Benin district, which had previously been in the care of the Niger Delta
Pastorate Church. Bishop James Johnson had started Anglican missionary work
there in 1902. But it was remote from the main centres of the Delta Pastorate,
and after Bishop Johnson's death in 1917, a commission of inquiry, led by
Melville Jones, recommended its transfer to the Yoruba mission. He visited
the area in November 1918 and was impressed by what he found. He preached
to a congregation of six hundred in Benin City itself, and there were twenty-
five out-stations in the immediate neighbourhood. Sapele and Warri, to the
south of Benin, each had large churches, good Sunday congregations and a
number of out-stations; but the only trained Anglican workers in the whole
region were two African clergy, one catechist and two schoolmasters. After its
union with the Yoruba mission, a European missionary, the Rev. R. Kidd,
was appointed superintendent of the Benin district.

In the longer-established Anglican church centres of western Nigeria the
decade 1910–19 was a time of consolidation, despite the disturbing effects of the
African Church Movement (see above, p. 37ff). The district church councils in
Lagos, Abeokuta and Ibadan had been virtually self-supporting for some years;
and in 1911 provisional church councils were formed for the Onde and Owo
districts. In the same year, with the CMS parent committee's approval, a
patronage board was set up under the diocesan synod of Western Equatorial
Africa. Its purpose was to transfer responsibility for the deployment of African
clergy from the Yoruba mission to the district church councils. In 1912 Christ
Church, Lagos, was transferred to the synod with the intention of making it the
cathedral for the Yoruba part of the diocese. It was anticipated that suitable
churches in other parts of the diocese, such as St Stephen's Church, Bonny,
would serve as 'co-cathedrals'. The use of Christ Church had been the subject
of controversy a few years earlier. The suggestion that it should be developed
as a church for Europeans had met with strong opposition from some of the
parishioners led by Herbert Macaulay, grandson of Bishop Crowther. Its
transfer to the synod was a wise move, but suspicion that it might still be
Europeanized was slow to clear.[4]

The training of African evangelists, catechists and clergy had been listed as a
priority in 'A Working Plan for Yoruba Mission' drawn up by the executive
committee of the mission in July 1910. At that time there were two training
institutions – one at Oyo for schoolmasters and catechists; and the other at
Oshogbo for scripture readers. The Oshogbo training institution, opened in
1900, remained quite small. There were nineteen students in 1910 but numbers
rose steadily during the war years to reach a peak of thirty-six in 1916. It was
closed soon after the first world war. In 1911 Oyo training college, with new

buildings provided through the Pan-Anglican Thank-offering Fund, started a divinity class for the training of clergy. Soon afterwards the course for catechists was extended. A students' strike in 1913, ostensibly about the food provided at the college, appears to have been related to this lengthened course. Five students left as a result of it. In 1917 the college was affiliated to Durham University for a two-year course in preparation for a Licentiate in Theology. The college prospered under the leadership of Melville Jones and by 1918 there were eight-four students in residence. It was renamed 'St Andrew's College' in 1919.

The CMS Yoruba mission was cautious at first about accepting government education grants. In January 1910 its executive committee noted that a number of vernacular schools in the Ijebu district were applying for grants. These Ijebu schools were under the direction of the Lagos district church council, not of the CMS Yoruba mission. The mission committee was not at that time prepared to approve applications for government grants for its own schools in the interior because such grants would upset the scale of salaries for school-teachers. The parent committee of CMS encouraged the mission 'to co-operate with the government as far as possible'; and in 1914 Melville Jones appealed to the government to make provision, in its new educational code, for grant-aid on the basis of the general tone of the school and on the work of the staff. He thought that residual doubts about accepting government aid would be resolved if there was some guarantee that government inspectors would be sympathetic to Christian aims in education. The new code, issued in 1915, was welcomed by the mission executive committee. It recognized religion as 'a force in the formation of character and of good citizens which cannot be neglected without disastrous results'.[5] In 1917, with Bishop Tugwell's approval and support, the Abeokuta district church council decided to open most of its larger schools to government inspection, so making them eligible for grants-in-aid.[6] In 1918 Oyo training college received its first government grant of £400 per annum for the training of teachers. In 1919 Lagos Girls' Seminary, one of the three secondary schools under the Yoruba CMS mission, applied for a government grant for new buildings. Plans for this extension, made necessary by a rapid growth in the number of pupils during the war years, had been approved by the CMS parent committee at a total cost of £5,500.[7]

In 1916 Lagos grammar school received a European missionary, the Rev. E. J. Evans as headmaster. In the fifty-seven years of the school's life there had always been an African headmaster. Melville Jones had been urging such an appointment for several years. He thought that a European headmaster would attract more pupils and would raise the standard of teaching in the school, but he recognized that 'race feeling might arise'. Evans was not in fact sub-jected to the kind of overt opposition which made Dallimore's task impossible at Freetown grammar school a few years earlier; but the appointment of a European was not popular.

There were two up-country developments in the education of women and girls in this decade. In 1912 Miss E. Downer started a girls' training school at Ijebu Ode with twelve pupils; a girls' boarding school was opened at Abeokuta in 1911. It foundered after a few months but was reopened in 1917 with thirty-four day girls and seven boarders.

During the first world war the CMS bookshop at Lagos extended its services to all parts of Nigeria. Its development was one of the significant new ventures of this period, and it owed almost everything in its early stages to the vision and energy of C. W. Wakeman. When he arrived in Lagos in 1906 as the new accountant of the Yoruba mission the bookshop was under threat of closure, but he was given charge of it as a spare-time activity. By placing book and stationery orders with publishers in Britain, he soon made it a chief supplier of schools and mission stations in West Africa.

By 1910 the Lagos bookshop had expanded considerably although the CMS mission committee was not yet persuaded that it merited the expense of a telephone. In that year Wakeman started publishing a monthly periodical, *In Leisure Hours*, which he continued to edit for thirty years. Its circulation was not large, and levelled out at about 1,300 copies monthly, but it proved a valuable ancillary to the bookshop. The setting up of some branch bookshops became a necessary part of Wakeman's policy of expansion. He found that Muslim traders and market women, twenty or thirty miles from Lagos, were selling Yoruba Bibles for 4s or 5s compared with the Lagos price of 2s 6d, and that they were charging 3d for exercise books which he sold for 1d. His answer to these inflated prices was a chain of new branches not only at most of the major CMS mission centres of western Nigeria, but in other areas as well. Between 1915 and 1920 such branches were opened at Ilesha, Ebute Meta, and Oshogbo; at Egbu, Awka and Port Harcourt in eastern Nigeria; and at Kano, Kaduna and Zaria in the northern provinces. This expansion meant a great increase in profitability, especially as the Lagos bookshop had become a chief source of supply for all educational books in Nigeria. It was inevitable, in a time of financial stringency, that the Yoruba mission should come to regard bookshop profits as a financial reservoir for general mission expenses. A resolution of the mission executive committee in 1911 proposed the use of these profits for missionary allowances, for 'special building work', and for other local expenses, as well as for the provision of more literature in the Yoruba language.[8] This short-sighted policy was to cause difficulties later (see below p. 60ff).

Lagos Diocese and the Yoruba Mission, 1919–42

On 18th October, 1919 Melville Jones was consecrated bishop of the new diocese of Lagos. His consecration was the first step in the division of the diocese of Western Equatorial Africa (see above p. 51). Bishop Tugwell continued in episcopal oversight over the Niger mission area for a time, pending the appointment of Bertram Lasbrey as Bishop on the Niger. Lagos diocese comprised the whole of the Yoruba country, and in addition Bishop Jones was given oversight of the Anglican congregations and missionary work in the northern provinces. It was a vast area to cover, and in 1925 Alfred Smith, who as archdeacon had worked for some years in the northernmost part of the Yoruba area, was consecrated as Assistant Bishop of Lagos with special responsibility for northern Nigeria. Even so the inclusion of the north within Lagos diocese continued to be regarded as a mistake by most of the CMS missionaries working there. In 1942, when a separate diocese for the northern provinces was again under discussion, one of them wrote:

A glance at the map shows that Lagos is not a good centre of administration even for the Yoruba country . . . much less for the cities in Northern Nigeria, 600 to 1,000 miles distant. Between 1933 and 1941 only one visit was paid to the North by the Bishop of Lagos, which indicates that in recent years Northern Nigeria has been a separate diocese in all but name.[9]

It would have been out of character in the inter-war period to create a separate diocese for the north, since there were scarcely a thousand communicants and only half a dozen clergy, two of whom were indigenous. Egypt and Gambia might, it is true, have served as precedents, but the political situation in northern Nigeria argued strongly against it. The doctrine of 'indirect rule', as applied to the Hausa states, made it difficult enough at first even for the assistant bishop to establish himself as more than an undesirable intruder. He hoped to make Zaria his headquarters in 1925 but the Zaria Resident made it clear that he was only prepared to accept Bishop Smith's presence in Zaria City as a temporary guest of Dr Walter Miller; and after a few months he moved to Kaduna and finally settled at Ilorin, a Yoruba city remote from all the other CMS mission centres in the north. It needs to be said that Bishop Melville Jones and the Yoruba mission executive committee lost no opportunity of pressing the claims of their colleagues in the north for missionary freedom; and it made sense, in terms acceptable at the time, that a numerically weak mission and church should be attached to a strong one. But it soon became evident that the oversight of the Bishop of Lagos would not be accepted easily by some CMS missionaries in the northern provinces.

In the major, Yoruba, part of the new diocese it was an advantage that the first Bishop of Lagos had been Bishop Tugwell's lieutenant for many years. He knew the country intimately. He loved Nigeria, and was one of those rare foreigners who appeared to find the climate congenial. He was able as bishop to pursue the lines of policy to which he had already committed himself as archdeacon. A constitution for the diocese was accepted without difficulty. Bishop Tugwell's 1906 constitution for the diocese of Western Equatorial Africa provided an obvious model, and it was taken over with scarcely more than verbal amendments. In 1924 the parent committee of CMS readily agreed to transfer to the diocese remaining rights in ownership of land and buildings for church properties in Lagos. These included Christ Church pro-cathedral, and the churches, parsonages and schools of St Paul's, St Peter's, St John's and Holy Trinity.[10] The foundation stone of the planned extension to Christ Church was laid by the Prince of Wales on 21st April, 1925.

As in most missionary dioceses where CMS worked during this period, acceptance of a diocesan constitution was followed by reconstruction of the local governing body of the mission. In April 1928 the parent committee accepted such proposals for its Yoruba mission. The executive committee of the mission was discontinued and replaced, as the local governing body, by the missionaries' conference. All missionaries out of probation were given a vote in the conference, together with all missionary wives with four years' service, excluding furlough, who had also passed the first language examination. Provision was made for the parent committee to nominate five Africans as members of the conference, and any African district superintendents were accorded voting membership. A standing committee of the conference was constituted for day-to-day administration, consisting of the bishop as *ex officio* chairman; the assistant bishops, the mission secretary and mission accountant as *ex officio* members; and, as annually elected members, two superintendents of CMS districts, two African members of the conference, two educational workers (one man and one woman), and one representative of women's work. The missionary conference met for the first time on 11th January, 1929.[11] This revised constitution for the mission was unusually conservative. It not only kept the mission structure intact but, by drawing into itself African represent-atives, tended to withdraw responsibility from the synod of the diocese. The parent committee pressed the bishop and the authorities of the mission to take further steps towards diocesanization. The 1931 missionaries conference discussed it but found that 'it raised many difficulties'. The bishop in a letter commenting on the discussion, mentioned two of these difficulties. There were CMS missionaries in 'Synod' areas, for example, McKay at Oshogbo; and there were CMS schools in Lagos and Ibadan. He thought the continuing existence of the missionaries conference was valuable, and that representatives of the diocesan synod might well be added to it. This hybrid organization of diocese and mission continued throughout the rest of the period.

Bookshop and Mission Finances

The rapid development of the Lagos bookshop and its branches (see above, p. 58) continued in the 1920s. Bookshop sales increased threefold between 1917 and 1921 and the net profit for 1921 was over £3,000. Orders were flooding in from mission stations and schools all along the west coast from Sierra Leone to the Camerouns, and the letterbox was cleared ten or twelve times a day. Fred Ward, who joined the bookshop staff in 1920, recalled the experiences and social conventions of that time:

I was soon domiciled in Caxton House on the Broad Street side of the compound, close to the printing press. There were no modern conveniences, but it had electric light. The power station was next door. . . . I chopped at the old mission house with the Wakemans, and at dinner it was then the custom to wear white evening kit. Mosquito boots were essential, and the old-fashioned khaki pith helmet was always worn during the sunniest hours of the day.[12]

Ward was sent from Lagos to assist in the opening of the bookshop at Port Harcourt, and five years later he supervised the opening of a new branch at Enugu. In 1930 he was sent to Freetown to open the bookshop with which his name is particularly associated.

In 1923 the extension of the Lagos premises, for which Wakeman had been pleading for several years, was made possible by the purchase of the Marble Hall site for £5,100. The extension was opened in May 1927. There were setbacks as well as progress. In the same month there was a disastrous fire at the Abeokuta bookshop, one of the earliest branches. The entire stock was destroyed, and it was not insured; but the expansion of business elsewhere made it possible to carry such losses without too great anxiety. By the mid-1920s the Lagos bookshop was not only self-supporting, but was underwriting the whole cost of 'European agency' in the Yoruba CMS mission, including the furlough allowances of missionaries.

In 1929 Wakeman was appointed secretary of the mission in addition to his duties as accountant, and J. R. Oliver, who had already been some years on the staff, was appointed joint bookshop manager. In the next year or two West Africa began to experience the dire effects of the world economic depression and in December 1931 Wakeman wrote to CMS headquarters in London saying that the bookshop funds could no longer support the mission on the scale of previous years. Receipts had fallen sharply as a result of the trade recession, and he urged the parent committee to take over the whole cost of European allowances, including furloughs, until bookshop finances were again stable. The parent committee demurred at first, but after further letters from Wakeman it agreed to do so.[13]

The setback to the Lagos bookshop proved to be only temporary, and in 1934 a sensible arrangement was made by which Port Harcourt and other Eastern bookshops then under Lagos were transferred to the Niger mission, which already controlled the bookshop at Onitsha; their amalgamation created the Niger bookshops organization (see p. 111). Wakeman welcomed this change. The eastern bookshops were proving difficult to run from Lagos, and he was confident that the production of vernacular literature would benefit by a concentration on the Yoruba and Hausa languages.[14]

In 1938 a Lagos bookshop management committee was formed with Wakeman, as mission secretary, as its chairman. By this time the bookshop was by far the largest retail business of its kind in Lagos. In 1940 it dealt with 16,000 orders and its total receipts were £80,000. It had eleven depots in Lagos itself and twenty-six branches in the interior. In 1942 the parent committee sanctioned the transfer of the Freetown bookshop to the CMS Sierra Leone mission. In twelve years Ward had built it up from nothing into a flourishing business.

The expansion of the missionary bookshops in West Africa into a major undertaking owed more to Wakeman than to anyone else in this period. He steadily resisted the denigration of bookshop work which he had encountered on his arrival in West Africa in 1906, and could never accept for it the role of a mere paymaster of the mission. A statement of the Yoruba mission executive committee, made during his time as its secretary, reflects his own conviction:

> The Bookshop is a missionary enterprise and its primary object is to assist in the spread of the Gospel and to extend Christ's kingdom. . . . The Bookshop is the handmaid of the Church and it exists to provide as far as it is able for the needs of the Church's work.

Inter-Communion and Reunion

Bishop Melville Jones had a keen personal interest in church unity and after the 1920 Lambeth Conference, on the basis of its famous 'Appeal to All Christian People', he encouraged the occasional interchange of pulpits with Wesleyan Methodist missionaries. But after the 1930 Lambeth Conference, his interpretation of Conference Resolution 42 earned him considerable unpopularity among some of the CMS missionaries in his diocese. It also brought a sharp rebuke, later retracted, from the general secretary of CMS, Wilson Cash. This incident is worth recording as an example of the way an honest attempt to interpret the intentions of the Anglican Communion could run into accusations of prelacy. Resolution 42 of the 1930 Lambeth Conference concerned the practice of inter-communion. While maintaining 'as a general principle that inter-communion should be the goal of, rather than a means to, the restoration of union', and bearing in mind the general rule of the Anglican Communion that 'members of the Anglican churches should receive Holy Communion only from ministers of their own church', the conference held that 'the administration of such a rule falls under the discretion of the Bishop, who should exercise his dispensing power in accordance with any principles that may be set forth by the national, regional, or provincial authority of the Church in the area concerned'. An explanatory note attached to the resolution said that the bishops felt bound to 'consider the difficulties created by present conditions, especially in some parts of the Mission Field' and they recognized that a bishop might 'under very strict regulations and in very special circumstances permit individual communicants to join with members of other Christian bodies in their Services of the administration of the Lord's Supper'.

Before the 1930 Lambeth Conference Miss E. F. Grimwood, Principal of the United Missionary Training College at Ibadan (see below p. 68), asked Bishop

Melville Jones whether the Anglicans at the college could have joint communion services with the Wesleyan Methodists in the college. He asked her to wait until after the Lambeth Conference, which he attended. On his return he agreed to a CMS missionary conducting a Holy Communion service for all students. He felt this was clearly covered by the Lambeth resolution. Then

> Miss Grimwood . . . asked that I would allow the Rev. E. C. Nightingale, a Wesleyan Minister, to conduct the next service. Letting my heart answer rather than my head, I agreed. Had Miss Grimwood written to me I should have thought the matter over, and very reluctantly would have had to refuse.

Though reciprocal inter-communion was the bishop's own personal desire, it had not been the custom of the United Missionary College; and therefore, after this one service with a Methodist celebrant, he could not agree to continue it in the light of the Lambeth Conference.

On 14th June, 1932 Cash wrote to the bishop, saying that he had heard from Wakeman that he had forbidden the lady missionaries along with others from going to a Wesleyan Holy Communion service. Cash took grave exception to such an episcopal ruling.

> The right of a Bishop over his priests [he wrote] is one thing, his authority to lay down a law on this question to lay folk is another. . . . We are a Church Society, but we do stand most emphatically for ultimate reunion with our non-conformist brethren, and inter-communion seems to us an essential step towards the great goal of unity.

He hoped that the bishop would not 'push us as a Society into open opposition to yourself'.

On 7th December, 1932, having received the bishop's account of the course of events, Cash agreed that he had made out his case 'convincingly and clearly'. The bishop, in view of the stir caused by his ruling, felt under obligation to consult the Archbishop of Canterbury about the interpretation of the Lambeth Conference resolution, and as a result he tightened his restriction on reciprocal inter-communion. On 1st March, 1934 Wakeman wrote to H. D. Hooper, Africa secretary of CMS, to say that the measure of inter-communion which the bishop had previously sanctioned was sanctioned no longer and that both Union Colleges (in Ibadan and Lagos) were in danger. 'Neither they nor we would have embarked on union schemes had we visualized the possibility of a breakdown in connection with inter-communion.' Cash felt this was going a bit far. Inter-communion had never been made a condition for co-operative schemes for missionary institutions in other parts of the world, and he did not see why it should be so in Nigeria. He wrote a note to Hooper saying that he found Wakeman's position 'very difficult', and that he did not feel that CMS could go beyond what the Lambeth Conference had sanctioned.[15]

The Ogboni Cult

The bishop had another difficult problem of church discipline on his hands in 1934. The Ogboni was an ancient secret society. Dr Ayandele describes it as 'deeply rooted in Yoruba country, but most prominent among the Egba and Ijebu'. In earlier times it served as a check on the absolute rule of the local chief or king and fulfilled the role of a popular court of appeal against tyranny. The British administration, however, regarded it as dangerous, and in 1892 Sir Gilbert Carter had taken a personal hand in the destruction of the Ogboni 'house' in Ijebu-Ode. In 1914 some African Christians, including the Principal of the Wesleyan High School in Lagos and an Anglican clergyman, the Rev. T. A. J. Ogunbiyi, founded the Christian Ogboni Society.

Jacobson Ogunbiyi deserves more than a passing mention. His father, Chief Jacob Ogunbiyi, was the first indigenous chief of Lagos to be converted to Christianity, and built the first 'Native Pastorate' church in Lagos. Jacobson came under the influence of Bishop James Johnson. He spent three years at the CMS training institution in Lagos and after a few years as a teacher in Ondo went to Fourah Bay College, Sierra Leone. In 1900 he attempted to found a Christian Ogboni Society but was discouraged from doing so by other Anglican clergy. In 1912 he visited England and appears to have been equally impressed by the Keswick Convention and English freemasonry. He was the prime mover on his return in founding the Christian Ogboni Society. He found scriptural justification for the cult in a passage from Ezekiel in which the word *ogboni* occurred in the Yoruba Bible, and in one from Nehemiah (10.29) about oath-taking. He became convinced that the Ogboni cult, in a christianized form, would produce a more binding fellowship than the rather loose brotherhood of the normal church congregation; and that the 'six degrees' of the Christian Ogboni Society would provide a more satisfying hierarchy than either the foreign Masonic lodges or the order of ministry in the Anglican Church. The display of the Bible in Christian Ogboni rituals was no doubt inspired by a similar use in the European Masonic lodges. The declared programme of the society was 'the amelioration of our race and the uplifting of our brethren in the interior'. Both Bishop Tugwell and Bishop Oluwole were unhappy about it and tried to persuade Ogunbiyi to give it up. This he did for a time. He was appointed pastor of St Paul's, Breadfruit, Lagos, where James Johnson had ministered for many years, and was also appointed by Melville Jones as Arch-deacon of Lagos. In 1929 the bishop withdrew his licence as archdeacon and Ogunbiyi thereupon founded his own church at Ikeja, and resumed his Ogboni activities in a Reformed Ogboni Fraternity.

Bishop Melville Jones shared his predecessor's concern about the spread of the cult among Anglican clergy and church members. In September 1934 he wrote about it to Canon S. V. Latunde, Principal of Ibadan Grammar School and secretary of the Lagos diocesan synod. The placing of the Bible in a calabash, with the use of the words 'dare you look at it?' were open, he said, to 'very grave objections'. His letter warned clergy of the diocese not to extend the hospitality of their churches to the Ogboni Society. This was no doubt aimed at Ogunbiyi himself, for he was a popular preacher and was frequently invited to take part in Sunday services. The bishop sought Canon Latunde's help in counselling clergy to abstain from taking part in the operations of the society.

The bishop's counsel had some effect, but was not followed by all clergy. The Reformed Ogboni Fraternity, with Ogunbiyi as its general secretary, spread beyond the Yoruba people and found a ready response among the educated Ibo and Hausa at a time when Nigerian nationalism was gaining strength. Under its new name it ceased to confine membership to Christians, but a good many African church leaders, including Anglicans, continued to belong to it, as a form of indigenous freemasonry not incompatible with their Christian profession.[16]

New Missionaries in the 1930s

It is evident from the missionaries' annual letters in the mid-1930s that a younger generation of CMS missionaries had begun to find their feet; and they tended to be critical of the existing leadership in church and mission. 'We are in an absolute whirlpool of new movements...,' one of them wrote in 1935, 'our pastors and our Bishop are really too old, for the most part, to cope with the vigorous life of this Colony. ... At the moment, we are in the stage of being pleased with any particular function or event if it can be described "as being as good as last year".' In 1936 another missionary reports that the bishop's stand against the Reformed Ogboni cult had caused much ill-feeling, at a time when nationalism had been stirred up by the Italian invasion of Abyssinia.

There was a growing concern among younger missionaries about the role of the European missionary in the Nigerian church.

The time is gone by, at any rate in Lagos, when what the European said was right because he said it. ... We have got to be right because we are right, and not because we are white, and to be willing to acknowledge when we are wrong.

From such openness, she believed, there would grow 'a church which is a fellowship, and not a hierarchy with the European at the top because he is a European'. The same writer regretted the lack in the church of responsible and wise leaders, and of young men and women under forty.[17]

No doubt these comments represented the ebullience of a new generation of missionaries, not yet burdened with the major responsibilities of leadership; but their dismay about the static character of the church in Lagos diocese was taken seriously by the authorities of CMS in London. On 1st April, 1938 Wilson Cash wrote to Bishop Melville Jones drawing attention to the Society's rule by which its missionaries retired at the age of sixty-five. 'The Society feels', Cash went on to say, 'that the time has come when you ought seriously to consider resignation. . . . If the Archbishop [of Canterbury] felt that the Society was wrong in suggesting your resignation now, we would at once revise our opinion, and loyally accept any decision that His Grace might make.' It was a difficult letter to write, and a distressing one to receive; but in writing it the general secretary of CMS was not acting with undue haste. The suggestion of resignation had already been made verbally to the bishop by Yoruba missionaries with the knowledge and approval of the headquarters secretariat. On 1st July, 1938 Archbishop Lang wrote to Cash saying that he had a frank talk with the bishop and Mrs Melville Jones, and that he, 'and especially she', were hurt by what they thought was 'the rather peremptory way in which the wish of CMS was conveyed to them . . . but I think I was able to mollify them a good deal'. The Archbishop suggested that Bishop Melville Jones should remain in office until the 1940 Lambeth Conference. Canon Leslie Vining, who was already in mind as his successor, could be consecrated before that as assistant bishop in Nigeria, and would thus be eligible to attend the Lambeth Conference. Because of the second world war the conference was postponed, and did not take place until 1948. Bishop Melville Jones retired, still with evident reluctance, in 1940. He and Mrs Jones continued to live in Nigeria. The CMS secretariat had made it clear that they were against their doing so, but the Archbishop was not prepared to dissuade them.[18] They had given exceptionally long service as missionaries in Nigeria – the bishop for forty-seven years and his wife for fifty. Neither of them were happy at the prospect of retirement in England. The bishop died in 1941 and Mrs Jones in 1947. They had seen the Anglican Church in western Nigeria grow through its adolescence to maturity, and at St Andrew's College, Oyo and later in Lagos they had given themselves without stint in its service. The bishop's work is happily commemorated in Melville Hall, Ibadan, where African clergy receive the final stages of their training.

Church Growth in the 1930s

The growth-rate of the Anglican Church in western Nigeria slackened in some areas in the 1930s, but in the Ekiti district it was still maintained. Archdeacon Dallimore reported that, between 1931 and 1937, 8,800 baptisms had taken place in the district, and 2,000 had been confirmed; thirty new churches had been built, thirteen new schools, and fifteen teachers' houses. The larger elementary schools, grant-aided by the government, each had a cluster of village schools around them and the headmaster of the main school was responsible for the whole group. In 1937 a school of instruction in the spiritual life was held in all parts of Dallimore's archdeaconry. An annual retreat for clergy had been started, 'through the kind assistance of clergy in the diocese of Liverpool'.[19]

A new venture in pastoral care in the Yoruba mission was the appointment in 1937 of the Rev. W. H. A. Cooper as 'district missioner'. He arrived in Nigeria in 1939. He ran study circles for English-speaking Africans in Lagos and conducted short missions in the interior through an interpreter. After the first six months he wrote: 'The more I travel the greater I realize the difficulties to be . . . yet my conviction grows that the only effective solution must be radical – individual conversion, individual faith, individual training and service.'[20] It was a common concern of missionaries, faced with 'third-generation' problems, to do all in their power to present the challenge of deep Christianity as widely as possible. A new venture with this purpose, the annual 'bishop's camp' for evangelists and teachers who had no previous formal training, was launched by Bishop Vining. The first of these camps was held in 1941 and it was attended by a hundred and thirty teachers.

Missionaries in Education, 1920–42

Dr Ayandele and other African historians have commented on the tension between missionary aims in education and the motives of those who entered the schools and colleges which they ran. More often than not, what parents and their children wanted from missionaries was a good general education on Western lines. It is not surprising, therefore, that difficulties should arise and harsh judgments be passed when this objective appeared to be secondary. In 1923 the diocesan synod appointed a commission of inquiry about 'the staffing, curriculum and discipline' of Lagos grammar school. The Rev. E. J. Evans, principal in 1916, was able to show that reports on the school had been more satisfactory since his appointment six years earlier, but as principal he was inevitably the focus for African criticism. He left the grammar school in 1924 to become supervisor of the elementary schools of the Yoruba mission, for which post the government provided a salary.

In 1927 the Rev. A. G. Fraser, Principal of Achimota College, Gold Coast, was asked by the parent committee of CMS to make a confidential report on the Society's educational policy and work in Nigeria. Fraser's report was forthright alike in praise and blame. Of one school he wrote: 'The headmaster is interested in politics in the town and pays the smallest possible attention to his school.' He thought the Rev. C. W. Jebb was doing first-rate work at Owo, though with bad equipment. He was particularly impressed by Ibadan girls' school (known as Kudeti girls' school from 1928). He recommended it for the highest grade of government grant. On St Andrew's College, Oyo, he reported that the Rev. George Burton, Melville Jones' successor as principal, was 'keeping up-to-date and thinking hard'. He formed an unfavourable impression of CMS girls' school, Lagos and he commented on its lack of a Christian atmosphere. The Bishop of Lagos wrote to London to say that Fraser's strictures 'were far too sweeping', and that they did not coincide with his own impression of the Lagos girls' school, nor with those of a government inspector who had visited the school shortly after Fraser.[21] The school attained full secondary status, and qualified for a government 'A' grant in 1929.

Co-operative educational work between CMS and the Wesleyan Methodist Missionary Society was first proposed in 1928. The principals of the CMS girls' school and grammar school, and the Wesleyan boys' and girls' schools in Lagos produced a memorandum which proposed that they should reorganize their schools on a boarding basis at Yaba, a suburb of Lagos. In 1930, with the help of the government Director of Education, the proposal took further shape with plans for a combined school at Yaba. To start with, four European members of staff would be needed, to be replaced later by Africans with higher educational training. Its standard was to be that of a middle school, comparable to government schools at Ibadan and Umuahia, whose syllabuses would serve as a guide. The government proposed a building grant of £6,000. Wakeman was worried about the financial implication of the project. He did not think the new school could carry seventy-five per cent of the salaries of the four European members of the staff, even after allowance was made for the pooling of government grants to the existing schools. It took several years to sort out the problems of finance and staffing but the school opened in January 1933 with the name Igbobi College and with a Methodist, the Rev. J. A. Angus, as principal. It developed on English public school lines to become one of the major schools of Lagos.

Another co-operative scheme, dating from the same period, was the United Missionary College at Ibadan. In 1929 WMMS drew up plans, for discussion with CMS, about a joint women's teacher-training college. It was proposed to open the college with twelve students nominated by CMS, and five by WMMS; the cost of maintenance (after allowing for government grants, fees, etc.) would be borne in the proportion of three parts CMS to one part WMMS. The former undertook to find £1,250 towards the initial costs, and WMMS £250. This proposal, slightly modified in detail, was warmly accepted by CMS and in December 1932 the parent committee agreed to a constitution for the college. It provided for a governing body of thirteen members, eight nominated by CMS and five by WMMS. It undertook to provide two European members of staff to be paid from college funds, but was not prepared to accept any responsibility for running costs. By 1938 the United Missionary College was well-established, with sixty-two students in residence.[22]

One of the best pieces of educational work, in the broadest sense, undertaken by CMS missionaries in this period was the Girls' Training Centre at Akure. It started in the 1920s and provided a well-balanced course of instruction for girls preparing for marriage with catechists and other church-workers. A girls' day and boarding-school, with emphasis on domestic science, was started at Benin by the Rev. W. J. and Mrs Payne, in 1935.[23]

The continuing tension produced by diverse educational aims may be illustrated by a comment from the Rev. C. G. Thorne shortly after he took over the headship of Lagos grammar school in 1935. By then there were 350 boys in the school and sixteen African members of staff.

> The Local Government Education Department's Syllabus, [he wrote] is far better, as being more truly educative; but if we do not prepare our boys for the Cambridge Local, attendance would fall off at once, and so would fees *per se*, and we could not finance the school.

He regretted that the influence of the staff on the boys was far less in a day school than in a boarding school; but real results were obtained by talks at morning prayers, confirmation classes, and scripture teaching. Miss Margaret Potts noted the same kind of difficulties in day-school education at Lagos girls' school.

> In the case of many of the day-girls, home influence runs counter to the influence of the School, and is stronger because it is exerted for seventeen hours out of the twenty-four every day, and in the holidays and at weekends. Lagos has a veneer of European civilization, but the primitive is very near the surface. . . . It is easy to feel that the task is a hopeless one, which it would be of course without the power of God working with us.[24]

Medical Mission

The Yoruba mission was unique among the larger CMS missions in having no hospital until 1936 and no resident doctor until 1937. In the pioneer days missionaries had started dispensaries at Abeokuta and Ibadan, but the first step towards a more professional medical mission was taken in 1928 when Bishop Melville Jones invited Sister Mary Elms to visit his diocese and to initiate maternity and child welfare work. She had recently retired from Iyi Enu hospital in eastern Nigeria and by her achievements and writing had earned a unique reputation in this field in West Africa (see Eastern Nigeria, p. 99). She stayed eighteen months, but it was not until 1936 that a small maternity home was opened by Mrs Payne in Benin City.

Archdeacon Dallimore had pleaded for some years for a mission hospital up-country in western Nigeria, and in 1935 the parent committee sanctioned an appeal for £2,000 for building such a hospital at Ado Ekiti. It was made clear that the expenses must be met from government grants and from money already collected. In September 1936 the Governor of Nigeria opened the small twenty-bed hospital at Ado. Mrs Dallimore had supervised welfare work there for some years previously and she took charge until Dr Hilary Gunton arrived in January 1937. At first Dr Gunton had the help of only one trained nurse from Iyi Enu hospital. During the first year there were some three to four hundred in-patients, a hundred and twenty midwifery cases, and some six hundred out-patients. She was a surgeon and she had intended to specialize in surgery; but after a few months in Ekiti the appallingly high rate of infant mortality in the district impelled her to concentrate on maternity training and infant welfare. In 1940 Dr Eva Weddigen took over the hospital. She had formerly served with the Basel Mission and was well-versed in tropical medicine.[25] Four out-station clinics were started, and in July 1942 the CMS medical committee accepted responsibility for the Yoruba medical mission.

It will have become evident from the foregoing account that the period 1910 to 1942 was a difficult one for the Anglican Church and mission in western Nigeria. The day of the pioneers was more remotely in the past than for any mission area in tropical Africa except Sierra Leone and the problems of 'third generation Christianity' were more acute in consequence. But new missionary enterprises were not lacking, and Archdeacon Dallimore in Ekiti, Miss Jessie Mars at the Girls' Training Centre at Akure, and C. W. Wakeman during his long service in Lagos were doing more than faithfully transmitting a tradition of missionary service inherited from the past; they, with their younger colleagues, were exploring new forms of missionary relationship to a mature African church.

NOTES

1. E. A. Ayandele, *The Missionary Impact on Modern Nigeria, 1842–1914*, Longmans, 1966, pp. 68, 69, 156, 157.
2. *CMS Gazette*, 1917, p. 158.
3. G3/A2/P5, 1913/60.
4. P5, 1911/32 v, 108; 1912/135; also Ayandele, op. cit., pp. 248–9.
5. CMS *Annual Report*, 1914–15, p. 37.
6. *CMS Gazette*, 1917, p. 226.
7. P6, 1919/xvi.
8. P5, 1911/70.
9. G/Y/A2/3, L. C. Hickin to M. A. C. Warren, 24th August, 1942.
10. P6, 1924/xviii.
11. P6, 1928/11, ii.
12. From notes on West Africa CMS bookshops, lent by H. B. Thomas.
13. ibid.
14. P6, 1934/35.
15. G/Y/A2/4, W. W. Cash to Bishop of Lagos, 14th June, 1932; Bishop of Lagos to Cash, 1st July, 1932.
16. GY/A2/3, Bishop of Lagos to Canon S. V. Latunde, 5th September, 1934. See also Ayandele, op. cit., pp. 267ff.
17. *AR* (MS), 1935–36, p. 6; 1936–7, pp. 8, 10. The writer was Miss M. I. Potts.
18. G/Y/A2/3, letters cited.
19. *CMO*, Archdeacon H. Dallimore, 'Aftermath of the Prophet Movement', October 1938, pp. 220–22.
20. *AR* (MS), 1939–40, p. 10.
21. P6, 1927/32, 39; 1928/36.
22. P6, 1930/33; 1932/xiva.
23. P6, 1934/44.
24. *AR* (MS), 1935–6, p. 9.
25. *CMO*, 'Builders of an African Hospital', February 1941, p. 4.

Northern Nigeria

There is no understanding of the development of the CMS northern Nigeria mission otherwise than in the context of those political events which followed upon the establishment of the British protectorate in 1900.

British influence had been slowly penetrating the area under the dynamic leadership of Sir George Goldie of the Niger Company. The scramble for Africa set in train by the Congress of Berlin 1884–5 meant that political intervention was bound to follow commercial penetration. In the sequel, on January 1st, 1900, Colonel Lugard hoisted the Union Jack at Lokoja and proclaimed a British protectorate.

As high commissioner Lugard had at his disposal to enforce British rule over an area of 254,000 square miles a total force of fifty-eight British officers, eighty-eight British NCOs and rather less than 3,000 African soldiers. His civil administrators by the end of the first year numbered nine political officers. With this exiguous force Lugard had to enforce peace and secure it in the face of overt resistance and universal suspicion.

These circumstances determined policy. Lugard was clear that only by reassuring the local emirs that their own privileges were not threatened, and that interference with their political authority would be minimal, could British rule be established. This meant the policy of indirect rule through the native authorities, a British Resident in each emirate being essentially an adviser.

Lugard realized that religion was the most sensitive area, and the one in which suspicions and mistrust were most liable to produce armed revolt. He therefore laid down that there would be no interference with religion. For his own part, this did not mean any permanent refusal to allow access to Christian missions. Indeed his friendship with and deep respect for the CMS pioneer missionary, Dr Walter Miller, demonstrated this beyond doubt. All Lugard asked was that in the early years of British occupation the missionaries should be mainly concerned with the pagan areas, and that in Muslim areas they should have in mind the not unnatural suspicions of the Muslim inhabitants.

Dr Miller, without compromising his evangelistic objective, recognized the wisdom of Lugard's policy and co-operated with it.

The main difficulties which Miller and other missionaries had to face came when Lugard left in 1906 to become Governor of Hong Kong. Those who took over responsibility in northern Nigeria proved wholly unsympathetic to Christian missions, viewing them as a menace to security and peace.

This was the context of the relations of missions and government in northern Nigeria from 1906–30.

In 1910 northern Nigeria was one of the three CMS missions which, with the Niger Delta Church and the district church councils of Lagos, Ibadan and Abeokuta, constituted the Anglican diocese of Western Equatorial Africa. The mission headquarters was at Lokoja, a cosmopolitan town near the confluence of the Niger and Benue rivers. Apart from the Lokoja district there were three widely separated areas of mission in the northern provinces: (1) in the Nupe country north-west of Lokoja, at Bida, the chief town, and at Katcha on the Baro-Kano railway which was nearing completion in 1910; (2) on the Bauchi, or Jos, plateau. There, well to the north of the river Benue, there were two stations manned by the Cambridge University Missionary Party; (3) in the Hausa states, with headquarters at Zaria, near the southern edge of the Hausa-land plains.

Lokoja had been a CMS mission centre since the Niger expedition of 1865, with continuous residence of a European missionary from the 1890s. All the other mission stations named had been occupied within the last seven years, between 1903 and 1910. The total Christian community associated with CMS in 1910 was reckoned as 310, of whom 204 were baptized and 113 were communicants. Nearly all of these were in the Lokoja area, and most of them southerners. By 1942 the total Christian community had risen to 11,891, but less than a thousand of these church members were indigenous to the north. The great majority were southerners who had migrated to the north and who were, for the most part, under the care of African clergy, also from southern Nigeria.

The problem of oversight for the widely-separated and thinly-held mission areas was a vexing one. Various solutions were proposed. Should they be placed under the oversight of the much stronger CMS Yoruba mission? Should the mission in the Muslim Hausa states be developed in separation from Lokoja, with which there was normally little contact? The problem was complicated by the differences in temperament, and in ideas of missionary strategy, between the two senior missionaries, T. E. Alvarez, mission secretary at Lokoja, and Dr Walter Miller at Zaria. Alvarez was an Oxford graduate who joined CMS for service at Fourah Bay College in 1893. He was conscientious, one might think inordinately so from the length of the minutes of the mission executive committee. He had been asked by the CMS parent committee in 1907 to 'organize' the northern Nigeria mission and that involved, as Alvarez saw it, attempting to organize the work of Walter Miller. Miller was essentially a pioneer, with his own methods and approach. He did his best work in freedom and isolation. He tended to regard the Lokoja committee as a nuisance.

The tension between these two able and devoted missionaries, and their differing views as to the best strategy to be followed in the CMS mission in northern Nigeria, aggravated human relationships for the next thirteen years, tragically arresting the progress of the work. But behind the clash of person-alities lay a practical problem of administration. Was the mission in the north to be administered as part of the mission in the south or as a separate entity? In insisting that it must be a separate entity, Miller was right. The whole setting of the two areas was fundamentally different, a fact which it took both head-quarters and the missions or authorities in the south too long to recognize.

In March 1924 a workable solution was at last found. A conference at Zaria, chaired by the Bishop of Lagos, decided that amalgamation with the Yoruba mission was impracticable. The ultimate aim must be a separate diocese for northern Nigeria. Meanwhile there should be a suffragan bishop who would act as secretary of the mission and have his headquarters at Zaria. Local committees would be formed for each district (Hausa, Nupe, Bauchi, and Lokoja) and a central committee for the whole mission, meeting at least once a year. The local committees would have a considerable range of executive powers, such as the framing of estimates, locating workers, and corresponding with the government on local matters. The central committee would receive reports from them and exercise general supervision. The parent committee accepted this solution (12th November, 1924); recognized the proposed central com-mittee as the CMS local governing body; and nominated, as superintendents of the four districts, Miller for Hausa, Alvarez for Nupe, Thompson, the West Indian missionary, for Lokoja and C. H. Wedgwood for Bauchi.[1]

CMS, far from being the only Christian missionary society in northern Nigeria, was numerically much smaller than the Sudan United Mission and the Sudan Interior Mission, especially towards the end of the period. Good relations were maintained between the societies and 'comity' arrangements were made and kept; for example in the Bauchi plateau area, until 1930 when CMS handed over its stations there to SUM, inter-mission conferences were held from time to time. There was one such conference at Lokoja in July 1910, attended by representatives of CMS, SUM, SIM, and of the Canadian Mennonite Mission. Resolutions were passed on matters of common concern. It was agreed that in mission schools the vernacular was to precede English as the medium of instruction; that African Christians should be dissuaded from wearing English dress and using intoxicants; and that the only valid basis for government restrictions on the freedom of missionaries to evangelize willing listeners was the necessary preservation of law and order. A series of larger inter-mission conferences was held at Miango from 1926 onwards. At the first of these there were representatives of the Dutch Reformed and Southern Baptist (USA) missions as well as those of CMS, SUM and SIM. A 'Council of Missions' was formed for northern Nigeria, and a warm welcome was given to the constitution proposed by SUM for a United Church of Africa. The 1930 Miango conference reaffirmed the desire to form a united church, and a federation of missions was proposed with the council of missions to act as its executive body. The Rev. Guy Bullen, CMS mission secretary, felt obliged to oppose it at the 1932 Miango conference:

> When the representative of one society said he had no objection to African laymen administering Sacraments, I felt I must remind the Conference that ordained missionaries of the CMS had a loyalty to the Church in which they were ordained as well as to the Society in which they were working.

The proposed federation was not put into effect, but the search for unity in these inter-mission conferences played a valuable part in the preparation of a union scheme for the whole of Nigeria.[2]

Relations with the Government

What has already been noted as to the policy of the government must now be followed in some greater detail. The British administration in northern Nigeria committed itself to supporting the wishes of the Muslim emirs and their subjects in relation to Christian teaching and preaching. No less determined were the missionaries in the north, backed by Christian public opinion in Britain, to challenge the restrictions which the government placed on their freedom to evangelize. This controversy occupies a great deal of space in mission records for this period, and its broad outline has been sketched already (see above, p. 71). What concerns us here is the effect it had on the plans for missionary advance made locally by the CMS missionaries in northern Nigeria. None of them was prepared to accept Zaria indefinitely as the only CMS station in the Hausa emirates; but they saw that it would be all too easy to be manœuvred by the government into accepting mission sites in other Hausa towns which were virtually useless for evangelism because of the restrictions placed upon their use. It was this that gave a critical importance to the lengthy negotiations for a mission site in Kano.

Kano, an ancient Hausa city with mud walls of gargantuan breadth and length, was the chief commercial centre of the north. Early applications for a CMS mission site there had been deferred until the railway reached the town in 1911. In December of that year Alvarez filed an application for the lease of a plot of land in the *sabongari*, the 'foreign' quarter where an increasing number of Africans from southern Nigeria had come to live. He knew it would be hopeless to expect a mission compound within the walled city under existing conditions, but the site was close outside the 'most favourable' town gate. He went there in January 1912 and building was started on the site. Six months later

(14th June, 1912) an Under-Secretary of the Colonial Office wrote to CMS headquarters disapproving of the lease, and an alternative site was suggested in the European quarter of Kano. Alvarez was disposed to accept the alternative as better than nothing, and the parent committee supported him against other missionaries who thought it would be no good. Sir F. D. Lugard, the Governor-General of Nigeria, had promised a decision after visiting Kano himself, and he wrote from there to CMS, London (10th January, 1913) saying that, in view of the objections of the Resident and the people, he could not give permission for CMS work in Kano. The missionaries found this hard to accept after waiting so long, but the Emir of Kano had apparently objected to Christian preaching, even in the European quarter of the town. Two years later in March 1915 Melville Jones visited Kano, encouraged by a note from Lugard that an application for a site in this area could now be made; but he found the Resident 'anti-missionary' and averse to making any concessions. Permission to open a dispensary was refused; requests from Muslims for Christian teaching could not be accepted; and there must be no evangelization from door to door. On these terms there seemed little point in applying for a site, but negotiations continued in a desultory way for another four years until in 1920 a site outside the walls was assigned for a missionaries' house and bookshop. The Rev. J. F. and Mrs Cotton went to Kano in 1921, and from there organized Christian bookshops in other towns of the north.

The difficulty of getting mission sites in the large Hausa towns forced the missionaries to explore other ways of advance. In 1913 when the CMS Yoruba mission began taking a special responsibility for the Hausa area, Archdeacon Melville Jones suggested two points of concentration which, he hoped, would avoid restriction by the government: (1) evangelization by Hausa Christians in villages north-east of Zaria, supported by Zaria church collections: (2) an attempt to reach the *Maguzawa* (i.e. non-Muslims in the Hausa states) by Hausa-speaking European missionaries. The second project soon ran into trouble. H. S. Goldsmith, Chief Secretary at Zungeru, wrote (29th September, 1913), to say that the government would feel bound to oppose it. The Maguzawa were scattered among the Muslims. If missionaries attempted to evangelize them they would find it difficult to turn away Muslim inquirers, and the government would be misinterpreted as allowing Christian preaching to Muslims. Melville Jones sent Goldsmith's letter to the parent committee, urging a 'strong approach' to the Colonial Office with support from the Edinburgh Conference continuation committee.

The parent committee did what it could to help. In May 1915 it appointed a sub-committee on 'Difficulties with the Nigerian Government' which met four times in the following winter and reported on 26th January, 1916. Its report asked for a recognition by the government of freedom of conscience, without forcible maintenance of religion. If the use of Muslim officials and Islamic forms of administration were unavoidable in pagan districts, they should not be

employed in such a way as to favour Islam and repress Christianity, and the
local vernacular or English, not Arabic, should be used for administration
purposes. The sub-committee thought it right to contest the '400 yards rule'
which required mission buildings to be at least this distance from African houses.
It requested the removal of legal restrictions on Christian preaching. Missionaries should inform the appropriate government officials of their movements.
It thought that other premises should be found for the mission school at
Kataeregi (on the Baro-Kano railway, north-east of Bida) which had been
dismantled by the assistant Resident and for which the lieutenant governor had
refused permission to rebuild. The Colonial Office insisted (16th February,
1917) that the present restrictions were political, not religious. It quoted
Lugard's opinion that it would still cause trouble to send African Christian agents
to towns and villages outside recognized stations. The Colonial Secretary would
ask the governor-general to report and give his views on the matters raised, at
the end of the war.

Relations took a turn for the worse in 1917. The Resident at Zaria refused
Miller's request for more land to provide a bookshop on the cramped mission
site inside the walls. He also made it clear that permission to live in the city was
a personal concession to Miller, and that it would not be extended to other
CMS missionaries when he left. The parent committee was ready to accept an
alternative site outside the walls, and did so twelve years later; but 1917 was
not a good time for negotiations. Lugard and some other senior officials thought
Miller could be trusted to honour the regulations in the spirit if not in the letter;
but considerable resentment was caused when the Rev. H. Earnshaw Smith,
who had joined Miller at Zaria in 1914, claimed the same freedom for itinerant
preaching in Zaria Province. Early in 1918 the parent committee requested its
missionaries in northern Nigeria not to embarrass the government.

In 1919 Lugard retired from Nigeria. He was succeeded as governor by Sir
Hugh Clifford, who had for the past seven years been Governor of the Gold
Coast. In the same year Melville Jones became Bishop of Lagos and he and
other CMS missionaries were hopeful that at last they would be allowed greater
freedom in the Hausa states. This hope was diminished considerably after the
bishop's interview with the new governor in March 1921. Clifford was not
prepared to allow new sites for district missionary work. Zaria could remain as
the only CMS centre; but African mission agents would be allowed to travel,
and bookshop sites could be taken up in addition to the one in the *sabongari*
of Kano. Clifford, in a long letter on 11th February, 1922, explained his policy.
In it he quoted a letter which Lord Milner, Secretary of State for the Colonies,
had sent him in 1919 at the time of his appointment. It divided northern
Nigeria into three categories: (*a*) *the Muslim emirates*, where the government
had promised no interference with Islam; (*b*) *pagan districts under the Muslim
emirates*, where missionary work could be allowed among the large tribes;
(*c*) *independent pagan areas*, where missionary work was to be encouraged if

there were only a few Muslims. The Maguzuwa, said Clifford, came under the first heading, because the majority of the population was Muslim with only a few scattered pagans. The same ruling covered the non-European reservations in Hausa towns. He maintained that the co-operation of the emirs with the government was only possible if Muslim religion and law were upheld and missionary work excluded. He thought that a resolution of the Lagos diocesan synod in 1920, condemning the emirates on the score of oppression, came near to dictating to the government. It had made the emirs hostile to the extension of missionary work.

The bishop in his reply to the governor's letter said that he must criticize when the British administration appeared to be wrong. He felt that mission should not be excluded among Muslims. He agreed that indirect rule was the only feasible policy at present but he thought the danger of rebellion was overrated.

Clifford continued to follow a rigid policy of exclusion in the Muslim areas. In his address to the Nigerian legislative council in 1924 he put emirs and administrators on their guard against those who would influence them to permit Christian missionaries to proselytize in predominantly Muslim territory. On the other hand, he made it clear that the 'pledge' given by Lugard to the emirs in 1900 did not give Muslims exclusive rights to proselytize in the 'pagan' areas of the north. The Bishop of Lagos, ever watchful, asked the parent committee to challenge the first point in the governor's speech. He suggested asking the advice of J. H. Oldham and of Henry Carr, the African chancellor of his diocese. Carr's advice was to go gently with the governor and to offer medical missionary work in the Muslim areas in the hope of greater freedom later. This in fact proved to be the way forward, but it only became possible after a change of governor and a change in missionary leadership. On 15th August, 1931 the new governor, Sir Donald Cameron, met the Rev. Guy Bullen (CMS secretary for northern Nigeria) and representatives of the Sudan Inland Mission and the Sudan United Mission. The governor said that he would not influence emirs against missionaries and would try to inculcate toleration, but it would be unwise to hurry. Public preaching could be allowed in the quieter places, if approved by the administration; and the visiting of houses could be permitted where there was a definite invitation to missionaries, or prior indication that their visit would be welcomed. These points were incorporated in amended terms for a certificate of occupancy for mission sites issued in May 1932, and on this basis the parent committee authorized application for further sites. In the case of CMS these new sites were used primarily for medical dispensaries. In his address to his legislative council in February 1933, Cameron said that the time was past when indirect administration could be regarded 'as a sacred and mysterious art peculiar to Nigeria and understood only by a chosen few. We have advanced now to the stage when the curtain is being gradually withdrawn and I hope will be fully withdrawn within a comparatively brief

period.' It was against this background of government policy that Bullen wrote:
'It can be truthfully said that the bigger Emirates really are beginning to be
accessible. An appeal for men (for Muslim areas) ten years ago might have been
met with a "Where are they going?" Today we have the reply.'[3]

The Hausa Band

Early in 1922 Miller offered to resign the superintendence of the CMS Hausa
mission to a younger man. He hoped it would be Earnshaw Smith. He hoped
also to continue working in northern Nigeria as an independent missionary
'in harmony with CMS'.[4] His sister Ethel had been doing so for some years, and
it was not surprising that Walter Miller should covet similar freedom for
himself. His offer of resignation was not taken up at the time. Earnshaw Smith
was back in England as head of the Cambridge University Mission Settlement
in Bermondsey, and it was doubtful whether, on health grounds, he could return
to Nigeria. No other suitable successor was in sight; but the need for a new
missionary strategy in northern Nigeria, and other Muslim areas, was beginning to be felt at CMS headquarters.

In the Michaelmas term 1923, G. T. Manley, the Society's Africa secretary,
visited Cambridge. He met a small group of men who were already persuaded
that God was calling them to offer their lives for missionary service among
Muslims. One of them recalled Manley's visit in these terms:

> His specific appeal was for a band of men for Transjordan in three or four
> years' time and for Northern Nigeria, ready rather later. Transjordan was
> out of the question as we could not be ready in time: but the way in which
> he developed the idea of a push in the Muslim-speaking Hausa emirates
> of Northern Nigeria seemed to point to just the very thing we had visual-
> ized.

By March 1924 a 'Hausa Band' had been formed by this Cambridge group.
Its first members were: Guy Bullen and W. H. Oswald, preparing for ordination
at Ridley Hall, Cambridge; Norman Cook, in medical training (his father was
J. H. Cook, formerly of Uganda and by then the Society's physician at headquarters); and Max Warren, in his first year at Jesus College. These four
decided to offer to CMS with the strong conviction that they should work as a
team, and they had some difficulty in persuading the candidates' department
and secretariat at Salisbury Square that this conviction was integral to their
offer.

> They asked us [Warren wrote later] to enlarge our offer of service to include
> the whole of Northern Nigeria, 'pagans' as well. We guessed at the time what
> this would probably mean: namely, that the band would be split up, indi-
> viduals drafted as recruits to various missions.

In the end they agreed to make an open offer for northern Nigeria, 'with stress on Muslim work'.

In June 1924 a conference of missionaries was held at Zaria, presided over by Bishop Melville Jones. It drew up plans for the reorganization of the Nigeria mission on the assumption that recruits would be arriving in the next year or two. Reports of this conference encouraged the Band to think that they would be kept together; but a letter which Bishop A. W. Smith wrote to Wilson Cash after the conference (29th June, 1926) makes it clear that he was not prepared at that stage to treat the offer from the Hausa Band as restricted to the Hausa states. He thought that because Oswald was not musical he would find the tonal Nupe language too difficult: but Wedgwood was the only ordained missionary on the Bauchi plateau and he was opening up new work among the Sewaya tribe, many of whom understood Hausa. The bishop evidently thought that if the new recruits were all prepared to learn Hausa they could be deployed individually to any area of the north where Hausa was spoken. Bishop Smith was himself feeling the weight of the restrictions already described. 'The Government,' he wrote, 'regard all missionaries in Zaria, apart from Dr Miller, as here on sufferance.' Itineration in the Hausa states was possible but 'recruits could not do it without an experienced man to speak for them'. At the end of the letter he said:

> We will keep faith with them (i.e. the Hausa Band) if only they will trust us, and will only remember that the northernmost provinces of Northern Nigeria will be kept as a close preserve for Islam if the senior political men can have their way.

Bullen and Oswald, after serving curacies in England, arrived in Zaria in November 1926. Oswald was sent almost at once to help Wedgwood in the Bauchi plateau.

The Hausa Band accepted this disappointment, though not without protest, and continued its recruiting campaign. Its occasional paper, *Crusade Report*, kept well-wishers informed of the names and progress of volunteers and of the state of the Band's special fund for supporting them in northern Nigeria. In 1926 Handley Hooper returned from Kenya to succeed Manley as Group III (Africa) secretary at CMS headquarters. He was quick to appreciate that they were an exceptionally gifted and dedicated team, and that the Society should take them into its confidence. He counselled them 'to keep finance balancing your offers of recruits' and made it clear that if Warren was to get to Nigeria in 1927 it would have to be on special funds. 'I want 108 recruits for the Africa Group, of whom only eight can be provided on the budget, and therefore we must try every possible source of independent support.' In August 1927 the *Crusade Report* announced that money was in hand for Warren's stipend and early in December 1927 he arrived in Zaria. Soon after his arrival he described a typical day, much of it spent in teaching at the CMS school.

5.45 alarm. Prayers, 6.30. Ten minutes' Swedish drill. A very light breakfast with butter that tastes like gripfix, only not quite so nice. 1–1½ hours quiet time. 8.30 – 9.0, all forms, Bible reading, distinct from Scripture teaching. School till 10.30. 10.30 – 12.0 free time, learning Hausa, supervising cleaning of rooms, receiving visitors. Lunch . . . rest after. School 2.30 to 4.0, emerging in a state of absolute perspiration, therefore we play hockey.

In a further section of the same letter he described a lantern-lecture in Zaria attended by four hundred people: 'This took place in a big Muslim city in which our presence is represented, by the government, as an insult to the Muslims, a personal affront to the Emir, and a general danger to the public peace.'

By 1928 Bullen was proving himself a leader of mature judgment and a negotiator whose tact and patience were already beginning to show results. He was determined to secure new strategic mission sites; and if the price to be paid for them was to move the mission headquarters out of the walled city of Zaria, he was ready to press for a move. In February 1928 Bullen and Warren made a long trek in the mission's Ford car and explored a good deal of Kano Province, always with possible mission sites in mind. In July Miller took Warren with him to Kaduna to discuss with the lieutenant-governor the terms for the new Zaria site. A spacious square mile was promised, its nearest point being only half a mile outside the town walls, and 'close to the part of the city where our influence is strongest'. A 'gentleman's agreement' was reached between the CMS mission and the government that the existing compound within the city could still be used as a dispensary; and the government offered compensation, which Miller considered generous, for surrender of rights in it.

On furlough in 1928 Guy Bullen was married to W. H. Oswald's sister, May. She was a qualified doctor and, as the fourth member of the Hausa Band to reach Nigeria, she was soon making her contribution in the development of the medical mission in Zaria while her husband, among much else, completed plans for the move to the new – Wusasa – site outside the walls. In the Hausa Band occasional paper for July 1928, by then rechristened *Northern Nigeria*, Miller explained the reasons for the move. The compound within the city had become too cramped for the growing requirements of church, school and hospital. The church was over-full. Forty-four boys were being taught in a building designed for twenty. The grant of the old site from the Emir of Zaria pre-dated the government's ruling that Europeans could not live in 'native' cities, and it was better for young men to have a clean slate with the government. It was generous of Miller to write in these positive terms about the move for he was far from persuaded that it would help the mission to be more effective. 'I am prepared for a considerable set-back' . . . he wrote in the February 1929 issue of *Northern Nigeria*. 'Islam leads to apathy, and people who might walk half a mile for medicine would rather suffer and die . . . than walk three miles.' These forebodings were not justified. The medical side of the mission developed rapidly under May Bullen and Norman Cook (see below, p. 83). A fine new church was built on the Wusasa site between November 1929 and April 1930 and was dedicated by Bishop Alfred Smith on Easter day that year. Although twice the size of the old church it was soon full.

Warren was unable to share in these new developments directly. Early in 1929 he was invalided home and was desperately ill for many months. But as soon as he was able to dictate letters and receive visitors he was deeply involved once more in the work of the Hausa Band, holding the team together, recruiting new members, and writing to persuade the CMS secretariat that a concentration in Zaria was the soundest policy, and that the Bauchi plateau was not an acceptable alternative sphere for C. G. Thorne, the next recruit in line. Early in 1930 the Band's relations with CMS headquarters were strained for several months because of differing interpretations of the Band's financial commitment. The Band had originally put up £180 per annum for each recruit from sources outside CMS special funds: but by the late 1920s it appeared that this did not cover such items as cost of passage, equipment, and pension contributions. This meant that recruits found by the Band still came within the Society's annual quota of new missionaries, with consequent delays in passage to Nigeria. In the end the Band agreed to find £300 per annum from its own resources for future recruits, and on 4th April, 1930 Warren wrote to Bullen saying that it seemed to him that the storm had been weathered:

I am absolutely certain that if we play the game Hooper will see us through. . . . I feel as never before that we have got an Africa Secretary for whom Northern Nigeria is not just an office file but a living reality.

Like the Ruanda Council, with a similar financial arrangement within CMS, the Hausa Band was gravely handicapped by the great depression of 1929–32, and Leonard Hickin who was to have followed Thorne to Zaria in 1930, had instead to go to Egypt for several years, though on the understanding that northern Nigeria would be his field of missionary service eventually.

Under Bullen's inspiring leadership in the field the Wusasa site developed as a comprehensive mission centre in a way that the former site inside Zaria could never have done, and it became the springboard for advance into other Hausa emirates, previously closed to Christian missions. Cotton was invalided home from Kano in 1929, and after complicated negotiations, and under restrictions that irked him, Miller developed a new mission site outside Kano. In November 1932 he paid a return visit to Zaria. Bullen had been somewhat anxious about the outcome of this visit, since it was he who had insisted on Miller's moving from Zaria three years earlier: but he reported that the visit had been 'a great success and has done much good'. In 1932 Thorne, at his own request, transferred to the Yoruba mission and became headmaster of Lagos grammar school. Oswald also had moved to the Yoruba mission when the Bauchi plateau area was transferred to the Sudan United Mission in 1920 (see below p. 85) but in 1933 Hickin arrived and after a short time in Kano and Lokoja joined the Wusasa team. On St Luke's Day, 1935, Guy Bullen was consecrated in St Paul's Cathedral as Assistant Bishop in Egypt and the Sudan. Shortly before he left Nigeria he summed up the policy of the Hausa mission as exemplified at Wusasa:

> We aim at a church where God is really worshipped in spirit and in truth. We aim at a school where Christian character will be developed. We aim at a hospital where love may be manifested in action.

Of that school it is worth recording that one who made an outstanding contribution to its efficiency was Mary Locke, a trained teacher, who administered the school from 1925 to 1944; but the wider fulfilment of these aims belongs largely to a period later than 1942, for which the Hausa Band, under Bullen's leadership, had done some excellent groundwork. Their team pattern fitted the opportunities of the 1930s; but Walter Miller's dedication and achievement as a lone missionary in the northern emirates remained an inspiration to many.

The true monument to Walter Miller's thirty-four years as a missionary in northern Nigeria was the school which he founded. Although the original intention to make it a school for the sons of chiefs, was shipwrecked on the twin rocks of Muslim suspicion and official prejudice, Miller remained undefeated. He made the school a centre for a liberal education, with English as the medium of instruction. From this small school there has come over the years a steady stream of men of great ability and with a fine capacity for leadership. That so small a school should prove the source from which in due course would come a federal Nigerian head of state, a vice-chancellor of the Ahmadu Bello University in Zaria, a federal commissioner for Mines and Power, a principal of the School of Pharmacy, a chief agricultural officer for the North Central State, all of them convinced Christian men, as well as many others, is some measure of the far-sighted vision of Walter Miller. He retired from being a CMS missionary in 1935; but from 1900 until his death in 1952 northern Nigeria was the only place where he felt at home. In England he was always fretting to get back there. In Tripoli at the turn of the century he fell in love with the Hausa language and came to speak it with complete mastery. Mr Eric Hussey, in a foreword to Miller's autobiography, *Reflections of a Pioneer*, says that he

> conceived it to be his duty to learn to speak Hausa so that some day he should not be detected, when speaking in the dark, by a native of the country. He was commonly reputed to have achieved that standard . . . and he is probably the only European of whom it could ever truly have been said.

His application of this linguistic gift to a new translation of the Bible into Hausa was natural, and he spent much of his later years on completing it. But he used it also to get closer to the Hausa people whom he loved and served; and he coveted their gifts for the kingdom of Christ and for a united Nigeria.

It was an Ibo, Hon. Eyo Ita, in an article written soon after his death, who called him 'one of the greatest sons of Nigeria'.[5]

The Northern Nigeria Medical Mission

The first CMS hospital and dispensary in northern Nigeria was started by Dr J. C. Fox, at Kabwir on the Bauchi plateau in 1913. He had as his first helpers Africans who were untrained and for the most part illiterate. In 1917 he went to England to join the Royal Army Medical Corps, leaving in charge a dresser whom he had trained. After the first world war he returned to Kabwir but within a few months, in August 1919, he died of blackwater fever. No doctor could be found to replace him, and for ten years the Northern Nigeria Medical Mission was officially discontinued. Walter Miller, although qualified as a doctor, was absorbed in work of a non-medical kind; and although he and his colleagues at Zaria ran a dispensary which he sometimes referred to as 'our hospital' it never developed beyond the primitive stage until May Bullen arrived in 1928. Miss D. M. Saunders, who was a certified midwife, had come to Zaria from the CMS Palestine mission in the previous year and she and Dr Bullen began to develop medical work, as far as conditions of space allowed, before the move to Wusasa; but it was only after the move that expansion could begin. In January 1930 the CMS medical committee made an initial grant of £50 for the reopening of the Northern Nigeria Medical Mission, and a Medical Mission Auxiliary grant to Miss Saunders' allowance. In 1931 the building of men's wards and a doctor's house on the Wusasa site was authorized and in 1932 the in-patient accommodation was increased from twenty-five to forty beds.

The rapid development of the medical mission in the early 1930s owed most to the vision and energy of another member of the Hausa Band, Dr Norman Cook. He started branch dispensaries at Funtua in 1931 and at Maska, in the Katsina emirate, in 1932 with funds supplied by the Boys' Brigade in Britain. The Emir of Sokoto visited the Maska clinic and was so impressed by the work it was doing that he asked Cook to start a similar clinic in his emirate; it was opened at Chafe, forty-five miles from Funtua, again with support from the Boys' Brigade. On 11th May, 1933 Norman Cook died of septicaemia contracted, it was thought, in the operating theatre. He was a man 'who brought to everything he did life and enthusiasm'. Within a few months of his death his brother Dr Bertram Cook had taken his place as superintendent of the Northern Nigeria Medical Mission, and he was joined by Dr A. L. Craddock in 1938 and Dr H. A. Kelsey in 1940. A memorial fund to Norman Cook provided the means to open a further branch dispensary at Bakori on the railway line from Zaria to Kano.

In the mid-1930s Wusasa hospital became a government-recognized training centre for midwives, and the out-station clinics attracted an increasing number of patients. In 1936 attendances at Maska, Chafe and Funtua totalled 33,000, four times as many as at the base hospital at Wusasa. The charging of fees for medical treatment worried some of the medical staff. 'How can we teach the love and compassion of Christ,' asked Miss Saunders in an annual letter, 'while we haggle for fees and are harassed by every shilling we spend?' In his 1939 annual letter Cook described the aims of the medical mission. It sought to concentrate on services for which the government was at the time unable to take responsibility. The work 'flowed in four main channels': (1) house-to-house visiting in Zaria city: (2) women's work, and welfare clinics for mothers and children: (3) out-station, village dispensaries: (4) the leprosy treatment colony.

The medical mission had become involved gradually in the treatment of leprosy. In 1932 a government leprosy treatment centre was moved closer to Zaria, in order to benefit from Norman Cook's oversight, and in 1937 the government requested CMS to take over full responsibility for its development. Freedom for religious teaching was guaranteed provided that it was not made compulsory. The medical mission accepted this responsibility with funds provided from several sources. During the first fifteen months (1937–38) the total cost of £713 was met by £413 from the Native Administration, £100 from the Mission to Lepers and £200 from CMS, partly by special donations. The British Empire Leprosy Relief Association shared with the Native Administration the cost of the buildings and the colony's car. By 1939 there were 170 patients in the colony and numbers were still growing.

Sister N. Protheroe, a new arrival in 1940, described Wusasa hospital as much like a cottage hospital in England. By then nurses and dressers from the out-station clinics were being brought into Wusasa every few months for refresher courses. The distance of the hospital from the centre of Wusasa was still deplored by some missionaries. One annual letter in 1941 commented that it was five miles from the Hausa people it was seeking chiefly to serve, and six miles from the southern community near the railway station. But by that time the revived Northern Nigeria Medical Mission had already proved itself as 'the great breaker-down of prejudice' which a decade earlier the Hausa Band had hoped for. Churches and schools were established in connection with the dispensaries at Maska, Chafe and Bakori. St Andrew's Church, Bakori, was built as a memorial to Mrs Varley Roberts, one of the early supporters of the Hausa Band. A small church at Chafe, with money from the Life Boys in England, commemorated Norman Cook. Both were dedicated in 1939 by Leonard Hickin. The schools at the medical out-stations developed as 'feeders' to the Zaria CMS middle school.[6]

The Bauchi Plateau

Mention has already been made of the Cambridge University Missionary Party and their work on the Bauchi, or Jos, plateau. The CUMP, like its later counterpart the Hausa Band, was a largely self-supporting group within CMS.

Their mission area was one in which 'pagan' tribes had resisted, with varying degrees of effectiveness, the Fulani advance from the north in the nineteenth century. The hope that they would prove more responsive to the Christian message than the Muslims of the Hausa states proved to have little substance. The Mhagavul tribe around Panyam were called *Sura* by the Hausas. It was a term of contempt which was little deserved. They had fought off numerous attacks by the Hausa cavalry and held tenaciously to their tribal religion and customs. Their response to Christian missionaries was guarded and suspicious and it was eight years before any of them accepted baptism.

In 1910 there were four CUMP missionaries on the Bauchi plateau, the Revs. G. T. Fox, C. H. Wedgwood, J. W. Lloyd, and Dr J. C. Fox, the first and last named being sons of Prebendary H. E. Fox, Honorary Clerical Secretary of CMS. In February 1910 Lloyd reported that he and John Fox were about to open a new mission station among the Angass tribe. The language was much like Sura and the chief and people were friendly. Kabwir, the site chosen, was below the main plateau, about 2,000 ft. above sea level. In 1915 the first baptisms were administered, of two men at Panyam and twelve at Kabwir; and in the same year Wedgwood reported (20th March, 1915) that government approval had been given for building on a site at Amper (or Per) a few miles from Kabwir. Lloyd went to work there but a year later he caught blackwater fever and died at Kaduna on 22nd October, 1916. In spite of their height these plateau stations proved far from healthy for Europeans. George Fox died in 1912 and his brother John in August 1919. Of the four CUMP missionaries of 1910 only Wedgwood survived to work through another decade before returning to a parish in England in 1929. There were reinforcements, notably the Rev. Ernest Hayward and his wife (1911) and Miss Elsie Webster (1919). In 1922 Wedgwood described the situation as still 'tough'. African evangelists were being trained, but insistence on monogamy as a condition of baptism had produced a crisis among adherents of the mission. Church membership remained small. Oswald found fifty baptized Christians at Panyam when he arrived in 1926.

In April 1929 Wedgwood wrote to the parent committee of CMS suggesting that the Bauchi plateau mission stations should be transferred to the Sudan United Mission. He gave three reasons: (1) the Society's retrenchment policy, which precluded adequate reinforcement; (2) the advance of SUM and SIM in surrounding areas; (3) the 'uncertain income' from personal supporters of CUMP. The parent committee were prepared to transfer Kabwir but temporized about the transference of Panyam. It was the strongest centre, and the missionaries there had made it clear that they were against the transfer. In August 1929 the secretary of SUM wrote to say that his committee were prepared to consider taking over the CMS stations provided all were included, and no conditions laid down about continuing Anglican leadership. They intended to work with Church of England missionaries at the outset, but could not pledge themselves to do so indefinitely as it was the aim of SUM to create an African united church.

The CMS Africa committee approved the transfer to SUM in January 1930, on the understanding that there would be no sudden changes of policy and method. Oswald moved south to serve in the Yoruba mission. The Rev. Henry Miller, Walter Miller's adopted African son, was appointed pastor of Hausa congregations in connection with SUM and Miss Webster continued her effective work at Panyam for many years as a 'loaned' CMS missionary.[7]

The Nupe, Lokoja and Bassa Districts

Bida, the main city of the Nupe people, was renowned for its brass, silver and metal craftsmanship. CMS missionaries, the Rev. J. L. and Mrs Macintyre, were stationed there in 1903. The annual report describes them as 'shut in by a "solid wall of opposition", and it is almost impossible to induce the people to listen to the Gospel unless some attraction such as the lantern or the phonograph is offered them'. Macintyre attributed the lack of response mainly to fear. 'When a Nupe is asked to do anything he is afraid of three different sets of people: first his relatives; second the lord whose dependent he is; and third the king.' Katcha, south-east of Bida, became a CMS centre of mission in 1909 when Mr A. E. Ball was stationed there. His attempt to start a school met with little response, but a dispensary proved popular. In 1910 Bishop Tugwell and his advisers allocated £400 from the Pan-Anglican Fund for a training institution for evangelists at Katcha. Macintyre was appointed Archdeacon for Northern Nigeria in 1912 and a year later transferred to Palestine. Ball succeeded him as superintendent of the Bida district. Nine young Africans were baptized in September 1912 and Ball saw many other signs of a changing attitude to the Christian message. He reported large congregations in village churches in the neighbourhood of Bida. Ball resigned in 1914, unsettled by the lack of accommodation for his wife and by the uncertainties, mentioned earlier, about the leadership and oversight of the northern Nigeria mission. The Rev. N. C. Orr, who followed Ball as superintendent missionary, saw some progress in the Nupe mission, but he too felt frustrated by the lack of reinforcements, and by the isolation of this section of the mission, and by the continuing restrictive policies of the government, which did not affect the Hausa states only. On 19th February, 1923, Orr and two other CMS missionaries who had served in the Nupe district – the Revs. A. Beaghen and C. H. Williams – met G. T. Manley at CMS headquarters. There was talk of reinforcements – two missionaries permanently at Bida and two elsewhere in the district; of building a missionary's house at Bida; and of increasing the pay of African mission agents. The reinforcements, as so often during this period, were not immediately forthcoming; and the reorganization of the northern Nigeria mission made at the 1924 Zaria meeting was not acceptable to Orr and Williams, who resigned in 1925. Alvarez moved from Lokoja to Katcha as superintendent of the Nupe district; and the Rev. C. N. Daintree, who had been stationed at Bida since 1921, worked his way through the vexations and set-backs to become an accomplished trainer of evangelists. By 1932 there were fourteen out-stations in the district and eighteen evangelists who divided their time between oversight of these village centres and itinerant evangelism.[8] A hostel for the sons of Nupe mission agents and village teachers was opened at Bida in 1933 and named after Daintree.

The first Nupe to be ordained into the Anglican ministry was Daniel Tsado Sheshi, made deacon in January 1935. Alvarez described the ordination as something of an experiment, aimed at assisting the mission policy of keeping Christian converts on their own ground and out in their villages.

In the Bassa district, across the Niger from Lokoja, there was a greater response than any area of the north in the 1930s. Bassa was one of the regions where the Aladura (Prophet) movement made great impact, and Miss K. E. Ritsert and Miss Christine Matthews were transferred from Lokoja to Kpata in 1931 to work among those influenced by it. Miss Ritsert started medical work in a small dispensary and in 1934 Miss Matthews opened a maternity and child welfare clinic. It proved difficult to confine its scope. People with all sorts of complaints came to it and many called it 'the hospital'.[9]

In *The Church Missionary Outlook*, January 1936, Miss Matthews gave an encouraging progress report from Kpata.[10] The traditional religion of the people by then had been largely superseded by Islam, but nearly a hundred village churches had been built, mostly very simple structures of mud and thatch. In Kpata itself Muslims and other non-Christians had helped to build a large church, ninety feet long. By the end of 1935 it had a regular congregation of two hundred and fifty people. There were only seven paid African church workers in the Bassa district, but the total number of regular worshippers was about eight thousand. Miss Matthews described an instruction class which she ran for great-grandmothers; and she kept open house for adolescent girls who fled to her for shelter in order to avoid enforced marriage to a Muslim or pagan husband.

Self-support was still a distant goal for the Anglican churches in this area. In 1939 CMS grants for general mission purposes in the Lokoja, Bida and Bassa districts were reduced from £999 to £654 per annum. Alvarez described the results of this cut in grants as devastating. In the Bida district it meant that ten African evangelists had to be dismissed, and twenty-three classes of instruction and ten base stations had to be closed. In the Lokoja and Bassa areas twelve evangelists were given notice for the same reason and seven base stations and thirty instruction classes closed. It seemed a tragic waste of man-power, as all the evangelists concerned had received from nine months to two years training. It appears to have been one of the fairly rare cases where the Society's general mission grants were being used extensively for purposes which in the view of headquarters should by that time have been covered by local church offerings; but for Alvarez, now very close to retirement, and caring deeply about those who had to be dismissed, it was hard to bear.

Alvarez retired at the end of 1940, after forty-seven years of missionary service in West Africa. An Oxford graduate, he began this long stint as vice-principal of Fourah Bay College. After five years he volunteered for pioneer missionary work among the Yalunka people in the far north of Sierra Leone. Canon M. D. Showers, who worked with him there, remembered him as 'a difficult man to please, but kind'. Then from 1901, apart from six years in the Niger mission, he had served continuously at Lokoja or in the Nupe district, for long periods as secretary of the northern Nigeria mission and latterly as a district superintendent. His travels in 1906 opened the way for the Cambridge University Missionary Party on the Bauchi plateau, and he had always hoped to return to pioneering missionary work in the Hausa emirates; but he was the kind of 'anchor-man' on whom a missionary society comes to rely. Almost inevitably, he came to be known as 'the lay bishop'. The tribute paid to him in the committee minute on his retirement would include many others who like him, were obedient in their missionary calling:

> Humbleness of mind and saintliness of character marked all his service, and the growth of the Church in West Africa during the last fifty years is witness to the blessings which God has given to the self-sacrificing labours of CMS missionaries of such qualities and devotion.

NOTES

1. G3.A9/P1, 1911/33-38; 1912/4-21; 1913/11, 41, 61, 70; 1915/33; 1923/8, 10; 1924/16.
2. A9/P1, 1910/75; 1927/1,2; 1930/17; *AR* (MS) 1932-3, pp. 21, 22.
3. A9/P1, 1912/3, 71, 112; 1913/30; A2/P5, 1913/74, 77, 80, 119 (about Maguzawa); A9/P1, 1916/3; A2/P6, 1922/20, 21; A9/P1, 1924/17; 1931/24, 31; 1932/30; P2, 1933/8, 9.
4. A2/P5, 1922/12.
5. *Hausa Band Papers* (lent by M.A.C.W.). Warren to A. W. Smith, 14th September, 1927; Smith to Cash, 29th June, 1926; Warren, circular letters, 13th–27th December, 1927; 17th April, 1928; 28th July, 1928; *Northern Nigeria*, No. 18, February 1929, p. 4; Hooper to Warren, 5th February, 1930; E. D. K. Wood to Hooper, 8th February, 1930; Warren to Bullen, 4th April, 1930; *Guy Bullen*, by his Friends, Highway Press, 1938, p. 89; W. R. S. Miller, *Reflections of a Pioneer*, CMS, 1936, foreword by Eric Hussey; Hon. Eyo Ita in *Nigerian Review*, August 1952.
6. H. Anderson, MS 'History of CMS Medical Missions', pp. 305, 436; *AR* (MS) 1937-8, p. 9; 1938-9, pp. 21, 22; 1939-40, pp. 15, 17; 1941-42, p. 9.
7. A9/P1, 1929-18-42; Africa Committee minutes 28th January, 1930.
8. *CMO*, T. E. Alvarez, 'Thirty Years in Northern Nigeria', June 1932, pp. 116-18.
9. *AR* (MS) 1931-2, p. 26; 1936-7, p. 18.
10. *CMO*, C. Matthews, 'Prayer in the Basa Country', January 1936, pp. 8-10.

Eastern Nigeria

The decade 1910–20 was one of immensely rapid expansion in the number of Christian adherents in southern Nigeria, but in the eastern region the rate of growth was roughly twice as fast as in the western region. The comparative figures, on one estimate, are

	1910	1920
Eastern	18,500	514,395
Western	17,000	260,500[1]

Various reasons have been put forward for this difference in growth-rate. They include (1) the effect of the social organization of Yoruba and Ibo peoples respectively; the former favouring early growth, the latter a more rapid growth at a more mature stage: (2) a pervasive, though somewhat superficial, spread of Islam in Yorubaland which tended to slow down the Christian advance; whereas in Iboland the advance of Islam was negligible. The CMS share in this expansion in the eastern region between 1910 and 1920 was much smaller than that of the Roman Catholic and Qua Iboe missions; but enough was happening through its agency to give missionaries' letters a certain breathlessness, in which thanksgiving for the wonderful response to Christian teaching was balanced by a fear that much of this response was superficial. 'Mass movement' was a term frequently used, but it was variously qualified. The Anglican Church was organized in two sections: the Niger district of CMS and the Niger Delta Pastorate Church. It will be best to trace their history separately until 1922 because during this time they had few dealings with each other.

The Niger Delta Pastorate Church 1910–22

Under a constitution approved by the CMS parent committee in 1896 and by the Archbishop of Canterbury in 1897, the Delta Pastorate church was a self-governing and self-supporting African church led by Archdeacon Dandeson

Crowther. The first article of the 1897 constitution described it 'as a branch of the Church of England . . . under the episcopal supervision of the Bishop of the Church of England within whose diocese, for the time being, the Delta of the Niger is situate'. This cumbersome phrase reflects both the estrangement that followed the 1890 'purge' of the Niger mission and the sustained efforts of Archdeacon Dobinson and Bishop Tugwell to find a way of reconciliation between the CMS and the Delta church. From 1906 the CMS in eastern as well as in western Nigeria had been organized under the diocese of Western Equatorial Africa, and Bishop Tugwell hoped that the Delta church would accept incorporation in the diocesan framework. By 1910 Archdeacon Crowther was prepared for this to happen, and the necessary consent for a change in the 1897 constitution was given by the CMS on 10th May and by the Archbishop of Canterbury on 16th August, 1910. In 1912 the Delta church conference accepted the diocesan constitution, and considerable internal reorganization followed. From the beginning of 1913 the Delta church conference was replaced by a church board; and district church councils were gradually formed, on the same pattern as the rest of the diocese. The archdeacon toured the churches of the Delta explaining what was involved and establishing district councils. On 26th February, 1913 the Niger Delta church board unanimously adopted a constitution for itself 'in pursuance of the Constitution of the Synod and other Regulations for the Diocese of Western Equatorial Africa'. Bishop Tugwell read a letter from Archbishop Randall Davidson at this meeting, which foresaw a great future for the Delta church and expressed the cautious hope that 'the Native Pastorate, headed in due time by a Bishop of African descent, will be able in the Providence of God to do more for the people of that region than can ever be done by those who are not themselves of African birth or upbringing'.[2] Another thirty-nine years were to pass before E. T. Dimieari was appointed first Bishop of the Niger Delta diocese. It is not surprising that African church leaders felt that the process of appointing a diocesan successor to Bishop Crowther was painfully slow.

In April 1913 the Delta Pastorate church celebrated its twenty-first birthday. It was by that time constituted in five districts – Bonny, Opobo, Okrika, New Calabar and Brass. There were only two clergy from the Delta itself, Anthony O. Ockiya and Moses A. Kemmer, both ordained by Bishop James Johnson at Brass in 1911. Sierra Leonean clergy continued to provide most of the leadership for some years to come. The church membership statistics for 1913 were: communicants 1,564; baptized members 7,211; inquirers 3,784. It had a number of schools chiefly concentrated in Bonny, including the Female High School founded in 1904 with Mrs E. M. George, a Sierra Leonean, as the first principal; and a boys' boarding school popularly known as 'The Bishop Crowther Memorial School'.

In 1912 a theological institute was opened, also in Bonny, for the training of clergy and catechists. Archdeacon Crowther had been working hard to raise money for it for several years. In 1910 he visited England to raise the £700 still needed for an endowment of £2,000. Bishop Tugwell assigned to it £400 from the Pan-Anglican Thank-offering Fund, and SPCK contributed part of the building costs. The Rev. F. M. Renner, a Sierra Leonean, was the first principal. The curriculum in preparation for the diocesan teachers' certificate was described by Mr E. M. T. Epelle as rather ambitious. It comprised the 'Scriptures (the Pentateuch and the Gospels), Prayer-Book, Greek Grammar, Greek Testament, Latin Grammar, English Grammar and Composition, Arithmetic, Algebra, Mensuration, Euclid, School Management, Elocution and Sermon Making'. The Bonny district church council served as the governing body of the institute.[3]

In 1915 the Delta church was severely shaken by the movement associated with Garrick Braid (see p. 38). Two pastors, one of them Moses Kemmer, joined the movement. Many of the keener church members as well as catechumens were attracted by some of its tenets. At the Delta church board session in February 1916 Bishop James Johnson felt it necessary to denounce the seceders as 'heretic and schismatic'. Not all the lay members of the board were prepared to follow the bishop's lead. A number of resolutions were taken which praised the good in the movement as well as condemning the evils. The ownership of church property occupied by seceding groups caused the board a good deal of anxiety, and it appointed a deputation to the appropriate government officials where churches or schools had been taken over by Garrick Braid's supporters. Most of these properties were recovered eventually, but law-suits continued for a long time, especially in the Opobo district where the movement was most influential. Many of the seceders also returned to the Delta church in the course of time, but a great deal of unrest and uncertainty had been caused, and the 'Christ Army Church' continued to find recruits from among the Anglicans of the Delta.[4]

Bishop James Johnson died in May 1917 and soon afterwards Bishop Tugwell appointed a commission 'to inquire into and report upon the causes and results of the recent disturbances in connection with the Delta Church'. The members of the commission were Bishop Isaac Oluwole, Archdeacon Melville Jones, and Mr. Henry Carr, the chancellor of the diocese. They visited all the main church centres. In their report they noted the long-standing grievance due to the virtual restriction of the ordained ministry to Sierra Leoneans. They recommended the strengthening and enlargement of the theological institute at Bonny as a training-ground for truly indigenous pastors; the division of the diocese of Western Equatorial Africa so as to ensure closer episcopal oversight; a regular system of advancement and a fixed scale of salaries for catechists and other church employees; the establishment of a district sustentation fund; the introduction of the 'union' Ibo prayer-book and hymn-book; firm adherence to the marriage ordinance for all church members; a longer period of preparation for catechists; the registration of mission sites and properties;

and the transfer of the Benin mission from the oversight of the Delta church to the CMS Yoruba mission.

The parent committee of CMS was unable to accept the threefold division of the diocese which the commission proposed because of its financial implications; but, as already recorded, it did accept the proposal for transferring the Benin mission to Yoruba oversight, and it proposed the affiliation of the Bonny theological institute to the CMS training college at Awka in the Niger mission of CMS, giving it a preparatory rather than an independent role in the training of clergy. Other proposals of the commission were followed up locally. For example, in an attempt to reorganize the finances of the Delta church, each district was required to present a balance sheet for the 1920 session of the church board. Bishop Tugwell presided at this session, and he obtained unanimous support for a resolution creating a central church endowment fund, based on a two per cent charge on the annual income of each district. In spite of the board's approval, the central church fund proved ineffective.

On 24th June, 1920 Adolphus Williamson Howells, a Yoruba, was consecrated assistant bishop. It was Bishop Tugwell's intention that Bishop Howells should be clearly identified with the Niger Delta church. He hoped he would reside in the Delta, acquire the Ibo language, and associate himself closely with the training institute at Bonny. On 7th May, 1920 Melville Jones, by then bishop of the new diocese of Lagos, urged that Bishop Howells should not have a permanent house in Lagos. The Niger delta must be his home base. A curious piece of history lies behind this request. Bishop Crowther, although indefatigible in travel on and around the Niger, always had his home in Lagos, and Bishop Johnson did so for much of his episcopate. Melville Jones evidently felt that in view of the division of the diocese into eastern and western sections, it would be anomalous to continue this tradition. In the end a house for Bishop Howells' family was rented in Lagos for six months only, while he himself looked for a suitable place in the lower Niger area. In September 1921 he selected Aba, on the railway north of Port Harcourt, as his episcopal headquarters. It was not in the Niger Delta church area, but it was close to it and reasonably accessible.

Bishop Howells presided for the first time at a session of the Niger Delta church board in March 1921. He created a favourable impression by including in his address a reference to the need for a truly indigenous clergy. Further disturbances broke out, towards the end of 1921, in some of the oldest church centres – Bonny, Opobo and Okrika – about the continuance of 'foreign' (i.e. Sierra Leonean) pastors; but in February 1922, on a mandate from the Archbishop of Canterbury, Bishop Howells ordained two indigenous clergy, Ebenezer Jumbo (who changed his surname to Dimieari) and Alfred Spiff. The ordination took place in St Stephen's Church, Bonny.[5] The Delta church had begun to feel that its right to self-determination was at last being recognized, and was therefore more ready to co-operate with the CMS Niger mission to the north.

The CMS Niger Mission 1910-22

In 1910 the mission had five main stations – Onitsha (1857); Asaba (1875); Awka (1904); Egbu (1906) and Patani (1907). The first considerable extension of the mission in the next decade was to the west of the Niger among the Igabo or Isoko people.

Isoko country, in the north-west corner of the Niger delta region, is swampy and at the end of the wet season two-thirds of the land is water-logged. Most of the Isoko clans trace their ancestry to emigrants from Benin city, but a smaller number originated in Ibo country on the eastern bank of the Niger. It was a remote area, difficult of access, but in 1908 the Royal Niger Company opened a trading post there and not long afterwards Christianity was introduced to the Isoko people by a non-Christian, Eda Otuedon. In July 1909 he was sent to the Isoko town of Uzere as clerk to the native court. His home was near Warri, and he had heard Bishop James Johnson preach there. For a few years he had attended the CMS church in Benin, though without being baptized. In 1910 Otuedon began to hold meetings in the court-house at Uzere every Sunday morning and afternoon. He read the Bible and taught hymns in English to the score or so who came to the meetings. His message was that God had sent his Son to save all people; the whole truth about God was to be found in the Bible; and it was not possible to become civilized until one became a Christian. Although himself a polygamist, and for this reason held back from baptism, he taught that Christians could only have one wife. From his preaching a small group of inquirers was formed, and interest in Christianity began to spread to other Isoko villages. The Rev H. Proctor, the CMS missionary at Patani, heard of this movement and in August 1911 the executive committee of the Niger mission authorized him and the Rev. J. C. R. Wilson to make an exploratory tour of the area, and by July 1913 the Rev. J. D. Aitken, another CMS missionary, had started visiting the Igabo people. In the next six years the response was remarkable. In 1919 alone 1,150 baptisms took place in the Isoko districts, over half the total for the whole Niger mission; and the number of adherents was by then estimated as 12,500. Aitken had very little skilled help, only one pupil-teacher and two 'Standard IV' evangelists. He preferred not to call it a mass movement, but rather 'a preaching of the Gospel by those who first heard'. In his annual letter for 1919 he wrote:

Now that a catechism . . . has been introduced and reading and writing are being taught, the attention of the convert has been turned from carrying the message to learning these things, with the result that extension has almost stopped.

He missed the spontaneous response of a year or two earlier when he had written:

Groups of twenty or thirty at a time (men and women), have come to stay in Patani for a week, bringing their food and finding their own lodging, to receive daily instruction, and now in their hundreds they are asking for baptism.[6]

By 1921 Aitken was long overdue for furlough, last taken in 1917; the African Church Movement was creating difficulties; and in March of that year the Rev. M. C. Latham was sent from Awka to help him. In 1923 Latham died of blackwater fever and Aitken resigned after twenty-five years' service. The committee minute on his retirement noted that 'the remarkable spread of Christianity among the Igabo' owed much to his evangelistic zeal and to his work as a translator. By 1925, when a provisional church council was formed for the Isoko district, there were seven thousand baptized Christians and eighty-five churches.

The other main area of extension during the first world war was at the north-eastern corner of the CMS Niger mission sphere, in the Udi coalfield. On 1st September, 1916 Bishop Tugwell sent a telegram to CMS headquarters: 'Immediate extension Udi urgent.' A letter followed explaining that the people wanted CMS teachers and that local chiefs were ready to provide sites for buildings. Spheres of missionary occupation had been arranged with the Primitive Methodist mission. The Roman Catholics and the Muslims in the area did not 'command confidence' in the people. The parent committee replied that no recruits were currently available for development in the Udi district, but it recognized that this area was an important link between northern and southern Nigeria. In July 1919, when there was still no prospect of a European missionary for Udi, the mission executive committee discussed the staffing problem generally. G. T. Basden found his position impossible. He was acting-secretary of the mission during S. R. Smith's furlough; superintendent of five districts; general manager of three hundred schools with twenty thousand pupils, and acting-principal of Awka training college. The committee proposed that unless there was a prospect of six new men by the following July, the work of the mission should be curtailed by (a) handing over the southern district to the Qua Iboe mission; (b) handing over the Udi district to the Primitive Methodist mission; (c) handing over the area west of the Niger to the CMS Yoruba mission. The parent committee recognized that the Niger mission was seriously under-staffed, and gratefully accepted Bishop Tugwell's offer to stay on as bishop in eastern Nigeria until the end of 1920, and thereafter to remain on the Niger in whatever capacity was useful until reinforcements arrived.

In 1921 the situation began to improve. A European recruit, E. F. Wilkinson, was promised to Awka, and two West Indian clergy, R. A. Llewellyn and W. L. Brown, were appointed, the former as tutor at the training college and the latter for district work. Looking forward to the formation of the new Niger diocese, Bishop Tugwell hoped that the new diocesan bishop and Bishop Howells would between them superintend the districts, leaving CMS missionaries free to concentrate on evangelism and education. He thought the Udi area was a suitable base for the next phase of extension. Its value would be enhanced as the Port Harcourt-Enugu railway line was extended northwards to meet the Lagos-Kano line.[7]

Co-operation in Education 1910-22

In eastern Nigeria, as elsewhere in tropical Africa, government education grants were to prove the chief means of maintaining a far larger field-force of European missionaries than would otherwise have been possible. But the CMS Niger mission was no exception in finding the first stages of co-operation with the government difficult. On 3rd June, 1910 S. R. Smith, secretary of the CMS Niger mission, wrote at length on the subject. Mr Proctor's name, he said, had been withdrawn from the provisional board of education. The board had 'done little or nothing' and the interests of the CMS mission were sufficiently safeguarded by the presence on it of Bishop Oluwole and Mr Henry Carr. Missionaries were happy, Smith continued, to leave to the government the establishing of English-speaking schools for Africans; but rather than have the evangelical character of the mission schools destroyed, and an English atmosphere introduced, they would prefer to devote themselves solely to education in the vernacular. The executive committee of the mission, debating educational policy in January 1911, took the same line. The purpose of the training college (at Awka) was to equip evangelists, teachers and pastors. If higher grade classes were started at Onitsha grammar school, preference should be given to those training as catechists. All other secondary education should be under the government or the Native Anglican Church; but in some places, such as Onitsha, Christian hostels under mission auspices might be useful.

Bishop Tugwell was less conservative in this matter than the Niger mission committee. He wished to see a mission secondary school started at Onitsha and to move the training college from Awka to Onitsha. He noted that the Roman Catholic missions had received £1,077 in government education grants in 1908, and that they had three schools, with 870 scholars, at Onitsha. Archdeacon Dennis and S. R. Smith supported the bishop in his desire for a boys' secondary school at Onitsha, and in 1913 they judged that the climate of opinion was favourable for starting it, as some Roman Catholic schools had been closed temporarily because of local resentment against the marriage discipline imposed by the Roman mission priests. In December 1913 a West Indian CMS missionary was installed in the old mission compound at Onitsha, with about a hundred boys as the nucleus of an 'upper' school. Permanent buildings had to wait another seven years. Money collected locally for this purpose in 1914-15 was returned to the donors when it became clear that the parent committee could neither find a missionary recruit to take on the headship nor help with a building grant. But fund-raising began again in 1919. Archdeacon Dennis had died two years earlier when the ship in which he was returning to England was torpedoed, and it was decided to associate his name with the school. Local chiefs promised

£1,000 and district church councils guaranteed a further £1,000 for the school buildings. Construction began late in 1920 and was finished in 1923 at a total cost of £6,000.

Acceptance of government grants for CMS mission schools did not come quickly or easily. In 1914 the mission executive committee still showed a five to one majority against it. The reasons given against acceptance were: (a) the 'conscience clause' allowing withdrawal of children from religious instruction on parental request; (b) the unsuitability of the government's education code to mission schools, especially in its preference for English rather than the vernacular as the medium of instruction; (c) the likely effect of government inspection of schools, directing expenditure to more elaborate equipment; (d) the government's emphasis on 'unduly secular subjects' and its insistence on 'burdensome clerical work'. Bishop Tugwell held steadily and patiently to the conviction that mission-government co-operation in education was desirable and he knew he had the support of the parent committee of CMS. The mission executive committee slowly came round to his point of view. In July 1919 it accepted the recommendation of the Niger mission education board that government grants should be sought for five or six elementary schools under trained African masters, selected on a written guarantee that they remain in charge of the same school for at least three years. The committee also agreed at the same meeting that the syllabus in their schools should be aligned with the government's educational code. Three years later, in 1922, it was decided to apply for a government grant for Awka training college.[8]

Bookshops and Literature, 1910–22

By 1910 the earlier translations of the Bible into the Ibo language were under revision, and an inter-mission conference had found in Archdeacon Dennis a translator of marked ability and single-mindedness. He had already been largely responsible for a 'union' version of the New Testament, and in May 1909 he started work on the Old Testament. For the next two years he remained at Egbu, largely relieved of other duties, his wife acting as his typist. The progress reports in his journal are worth quoting: 'We go on much the same day after day . . .' he wrote on 4th March, 1910. 'The translation progresses slowly, but every day brings us nearer the end, and I don't think I could ever grow tired of the work.'

A year later, 14th April, 1910, he was about half way through, making good progress in I Chronicles. He and his wife worked steadily at it for the rest of the year, most of the time they were the only Europeans at Egbu. 'No news of the Bishop or the Spencers,' he wrote on 1st October; 'It is possible the Bishop may give up his intention of visiting us altogether now that so much time has been lost. I don't think we have ever before felt quite so isolated.'

On 16th May, 1911, exactly two years after starting, the work was finished.

'The total number of foolscap pages of MS is 3,025 and that means about 2,500 pages of typed matter. Thank God for the health and strength vouchsafed during the two years of close application.'[9]

It was one thing to translate. It was quite another thing to get the union Ibo version accepted as the standard version. During the next few years Dennis had to fight for its acceptance. An earlier Ibo translation, the Onitsha version, was the standard textbook in CMS schools, and there was an 'adapted' Onitsha version which brought it nearer to Dennis's new translation but not, in his view, near enough. In January 1912 the Niger mission executive committee asked the British and Foreign Bible Society to grant 4,000 copies of the 'adapted', or 4,000 copies of the 'Onitsha' New Testament, as the union version was not likely to be acceptable. Dennis, who was in England on furlough, sought the approval of the parent committee for a scheme to promote the union version. He recognized that there was a good deal of conservatism, and he wanted to travel round the Ibo country to popularize it. This he did, with excellent effect, in the next year or two. At a meeting of the mission executive committee in July 1914 there was a greater readiness to recognize the harmful effect of keeping different Ibo versions of the Bible in use, and appreciative comments were made on Dennis's work. Bishop Tugwell asked him to lecture on the history and purpose of the Union version to the students at Awka training college, and to mission agents. The parent committee, endorsing the minute of appreciation about the work of Archdeacon Dennis, urged the Niger missionaries 'to work towards securing the universal use' of the Union Ibo Bible. By the end of 1919 its acceptance within the Niger mission was virtually complete. Bishop Tugwell reported to London (12th December, 1919) that 75,000 copies of the Union Ibo Bible, or sections of it, had been sold since 1913, and he paid further tribute to Dennis's achievement and to the consistent help given by the BFBS in promoting the new version.

Dennis was not the only member of the CMS Niger mission to give himself to translation in this period. The Rev. H. Proctor completed a version of the Book of Common Prayer in the Brass language in 1910, and in 1911 his 'Ijo Primer' was sent for printing to the SPCK. Bishop Tugwell asked the parent committee to delay printing Proctor's version of St Mark in Ijo in view of a possibility that a 'Union' Ijo version of the whole New Testament would be prepared before long. A conference of translators from several missions in the Ijo language area was held later in 1911. The time for individual translators was passing, and the advantage of inter-mission co-operation in translation was increasingly recognized.[10] From 1913 onwards correspondence about literature between the Niger mission and the parent committee tends increasingly to be about bookshops rather than translations.

A bookshop had been started at Onitsha in 1896 by J. N. Cheetham and, as mission secretary and treasurer, he continued to devote a considerable part of his time and energy to its development until his retirement in 1931. By 1914 its business had expanded considerably and the parent committee approved the appointment of F. E. Wilcock as a missionary on special agreement to assist Cheetham who was by that time much involved in school organization and finance. In the same year new premises for the Onitsha bookshop were completed with the help of a £300 loan from the parent committee carrying 5 per cent interest and repayable by instalments. Although the bookshop had a separate bank account in London the sanction of the parent committee was still required for even minor items of expenditure, such as £40 to complete the fittings and guttering of the new building. The Onitsha bookshop did not have the resources at this time to establish branch depots in any number and it tended to rely on superintendent missionaries as salesmen in their districts; but one branch was opened at Egbu in 1917 (it moved to Owerri six years later) and in the same year a site was secured for a bookshop in Port Harcourt. This was opened in January 1920 in a two-storied wooden house with a stockroom and shop on the ground-floor and rather primitive provision above it for missionaries in transit. In its early years the Port Harcourt bookshop relied heavily on financial aid from its flourishing counterpart in Lagos.

In 1922, owing to a misunderstanding which was cleared up later, the stock of the Onitsha bookshop, valued at £5,000, was treated by the parent committee as capital available for general mission purposes, and the Niger mission committee agreed to its proposal that £2,000 from these 'accumulated profits' should be paid into the CMS general fund, and that a further £500 should be used to underwrite the cost of passages and outfits for Niger missionaries.[11] Neither the London headquarters nor the local mission committee were quite at ease with the concept of a money-spinning enterprise of this kind, and the much greater profitability of the Lagos bookshop in the early 1920s provided an unfortunate precedent from the standpoint of the Niger mission. The Onitsha bookshop was in no position at that time to sustain the finances of the mission.

Medical Mission up to 1922

In the 1890s H. H. Dobinson had started medical work at Onitsha of a very simple kind. 'Almost all comers alike were treated with carbolic acid externally or salts inwardly.' Dr A. E. Clayton and Dr C. F. Harford-Battersby served for a time in the Niger mission at the turn of the century, and in 1902 Sister Mary Elms began her long and devoted service as a medical missionary at Onitsha. In 1908 Dr A. E. Druitt and his wife, who was a nurse, opened a small hospital at Iyi Enu six miles from Onitsha. It was soon attracting more patients than they could look after.

We have just had twenty men from Owerri, [Druitt wrote in 1910] bringing with them several sick, but we have no vacant beds, and no opportunity to operate, having already more patients than we can accommodate properly. Another batch of fifteen men came a seven days' journey, obliging us to take in three for operations. . . . The women's side has been enlarged to twenty-five beds, and even now some are sleeping on the floor, and two beds have been put up in the laundry.

In 1912 Druitt was joined by Dr R. Y. Stones and they started several branch dispensaries before volunteering for war service in 1914. Miss Elms carried on without a doctor, running the thirty-seven-bed hospital, including six cots for children, until a delayed furlough in 1919. In December 1918, shortly before she left for England, she wrote a letter to CMS headquarters which indicated the kind of strain imposed upon her during the years of war. It was not correct, she said, to talk of 're-opening' Iyi Enu hospital. It had never been closed. She had been sister-in-charge since 1916, running a large dispensary and two crowded hospitals with the help of four African dressers and four trainee nurses. The work had been highly commended by the government.

On return from furlough Miss Elms had a missionary recruit, Miss M. E. Margerison, to help her, but by 1921 she was on the verge of a breakdown and the hospital was under threat of closure. The native church council of Onitsha and the mission executive committee were quick to protest against this. S. R. Smith suggested that it would be wrong to give priority to the development of medical missionary work in the northern provinces when premises and medical stores were already there to be used at Iyi Enu. All that was needed was a doctor. Smith, by then archdeacon, and Miss Elms discussed the future of the hospital with the Africa secretary at CMS headquarters on 15th September, 1922. They both emphasized the need for a medical mission at Iyi Enu and they were confident that with a doctor in charge it would become completely self-supporting. The buildings and equipment were valuable assets, and it was a good centre both for southern Nigeria and for work among Muslims. On 3rd October Group III committee agreed that the hospital should remain open until a doctor became available, provided that another nurse could be found to help Miss Margerison.[12]

The Niger Diocese 1922-42

On 25th January, 1922 Bertram Lasbrey was consecrated in St Paul's Cathedral as Bishop on the Niger. He used to explain the curious title of his see, 'on' not 'of' the Niger, as factual because the river for two-thirds of its length was in French colonial territories and outside his diocese. He arrived at Port Harcourt in March. The Niger Delta Pastorate church board was in session there and was thus the first of the two sections of his diocese to welcome him. It was an important encounter, because the future integration of the diocese depended a good deal on Lasbrey's capacity to win the confidence of the leaders, both clerical and lay, of the Delta church. The new bishop evidently made a good impression, but the process of integrating the diocese required many years' hard work, much patience, and administrative skill. A description of the

diocese which Bishop Lasbrey wrote in 1925, for a Church Assembly Missionary
Council survey, sums up his first impressions and his hopes:

> The Diocese of the Niger is divided into two parts or archdeaconries, the
> northern one comprising the area in which the CMS operate, the southern one
> that in which the Niger Delta Pastorate operate. There are other large areas
> where the Church of England has no work. . . . What we look upon as our
> sphere includes the large majority of the Ibo tribes, the Ijaws and the Isokos
> or Igabos, and has a population of four and a half to five million. It is the
> most important and richest part of East Nigeria, and contains Port Harcourt,
> Enugu, Aba and Onitsha – in fact all the centres of any importance except
> Calabar.

He goes on to describe the two parts of the diocese in detail:

1. *The Niger archdeaconry* is divided into eight districts, each containing about
seventy churches, a good few of them having congregations of over five hundred,
but most ranging from a hundred-and-twenty to two hundred. Each district
is in charge of a clergyman, usually an African pastor. Each church is in charge
of an evangelist or catechist, except in the Isoko district, where agents are very
few. All African clergy, catechists, evangelists and ungraded teachers are
entirely paid by the native church, which also meets all expenses connected
with pastoral and evangelistic work, all church and school buildings, pastors'
houses, etc.

2. *The Delta archdeaconry* contains eleven districts of varying size but aver-
aging fifty-eight churches in each district. The whole archdeaconry is entirely
self-supporting, and, with the exception of the bishop, is without European
help. The 'fourfold aim' of the church in the Niger diocese is: (i) to evangelize
the whole Ibo country, of which 'a largish area remains almost untouched';
(ii) to improve very greatly the educational work of the mission, in which the
enlargement of Awka training college is a first requirement; (iii) to staff and
equip adequately one efficient hospital; (iv) to extend considerably the women's
work in both archdeaconries.[13] Lasbrey proved himself to be one of the outstanding episcopal administrators of his generation, and in the twenty years
that remained for him as Bishop on the Niger these aims were largely fulfilled.

The Extension of the Mission, 1922-42

The Delta Pastorate church had taken to heart Venn's dictum about self-
extension as well as self-government. E. M. T. Epelle gives a full account of its
'interior mission' in chapter four of his history of *The Church in the Niger Delta*
(1955). By 1918 the mission area covered 'a considerable part of the political
districts of Aba and Bende in Owerri Province', and a provisional church
council was inaugurated at Umuahia in July of that year. The council was made
responsible to the Delta church board; and the Rev. J. M. A. Cole, the Yoruba
superintendent of the Okrika district, was appointed by the board as general

supervisor of the interior mission and ex-officio chairman of the council. The Umuahia division was given a resident pastor, the Rev. M. D. Showers, and the first confirmations were held at Umuahia in 1923. The Aba mission station of the Delta church was the result of evangelism by Opobo church members. Central schools were opened in a number of places and a training institute for evangelists, with the Rev. S. S. Williams as its first principal, at Ihie. Showers and Williams were both Sierra Leoneans and both served for over thirty years in eastern Nigeria before returning to Freetown. By 1925 there were three hundred mission stations in the 'interior mission' area; and the Delta Pastorate church board opened a central training fund which assisted students in preliminary training at Ihie and also awarded scholarships for more advanced training at Awka. After the constitution of the Niger diocesan synod in 1931 seven of the interior mission districts qualified to send representatives to the synod, and the provincial church council was thereupon dissolved.

This development of the Delta church is an index of successful evangelization, carried out for the most part not by trained and paid agents but by Christians of the Delta church in the course of their trading inland. Most of the old coastal church centres of the Delta church became parents of some mission area until the number of established congregations required that they should be separately organized. Judged by European standards there were some deficiencies in organization, but the Delta church grew for the most part by the simple witness of Africans as they handed on their own faith. In 1931 the Delta Pastorate church board recorded a baptized membership of over twenty-seven thousand with more than five thousand, six hundred communicants. Seventeen African clergy were serving in fifteen districts.[14]

Comparable figures for the CMS Niger mission in 1931 were: baptized members, thirty-nine thousand; communicants, about ten thousand; forty-four European missionaries, ordained and lay; and about twenty-five African clergy. The growth of a church of this size had not been achieved without set-backs and anxieties. In 1922 the parent committee of CMS, faced with the need for severe retrenchment in all its missions, had suggested that the superintendence of missionary districts should be handed over entirely to the African church, as organized in the district church councils, and that European missionaries not engaged in training evangelists and catechists should be withdrawn. The mission executive committee reacted sharply. Such a withdrawal was an open invitation, in their view, to the Roman Catholics and 'the African polygamous churches' to absorb the congregations formed through the CMS, and promising work would be ruined. S. R. Smith was convinced that the African church could not support the West Indian agents without the Society's help and that it was itself 'weak in superintending capacity'. He suggested that the missions' general expenses, the chief target for retrenchment, could be cut in other ways. For example, district church councils could be urged to increase their support; and government grants could be accepted for Awka training college and Onitsha girls' school. There was, Smith maintained, a strong desire on the part of the African church to retain both the West Indian agents and the European missionaries.

The death of Latham, and the resignation of Aitken in 1923 left the Niger mission with only four European clergy, only one of whom was engaged in pastoral work; but by 1925 the parent committee seems to have accepted the need for strengthening the mission with more Europeans. In the summer of that year three new recruits sailed from England – R. E. Walker, located to Awka college for teacher-training; the Rev. B. J. S. Watkins, to the grammar school, Onitsha; and the Rev. T. H. Houghton to assist the Rev. O. N. Garrard, the district superintendent at Patani. Houghton died within two years, leaving Garrard once again as the only European missionary in the Isoko district, in which by that time there were nearly a hundred churches and many schools. Archdeacon Basden wrote to London (17th August, 1927) suggesting that if another missionary society could be found to carry on the Isoko work, it should be invited to do so. Garrard, he said, would be willing to work under the Bible Churchmen's Missionary Society. Garrard was invalided home later in 1927, and Daws was transferred from Enugu to give the parent committee time to decide on the future of the Isoko mission. Bishop Lasbrey pressed the claims of the Niger mission at CMS headquarters. The need for European recruits was desperate. In the last five years, during which the smaller Kenya mission had doubled its European staff, the Niger mission staff had been greatly reduced, except at Iyi Enu hospital; and the mission had received no building grant for years 'in spite of generous money sent home'. Early in 1928 the mission executive committee received a report from Daws about the great opportunity in the Isoko country. There were, he said, only twenty-four low-grade teachers to serve the needs of one hundred and four churches; and six or seven European men and three or four women were needed there at once. On the strength of this report, the mission committee took the drastic and unusual step of sending a cable to London saying that supervision of the Isoko district had ceased on 1st February, 1928.

H. D. Hooper, the Africa secretary at CMS headquarters, sought to clarify the position in a memorandum, 'European Personnel in Isoko Country: an Issue of General Policy'. The spontaneous growth of the Isoko church had been, he said, too rapid to allow the Niger mission to cope with the training of African leaders. The few Europeans had been overworked. The parent committee must either provide adequate staff or agree to its transfer to another society, such as the Qua Iboe mission; alternatively, the Niger Delta church might be asked to take over. Three years later, in 1931, the staffing of the Niger mission had improved considerably. Two missionary recruits, J. W. Welch and J. W. Hubbard, had arrived from England in the previous year. Mr and Mrs J. W. Jackson were on temporary loan for Isoko from the Yoruba mission, and Garrard and Daws had returned. The supervision of the Warri,

Burutu and Sobo areas was transferred in 1931 from the Yoruba mission to the Niger mission. This was a sensible move as these districts were adjacent to Isoko and remote from Lagos. In April 1934 Welch reported enthusiastically on the prospects of the schools and churches in the Sobo country. District church councils were formed for Sobo in 1935 and for Warri in 1938.[15]

Meanwhile the other extremity of the Niger mission area, the Enugu district, had witnessed the same kind of spontaneous growth which had taken place in Isoko a decade earlier. In 1927 Agnes Nwokoye, wife of an interpreter to a district officer, had started evangelistic meetings at Nsukka, forty-two miles from Enugu. African teachers were sent there in 1932, and in 1933 J. W. Jackson was transferred there from Isoko. He was joined by his wife after a few months, and she opened a dispensary and started an infant welfare centre. By 1936 there were fifty churches in the Nsukka district with a vernacular school attached to each of them. F. E. Wilcock was finding a similar response in the Udi coalfield area where previously results had been small. By 1939 St Peter's Church, Enugu, under an African pastor, the Rev. Daniel Okechuku, had a regular Sunday morning congregation of twelve hundred. The advance in some areas, including the Nsukka district, was too rapid to ensure adequate teaching of converts, and Wilcock (Archdeacon of Onitsha from 1938) reported in 1941 that there had been some falling off after the 'mass movement' a few years earlier. All the same, when the Niger mission celebrated its centenary in 1942 there was much to praise God for. The church in connection with the mission had grown marvellously in the 1930s. The diocesan synod by then represented fifteen hundred congregations, and there were fifty thousand pupils in mission schools. Best of all, the separation between the Niger mission and the Delta Pastorate Church was a thing of the past, happily forgotten in a new spirit of unity in the Niger diocese.

Epelle, who does not hesitate to use the word 'reunion' for this reconciling process, lists seven contributory reasons for it: (1) the constitution of district church councils across the former boundaries of the Niger mission and Delta church; (2) the common involvement in education (the first diocesan general manager of schools was chosen from the Delta church); (3) co-operation in evangelism (the organization of evangelistic bands from 1920 onwards brought clergy and laity from both sections of the diocese into close contact); (4) the common use of diocesan institutions, such as Awka training college and St Monica's School; (5) increasing contact in the field of women's work, particularly through the Mothers' Union and the Diocesan Women's Conference; (6) the common use, by both sections of the diocese, of the Union Ibo Prayer Book; (7) the fellowship in adversity which brought help when it was most needed. Epelle gives, as an example of this, the way Bishop Lasbrey brought with him CMS workers for a mission to the church at Brass when it was gravely threatened by apostasy. At the Jubilee celebration of the Niger Delta Pastorate Church in 1942 full credit for the reconciliation was given to Bishop Lasbrey.

He had seen the integration of the diocese, not as an end in itself, but as the outcome of co-operation in evangelism which required the energy and varied skills of all church members. Among the European missionaries, Proctor and Aitken in the earlier part of the period, Jackson and Wilcock in the 1930s and 1940s, ably supported the bishop's purpose 'to evangelize the whole Ibo country'.

Wilcock, a shy, soft-spoken man, was remembered by Africans as an outstanding Ibo speaker and evangelist, who would often win a hearing by playing his accordion. He was always among the first to pay tribute to his African colleagues for the great advances made in the Niger diocese in the 1930s.

Archdeacon G. T. Basden retired in 1936. He had served in the Niger mission since 1900, first as a pioneer missionary, then as first principal of Awka training college. In 1925 he succeeded S. R. Smith as mission secretary, and from 1931 was secretary of the diocesan synod. He had often been desperately overworked, but he kept his patience, and had a clear sense of priorities; not only in the field of education, but in the development of the medical mission at Iyi Enu and Oji River (see below pp. 108ff.) he had fostered institutions for the sake of their usefulness to mission, as means and not as goals. He had a knowledge of the Ibo people and customs which was unrivalled among Europeans of his generation, and government officials used his writings gratefully. In retirement until his death in 1946, he and Mrs Basden kept open house for West Africans in England; and he served on a number of the Society's committees.

On 5th January, 1938 Archdeacon Dandeson Coates Crowther died at the age of ninety-three. As a young man he had accompanied his father on many hazardous journeys, and his leadership of the Niger Delta Pastorate Church for nearly half a century made unremitting demands on his courage as well as his patience and wisdom. Bishop Gelsthorpe wrote of his closing years:

> To the end he retained his memory and to a great extent his shrewd judgment concerning character and events. . . . It was no uncommon thing to see two sides of a palaver standing before him. He would listen to each side in turn, just asking now and then a shrewd question. Then at the end he would, as it were, retire into himself, and then come out with a neat, clear decision. I know of no-one whose decisions were regarded as so final by both sides.[16]

Educational Work in the Niger Diocese, 1922–42

Bishop Lasbrey put education next to evangelism in his list of priorities for the Niger diocese, with 'the enlargement of Awka Training College as a first requirement'. The college received its first government grant in 1923. Application for it had been made on the bishop's initiative. In 1925 an extension programme of new building was sanctioned by the CMS parent committee at an estimated cost of £6,000, from money already in the bishop's hands and on the promise of a building grant from the Nigerian government. The new buildings were finished in 1928, and the government refunded fifty per cent of their cost to the diocese. The old buildings were kept in use to house thirty students. In July 1928 the Rev. Morris Gelsthorpe succeeded Basden as principal. By 1930 there were sixty students taking a four-year course of teacher-training; thirty more were training as junior catechists; and ten were in the divinity class, training to become senior catechists or clergy. Two 'annual letters' from missionaries at the college show the kind of policy decisions that constantly had to be made. In 1936, G. E. I. Cockin, member of the college staff in charge of the practice school, wrote of the conflict of duties, familiar to all concerned with the training of teachers, between what is best for them as students and best for the children whom they taught. 'In practice, of course, one usually has to arrive at some compromise.' In 1939 B. J. S. Watkins, Gelsthorpe's successor as principal, wrote of the strong desire of African clergy and laity to affiliate Awka training college to Durham University for a degree course. He appreciated the reasons for it, but 'as a missionary,' he wrote, 'I feel that this demand for higher education is at present crowding out, in the minds of African church leaders, the needs of the unevangelized, illiterate majority of the people of this teeming country, to supply which the college was founded'.

This conflict of interest between a direct missionary purpose in education, and the natural desire of Africans to obtain through the mission the best that Western education could provide was not confined, of course, to Awka training college; nor was it easily or permanently resolved. In the 1920s the Nigerian government was for the most part content to co-ordinate, and to assist financially, the educational provision of the missionary societies; but its insistence on even minimal standards of efficiency as a condition for grant-aid was sometimes regarded by missionaries as unwarranted interference, particularly the government requirement of school staffing at a level for which it was often difficult to maintain the necessary flow of recruits. 'The mission,' Basden wrote (10th March, 1926) 'feels bull-dozed into the education scheme from home, therefore the Parent Committee must meet the situation.' The particular issue at the time was new government regulations due to come into force in 1927, requiring more thorough supervision of grant-aided mission schools. The government were prepared to pay for European supervisors at missionary rates, and eighty per cent of the salaries of African supervisors, but Basden was still worried: 'If missionary supervisors are to be paid by the government, they will be government officials. Why then can they be paid only at missionary rates?'

As has already been noted (see Western Nigeria, p. 67), A. G. Fraser, Principal of Achimota College, paid an extended visit to Nigeria in 1927 to advise on CMS schools. He thought Basden was a 'passive resister' to all progress in missionary education, and that he wanted 'to reduce all supervisors to helpless nonentities'. Fraser also made unfavourable comparison between the schools of the CMS Niger mission and those of the Presbyterian and Primitive Methodist missions in eastern Nigeria; and he appears to have blamed Basden for the difference. This seems somewhat unfair. Basden, as mission secretary, conceived it his duty not to take on more responsibilities than the existing mission staff could maintain until the home church, through the parent committee, supplied reinforcements. As already described, in the years 1926–9 the Niger mission was going through a severe staffing crisis. Basden felt it to be inappropriate, and a misuse of depleted staff, for a missionary such as E. F. Wilkinson to be removed from Awka for 'purely office-work'; and he felt the parent committee of CMS was requiring him as mission secretary to co-operate with the government in education on terms which meant further financial duress for the Niger mission. The Society, for its part, was finding great difficulty in recruiting the qualified educationists for whom government grants were available in all its tropical African missions. It had to balance the requirements of one mission against another, and it had to husband its perennially inadequate resources.

Gradually the tension eased. Recruitment of educational missionaries was helped by the assurance given in 1928 by the Board of Education in England that service in grant-aided and government-inspected schools in colonial territories would count for pension rights under the Teachers' Superannuation Act of 1925. Missionary misgivings about co-operation with the government tended to diminish when it was seen that those who came out on government grants remained in the full sense missionaries of the Society. The Nigerian government was, for its part, reassured by the quality of the new generation of educational missionaries, such as G. E. I. Cockin (later first Bishop of Owerri) and J. W. Welch (later Director of Religious Broadcasting, BBC), and their evident concern for proper supervision of mission schools.

Thus reassured, the government was not ungenerous to the Niger mission. For example, when in 1938 in the Isoko mission area, the demand for village schools was still out-running the supply of teachers of adequate calibre and training the education department agreed to the temporary employment of twenty vernacular teachers who had not passed the 'first school leaving certificate', and were therefore not technically eligible for registration as teachers, provided they passed in the following year. 'Many, I know, will fail,' wrote the Rev. J. M. Carr; he thought the only solution for the Isoko areas was to start a junior training institution. By 1941 a training-course at Oleh was well-established, with twelve Isoko and two Urhobo students taking a three-year course, with a year's teaching practice after the second year.

In 1940 the Nigerian Board of Education discontinued the first school-leaving examination, previously taken at Standard VI, and granted certificates instead to all boys with seventy-five per cent attendance. This was not welcome to many Africans, for whom the school-leaving certificate had once been the gateway to government or commercial posts: but the supply of school-leavers had by 1940 outstripped the demand in these occupations and many Standard VI leavers were reluctantly returning to village life. The Niger mission's response to this new situation was to appoint Mr Kenneth Prior, a member of the Awka staff, as mission agriculturalist. The development, under his leadership, of a farm school for Standard VI boys, and an agricultural course for all schoolmasters, was in line with government policy and the actual needs of the community.

Apart from the teacher-training at Awka, the educational commitment of the Niger mission was almost entirely in the field of elementary education, and by 1942 there was still only one boys' secondary school in the Niger diocese, the Dennis Memorial Grammar School, Onitsha; and one major girls' school, St Monica's at Ogbunike, eleven miles from Onitsha.

The Dennis Memorial Grammar School, after the delays and setbacks already described, opened in February 1925 with thirty-five boarders and fifty day boys. By 1930 there were a hundred boys, including thirty boarders. In 1937 the Rev. C. A. Forster, who had guided the school through its early development, was appointed general manager of schools in the Onitsha archdeaconry. He was succeeded as principal by Mr E. D. C. Clark. By then the number of boys had grown to 270. Most of the boys were Ibos, but there was a growing minority from other tribes. At the outbreak of the second world war the school was still growing (330 boys in 1939) and Clark, with a depleted staff, found it increasingly difficult to maintain spiritual contact either with the staff or with the boys. Clark's answer was to restrict entry in terms of its missionary purpose.[17]

St Monica's School was described by A. G. Fraser in his confidential report in 1927 as 'good, but unprogressive'. A government supervisor's report of the same period was more positive in its praise but noted that the European staff were never off duty and were thus in danger of over-strain. This report was more just to Miss P. M. Row's headship. A woman of great mental and physical energy, though not professionally qualified, she was a pioneer of women's and girls' education in eastern Nigeria. She set high educational standards and girls trained by her became strong church leaders as wives of catechists and pastors. During 1927 the school temporarily lost its government grant for lack of a qualified teacher on the staff, and in the late 1930s the dangers of under-staffing and over-work were again evident. In 1937 Miss Janet Clarke, soon to succeed Miss Row as principal, wrote of the lack of time 'to get to know people as friends. It has been as much as we could do to get our lessons prepared and our books corrected for the next day.' Miss Marjorie Hill made a similar point a year later:

> Government examinations loom so large that you are apt to turn into an efficient business woman, and nothing else. . . . Something more will have to go for the staff to have a spirit of leisure, rested minds, and time to make and maintain personal contacts.

The remedies soon being applied, a gradual cut in numbers and a reduction in the hours of school work, were not welcomed by some of the African members of staff. The evident lack of shared missionary purpose made Miss Hill wonder whether it would not be much more worth while if all Europeans concentrated on training teachers and leaders, and left the masses for a time: 'They hardly touch them as it is.' In 1941 Miss Clarke wrote more hopefully. The African members of staff were taking more responsibility and showing more initiative. 'The prefects are also very helpful, and more or less run their own houses, making their own rules, supervising the garden work, and making us feel very hopeful about the prospects of self-government in the future.'[18]

Common concern among the missionary bodies working in eastern Nigeria for the training of teachers, especially of women teachers, led to the formation of a united (teacher training) college in 1938. Its purpose was to provide higher elementary certificate training for girls. In the first group of students, thirteen came from CMS schools, twelve from Church of Scotland, and a few from the formerly Primitive Methodist mission. The college was temporarily housed at Arochuku but it moved after a few months to Umuahia. The new buildings were completed there in October 1939, on a site overlooking a steep valley. The curriculum included agriculture, under Kenneth Prior's direction; and pottery, weaving, basketry and netting were taught by village women. When the chapel was almost finished and a date fixed for its dedication, a tornado wrecked it; but voluntary helpers repaired the damage in time for its opening on the appointed day. Anglican, Presbyterian and Methodist elements of worship were incorporated in the dedication service.

By 1940, through the initiative of Miss W. B. Yeatman there were twenty-nine girls' vocational schools in the diocese. They had no educational pretensions. The staff normally consisted of an African matron and a girl who had just left school, neither of them with any formal training. But these vocational schools were, by 1941, training some seven hundred girls at a time to become Christian wives and mothers.[19]

In 1940 under Miss Hill's guidance, the girls' training home at Egbu Owerri developed into an elementary training centre for women teachers. She started with twenty-one students, most of them with pupil-teacher experience. The two-years' course prepared them for the government elementary teachers' certificate. Miss Hill also helped to organize religious classes in villages within cycling distance of Egbu Owerri. These classes, run by mission agents and catechists, were intended for older children and illiterate adults, but under social pressures were tending to become infant and junior schools, serving as 'feeders' for the central school of the district.

Medical Mission, 1922–42

Bishop Lasbrey's third aim for the Niger diocese was 'to staff and equip adequately one efficient hospital'. The prospect of making Iyi Enu such a hospital was not bright when he arrived in his new diocese. The hospital was largely in ruins. S. R. Smith reported that the women's ward had collapsed and that Sister Elms was on the verge of another breakdown. But rebuilding in concrete, not beautiful but serviceable, was completed in the latter part of 1924; and in 1925 Dr Sybil Batley arrived, the first doctor in the Niger mission since the early part of the first world war. Two years later she was joined by Dr Jessie Horne. In April 1926 Mary Elms finally left Nigeria. She had kept Iyi Enu going against almost impossible odds; and by her writing and teaching she had prepared the way for a reformation in village hygiene in the Onitsha area which was already showing results in a reduction of infant mortality. She had also won over the years the sympathy and support of government officials. The Governor of Nigeria visited the hospital in 1926 and promised a grant to cover the salary of a woman doctor and a nurse and an additional equipment grant.

In 1929 a government grant of £1,000 was secured for building a new maternity block, and during the furlough of the two women doctors, Dr Mackay, the Senior M.O. for Onitsha, came daily to supervise the work of the hospital nursing staff. A third woman doctor, Margaret Roseveare, arrived in February 1931 and in April the new maternity block, later to be named after Mary Elms, was opened by the Director of Medical Services in Nigeria. The maternity centre received government recognition in 1932 as a training-school for Grade I and Grade II midwives. Five years later new wards were built bringing the number of beds up to 170, and the hospital Chapel of the Divine Compassion was dedicated on 9th May, 1937. With 47,000 out-patient treatments and over 3,000 in-patients a year, the hospital could be said to have reached the target of efficiency and usefulness which Bishop Lasbrey had set twelve years earlier. And other medical services were also developing alongside Iyi Enu hospital from the mid-1930s.[20]

On 18th July, 1933 the standing committee of the Niger mission held a special meeting to consider two new projects. The first was the appointment of a woman doctor to travel round the Ibo country, developing the opportunities Mary Elms had opened up in the field of village hygiene, and maternity and child welfare. Government grants had already been promised for this. The second project, initiated by the government, was for a leprosy treatment centre in Onitsha Province to be run by the CMS mission. Both schemes were approved by the committee, the latter subject to help being available from the British Empire Leprosy Relief Association and the Mission to Lepers, and the provision of an additional doctor by the parent committee. Both projects were started in 1934. Dr Roseveare began itinerant work in Owerri Province. Owerri itself, sixty miles south of Onitsha, had long been a sizeable African town and four miles away at Egbu Owerri there had been a CMS mission station since 1906. There was a large mission primary school there, and the girls' training home already mentioned. Dr Roseveare made Egbu Owerri her headquarters. Her staff consisted of 'a male dresser and a midwife, both trained at Iyi Enu, a driver and mechanic, an interpreter, a cook and a steward'. Transport was a government-provided 30 cwt. Albion lorry. At first a fortnight was spent in turn in each of four centres. In 1939, after five years of this exhausting work, Dr Roseveare reported that on the eastern side of the Niger there were fourteen CMS maternity centres, each with a labour theatre run by a midwife, wards for from eight to twenty women and babies, a verandah and an outside kitchen and storehouse. The pastor of the district was responsible for building the centre and for its upkeep and equipment, and also for the salary of the midwife. Fees of 5s from each patient who could afford it were paid into local church funds.

The second project of 1933, the leprosy settlement, naturally took longer to get going. Basden's description of the way it started is worth quoting. In March 1933 the Director of Medical and Sanitary Services for Nigeria had been visiting the small government leprosy treatment centre at Onitsha. His car broke down and he spent the night with the Basdens at the mission house. The director was far from satisfied with what he had seen of the existing centre, and he and Basden were soon talking in terms of a CMS leprosy colony with strong government support. The project received parent committee sanction in 1935.

The site chosen was on the Oji River, forty miles north of Onitsha. Dr David Money was appointed medical superintendent, with Mr Len Parker, a Toc H worker, as his assistant. The settlement opened in the latter part of 1936 with sixty patients. Such numbers were hardly significant in view of Money's estimate of ten thousand lepers in Onitsha Province. By 1942 the number of in-patients had risen to seven hundred and the number of patients registered as under treatment at the clinics in surrounding districts was twelve thousand, exceeding Money's earlier estimate of actual cases. Oji River was by then as well-known as Iyi Enu as a place of healing, and leprosy patients were coming from great distances. From 1939 a system of different treatments was operating – segregation in the Oji River Settlement for severe and infectious cases; free treatment at the nearest clinic for others. 'We have now come to the time,' Dr Money wrote in 1940, 'when discharges of patients from the settlement as "recovered" is a normal event.' A number of non-infectious patients acted as nurses and helped in the operating theatre, dressing ulcers and giving injections. When Dr Harold Anderson, CMS medical secretary, visited Oji River in 1944 he was impressed by the size of it, extending over two square miles. 'One can only speak in terms of the highest respect,' he wrote, 'for the perfect organization which has been built up in the last nine years.' By then all the administrative positions in the settlement were held by Africans, the majority of them leprosy patients. It was closed down in the 1960s for the best of reasons – treatment of leprosy had been so successful that large-scale segregation treatment of the disease was no longer needed.[21]

CMS Niger Bookshops, 1922–42

The bookshops, which developed rapidly in the 1920s, performed two important functions in the new Niger diocese. First, the main centres and the increasing network of branch depots provided teachers and pastors with the bibles, prayer-books, and school textbooks which they needed; second, their steadily rising profits, as the volume of business increased, financed missionary projects which would otherwise have languished. Cheetham resigned from his bookshop work in 1928 to specialize in the writing and production of Ibo literature, though he remained mission accountant. The availability of bookshop profits for general purposes in the Niger mission came under review in 1933. Basden wrote to CMS, London (12th December, 1933), to point out that the 1922 agreement on this matter was based on a misunderstanding. The value of the stock had been treated as cash-in-hand; and although this had been pointed out earlier, and its significance had been accepted by the parent committee, request was now being made for £200 per annum from bookshop profits. Basden's explanation was accepted, and the minute of 1922 was rescinded.

In February 1934 the Niger missionary conference approved a proposal that Port Harcourt and certain other Ibo bookshops, for which Lagos had been responsible since 1917, should be taken over by the Niger mission and amalgamated with the Onitsha bookshops. It was agreed that 50 per cent of the net profits should be earmarked for repayment of a loan from the Yoruba mission; 25 per cent kept as a reserve fund; and 25 per cent made available for mission purposes approved by the parent committee. The terms were slightly modified in October 1934 and the name changed to 'CMS Niger Bookshops'. Their indebtedness to Lagos had been repaid before 1942.

Port Harcourt became the chief bookshop centre in the later 1930s, with T. W. Collins as manager, and G. W. Pearman and R. N. Bubb as assistants. By 1936 it had ten branch depots, and three more were opened in 1937. The turnover for 1939 was £30,000.[22] 'Bookshop work nowadays,' Pearman wrote in 1937, 'is just as specialized as educational or medical work and calls for people with just as much ability.'

'Diocesanization', 1922–42

The development of diocesan structures in CMS missions was a common feature in the 1930s. In some cases it meant little in terms of church life or missionary purpose. The real centre of ecclesiastical power remained, in many areas, with the local governing body of the mission, of which a European diocesan bishop was normally the chairman. This was not the case with the Niger diocese. From its inception in 1922 it had to work for the removal of the time-hardened barrier between the CMS mission and the Niger Delta Pastorate Church. This was a unique situation, and it provided the new diocese with a specific task which helped its rapid development; and the diocese had in Bishop Lasbrey a leader determined to effect the reconciliation as rapidly as possible. The parallel development of district church councils in the two sections

of the diocese, already described, proved useful. The huge rural deaneries of
East Africa would have increased the problems of integration. An infra-structure
of comparatively small districts was more flexible. The only missionary institutions not under the direction of district church councils were Awka training
college, St Monica's School, and the Dennis Memorial Grammar School, and
all three were well used by the Delta Pastorate Church by the end of the 1920s.

A draft constitution for the diocese, previously accepted by the appropriate
local bodies, was approved by the CMS parent committee in May 1929. It was
closely modelled on Bishop Tugwell's 1906 constitution for the diocese of
Western Equatorial Africa. On 29th August, 1929 it was accepted by a diocesan
representative assembly at Christ Church, Onitsha Waterside. Basden welcomed
the delegates from the Delta church. Recalling the differences that arose over
forty years before at Onitsha, he suggested that nothing could be more fitting
than a reunion in the very place where the rupture had occurred. Bishop Lasbrey
then described the function of a diocesan synod and its method of voting by
three houses: 'Should the majority of the Laity be opposed to a motion before
the Synod and vote against it, it would fail. The result would be likewise if
rejected by either the Clergy or the Bishop.' The synod would normally meet
once a year and would appoint various boards to carry on its work between
sessions. The bishop then went on to describe the goal of missionary work,
in terms of the 1928 Jerusalem Conference Report, as 'the settlement of a native
church under native pastors upon a self-supporting system'. The formation
of the synod would be a great step towards the independence of the church,
independent, not in doctrine, but in its ability to stand on its own feet, co-operate
with other churches, and able to make its own spiritual contribution to the
whole church. Such an independent church, internally united, must make itself
responsible for the evangelization of the whole country.

After the bishop's address the proposed constitution was read section by
section, first in English, then in Ibo. Bishop Howells thereafter moved the
adoption of the constitution, and the motion was seconded by Chief Lawrence
Onwudiwe. After further speeches the constitution was unanimously approved,
and all present rose and sang the doxology. The constitution of the synod came
into force on 1st January, 1931. The CMS missionary conference, newly constituted as the local governing body of the Niger mission, was accepted by the
synod at its first meeting as one of its constituent committees. It would remain
responsible for the control of movements of missionaries, for mission-worked
institutions, and for finances provided by the parent committee of CMS. The
synod was not authorized to withdraw any power from the missionary conference without the Society's approval. Under the synodal constitution all
existing mission property passed to the synod except the grammar school, St
Monica's School, Awka training college, and Iyi Enu medical mission. Three
synod trustees were appointed – the bishop, the chancellor of the diocese (Sir
Kitoyi Ajasa, OBE) and the secretary of the synod (Basden). In the next few

years the agreed transfers of property were made by the CMS to the synod.[23]

The membership structure of the Anglican Church in the Niger diocese was succinctly described in a *Report of the Council of the Niger Diocese on Reunion in 1932*, Appendix 2.

There were four classes of church members: enquirers, catechumens, confirmation candidates, and communicants. Classes for each of the four groups were held at each station once a week. Enquirers in order to become catechumens had to have a good knowledge of the Ibo Primer, of the religious knowledge given in prescribed textbooks, and of the Apostles' Creed, the Lord's Prayer and the Ten Commandments. Candidates for baptism were required to read St Mark's Gospel; and confirmation candidates the four gospels and the daily Scripture Union portions. The minimum time of instruction for enquirers and catechumens was one year, and for confirmation candidates two years. The ministry of the church consisted of lay agents, many of whom had no training except what they picked up from senior agents or in agents' weeks when they received some instruction in doctrine. Then there were evangelists (or third class catechists), second and first class catechists, lay readers, deacons and priests. The normal period of training of deacons for the priesthood was two years.

Each church had its own church committee; each district consisting of from forty to four hundred churches, arranged in groups of five or six, had its own district church council and was in charge of an ordained minister.

There was nothing unique about these diocesan structures; they could be paralleled in many other areas during the period of transition from 'mission' to 'church' forms of organization. What was distinctive in the development of the Niger diocese during the 1930s was the thoroughness with which administrative arrangements and ecclesiastical discipline were made to serve church growth and evangelism. It was Bishop Lasbrey's gift and lasting achievement to inspire structures with spiritual meaning and relevance, with the result that his diocese was more truly a unit of the universal church than any other Anglican diocese in tropical Africa during this period.

NOTES

1. E. A. Ayandele, *The Missionary Impact on Modern Nigeria, 1842–1914*, Longmans, 1966, p. 343.

2. G3/A3/P5, 1910/58, 87; 1912/122, 123, 124. See also E. M. T. Epelle, *The Church in the Niger Delta*, Port Harcourt, 1955, p. 50.

3. Epelle, op. cit., p. 49.

4. ibid., pp. 51–3.

5. ibid., pp. 53–7. See also P6, 1920/12, 24, 25, 29; 1921/38; 1922/26.

6. *Nigeria the Unknown*, CMS, 1918, p. 44. See also *IRM*, 'An African Tribe in Transition', James W. Welch, October 1931, pp. 556–74.

7. P6, 1919/49, xvi; 1920/20, 47; 1921/15.

8. P5, 1910/69; 1911/32; 1913/25, 41, 83, 91; 1914/1, 22; 1915/71; 1916/49; 1917/33, xvii; 1918/10, 12; 1919/49; 1921/9.

9. Acc. 89, Journal of the Rev. T. J. Dennis, 1906–17. The Rev. Julius Spencer was the African pastor at Asaba.

10. P5, 1912/34, 71, 93, 94; 1914/45, xxi; P6, 1920/2; P5, 1911/i.

11. P5, 1913/24; 1914/10, iv, 12, vii, 16; P6, 1916/71, xlvi; 1917/xii, 39, xix; 1918/10, 12, iii, 28; 1922/40, xx.

12. Anderson MS. pp. 114–16, 169–71; P5, 1910/34, 83; P6, 1919/10; 1922/43, xxi.

13. *The Call from Africa*, World Call Series, Press and Publications Board of the Church Assembly, 1926, pp. 122–8.

14. Epelle, op. cit., pp, 63–82.

15. P6, 1922/10, 29; 1924/8; 1927/59, 68, 74; 1928/25, 59; 1932/27A; 1934/42, 51.

16. *CMO*, J. W. Jackson, 'How the Gospel came to Nsukka', May 1936, pp. 105–6; *AR*(MS) 1938–9, pp. 29f.; Epelle, op. cit., pp. 83–92; F. E. Wilcock MS 'Diary of a Diocesan Missioner'.

17. P6, 1923/13; 1925/xviii; 1928/35; *AR*(MS), 1936–7, p. 27; 1937–8, p. 31; 1940–1, p. 14; 1941–2, p. 17; 9/Y/Ag/4/1, Report on Missionary Education in Niger Diocese, April 1930; P6, 1926/3, 7, 54; 1928/12; 1925/14.

18. P6, 1928/56; 1930/19; *AR*(MS) 1937–8, p. 25; 1938–9, p. 36; 1941–2, p. 16; P6, 1927/76.

19. *AR*(MS) 1939–40, pp. 23, 24; 1940–1, p. 25.

20. Anderson MS, pp. 306, 448; P6, 1923/32; 1926/40; *CMO*, 1939, p. 223; P6, 1933/56.

21. P6, 1933/54; 1934/29; *CMO*, May 1937, p. 113; Anderson MS, pp. 452–60; *CMO*, 1936, p. 126; *East and West Review*, 1939, pp. 236–45.

22. P6, 1934/9, 26; *AR*(MS) 1937–8, p. 33. See also H. B. Thomas, MS Notes on West African Bookshops.

23. P6, 1928/58; *The Synod of the Diocese on the Niger: Constitution, Principles and Regulations*, 1930, pp. 3–11; P6, 1930/19, 20, 23; 1931/37, 73.

PART TWO

East Africa

East Africa: Introduction

East Africa is most commonly defined as embracing the mainland countries of Uganda, Kenya and Tanganyika (Tanzania) and the off-shore islands of Zanzibar, Pemba and Mafia. It comprises an area of 682,800 square miles including 38,860 square miles of water. For the purposes of this history East Africa is also taken to include Ruanda (Rwanda) and Urundi (Burundi) which formed part of German East Africa for thirty years before the first world war. During the period 1910–42 CMS missionaries were at work in all the mainland territories.

The European intrusion into this region in the mid-nineteenth century is described by the African historian B. A. Ogot as 'the last in a long process of invasion and cultural diffusion going back to the fifteenth century and even beyond'. This process included Portuguese dominance of the coast for two hundred years from the end of the fifteenth century, followed by a similar period of dominance by the Omani Arabs, and waves of Nilo-Hamitic migration from the north-east which led to a fusion of Hamitic, Bantu, and Nilotic cultures, especially in Uganda.[1]

In the European scramble for East Africa the administrators followed the missionaries, explorers and traders, and 'spheres of influence' were established which later became colonies or protectorates. Following the Berlin Conference of European powers, 1884–5, Britain and Germany agreed to recognize the authority of the Sultan of Zanzibar over Zanzibar itself, the smaller offshore islands and a coastal strip ten miles deep. They also agreed on a boundary between German and British spheres of influence which remains the frontier between Kenya and Tanzania. By an Anglo-German treaty of 1890 this line was extended across Lake Victoria westwards.

By the Treaty of Versailles following the first world war Germany was forced to renounce all her claims to overseas possessions, and it was decided that former German dependencies should be administered by mandates assigned to one or other of the victorious allies. The mandate for German East Africa was given to Britain except for Ruanda and Urundi, west of Lake Victoria, which was assigned to Belgium. The British mandated territory was renamed Tanganyika. Kenya was given the status of a colony in 1920 and Uganda remained a British protectorate throughout the period under review. Occupation of these three territories, together with Zanzibar, which had been recognized as a British protectorate by the Berlin Treaty in 1890, gave Britain a dominant position in East Africa. The possibility of federation, or 'closer union', for British East African territories was debated throughout the colonial period. As early as 1893 in his book, *The Rise of our East African Empire*, F. D. Lugard proposed a single administration, with a governor resident in the Kenya Highlands assisted by commissioners stationed on the coast, in Zanzibar and in Uganda. After the first world war, with Tanganyika now included in the British sphere, successive colonial secretaries at Westminster sought to implement a scheme for federation. Article 10 of the British Mandate for German East Africa, 1922, authorized the Mandatory 'to constitute the territory into a customs fiscal and administrative union, or federation, with adjacent territories under [British] sovereignty or control', provided that such measures did not infringe other provisions of the mandate which sought to safeguard the welfare and encourage the development of the indigenous population.[2]

A British government commission headed by Mr W. B. A. Ormsby-Gore, reporting in 1925, found little evidence of support for the idea of federation in East Africa itself and much evidence of opposition to it. 'Africans in Uganda, Europeans in Kenya, everyone in Zanzibar, and most Indians opposed it.'[3] The Ormsby-Gore commission concluded that federation could not be imposed from without, but it suggested periodic meetings of the governors, and of officials in charge of various departments to discuss such common concerns as communications, land and labour. All this happened. The first conference of governors was held in 1926, and some common services were established between the three mainland territories. For example, a Postmaster-General was appointed in 1933. But full-scale federation proved elusive. There were further commissions in the later 1920s, and in 1930 a joint select committee of both Houses of Parliament was appointed, on Lugard's instigation, to examine the whole question of closer union in East Africa. It heard a great deal of evidence. It noted the opposition of witnesses from Tanganyika and Uganda to any closer association with Kenya. It noted the plea of Africans from all three territories against any insertion of an intermediate authority between the several territorial governments and the British parliament. Reporting in 1931, the select committee advised against any radical move towards political federation or even economic union, and the British government informed the Permanent Mandates Commission that 'the time was not yet ripe for any far-reaching steps in the direction of political and constitutional union of any of the territories concerned'.[4] By the mid-1930s a resurgent Germany with a stronger voice in international affairs insisted that the mandated status of Tanganyika ruled out the possibility of its entering a federation with British colonies and protectorates. Eventually it came to be accepted that an East African federation, ahead of African majorities in the legislatures of the several territories, would be inimical to African interests.

The long search for, or as it seemed to many Africans, the threat of, federation had important repercussions in the ecclesiastical sphere. An Anglican province for East Africa was suggested by Archbishop Randall Davidson of Canterbury as early as 1914. He addressed a memorandum to the diocesan bishops of East Africa urging the value and importance of forming a province. He saw the danger of two separate forms of Anglicanism developing in East Africa, in line with the ethos of the CMS in Kenya, Uganda and central Tanganyika, and of the UMCA in southern Tanganyika and Zanzibar. The Archbishop's plea was reinforced by Resolution 43 of the Lambeth Conference in 1920 which encouraged the gradual development of new provinces and held it to be 'undesirable that dioceses should remain indefinitely in isolation, or attached only to a distant Province'.

There were formidable difficulties in the way of forming an East African province in the inter-war period. Geography as well as diverse churchmanship told against it. It was a huge area and communications were still poor. When Bishop J. J. Willis first put forward the suggestion of a province in the Uganda diocesan synod in 1921 almost all the African members disapproved it on the grounds of the 'Romanizing' tendencies of the diocese of Zanzibar. But in 1923 the Mombasa diocesan synod pleaded with Uganda to reconsider it, and in July 1927 a conference met to explore the possibilities under the chairmanship of the Bishop of Northern Rhodesia. The conference met in an atmosphere of hope and reconciliation. 1927 was the Jubilee year of the CMS Uganda mission and several of the UMCA bishops had shared happily in the celebration as guests of the Church of Uganda. But as Bishop Willis recalled, the Baganda were full of fear of the Federation 'believed to be contemplated by the government, which would rob them of their independence and bring them under the heel of the European minority in Kenya'.[5] These fears were at least temporarily assuaged and the Uganda synod accepted the proposals of the conference to form an East African province. It was the Mombasa synod that rejected it, chiefly on the grounds of incompatible views of churchmanship. But at a critical stage the prospects, and fear, of a political federation had an importance which Bishop Willis tended to underestimate. An ecclesiastical province was achieved shortly after the several territories became independent in the early 1960s; but political federation proved as elusive as under colonial rule.

In East Africa, as in West Africa, the normal context in which the Christian missionaries worked was that of traditional African religion, which they frequently described as 'paganism' or 'animism', but throughout tropical Africa in the colonial period Islam was spreading with dramatic effect as a missionary faith alongside Christianity. In West Africa its progress was from the interior towards the coast; in East Africa it was from the coast inland. The means of its penetration were similar – the unofficial missionary work of Muslims who served as guides, interpreters, clerks and minor officials of colonial governments, as well as traders. The strongest penetration of Islam in East Africa during this period was in Tanganyika, where twenty-seven per cent of the population was claimed to be Muslim by the early 1950s. In Uganda and Kenya the figure was much lower, between three and five per cent of the population. Professor Spencer Trimingham, who has made detailed studies of the spread of Islam in both East and West Africa notes a number of differences between the two regions. For example, Islam in East Africa has the characteristics of a foreign religion, with Muslims forming distinct communities in the coastal areas, and with its village clergy detribalized, whereas in West Africa they remain fully associated with the people they serve. The result has been a distinctive Islamic Swahili culture near the coast and in the offshore islands, and a weak diffusion of Islamic religion in the interior, where Muslims can scarcely be distinguished from pagans. The rising tide of Muslim advance into the interior, which gave so much anxiety to Christian missionaries in the inter-war period, seems to have spent itself after about 1930 and Islam proved itself at least as ill-equipped as Christianity to deal with the rising tide of African nationalism. Even in Swahili society 'religious life rests upon a double structure, the animistic underlayer and the Islam superstructure'.[6]

NOTES

1. B. A. Ogot, 'The Movement of Peoples in East Africa' in *Africa Past and Present*, Éditions Présence Africaine, Paris, 1964, pp. 36–48.
2. T. Walter Wallbank *Contemporary Africa*, Princeton, 1956, p. 116.
3. A. J. Hughes, *East Africa, the Search for Unity*, Penguin African Library, 1963, p. 215.
4. Hughes, op. cit., pp. 218, 219.
5. Willis MS, pp. 191–7.
6. J. Spencer Trimingham, *Islam in East Africa*, Edinburgh House Press, 1962, p. 32.

Kenya

The Country and its Peoples

The name Kenya is a Europeanized version of Kere-Nyaga, the name given by the Kikuyu tribe to the 17,000 foot mountain in its central highlands.[1] The territory, 225,000 square miles, is approximately the size of Spain and Portugal combined.

From 1895 to 1920 Kenya was a British protectorate, and thereafter a Crown colony. It became an independent state within the British Commonwealth in 1963. It retained the boundaries constructed by Western powers at the height of the colonial period. Thus its southern boundary, from the Indian Ocean to Lake Victoria, dates from the Anglo-German agreement of 1886; its western boundary with Uganda dates from 1902; and the north-eastern boundary with the Republic of Somalia from 1925. During the period 1910–42 a coastal strip, approximately ten miles in depth, remained the property of the Sultan of Zanzibar for which the colonial government of Kenya paid an annual rent.

Britain's early interest in Kenya was little more than a by-product of the Uganda railway built with Indian labour and British finance between 1895 and 1901. The British Foreign Office at that time regarded it as 'a valueless, sterile region'.[2] But this estimate changed dramatically when the railway reached the central highlands around and to the north of Nairobi. Here were fertile soil and a congenial climate that set Englishmen dreaming of the imagined summers of their youth. The highlands appeared also to be largely unoccupied; and the absence of powerful African chiefs in the neighbourhood led to the further mistaken conclusion that there was no sophisticated and coherent tribal life thereabouts, and that the occupation of this delectable area for European development would remain unchallenged. The unhappy long-term result of these misconceptions is only too well-known. The Mau Mau outbreak of 1952–55 which cost ten thousand lives, nearly all of them African lives, might have been avoided if certain facts had been ascertained before white settlement

schemes got under way. The population of the Kikuyu tribe had been savagely
cut down in the 1890s by an overlapping series of disasters – rinderpest, smallpox, drought and locusts; in such circumstances, and given a tribal tradition
of shifting subsistence farming, it was not realized that land apparently unoccupied was still looked upon as the property of the tribes; likewise there was
little appreciation (until the publication in 1938 of Jomo Kenyatta's anthropological study, *Facing Mount Kenya*) of the subtler forms of tribal coherence
among the Kikuyu – notably the social significance of the 'age-sets' and the
cultic significance of Mount Kenya itself. A true appraisal of the situation was
made more difficult by the fact that it was the least settled section of Kikuyu
society with whom Europeans first made contact; this was in the Kiambu area
where the complex system of land tenure and political organization was less
advanced than in the heartlands of the tribe to the east of the Great Rift
Valley.[3]

The total African population of Kenya was estimated at a little over two
million in the 1911 census. It reached three million in 1922 and three and a
quarter million by 1939.

The Kikuyu of the central highlands, though the largest tribe (1,750,000 in
1963) is by no means the only large tribe in Kenya. Other Bantu-Nigrotic
tribes are the Swahili (a million strong in Kenya and Tanzania in 1963), the
Kamba (600,000) and the Baluyia of Nyanza. The largest of the Nilo-Hamitic
tribes are the Joluo (800,000) and the Masai (180,000) both overlapping
the Kenya-Tanganyika border in the period under review. The Kamba, concentrated mainly to the east of Nairobi in central Kenya, and the Kikuyu speak
mutually comprehensive languages.

Not only in the growth of population, but in every aspect of Kenya's social,
cultural and economic life, the years 1910–42 were a time of immensely rapid
development.

Mombasa on the coast had been a large Arabized town for centuries; but
Nairobi in 1910 was 'a little cluster of bungalows and sheds whose tin roofs
winked like heliographs'[4] and rhinoceros would occasionally interrupt the race-
meetings of the early white settlers. It would be difficult to exaggerate the
irrationality and the violent emotions of the early colonial period. The settlers
were already politically active, and putting forward ideas of white self-government for Kenya. Winston Churchill noted, on a visit in 1907: 'Every white man
in Nairobi is a politician; and most of them are leaders of parties.'[5] The Indians,
outnumbering the Europeans by four to one, were determined to have a comparable share with them in the government of the country, and greatly resented
white pressure on the government to keep them out of the Highlands, or to
limit immigration.

The first major political confrontation in Kenya during the period was due
to Indian pressure for political recognition and white settler resistance to it;
and, ironically, the first clear statement of African political rights was made

in a White Paper (Cmd. 1922) presented to the British parliament in 1923 entitled *Indians in Kenya*. The second paragraph of Part II of the White Paper included the famous statement:

> Primarily Kenya is an African territory, and His Majesty's Government think it necessary definitely to record their considered opinion that the interests of the African native must be paramount, and that if and when those interests and the interests of the immigrant races should conflict, the former should prevail.

White settlers' hopes of early self-government were deflated with the statement that 'His Majesty's Government cannot but regard the grant of responsible self-government as out of the question within any period of time which need now be taken into consideration'. Provision was made for five elected Indian 'unofficial' members on the legislative council and one Arab, both on the basis of a wide communal franchise; and for the nomination of an additional unofficial member, preferably a missionary, to advise on matters affecting Africans.[6]

Missionary spokesmen tended to regard Indian aspirations with anxiety. Canon H. Leakey, a CMS missionary, who was later to serve on the legislative council as representative of African interests, spoke of the Indian demands for equal representation with Europeans as 'highly detrimental to African interests'. Bishop J. J. Willis of Uganda was more explicit:

> Indians [he wrote] had no experience of domestic government, and it would be wrong for representatives of two completely different civilizations corporately to administer African races alien to both. No claim for Indians can be put forward which cannot, with far greater force, be advanced for Africans in their own country.[7]

The 'paramountcy' of African interests, so firmly stated in the White Paper of 1923, was interpreted and qualified by successive colonial secretaries and commissions. Little was done during the period under review to hasten direct African representation on the legislative council. The missionaries nominated to represent African interests did so conscientiously, but the continuance of indirect representation was openly questioned by Archdeacon W. E. Owen and others.[8]

African apprenticeship in politics during the colonial period was served chiefly in tribal associations such as the Young Kikuyu Association founded by Harry Thuku in 1921, replaced later by the Kikuyu Central Association led by Jomo Kenyatta and Jesse Kariuki. In the later 1930s other tribal associations were formed such as the Ukamba Members' Association and the Taita Hills Association. In face of Italy's threat of invasion in 1940, the Kenya government proscribed these organizations on precautionary grounds. Their leaders were interned and their papers seized.[9]

Missionary opinion about the associations was divided. One annual report (1929–30) described KCA as 'a political organization to which most of the leading Kikuyu Christians belong and which, with many of them, comes before the

Church'. KCA was criticized in the same report for defending customs, such as female circumcision, which missionaries and many leading African Christians were seeking to discourage. Some missionaries, on the other hand, regarded the development of such organs of African opinion in political and social matters as valuable, and Archdeacon W. E. Owen of Kavirondo founded and led the Kavirondo Taxpayers Welfare Association until 1936. KTWA occupied an equivocal position between protest and desire to co-operate with the government. By the end of the period missionary leadership was no longer welcome to the Africans, but in Nyanza Province particularly it had helped to articulate local grievances and aspirations and this, in Owen's view at least, was a proper part of the missionary's task in a British dependency.[10]

It is not possible to trace in detail the complex history of Kenya's political development during the period 1910–42. For a full account the reader is referred to three books; a lively contemporary account, up to 1926, by a former Director of Public Works, W. McGregor Ross, entitled *Kenya from Within* (1927); George Bennett's *Kenya: A Political History of the Colonial Period* (1963) and Roland Oliver's *The Missionary Factor in East Africa* (1962), particularly Chapter Five, pp. 231–92. Missionary involvement in a number of social questions, for example, labour on European farms, ownership of land, female circumcision, marriage customs, will be treated later (see pp. 163–70).

Other Religions

Two of the great ethnic religions, Hinduism and Islam, were strongly represented in Kenya among minority racial groups. Most of the Muslims in East Africa belonged to one of the three *Shi'a* sects – Ismaila Khoja, Bohra and Ithna'ashri. The Khoja sect was most strongly represented among the Indians in Kenya, and photographs of the Aga Khan, the head of the sect, were frequently to be seen displayed in their shops. Many of the Indian Hindus belonged to the reformist society, Arya Samaj. There was little Christian missionary work among either Muslims or Hindus. The European missionary tended to regard the Indians as alien intruders, and to concern himself exclusively with the indigenous Africans.

Other Christian Missions and Churches

Early Roman Catholic missions were chiefly among the Goanese of whom there were four thousand in Kenya by 1931, mostly cooks and clerks, but by the 1950s there were over seventy thousand Roman Catholics in Kenya, and over thirty thousand catechumens. The chief societies and mission stations were the Holy Ghost Fathers (French) at Mombasa (1892) and Nairobi (1899); St Joseph's EMS [Mill Hill Fathers (British)] at Kisumu and Mumias from 1903 onwards; the Mission of the Consolata (Italian) from 1902, mostly in the

Highlands. In 1927 Mgr Arthur Hinsley, Rector of the English College at Rome, was sent to investigate Roman Catholic missionary work and he returned shortly afterwards as Archbishop residing at Mombasa. He was transferred to Westminster in 1935.

Among non-Roman missions the CMS was the largest, but the range of Protestant missions was far greater than in Uganda. Philp (1936) gives details for 1934 for fifteen such missions.[11]

The Africa Inland Mission was, next to CMS, the most widespread and had the greatest number of missionaries. It began work at Mombasa in 1895. It had an outstanding missionary leader in C. E. Hurlburt who first visited Kenya in 1898 and came to stay in 1910, establishing AIM headquarters at Kijabe. Its nineteen stations were spread throughout Kenya apart from the coastal district.

The Church of Scotland mission dates from 1891 when Dr James Stewart of Lovedale, leading an independent mission sponsored by Sir William Mackinnon, established a station at Kibwezi among the Kamba tribe, two hundred miles from the coast. It moved to Kikuyu in 1898 on the border between the Kikuyu and Masai tribes; a year later CMS began work at Kabete only five miles away, creating 'comity' problems for the future. In 1901 the mission was adopted by the Church of Scotland. Henry Edwin Scott, a great missionary who revised the agricultural policy of his predecessors, began educational work at a second centre, Tumutumu, near Mt Kenya in 1908. H. E. Scott worked in close co-operation with Hurlburt and Leakey (CMS) in the Kikuyu area. He was succeeded, on his death in 1911, by Dr J. W. Arthur. The policy of the Church of Scotland mission, unlike that of CMS and AIM, was to concentrate its work at a small number of large stations.

The American Friends' Industrial Mission began work in Kavirondo with three missionaries in 1902, slightly ahead of the CMS and the Mill Hill Fathers. The Christian community associated with the Friends' mission grew rapidly, to number thirty thousand by 1934.

The Seventh Day Adventists concentrated their work in south Kavirondo and the Salvation Army in north Kavirondo. The Methodist mission worked chiefly in the coastal area. Two other Anglican societies had missions in Kenya during the period. The Bible Churchmen's Missionary Society began work in the Turkana (Northern) Province in 1923, in Poko and Nandi territory; and the Colonial and Continental Church Society maintained two whole-time chaplains in Nairobi and subsidized five others in the central highlands ministering to Europeans.

The Anglican Church

When the diocese of Eastern Equatorial Africa was divided in 1897 Bishop Alfred Tucker elected to continue his episcopate as bishop of the new diocese of Uganda.

William George Peel, who had served for nineteen years as a CMS missionary in India, was nominated the first Bishop of Mombasa, and remained in office until his death in April 1916. The extension of Anglican missionary work into Kikuyu territory and into German East Africa (later Tanganyika) owed much to his initiative.

After a lengthy interval another CMS missionary in India, R. S. Heywood, was consecrated Bishop of Mombasa as Peel's successor in April 1918. He retired in 1936, and was succeeded in turn by R. P. Crabbe. Crabbe had served in West Africa some years earlier as chaplain to the Bishop of Sierra Leone from 1911 to 1914.

There were two modifications of diocesan boundaries during the period. In 1921 the Nyanza province of Kenya Colony, previously included in the diocese of Uganda, was transferred to the diocese of Mombasa. This transfer was the subject of protracted negotiations between the two diocesan bishops, Willis of Uganda and Heywood of Mombasa, and the Archbishop of Canterbury over a period of nine years, 1912 to 1921.[12] The two dioceses were at very different stages of development, and it required nice judgment to decide when the gain to the diocese of Mombasa of the vigorous church life of Kavirondo would outweigh the advantage Kavirondo received from continued association with the diocese of Uganda and its value as a buffer against Islam.

The other change of diocesan boundaries was the formation of the diocese of Central Tanganyika in 1927. By then the time was ripe for the hiving off of the former CMS mission area in German East Africa into a diocese of its own; and the promise of substantial support from Australia in money and missionary personnel appeared to guarantee a strong start for the new diocese.

The way forward from a mission to a diocesan structure was more compli- cated in Kenya than in Uganda, owing largely to the regional development of the CMS mission. The diocese of Mombasa, after 1927, virtually consisted of three areas of CMS work: the old coast mission, including the Taita hills region; the Kavirondo mission, pioneered from Uganda; and the mission in the central highlands and Nairobi area, which developed greatly in the period under review. In 1922 district missionary committees were set up for each of these three areas. Bishop Heywood was by that time feeling his way forward to a diocesan con- stitution and synod. In August 1923 he wrote to CMS headquarters saying that he thought the synod should meet towards the end of 1924 and accept whatever constitution was agreed upon, tentatively and without compulsory powers, for three years. The synod met 9th to 12th September, 1924. Membership con- sisted of the bishop, the four archdeacons, three honorary canons, twenty-five priests, one deacon, twenty-six lay delegates (men and women) elected by the missionary districts, twenty-one members elected by the Europeans and Asiatics, and six co-opted by the bishop – a total of thirty-five clergy and fifty- three laity. Many of the missionaries remained unconvinced that diocesanization on the thoroughgoing Uganda model would work in Kenya. The executive committee of the mission, meeting in December 1931, received a report from a sub-committee appointed to look into the matter and to make proposals; but the report was brief and negative: it felt unable to make any practical suggestions. A senior missionary, writing three years later, spoke for many of his colleagues. He agreed with diocesanization in principle, but did not agree with its application to Kenya where it raised more difficulties than it solved.[13]

One difficulty in the integration of the diocese related to its cathedral. The synod of 1924 unanimously decided that a second cathedral at Nairobi was necessary. This surprising proposal, which was soon to be implemented, reflects the regional separation referred to earlier: it also reflects five years of unhappy tension about the arrangements for services in the cathedral at Mombasa. The cathedral site at Mombasa had been secured by Bishop Tucker, and the building had been done under Bishop Peel's direction at a cost of £4,400, all but £400 being contributed by the CMS from a special fund in memory of Bishops Hannington and Parker and the Rev. Henry Wright. On 12th May, 1919, the cathedral church wardens wrote to the parent committee complaining that the CMS was at present fixing times for African services without reference to the minister acting as European chaplain. The position of the European congregation was difficult since Bishop Peel, some eighteen years before, had handed over the European church and it was occupied by CMS offices. The European congregation wished to be free to appoint a chaplain of their own choice, not necessarily a CMS missionary. They wanted their own furnishings – it was 'not a matter of ritual, but of wear-and-tear, cleanliness, etc.' Structural repairs were urgently needed, and unless the cathedral was kept thoroughly clean there was a danger to health. The Bishop of Mombasa urged the parent committee to leave the matter to be settled locally.[14]

In 1932 the executive committee of the Society in London, on the advice of its ecclesiastical committee, agreed to hand over Mombasa cathedral to the diocesan trustees, provided that proper arrangements were made for both the African and European congregations and that 'CMS principles' were observed. The bishop, or a member of the cathedral staff appointed by him, would be dean of the cathedral with a committee for each congregation, and a joint committee to deal with all questions relating to ornaments and use. It was suggested that cathedral churches in Nairobi and Mombasa have equal status in the diocese.

Retrospect, 1844–1910

The pioneering days of the CMS in Kenya are among the best known in the annals of the Society. Johann Ludwig Krapf settled in Mombasa in May 1844, hoping to make contact with the Galla people whom he had sought unsuccessfully to reach from Abyssinia. On 13th July his wife Rosine died of fever, and Krapf wrote to the CMS committee the message which proved a badge of courage to many who followed him:

Tell our friends at home that there is now on the East African coast a lonely missionary grave. This is a sign that you have commenced the struggle with this part of the world; and as the victories of the Church are gained by stepping over the graves of her members, you may be the more convinced that the hour is at hand when you are summoned to the conversion of Africa from its eastern shore.[15]

Krapf's name is, somewhat unfortunately, linked with the idea of 'a chain of mission stations' between East and West Africa. His prophetic vision was no more limited by this project than the vision of Cecil Rhodes was limited by the project of a Cape-to-Cairo railway. His more strategic concern was 'that the coast mission must have a broad basis towards the west',[16] which accords with Henry Venn's instructions to Krapf on the eve of his return to Africa after furlough in 1851, 'not to settle down at one place . . . but to launch out far and wide witnessing to the Truth in successive tribes and countries'.[17]

When, almost a century later, Wilson Cash visited East Africa as general secretary of the Society, and described what he found – 'not a chain of mission stations . . . but rather a network of mission centres, interlaced and knit together in the fellowship of the church' – he was witnessing the fulfilment of Krapf's wider vision.[18]

The story of the early developments in Mombasa Island, in the Taita hills (from 1883), at Taveta (1885) and in Giriama territory near the coast cannot be retold here. Many of the second wave of pioneers were at work still in 1910, notably J. A. Wray, H. K. Binns and Douglas Hooper. It was only in the first decade of the present century, sixty years after Krapf's arrival, that the Society's area of evangelization extended inland much beyond the Taita Hills, a hundred miles inland from Mombasa.[19] The first CMS up-country station was opened at Kabete in 1903, followed by a start at Weithaga in the same year, and Kahuhia in 1906. The station at Maseno and the beginning of CMS work in Nyanza also date from 1906. By 1910 the strategy of mission pointed away from the coast to the Highlands and Nyanza, but the 'coast mission' had its own vital part to play in the growth of the Anglican Church in Kenya. It will be convenient, and in line with the way the missionaries of the period thought of their work, to chronicle developments in the three areas separately, and then to consider certain aspects of the mission under the general headings of medicine, education, comity and co-operation, literature, social witness.

The Coast, 1910–42

In 1911 G. W. Wright wrote optimistically of Mombasa as a centre of mission – a rapidly growing town, with good commercial prospects from its fine deep-water harbour of Kalindini and as the terminus of the Uganda railway, and increasingly a meeting-place of the nations. The cathedral congregations, both English and Swahili, were increasing. The Buxton High School, like the cathedral on the main road on the east side of the island, had doubled its daytime numbers between 1906 and 1910, and was also serving as a night-school. Mzizima hospital, on the northern end of the island, opposite Frere Town on the mainland, had become widely known and used in its eighteen years of existence; and the mission hall, also dating from 1892, was being used as a dispensary as well as an evangelistic centre, with a hundred outpatients visiting each day. As an illustration of the cosmopolitan character of Mombasa, and the evangelistic opportunities derived from it, he noted that among twenty young men recently admitted as catechumens only three were Mombasa-born. 'The others were from Taita, Tana, Kenia, Nyanza, and Kilima Njaro.'[20]

One of three married missionaries who made up the small team on Mombasa Island in 1910 was Dr R. K. Shepherd. Remembered as a 'man of incredible energy and great ability', Shepherd had taken charge of the Mzizima hospital in 1905. He continued working in and around Mombasa until 1922, but the hospital was already running down when it was requisitioned by the government in the first world war. It had not proved possible to develop extensive contact with, and service of, the Arab community. After prolonged negotiations the whole property was made over to the government in return for a cash payment to CMS of £9,000 and a nineteen and a half acre plot in the Manyimbo district on the west side of Mombasa Island. The first intention was to rebuild the hospital on this plot, but when it was realized in 1921 that the cost of new buildings would far exceed the money in hand, the project was abandoned. Eventually, after a proposal to use the Mzizima balance for the new Maseno hospital in Nyanza[21] had been turned down, the greater part of it (£5,000) was used for the building of Kaloleni hospital (see below).

The Buxton High School, opened by Mr Victor Buxton on Mombasa Island in 1904, had enrolled a large proportion of Indian boys by 1911, and in October of that year some leading members of the Indian community in Mombasa complained to the government about the compulsory Christian teaching given in the school. They also made more general charges of inefficiency. The headmaster, S. A. Martin, began negotiations with the newly-formed Kenya Education Department for grant-aid on the basis of a 'conscience clause' allowing for withdrawal from Christian teaching. In 1914, however, CMS decided to continue the Buxton High School without either conscience clause or grant. Wright succeeded Martin as principal in 1919 and the school settled down with elementary status and a commercial bias, and a smaller proportion of Indian boys than at first. In 1929 plans were made to move the school to the Manyimbo plot, but in fact the girls' school moved there first in 1931. In 1936 the two schools merged for a time as an experiment in co-education. It was still working satisfactorily two years later.[22]

In the 1930s a small mission hospital on Mombasa Island was started for Indian women and children by Dr Alma Downes-Shaw, formerly a CMS missionary in Uganda. Dr Downes-Shaw, whose only assets were 'her strong faith, £10 and a bicycle',[23] began work in Mombasa in the spring of 1935 in the old disused mission hall. She was joined in the same year by Miss D. Minshall. Better quarters were found, with accommodation for twelve women and eleven children without financial commitment on the part of CMS. Some missionaries were critical of Dr Downes-Shaw's methods at first. They objected to European and non-European members of the hospital staff eating their meals together. But the hospital weathered its early troubles, and there were 3,300 out-patient attendances in the first full year.

In Frere Town, on the mainland, H. K. Binns was still at work in 1910, after thirty-four years of service on the coast. In that year he was appointed Archdeacon of Mombasa. J. E. Hamshere succeeded him in this office three years later, but Binns continued work in Frere Town until 1922. A fluent preacher in Swahili, and an enthusiastic builder and gardener, he regarded furloughs as an unnecessary interruption of a full and busy life. In 1911, under pressure to take leave due to him in England, he said he had no intention of leaving Africa. His health, he maintained, was not likely to be worse in Africa than elsewhere, and he could not be happy in England. The committee minute on Binns' retirement in 1922 said of him: 'No missionary had closer touch and sympathy with the African people and few have exercised more varied gifts and talents.'

Hamshere, Archdeacon of Mombasa from 1914 to 1928, continued as principal of the Divinity School; and from 1920 he was also given charge of the congregation gathered by the mission in Frere Town. The number of ordinands in the Divinity School was growing steadily. As most of them came from the Highlands and Nyanza, the case for moving the school up country was strengthened.[24]

In 1929 the Bishop of Mombasa and the executive committee of the CMS Kenya mission began planning a move to Limuru, twenty miles from Nairobi, where land was being offered on a 999 years' lease at £8 to £10 per acre. Mr Ernest Carr, a retired British businessman, offered the Society part of the land he had recently acquired there. The parent committee agreed to a £2,000 loan after selling the Frere Town property; and in 1930 H. J. E. Butcher, who had recently succeeded Hamshere as principal, took the Divinity School to the Highlands.

This move marked the end of the long CMS missionary occupation of Frere Town, but the Anglican Church there held together under African pastors. Rabai, another of the early CMS mission centres fifteen miles inland from Mombasa, had no resident missionaries between 1922 and 1943 but the congregations in the area were well cared for by two African clergy, Timothy Mapenzi, who died in 1925, and Samuel B. Kuri, who was made a canon of Mombasa cathedral in 1934. Butcher visited Rabai from Limuru in 1938 and found the church 'very much alive'.[25]

Strategically it was no doubt desirable to build up the missionary force in the Highlands and Nyanza, but it is not surprising that some of the few missionaries who remained in the Mombasa area felt marooned and were apt to complain at times about the demands made on their time by missionaries from up country arriving and departing, and sometimes waiting for a boat for weeks on end.

The dispersal of missionary forces from the coastal region is happily not the whole story. During the period Kaloleni became established as a strong centre of mission in southern Giriama. In 1910 there were only two missionaries at Kaloleni: Miss Florence Deed (1893–1937) and Miss M. L. Mason (1897–1921). Bishop Peel took them both with him during 1910 on a *safari* that covered much of the area occupied by the Giriama tribe. They were looking for a more promising site for a mission centre for the region, as Kaloleni had a capricious rainfall and poor communications; but they were unable to find anywhere better. Miss Deed and Miss Mason continued alone for some years, having to leave for several months in 1914 on account of a rising of the Giriama tribe against the government. Teacher-training was started on a modest scale in 1920. In 1922 H. T. Harris moved from Rabai to open a vocational school with a grant-in-aid from the government. Miss Deed had established a reputation as a gifted linguist, and was increasingly occupied with Kigiriama translation work. In 1928 the Normal School (teacher training) moved to Kaloleni from Mombasa with Miss E. Bodger as principal; and in 1929 the first resident doctor arrived, Dr K. W. Allen. Under his guidance plans for transforming the dispensary into a well-equipped hospital were carried through speedily, helped by the £5,000 secured for this purpose from the Mzizima hospital fund. Continuity was preserved by calling it the Edwards Memorial Hospital after a CMS pioneer doctor in Mombasa, C. S. Edwards. The problem of an adequate supply of water in an arid region was solved by sinking a well, which proved excellent in capacity and quality.[26]

The case for a mission hospital at Kaloleni was strong. In 1931 Dr Allen reported that ninety per cent of the boys at the mission school had bilharzia, and his report in 1934 underlined malnutrition as a cause of much of the illness in the district. In 1935 Miss Amy Sparrow arrived as hospital sister. When H. D. Hooper, Africa secretary of the Society, visited Kaloleni in 1937 he was particularly impressed 'by the ordered purpose and activity in all departments'. Following his visit, plans were worked out for a ring of out-station dispensaries such as Dr K. G. Fraser had developed around Lui in the southern Sudan. Six of these out-stations had been established by 1944. By then Dr W. H. Kirkaldy-Willis (1941–56) had taken over as hospital superintendent, and had started a small leper camp which developed considerably in later years.

By the end of the period Kaloleni had become an all-purpose mission station approximating more closely to the large establishments typical of the CSM at Kikuyu and the AIM at Kaimosi. The primary school flourished under K. E. Stovold from 1932 to 1938 and Alfred Stanway (later Bishop of Central Tanganyika). Not all the missionaries were happy about this large establishment.

Stovold saw a danger that the growing African church would become too dependent on European leadership; and M. G. Capon, in his annual letter in 1935, questioned whether it was right for six missionaries to be stationed at Kaloleni without freedom to itinerate.[27] Capon was at this time stationed at Vitengeni, fifty miles by road from Kaloleni. Much earlier, in 1911, Vitengeni had been selected as the site for a central school to serve a wide area of Giriama territory, but the plan had been halted by the Giriama rising of 1914. The problem of penetration much beyond strong centres such as Kaloleni remained vexatious. The intense conservatism of the Giriama tribe combined with a lack of missionary staff free from institutional responsibilities, made progress in evangelism and church-growth painfully slow.

It was slow too among the Digo people to the south-west of Mombasa. There was no resident missionary in this region after 1904 when George Burns left there to begin his outstanding ministry in Nairobi. G. W. Wright in Mombasa sought to lay responsibility for mission among the Digo on the cathedral congregation; and in the years 1911–14 he himself paid several visits, accompanied by catechists from Mombasa. Thirteen village schools were started, but continuity of oversight proved difficult. Islam was progressing more rapidly than Christianity. In 1919 when Bishop Heywood made his first tour of the Digo region with Archdeacon Hamshere he reported 'little progess, due to lack of supervision'. In the late 1930s Canon W. H. Hillard of Mombasa cathedral wrote of renewed attempts to evangelize the Digo people.[28]

In the Taita Hills, a hundred miles or so north-west of Mombasa, the people were more responsive than the Giriama and Digo, and the long service of several missionaries – J. A. Wray (1882–1912), R. A. Maynard (1895–1929), Miss Ada Drake (1901–21), V. V. Verbi (1895–1929) and Miss M. H. Murray (1920–57) helped to ensure continuity in the pastoral care of converts. Immanuel Church, Wusi, built by F. H. White, was consecrated by Bishop Heywood in 1935.

In 1937 the coastal Normal School for teacher-training moved from Kaloleni to Wusi under P. G. Bostock, who also was given pastoral charge of the Taita Hills and Taveta. There had been no resident missionary since 1934, and he found much to do, supervising eighteen out-schools and leading teams of witness.[29] In 1942 Miss Bodger followed him from Kaloleni to take charge of the girls' boarding school at Wusi.

Two African clergy contributed much to the steady growth of the church in the Taita Hills – Jonathan Kituri who retired in 1942; and Jeremiah Kiwinda.

Taveta, on the Lumi river to the north of Mount Kilimanjaro, had seven resident European missionaries at the turn of the century, but it had ceased to be a place of missionary residence before 1910. For a time Taveta was placed in the care of the Bishop of Central Tanganyika, but was restored to Mombasa diocese in 1937. In 1938 two trained Wataita teachers were sent to build up its schools.[30]

The Highlands, 1910–42

The year 1910 is very close to the beginning of the story of the Anglican Church in the Kenya Highlands. The first baptisms had taken place at Weithaga only two years earlier when eight young men were baptized, including the son, nephew and adopted son of Chief Karori. In 1910 two new CMS stations were started, in the territory of the Ndia people, at Kabare and Embu, a hundred miles or so north of Nairobi. The rapid development of so many pioneer missions in the Highlands overstrained the Society's resources in available man-power; and some of the early centres of mission proved impossible to maintain.

This proliferation of 'one-missionary' stations was in marked contrast to the policy of concentration adopted in the same area by the Church of Scotland mission, and came in for considerable criticism in later years. The impression given by the early entries in the log-books of these CMS Highland stations is not, however, of a clearly-formulated policy of wide dispersion, but of opportunism. If a chief was willing to receive a missionary in his district, and if land was made available a start was made, often with more than half an eye on Roman Catholic missionaries looking for sites in the same neighbourhood. It is possible that the CMS method owed something to the parochial system of England, as the Scottish system of larger units owed something to the Scottish presbytery; but if so it was, on the part of the Anglican mission, largely unconscious. Bishop Peel, as 'mission director' was living four hundred miles away at Mombasa; his visits were not frequent: he trusted McGregor and the other pioneers to get in where they could.

Progress in the Highlands was slow before 1914, but after the first world war it was very rapid. In the Highlands, as in Nyanza further west, the breakthrough owed a good deal to mission units in the Carrier Corps. The numbers of young men involved in this form of war service was far greater than the baptisms recorded in the Highland stations up to that time; and fear of press-gang methods no doubt explains their eagerness to join mission rather than government units. H. D. Hooper, who was directly involved with recruitment for the Carrier Corps, was probably not wrong in seeing it as the first real opportunity for evangelizing the Highlands, and at the end of the war the prospect was bright. In November 1918 Hooper wrote: 'Everywhere signs of recovery are evident. War-time government restrictions on out-schools have been removed. Good harvests have restored energy.' Retrenchment was soon to bear down with crippling effect on other missions of the Society, but the Highlands mission was already too buoyant to be seriously hurt by it; and, in the lean, early years of the country stations, George Burns in Nairobi had already met with a remarkable response to the proclamation of the gospel which gave heart to other missionaries in the Highlands proper.

Burns, an Australian, had come to Frere Town in 1899. In 1906, still a layman, he was posted to open a station at Nairobi and remained there until his retirement in 1932. He was ordained deacon by Bishop Peel in 1910, and priest in 1912. In 1915 he was made an Honorary Canon of Mombasa. He served on the Kenya legislative council as a representative of native interests and was awarded an OBE in 1926. The first baptism took place in Nairobi on 27th September, 1907. Writing in 1910 Burns estimated the population of the town as already twenty-five thousand, forty per cent European and ten per cent Indian. A European chaplain, P. A. Bennett, had been appointed to Nairobi in 1902 several years before Burns arrived to minister primarily to Africans. They were soon accepting his ministry in considerable numbers. One hundred people usually assembled for the weekly prayer-meeting, and twice that number for classes for catechumens and inquirers. Writing three years later he noted that representatives of all the tribes within a hundred miles of the railway were always coming and going. This ebb and flow made it impossible to have a regular school curriculum. He taught one large group in the day-time and another in the evening. The church building was enlarged in 1913 but was still too small for the rapidly growing number of those attending Sunday services. By 1916 the regular Sunday congregation in Nairobi was fifteen hundred in two sittings – 'nearly half Kikuyu and thirty-five per cent Kavirondo'. Five hundred people were now attending the Friday prayer-meetings. A new church was finished in 1924 and the old tin-roofed St Stephen's Church was re-erected in Pumwani, the African area of Nairobi. On the site of the old church a new women's school was built.[31] The response to Burns' teaching in Nairobi was quite without parallel in the coast region. It meant catering for large numbers of enquirers who wanted education, recognition, and Christian teaching (often in that order of priority) in a restless, rapidly growing town. Burns was the first to admit that educational standards were low. 'From the purely scholastic point of view,' he wrote in 1931 of the six schools comprehensively called CMS Nairobi School, 'they are hardly to be classed as schools at all' but as evangelistic agencies they were invaluable in a cosmopolitan area.[32] Perhaps, too, in a rigorous test of content and apprehension, Burns' evangelism would have been found wanting. Stories still circulate of how many an African, when asked about his religion, would reply 'Burnsi'. His preaching and evangelistic strategy were millenarian – he was determined to convert and baptize as many Africans as possible 'before the Lord's return'.

In his old age Burns was troubled by the thought of the large numbers he had baptized in view of the many lapses from church membership and the low moral standards among those he had taught. But the growth of the Anglican Church in the Kenya Highlands owes more to Burns' long ministry in Nairobi than to any other single factor; and in spite of the strong personal quality of his ministry, he laid foundations on which others could build. For many years he was the only CMS missionary in Nairobi; and then for most of the decade 1915–25 he and Miss E. Lockett were the only two listed. By 1930, however, he was one of sixteen CMS missionaries stationed there, including the staff of the bookshop and mission headquarters. A. R. Pittway, who succeeded Burns in 1932, reported three years later that he had about fourteen hundred people under instruction for baptism.[33]

The CMS Nairobi bookshop was opened in 1924 as a modest adjunct of the mission office, and was managed by the mission accountant, F. C. Smith. In 1933 the undertaking became a registered business and was then separated from the mission office. It remained however answerable to the Kenya mission executive and its ultimate ownership by the Society was recognized. C. G. Richards joined the bookshop in 1935 and by the 1940s had taken over the managership. Under his enthusiastic guidance the war years 1940–5 saw great developments, particularly in the publication of simple English and vernacular books, while a network of strategically placed depots was provided to serve a wide range of educational needs.

In 1927 the twin-towered All Saints Church became the second cathedral for the diocese of Mombasa. It was built to meet the needs of the growing Christian community of Nairobi – European as well as African.

Kabete, now a suburb of Nairobi, was originally planned as a rest-place for missionaries from the coast, but from 1902 to 1930 Harry Leakey exercised a ministry there as long and distinctive as that of Burns in Nairobi. In recruiting his early classes of inquirers, gifts such as sheets and soap were not uncommon. Kabete was not strategically well-placed as a centre of mission, and the numbers of inquirers and baptisms were not comparable to those of Nairobi; but T. F. C. Bewes, coming to work there in 1930, wrote of the crowded congregations in the small church every Sunday, with two to three hundred sitting outside; and an average attendance of two hundred in the Sunday School.[34]

Moving away now from the Nairobi neighbourhood to the group of stations close to Mount Kenya, Weithaga will always be associated with the name of A. W. McGregor. He opened the station in 1904 and, apart from two years away on war service, it remained his post until 1924. By then he was sixty, and he was asked to take charge of Nakuru 'and to work among farmers in that district as his strength permits'. He finally retired in 1927. Like Leakey, McGregor is remembered for his toughness with parents who tried to take their sons away from him. Canon Paul Mbatia, the first divinity student from Weithaga, described how in about 1906, his family tried to remove him forcibly; but McGregor 'calmed them down by threatening to take the matter to Chief Karori'.[35] The Rev. Shadrachi Mliwa, whom McGregor brought with him to the Highlands from Taveta, described him as 'a wonderful singer, a kind man . . . who had great influence around Kahuhia, Weithaga and Kathukeni'. McGregor laid down strong foundations for the church in the Fort Hall area. Canon E. W. Crawford, returning to Weithaga in 1930 after twenty years elsewhere, was impressed by the changes he found there. He noted that there were six thousand names on the register, baptized or under instruction for baptism, and twenty out-schools. In 1935 the foundation stone of a new church was laid. It was consecrated by Bishop Crabbe on 5th June, 1937. By that time Weithaga was the centre for over forty out-schools. There was an annual training-week for the village teachers, but in 1937 a government inspection detected lack of supervision, and grants were reduced.[36] But 'out-school' was a comprehensive term for a village centre for worship, evangelism and pastoral care as well as for formal education, and the work of Miss Wiseman and Miss Rickman among women and girls in the later 1930s deserves special mention.

Kahuhia has special links with the Hooper family. Douglas Hooper was there from 1909 until shortly before his death in 1917; his son Handley from 1916–26 when he was appointed Africa secretary at the Society's headquarters; and his grandson Cyril served at Kahuhia and Maseno from 1937 to 1957 when he too joined the headquarters staff in London. Douglas Hooper's health had broken down in Giriama, but in his years at Kahuhia he filled a long day from four in the morning till eight at night and felt no need of holidays. 'This old crock of a body is generally at work all day long with three breaks of twenty minutes for meals. Furlough must not be the form my thanksgiving takes.'[37] Livai Gacanja Ngumba recalled Douglas Hooper's popularity among the Kikuyu:

> He led the best spiritual life I could think of . . . a wonderful man, partly because he was a rich man and yet would not show it off; and partly because he could adapt himself in all spheres of life, disregarding the colour of people.[38]

Douglas Hooper was an individualist, utterly dedicated, ascetic in his self-discipline, and expecting the highest standards in others. He was impatient sometimes with the diocesan and mission authorities. He took strong exception, for instance, to a new diocesan service for the admission of catechumens, and refused to use it. In his strength and in his limitations he was a typical pioneer. His son Handley brought different gifts to a new situation.

By 1925 Kahuhia was a thriving church centre, with a normal school for teachers, a technical school, a girls' boarding school, an adult day school, and a dispensary with an African in charge of it. All these institutions were quite small but eighty-nine adults were baptized in the first nine months of 1924. Handley Hooper wrote in his annual letter that it had been an uneventful year, but he added that 'uneventfulness is one of the healthiest signs of growth'. The African church elders were beginning to see themselves as leaders of a permanent Christian community – 'as stewards of Christ, and no longer as protégés of an individual missionary'.[39] In 1930 the congregation at Kahuhia was building a new church, a common sign of growth. In 1935 W. H. Cantrell at the Normal School wrote of the 'grand opportunity for helping a very wide area' presented by the boys from many stations who were in training there. L. J. Beecher wrote of increasing pressure on places in the small boys' boarding school and of boys 'once in, being not too willing to leave'. Miss Soles, on the contrary, found continuity of training made difficult at the girls' school because the older ones were constantly leaving to get married, and the younger ones interrupting their training for the initiation rites.[40] In 1937 Martin Capon, Principal of the Normal School at Kahuhia, wrote of it as a truly co-operative venture, with a Presbyterian as the other member of the staff, and four different missions represented among the students.[41]

Embu, the most northerly of the CMS Highlands stations in Kenya and the furthest from Nairobi, was, like Kahuhia, opened by Dr T. W. W. Crawford, the elder brother of E. W. Crawford. When he went there in 1910 he found the local chief friendly. A sensitive account, *By the Equator's Snowy Peak*, by his wife, E. May Crawford (CMS, 1913) conveys something of the atmosphere of these pioneering years. But lack of missionary staff did not allow a missionary to remain there on a permanent basis until April 1915 when the Comelys arrived to begin a notable ministry of twenty-three years. Mr Comely reorganized the dispensary and the small in-patient hospital built by Dr Crawford. He also started farm-training on twenty-five acres of land. In 1925 he was able to report that the opposition met with ten years earlier had almost died out. By 1931 the number of out-schools connected with the Embu CMS station had risen to thirty-six, served by thirty-three teachers wholly paid, and four partly paid, from local church funds. Congregations of seven hundred to a thousand crowded in and around the church each Sunday, and Mrs Comely had a class of two hundred and fifty women on Sunday afternoons.[42] In 1931 she started an orphanage for mothers and babies with support from the National Church Council.

Kabare was open by E. W. Crawford in June 1910. He and Mrs Crawford lived in a mud hut at first. With the help of a catechist, Joseph Munyao, they started a school. When the Crawfords returned after two years' absence, in 1913, relations with a local chief became difficult, and later a rumour spread about that those who became Christians 'would never be allowed to eat cold food or to marry'. Gradually confidence was gained and in 1924 a 'strong and representative' church council was formed, taking responsibility for the maintenance of village schools and their teachers. By 1930 there were two thousand adherents on the books. Four years later H. J. Church reported that twenty out-schools were established, divided into six groups with a trained sector teacher for each group.[43] But work at Kabare remained heavy-going and a report in 1937 described it as 'a very backward district'.[44]

The CMS station at Muitira, opened by B. Laight in 1911, suffered like Embu and Kabare in their early days from lack of continuous missionary residence and there was some opposition from a local chief. The first inquirers at Muitira were admitted on 30th June, 1917 and the first baptism was administered on 29th February, 1920. In 1930 W. H. Hillard wrote of 'continuing opposition from heathen priests and headmen' but new readers were coming forward. In 1935 a new church was built to seat eight hundred people. The

Kathukeni CMS station, opened by A. E. Clarke in 1913, also experienced early opposition from the local elders, but a pastorate was formed in 1922, and in 1926 a new church was built, being enlarged ten years later.

'A large number of small stations that proved difficult to staff' – that is a fair picture of the CMS evangelism in the Highlands of Kenya in the first two decades; but as these brief accounts of each station have shown, a church had begun to take root in the 1920s. The Society's general secretary, Wilson Cash, wrote after a visit in 1937: 'In a lean period of restricted income almost every mission station has shown a marked advance.'[45] He attributed this advance largely to young missionaries. In the Highlands, as at the coast, the young church that grew up in connection with the CMS in Kenya was fortunate in the recruits of the 1930s – to mention only a few, Leonard Beecher (1930), Peter Bostock (1935) who like McGregor came to the highlands after apprenticeship in the Taita Hills; Harvey Cantrell (1931) and Cecil Bewes (1929) both to serve later on the headquarters staff, the latter as Africa secretary from 1949 to 1959; H. J. Church (1933), Martin Capon (1931), Kenneth Stovold (1931), Charles Richards (1935), and Elisabeth Richards (m.1939). This present record is indebted to the four last named for their writing on missionary history in Kenya, not all of it published.

The spiritual revival which started in Ruanda began to spread to the Kenya Highlands in 1937–8 largely through the agency of Dr Joe Church and a team of African evangelists. They met with a good response at Kabete and Kabare. A convention at Muitira was attended daily by fifteen hundred to two thousand for a whole week. Capon, who by this time had succeeded Butcher as Principal of the Divinity School at Limuru, worked closely with an African pastor, O. Kariuki,[46] in following up the mission with Bible courses and conventions.

Nyanza, 1910–42

The area of Kenya lying to the east of Lake Victoria was called 'Kavirondo' by Swahili traders. This regional name was adopted by Europeans, and until about 1910 the two main tribes of the region, the Joluo and the Baluyia were known indiscriminately as 'Wa-Kavirondo'.[47] CMS reports dropped 'Kavirondo' in favour of 'Nyanza Province' as the heading for its western Kenya missions from the time of their transfer to the diocese of Mombasa in 1921; but the older names continued in use for a long time. In this densely populated area the Joluo, a Nilotic people, live mostly in the lakeland plain, and the Bantu Baluyia on the largely treeless escarpment rising eastwards from the plain.

'Every party of missionaries going through from the coast to Uganda appealed to CMS to take up work among the tribes through whom they passed'.[48] These appeals received an answer in 1904 when Bishop Tucker visited Nyanza with J. J. Willis and another Uganda missionary. Willis volunteered to return there. In 1905 he chose Magarole as the first site for a mission centre, but moved in the following year to Maseno, about seventeen miles from Kisumu on the Kavirondo Gulf of Lake Victoria. He remained the inspirer and leader at Maseno until his appointment in 1912 as Bishop of Uganda.

The first baptisms in the Anglican Church in Nyanza were administered on 30th January, 1910, when fifteen boys from the school were baptized. Willis had opened the school in 1906 with four small boys, sons of Luo chiefs. Such a school for chiefs' sons was part of his general plan of compaign based, as he claimed, on 'the model of Iona', but his experience of Mengo High School provided a less remote model. The school grew rapidly and by 1911 there were one hundred and twenty boys. Miss Edith Hill started a girls' boarding school at Maseno in 1914. In 1924 H. S. Hitchen, who succeeded John Britton (1917) as principal of the Maseno boys' school, brought with him a number of Baluyia boys from the second CMS station, Butere, twenty-five miles away. When Hitchen returned to Butere after only a few months to organize village schools, he was succeeded by Canon J. S. Stansfield. Stansfeld, who had done remarkable work among boys in the East End of London before becoming Vicar of St Ebbe's, Oxford in 1912, volunteered to CMS at the uncommon age of seventy. In his short time at Maseno he made many friends, but the government was pressing at this time for fully-trained educational staff in grant-aided mission schools, and an education department report on Maseno school was critical of the quality of the teaching and the conditions under which it was given, noting with dismay that six African teachers were taking four classes in one room.[49]

The needful reforms were soon put in hand by a new principal, E. Carey Francis who, in his twelve years at Maseno school (1928–40), transformed it into one of the outstanding schools of East Africa. In his early years boys went on to the Alliance High School, Kikuyu (of which Francis was later to become principal) for secondary courses, but in 1938 Maseno school was itself given secondary status. In 1939 Carey Francis noted that, as a result of this change, forty out of two hundred and sixty boys were staying at Maseno school for five years instead of three. Teacher-training began at Maseno in 1920 under J. C. Hirst. He had forty pupils by 1922, many of them married men who had already worked as teacher-evangelists in village out-stations. Hirst retired on health grounds in 1925. In 1934 the government encouraged CMS to specialize in teacher-training at Maseno.

Medical work was early established at Maseno on the simple lines common to most pioneer mission stations, but it was not until 1921 that the present hospital was started by Dr R. Y. Stones with Miss J. E. Hillier as nursing sister. They worked in mud huts, while F. H. White, technical master at the boys' school, got to work on permanent buildings. The building of the hospital was largely financed from British Red Cross funds as a memorial to men from Nyanza who had served during the first world war in the King's African Rifles and the Carrier Corps. Medical work grew during the 'twenties under Drs

E. W. Fitzpatrick and D. S. Dixon; and Dr F. N. Green served with faithfulness and evangelistic zeal from 1930 to 1945.

At first CMS confined its work in Nyanza to the Joluo people, having agreed with the Friends Industrial Mission to do so in 1905, but a number of other non-Roman missions had come in which did not observe such 'comity' arrangements, and in 1912 the executive committee of the Uganda mission sent Walter Chadwick, the chaplain at Entebbe, with three Buganda evangelists to begin work among the Baluyia of north Kavirondo. Chadwick chose Butere, twenty-five miles north-west of Maseno, as the most suitable site, observing the government's ten-mile rule of distance between mission stations. He was soon joined by his sister, Miss Lisette Chadwick. In 1915 he was appointed Archdeacon of Kavirondo, but he died of blackwater fever on active service two years later. Lisette Chadwick remained at Butere for another nine years until her retirement in 1926. Mrs Richards writes of her gifts 'as a teacher, musician and linguist'. With some misgivings, Miss Chadwick took frequent charge of the dispensary. 'The worst of it is,' she wrote in 1919, 'that now people look on me as more or less of a doctor and keep on coming at all hours of the day when it is most inconvenient; but of course you cannot arrange that people should be ill only between 8 and 9 a.m.'[50]

In 1918 W. E. Owen, Chadwick's successor as archdeacon, had arrived at Butere with his wife and three sons. He had already been a missionary in Uganda for fourteen years, and for the last twenty-seven years of his life he was to identify himself with the life and aspirations of the peoples of Nyanza in a way that made him the hero of more than one generation of missionary recruits. Like the Chadwicks, Owen came from Northern Ireland and had worked for a time in the CMS office in Belfast before training at Islington.

An enthusiastic archaeologist and geologist, a skilful administrator, and a formidable champion of the oppressed, Owen kept alive for a little longer the image of the omnicompetent missionary. He could turn his hand to anything. He was tough and not without guile in his dealings with the powerful, and impenitent about the 'rows' in which he involved them; but he was wonderfully patient and gentle with those who had no power. He ran the dispensary at Butere with Miss Chadwick's help, compounded medicines, delivered babies, applied dressings, and when bubonic plague broke out in the district in 1919 he made repeated journeys on his motor-cycle to fetch serum from Kisumu, and it is estimated that he inoculated eleven thousand people in less than four months.[51] In 1919 the largest school-church in the Butere area was blown down in a violent hail-storm, and he was soon at work, planning and supervising the building of a new permanent church.

Owen's work as archdeacon inevitably took him far afield from Butere, and the building up of the church in the district was largely the work of A. J. Leech (canon of Mombasa, 1935) who came to Butere in 1913. Leech was a meticulous, somewhat eccentric person 'who combined . . . a strong sense of his authority as priest and a natural extreme diffidence and modesty'.[52] He never spared himself, and expected the same standards of self-discipline in others.

Butere had a grant-aided boys' boarding school from 1921, at first under the direction of Miss E. B. Downer. As already recorded, H. S. Hitchen took the boys from this school to join forces with Maseno school in 1924, returning in 1925 to develop the Normal School at Butere which prospered as a centre of teacher-training. A girls' boarding school was built in 1936, with Miss Grace Camm as principal from 1940.

As the CMS mission in Nyanza gained strength the disadvantages of Maseno as a centre for evangelism became more evident, since it was on the eastern boundaries of the Joluo tribal territory. In 1919 Ng'iya, due west of Maseno, was chosen as the site for a second station for the Joluo. H. O. Savile built a missionaries' house there and A. E. Pleydell returned from furlough in October 1921 to become the first resident missionary. He is remembered as 'a gentle, lovable, self-effacing person'. A characteristic gesture of his arm reminded the Luo people of the way an elder uses his fly-whisk made out of a cow's tail, and so he earned the nick-name 'Orengo' by which he was universally known among Africans. He acquired an extensive knowledge of the Luo language and its proverbs, largely from the children and old women with whom he was quick to make friends. When he first arrived at Ng'iya his reputation had run ahead of him and he was given a hilarious welcome with large crowds and a band.[53] In 1923 Miss Fanny Moller arrived in Ng'iya to begin her distinguished service to girls' education in Nyanza. Most of the money for the first girls' school came, like Miss Moller herself, from Australia, and another Australian CMS missionary, Miss Mercia Wray, joined her in 1925. She helped at the school but was chiefly occupied with the dispensary and maternity welfare.

A new girls' boarding school in Ng'iya was opened in September 1932 by G. E. Webb, the government inspector of schools for Nyanza, to whom the development of girls' education in Nyanza owes much.

Medical work at Ng'iya was only on a small scale. The Pleydells ran a dispensary in the early days, and when Miss Wray came a small maternity ward was built with the help of a government grant. A permanent church was consecrated by Bishop Heywood in 1935; and Archdeacon Owen, who lived at Ng'iya during his last years in Nyanza, enjoyed demonstrating his skill as a builder with murram blocks.

Kisumu, as the original Lake Victoria terminus of the Uganda railway (1901) and a main port for lake steamers, was the communications centre for the Nyanza group of mission stations. Bishop Tucker consecrated a small church there for African and European use in 1907. Three years later the government made a grant of three acres of land for the purpose of building an African church and school. In the same year, 1910, F. H. Wright went there as resident missionary and chaplain to the European community. Wright was one of the 1895 party of missionary recruits who walked up from the coast to Uganda; Miss Lisette Chadwick was in the same party. He remained at Kisumu until his retirement in 1924, acting in his later years as secretary of the Kavirondo district committee of Mombasa diocese. After Wright's departure an African pastor, Reuben Omulo, had pastoral charge of the church in Kisumu and the CMS annual reports in the late 1920s frequently praised his work.

By the later 1930s the Anglican Church in Nyanza had grown remarkably, from a baptized membership of fifteen in 1910 to one of over fifty thousand in 1935. Some missionaries, notably Carey Francis, were outspoken in their anxieties about this development. 'The Church is an immense baptizing machine,' he wrote in his annual letter in 1934; and two years later: 'The Church holds up no challenge, no higher ideal; has its Church Council, divides its collections, condemns the polygamists and goes on in the same old way.'[54] Writing in 1939, however, Archdeacon Owen was more hopeful. He saw signs of the revival which had begun in Ruanda beginning to spread to western Kenya, and he was ready in defence of the numerous little churches 'that are centres of community life no matter how inefficient they may appear to be'.[55]

In the foregoing accounts of the development of the three CMS areas of mission in Kenya it is noticeable that the numerical expansion in the Highlands and Kavirondo was of a quite different order from the coastal region proper, and even of the Taita Hills. There was a far greater readiness up-country to accept what the missionaries had to give. One factor leading to this greater response was the widespread expectation that the missionaries held the key to the new situation created by colonialism. Certainly they stood apart from the settlers' community; and could be seen to do so. Some more detailed account of how and why they did this forms the substance of the rest of this chapter.

The Search for Christian Unity in Kenya

I. Proposals for Federation, 1908–18

By the Treaty of Berlin, 1885, Britain and Germany gave specific guarantees of freedom of conscience and religious toleration in the part of East Africa covered by their agreement. The guarantee included 'the free open exercise of all forms of worship, the right of constructing buildings for Divine Service and the organization of Missions, to whichever kind of worship the same may belong'.[56] This open policy, combined with the construction of the Uganda railway, made East Africa a natural outlet for the missionary zeal of small sects which might well have failed to gain admittance to other fields. By 1903 there were four Protestant missionary societies at work in the immediate neighbourhood of Nairobi, and by 1908 at least six in the heavily populated area near the railhead at Kisumu in Nyanza.

A laudable attempt was made by some of the missionary bodies to limit competition by dividing the accessible areas into 'spheres', in each of which one mission only would have the right to develop its work, but these comity agreements were only partially successful. The main mission centres tended to be very close together near the railway; the boundaries between the spheres were sometimes drawn with little regard to the terrain, and not all the missions were prepared to bind themselves to observe them. Further, the increased mobility of the population, especially among young men seeking work in the growing towns, made the policy of mission spheres very difficult to operate.

It was to meet this situation that J. J. Willis, recently appointed Archdeacon of Kavirondo, convened a conference of representatives of several missions at Maseno in 1908. It had the limited aim of avoiding overlapping and confusion of missionary effort in Nyanza. But in his urgent concern for greater co-operation between missions Willis also had in mind the rising tide of Muslim influence spreading inland from the East African coast. In halting the advance of Islam, Kenya, from the standpoint of Christian mission, had a peculiar strategical importance.[57] In Kenya also, to a far greater degree than in Uganda, Western secularism and materialism were already contending for the 'soul of Africa'. It could only be countered, Willis believed, by a strong indigenous African church. 'But so long as Christianity was speaking with a divided and uncertain voice, so long would its message be frustrated and the conversion of the African delayed.'[58] The Maseno conference agreed on a system of missionary comity for the region, and began to work out a common policy about language problems. But a conference at Kijabe, the AIM headquarters in the Highlands, later in that year looked at the problems of Kenya as a whole and sought ways of encouraging 'the growth of what is common between the different branches of the Church of Christ'.[59] By now Willis had found a strong ally in Dr H. E. Scott, head of the CSM at Kikuyu. A further conference at Kijabe early in 1909 affirmed 'the development, organization and establishment of a united self-governing, self-supporting and self-extending Native Church as the ideal of our Missionary Work'.[60] A larger and more representative conference met in Nairobi from 7th to 11th June, 1909. Its membership included missionaries of the Africa Inland Mission, Seventh Day Adventists, the Friends Africa Industrial Mission (Kaimosi), the CMS, the Church of Scotland mission, the United Methodist mission (Mombasa) and the English Friends mission (Pemba). Willis read a paper on 'The Desirability of a single Native Church in British East Africa'. He had been encouraged by the Report of the Lambeth Conference, 1908 (especially Resolutions 58, 75), to think that the highest authorities of the Anglican Communion would give their blessing to local efforts towards the closest co-operation between the churches, and to the exploration of the possibilities of reunion based on the 1888 'Lambeth Quadrilateral'. Willis realized from private conversation with Dr Scott and with the Rev. C. E. Hurlburt, Director of the AIM, that there was scarcely any chance of the fourth term of the Quadrilateral, 'the historic episcopate' being accepted as a basis of negotiations for a united church. For this reason the idea of a 'federation of missions' began to take shape as a first step towards church union. Federation was not a wholly new idea. The Centenary Missionary Conference at Shanghai in 1907 had proposed it. But it had a particular relevance to the inter-mission problems of Kenya.

The findings of the Nairobi conference were sent back to the home authorities of the missions concerned. In the case of the CMS they took the form of a 'Memorandum on the Proposed Union of Native Churches in British East Africa', drawn up by the CMS representatives at the conference – J. J. Willis, J. A. Wray, and K. St A. Rogers. The memorandum[61] was divided into three sections:

1. *A Proposed Constitution for a United Church*, based on the Lambeth Quadrilateral, but substituting for the historic episcopate 'a regularly ordained and properly safeguarded ministry'. The proposed constitutions included a scheme for church government with a pyramid of parochial councils, district councils, and a synod. The CMS representatives said in their memorandum that they realized this was not practical at present.

2. *A Federation of Missionary Societies*. This, the representatives hoped would be effected 'in the immediate future'. The federation would be based on a common acceptance of the Holy Scriptures 'as our sole standard of faith and practice'; and of the Apostles' and Nicene Creeds 'as a general expression of our common faith'; on the recognition of a common membership; on the regular administration of the two sacraments, Baptism and Holy Communion; and on a common form of church organization. A representative council of the federation would be formed, but its function would be 'wholly advisory'.

3. *Recommendations*. These included (i) *Comity*. Societies to agree to respect each other's 'spheres'. Townships to be regarded as neutral spheres. (ii) *Ministry*. For the present all Europeans who were recognized as ministers in their own churches to be welcomed as visitors to preach in other churches; African candidates for the ministry to 'be duly set apart by lawful authority, and by the laying on of hands'.

The salient features of the Kikuyu conference of 1913 were thus already worked out by the Nairobi conference of 1909, and its drafting committee. 'Cautious, but not discouraging' might describe the wider Anglican reaction to the project. Bishop Tucker of Uganda, for example, thought federation would be a help to the smaller societies, and he was glad to see that the proposed representative council was to be purely advisory.[62]

Bishop Whitehead of Madras wrote in his diocesan magazine: 'I do not think there is anything in this scheme that differs in principle from what has been done in India during the last thirty or forty years.'[63]

The matter was referred to the Society's ecclesiastical sub-committee, and its recommendations were incorporated in a resolution confirmed by general committee on 8th November, 1910.

The resolution referred back to a CMS committee memorandum of 1901 on 'The Constitution of Churches in the Mission Field',[64] and encouraged the authorities in the Society's missions in British East Africa and Uganda 'to do what in them lies to foster the spirit of unity, and to advance such measures of co-operation as they may from time to time conclude to be wise and capable of practical application', but on the following conditions: (1) all suggestions made to or by the missionaries of the Society must be submitted to the Bishops of Uganda and Mombasa 'whose concurrence would be essential to the efficient adoption of any proposal'; (2) the ordinary powers of the governing bodies in each mission were not to be exceeded without special reference to the parent committee; (3) the existence of the strong and stable church in Uganda must be recognized as an important factor in the problem to be dealt with, the parent committee being of opinion 'that the fruits of the Society's other Missions in East Africa should, in all likelihood, be some day brought into one organization with the Church in Uganda'.

The resolution gave cautious approval to the proposed federation, 'it being understood that each Mission retains for the time being its independent management and its liberty to withdraw from the federation at any time, should occasion arise'. The committee was not yet ready to express any opinion about the future constitution of a united church, nor was it ready to ask the ecclesiastical authorities of the Church of England to do so. 'The principles involved will be very far-reaching, and the circumstances to which they will need to be applied have at present developed to only a very small extent in British East Africa.' When the time came for such wider consultation 'it should be by the Bishops in East Africa rather than by the Committee of the CMS, or, if by that Committee, then only at the request of the Bishops concerned'.

The cautious tone of the CMS parent committee's resolution of 1910 is understandable. Quite apart from questions of ecclesiastical authority, the committee had been asked to pronounce on two quite different proposals – one for an African united church and the other for a federation of missionary societies working in Kenya. The connection between these two proposals was far from clear. In private conversation with Willis, F. Baylis, the Society's Group III (Africa) secretary, and C. C. B. Bardsley, the general secretary, gave it as their opinion that the only possible united church would be one within the Anglican Communion; they could see no prospect of a native church emerging from the proposed federation.[65]

Meanwhile events in Kenya underlined the difficulties of the double approach. A committee appointed by the 1909 Nairobi conference worked out a general scheme for missionary federation, and drew up in some detail a draft constitution for its organization. This was brought before a further conference at Nairobi in January 1911, but no agreement was obtained. Willis attributed this temporary failure to the absence of Dr Scott, who had died in 1910, and to the difficulties commonly met with when the attempt is made 'to translate broad principles into concrete and detailed action'.[66] But there were deep underlying differences of ecclesiology between 'church' missions such as CMS and CSM and the 'undenominational' missions, particularly those of American origin. These differences had now started coming to the surface.

The large and representative conference which met at Kikuyu in June 1913 was not, in Willis' view, a rash venture into uncharted territory but a last effort to translate the 1909 proposals into practice.

He had recently succeeded Tucker as Bishop of Uganda but it was natural that, with Nyanza still within his diocese, he should come to the conference; and, being there, that he should be elected its chairman. Opening the discussion on federation he made it clear that the basic issue before the conference was federation not union:

> We must look forward to one Church. . . . This work cannot be done by the missionaries, only the natives of the country can effect it; but missionaries can prepare the foundations. The question for us today is, how far can we get on converging lines, which in the future shall lead to one United Native Church?[67]

The basis of federation as proposed at Kikuyu in 1913 followed closely the proposals of the Nairobi conference of 1909, but a new clause was added affirming 'belief in the absolute authority of Holy Scripture as the Word of God, in the Deity of Jesus Christ, and in the atoning death of our Lord as the ground of our forgiveness'.

The constitution of the federation included provision for a common form of organization to be adopted by all missions in the developing native churches; and for a positive preparation of native Christians for church union by (a) similar forms and usages in public worship. (A form of service very like Morning and Evening Prayer in the 1662 Book of Common Prayer was put forward in outline with a recommendation that it be used sufficiently often to enable members of all the churches to become familiar with a common order; it was still in use by Anglicans and Presbyterians throughout Kenya in the 1960s.); (b) letters of commendation for members of one church temporarily residing in the area of another church; (c) acceptance of a common standard of church discipline; and (d) a common course of instruction and preparation for catechumens and African ministers of all churches.

The proposed constitution contained a number of resolutions which caused anxiety in some Anglican circles both in Africa and elsewhere where the scheme was studied. Resolution 1, concerning the ministry, laid it down that for the present 'all recognized as Ministers in their own Churches shall be welcomed as visitors to preach in other Federated Churches'. Resolution 6, concerning the sacraments, stated that 'the Sacrament of the Lord's Supper shall not be administered to anyone who is not a full member of the Church to which he belongs'. Resolution 7, under the same heading, provided that 'members residing temporarily in other Districts should be supplied with cards on which the Minister of the Church visited shall record attendances at Communion'.[68] Section IV of the constitution provided for the setting up of a representative council of the federated societies 'until the Synod of the Native Church shall come into existence'.

The constitution was signed by representatives of AIM (and of the Independent Nilotic Mission shortly to be amalgamated with the AIM); the CMS; the CSM; and the United Methodist mission. Members of other missions represented at the Kikuyu conference – the Gospel Missionary Society, the German Lutheran mission, the Friends' Africa mission, and the Seventh Day Adventists – expressed sympathy with the main objects of the proposal but for varying reasons found themselves unable to sign the constitution.

At the close of the conference a service of Holy Communion was celebrated in the chapel of the Church of Scotland mission at Kikuyu; Bishop Peel was invited to be celebrant and the Book of Common Prayer rite was used; delegates were invited to communicate; and the great majority, apart from members of the Society of Friends, did communicate.

The strenuous controversy that followed the 1913 Kikuyu conference belongs to the wider history of the ecumenical movement rather than to a chronicle of CMS operations in Kenya. It must be mentioned here in brief, however, to explain the terms in which CMS missionaries in East Africa were to continue their search for inter-mission co-operation and church unity.[69] Public attention was first drawn to the conference in the British press by a letter in *The Scotsman* on 9th August, 1913. Written by Dr Norman Maclean, who had been present as a visitor, the letter described its proceedings, including the 'open' service of Holy Communion, enthusiastically and concluded that the missionaries in British East Africa had 'solved the problem of how to coalesce Episcopacy and Presbyterianism'. His letter failed to explain that the proposals were only tentative. Four days before this letter appeared Bishop Frank Weston of Zanzibar had written to the Archbishop of Canterbury expressing grave concern at the reports he had received about the conference and saying that, if they were confirmed, 'there is no shadow of doubt that this diocese will refuse communion with the dioceses of Mombasa and Uganda'. Weston wrote again to the Archbishop on 30th September, urging him to summon a synodical court to investigate the matter, and suggesting that if this was not done he might have to resign his see on the ground that heresy had been condoned 'in the sight of the Missionary Churches in East Africa, who do not see things as we Englishmen see them'.[70] This letter was accompanied by a formal indictment of Bishops Peel and Willis 'for the grievous error of propagating heresy and committing schism'. A third letter from the Bishop of Zanzibar to the Archbishop dated 29th October was more moderate in tone. Bishop Willis was staying with him, and had explained certain points and it was now necessary, he said, to amend his appeal. But he was still not satisfied that episcopacy had been taught in the Kikuyu conference as the vital foundation of the church or that the sacramental system had been given its right place.

A resolution of the general committee of the CMS, 9th December, 1913, noted that there was no intention to take any steps involving alteration of the present ecclesiastical status of the missions; and gave general approval to 'the continuing search of the Bishops of Mombasa and Uganda, and their brethren, for further advance on the path to reunion'. A further resolution of 30th June, 1914 gave tentative approval to the local governing body of its BEA mission entering the proposed federation subject to the concurrence of the Bishops of Uganda and Mombasa and without prejudice to any ecclesiastical ruling 'that hereafter may be made'.[71]

Meanwhile the Kikuyu matter had become a *cause célèbre* in the British press. Stock noted no less than thirty columns of letters about it in *The Times* between 17th December, 1913 and 6th January, 1914.[72] On 9th February, 1914 the Archbishop of Canterbury published a full statement. He was not prepared to allow a trial of the Bishops of Mombasa and Uganda for heresy and schism, as the facts before him gave no grounds for this: but he proposed to summon the Consultative Body of the Lambeth Conference to meet in July 1914 to advise him in particular on two questions: 'Do the provisions of the proposed Scheme contravene any principles of Church Order. . . . If so, in what particulars?'; and was 'the action of the Bishops who arranged and conducted the admittedly abnormal Holy Communion Service consistent or inconsistent with principles accepted by the Church of England?'[73]

The Consultative Body met for four days, 17th to 21st July, 1914, with the Archbishop of York (Dr Lang) as its chairman. Its conclusions were unanimous. Anything approaching federation must be sanctioned by the Lambeth Conference: qualified approval was given to the invitation of missionaries of other societies to preach in Anglican pulpits: but any encouragement of Anglicans to communicate in non-episcopal churches was not consistent with the principles of the Church of England, nor, if accepted as a precedent, was the closing service of Holy Communion at the Kikuyu conference.

The Consultative Body's report was not published until Archbishop Davidson was ready with his own answer which, due to the outbreak of the first world war, was not until Easter 1915. The Archbishop found it less necessary than the Consultative Body had done to hedge round the interchange of pulpits with episcopal inquiry about the individual standing and attainments of non-Anglican preachers; and he was positive in his opinion that 'a Diocesan Bishop acts rightly in sanctioning, when circumstances seem to call for it, the admission to Holy Communion of a devout Christian man to whom the ministrations of his own Church are for the time inaccessible'. But 'a corresponding readiness to bid the members of our Church, when temporarily isolated, [to] seek the Holy Communion at the hands of any Christian Minister though not Episcopally ordained . . . [is to] run the risk of creating serious confusion'. The Archbishop was glad to be able to say that this question was of an academic rather than a practical kind since the Bishops of Mombasa and Uganda had no wish or intention to give that advice to African Christians, belonging to their dioceses.

As to the holding of the joint Communion Service, the Archbishop pointed out that this was 'far from being the first time that in the Mission-Fields of Africa or of the Far East' such an open Anglican Communion had been held; but it only confused matters to equate occasional hospitality with the kind of service that might be acclaimed as a 'demonstration'. He believed 'that we shall act rightly . . . in abstaining at present from such Services as the closing Service held at Kikuyu'.[74]

The standing committee of the Kikuyu conference met at Nairobi in December 1915. Certain modifications to the scheme were proposed, notably the use of the word 'alliance' instead of 'federation'. Nothing was finally decided. The main questions referred back for further consultation were (a) the question of the full validity of baptism administered in any area of allied missions and (b) the autonomy of each mission in its own sphere as to making total abstinence a *sine qua non* of admission to the catechumenate. Mr Hurlburt wrote to Bishop Willis about these matters in April 1916. He required an answer from CMS about the liberty for Anglicans attending Baptist churches to be immersed (i.e. rebaptized) if they so desired and about the exclusion of non-teetotallers from full membership. The ecclesiological gaps between Anglican missions and the interdenominational missions were increasingly evident. But it is only fair to note that Hurlburt's concern was to protect the right of Christians to change denomination. Bishops Willis and Peel tended to act as though church union had been established.[75]

In July 1916 the CMS Kenya missionary conference heard reports of two letters. One from Dr Arthur of the CSM agreeing that total abstinence from alcohol should not be a condition for baptism; and the re-baptism of those baptized in infancy should not be practised: and another from Mr Hurlburt of AIM saying that his society could not give way on these points. The prospects of a united church within the foreseeable future seemed poor indeed; and the hopes of some form of 'federation' or 'alliance' had diminished considerably.

They were revived from an unexpected quarter. Early in 1917 the government of the protectorate was faced with the urgent task of providing forty thousand porters for war service in German East Africa. Four of the missions represented at the Kikuyu conference (CSM, CMS, AIM, and GMS) decided to co-operate in recruiting a Mission Carrier Corps. Some two thousand volunteers from the various mission stations assembled at Kikuyu in April, half of them from CMS stations, and were formed into a battalion. Dr Arthur was in command with the rank of captain and eight other missionaries, including H. D. Hooper of CMS, served with the Corps during the later months of 1917. Dr Arthur, writing of this experience, claimed that it did much to bring home the reality of their oneness in Christ Jesus to all concerned in it and prepared the way for fresh efforts towards unity when the war ended.[76] Plans were laid for a further conference to assess the possibilities of further progress towards federation in the light of the reactions of the various home authorities of the missions in

Kenya; and of the new experiences of oneness in Christ which war-time experiences in East Africa had brought.

After careful preparation, including an invitation to Bishop Weston to attend it, a second Kikuyu conference was held from 23rd to 26th July, 1918. It was larger than the 1913 conference. A hundred delegates and visitors assembled, and Bishop Willis, after R. S. Heywood, newly-appointed Bishop of Mombasa had declined, was again elected chairman. Bishop Weston, accompanied by Canon Malcolm Mackay of the UMCA, attended as a visitor, and on the first full day of the conference was invited to address the delegates, and was listened to 'with eager attention'.[77] Weston put forward his views of the controversy which had arisen about the 1913 proposals and outlined his own scheme for a united church. Unity, he suggested, must be based on a common acceptance of episcopacy – 'of the fact that Episcopacy has always existed, and is today in possession of the far greater part of Christendom'; and a common acceptance of the principle of sacramental grace – the gospel sacraments to be used by all, and all bodies to admit the liberty of Christians to use 'those other rites' which Bishop Weston himself called sacraments. Episcopacy need not be monarchical. Bishops should be freely elected and rule synodically with the clergy and laity. If non-episcopal bodies would accept some such proposals as these and 'consent to some form of Episcopal Consecration and Ordination so as to enable them to minister, by invitation, in episcopal churches, he for his part would gladly come before any of their congregations, and accept any form of popular recognition.'[78] He laid stress upon the necessity of freedom in worship and 'did not hide from the Conference the wide tolerance it must exercise if it desired to include Zanzibar Diocese in its scheme of re-union'.[79]

The conference was placed in something of a quandary by Weston's proposals. Many of the delegates saw hope of a workable scheme of missionary alliance in Kenya. Their minds were now set on this, and they found it difficult to relate it to Bishop Weston's scheme. He proposed an organic union of East African Churches on conditions which, for most of them, raised novel problems. After an agreed adjournment, in which the delegates conferred in their own groups, the non-episcopal missionaries gave their opinion that the solution proposed by the Bishop of Zanzibar was not possible at present.[80] Hurlburt, as their spokesman, summed up their anxieties about it. First, they might find themselves in relation with some who, 'though nominally agreeing with this basis, were really tending towards at least some doubt of the integrity of Scripture and the deity of our Lord'. Second, they had reason to expect an attempted union of all churches based on compromise, which would fail to bring the proposed united church into any real fellowship. Third, they felt that 'no ritual which would take the place of personal communion, and no ecclesiastical control which limited personal liberty in vital things, or failed to honour the authority conferred by their own Churches, was possible'.[81]

Hurlburt made it clear, however, that his own society and those who took the same point of view as he had expressed, were willing to go ahead with the proposal for an alliance. It is a pity that some of the positive aspects of Weston's proposals, particularly the necessity of comprehension and liberty in un-essentials, were not explored more fully by the conference, even at the risk of losing AIM support. Willis described the Bishop of Zanzibar's contribution to the discussion as 'remarkable' and said that in the five days of the conference he 'entirely won the hearts of many who must have widely differed from him'. Weston's biographer gives a less happy picture:

> Frank took little part in the discussions at Kikuyu . . . the point that struck him most forcibly was the futility of the proceedings. Here were a hundred delegates belonging to many sects, and they had met together to plan the African Church of the future, and not a single African was present.[82]

The comment is not wholly just. The up-country missions in Kenya were most of them of very recent foundation, some only within their second decade, and there were as yet no African clergy except at the coast. It was partly because of this absence of Africans that both Kikuyu conferences regarded their work as preparatory only – to open the way for unity 'for the sake . . . of those African Christians to whom our controversies are as yet unknown'.[83]

On the last day of the conference, 26th July, 1918, the constitution of the alliance was signed by delegates on behalf of the CMS, the Church of Scotland mission, the Africa Inland Mission, the United Methodist Church mission, and the British and Foreign Bible Society. The Bible Society later withdrew from participation as a constituent member of the alliance on the grounds that it existed to serve other missionary societies in a special way. The Bishops of Mombasa and Uganda signed on behalf of the CMS in spite of a formal pro-test by the Bishop of Zanzibar that they should not do so. The changes in the constitution since 1913 were not extensive. The basis of the alliance, as amended, omitted any reference to a recognition of common membership between the churches and to a common form of church organization. Section IV of the constitution – 'Method to be Adopted by Each Allied Society within the Sphere' – required a minimum course of instruction to the catechumenate; a course of instruction for those baptized in infancy before admission to Holy Communion; and a prescribed course of instruction for all future candidates for the native ministry. Section V, 'Relating to the Non-Allied Societies', advocated co-operation with them where possible. Several such societies, including the Friends Africa Industrial Mission, the Seventh Day Adventists, and the Gospel Missionary Society, expressed a desire for such reciprocal relationship. Section III of the constitution of the alliance made it clear that the representative council was to be 'wholly advisory' and 'to exercise no control over the Allied Societies or Churches'. The council was formally constituted with the Bishop of Mombasa as chairman, the Bishop of Uganda and Mr Hurlburt as vice-chairmen, and Dr J. W. Arthur as secretary.

2. The Alliance at Work, 1918–35

The representative council did good work, especially in its early years, as spokesman of the missionary bodies to the government of Kenya on matters affecting the welfare of Africans, especially in educational and medical policy. In 1919 it approved a scheme prepared by its theological board for the training of evangelists and catechists on parallel lines with hope of joint training eventually. A committee of reunion was appointed by a further Kikuyu conference and met at Nairobi in November, 1922. Its report recommended that the aim of the alliance should be the organization of the uniting churches into a United African Church in Kenya Colony which would be autonomous in its government, though 'it should regulate its acts by the necessity of maintaining fellowship with the Church Universal'; and when and where possible it should join up with united African churches formed in other parts of Africa. The substitution of the word 'African' for 'Native' in the title of the proposed united church was token of a new sensitiveness towards African dislike of the word. It also left the door open to membership for European citizens of Kenya.

In February 1926 one more united conference of missionaries was held at Kikuyu. Its first concern was the establishment of the Alliance High School which opened at Kikuyu on 1st March in that year. Its discussion ranged widely over current problems; it set up a committee to scrutinize a Native Land Bill and to watch its progress; it made representations to the government of the colony about Sunday work; it recommended the setting up of maternity centres in the African Reserves; and it ratified the constitution of the Kenya missionary council. The council had been formed on 24th April, 1924 with representatives from the allied societies and some half dozen others.

In January 1926 the representative council of the alliance issued a 'Memorandum on Co-operation'.[84]

It recalled the formation of the alliance eleven years earlier and summarized 'the principal matters agreed on by the four Societies', at that time. It regretted difficulties which had arisen 'of late years when African Christians of one church have begun to settle in considerable numbers in portions of the sphere occupied by another church'; and the council had therefore decided to suggest certain modifications of the 1918 agreement. The first four modifications concerned the 'sphere' system particularly 'in the case of areas where Church consciousness and organized Church life are developed', and where 'latitude may be allowed and the desires of African Christians themselves taken more and more into consideration'. In townships every effort should be made to avoid the erection of competitive buildings for public worship, and church buildings should be made available by mutual arrangement for joint services, and for the services and classes of other churches represented in the alliance. In 'Non-Native Areas' (e.g. European farms and forest lands) where more than one church was represented, 'spheres' should be abrogated, but the principles proposed for townships should apply. In the reserves where a considerable number of African Christians, belonging to one of the allied missions, were living in the sphere of another they should be given corporate recognition.

Modification of 'comity' along these lines was by 1929 overdue. There had been considerable tension between the CMS and the Church of Scotland ever since 1911 in the Kabete area, and in relation to Nairobi itself.[85] In 1926 the CMS Kavirondo district committee heard a plea for the reconsideration of the policy of mission spheres 'in view of the Africans' demand for their abolition and the partial breaking down of the system'.[86]

The representative council's memorandum recalled the original purpose of the alliance – 'to endeavour to avoid the production of denominational rigidity and to promote the possibility of real union in the African Church'; and it drew attention in particular to two recommendations: '(a) It is recognized that a baptized communicant member of any Allied Society is eligible for appointment to the Church Council or as an officer of the Church with which for the time he is identified. (b) It is recognized that visiting communicant members should be admitted to communion in Churches of the Alliance, without necessarily conforming to the special discipline of the church they are visiting, provided they are in full communion with their own church at the time.'

These recommendations were, on one level, a last, and almost despairing attempt to work through the organs of the alliance towards that real union of the African church which seemed as elusive as ever. The differences in church polity were little eased. Anglican rules continued to stand in the way of reciprocal hospitality to communicants. In 1929 Anglican missionaries went 'beyond authority' in implementing proposals of the 1922 Kikuyu conference about joint ordinations. One Anglican priest took part with a Baptist and a Methodist in the laying-on of hands at a Church of Scotland ordination at Kikuyu; and two priests did so on a similar occasion in the same year at Tumutumu. No reciprocal invitations, however, were given for Anglican ordinations; and in 1935, when the Bishop of Mombasa and three Anglican priests were present at a Presbyterian ordination service, they took no part in the laying-on of hands.

Between 1929 and 1932 the council of the alliance was much occupied with the female circumcision controversy[87] and the problem of the independent schools and school-churches that grew out of it. It became evident that a common policy on moral questions, written into the 1913 federation proposals, was as difficult to obtain as an agreement on matters of church order. The alliance virtually came to an end in 1935 when, at a joint meeting of the representative council and the Kenya missionary council, it was resolved that there was no longer any need for the former body 'because of the development of its offspring'. Between 1935 and 1943, when the Kenya Christian council was formed, a committee of reference met occasionally to watch the interests of the alliance. In 1941 it recommended that missionary 'spheres' should be abandoned, but that no mission should open any station to be staffed by Europeans in an area not previously occupied.

A new initiative towards church union was made in 1931. Following the encouragement given by the Lambeth Conference that summer to the South India Scheme of Church Union, Bishop Heywood invited other churches to join with members of the Mombasa diocesan synod in exploring the possibilities of advance on the lines of South India. A committee on church union, appointed by the respresentative council of the alliance, met twice in 1932, in June and October. Anglican, Presbyterian and Methodist missions were officially represented. Members of the AIM were present, but felt unable to take part as voters in view of the interdenominational and international character of their mission. The June meeting of the committee recommended that unity should be sought on the doctrinal basis of the alliance, with the additional acceptance of some form of episcopate, without commitment to any one theory of apostolic succession and without calling into question the validity of non-episcopal ministers now functioning. Local autonomy in church discipline would continue; and the united church must maintain 'full inter-communion and fellowship with all the churches overseas through which she has received the message of salvation'.[88] In July 1933 the committee drew up a document entitled 'Church Union in East Africa. Proposed Basis of Union'. It followed the South India statement closely. The uniting churches were asked to accept as part of the basis of union, the threefold ministry of bishops, presbyters (priests) and deacons in a constitutional form such as should preserve historic continuity and at the same time safeguard the cherished traditions of all the uniting churches: and to agree 'that it is their intention and expectation that eventually every member exercising a permanent ministry in the united church will be an episcopally ordained minister'.

A continuation committee, meeting in Nairobi on 30th October, 1936, had before it a memorandum prepared by Bishop Heywood and G. M. Calderwood entitled 'A Sketch of a United Church', which summarized the results of four years' work. It envisaged a thirty year period of growing together of ministries during which all ordinations would be episcopal. The South India 'pledge' respecting the different traditions of congregations would operate. The memorandum suggested that one essential condition for the attainment of complete unity was that all members of the united church should be willing and able to receive communion equally in all of its churches. Freedom of opinion on debatable matters and respect for even large differences of opinion and practice would be required. The compilers gave their opinion that 'at least three dioceses should be formed in Kenya itself'.[89]

After 1936 no progress was made for many years. The dragging out of the South India negotiations discouraged the hope of achieving anything quickly in East Africa. Then came the second world war, and the union proposals were an early casualty. But there were long-term reasons for the failure to achieve unity in Kenya. The range of church politics represented in the Kenya missions was wider than those which achieved union in South India in 1947. It is possible that the Anglican, Church of Scotland and Methodist missions could have carried through a union scheme if they had gone forward alone. But it would have come too early in the life of the church in Kenya to have been other than a 'mission-imposed' union. It may yet be shown that the long search for union in East Africa, with all its frustrations, served the future church better than a quick achievement in which Africans had taken no active share. As things turned out, the alliance of missionary societies was able to speak effectively on matters of social justice and prepare the way for one of the most effective national Christian councils of the post-war period; and the steady concern, among senior missionaries, for organic unity made Kenya a testing-bed for alternative methods of achieving it, to which the whole ecumenical movement remains indebted.

Missionaries in Education, 1910–42

The annual letters of missionaries towards the end of the 1930s make frequent reference to nominal Christianity. Several of these letters relate this lack of force and fire in the still young Anglican Church to the growth of missionary institutions. 'We are fast leaving the ways of St Paul,' wrote one missionary, 'and building up large institutions. . . . These institutions make the European missionary *essential* and not advisory.' Another letter was equally forthright: 'Some of us are beginning to realize the danger of the spiritual and pastoral side of the work becoming subordinated to the educational. . . . We are turning out vast numbers of half-educated baptized pagans.'[90]

As an earlier generation of missionaries had looked on the practice of medicine as a deviation from the primary task of evangelism, so now, for some at least, the 'educational missionary' appeared to be the prisoner of a system over which he had lost control. Much of the criticism was no doubt due to a misunderstanding of a new situation; and in the period under review the doubts of most missionaries were resolved. But in Kenya, as elsewhere, the transition from a near monopoly in education to one of sometimes exacting partnership with the government was not easy.

Before 1911 the provision and maintenance of schools for Africans in Kenya was almost entirely the concern of missionaries. In 1908, for example, the total government expenditure on African education was £950, of which all but £200 consisted in grants to missionary bodies.[91] But in 1911 a government education department was constituted, with Mr J. R. Orr as the first Director of Education. Orr believed that Africans learned through hands rather than eyes and he became an enthusiastic advocate of 'industrial' education for Africans. His views proved unacceptable to some Africans, but until 1925 the instruction in all schools in Kenya, whether mission or government, was basically of this character. Medical training for hospital dressers was included. In 1918 government grants-in-aid, previously limited to a capitation grant for each indentured apprentice, were extended to apply in addition to the training of teachers and to assisting 'literary' education in institutions which were already receiving grants. Grants were later applied to the systems of village schools linked with existing aided institutions. The basis was also changed. Capitation grants continued to be made, but capital grants were also provided for buildings and for certain equipment up to one-third of the certified cost. For the purpose of such grants-in-aid a 'school' was defined as not less than ten pupils receiving regular instruction, provided such instruction was not wholly, or mainly, religious. No grants were available for specialized training for the ordained ministry or for religious orders. Payment of grants was made dependent on annual inspection by government inspectors.[92]

In Kenya, as in many other territories, government grants-in-aid to mission schools were accompanied by the provision, generally known as 'the Conscience Clause', whereby pupils whose parents did not wish them to receive religious instruction normally given in the school were excused from it. Inevitably some senior missionaries regarded this as an intolerable restriction of their freedom to proclaim the Christian faith and to give Christian instruction to all pupils in their care. One CMS missionary in 1924 wrote to London headquarters saying that he could not accept the conscience clause. He realized that non-acceptance might involve his resignation from his present post as a general missionary in charge of a 'station'; if that was the case he would be prepared to take up work among Indians in Kenya.[93]

The great majority of missionaries, however, were prepared to accept the working of the conscience clause as explained at the annual missionary conference at Nairobi in September 1924: (a) the first half of the daily time-table in African schools to be available for religious instruction; (b) adherents of any religion to be expected, though not compelled, to attend R.I. given by a teacher approved in writing by the authorities of their religion; (c) other pupils to be allowed to attend such instruction unless objection was formally lodged; (d) those excused from R.I. to be given other occupation during the time in which it was being given.[94]

The Bishop of Mombasa explained in a letter to London headquarters that the conscience clause was 'part of a much wider concordat with the Government'. It was a definite admission by the government of the principle that religious instruction is most desirable, and to be encouraged in all schools, 'though they are bound to state that it is not compulsory'. Thus, he argued, 'it is not negative in the main but markedly positive'. The bishop's view of this matter won general acceptance.

In 1926 the government grant for European staff was raised to four-fifths of the approved rate of salary plus allowance for passages; and grants for maintenance, permanent equipment and new building were authorized. In 1929 Mr H. Scott succeeded Orr as Director of Education. Scott, with long experience of South African education, was inclined to be critical of his predecessor's emphasis on industrial education. In 1934 the apprentice indenture system was dropped. The world depression of 1929–33 hit Kenya severely and led to considerable cuts in government expenditure. The African community was thrown back on its own resources through the local native councils which, under an education ordinance of 1924, had begun to levy rates for educational purposes. In spite of the setback caused by the depression, government expenditure on African education in 1934 was £76,770.

The process of adjustment on the part of missionaries to this greatly increased government share in education was inevitably slow. It seemed to the CMS local governing body in Kenya that the parent committee in London was too ready to look on government educational grants as providing a solution to the general problem of financing the mission. Rogers, the secretary of the Kenya mission in the 1920s, felt it necessary more than once to point out that the intention of government grants was not to relieve the Society of any part of the salaries of the missionaries in educational posts, but to build up a more efficient staff in the schools.[95] The executive committee of the mission (November 1925) was prepared to credit government grants to the parent committee only on the understanding that it would regard them as a contribution to the upkeep and equipment of the schools, to the salaries of the African staff, and to boarding expenses and cost of repairs.[96] It was understood in Kenya, as elsewhere, that CMS missionaries in whole-time education should receive the same basic missionary stipend as other missionaries, whatever method of payment was adopted for government grants.

The anxieties of missionaries about the possible abuse of the grants system was allayed to some extent when the Society's Africa committee, in May 1926, sanctioned an appeal for £10,000: £5,000 to match grants for a similar amount for school building and £5,000 for houses for European staff, the houses to be erected without grant aid and therefore remaining entirely at the disposal of the Society. Some new giving from the home constituency of the Society for its expanding educational work in Kenya was felt to be important for the future relationship of the mission and the Kenya government in education.

In 1931 a special committee appointed within the Kenya mission worked out a 'pool' system for the allocation of government grants,[97] and in 1933 Pitt-Pitts, the mission secretary, worked out a more comprehensive plan 'for all our school revenues from all sources'. His view was that central funds should be primarily used for payment of the salaries of European teachers. He hoped that local native councils would become increasingly responsible for teachers' salaries in sector schools and for those of African staff in the primary schools; and that mission funds would carry the whole cost of building, equipment, and the general management of schools.[98]

In June 1930 a high-level three-day conference on Christian Education in

East Africa was held at CMS headquarters in London. It considered at length the difficulties that had arisen in co-operation between missions and the government in the educational field, and concluded that the difficulties were due in the main to defects in missionary organization rather than to a government policy that was inimical to partnership with the missions. It saw need for the appointment of an adviser on missionary education comparable to that of Monsignor Hinsley for the Roman Catholic missions in East Africa. Ideally there should be separate advisers for Kenya, Uganda and Tanganyika, but that might not be possible at once. The conference agreed to nominate Mr J. W. C. Dougall, of the Jeanes School, Kabete, for this important post. Mr J. H. Oldham, secretary of the International Missionary Council, carried forward the negotiations. The CMS agreed to find £300 per annum for five years towards the salary and expenses of an educational adviser; and Dougall was appointed from September 1932 with the title 'Educational Adviser to non-Roman Missions in Uganda, Kenya, and Tanganyika'. He was succeeded by Mr L. B. Greaves, a Methodist, in 1936.

In a pamphlet published in 1936[99] he attempted to answer the criticisms of missionary education made by Professor Julian Huxley. In an influential book, Huxley had contended that 'with few but notable exceptions, missionary endeavour puts conversion far above education, concentrates as much as possible on religious teaching, and often – though this attitude is decreasing – sees in secular education merely a bait with which to angle for souls'.[100] Dougall was able to show that this criticism, though containing a measure of truth, had never been typical of missionary education as a whole and was increasingly less true. He drew particular attention to the problems of village or bush schools in which the great majority of the children attending schools in Kenya and Uganda were being educated, the vast majority of them being unaided church schools or catechetical centres. The training of teachers for these schools left much to be desired. 'We are using as teachers,' he said, 'men who have no gift or calling as teachers but look upon teaching as a temporary means of obtaining the further literary education they so desire.'[101]

A CMS missionary in the Kenya Highlands, Miss M. C. M. Rickman, writing in 1938 filled out the picture for village schools in the Weithaga area. The teachers who conducted services and ran the village schools were usually 'untrained, underpaid, or unpaid'; the school itself 'may be a dark mud hut with a cow-dung floor, tree trunks for forms, and no equipment but an old blackboard. . . . An overworked missionary, who is not a trained teacher, endeavours to supervise by perhaps one visit per term.' Such schools were of course outside the range of government grants: and in most cases they were not initiated by missionaries who were in fact trying to restrict their number. They were the spontaneous expression of a demand for education by the villagers themselves. Miss Rickman describes how she went with Mr Harvey Cantrell to the opening of a new school in the Weithaga district in 1937:

When we arrived we found the whole hillside black with people; the local chief, a very advanced young man who has been to England, was there as well as the local elders and teachers from neighbouring schools. The new building, which was of a superior type (tin roof, cement floor, and bamboo walls) was packed to fullest capacity very early. Finally the enrolled pupils were marched in and sat *on* our feet! The building was decorated with paper chains, coloured streamers and balloons with comic noses. No one thought them the least incongruous to the full Order for Morning Prayer and sermon which was the opening ceremony, followed by a feast for all. After the feast I managed to get a short talk with the teacher, a Christian man with no training and very little education, and arranged that he should come in for the teachers' week in the next holidays. Unfortunately he is too old to profit by a teachers' training course, and yet he can hold that school together better than a younger man with higher qualifications.[102]

The government Jeanes Teacher Training School at Kabete was bringing valuable and increasing help to the mission village schools at this time and missions had their own teacher-training projects, such as the vacation courses which Miss Rickman described: but the main responsibility for village schools remained for the most part with the 'station' missionary who did what he could to encourage untrained teachers to achieve a higher standard. In the late 1930s supervision, in groups, of village schools was being taken seriously: for schools that proved themselves small grants were sometimes made available from mission funds towards teachers' salaries and equipment. The profits of the Nairobi CMS bookshop were usefully applied for this purpose.

In 1942 twenty-five CMS missionaries in Kenya, thirteen men and twelve women, were engaged in full-time educational work. The disproportionate lack of educational opportunities for women and girls had been a frequent subject of discussion at meetings of the mission executive committee in the 1930s and effective steps were taken in the Highlands district to remedy this.

Opportunities of higher education for those who were being trained as clergy were still lacking in the inter-war period. B. Ogot appears to attribute this to a conscious policy on the part of the missionaries. '[Africans] would feel frustrated and bitter if, after training, they were not given responsibility. The Missionaries therefore continued to run the church in their own way.'[103] This is scarcely fair to the missionaries of this period. It has to be remembered that up-country Kenya was at least thirty years behind Uganda in church development. The timing of the first ordinations to the diaconate and priesthood in relation to first missionary occupation does not suggest any deliberate policy of delay in the development of the indigenous church. Missionary letters and the Highland station log-books suggest that the training of Africans in responsibility as catechists and teachers was taken with full seriousness. But it is certainly true that the first generation of African clergy in Kenya was small compared with the first generation in Uganda, and there were few among them with a secondary education.

The policy of a self-supporting church, admirable in other ways, worked against an educated clergy. Until 1944 any pastorate committee which wished to nominate a candidate for the ministry was made responsible for the cost of his training, and a system of quotas levied on the pastorates provided for the general cost of the divinity school. The stipends of evangelists remained dependent on the contributions of congregations, and their payment remained uncertain in the thirties. Older clergy remember how for months and sometimes years they were unpaid. They lived on the produce of their own little plot of land. The status of clergy, compared with teachers, was not one that encouraged recruitment among boys with a secondary education. It is also true that the institutional provision for clergy training was not given the priority one would expect. The divinity school, at Mombasa until 1930, was a long way from the centres of most rapid church growth in Kenya. Both before and after the move to Limuru the divinity school was inadequately staffed. It was only towards the end of the 1930s that provision of staff and buildings began to measure up to the requirements. If there were weaknesses in this field of missionary responsibility, they can in part be attributed to the failure of hopes for a united ministry based on united training which had been fostered by the Kikuyu conferences.

Even so, it was in the educational field that the alliance of missionary societies made its most enduring contribution – in the Alliance High School at Kikuyu which opened with sixteen pupils on 1st March, 1926. The first principal was Mr G. A. Grieve of the Church of Scotland mission. For the first few years the school was run with the direct oversight of the council of the alliance, but in 1929 a board of governors was appointed. Mr Carey Francis, a CMS missionary, was appointed as the second principal in 1940. Many of his senior boys from Maseno had already found their way there in the 1930s. A high proportion of the boys leaving the Alliance High School went on to further education at Makerere College in Uganda, which in 1938 took the first steps to becoming the University College of East Africa.

A comment by Professor Roland Oliver about the missionary share in education in East Africa can be fairly applied to efforts of the CMS Kenya mission. 'The fact that the majority of the Africans who reached the new professional status owed their rise to mission schools gave to Christianity an influence which far surpassed the numbers of its adherents, while the continued identification of the missions through their schools with that which was in African eyes most progressive and most liberating must be accounted a powerful reason for the remarkable extent to which African Christians remained loyal to the traditional forms of the religion even under the pressure of rising nationalism.'[104]

Missionaries in Medical Work, 1910–42

Medicine had a smaller role than education in the development of CMS missionary work in Kenya. All the larger societies had some share in it but only the Church of Scotland mission insisted on having a qualified doctor at each of its stations. This comparative lack of development in the medical field was due partly to the timing of missionary expansion up-country into the Highlands and in Nyanza. By the early 1920s the government of the colony had developed a vigorous medical policy, with resident medical officers spread throughout the more populous parts of Kenya. Dr Ernest Cook, visiting Maseno from Mengo in 1925, advised against the development of a large mission hospital partly because no less than twelve MOs were on the way to Kavirondo.[105] Opportunity for the kind of pioneer medical work which was distinctive of Christian missions in other areas was thus lacking in Kenya, although some able doctors served there in the period – notably Shepherd (CMS); Bond (FAM) at Kaimosi in Nyanza; Kenneth Allan (AIM) at Kijabe in the Highlands; and R. Y. Stones (CMS) in the pioneer days at Maseno.

Government economy measures after the first world war encouraged for a short time a system of medical grants-in-aid to missions. They were a very small item compared with the educational grants, and were never more than a temporary expedient; but a building grant of £3,950 in 1920 helped Maseno hospital into being – a small hospital and dispensary was specified as a condition for the grant, with a training school for medical assistants.

One of the early projects of the alliance of missionary societies was a Kikuyu medical school, but the government medical department had its own plans for a training school, and the CMS medical committee found itself unable to recommend joining in the alliance scheme owing to lack of suitable staff and funds. The alliance decided instead to concentrate on the development of a good secondary school at Kikuyu.

The local governing body of the CMS, partly no doubt through lack of missionary doctors serving on it, partly because of fairly continuous problems of staffing and finance, was not friendly to the development of mission hospitals in Kenya. It objected to the Mzizima hospital fund being applied to Maseno, preferring that it should be used for medical or other needs in the Highlands or in the coastal region where it had originated. In 1923 the mission secretary, Rogers, reported that the location of Dr Fitzpatrick to Maseno had been received by the local governing body with some feeling of resentment. Nyanza was still thought of as part of the Society's Uganda mission and 'Uganda receives prior consideration over Kenya'.[106] When, however, Fitzpatrick was moved in 1924 to the Highlands as medical superintendent of six dispensaries in the Kikuyu tribal area, his desire to build a hospital at Kabare in relation to these dispensaries ran counter to the views of the local governing body. The doctor resigned, and Kabare reverted to an ordinary dispensary.

In spite of the coolness of the local governing body towards its development, and an adverse report from Dr Ernest Cook in 1925, Maseno hospital established itself, with considerable help from Dr Ross, the government MO at Kisumu. Under Dr D. S. Dixon, Dr Stones' successor in 1927, a twenty-five bed maternity block was completed. In 1929 Dr L. M. Cranage, its first woman doctor, arrived and in 1930 Dr Norman Green, who was to give long and distinguished service there. Early in his time Dr Green and Miss Guyler, sister at Maseno hospital, were involved in a court case which received wide publicity at the time. It is noticed here as an example of the tensions that arose in Kenya between missions and government in the medical field.

In 1933 an African boy who was a patient at Maseno hospital died under an anaesthetic in the course of a minor operation performed by an African assistant. Dr Green and Miss Guyler were charged with manslaughter. Although the charge was later modified, there was, so the mission secretary reported, a good deal of public criticism by the local medical profession in Nyanza, who complained about people doing jobs for which they were not qualified. The trial was fixed for 7th July, 1933 and Sir Albert Cook and Dr Stones arranged to be present at it. Miss Guyler was found guilty of negligence and the sentence was deferred. In Dr Green's case, on a charge of 'criminal rashness in medical practice', judgment was reserved.

Sir Albert Cook wrote to the mission secretary on 13th July, 1933:

If we take the judgment *au pied de la lettre* it means that every Branch Dispensary and Maternity and Child Welfare Clinic connected with either our own or any other missionary society in Kenya Colony is illegal. If you want to be on the safe side after this ruling, you must close all dispensaries throughout your mission.

He advised that the government medical service should be asked to appoint an examining body and issue licences for native dressers, anaesthetists, and operations in minor surgery. If no satisfaction was obtained, an appeal should be made to public opinion to alter the law.[107] Cook's warning carried great weight but anxiety was reduced quickly by a letter from Owen on 14th July saying that 'the Senior Medical Officer at Kisumu has given an understanding that he will accept full responsibility for the continued running of our dispensaries at Butere and Ng'iya pending further negotiations with the Government – provided there are no extensions or developments'. On 26th July Miss Guyler was sentenced to a nominal fine of 1s, and the magistrate agreed to see Miss Guyler with Archdeacon Owen afterwards. The mission secretary wrote of the 'intense relief' at this outcome, but Dr Green had to appear before a medical board in October and the removal of his name from the list of acting doctors in Kenya was a distinct possibility. Fortunately it did not happen. He remained in charge of the hospital to give valuable service for many more years, and the repute of the hospital locally appeared to suffer little from the court case.

Dr Green's own account of the matter must in fairness be added:

The trouble arose through my having permitted a few very minor (circumcision) operations to be performed during my absence from the hospital; and because one of the natives died under the anaesthetic, owing to his suffering from a very rare form of heart disease which, as proved in Court, is undiagnosable during life. My great sin was that I allowed the anaesthetics to be given under the sole supervision of Sister Guyler who, in my considered opinion, is more efficient and reliable at this work than at least 50 per cent of qualified medical practitioners. Had a qualified doctor been present (however inexperienced in anaesthetics) no prosecution apparently would have resulted.[108]

Missionary Participation in Politics and Social Problems, 1910–42

CMS missionaries in Kenya, as elsewhere, were for the most part patriotic Englishmen, conservative in their political views, middle-class in their social habits of thought, as most of the settlers and government officials were. They viewed their calling primarily as that of evangelists, entrusted with a gospel of personal salvation. To expect them to have shown a degree of social awareness and political acumen unmatched by the evangelicals of their generation in Britain is unreasonable; but not a few of them learned in the hard school of Kenya politics that the prophetic witness of an Amos or an Isaiah was sometimes called for: and they did not shrink from the task. W. E. Owen's acute perception of political realities would have been rare among clergymen of his time in any country; but he did not stand apart from his fellow-missionaries as a lone radical. His method of getting a case heard sometimes embarrassed them; but for the most part his clear-sightedness was a gift which they appreciated, and his lead was more frequently followed than opposed in the local councils of the CMS in Kenya.

In 1921 Owen wrote an article in *The Church Missionary Review* entitled 'the Missionary in Politics' which sums up his philosophy in this field of Christian witness:

> The British subject in a British dependency has . . . [an] inalienable right to be interested in the political development of a subject race. . . . He must justify his non-use of his powers, rather than the principle of his use of them.

In answer to the objection that such intervention in political matters puts the society in which he serves at risk, he made this memorable comment:

> It is dangerous to be alive at all and we must all take risks daily. . . . The society can safeguard itself by requiring of its agents allegiance to whatever native policy it has enunciated. . . . It can request any agent to retire who involves the society to its detriment.[109]

It is to the credit of the CMS, that in spite of considerable pressure to 'discipline' Owen, a request to him to retire was never seriously contemplated. Near the end of his life he himself offered to retire, but the offer had nothing to do with his political activities. He did so in order to save the Society the cost of his missionary allowance at a time of acute financial difficulty, hoping to be allowed to continue in Kenya on the smaller missionary pension.

A full review of missionary activity and initiatives in political and social issues in Kenya deserves more space, and requires more specialized knowledge, than can be supplied here. The notes that follow are merely samples of missionary involvement in these issues in Kenya from 1910 to 1942. A concentration on the part played by CMS missionaries must not, of course, be taken to imply that other societies were less active or less concerned.

1. Compulsory Labour

On 23rd October, 1919, a printed circular was issued over the signature of the Chief Native Commissioner, John Ainsworth, and headed 'Native Labour required for non-native Farms and other Private Undertakings'. It required all government officials in charge of 'native areas' to exercise 'every possible lawful influence' in recruiting labour for these purposes. African chiefs and elders were to consider it part of their duty to advise and encourage all unemployed young men in the areas under their jurisdiction to go out and work on the plantations. District commissioners were to keep a record of the chiefs and headmen who proved helpful in this matter, and also of those who were unhelpful.

This labour circular drew a prompt response in what came to be known as the 'Bishops' Memorandum'.[110] It was in fact the joint comment of the Bishops of Mombasa and Uganda and of Dr J. W. Arthur, head of the Church of Scotland mission. The memorandum sensed a change of government policy in the circular. 'Hitherto the government has steadily refused to compel natives to work for the private benefit of Europeans.' Now, although technically compulsion was not required, the tone and some of the wording of the circular implied it. There were several lapses from 'should' to 'must'. It did, in effect, introduce compulsory labour. It assumed, wrongly, that the choice lay between useful work done for Europeans and idleness in the reserve. 'The native has his home, his crops, his plans for development. The demands on his time may not be constant, but they are insistent.' The decision to 'encourage' women and children to labour seemed to the three missionaries 'a dangerous policy'. But they were not prepared to regard compulsion as itself an evil and they would favour some form of it, 'at any rate for work of national importance', with certain safeguards. The safeguards included: a frank recognition of compulsion and its legalization; such compulsory labour to be confined to able-bodied men; proper working conditions to be guaranteed by the government; the terms of employment to be limited and defined; compulsion to be exerted uniformly; reasonable exemptions to be allowed; and its use to be confined as far as possible to government work. The bishops and Dr Arthur did not hide their anxieties. Compulsion was 'certain to be intensely unpopular with the natives', but they believed it to be necessary in present conditions.

Bishop Frank Weston of Zanzibar was more forthright than his brothers of

Uganda and Mombasa. In a pamphlet entitled *The Serfs of Great Britain, being a sequel to the Black Slaves of Prussia*, Bishop Weston made it clear:

> that some of us who are missionaries will not agree to any such policy. We regard forced labour, apart from war, as in itself immoral; and we hold that forcing Africans to work in the interests of European civilization is a betrayal of the weaker to the financial interests of the stronger race.[111]

The matter was taken up in England and the offending circular was attacked in a House of Lords debate on 14th July, 1920. The same day a supplementary circular was issued by the Governor of Kenya which adopted several, but not all, of the safeguards proposed by the 'Bishops' Memorandum'. It required that if women and children were employed they must be allowed to return home the same night. Chiefs were warned not to use favouritism or oppression in recruiting labourers; nor were they to bring pressure to bear on those whose labour was needed for the cultivation of their own land in the reserves. In 1921 Winston Churchill, newly appointed Secretary of State for the Colonies, issued a White Paper (Cmd. 1509, 1921) which laid down that (1) there was to be no recruiting of labour for private employment beyond supplying information as to sources of labour for voluntary recruitment; (2) labour on government works (to which Africans had been liable for six days a quarter since 1912) was only to be required when absolutely necessary and the exercise of powers under the ordinance requiring such labour must have the prior approval of the Secretary of State.[112] At a meeting of the Convention of (Settlers) Associations in October 1926 the governor, Sir Edward Grigg, reaffirmed the policy of the White Paper:

> The Government neither can nor will produce labour from the Reserves by compulsion of any sort. . . no policy is justifiable which does not give to the native the fullest opportunity of developing the areas secured to him.[113]

Compulsory unpaid labour on public works in the reserves continued to be a cause of hardship. Early in 1930 the local governing body of the CMS asked the Kenya missionary council to review the whole question, and proposed that the African local councils should be made responsible for raising and expending the funds necessary for the proper performance of public works in the reserves. A government White Paper issued later in the year went far towards allaying their anxieties.[114]

2. The Ownership of Land

Grants of land to European settlers under the Crown Lands Ordinance of 1902 had already begun to get out of hand by 1904, when the protectorate government first accepted the idea of reserving certain areas of Kenya for Africans to prevent further dispossession by Europeans. These reserves were not formally gazetted until 1926. The Native Lands Trust Ordinance of 1930 included a declaration that the reserves were 'set aside for the benefit of the native tribes for ever' and placed them under a Native Lands Trust Board, consisting of government officials, and two non-official members of the legislative council, one of whom would represent native interests. In 1931 the Joint Select Committee of both Houses of Parliament (appointed to deal with the matter of the closer union of East African territories), required that an authoritative inquiry be made not only about the security of the reserves but about their extent, in view of present and future needs of Africans. Accordingly, a Land Commission under the chairmanship of Sir Morris Carter was appointed in 1933.[115]

While the Carter Commission was still taking evidence gold was discovered at Kakamega in the Kavirondo reserve. The guarantees made in the Lands Trust Ordinance of 1930 were put to the test. In July 1932 one missionary saw seven European mining camps from one vantage point. By the next spring there were 'well over 1,000 prospectors, spreading their activities over 700 square miles of the reserve'.[116] Owen was on the alert, scenting the danger of alienation of land in the Kavirondo reserve, without proper inquiry and consultation. He wrote to the London headquarters of CMS on 14th April, 1932, 'Gold is likely to raise a major problem'. The information given in his letter was passed to J. H. Oldham with the request that he should consider what action was called for to safeguard the interests of the native population. Oldham found formidable allies in the Archbishop of Canterbury and Lord Lugard. The Kenya missionary council, meeting on 23rd February, 1933, thanked Owen and the CMS for the prompt action they had taken and for the protest they had initiated. It also thanked the archbishop and Lord Lugard, and asked for 'the continued exercise of constant vigilance from those at home'. In May 1933 the executive committee of the CMS Kenya mission appealed to the Kenya government to take no further steps about leasing land at Kakamega until the Carter Commission had reported. 'We view with grave anxiety,' it said, 'the dislocation of native life and customs which will arise from even a well regulated invasion of Europeans into a native reserve so large and in parts so thickly populated.' They urged that, if opening up the land for gold prospecting was inevitable, it should be done gradually.

> We would further urge, as we have done in the past, the principle of land for land, in which we believe our national honour is involved, shall be maintained in every case in which land is excised from the reserves.[117]

In January 1934 the mission secretary, Pitt-Pitts, reported that the decision had been made to open up the reserve for gold-mining in February, but he quoted Owen as saying that the new mining ordinance embodied points he had made in evidence before the Morris Carter Commission, and that Owen was assured that every care would be taken not to give handles for complaint.[118] Later in the year Owen, addressing the CMS Africa committee in London, said that if gold had to be got out, he felt that everything possible was being done to safeguard native rights and interests. The Native Lands Trust Ordinance was amended in 1934 on the advice of the Carter Commission. Land required for mining might be temporarily excised from the reserve by the governor, with the consent of the local native council and the occupants. These had the right to receive compensation and accommodation in an area of equal size and value which must be added to the reserve for the duration of the lease. Alternative safeguards were suggested, but in all cases the natives concerned must be given the opportunity to express their opinion.[119]

Two years earlier a land dispute in the Kavirondo reserve had a tragic outcome. While Owen was on furlough in 1932, a Luo deacon in the Anglican Church at Butere, Alfayo Odongo, had been establishing a Luo group on Bantu (Luyia) land at Musanda. There was a school building on this land formerly used by both clans. Alfayo Odongo and about ten others were evicted from Musanda. The anger of the dispossessed was turned upon Archdeacon Owen.[120] The trouble came to a head in January 1933. Owen and A. J. Leech went to call on Alfayo on January 6th, to reason with him and to warn him of the danger he was in personally. A few days later the Baluyia moved against Alfayo and his group and he and ten others were massacred. The followers of Alfayo formed themselves into a separate sect, the *Dini Ya Roho*, 'The Church of the Holy Spirit', the forerunner of one of the much larger break-away groups of a later period.[121]

Owen wrote at length to the secretary of the Land Commission on the problem 'how to attain re-distribution of population without making any break with the clan and tribal system'. There were three types of hereditary land holding within the clan – as freehold; as 'absorbed families' over several generations; and as tenants cultivating the land of relatives, who feared to register as tenants in case this would operate against eventual absorption of the land they occupied. He recognized that a certain amount of land-grabbing went on between clans within the same tribe, or from other tribes, but traditional rules of land-tenure were so complicated that 'a general scale of individual tenure was absolutely premature'. The tribal system must be modified, but only gradually. Five years was not too long for proposals to be before the tribes.[122]

3. The Emancipation of Women and Girls

A visitor to the Highlands of Kenya in the 1960s could still be disturbed by the sight of Kikuyu women bearing enormous loads of wood on their bowed backs with harness across their temples. It is not surprising that European missionaries should have set themselves from the first against tribal customs that appeared to degrade womanhood: that they should rejoice when they found among their Christian converts those who recognized these traditional customs as degrading; and that they should grieve at the 'backsliding' of those who, after baptism, found the pull of these customs to be stronger than the newly-learned and imperfectly understood standards of westernized Christianity to

which the missionaries had introduced them. Two examples will be given of the
stand missionaries made against tribal custom: 'female circumcision' and
'forced marriages'.

The Kikuyu custom of circumcising girls at the age of eleven or twelve, a
puberty rite performed in public, was deplored by almost all missionaries.
But there was a considerable difference of opinion between the missionary
societies, and individual missionaries within the same society, about the best
method of eradicating a custom which was believed gravely to increase the
pains and perils of childbirth and to render the woman's part in sexual intercourse a mere passive reception of the desire of the man. Almost from the
start in the Church of Scotland mission at Kikuyu, and by the first world war
in other Church of Scotland and AIM mission stations, rejection of the rite was
made a condition of church membership; but until the late 1920s there was
no open persecution of Christians who thus departed from tribal custom.[123]
Between 1929 and 1933, by which time the Christian churches in the Highlands
had grown greatly in membership, there was a strong tribal campaign in defence
of the custom, which led to a rapid decline in church and school attendance.
When the reaction began the Anglican Church in Kenya had no general
policy in relation to the custom. Individual missionaries were left to take their
own line. J. Comely, CMS missionary at Embu, wrote in the Station Log Book,
4th October, 1929: 'Led by prayer to make a definite stand in the matter of
Female Circumcision.' Parents, he decided, would be encouraged to bring their
daughters to a special service in church, and to announce that they wished to
renounce the practice for their daughters, and to claim the help of the church
in meeting opposition.[124]

At this time the Kikuyu Central Association was using the circumcision issue
as a main platform. Comely took the logical step of banning the KCA for church
members, but he received no support from the Bishop of Mombasa. There was
clearly need for an agreed policy for the CMS mission, and in January 1930 the
executive committee of the mission endorsed a resolution of its Highlands
district committee asking the bishop to meet all the Kikuyu-speaking clergy
to consult with him 'on the question of how to put an end to female circumcision
among church members'.

The clergy had previously asked the bishop to issue a pastoral letter clearly
stating the rule of the church in the matter and this letter had been circulated
to all members of the pastorate committee.[125] In his pastoral letter the bishop
had stated 'the rule of the Church' as follows: heathen practices connected
with the custom were to be abandoned; anything public was to be strictly.
prohibited; any operation involving physical injury was strongly to be condem-
ned. But the direction stopped short of absolute prohibition. The bishop held
that only through gradual education could the practice be expected to disappear.
Many of the senior missionaries welcomed the line taken by this letter. Leakey
described it as most helpful. 'While not taking the same line as the CSM. . .

CMS has made it perfectly clear that they are as opposed as any of those missions to their adherents contemplating female circumcision.'[126] But some missionaries of the Society, notably Comely, did not believe in a policy of gradualness, and excommunication of those involved in the practice seemed, to some, necessary for an effective stand.

On 12th October, 1931, the bishop issued a further circular letter to all clergy and members of pastorate committees. He said that he could not sanction the excommunication of persons who acted within the limits of diocesan regulations: but that no-one should be eligible to be a member of a pastorate committee who was not ready to observe the ruling. The letter reaffirmed the terms of his earlier pastoral letter as the rule for the whole diocese: but he addressed himself separately to those clergy and pastorate committee members 'who are prepared at once to take the stand and condemn the custom entirely'. To them he said that if clergy refused to baptize infants of people who would not abide by the decision, the pastorate committee would have his support. The Embu pastorate committee, under Comely's leadership, accepted this part of the letter as addressed to their situation. Baptisms were refused, and the results were distressing. Comely reported in 1931 that thirteen out of thirty-eight schools in the pastorate were closed and that eighteen out of sixty-six teachers had left. One school-church with a normal Sunday congregation of five hundred found it reduced to about twenty.[127] The losses in Church of Scotland and AIM missions were much greater, and the growth of the Independent Schools Movement in the early thirties was directly related to the circumcision issue, though this was not its sole cause. In 1934 there was some movement back to the church; and in that year CMS was asked to accept three candidates from the Kikuyu Independent Schools Association for further training at Limuru. CSM and AIM were of course consulted,[128] and it says much for the charity of these hard-hit missions that they agreed to this, provided that these and any other applicants accepted formally the discipline of the Anglican Church.

In the later 1930s Owen fought a long and often lonely campaign, in the *Manchester Guardian* and in the local East African press, to draw the attention of the Kenya government to the suffering caused by marriage customs in Nyanza Province. Contracts of marriage were often made, he contended, for young girls against their wishes, and he became personally involved in numerous cases of inhuman cruelty to brides who had run away from husbands whom they had never wished to marry. His publishing of the evidence drew support from unexpected quarters. Jomo Kenyatta, who at the time was working in England as General Secretary of the Kikuyu Central Association, wrote to the *Manchester Guardian* saying: 'I join with him in raising my voice in protest against this masculine form of oppressing women regardless of race'; but he qualified his support by saying that it would be unfair for anyone to create the impression that such behaviour is tolerated by tribal authority among the Kavirondo or any other African races in Kenya.[129]

By 1939 Owen had formulated proposals for government action in the matter of forced marriages which he hoped would apply to all African dependencies. (1) No contract of marriage or betrothal to be made for any girl aged fourteen or less; (2) no contract to be made for a girl aged over fourteen without her consent; (3) any person who causes any girl or woman to enter a marriage against her will shall be guilty of an offence at law; (4) no contract arising out of a forced marriage (i.e. marriage without the consent of both parties) shall be enforceable in any court of law.[130] A local district commissioner wrote to Owen in May 1939:

> It remains our belief that forced marriages are rare: but we do not dispute that fathers or guardians sometimes bring an undesirable amount of pressure on their daughters to persuade or compel them to marry husbands they would not have chosen.

The letter revealed that a meeting of district commissioners at Kisumu in 1937 had recommended (a) compulsory notification and registration of intentions to marry; (b) compulsory registration of marriage; (c) voluntary registration of the bride price. These recommendations had been dropped, however, because 'of the degree of alteration which they underwent at the secretariat'.[131]

One letter which Owen treasured and kept in his file on forced marriage, was written by Winifred Holtby, the novelist. After offering to take up the question with the British Commonwealth League, she continued:

> I feel that so many of these customs which cause real suffering are retained partly because of the influence of anthropologists who are so anxious that ancient tradition should not be destroyed, and lose human values through their scientific interests. . . . Since I knew of all you are doing, I have regarded all missionary effort with greater respect, and in doing so have found far more to admire than I imagined.[132]

NOTES

1. A. Marshall Macphee, *Kenya*, Ernest Benn, 1968, p. 23n.

2. *The Times*, 12th December, 1963, Special Kenya Supplement. Article by Margery Perham.

3. Kenneth Ingham, *A History of East Africa*, Longmans, 1962, p. 55.

4. Elspeth Huxley, *The Mottled Lizard*, Chatto & Windus, 1962, p. 14.

5. Winston Churchill, *My African Journey*, Holland, 1908, p. 21.

6. See W. McGregor Ross, *Kenya from Within*, Allen & Unwin, 1926, pp. 382, 384.

7. Letter in *The Times*, 25th April, 1923.

8. Roland Oliver, *The Missionary Factor in East Africa*, Longmans, 1962, p. 259.

9. George Bennett, *Kenya: A Political History of the Colonial Period*, OUP, 1963, p. 96.

10. *CMR*, W. E. Owen, 'The Missionary in Politics', June, 1921, pp. 135 ff.

11. Horace R. A. Philp, *A New Day in Kenya*, World Dominion Press, 1936, Appendix.

12. G3/A5/P7, 1912/14, 37, 38, 52.

13. A5/P8, 1923/64; 1924/87; 1932/16; *AR* (MS) 1934-5, p. 45.

14. P8, 1919/48, 56; 1920/33, 34.

15. Stock, Vol. I, pp. 461, 462.

16. See Oliver, op. cit., p. 6.

17. Stock, Vol. II, p. 132.

18. *CMO*, W. W. Cash, 'My Tour in Africa', January 1938, p. 1.

19. M. G. Capon, *Towards Unity in Kenya*, Nairobi, 1962, p. 4.

20. *CMR*, G. W. Wright, 'Mombasa – Its Position and Possibilities,' May 1911, pp. 295ff.

21. P8, 1921/12; 1922/12, 21.

22. *AR* (MS), 1938-9, p. 49.

23. K. E. Stovold, *The CMS in Kenya, Book I. The Coast, 1844-1944*, Nairobi, n.d. p. 72.

24. P8, 1926/96.

25. *AR* (MS), 1938-9, p. 50.

26. Stovold, op. cit., p. 70.

27. *AR* (MS). 1934-5, p. 49 (cf *AR* (MS), 1938-9, p. 52).

28. *AR* (MS), 1937-8, p. 38.

29. *AR* (MS), 1938-9, pp. 53, 54.

30. ibid., p. 54.

31. P8/1925/68.

32. *AR* (MS) 1930-1, p. 79.

33. *AR* (MS) 1934-5, p. 52.

34. *AR* (MS) 1930-1, p. 83.

35. Limuru MSS.

36. *AR* (MS) 1937-8, p. 47.

37. P7, 1917/35.

38. Limuru MSS.

39. *AR* (MS), 1924-5, pp. 42, 43.

40. *AR* (MS), 1934-5, pp. 57, 58.

41. *AR* (MS), 1937-8, p. 37.

42. *AR* (MS), 1930-1, p. 89, 90.

43. *AR* (MS), 1934-5, p. 61.

44. *AR* (MS), 1936-7, p. 56.

45. *CMO*, W. W. Cash, 'My Tour in Africa, January 1938, p. 3.

46. *AR* (MS), 1940-1, p. 32. O. Kariuki later became Bishop of Mount Kenya.

47. J. M. Lonsdale, 'Politics and Society in Kavirondo, 1894-1945' (MS).

48. C. G. Richards, *Archdeacon of Kavirondo*, Highway Press, Nairobi, 1947, p. 10.

49. Elisabeth S. Richards, *Fifty Years in Nyanza, 1906-1956*, p. 21.

50. ibid., p. 33.

51. C. G. Richards, op. cit., p. 14.

52. E. S. Richards, op. cit., p. 30.

53. ibid., p. 40ff.

54. *AR* (MS), 1936-7, p. 58.

55. *AR* (MS), 1939-40, p. 51.

56. Capon, op. cit., p. 3.

57. J. J. Willis and others, *Towards a United Church, 1913-47*, Edinburgh House Press, 1947, p. 22.

58. ibid., p. 23.

59. Capon, op. cit., p. 11.

60. *Towards a United Church*, p. 24.

61. P7,1910/57.

62. P7,1910/78.

63. Stock, Vol. IV, p. 414.

64. See Stock, Vol. IV, pp. 402–3.

65. G/AM/6/25, 26, memo of interview, 28th September, 1911.

66. *Towards a United Church*, p. 27.

67. See Capon, op. cit., p. 12.

68. *Proposed Scheme of Federation of Missionary Societies Working in British East Africa*, pp. 4, 6.

69. It is well summarized in Bell, *Randall Davidson*, Oxford, 3rd ed., 1952, Ch. XLII.

70. ibid., p. 693.

71. P7, pp. 461–2.

72. Stock, Vol. IV., p. 414.

73. Bell, op. cit., p. 698.

74. ibid., p. 707–8; Stock, Vol. IV, pp. 419, 420.

75. The author is indebted to the Rev. Gavin White for this, and other, insights.

76. *CMR*, H. D. Hooper, 'Kikuyu Churches in United Action', June, 1919, pp. 15ff.; J. W. Arthur, *Towards a United Church*, p. 53.

77. *Towards a United Church*, p. 55.

78. Quoted Capon, op. cit., pp. 21–2.

79. *Kikuyu, 1918: Report of the United Conference of Missionary Societies in British East Africa*, pp. 7, 8.

80. *Towards a United Church*, p. 58.

81. *CMR*, J. J. Uganda, 'The Principle of Alliance in Missionary Work', March, 1919, pp. 7ff.

82. H. Maynard Smith, *Frank, Bishop of Zanzibar*, SPCK, 1926, p. 169.

83. *Towards a United Church*, p. 58.

84. Representative Council Minutes (Nairobi CMS Archives).

85. See for example P7,1911/24, P8,1919/, 1, 2.

86. P8,1926/91.

87. Capon, op. cit., p. 34, and see above, pp. 167–70.

88. ibid., p. 52.

89. ibid., pp. 90–6, where the statement is printed in full.

90 *AR* (MS), 1937–8, p. 35.

91. Philp, op. cit., p. 171.

92. *African Education in Kenya*, September, 1949. The report of a committee appointed by the government of Kenya under the chairmanship of Archdeacon L. J. Beecher.

93. P8, 1924/117.

94. P8, 1925/1.

95. P8, 1922/61; 1925/153; 1926/17.

96. P8, 1925/51, 151.

97. P9, 1931/52.

98. P9, 1933/92.

99. J. W. C. Dougall, *Missionary Education in Kenya and Uganda: A Study in Co-operation*, IMC, 1936.

100. J. S. Huxley, *Africa View*, Chatto & Windus, 1931, pp. 327, 328.

101. J. W. C. Dougall, *The Relation of Schools and Colleges to the Life of the Growing Church*, CMS, 1932, p. 8.

102. *CMO*, M. C. M. Rickman, 'The Crest of the Wave', February, 1938, p. 32.

103. F. B. Welbourn & B. A. Ogot, *A Place to Feel at Home*, OUP, 1966, p. 22.

104. Oliver, op. cit., pp. 280, 281.

105. P8, 1925/102.

106. P8, 1923/91.

107. P9, 1933/124, 134.

108. *AR* (MS) 1933-4, pp. 66, 67.

109. *CMR*, 1921, pp. 135ff.

110. Ross, op. cit., pp. 103-5. (See also *CMR*, J. J. Willis, R. S. Heywood and J. W. Arthur, 'Native Labour in East Africa', June 1920, pp. 142ff.)

111. *The Serfs of Great Britain*, London, 1920.

112. P8, 1921/81, letter from J. H. Oldham.

113. *AR* (MS) 1926-7, p. 42.

114. P9, 1930/89.

115. Lord Hailey, *An African Survey*, Oxford, 1938, pp. 742-55.

116. *CMO*, E. Carey Francis 'Gold in Kavirondo', May 1933, pp. 92-4.

117. P9, 1933/109.

118. P9, 1934/18.

119. Hailey, op. cit., p. 754.

120. *AR* (MS), 1932-3, p. 43.

121. See Welbourn & Ogot, op. cit., pp. 47, 48.

122. Owen MSS, (Acc. 83/O2), letter of 2nd September, 1932.

123. F. B. Welbourn, *East African Rebels*, SCM Press, 1961, pp. 135ff.

124. CMS Archives, Nairobi.

125. P9, 1930/21.

126. P9, 1930/23.

127. *AR* (MS), 1931-2, p. 37.

128. P9, 1934/104.

129. Owen MSS (Acc. 83/O16), letter of 29th November, 1935. Owen replied (2nd January, 1936) that 'tribal authority does tolerate such behaviour'.

130. *The Weekly Telegraph*, 20th May, 1939, article by Michael Woodstock.

131. Owen MSS, ibid., letter from the diocesan council, Central Kavirondo, 11th May, 1939.

132. Owen MSS, ibid., letter from Winifred Holtby to Owen, 29th August, 1935.

Tanganyika

The Country and its Peoples

Tanzania is the largest of the East African territories which were for a time under British rule. The island of Zanzibar was declared a British protectorate by an Anglo-German treaty in 1890. By the same treaty Germany abandoned all claims to mainland territory north of latitude 1° south which crossed Lake Victoria to the boundary of what was then the Congo Free State. South of this line the German sphere included the present mainland area of Tanzania. The League of Nations mandate assigned to Britain for Tanganyika Territory in 1919 was continued after the second world war under the United Nations until 9th December, 1961 when it became an independent state within the British Commonwealth.

Tanzania contains within its borders the extremes of topographical relief for the whole continent of Africa – the highest mountain, Kilimanjaro (19,340 ft) near its northern border with Kenya; and the deepest trough, beneath the waters of Lake Tanganyika. With the three great lakes, Victoria, Tanganyika, and Nyasa partly or wholly within its borders, about six per cent. (20,000 square miles) of its land is covered by inland waters. Its main geographical features otherwise are a coastal plain ten to forty miles wide; a belt of forest and irregular mountains rising inland from the plain; and a vast inland plateau ranging from 4,000 to 7,000 feet, with an occasional outcrop of higher mountains, such as the Usambara range, rising to 9,000 feet. The density of population is lower than Kenya; but population rose rapidly after the first world war from just over four millions in 1913 to five millions in 1931. (It almost doubled in the next thirty years to reach nine and a half millions in 1961.) Nearly all its inhabitants are African. The immigrant and expatriate population in the colonial period remained much lower than neighbouring Kenya. In 1931 the figure for Europeans was 6,631 (British 3,067; German 1,333; Greeks 633); Asians were slightly more numerous though still a minute proportion of the whole population (Indians 9,411; Goanese 798; Arabs 4,041).

The African population during this period was divided among some hundred and twenty tribes. The majority were classified as Bantu, although there were some peoples of Nilotic and Hamitic origin. There was no dominant tribe comparable to the Kikuyu in the Kenya Highlands, but fourteen tribes made up about half the population; among the largest were the Sukuma (600,000) living to the east of Lake Victoria; the Nyamwezi (350,000) in Tabora Province; the Chagga (156,000) on the southern slopes of Kilimanjaro; and the Gogo (182,000). The pastoral Masai spread well down into Tanganyika across the border with Kenya. A hundred or so languages were spoken at this time but by the mid 1930s Swahili, encouraged by the government as the standard language, was spoken more or less over the whole country.[1] Missionaries were normally expected to learn a tribal language, but they could not do without Swahili.

The German administration suppressed the slave-trade and began to open up the interior with roads, railways, and telegraph; but Tanganyika suffered more than any other East African territory from the effects of the European invasion. Tribal risings against European rule were more frequent than elsewhere, and were put down more ruthlessly. After the suppression of the Maji-Maji rising of 1905–7, the German administration adopted more liberal policies under the direction of Dr Dernburg who was German colonial secretary from 1907–10. He encouraged the growth of cash crops by Africans and the development of African education. In the western area of Bukoba, Ruanda and Urundi 'indirect rule' through African tribal authorities was to some extent retained in the German period; but over the greater part of the territory the German colonial administration was of a para-military character, taking little account of tribal boundaries. Before the first world war the country was divided into twenty-one districts, each under a German officer. Sub-districts consisting of groups of villages, were administered by an *akida*, usually an Arab or a Swahili, who was the effective power in local government. Each village was in charge of an official known as the *jumbe*. The *akidas* were frequently corrupt and oppressive.

The first world war had a devastating effect on Tanganyika. Elsewhere in Africa the fighting had practically finished by the end of 1915, but it lasted there until the Armistice in November 1918. This was largely due to the military genius of General von Lettow-Vorbeck. Although he lacked supply routes from the sea, he succeeded in keeping large allied forces in East Africa. By the end of 1916 British and Belgian troops had occupied the northern part of the country and a provisional civil administration was established under Mr (later Sir) Horace Byatt: but it was not until November 1917 that von Lettow-Vorbeck's force was driven across the Rovuma river into Portuguese territory; and at the time of the Armistice he was on the offensive again in Northern Rhodesia. The military campaign in East Africa cost Great Britain £72,000,000, but the misery caused in human suffering and loss of life was immeasurable. Under pressure of the military campaign the efficient German sanitation arrangements broke down. Tropical diseases spread to areas where they had previously been unknown. Tens of thousands in the African carrier corps died of malaria and dysentery. Disease and famine ravaged the whole country and the influenza epidemic of 1918–19 carried away many more thousands of easy victims. Sir Donald Cameron, later to be Governor of Tanganyika, wrote of this time:

> Chiefs were without people and people without chiefs. Thirty thousand natives were said to have died of famine. . . . Amongst those remaining great numbers had pawned their children for food, husbands had left their wives, mothers had deserted their children, family life had very nearly ceased to exist.[2]

In 1919 Byatt was appointed administrator of the whole territory, and in 1920 under the Tanganyika Order-in-Council he was appointed governor. A High Court of Justice was established, with civil and criminal jurisdiction. By 1920 all the Germans in the territory were repatriated and all German property was sold in the open market at bargain prices in a time of severe economic depression. Much of this property, in Dar es Salaam and in the settler estates in the north-east highlands, was bought by Indians.[3] The property of the former German Christian missions was excluded from sale under section 436 of the Treaty of Versailles, and it was handed back in July 1925.

The peace treaties deprived Germany of all her former colonies but there was a genuine desire among the victorious powers to express in some way their common conviction that the age of raw imperialism was over. A system of mandates was devised by which the European country administering an African or Near East territory was made responsible to the League of Nations. There were two types of mandates: under type A, evolution towards independence was to be actively encouraged: under type B, where independence was not foreseen except as a very distant goal, the mandatory power undertook 'to promote the material and moral well-being and the social progress of the inhabitants'. Annual reports were to be made to the League and a Permanent Mandates Commission was appointed with a watching-brief on the League's behalf. The British mandate for Tanganyika was type B. It included the suppression of slavery and the slave-trade; the regulation of forced labour; and the control of the liquor traffic. The sale of land to expatriates, without government permission, was forbidden.[4]

The terms of the mandate, combined with persistent pressure from Germany for the return of the territory, prevented any large post-war influx of European settlers in Tanganyika. Under section 8 of the mandate it was laid down that 'the mandatory shall ensure the complete freedom of conscience and the free exercise of all forms of worship which are consonant with public order and morality'. Missionaries who were nationals of states within the League of Nations were to be allowed to enter, to travel, to acquire property, to erect religious buildings and to open schools subject to the responsibility of the mandatory to exercise control for the maintenance of public order and good government.[5] This 'missionaries' charter' formed the basis for good relations between missions and government which were a feature of the inter-war period in Tanganyika.

Under Sir Horace Byatt's governorship (1920–5) Tanganyika recovered fairly quickly from the disastrous effects of the war. By 1925 exports had doubled from the immediate pre-war period; and from 1923 Tanganyika no longer needed British grants-in-aid. But Byatt was criticized, not least by his successor Sir Donald Cameron, for a *laissez-faire* attitude in the administration of the territory. Many of the German practices and laws remained in force; and some of the *akidas* appointed in the period of German rule remained in charge of local government: there was great variety of practice from one district to another. Cameron was one of the great administrators of the colonial period. He declared his policy soon after his appointment in the 1925 Report to the League of Nations: 'It is our duty to do everything in our power to develop the native on lines which will not Westernize him and turn him into a bad imitation of a European.' He gave real authority to the traditional African rulers and scope for tribal development, while keeping the ultimate local power in the hands of his administrative officers. The territory was divided into eleven districts, each with a district commissioner. Under the Native Authority Ordinance of 1926, the chiefs were made responsible for the maintenance of law and order and were given limited legislative powers (e.g. to check illicit brewing); they were also empowered to collect hut and poll taxes from which they were paid a salary in place of customary tribute. In 1929 a Native Courts Ordinance removed African courts from the jurisdiction of the High Court. But the central government remained firmly in the hands of expatriates. The legislative council, formed in 1926, consisted of the governor, thirteen officials and up to ten unofficial members, nominated by the governor. Two Asians (and from 1929 three) were invited to serve, but Cameron maintained that African interests were represented by the governor, the chief secretary and the secretary for native affairs. Although he claimed later that he intended to keep places available for Africans, no Africans were nominated to the legislative council until 1945 or to the executive council until 1951; and all these were chiefs.[6] The effect of Cameron's 'retribalization' of local government, and of the parallel development of African and non-African institutions, was to deprive the younger educated Africans of any early apprenticeship in political responsibility. The Tanganyika Africa Association, founded in 1929, had little scope for political development. This society reached across tribal divisions but it consisted mainly of teachers and civil servants, and it attracted no popular support.

The government developed a system of education in co-operation with the Christian missions on a similar pattern to Kenya and Uganda. (See below, pp. 196ff.)

Tanganyika was far less troubled than Kenya with problems of land tenure, and after the first world war the troubles that arose were due more to Asian than to European acquisitiveness. In 1923 a Land Ordinance declared the whole land of Tanganyika to be public – 'that is, under the control and subject to the disposition of the Government'; but it was to be held and administered for the use and common benefit of the natives of the territory. The main crops in the 1930s were millet, maize, rice, bananas, sisal, cotton, and coffee. Diamond mines near Mwanza, south of Lake Victoria, employed about five hundred Africans, but there was as yet little industrial development. Forced labour was not permitted under the mandate for private employment, but there was some government recruiting of labour for schemes such as the coffee-plantations in Bukoba Province in 1929. In the period of British rule African co-operatives for coffee-growing in the Kilimanjaro area were encouraged.

The Advance of Islam

In Tanganyika, as in Kenya, the rapid advance of Islam gave a sense of urgency to the Christian mission. In Zanzibar and along the East African coast the Muslim faith had been established for a millennium, but during the period of European rule it spread inland over the whole territory.

The European occupation, however, gave to the superior Swahili population something of the same prestige as it gave to the Baganda, and thus carried a militant host of Muslims from the coast to the interior.

Primitive animism showed little resistance to the advance of Islam.

Their understanding of the Koran might be imperfect, their observance of religious practices might be meaningless; but to the pagan African it would at once be apparent that membership of the great brotherhood of the faithful would confer at least that sense of sophistication, which, in his tribal parochialism, he so signally lacked.[7]

Under the mandate the official census of 1924 registered 1,276,000 Muslims in Tanganyika, and only five years later in 1929, 2,100,000. Christian missionaries judged these figures to be greatly exaggerated, but Dr Richter (1934) reported that in the space of two years, in a population of 58,000 in the Pare Mountain area, at least 30,000 had gone over to Islam; and that at one place in the Chagga tribal area in 1927, 700 Roman Catholics had been re-baptized into Islam. The advance of Christian missions in Tanganyika was achieved in the face of formidable competition.

The Christian Missions

By 1938 ten per cent of the population of Tanganyika had some Christian allegiance – the hard-won fruit of many missionary societies and groups, mostly

French, German and British.[8] At least half the number of Christian adherents in the period were Roman Catholics. The pioneers among Roman Catholic missions were the French Congregation of the Holy Spirit (the Holy Ghost Fathers). They reached Zanzibar in 1863 and did notable work there among freed slaves. In 1868 they extended this work to the mainland at Bagamoyo, which soon became the main centre of the mission. In 1910 the Apostolic Vicariate of Bagamoyo was divided into the two vicariates of Bagamoyo and Kilimanjaro. By the early 1930s the number of baptized Roman Catholics in these two vicariates was approaching 60,000, and there were about 300,000 children under instruction, mostly in small 'bush' schools.

In 1878 Cardinal Lavigerie's 'Société des Missionaires d'Afrique' (the White Fathers) began work at Karema on Lake Tanganyika. By 1929 four vicariates were established in the western half of the country with a baptized church membership in the early 1930s of over 88,000.

In the south-east of Tanganyika the pioneer missionaries were German Benedictines of the Order of St Ottilien from Bavaria. The work spread from Dar es Salaam (1888) over a wide area southwards to the Rovuma river and inland to Lake Nyasa. In 1922 Swiss Benedictines took over the part of this region around Dar es Salaam and in 1931 the Italian Consolata Fathers were brought in at Iringa.

In the early days the Roman Catholic missions required only a very short catechumenate of one month before baptism, but following a conference of East African bishops in 1912 a three-year period of preparation for baptism was required. The missionary strategy changed slowly from that of the freed-slave settlement to a widely-spread system of African education.

Protestant Missions

Next to the Roman Catholic Church it was, as one might expect, German Lutheran missions which played a dominant role in the evangelization of Tanganyika before the first world war. When these missions were allowed to return in the 1920s they consolidated the work they had begun earlier with remarkable results. The Christian community associated with these missions rose from 20,000 in 1914 to 92,000 in 1938.

The first Lutheran mission to enter Tanganyika was the 'Deutschostafrikanische Missions-gesellschaft zu Berlin', (Berlin III), an imperialist foundation which started at Dar es Salaam in 1887 with the avowed aim of educating Africans to work on the German plantations.[9] It was reorganized with a stronger evangelistic purpose in 1891 and became widely known as the Bethel mission, working chiefly among the Shambaa tribe in the Usambara hills and later in Bukoba on the western shore of Lake Victoria. In 1891 the original Berlin Missionary Society (Berlin I) and a group of Moravian missionaries entered the East African field together. They chose deliberately to work in areas remote

from secular European interests: the Moravians expanded north and west from
the northern end of Lake Nyasa towards Tabora; and the Berlin society worked
eastwards across the coastal plateau towards Dar es Salaam. Both societies were
well-established on these lines of advance by 1914. The Leipzig Evangelical
Lutheran Mission Society entered the Chagga district near Kilimanjaro in
1892, later extending their work southwards to the Pare Hills. In 1911 the
Neukirchen mission began work among the Ha tribe to the east of Lake Tanganyika, returning to the same field in 1928.

There were a few non-Lutheran Protestant missions working in Tanganyika
during the period. In 1909 the Africa Inland Mission took over the lone CMS
station at Nassa in Usukuma and had six stations among the Sukuma tribe
in the 1930s. Seventh Day Adventists from Germany worked in the Pare hills
and on the eastern shores of Lake Victoria. From 1926 American Lutherans
(Augustana synod) were at work in Tanganyika, and an American Pentecostal
mission from 1930.

Anglican Missions

Of the two Anglican missionary societies working in Tanganyika, the Universities' Mission to Central Africa[10] was first in the field. Their first base in
Tanganyika was at Magila, in the territory of the Bondei tribe from 1873. A
year later Bishop Steere established a group of freed slaves at Masasi, a hundred
miles inland from Lindi. By 1914 the society had flourishing centres of mission
in Nyasaland and had started in Northern Rhodesia, but in Tanganyika it was
still 'a pair of disconnected archdeaconries', based on Magila and Masasi three
hundred miles apart. After the first world war growth was rapid especially in
the southern archdeaconry which in 1925 was constituted a separate diocese of
Masasi. By the middle 1930s the church that had grown from the UMCA's work
in Tanganyika had a baptized membership of 41,000 and some 450 schools.
It was by that time the strongest and most widespread non-Roman missionary
church in the southern part of the country.

The CMS mission in Tanganyika was a by-product of its Uganda mission.
The first CMS party (1876) decided to approach Uganda by the long Arab route
to the southern shore of Lake Victoria, starting from Bagamoyo. Mpwapwa,
two hundred and fifty miles inland, was selected as a support station for the
Uganda mission, and the neighbouring districts of Usagara (later to be known
as Ukaguru) and Ugogo became the main areas of CMS mission. In 1880 a second
station in the Usagara hills was opened at Mamboya. In 1900 Bishop Peel paid
his first visit to the mission which was extended in that year to include Berega
and Mvumi, and in 1901 Buigiri twenty-five miles north of Mvumi. In 1904
the Mpwapwa station was moved ten miles north to Kongwa.

The early years of the CMS mission were far from easy. The German administration was not unfriendly, but the mission tended to be a poor relation of the

CMS missions further to the north in Kenya and Uganda; and even after the division of the diocese of Western Equatorial Africa in 1890, episcopal oversight was still remote and the response was small. By 1910 it was more promising. The CMS annual report for that year claims that the mission was 'gradually increasing its grip on the younger generation'. By that time many of the pioneers had departed, but Dr E. J. Baxter, who had joined the mission in 1877, was still serving. A colourful and somewhat eccentric man, he had strong views about the need for ample protection against the African sun. He used to wear a circlet of champagne-corks on his sun helmet to deflect the sun's rays, and he equipped his donkey with two pairs of trousers as protection against the tsetse fly. David Deekes, another hardened campaigner who was still serving in the mission, had been with Mackay when he died. He enjoyed telling younger missionaries of the cheese with which he had once entertained H. M. Stanley – so tough and ancient that it had to be carved with an axe. The Christian community associated with CMS was still quite small. Statistics for 1910 gave a baptized membership of 810 with 97 catechumens. But, as with other missions in German East Africa, there was a sudden increase in response in the years immediately before the first world war.

J. H. Briggs describes the area of CMS mission at that time as embracing the whole of the country of the Wakaguru and Wagogo tribes, an area of about three hundred miles from east to west and one hundred and fifty miles from north to south. The Wakaguru in the eastern, and the Wagogo in the western part of this area spoke different Bantu languages. Ukaguru was a land of mountains and valleys, well-watered, with plenty of fine forest land; Ugogo was a land of wide plains free of trees except for the ubiquitous baobab. The dry season lasted for eight months of the year.[11]

The CMS Mission, 1910–17

The first entries in the précis-book for 1910 have an old-world flavour. The executive committee of the German East Africa mission decides that the donkeys shall be moved from Berega to Buigiri, and renews its request to London headquarters to send out artisans 'in view of the great claim on time and strength of an evangelistic missionary in building and repairing buildings which could be done more efficiently and economically by artisans'.[12] Although the donkeys were soon to be replaced by petrol engines and craftsmen were sent out eventually, evangelistic missionaries continued to design, erect and repair buildings for many years to come.

The mission felt threatened at this time not only by the advance of Islam into the interior, but by uncertainty about its own future. Directives from London on the necessity of retrenchment always made the smaller CMS missions uneasy, but some reassurance was given by a 'declaration' approved by the Group III committee on 7th February, 1911:

In view of the grave urgency of missionary work in Usagara-Ugogo, as an important link in the chain of stations by which alone it can be hoped that the advance of Islam may be stayed in German East Africa ... the Committee recognize their responsibility to do their utmost to maintain this field and to strengthen it as God may enable them.

The declaration stated that there was no present intention of abandoning the work 'unless it be by the method of handing it over, on terms not unfavourable to CMS, to some other Missionary Society at least as well able as themselves to carry it on effectively'.

Stimulated, no doubt, by this declaration and by signs of a growing response in the Buigiri district, the missionaries at their general conference in August 1911 unanimously supported a proposal from Dr Westgate to place a European missionary at Dodoma; and the executive committee of the mission named five candidates for ordination to the diaconate. Largely because of the CMS policy of self-support, it was to be another ten years before any Africans were ordained. Bishop Peel wanted to ordain them earlier.

The growth in church membership inevitably raised questions of church discipline. In December 1911 the Bishop of Mombasa wrote to London seeking advice about this. It had been found helpful, he said, for missionaries to continue the tribal custom of exacting fines on church members for fornication and adultery, such fines being imposed by the church councils on the authority of the bishop.[13] In a further letter, after consultation with the Bishop of Uganda, Bishop Peel said they were agreed about the policy of following tribal custom in the treatment of such offenders, with proper Christian safeguards.[14] The Society's ecclesiastical sub-committee gave its advice in March 1912 in a memorandum on church discipline. General approval was given to the payment of fines by offenders, payable to the injured parties and equivalent in amount to fines imposed in the tribal community. The sub-committee thought it undesirable for the church as such to be collecting fines. Ostracism should be a normal part of the punishment. Any discipline should in any case be carried out under the direct authorization of the bishop.[15]

Another range of disciplinary questions came before the executive committee in March 1912. The committee noted the bishop's ruling that marriages should only take place in church where both parties were Christians: and that a missionary in charge of a station may use his discretion in divorcing a partner who had had a *baraza* wedding. No one upon whom the 'greater excommunication' had been imposed should be allowed to live within a quarter of a mile of mission property.[16]

In November 1912 plans were well advanced for opening a new station at Muhalala. It was a strategic point for checking the advance of Islam; and the executive committee of the mission were convinced that unless a new centre was developed in north-west Ugogo the whole area might transfer from CMS to the Roman Catholic missions already working there.[17] Although these arguments bore no immediate fruit because of the war, Muhalala was the first new station to be opened after it, in 1921. A few months later it was moved to Kilimatinde five miles away, because a swamp made Muhalala difficult to approach from the plains.

In November 1913 the bishop ordained three missionaries, J. H. Briggs, David Deekes, and E. W. Doulton as deacon and priest on successive Sundays. He gave as his reason for 'the double ceremony' the fact that he did not expect to be in German East Africa again until July 1916. All three candidates had studied all subjects necessary for the priest's examination, and had undertaken 'to keep up their Greek'.

The statistics of the German East Africa mission for 1913 (the last to be compiled for six years) tell their own story of expansion and advance in the three-year period from 1910.[18]

	Native agents	Communicants	Total Adherents	Adult Baptisms (Year)	Scholars
1910	40	217	907	22	3,989
1913	211	581	4,271	134	17,202

It needs to be said that 'scholars' in the statistics of this period, is a comprehensive and elastic term. It would include men and women, as well as boys and girls, who were receiving a few hours' teaching each week. Dr Westgate's estimate, in round figures, for the strength of the Christian community associated with the CMS mission was '1,000 baptized and 4,000 catechumens'. Miss Peel, who accompanied her father on his 1913 episcopal visit to the territory, made a map of the mission in which she marked in 370 'out-stations' where some teaching was being given. The number of out-stations had risen to 400 by the time war broke out in August 1914.

The German East Africa mission was the only CMS mission in non-British territory in tropical Africa, and the outbreak of war meant that the missionaries became enemy aliens overnight. There were fourteen of them on the station at the time. For months no definite news was received about their health or whereabouts. The first letter to come through was received by Mrs Westgate from her husband a year after the war began. Writing in June 1915, Dr Westgate said that a number of UMCA missionaries were interned with the CMS party, and that he had been steadily at work on translating parts of the Old Testament into Cigogo. Anxiety for the welfare of the missionaries remained until a telegram, dated 9th October, 1916, was received from Kampala: '14 Testimony missionaries safe at Tabora.' ('Testimony' was the telegraphic code-name for CMS.) They had been liberated by Belgian forces who entered Tabora on the 18th September soon after its evacuation by German troops. At first they had been allowed to stay in their mission-stations, but in May 1915 they were all interned and taken to Kiboriani. Later they were moved to Buigiri and in

April 1916 to Tabora. The discipline at Tabora had been 'rigorous' and false charges of espionage were made against missionaries.[19]

It appears that Dr Westgate had been singled out for questioning and had a rough time. He had resigned from the mission in 1914 on appointment as field-secretary of a new Canadian missionary society and it was now clear that he must take up the appointment which had been held open for him. His leadership in the mission had been outstanding, particularly in relation to the establishment of a divinity school and teacher-training institution at Kongwa.

Reconstruction, 1917–26

The CMS mission in the former German territory, soon to be renamed Tanganyika, was restarted in February 1917 when two missionaries established a temporary headquarters at Kongwa. One of them was Canon K. St A. Rogers, the secretary of the British East Africa mission. The other was the Rev. Ralph Banks who had been accepted for service in the German East African mission before the war broke out, but who had been held up at Mombasa since December 1914. They took charge of a group of refugees – catechists and their wives – who had been interned with the missionaries at Tabora. They found distressing famine conditions everywhere and did what they could to provide seed-corn, ground-nuts and other foodstuffs. Transport was very difficult. The porters were weak through lack of food. But from Kongwa, conveniently situated for reaching both the Ukaguru and Ugogo sections of the CMS mission, Rogers and Banks travelled round as best they could, and found much encouragement in spite of widespread distress. They reported from Mpwapwa that the African congregations had held together through the months of war under their teachers and catechists. Little damage had been done to mission property in the district, but all Cigogo New Testaments and prayer-books and most of Dr Westgate's manuscript translations had been destroyed. At Mamboya, the work had been kept going and the mission buildings were 'in fairly good condition'.[20] Labour recruiting agents had exempted senior catechists at the mission station. Banks, in another letter, described the good welcome given to him at Zoyisa. The dispensary was open and there were three hundred children in school, well-cared for by two African teachers, in eight classes. Over four hundred people attended Morning Prayer on Sunday.[21] The small Anglican church in Central Tanganyika had survived the ordeal of war conditions more severe than in any other part of East Africa, and the African church workers were now proving themselves in the work of reconstruction, both spiritual and physical.

Meanwhile in London, on 23rd January, 1917, there was a conference on the future of the mission. Five of the missionaries on furlough met with G. T. Manley, the Group III secretary at Salisbury Square; and together they made a number of decisions and suggestions. They decided that Rogers should be asked to stay in the former German territory until the autumn of 1917, by which time

the first of the old staff were expected to have returned; and the parent committee agreed to sanction a special £5,000 appeal for the reconstruction of the
mission.[22]

In this discussion, and for some years to come, a number of senior missionaries were keen to take over the former German Lutheran missions – partly
to give European oversight to the Christian communities associated with them;
partly because they were convinced that unless CMS stepped in, the Roman
Catholic missions would quietly take over. The British Colonial Office made it
clear that no financial assistance could be expected if CMS were to take over
any German mission-stations; but British missionaries of reputable societies
would be welcome in the territory for the remainder of the war. J. H. Oldham advised caution. With his customary prescience and exceptional knowledge
acquired as secretary of the International Missionary Council, he expected German missionaries to be allowed back within a few years. (See below pp. 193ff.)

By the autumn of 1919 all the senior missionaries had returned and in
November Bishop R. S. Heywood, Peel's successor as Bishop of Mombasa,
presided over a general conference of missionaries at Kiboriani. The conference
agreed that the teaching of English should be encouraged in all schools and all
the mission stations. In confident mood, the conference asked the parent
committee for £1,000 for the reconstruction and expansion of the work of the
mission; for £2,000 in order to build a hospital and doctor's house; and for
more European staff. These requests, typical of many that were made in the
immediate post-war period, were not granted. When, a few months later, the
parent committee proposed that the mission should expand northwards to link
up with Taveta, and hinted that it might also take responsibility for new work
in Ruanda, the answer was firm. The executive committee of the mission
referred back to the unfulfilled requests of August 1914. Without additional
staff any expansion beyond their present field of operation was impossible.[23]

The 1920 statistics of the mission showed that all the ground lost during
the war had been made up. Baptized church members had increased to 2,460,
and the numbers in schools had grown to 18,746 compared with 17,202 in 1913.[24]

In 1921, along with other missions of the CMS, the Tanganyika mission was
asked by the parent committee to propose a scheme for the reduction of salaries
by twenty per cent. At first the local governing body found itself unable to
suggest a scheme by which so large a reduction could be achieved, but eventually
it accepted the necessity of a twenty per cent reduction from October 1921.

Two Africans connected with the mission, Haruni Mbega, and Andrea
Mwaka, were made deacon by Bishop Heywood in 1921. A minute of the
parent committee (November 8th, 1921) took exception to the bishop's action in
ordaining Africans without prior consultation. The bishop explained that there
was no intention of making the Society responsible for their stipends.[25] The
mission secretary, J. H. Briggs, wrote in support of the bishop's action. He
explained that the appropriate native church councils had agreed to support

the two deacons, and therefore it had not been thought necessary to ask for the parent committee's sanction for their ordination. The two deacons were not priested until March 1924, after a period of further training.

In April 1922 the parent committee approved a scheme for 'The Regulation of Pastorate Committees and Church Councils in the Tanganyika Mission'. Each pastorate, defined as one or more congregations, was to have a committee consisting of the African pastor or quasi-pastor; the superintendent missionary of the district; and at least four baptized church members elected by subscribers to the church funds. The pastorate committee was to meet at least once in every three weeks. Its duties were to collect and disburse money received from central church funds; to prepare annual estimates of needs, and of subscriptions and other funds available locally to meet these needs; to repair pastors' houses and schools; to provide everything necessary for divine worship; and, at the first meeting each year, to elect two delegates to a central church committee. Two such central committees were envisaged, one for each of the two main districts of the mission; but a revised scheme, approved by the parent committee on 8th January, 1923, amalgamated them in a single council with the bishop as *ex officio* chairman, meeting at least once a year. The business of the council included payment of African clergy and other agents from pastorate contributions and parent committee grants; consultation about the formation of new pastorates; and nomination to the bishop of all candidates for Holy Orders, whether African or European. These regulations were a significant step forward from mission to church in Central Tanganyika.[26]

Ralph Banks, in an unpublished sketch of the history of the mission and church in Central Tanganyika, recalled the years 1924 and 1925 as a time of 'constant struggle against difficult circumstances and serious losses of staff'. There was renewed anxiety about the transfer of CMS work in Tanganyika to some other society; UMCA had offered to take over earlier, but now there was another Anglican society directly interested in the possibility. On 16th June, 1925 Bishop Heywood of Mombasa wrote 'strongly deprecating' the intention of such a transfer, but saying that if it had to happen the only possible society was the BCMS. In December 1925, Dr Daniel Bartlett, the BCMS secretary, indicated his committee's interest.[27] Bishop Heywood pressed upon the parent committee the importance of some guarantee of continuity in educational policy, particularly in co-operation with the government of Tanganyika. Bartlett wrote on 29th December, 1925 to say that the BCMS committee regarded the policy for educational and industrial work, as outlined by the bishop, as 'bringing a new element into the field of operation which alters their attitude towards . . . taking over Tanganyika work'.[28] The negotiations ended there. Early in 1926 Bishop Heywood, after a visit to Tanganyika, reported 'the intense thankfulness' among the missionaries there that the parent committee 'had given up the idea of abandoning the mission'.

As in Kenya, not all the missionaries welcomed the new developments.

Are we justified, [one of them wrote] in sacrificing evangelistic work for educational when the staff is not sufficient for carrying on both side by side? . . . Candidates for baptism have been kept back, congregations have been unvisited and left without a teacher, medical work among the heathen has been closed down, native contributions have decreased, and all this in order to give twenty-six boys a better chance than they ever had before.[29]

The writer of the letter agreed that there was 'a terrible need for a higher standard of education in this mission' – but 'the problem remains'. This missionary spoke for many others. Acceptance of government grants inevitably restricted liberty of manœuvre. For those who saw education as something apart from, indeed in competition with, evangelism, the price was too high. For others who saw no sharp distinction of this kind, government aid meant the promise of a larger missionary staff after years of frustration.

Forming a New Diocese, 1926–31

Bishop Peel had recognized that the separation of the German East Africa mission from his diocese of Mombasa was desirable in the long run. After Peel's death in 1916 Bishop Willis of Uganda recommended to the parent committee of CMS the creation of a new diocese, with Tabora as its head-quarters.[30] Dr Eugene Stock, the Society's former editorial secretary, supported him and suggested an immediate appeal be made to the Archbishop of Canterbury to form a new diocese in German East Africa. It was the appropriate next step to the mission boundary agreements made under Archbishop Benson's guidance between UMCA and CMS.[31]

The next decisive steps were taken by Bishop Peel's successor, R. S. Heywood. After visiting the Tanganyika area of his diocese in the early part of 1926 he was persuaded that the time for separation had come. He had just moved his own headquarters from Mombasa to Nairobi to meet the claims of the rapidly growing churches in the Kenya Highlands and Nyanza, and the difficulty of supervising a distant mission, involving months of absence from Nairobi, was becoming even more obvious. He was convinced that any future development of government-mission partnership in education required a bishop resident within the territory, as were the Roman Catholic bishops and the Anglican Bishop of Zanzibar.[32] He suggested that the Australian CMS should be asked to nominate a bishop for the new diocese, and to help find his stipend in partnership with the CMS in London and the Colonial and Continental Church Society. This possibility was already being explored by Wilson Cash, the new general secretary of CMS, and the project developed rapidly. The parent committee gave its approval for Bishop Heywood to visit Australia on invitation from the Australian CMS and at their expense; and asked the general secretary to approach the Archbishop of Canterbury about the proposal for a new diocese and the appointment of its bishop.[33]

Bishop Heywood left Mombasa for Australia in December 1926. On 19th February, 1927 the Federal Council of CMS of Australia and Tasmania unanimously accepted 'responsibility for the proposed new Tanganyika diocese; the support of Australian missionaries now or hereafter there; and the relief of the Parent Committee from all mission costs save European salaries'. The Federal Council named the Rev. G. A. Chambers, general secretary of the CMS of Australia and Tasmania as a suitable bishop, and asked the parent committee of CMS in London to put his name forward to the Archbishop of Canterbury.

The Archbishop approved and Chambers began recruiting missionaries in Australia.

Meanwhile the English missionaries in Tanganyika needed assurance. One of them, though he welcomed the proposal as probably the best way out of a difficult situation, found in it further evidence of a long-held conviction that 'Salisbury Square would be glad to be rid of us'.[34] H. D. Hooper, G. T. Manley's successor as Africa secretary at Salisbury Square, wrote soothingly. Support for the English staff of the mission would continue from England for many years to come, while the Australian CMS aimed at complete support of their own missionaries and continued provision of their expenses. Meeting in April 1927 the executive committee of the mission expressed 'great thankfulness' that the Australian CMS had accepted responsibility for the Tanganyika mission and for the proposed new diocese. It considered that in view of this 'it would be a mistake to abandon any particular station, district, or institution'.[35]

Chambers visited all the main stations of the Tanganyika mission in July and August 1927 before going to England in the autumn for his consecration as bishop. It was agreed that he should thereafter return to Australia to secure reinforcements and financial support. In London in September he discussed plans for the future of the mission and the diocese with Wilson Cash. He asked for the appointment of J. H. Briggs as mission secretary at the earliest possible date. Cash suggested that Chambers should 'begin right away on diocesan lines, very simply' rather than contemplate a later transfer of responsibility from mission to diocese.

Bishop Chambers was consecrated by the Archbishop at Canterbury Cathedral on All Saints Day, 1927. He had hoped for consecration in Australia; but he had been reconciled to its taking place at Canterbury when he found symbolic value in it.

From Canterbury where Bishop Broughton many years before had gone forth to become first Bishop of Australia, I, an Australian, went forth to Africa as first Bishop of Central Tanganyika, to provide an outlet for Australian aspiration in fellowship with England.

This aspiration in fellowship was generously fulfilled in the next few years. 'Every state in Australia,' Bishop Chambers was able to write in 1931, 'has given of its best to the Diocese and during 1928 £11,000 was contributed (in Australia) for Tanganyika alone.'

The story of the early years of the new diocese has been well told by the bishop himself in *Tanganyika's New Day* (1931) and more recently by Mrs Nancy Sibtain and Mrs Chambers in *Dare to Look Up* (1968).[36] George Alexander Chambers, forty at the time of his consecration, proved himself an excellent choice as the first bishop of a missionary diocese. He had confidence and enthusiasm, and he was unusually gifted both as a recruiting-sergeant and money-raiser. The diocesan association which he launched at St Paul's, Onslow Square (where his father-in-law, Canon W. Talbot-Rice, was vicar) the day after his consecration was one of the most successful of its kind, both financially and in its fellowship. With it behind him he raised £16,000 in a few months in 1930 for projects outside the range of CMS grants. A 'Week's Good Cause' appeal which he gave on the BBC radio in November 1936 brought in £6,500 which he used to extend Mvumi hospital and to underwrite the cost of bringing out more nurses for the rapidly developing medical and welfare work of the diocese.

Bishop Chambers at times displayed the defects of his qualities in a way that endeared him to his friends and family at least in retrospect. His meticulous attention to detail made him fussy about such things as the composition of a group photograph or the cooking of a meal. He was a poor linguist, but a determined speaker and preacher in Swahili. He startled one of his congregations by charging them to 'have a potato', when the word he was after was 'self-control'. More seriously, his vigorous and sometimes rather casual recruiting methods meant that a rather high proportion of the thirty men and women who followed him from Australia to Tanganyika between 1927 and 1931 were not adequate for the demands of a missionary's life. One or two, to the bishop's dismay, revealed a deep-seated prejudice which made it impossible for them to continue, and others exhibited various symptoms of nervous strain. In later years he recognized the need for more careful selection and training of missionary recruits. His genius for money-raising sometimes created difficulty in finding worthwhile projects for which money was in hand; and the CMS supporting committees and secretaries, both in England and Australia, found it difficult to reconcile their enforced cheese-paring with the bishop's comparatively lavish expenditure. For all that, Bishop Chambers had great gifts which he dedicated to the service of Christ in Central Tanganyika, and he was able to look back at the end of his twenty years' episcopate with pride and gratitude at what had been achieved.

The bishop was enthroned in the newly-built church at Mvumi on 2nd November, 1928 and also at Dodoma on 4th November. The second enthronement took place in the government *boma* in the presence of the governor. Immediately after his enthronement the bishop inducted J. H. Briggs as Archdeacon of Dodoma, the former title, Archdeacon of Ukaguru-Ugogo being appropriately discarded from this time. A general conference of missionaries followed the enthronement from November 5th to 7th and no less than seventeen recruits from Australia were welcomed into its fellowship.

The conference, alive to the opportunities presented by such ample reinforcements after years of dearth, recommended that new centres of work should be opened at Morogoro, Ujiji and Tabora as soon as possible.[37] The executive committee of the mission, meeting immediately after the missionaries' conference, endorsed the bishop's decision to start work at Bukoba on the western shore of Lake Tanganyika and among the Wahe at Kasalo, forty miles from Kongwa.

Shortage of Funds

At a time of so much hope and promise, it was hard for the mission to have to face cuts in income; but the world slump had begun to affect missionary giving. The first pressure to be felt came from London. The parent committee decided that it would have to reduce the AOH grant to £700 for the year 1929 and to stop it altogether from the end of that year. Bishop Chambers called a special meeting of the executive committee to consider the effects of this decision. He explained that the Australian CMS had been very careful to say the AOH expenditure would be taken over – £1,000 a year to begin with. The main items under AOH grants were the stipends of African teachers, cost of missionaries' travel and of running dispensaries. These were the lifelines of the mission. Various proposals were made for cutting down expenditure, such as freewill offerings for medical treatment and definite fees for such treatment where possible; full support from district councils for their pastors, evangelists, and schoolteachers; no new out-stations to be opened without substantial support from the chiefs and people of the district; congregational offerings to be taken at baptisms, churchings and confirmations. The executive committee was fully aware that it would be no easy task to transform the mission-support of African workers, running at about £1,000 per annum, to self-support through the pastorate committees and the central church council; and it asked the parent committee in London to allow the bishop to make a special appeal when he visited England for the 1930 Lambeth Conference.[38]

The parent committee's answer to these proposals was not encouraging, and before the matter of AOH responsibility had been resolved Australia began to feel the full weight of the slump. In July 1930 Briggs reported to London that the Australian CMS had a large deficit and its commitment for 1931 would have to be reduced from £7,720 to £6,000.[39] The parent committee agreed to hold the AOH grant for the mission at £1,200 for the time being; and the decrease in grants from Australia was partially met by a ten per cent cut in all missionary salaries.

In 1932, as a further economy measure, the parent committee decided to retire three senior English missionaries at the end of their present tour of service. The local governing body pleaded as strongly as possible for the retention of Archdeacon Briggs, in view of his special gifts in the administration and conservation of missionary funds, and his involvement in the proposals for diocesanization of the mission.[40] This plea was accepted, but the two other missionaries left Tanganyika for parishes in England.

The financial crisis dragged on into 1933. In July the diocesan council (which had replaced the executive committee of the mission) expressed its discontents in a memorandum to the CMS Federal Council in Australia. It recorded its appreciation of the heroic efforts of those in Australia who were giving and organizing so generously, and of the timely help received during the year through special gifts from Tasmania and South Australia. At the same time, it claimed that Central Tanganyika was the only CMS area in the world where a local governing body was compelled to meet the cost of adverse rates of exchange. The memorandum listed all the economies that had been made locally, and suggested that since the Australian CMS had adopted not only the mission but the diocese as its special responsibility a greater sum than £4,150 out of its total income of £35,000 could surely be set aside for Tanganyika.[41]

The executive committee of the Federal Council of Australasia was evidently puzzled by the memorandum, and a little grieved. 'We know,' they said in comment, 'that our share is only a part of a great whole. Shall we tell Australia that to call Tanganyika an Australian diocese is only a misnomer?' It was not correct, in their view, to say that the diocese received only £4,150 per annum from Australia. The actual amount of contribution to the diocese and mission made in Australia was £6,128 per annum. This seems fair comment; and it says much for the Federal Council that they eventually agreed to conform to CMS practice in other areas. From July 1937 they decided to add the cost of exchange to their contribution.[42]

Such financial anxieties and discontents were common to most CMS areas of mission in the years 1929–33; it was a sign of strength that in the diocese of Central Tanganyika they were not allowed to stifle evangelism or seriously to hinder the growth of the church. The expansion of medical and educational work in the newly-formed diocese will be recorded later; but it is appropriate at this point to say something of the early development of diocesan life and institutions.

The Cathedral of the Holy Spirit at Dodoma was consecrated by the bishop on 15th July, 1933 and the Bishops of Uganda, Mombasa, Zanzibar, and Masasi shared in the service. The building was the work of local masons and mission carpenters to the design of N. J. Forsgate, one of the Australian missionaries, who was later to become provost of the cathedral. It was built of grey granite with an octagonal copper dome surmounted by a cross. Much of the woodwork was carved by boys of Dodoma Central School. The whole cost of the building was underwritten by a member of the Wills family of Bristol.

On the same day as the consecration of the cathedral, the constitution of the diocese was promulgated. It provided for a diocesan synod, consisting of the bishop of the diocese, assistant bishops, all licensed clergy and missionaries, and one layman elected from each pastorate. A diocesan council, which replaced the executive committee of the mission, was to serve as the standing committee of the synod. It consisted of certain diocesan officials appointed by the bishop, and ten members elected by the synod. These elected members included four lay-men who were not to be paid church agents. The constitution included provision for district and parish councils. It had been prepared over a number of years, largely by Archdeacon Briggs. The first senior appointments made under the constitution were: Archdeacon Briggs to be diocesan treasurer and secretary; the Rev. W. Wynn Jones to be diocesan education secretary; and Dr C. Wallace to be medical secretary.

The consecration of the cathedral was followed by a 'Week of Witness', from July 18th to 23rd, and the diocesan council held its first meeting from 27th July to 1st August, 1933. The bishop announced to the council that he had appointed as the foundation Canons of the Cathedral of the Holy Spirit two Europeans and two Africans – R. Banks, S. J. King, H. Mbega, and A. Mwaka. Canon Banks was given charge of the cathedral services and the oversight of education at Dodoma and Buigiri until his furlough in 1935. Canon Mwaka was given charge of the pastorate of Dodoma township. The council at its first meeting approved eleven names for submission to the bishop for ordination.[43] On the resolution of the central church council, the diocesan council approved maximum stipends for African clergy of thirty-five shillings a month for priests and thirty shillings for deacons.

The diocesan synod held its first meeting at Dodoma in August 1936. It gave general approval to revised plans for an East African province of the Anglican Communion, but the plan did not go through at that time largely because of opposition from the diocese of Mombasa.

Economies were still causing some hardship. In his annual letter for 1937 Banks reported severe wage-cuts for African workers, but the principle of self-support was being more readily accepted in the villages, and the church was growing. Writing from Kilimatinde in July 1938,[44] Banks reported 700 bap-tized church members in his district, and 1,768 pupils in fifty schools. Dr Wallace, also writing in 1938, described the work of a typical catechist. Normally he had the dual role of catechist and village schoolmaster. Usually he was recently baptized and could read and write only a little: but he attracted people and won converts 'by sheer force of character'.

The second world war did not, fortunately, involve Tanganyika territory in the same kind of disturbance and distress as the first; and, owing much to the effective leadership of Bishop Chambers, the integration of mission and diocese in Central Tanganyika was working well. An ordination on 3rd August, 1941, just before the second meeting of the diocesan synod, brought the number of

African clergy up to thirty. The meeting of the synod, planned to last two days, in fact went on for four. One of its major tasks was the amendment of the 'Diocesan Canons of Church Order' which dealt with such matters as the instruction of converts; standards required for adult baptism; infant baptism; confirmation; marriage, especially in relation to polygamy; relationship to the members of the other churches, etc. A contributory pensions scheme for African church workers, compulsory for clergy, but optional for teachers and others, was approved. One of the synod's main concerns was the extension of the mission to unevangelized parts of the diocese. It was agreed that effective extension would not be possible until the older parts of the diocese were self-supporting. The synod therefore requested all district councils to submit within six months schemes for complete self-support which would be considered by a sub-committee of six Africans and three Europeans before being passed to the bishop for approval.[45]

Inter-mission Relationships, 1910–42

Before the first world war the German East Africa mission of CMS was at some disadvantage in relations with other missions in the territory. Episcopal oversight was remote at Mombasa; and the number of missionaries (fifteen to twenty) was too small to give it the standing locally which was achieved by the other Anglican society in the territory, the Universities' Mission to Central Africa. It is not surprising, therefore, that inter-mission relationships tended to be embarrassing, even though the intention of the other party was one of generous goodwill.

No-one in this period sought more earnestly for good relations than Pastor K. Axenfeld of the Berlin I mission. He was a delegate at the Edinburgh Missionary Conference in 1910; and inspired by the vision and fellowship there he wrote from Edinburgh on 21st June, 1910, pleading for the strengthening of the CMS mission in German East Africa. He was convinced that if East Africa was not evangelized in the next generation it would be won for Islam. The implication of his letter was that it would be difficult for the German missionary leadership to resist proposals for expansion into the CMS area unless the CMS mission was quickly strengthened. The answer of the CMS Group III committee was not hopeful. They were grateful for Dr Axenfeld's concern, but they were unable at present to contemplate any considerable increase of staff.[46]

In 1911 the Leipzig mission suggested, as part of a wider plan, that CMS should take over their Ukamba station in British East Africa and that they should take over CMS work in the Usagara district. The Bishop of Mombasa could not agree to such an exchange. The Germans had failed for various reasons 'to get hold of the Ukamba people',[47] and this failure, in his view, lay behind the suggestion of an exchange. D. J. Rees, the mission secretary, was as firmly against it, and the parent committee decided not to pursue the matter.

In September 1911 Bishop Peel, Briggs and Westgate met representatives of Benedictine Roman Catholic missions to discuss the possibility of an agreement about 'spheres' in the Buigiri, Dodoma and Mvumi districts. Such discussions with Roman Catholics were unusual, but in this case some progress was made. In the spring of 1912 the mission executive committee was considering a draft agreement, for boundaries with the mission areas of the Benedictines and the Holy Ghost Fathers, which had been sent to Bishop Peel for his approval. But this was as far as it went. Early in 1913 Pastor Axenfeld informed E. W. Doulton that the Roman Catholic bishop had received orders from Rome that no such agreements were to be made with Protestant missions.[48]

A more promising inter-mission project may be accounted a war casualty. Dr Axenfeld was again its promoter. CMS was invited to join with the Berlin I and Moravian missions in joint theological training at Morogoro. The parent committee gave qualified approval, but suggested that in view of the mission's own plans for developing theological training at Kongwa participation in the joint training scheme should at first be quite small. Negotiations continued, but there was no great enthusiasm for the project among CMS missionaries. They felt Morogoro was too remote from their main centres of activity and they did not want to spoil their Kongwa scheme. The project was revived after the first world war when CMS was approached about the possibility of taking over the Basle mission station at Morogoro. The executive committee of the CMS mission thought it was only worth considering 'as a gift or on very favourable terms', because the Basle mission was a three hours' journey from, and 2,000 feet above, the railway station.[49] Another project which came forward for discussion in 1921 was that the CMS mission should take oversight of German mission stations in the Ilamba plateau. Once again J. H. Oldham advised caution on ecumenical grounds. He agreed to bring the suggestion before the Board of Trustees of German Property, but thought the 'ecclesiastical difficulty' would weigh against it. The goodwill of American Lutherans as well as the Leipzig mission would be necessary.[50]

It appears that in the late 1920s the local governing body of the CMS mission at this time was beginning to feel desperate about the possibility of expanding their area of work in the open post-war situation. Clearly they had expected that the transfer of territory from German to British administration would have enlarged their opportunities; but this was not happening. Briggs spoke of CMS being 'hemmed in' to the south by the Scottish mission at Iringa and to the north by the American Lutherans who were claiming the right of overseeing the German stations on the Ilamba plateau.[51] It was only with the accession of the large number of new recruits from Australia that the CMS mission felt able to break out of the disputed areas and expand westwards.

In 1929 Bishop Chambers took responsibility for opening a station in Bukoba, in spite of some opposition from German Lutheran missions. The bishop based his case on the invitation of '2,000 former adherents of CMS' in Bukoba. The

missionary situation in this area west of Lake Victoria was a complicated one
with an unhappy history (see Uganda chapter). It is clear that Bishop Chambers
was not fully informed about it; but he could reasonably claim that he was
answering a call for help from leaderless Anglicans in the Bukoba district. The
Rev. Martin White, of the South African Wesleyan Methodist Missionary
Society, wrote to Bishop Chambers in July 1928. His letter spoke of a 'large
group' of Anglicans in the Bukoba area who did not wish to place themselves
under any other mission than that of CMS. His mission had decided to leave
Bukoba, and he was himself about to leave East Africa. In September 1928
Bishop Chambers received a further letter, which Bishop Willis of Uganda had
been asked to forward to him, signed by seventeen evangelical Christians in
Bukoba who claimed to represent seventy-two churches. 'We, who were
baptized into the CMS,' the letter read, 'we want you to be our father.' In a
covering letter Bishop Willis outlined three possibilities for these 'orphaned'
churches: (1) that Uganda diocese should resume the responsibility it had
undertaken between 1916 and 1924; (2) that Bishop Chambers should visit
Bukoba to examine the possibilities of starting mission work there: (3) that
the Anglican mission should withdraw from any interest in the area and so
leave the field clear for the Bethel mission, which had returned to Bukoba after a
ten-year absence in 1926.[52]

In the light of this correspondence, Bishop Chambers' decision to visit
Bukoba was a fully responsible one. Unfortunately when he did so, in February
1929, he and Pastor E. Johannsen of the Bethel mission did not make a good
impression on each other. Johannsen, who had been in Bukoba and Ruanda
before the war, believed that Bishop Chambers' interest in Bukoba was related
to the current discussion about an Anglican province in East Africa. What
Bishop Chambers saw of the former Anglican Christians made him all the more
resolute to stake a claim in the Bukoba area. 'The people,' he wrote, 'are more
like the Baganda', and he had visions of Buhaya evangelists spreading out over
Tanganyika in the way the Baganda had done further north.[53]

In July 1929 he returned to Bukoba with a young Australian missionary,
L. J. Bakewell. The plan was to have two mission stations – one close to Bukoba
township and a hospital at Rubango thirty miles to the south of it. Bakewell
started work, and tried to co-operate with the Bethel mission; but there were
clashes between the Episcopalian and the German Lutheran groups; and
Lutheran missionaries in the north-east of Tanganyika joined with the Bethel
mission in Bukoba in protest to the International Missionary Council. J. H.
Oldham had not a great deal of sympathy with Bishop Chambers in this matter,
and he was supported by Wilson Cash, general secretary of CMS. They put
what pressure they could upon the bishop to withdraw from competing with
the Lutheran missions both in the north-east and in Bukoba. In October 1930
he agreed not to press for Anglican missionary work among Africans in the
Arusha-Moshi area, but he was not prepared to abandon his scheme for Bukoba.

In 1931, however, he reluctantly agreed to withdraw from the area in Bukoba north of the line 2° south latitude, provided that the Bethel mission would give up their claim to a mission site at Bugufi.[54]

In 1929, largely on the initiative of Bishop Chambers, a Christian council was formed for Central Tanganyika. Its aims were: (1) to foster the co-operation of missions in education, in the study of African languages and cultures; and in the provision of literature in these languages; (2) to promote harmonious relations and understanding between the different missions; (3) to represent the common interests of missions in questions involving relations with the government of the territory; (4) to consider such other matters affecting missionary work and native welfare as may be of common interest to the participating missions. The council included representatives of the Africa Inland Mission, the Augustana Lutheran Synod; the Berlin I, Bethel, Leipzig, Moravian, and Neukirchen missions; the CMS and the UMCA. The council proved its value particularly in the sphere of education.

As in Kenya, missionary 'alliance' led to exploration of the possibilities of a united church, and in 1934 Bishop Chambers presided over a church union conference at Mvumi at which six missions were represented. General approval was given by the conference to a basis of union for the church in East Africa as proposed by the continuation committee on church union in Nairobi in July 1933. No significant further progress was made in the period under review.

Missions and Government in Education, 1910–42

After the first world war, as already recorded, Bishop Heywood of Mombasa made co-operation with the government in education a priority in his oversight of the CMS mission in Central Tanganyika. In September 1921 he met the Director of Education, Mr S. Rivers-Smith, at Dar es Salaam and reported hopefully on the prospect of government grants-in-aid. The governor, Sir Horace Byatt, was discouraging. He wrote to the bishop (12th October, 1921) saying that probably a good many years must elapse before the government could come within reach of achieving its own educational aims. Until then its resources must be devoted to its own obligations, and there was no prospect of being able to subsidize the educational work of missions.[55] The bishop felt he had been let down rather badly. He wrote to the parent committee suggesting that the matter should be taken up by the Conference of British Missionary Societies.

Sir Horace Byatt's 'many years' were in fact cut down to a very few. A change of policy at the Colonial Office, owing much to J. H. Oldham; a more buoyant approach to the financial problems of the administration by Byatt's successor, Sir Donald Cameron; and the ability and enthusiasm of Rivers-Smith altered the situation within four years. In October 1925 an educational conference was held at Dar es Salaam between government officials and representatives of all the major missions. A sub-committee of the conference recommended government grants for teacher-training schools, girls' boarding schools, infant welfare training, central schools, industrial schools, elementary (village) schools and holiday schools. The Director of Education assured the missionary representatives that the 'conscience clause' currently proposed as a condition of government grants in Kenya was not contemplated in Tanganyika, but that the educational standards of village mission schools would have to come into line with government standards. Both CMS and UMCA would have a representative on an educational advisory committee for the territory.[56]

The mission executive committee lost no time in submitting to the parent committee a detailed plan for educational advance in line with the conference proposals. The main items of the plan were: (1) the provision at Kongwa of a 'normal school' for training schoolmasters, with a two-year course – provision also being made for the training of ordinands in the same institution; (2) a girls' boarding-school at Buigiri; (3) a central school for boys at Handali; (4) additional certificated staff to serve in a new central school and in the girls' boarding-school at Berega.[57] The scheme for government grants-in-aid to missionary education was quickly implemented. Briggs was able to report in November 1925 that grants to a total of £11,000 had been allocated for 1926; and the grants would be made on the strength of teachers' qualifications without waiting for examination results.

Co-operation developed smoothly at first from this excellent start, but in February 1927 the Tanganyika government published a native education ordinance which laid down tougher conditions for grants-in-aid. Under the ordinance all schools were to be regarded as under government supervision. No new school could be opened unless requested by the responsible body in a district, and in each case the provincial commissioner must satisfy himself that a school was needed and that the minimum staff was available. 'Bush schools' not conforming to the standards laid down by the government must be closed within five years. In all but the highest grades of primary schools instruction was to be given in Swahili. In central schools the four-year course was to be exclusively in English. No teachers were to work in government-assisted schools unless registered as first or second grade teachers. Religious instruction could only be given outside school hours.

The world economic depression was soon to affect the capacity of both missions and government to further their educational aims. The prosperity of the territory did not last into the 1930s, and the retirement of Rivers-Smith meant that his valuable initiatives in co-operation were withdrawn at a time when his wisdom and insight were badly needed. There was also some difference in educational aims between mission and government. The government believed it had the support of African opinion in working for high standards in 'literary' education along Western lines with as much English as possible. The missions were afraid of the kind of intellectual inflation which would produce an unhealthy caricature of 'white' civilization, and tended to think that industrial or vocational education, taking full account of African culture, would produce better long-term results; and they regarded the government syllabus as too academic; but by 1941 there was a new readiness by the government to recognize the value of all-round practical training.[58] The 1927 education ordinance was not applied in all its rigour to the bush schools. Eventually, through a system of selected sub-grade schools, the large majority of them did achieve registered status and qualified for grants-in-aid.[59] Higher up the educational ladder the Mvumi girls' school, under Miss Gladys Taylor, won high praise from the local community. Fathers were so impressed by its effect on their daughters that they put up their bride-price from seven cows to twenty-four.

During the 1930s the executive committee of the mission, and its successor, the diocesan council, made persistent efforts to remedy the 'defectiveness of missionary organization' which J. H. Oldham had singled out as the chief cause of difficulties in co-operation with government education departments in East Africa.[60] In September 1932, for example, the executive committee recommended the provision of school councils for all the boarding schools and teacher-training colleges of the diocese.[61] In August 1938 the diocesan council received from a sub-committee a memorandum on 'Educational Policy for the Diocese of Central Tanganyika'. It laid down the basis for a policy for education in co-operation with the government which was largely implemented in the next decade. At the bottom of the pyramid were the single village schools, standards I and II. These were to lead on to primary village schools, standards I to V, in suitable centres, giving special attention to handcrafts and African native industries. It was recommended that boarding-hostels be attached to these schools, as they would serve a large area. The number of primary schools was to be limited to the ability of the mission, with government grants, to make adequate provision for staff and equipment. The curriculum should not be exclusively 'vocational'. The memorandum proposed a permanent education committee for the diocese, to meet annually before the meeting of the diocesan council. The Rev. O. T. Cordell, as supervisor of village schools, had already done much to develop a network of village schools feeding primary schools at each of the main mission stations: and the organization of education was carried further by Canon Banks as supervisor and diocesan education secretary.

The Training of Clergy and Catechists

Brief mention has already been made of the attempt to establish a clergy-training institution at Kongwa in the years immediately before the first world war. Doulton, as mission secretary, had been pressing for it at the end of 1909, and early in 1912 the executive committee of the mission agreed that the mission house at Kongwa should be adapted and extended for this purpose.[62] In 1913 the parent committee appointed Dr Westgate as principal of the CMS training institution at Kongwa. The cost of alterations to the mission house (£225) had been already promised from Canada. For this reason, and on Dr Westgate's suggestion, it was given the name of Huron Training College.

A new two-storey building of native granite, begun in August 1913, was almost complete when the first world war broke out a year later; but the war, and Westgate's return to Canada in 1917, delayed the development of the college. In December 1919 Archdeacon Rees accepted the post of principal in succession to Westgate and served until his death in 1924. During the first three years seventy men, representing fifteen tribes, passed through the college, to serve as catechists and teachers. It was not until July 1926 that the executive committee of the mission was able to approve the completion of the buildings in accordance with the pre-war plans. The parent committee sanctioned a special appeal for this by the Bishop of Mombasa during his visit to Australia: and agreed that it should be named the CMS Training Institution, Huron Training College being no longer appropriate.[63]

In November 1928 it was decided that teacher training should be moved to the new diocesan headquarters at Dodoma, the Kongwa site being retained for the training of catechists and clergy. In 1930–1 there were forty-five students in training under the Rev. W. Wynn Jones. They included five students from the Moravian mission. At first most students had come from missionaries' houses, but later they came from village schools and from the central boys' school at Dodoma. The impression gained from mission records is that the training of evangelists and clergy suffered in Central Tanganyika as elsewhere in East Africa from lack of continuity in leadership, and from rather rapid changes of principal. The college at Kongwa was closed for a time in the later 1930s, but re-opened for short courses for evangelists in August 1941.

Medical Mission, 1910–42

Towards the end of his long service Dr E. J. Baxter had built a temporary hospital at Mamboya, but plans for a modern hospital there were halted by his retirement in 1912. Various suggestions were made about a new hospital site further west to serve the new areas of mission development. In 1919 Dr R. Y. Stones opened a temporary hospital at Dodoma, and the local governing body favoured Dodoma as the permanent site for a medical mission; but the government decided to build their own hospital there and the search for a permanent site for a mission hospital was resumed. In 1922 Dr Stones left Tanganyika for Maseno hospital in Kenya, and for the next six years there was no qualified doctor attached to the mission. Kilimatinde gradually gained favour as a suitable centre for the development of medical missionary work. There was a small leper settlement at Makutupora, about ten miles from there, which the government was prepared to hand over to the mission. In November 1928 the executive committee of the mission located Miss V. H. Hobbs to Kilimatinde for general medical work in preparation for a full-scale medical mission, and application was made for a government grant for her maternity work.[64]

In 1929 Dr R. M. Buntine arrived and, after making a survey of medical needs, recommended Kilimatinde as the site for a base mission hospital. At first it was thought that the former German fort could be adapted for this purpose, but this was turned down because the spirillum tick was found to be still active in the rubble. However, Buntine for a time used the upper floor of the fort as a temporary ward and operating theatre. Sister E. G. Hempel, in a manuscript account of the first twenty-five years of Kilimatinde hospital, pays tribute to Buntine's skill as a surgeon under primitive conditions, without trained African staff.[65] The Makutupora leper settlement was accepted as a responsibility of the mission, with an annual grant in aid from the government of £200.

Buntine wanted to start a leper treatment centre at Kilimatinde itself, and he appears to have gone ahead with this project without his colleagues' approval, making personal appeals for help to leprosy relief organizations without the customary consultation. On 28th March, 1931 he wrote to the Mission to Lepers, somewhat unwisely suggesting that money sent out for leper work might be appropriated in the field for other purposes. This supposition was stated by the executive committee to be 'absolutely untrue'; and Dr Buntine was asked to refrain from repeating such statements in future. The committee sent the doctor a memorandum on procedures and responsibilities in medical work. It is worth quoting as a comment on authority in mission and diocese as it was conceived at this time. The memorandum stated emphatically that funds available for leprosy in the diocese were at the bishop's disposal, 'as the Mission to Lepers understands'; that a fundamental condition of service in the CMS was that every worker should accord to the bishop his rightful place as head of the church in the diocese. All communications about leprosy work should be made through the secretary of the committee, acting for the bishop. The memorandum drew attention to Dr Cyril Wallace's appointment as medical superintendent of leper work in the diocese, including the Makutupora settlement, and requested Buntine to proceed no further with building a leprosy centre at Kilimatinde. He should confine his work to general medicine only at Kilimatinde hospital.[66]

Buntine returned to Australia in October 1932 for family reasons; but by that time the new buildings at Kilimatinde hospital were almost finished, and they came into use on 30th March, 1933. They had been planned by Buntine, in conjunction with Banks, the station missionary, who in April wrote of the relief it was 'to get away from the old German fort'.[67] In August 1933 Dr Wallace moved from Berega to take over Buntine's work at Kilimatinde. Two years later the diocesan council located him to the Makutupora leper settlement 'for research and for more intense medical treatment'.[68] The settlement developed considerably under his leadership. In 1937 he reported that thirty leper houses had been built, and twenty more were planned. A stone church was built at Makutupora, a gift from the Australian Mission to Lepers, and a number of small leper cottages with cement floors and corrugated iron roofs were given by friends in Northern Ireland.

In 1938 another doctor, Paul White, arrived from Australia and was located to Mvumi. In a very short time, with specially allocated donations from Australia, he developed a hospital there which replaced Kilimatinde as the main medical centre of the mission. A men's ward and operating theatre and a pathological laboratory were soon built. White succeeded Wallace as medical secretary of the diocese in 1939, but in 1940 he had to return to Australia owing to a breakdown of his wife's health. He had endeared himself both to missionaries and Africans and became well-known through a series of 'Jungle Doctor books' which achieved a wide circulation.

Infant welfare became an increasingly important part of the medical work of the diocese, and clinics for this purpose developed rapidly in the late 1930s. Statistics for 1942 show that, in spite of setbacks, medical missionary work had become an important part of the witness of the mission and diocese. In that year 116,000 out-patients were treated; 2,879 in-patients; 1,309 maternity cases, and African dressers carried out 6,701 pathological examinations. Mission funds provided £1,520 for the hospitals and the government grant, for seven hospital sisters, amounted to £892 10s od.

Literature and Bookshops, 1910–42

In the period immediately before the first world war, J. H. Briggs and E. W. Doulton were both engaged in translating the Old Testament into Cigogo, the language of the western part of the German East Africa mission, and upon the preparation of hymn-books and prayer-books in Cigogo and Swahili with the help of SPCK and RTS. This work continued after the war when there was urgent need for replacement as existing stocks had been largely destroyed.

In 1933 a joint committee on the revision of the Swahili prayer book and hymn book was set up by the dioceses of Mombasa and Central Tanganyika. There were considerable differences in orthography between Mombasa and Zanzibar Swahili, and the diocesan council of Central Tanganyika decided to delay reprinting their versions until the joint committee had reported.[69] In the following year, the diocesan council agreed to a reprint of the Mombasa Swahili prayer book for general use with the spelling altered to the Zanzibar form, and incorporating a new Zanzibar version of the Psalms. This was a temporary expedient while the work of preparing revisions in standardized Swahili went ahead.

Soon after the formation of the diocese in November 1928, the general conference of missionaries recommended the opening of a bookshop at Dodoma and at the same time asked the bishop to inform the Bishop of Zanzibar that the

CMS could not accept shared responsibility for a bookshop in Dar es Salaam. The bishop hoped for a loan from SPCK and W. E. Hoyle, manager of the successful diocesan bookshop in Uganda, warmed to the idea of opening bookshops not only at Dodoma but at Bukoba and possibly Moshi.[70] The negotiations with SPCK broke down; but in 1931 the diocese agreed to take over the local agency of the British and Foreign Bible Society. The Dodoma bookshop had only a short life. The turn-over and demand were not sufficient, apparently, to justify an inland bookshop at that time. In 1933 the bishop told the diocesan council that the Dodoma shop had been closed and its manager, L. Frost, had moved to Dar es Salaam to become assistant manager of the UMCA bookshop there. (It was taken over by SPCK five years later.) The bishop stressed the desirability of using the Dar es Salaam shop both for personal and school needs, as the mission and diocese would benefit financially.

The episode of the Dodoma bookshop is perhaps symptomatic of the strength and weakness of the young diocese of Central Tanganyika. With an enthusiastic and able bishop and a rapid influx of new recruits from Australia, a number of new projects were undertaken, not all of them viable in the long run. Such self-confidence was natural in the circumstances, but the long-term future of the diocese lay in co-operation with other Anglican dioceses in an East African province. The gradual realization that, without compromising its evangelical convictions, the diocese of Central Tanganyika could share in at least some common undertakings with the UMCA dioceses, laid the necessary foundation on which a future province could be built. The development of missionary education in co-operation with the government, to which Archdeacon Ralph Banks gave much time and skill over many years, ensured a Christian background for many of the future leaders of the country.

NOTES

1. For these and other statistics see D. Julius Richter, *Tanganyika and its Future*, World Dominion Press, 1934.

2. Z. A. Marsh and G. Kingsnorth, *An Introduction to the History of East Africa*, Cambridge, 1957, pp. 229, 230.

3. George Delf, *Asians in East Africa*, Oxford, 1963, p. 29.

4. A. J. Hughes, *East Africa: the Search for Unity*, Penguin, 1963, pp. 49–51.

5. Quoted Richter, op. cit., pp. 12, 13.

6. Hughes, op. cit., pp. 51–9.

7. Roland Oliver, *The Missionary Factor in East Africa*, Longmans, 1952, pp. 203, 204.

8. ibid., p. 234.

9. One of several Berlin societies, see Oliver, op. cit., pp. 165–7.

10. At first called the Central Africa Mission, then the UMCA for over a hundred years, it joined forces with the SPG in 1965 to form the United Society for the Propagation of the Gospel.

11. J. H. Briggs, *In the East African War Zone*, CMS, 1918, pp. 11, 12.

12. G3/A8, P1, 1910/1.

13. P1, 1912/4.

14. P1, 1912/15.

15. P1, 1912/12.

16. P1, 1912/16.

17. P1, 1913/4.

18. CMS *Annual Report*, 1910–11, p. 59; 1913–14, p. 62.

19. P1, 1916/18.

20. P1, 1917/19.

21. Banks MSS, 'History of the Diocese of Central Tanganyika', p. 11.

22. P1, 1917/7.

23. Banks MSS, minutes of mission executive committee 26th, 28th November, 3rd, 4th December, 1919 (23).

24. CMS *Annual Report*, 1920–1, p. xxvi.

25. P1, 1922/1.

26. P1, 1922/iv, x.

27. P1, 1925/40.

28. P1, 1925/43.

29. *AR* (MS), 1927–8, p. 68.

30. P1, 1916/27.

31. P1, 1917/20.

32. P1, 1926/20.

33. P1, 1926/22, 27, iii, iv.

34. Banks MSS, letter of 27th May, 1926.

35. P1, 1927/14.

36. G. A. Chambers, *Tanganyika's New Day*, CMS, 1931, Nancy de S. P. Sibtain, with Winifred M. Chambers, *Dare to Look Up: A Memoir of George Alexander Chambers*, Angus and Robertson, 1968, esp. pp. 41–87.

37. P1, 1929/1.

38. P1, 1929/27.

39. P1, 1930/22.

40. P1, 1932/31.

41. P1, 1933/20.

42. Banks MSS, diocesan council minutes, 1st–3rd September, 1937 (11).

43. P1, 1933/20.

44. Banks MSS, letter of 10th July, 1938.

45. Banks MSS, report on 1941 synod, p. 7.

46. P1, 1910/55; xxiv.

47. P1, 1911/8, 28.

48. P1, 1911/49; 1913/9.

49. P1, 1920/40, 17.

50. P1, 1921/34.

51. P1, 1921/31.

52. Carl-J. Hellberg, *Missions on a Colonial Frontier West of Lake Victoria*, Gleerups, Lund, 1965, pp. 206ff.

53. op. cit., p. 222.

54. op. cit., pp. 222–35.

55. P1, 1921/51.

56. P1, 1925/37, 38.

57. Banks MSS, report on CMS Tanganyika mission for 1925.

58. Richter, op. cit., p. 67; *AR* (MS) 1940–1, pp. 51–2.

59. Banks MSS, 'History of the Diocese of Central Tanganyika', p. 42.
60. P1, 1930/17.
61. Banks MSS, minutes of executive committee, 28th, 29th September, 1932, (17).
62. P1, 1912/16.
63. P1, 1926/7, viii.
64. P1, 1929/2.
65. Banks MSS, Miss E. G. Hempel, 'The Growth of a Hospital 1928–53', p. 8.
66. Banks MSS, minutes of mission executive committee, 8th to 12th April, 1932.
67. Banks MSS, letter of 22nd April, 1933.
68. Banks MSS, minutes of diocesan council, 10th to 14th May, 1935 (26).
69. Banks MSS, minutes of diocesan council, 27th July to 1st August, 1933 (13, 14).
70. P1, 1929/40.

Uganda

The Kingdom of Uganda is a fairy tale. . . . The scenery is different, the vegetation is different, the climate is different and, most of all, the people are different from anything elsewhere to be seen in the whole range of Africa.[1]

Winston Churchill wrote this after a visit to Uganda in 1907 when he was Under-Secretary of State for the Colonies. He summed up the first impressions of many less exalted visitors since that time. There is something 'different' about Uganda. The missionaries certainly felt it to be so.

In missionary circles Uganda became a symbol of all that the nineteenth century missionary movement hoped for and prayed for. The constancy of the pioneer missionaries such as Alexander Mackay, the fortitude of the young Baganda martyrs in 1885–6, the general openness to the proclamation of the Christian gospel; the rapid growth of a 'self-governing, self-supporting, and self-extending' African church – all these things gave the missionaries who served there a sense of privilege. There was no clearer instance in the colonial era of the cross preceding the flag.[2]

Uganda (from 1926 onwards) has covered an area of some 94,000 square miles, of which nearly 14,000 square miles are open water; thus, by African standards, it is a small country, with a land area less than that of England and Scotland together, fairly square in shape, approximately three hundred and fifty miles from east to west, and four hundred miles from north to south. Although its political and economic development has been orientated to East Africa, it is five hundred miles at the nearest point from the Indian Ocean, and its flora and fauna relate it rather to the centre and west of Africa.[3] It is for the most part highland plateau, 4,000 feet above sea level, essentially grassland and tropical savannah, with a mean annual rainfall of fifty inches. It is bounded on the west by the sharp, snow-capped Ruwenzori range of mountains; on its eastern border

with Kenya rises the great mass of Mount Elgon; to the south lies Tanzania;
to the south-west, Rwanda and Burundi; to the west, the Congo; and to the
north, the Sudan. Its southern boundary, crossing Lake Victoria at latitude 1°
south and continuing in a straight line to the Congo border, dates from 1890
and is a reminder of colonial map-making which has survived the colonial
period.

A tribal map of Uganda[4] shows the Victoria Nile as a main dividing line.
South-west of the Nile lie the Bantu kingdoms – Buganda in a broad wedge
immediately north and west of Lake Victoria; Bunyoro to the north-west of
Buganda across the Rivers Nkusi and Kafu; Toro to the west; and Ankole to the
south-west, south of Lake George and the River Katonga. North and east of the
Nile (apart from Busoga, nearest to Lake Victoria) the tribes are mainly Nilotic
(Lango and Acholi), Nilo-Hamitic (Teso and Karamoja) and in the west Nile
district at the north-west corner of Uganda, Nilotic (Alur) and Sudanic (Lugbara
and Madi). The 1931 census gave the races of Uganda as follows (figures
rounded to 1,000): Bantu 2,323,000; Nilotes 700,000; Half-Hamites 470,000.[5]
The population rose from 2,843,000 (1911) to 3,554,000 (1931) and more
rapidly thereafter to 7,189,600 (1963). A language analysis in the 1930s showed
that Bantu languages were spoken by 2,348,000 – Luganda by 950,000 (in
Buganda and Busoga); Lunyoro by 665,000 (in Bunyoro, Toro, and Ankole);
and Bantu dialects, more or less related to Luganda and Lunyoro, by some
418,000.[5]

The northern tribes of Uganda are traditionally cattle people, and the tribes
and kingdoms of the centre and the south are predominantly agriculturalist.
The richest soil is in Kigezi in the extreme south-west, and the poorest in
Karamoja territory in the north-east. Bananas were the basic food for the
Bantu peoples, and grain for the other tribes. But Uganda was changing so
rapidly to a mixed modern economy in the period 1910–42 that generalizations
of this kind progressively lost meaning. For example, the introduction of
cotton-growing into the west Nile district in the 1920s and cultivation of
tobacco in Bunyoro in the 1930s revolutionized the economy of those districts.
By 1942 the Karamoja were the only people in the protectorate who were
mostly living as they had always lived, but even there the introduction of cotton
was soon to alter the way of life for many. The railway and cotton were the
interdependent agents of rapid social change for central and eastern Uganda.

The Uganda Railway, so called until 1926, was started in 1896 and the first
locomotive ran into Port Florence (Kisumu), 587 miles from Mombasa, in
December 1901. Largely to serve the needs of cotton marketing, the Busoga
link railway of 61 miles was started in 1910 and completed in 1913. In 1928
a direct link was made between Jinja and Mombasa. Further extensions in 1928
and 1931 brought the railway to the capital, Kampala. The introduction of
cotton (1903) owes much to a CMS missionary, Kristen E. Borup, head of the
CMS industrial mission in Uganda. The first fifty-four bales of cotton were

marketed in 1904. By 1911–12 the annual product had risen to 20,433 bales, largely due to Sir Hesketh Bell's tough policy of uprooting and destroying all cotton plants that were not of the upland variety. Cotton became Uganda's chief export, and its efficient growth by Africans in small-holdings became a strong bulwark against the intrusion of European planters.

In the 1920s and 1930s a network of roads was laid down, and by 1934 there were 1,907 miles of main roads, under the care of the Public Works Department, and 5,500 miles of local roads under native administration. Encouraged by the roads mechanical transport grew rapidly. The first car was imported by Sir Hesketh Bell in 1908. By 1939, there were 6,000 cars in Uganda and 12,000 bicycles.

The early stages of the political development of Uganda in the period of British over-rule are complicated. On 14th May, 1872 Sir Samuel Baker took formal possession of Bunyoro in the name of the Khedive of Egypt. If Baker had been able to establish with Kabarega, Mukama of Bunyoro, the kind of trustful relationship which Emin Pasha achieved later in less favourable circumstances, the story of Uganda's political development might have been very different; but Kabarega's dream of recovering Toro and restraining Buganda was not realized, and he and his successors were to lose more territory to a Buganda backed by the British. It may be that in re-writing the history of the colonial period more justice will be done to Kabarega as champion of a proud and ancient people.[6] He was deposed by the British government in March 1898, and exiled with Mwanga, the Kabaka of Buganda, to the Seychelles. In 1923 he was allowed to return only to die at Jinja before reaching home. His son Kitahimbwe was also deposed by the protectorate government in 1902. Another son of Kabarega, Andareya Duhaga, was Mukama from 1902 until his death in 1924 when he was succeeded by his half-brother, Sir Tito Winyi. Although Bunyoro was allowed to keep its traditional institutions, the effective power from 1900 lay with the European collector, and later the district commissioner representing the Governor of Uganda. The intrusion of twenty Baganda chiefs into Bunyoro following the agreement of 1900 caused much resentment and agitation which came to a head in 1907. The Bunyoro agreement of 1933 restored some power to the Mukama, but it was Buganda that won the leadership of the Lakes Region for the whole of the colonial period.

'At the vital moment, the predominant element in Buganda, grouped in the new Baganda organism of the Christian party, associated with the British instead of rejecting them.'[7] On 27th August, 1894 an Order in Council made the Kingdom of Buganda a British protectorate, building on provisional treaties made earlier. In June 1896 the protectorate was extended to include Bunyoro to the north-west and Busoga to the east. Agreements with Toro (1900) and Ankole (1901) accorded them, like Buganda, the status of kingdoms.

Toro shared from the first with Buganda in such benefits of the *Pax Britannica* as the introduction of money and the promotion of local trade.[8] It was organized on the Buganda model with village and district chiefs responsible to the county chiefs who in turn were answerable to the Mukama. A British district commissioner advised the Mukama.[9]

In Ankole as in Toro the process of 'Bagandization' and the introduction of Christian teaching were also linked together.

East of the Victoria Nile there were no traditional rulers comparable to the kings of Buganda, Bunyoro, Toro and Ankole; and British administration was effectively established somewhat later. In 1919 an Authority Ordinance gave legal definition to the powers of chiefs elsewhere than in Buganda. By that time the system of administration had been stabilized and assimilated throughout the protectorate.

This political stability, and the manner in which it was achieved, was a significant factor in the success of the Christian missions and the growth of the Christian church. The special position of Buganda, and of the Kabaka's government within the protectorate, was also a favourable factor in the missionary situation. Under the Uganda agreement of 10th March, 1900, the three missionary societies working in Uganda at that time – the White Fathers, the CMS and the Mill Hill Fathers – were recognized as part of the Kiganda community and were given a total grant of 92 square miles of *mailo* land, later increased to 104 square miles. A close relationship developed between the Anglican missionary leaders and the Kabaka, H. H. Daudi Chwa, his chief minister Sir Apolo Kagwa, and many leading chiefs. The Native Anglican Church owed much to their patronage in the early days, and it was not until the 1930s that the privileged position both of the Baganda political hierarchy and the relationship to it of the CMS mission and the Native Anglican Church was seriously questioned. At an earlier stage the missionaries from time to time felt it necessary to make their voice heard in social issues, but these issues, which now demand attention, were on nothing like the same scale of divisiveness as in neighbouring Kenya.

Social Questions, 1910–42

One matter which caused anxiety was *compulsory labour*. Clause 14 of the Uganda Agreement, 1900, gave county chiefs the right to call out labourers for road maintenance for not more than one month in each year, in the proportion of one labourer for every three huts or houses. Also, until 1921, there was liability for paid labour for up to two months in a year on protectorate government public works. This compulsory labour was always unpopular and caused increasing resentment. Bishop Tucker was much concerned about this issue in 1910. He attributed the depopulation of Busoga (from 1,000,000 to 200,000) to forced labour as well as to famine and sleeping sickness. He had no doubt that the diminished marriage rate in Uganda was also due to forced labour.[10] The bishop protested to the acting-governor of Uganda and was assured on the point that most worried him – the supply of compulsory labour to traders was not approved or intended by the government. 'When a man has paid his poll tax and done his month's work on the roads he is free to work as he pleases.'[11] In 1920 the *Lukiko* (the Buganda council or parliament), on the initiation of the protectorate government, made the *luwalo* an individual obligation on all males over eighteen years, prescribing work for eight days in every quarter on public works projects. This could be commuted for 10s payment by men employed on longer contracts. Commutation became more and more frequent and incidentally provided the Buganda government with a considerable extra revenue,[12] but the *luwalo* obligation, commuted or otherwise, remained an irritant and it contributed to the growing resentment against the authority of chiefs in the 1930s and 1940s. In 1929 Archdeacon W. E. Owen of Nyanza wrote to the *Manchester Guardian* and the *East African Standard* protesting against the use of compulsory labour in laying the railway from Jinja to Kampala; but he was not supported by the Uganda CMS mission committee who were satisfied with the procedure in calling out this labour and claimed that there had been no complaints.[13]

In 1912 a special committee under W. Morris Carter was appointed by the protectorate government to advise on land settlement in Busoga, Bunyoro, Toro and Ankole. It proposed applying to these areas and others the *mailo* system used in the 1900 Uganda agreement. It was intended that the estates should be held in freehold and thus could be sold by the owners to European planters. The issue was an important one for Uganda in view of what was happening in Kenya. In 1923 the Colonial Office ruled that definite areas should be demarcated in which there would be no alienation of land to non-Africans; and chiefs were not, as in the Uganda agreement, to be granted private estates. In 1921 the *Lukiko* had ruled against permitting any further sale of land to non-Africans and this ruling was approved by the governor in 1922. In the early 1930s rights of alienation of land became an issue between the Kabaka, who published a pamphlet claiming that freehold implied freedom to sell to anyone, and the *Lukiko*, who held to their 1921 position. The governor, Sir Bernard Bourdillon, persuaded the Kabaka to fall into line with his council.[14]

Another land-holding matter, of considerable political importance, concerned the ownership of certain local sites by the *bataka* or clan-heads in Buganda. The Kabaka, H. H. Edward Mutesa, claimed justifiably that the 1900 agreement was a triumph for the 'new men' in power at the time. It changed the Lukiko from a levée, called at the Kabaka's pleasure, to an institution; and it 'totally ignored' the *bataka*.[15] The *bataka* were outside the ruling hierarchy, but in the early 1920s they began to press their claims. They founded the Bataka Association in 1921, and in the year following submitted to the Kabaka a list of properties which they claimed had been illegally seized by the chiefs in the land settlement. The matter eventually reached the Colonial Secretary, L. S. Amery, who censured the regents for the way they used their powers of land allocation during the minority of the Kabaka, but ruled that the present owners must remain in possession of the *bataka* estates.

In 1914 unwelcome attention was drawn to the CMS Uganda mission by an 'open letter' in *John Bull*, 10th October, 1914. It was addressed to Sir John Kennaway, the president of the CMS, accusing missionaries of exploiting land sold under compulsory development. Some missionaries in Toro had taken up leases of land. W. E. Owen, in an interview at CMS headquarters on 28th October, 1914, explained that the protectorate government let land on a three years' lease to be followed by freehold, if during the three years 10s an acre had been spent upon it. Owen, who wanted to test the issue, had written to the governor, who explained that for 640 acres he must have at least £2,000 guaranteed by his bankers and at his disposal for the benefit of this land. Owen thought it would not be possible for anyone to take up land who was not a resident in, or who had not at least visited Uganda, though there was nothing in the lease to this effect.[16]

Millar, the mission secretary, was a good deal worried by this matter before the *John Bull* open letter. 'When almost half the staff on the stations have taken up land,' he wrote (27th July, 1914), 'you can hardly wonder at outsiders finding fault with them.' The following January he thanked the parent committee for its support to the local governing body discouraging the practice. Most missionaries, he said, 'apparently have managers, and so do not look after the land themselves.'[17] A resolution of the parent committee made it clear that the principle that land should not be taken up by missionaries applied equally to land held by a missionary's wife, or by a missionary on behalf of his wife.[18]

Mention must be made of two constitutional crises in Buganda, each involving the resignation of a *Katikiro*, or chief minister. The first was in 1926 when Sir Apolo Kagwa was forced into retirement after sharp exchanges with J. P. Postlethwaite, Acting Provincial Commissioner of Buganda. The Kabaka was moving towards the same conclusion as Postlethwaite, but he did not wish to make the decision himself; he asked Dr A. R. Cook, head of the CMS hospital at Mengo, to advise the Katikiro's resignation. Cook refused to do so unless the Kabaka officially requested his opinion. Finally Sir Apolo Kagwa, under a mounting pressure of criticism, returned his staff of office. He died in the next year, 1927. He had been Katikiro for thirty-seven years, and the powers of his office had been enhanced by the 1900 agreement which made the Katikiro, and not the Kabaka, chairman of the Lukiko. He had been a stalwart supporter of the CMS from its early days in Uganda, and an outstanding leader in the Native Anglican Church. King's School, Budo, the Gayaza girls' high school, and the rebuilding of Namirembe cathedral (1911–19) owed a great deal to his personal interest and generosity.

Sir Apolo's resignation was perhaps inevitable. A new generation of protectorate officials was pressing for more efficient government, and the result of the constitutional crises was to establish the right of administrative officers to deal directly with Baganda chiefs, and not only through the Kabaka and his hierarchy.

In 1941 another Katikiro, Martin Luther Nsibirwa, was forced into resignation, this time by the Lukiko directly. The *Namasole* (Queen Mother), Lady Irene Drusilla, widow of H. H. Daudi Chwa, wished to marry a young commoner. In pre-Christian Uganda the re-marriage of the Queen Mother was unthinkable. There was a strong and immediate popular reaction against the marriage. Bishop Stuart and the leading CMS missionaries supported her right to do so. Very few of the Christian chiefs stood with them. Nsibirwa had the courage to do so, and the *Lukiko* put him out of office.[19] The *Namasole* was excluded from the court and deprived of her estates and allowance. The fact that she was the daughter of a clergyman of the Native Anglican Church told against her at a time of growing hostility to European influence.

By the early 1940s new strains and tensions were evident – resentment in the rest of the protectorate, particularly in Bunyoro, against the special position of Buganda under British over-rule: tension between the Lukiko and the protectorate government over administrative inefficiency in Buganda; discontent by the dispossessed *bataka*, and against the Buganda hierarchy; and by the younger generation in Buganda and elsewhere against chiefs and landowners. This was especially evident in 1942 among young Ugandans returning from military service in the Abyssinian campaign. The distinctive pattern of Westernization in Uganda, which had given the Christian mission an unusual opportunity, was being challenged with Western techniques of protest. Church membership began to decline under pressure of new political awareness allied to a reassertion of traditional tribal religion.

Traditional Religion

'Let Western minds make their inductive and precious generalizations; Africa, if she is true to herself, remains stubbornly inarticulate'.[20]

This warning by J. V. Taylor, a former Uganda missionary, later general secretary of the CMS, stands over anything that is now written on the subject of African traditional religion. Most, if not all, pioneer missionaries assumed that somewhere amid the complicated clusters of myths, legends and clan-rituals, there was some discernment, however obscured, of a 'high god' which would serve as a link with Christian theism. Some distinguished contemporary students of African religions support this assumption with detailed tribal studies. But F. B. Welbourn produces evidence for the contrary view. He argues that this apparent monotheism or henotheism 'is the result of assimilation, on the part of the old gods of the tribe to the God of Islam or Christianity' – the result of an understandable desire not to be outclassed by the intruders' claim to superiority in the field of religion as in everything else. He gives as an example the assertion by some Baganda that their many gods have never been the satellites of Katonda.

He recognizes the possibility that there may have been an original Creator-God, of whom Katonda, Muwanga and Ogulu may all be relics 'but recorded observations, over more than eighty years, cannot justify the claim that any of these was more than "the leader of the gods" – a role different from that of being their creator and absolute lord'.[21] In the light of Welbourn's comment and evidence one is bound to approach with caution such recent statements as F. P. Faupel's that 'the ancient religion of the Baganda, before the importation of the Sese Islands' gods, was monotheistic'.[22]

A more remarkable instance of the danger of monotheistic assumptions occurs in relation to the Acholi people of north-eastern Uganda. A standard work in the 1930s, following no doubt the best current opinion, states that 'the Acholi, Lango, Jopadola and Lugbara have essentially monotheistic religions, Jok, the supreme being of the Acholi and Lango, being regarded with a reverence which appears almost Semitic in spirit'.[23] More recently, however, p'Bitek Okot, himself an Acholi, has denied that there is one Creator-Jok, in the religion of his people – there are only many *jogi*. J. K. Russell, formerly Bishop in Northern Uganda, is firmly behind Okot.

> Jogi are not gods, still less God. They are . . . clan or chiefdom spirits which represent the corporate existence of the clan; spirits of known relatives; spirits of unknown persons and dangerous beasts. All are continuously and geographically present and intimately concerned with the day-to-day life of the clan . . . Jogi are not worshipped . . . They are invited to take their seats as aldermen rather than councillors, on the joint council of the living and the dead which regulates the affairs of the clan and the family group.[24]

Neither the Roman Catholic nor the Anglican pioneer missionaries used the work *jok* for God. In Lango and Acholi the former used *Rubanga* and the latter *Lubanga*. It would seem that both groups of missionaries, coming eastwards from Bunyoro, used the name of a subsidiary deity called *Ruhanga* around whose exploits Lunyoro creation myths gathered,[25] but the Acholi had no letter 'h' in their language. There was, however, in Acholi traditional religion a Jok called Lubanga, one of a group of dangerous spirits who was thought to be responsible for tuberculosis of the spine, and was therefore much feared and hated. So as Bishop Russell suggests, the use of Lubanga as the name for God by the early missionaries must have caused considerable bewilderment – though it did not prevent the very rapid growth of the Christian church among the Acholi in the 1920s and 1930s. (See Upper Nile chapter.)

Generalizations about a primitive, unchanging animism seem as liable to prove mistaken as generalizations about a primitive monotheism.[26] Taylor writes of the nature-divinities in the Yoruba pantheon and the *Balubaale* of the Baganda, including lords of earth and death, of rainbow, lightning and plague.

> It could be [he says] that all these represent an earlier, animistic stage in African religion before the great tribal ancestors and hero-gods took pride

of place. . . . It seems, rather, that these nature-divinities also are essentially human heroes whose power has become identified with that of a particular natural phenomenon that was at one time associated with them. . . . Nature worship is not characteristic of Africa in the sense that natural objects are peopled with non-human spirits.[27]

In a matter so complex, and in which a great deal of research is still going on, it is wiser to speak of pointers rather than conclusions, but perhaps it is fair to say this: (1) Ugandan tribes exhibit in their religious traditions most of the African spectrum from a genuine monotheism to polytheism; (2) at the mono-theist end of the spectrum there is no certain evidence of a widespread belief in a 'high god', belief in whom could ease the path to belief in the God and Father of the Lord Jesus Christ; (3) the insights of the African world-view are still dominant, as Taylor suggests, 'in the thinking of perhaps the majority of convinced and obedient Christians';[28] (4) and, again following J. V. Taylor, the revival of a neo-African culture, and the rejection of Western systems of thought and valuation, discernible in the late 1930s, has developed considerably since, and may go a great deal further. The assumption, however, that this movement will necessarily reject Christianity is no more valid than the earlier assumption that Christianity in Africa must hold to the traditional European modes of expression if syncretism and a drift back into 'paganism' are to be avoided.

The immensely rapid response of Uganda (not only of the Baganda) to the proclamation of the Christian gospel remains a mystery. Social and political factors favourable to this proclamation have been discussed above (pages 207, 208). Another pointer of great importance is the identification of the new religion with education – the designation of Christian adherents as 'readers' was much more than a convenient missionary term. It was an apt description of how the converts and inquirers thought of themselves. The fact that Roman Catholic and Anglican proclamation of the gospel in Uganda produced a response so similar in growth-rate and volume is also puzzling. It appears that the change from traditional direction to 'inner' direction in religion could as readily take the form of devotion to the Blessed Virgin as of a personal conviction by the Holy Spirit of sin, of judgment, and of salvation related primarily to the cross of Christ. The witness of the martyrs, both Catholic and Protestant, in the holocaust of 1885–6, to a God whose demands not even an absolute monarch could defy, was a powerful element in the building-up of the churches and it bound them together, even when active fellowship and co-operation were minimal; and though, by the 1930s, third generation *malaise* was all too evident, the martyr-tradition was kept alive. Apolo Kivebulaya, Musa Ali and scores of others continued to demonstrate in faithful lives that God can still be met with in history.

Islam, 'the religion of the Arabs', had initial successes in Uganda comparable with those of Christianity and approximately in the same period. Islam grew and spread, in Uganda as elsewhere, largely through Arab traders; and in Busoga in the 1920s the number of Muslims outnumbered Roman Catholics and were not far short of Protestant adherents (1921 census: Muslims 7,687; Protestants 9,687: Roman Catholics 3,816). The leader of Islam in Uganda was for many years Nuhu Mbogo, a brother of Mutesa I. After surrendering to Lugard in 1892 he was recognized as county chief of Butambala and received a land settlement under the 1900 Buganda agreement of twenty-four square miles 'for himself and his adherents'. He died in 1921.

Most African Muslims in Uganda are of the *Sunni* (Orthodox) school, but, stimulated by several visits from the Aga Khan, the Ismaili Khoja, a Shi'a sect, became increasingly prominent in the Asian community. The mosque on Kibuli Hill, Kampala, built by Mbogo's family became the nerve centre of orthodox Islam in Uganda. It is frankly Indian in design and symbolizes the important role played by Asians in the growing economy of Uganda. They came with the railway and spread widely as traders through the protectorate. Although not as numerous or politically significant as their fellow-countrymen in Kenya there were over twelve thousand Indians in Uganda by 1931, when the Hindus among them slightly out-numbered the Muslims.

Roman Catholic Missions

In February 1878 Pope Leo XIII approved Bishop Lavigerie's plans for a Central African mission, primarily to confront with the Christian gospel the encroaching forces of Islam. One of the four Vicariates Apostolic proposed by Lavigerie, the Nyanza vicariate, was entrusted to his own society of missionaries of Africa, the 'White Fathers'.

The story of the early days of the White Fathers' mission, and of the agony of the persecution of 1885–6, has been well told by Father F. P. Faupel in *African Holocaust*. In 1894 the Nyanza vicariate was divided. The eastern part, across the Victoria Nile, became the vicariate of the Upper Nile and was entrusted to the St Joseph's Society for Foreign Missions, Mill Hill, the 'Mill Hill Fathers'. The White Fathers retained the western part, now to be known as the vicariate of North Nyanza. In the same year, 1894, the area north of Lake Albert was included in the vicariate of Central Africa, and entrusted to the Verona Fathers. At that time there were only five Roman Catholic stations in Uganda, all of them in Buganda; but the missionary zeal of Baganda converts, and the dispersion which resulted from the persecutions and from the religious wars of 1888–92, provided conditions for the rapid expansion of both the Roman Catholic and the Anglican missions.

The pattern of expansion, in terms of first resident European missionaries, was almost uniform between Roman Catholics and Anglicans, and the number of adherents in the two churches also expanded at parallel rates. In 1915 each claimed a similar number of around 186,000 adherents. By 1931 the Roman

Catholic numbers for the whole protectorate had overtaken the Protestant (406,768 to 391,947) and by 1942 the gap had widened considerably – a fact of which CMS missionaries were painfully aware. In their appeals to London for more recruits, especially for 'pastoral' missionaries, the local governing body of the CMS mission frequently commented on the great superiority in numbers of the Roman Catholic missionaries.[29]

The parallel development of the Roman Catholic and Anglican churches in Uganda is symbolized in the two vast hill-top cathedrals of Kampala, both memorials to the martyrs of 1885–6. The astonishing joint gift and achievement of the Christian missions in Uganda can be read out of the 1931 census figures. Only forty-five years after the martyrdoms 23 per cent of the total population of the protectorate is counted as Christian, and of Buganda alone, 58.4 per cent.

Only a cynic could describe the intense rivalry of Anglican and Roman Catholic missions in Uganda as 'healthy'. Each believed the other to be so seriously defective in faith and practice as to be the enemy who must be worked against in the proclamation of authentic Christianity. Yet both gained by the almost complete absence in the protectorate of other competing Christian missions such as found their way into western Kenya in the early years of the twentieth century; and they slowly came to recognize their responsibility for the Christianization of Uganda as a joint one. In the sphere of education, including medical education, from the early 1920s onwards, they worked alongside each other – hardly in partnership, but in joint co-operation with the government department of education.

From the late 1920s other Christian missions began to appear in Uganda, though their representation remained small in comparison with the CMS, the White Fathers and the Mill Hill Fathers; for example, the Seventh Day Adventists were entering Buganda from 1927 and the African Inland Mission reached the west Nile district of Uganda in 1922. By agreement with CMS all the early AIM missionaries in Uganda were Anglicans. Another Anglican society, the Bible Churchmen's Missionary Society, after prior consultation with the bishop and the CMS, began work at Karamoja in 1933.[30]

Two African Breakaway Churches

In a country where the Christian church, in both its Anglican and Roman Catholic forms, had grown so rapidly it was perhaps inevitable that dissatisfaction with a dominant European leadership should find expression in African-led 'shadow' churches, providing an outlet for convictions and socio-religious aspirations which were not being met in the larger groupings. Two such breakaway churches were the *Malakite Church* (the *Abamalaki*) founded in 1913–14; and the *African Orthodox Church*, founded in 1929.

The Malakite Church, much the larger of the two, originated with Joswa Kate. He was one of ten lay evangelists set apart and licensed by Bishop Tucker in 1893. Soon afterwards he became convinced that recourse to doctors was derogatory to the sovereignty of God, who alone was the healer. His protest was based precariously on a few biblical texts, particularly in Deut. 18.9-11, where the word 'charmer' (AV) was rendered in the Luganda Bible by *omusawo*. The word was used elsewhere for 'doctor'. In 1889 Joswa Kate was given the important office of *Mugama* in the Buganda hierarchy of chiefs. The *Mugama* was the ritual father of the Kabaka, and had important duties as guardian of the tombs of the kings and at the installation of a new Kabaka. Following the Buganda agreement of 1900 he was allotted twenty-six square miles as an indication of the importance of his office. In 1912 Joswa Mugema wrote to the Anglican diocesan synod protesting against prayers for the doctors. In the following year he was joined by Malaki Musajjakawa, a landowner and certified teacher of the Anglican Church, who was engaged in controversy with the CMS over qualifications for baptism. Against the rule of six months' instruction before baptism, Malaki maintained that John the Baptist baptized freely without instruction; and that the apostles did the same and were commended by the Lord for doing so.[31]

On 20th May, 1914 Mugema wrote to the assistant district commissioner at Entebbe, saying that his group had now separated from the CMS and had built its own church at Kitale. In August 1914 he was turned back from the coming-of-age ceremonies of Kabaka Daudi Chwa at Kampala on refusing to submit to inoculation against plague. Another eminent chief, Semei Kakunguru, from Busoga, faced with a similar demand, threw in his lot with the anti-doctor group. It soon took on the characteristics of a mass-movement. By October 1914 over 9,000 had been baptized. In the 1921 census 91,000 were registered as Malakites in Buganda alone. The movement invites comparisons with the Donatists of the early Christian period. Both the Anglican and Roman Catholic churches lost a considerable number of adherents to the Malakites, and in the appeal to non-Christians they offered attractive short-term advantages – no literacy tests or catechumenate for candidates for baptism, and no requirement of sponsors; baptism was given on acceptance of the no-doctor formula and with the bare affirmation, 'God is Almighty'. The popularity of the sect was obviously enhanced by acceptance of polygamy, on the basis of Old Testament precedents and the absence of specific prohibition in the New.

The Anglican diocesan council was seriously concerned at loss of numbers, and instituted a campaign of 'instruction and enlightenment' as 'the best method of protecting Christian people, and of winning over the heathen who have been misled'.[32] In the decade between 1921 and 1931, the numbers of the *Abamalaki* declined somewhat. Protests against vaccination and inoculation continued, however. In 1929, following a violent attack on a European sanitation officer, Mugema and Malaki were deported. Malaki died soon afterwards, in November 1929, at Kitgum in the far north of Uganda. James Biriko (who had been a catechist in the Anglican church at Katara) succeeded as the religious head of the movement. He continued to lead it for many years from headquarters in Bugerere.

The African Orthodox Church began as a more direct protest against missionary paternalism. It was founded by Reuben Spartas. Archdeacon Daniell took him as a boy into his household at Mukono. Spartas later entered King's School, Budo, with a scholarship. In 1914 he joined the African Native Medical Corps and later the King's African Rifles. In the KAR he fell in with Obadiah Basajjakitalo, and they found much in common in their discontents and hopes of remedy. Although they remained Anglicans until 1924, they were disturbed by the respect of persons shown to Anglican clergy compared with Roman Catholic priests, and by the absence of ceremonial in the worship of the Anglican Church in Uganda. Together they started a private school. In 1929 Spartas announced that he had broken with the Anglican Church in order to found the African Orthodox Church which he described as 'a church . . . for all right-thinking Africans who wish to be free in their own house, not always being thought of as "boys" '.[33] The 1931 census registered 1,512 adherents of the AOC, organized in seven congregations. In the following year Spartas and Basajjakitalo were ordained priest by Archbishop Daniel William Alexander. By 1936 Spartas claimed, extravagantly, five thousand members in the Uganda protectorate with thirty centres, and twenty-three church schools. In 1946 the Orthodox Patriarch of Alexandria took the group under his wing and nominated Spartas as his Vicar in Uganda and Kenya.

The CMS in Uganda

Retrospect, 1877–1910

The story of the early days of the Anglican mission in Uganda has been told in some detail by Dr Stock, and more recently by Dr J. V. Taylor and Mrs Mary Stuart.[34]

Only at two points in Stock's narrative would questions appear to be raised by later research. The first relates to the total number of Christian martyrs in 1885–6. Stock's estimate – 'it was supposed two hundred in all' should probably yield, after extensive research by H. B. Thomas, F. P. Faupel and others, to Faupel's estimate of about a hundred.[35] The second point on which revision seems to be necessary is that of the role of Baganda teachers in the initial evangelization of Uganda. It is not that Stock or other writers of his time had any wish to denigrate or diminish the part played by indigenous evangelists. The whole system of plotting missionary advance in terms of 'stations occupied' by resident European missionaries at a given date breaks down in the case of Uganda, where the first proclamation of the Christian message seldom required a resident European. This lack of appreciation of the achievement of Baganda evangelists is due in large measure to sheer lack of knowledge. The facts are only

now becoming capable of a just evaluation, but the work of Roland Oliver,
J. V. Taylor, J. K. Russell, B. A. Ogot, Louise Pirouet and others gives a new
perspective on this matter. Writing of missionary expansion in Uganda up to
1914, Oliver sums it up thus:

> In nearly all these vast developments the foreign missionary expansion, both
> Catholic and Anglican, had followed and not preceded the expansion of the
> faith through indigenous channels. In most of these new districts missionaries
> came at the request of the peoples, and they came to consolidate bands
> of neophytes already gathered by unordained, very often unbaptized, African
> enthusiasts who had been in contact with Christian teachings at the older
> centres.[36]

The 'violent wind of Pentecost' was doing things in Uganda in the 1890s
which broke through the categories of normal expectation. It is not surprising,
therefore, that without any intention of falsifying history, initiatives were
sometimes attributed to, or even claimed by, missionaries, which in fact
belonged to the Africans with whom they were working. This is a hard thing
to get right and it may well be necessary, before a true and balanced picture is
obtained, to reassert, though in more modest terms, the positive and essential
role of such European missionary pioneers as Pilkington, Gordon, Baskerville,
Lloyd, Fisher, Tegart and Miller – but such re-assessment of African initiatives
was needed, and is still going on.

For most of the first decade of the twentieth century Bishop Alfred Tucker was
struggling to persuade his fellow-missionaries to commit themselves fully to
one self-governing church, African and European, in Uganda. Although, as
Taylor has pointed out, Tucker was a child of his time and tended to think of
the strength of the church in terms of its ordained clergy, he was passionately
concerned that missionaries should not think of themselves as the sole ini-
tiators, leading where Africans should be expected to follow. He saw this as a
constitutional question.

> If the work of the European Missionaries [he wrote] is carried on outside the
> limits of the native Church, there must be an outside organization. In that
> case the native Christian will not be slow to realize that the outside organiza-
> tion is the one which really settles whatever questions may be under dis-
> cussion in the Church, and that their own organization is more or less a sham.
> . . . To my mind, the true attitude and spirit of the missionary towards those
> to whom he goes is included in the words: 'Forget also thine own people and
> thy father's house.' Let him therefore throw in his lot absolutely with the
> natives, identifying himself as far as possible with their life, work and organiz-
> ation. Let him submit himself to the laws and canons of their Church. Let
> him not say to his fellow-Christians: 'Go that way or this, do this or that',
> but rather 'Let us go this way or that, let us do this or that'; and the result
> in my opinion, will be a real training of the native Church in the art of self-
> government.[37]

If the chronicle that follows of the years 1910–42 appears to concentrate unduly on constitutional matters, it does so in the belief that Bishop Tucker's question was the great question facing the CMS mission in Uganda during the period – namely, since the 1909 constitution of the church left the missionaries with an organization of their own, how could this organization be made to serve the purposes of identification, and not of over-rule? For much of the time over-rule seemed to be winning: only in the later 1930s did the will to 'identify' assert itself again with any strength.

Mission and Diocese, 1910–20

In 1909 the constitution for the Anglican diocese of Uganda, which Bishop Tucker had first put forward eight years earlier, was at length approved. It was a fairly elaborate structure – diocesan synod, diocesan council, district, ruri-decanal and parish councils, central women's conference, tribunals of appeal and reference, boards of mission and education; a theological board concerned with the training of clergy, lay readers, etc., and a board of finance. The missionaries were incorporated into this constitution, according to their status as clergy, laity, rural deans and so forth; but a local missionary committee, appointed by the parent committee of CMS, was formed to deal with specifically missionary concerns and services. This duality of control, though limited in range, gave rise to a number of vexing constitutional problems in the next few decades after 1910 – the problems, for example, of the division of authority between the bishop, the mission secretary and the missionary committee, in the matter of instructions to, and location of missionaries; and the relation of each authority, and of the individual missionary, to the parent committee in London.

One such problem arose in 1910 and had repercussions for several years afterwards. The Rev. F. Rowling (1893–1921) found himself in 1910 at cross-purposes with fellow-members of the translation committee – about Luganda orthography, about methods of committee procedure, and about the status of African advisers on translation. The dissension grew to such proportions that, apparently at Bishop Tucker's suggestion, the parent committee sent a telegram to Rowling, ante-dating his furlough and recalling him immediately.[38] Archdeacon Walker, the secretary of the mission, wrote to London to say that if this meant recall, Rowling should be allowed to know the reason for it. He should also have the right of appeal to the governing body of the Church of Uganda. Warming to his subject, the archdeacon inquired whether the parent committee in fact had the right to recall a missionary without consulting that body, and whether the telegram of recall should not have been sent to the secretary as representing the missionary committee. He also raised the question whether the bishop was still the director of the mission.[39]

The Group III committee (responsible for African missions of CMS) replied firmly on the constitutional issue. It remained within the powers of the parent committee to recall a missionary when they saw occasion, without consulting the synod, the effect of such a recall being, of course, to leave it open to the missionary concerned, 'if in any case it should seem well to sever his connection with the CMS and remain in the service of the Synod, if they are able to employ him, but not to remain a CMS missionary. Unconsidered action', said the committee, 'should, of course, be avoided, but it seems manifest that CMS are not in a position to maintain any missionary at his post against the will of the Synod, and, remembering the Constitution of the Synod, that must mean against the veto of the Bishop'.[40]

An invitation to take up language work in Kavirondo to which Mr Rowling had 'responded in admirable spirit', gave the bishop grounds for hope that the matter could be regarded as closed.[41] But on 11th October, writing from Ireland on furlough, Rowling opened up the constitutional question again. He asked whether the parent committee was prepared to protect missionaries against recall 'without notice, admonition, or hearing of any kind'; and he made it clear that he was not prepared to submit again to the authority of the Uganda translation committee without an alteration of its status and a guarantee of fair treatment.[42] Clearly the matter was by no means concluded. The Group committee sought the advice of the British and Foreign Bible Society on the points on which Rowling had been outvoted on the translation committee. On 31st December Rowling, in a further letter, quoted the constitution of the diocese, which 'makes a point of there being no racial distinctions in the Uganda Church'. If the Baganda were to have no active voice in the language question, then his name must be removed from the Uganda staff.[43] Six days later he wrote again, unable to agree that language work was not the work of the Uganda church. It should, he argued, be under the control of the diocesan council. This curious story had a happy ending, helped by a change of bishop. At a meeting of the Uganda missionary committee (4th March, 1912) the secretary was asked 'to convey to the Rev. F. Rowling the affectionate welcome of the Committee on his return to the Mission'. He remained for another nine years, until 1921, giving distinguished service as mission secretary, and as supervisor of the building of a new cathedral.

Lake Victoria is an efficient generator of thunderstorms and the visitor to Uganda can be disconcerted by the sudden power of these storms. On 23rd September, 1910, the large Anglican cathedral on the summit of Namirembe Hill was struck by lightning. The fire started about midday and spread rapidly. The walls remained standing, but the building was gutted. Built in 1902, it was a cavernous building, imposing for its size rather than its beauty; but its destruction was a grievous blow, particularly to Bishop Tucker. He spent much of the time on his last furlough before retirement appealing for funds to rebuild it. The Uganda missionary committee hoped that the new building would be undertaken by the Baganda and not by friends in England '[They] are going to rebuild the Cathedral themselves,' Millar wrote (25th October, 1910), 'raising the money in the next three years'; meanwhile they were hoping 'to borrow from the money the Bishop is raising in England'.[44] The response from the Baganda chiefs was certainly up to expectation: 'each Anglican chief undertook to contribute a third of his income for three years, and some continued to do so when that time was over'.[45] The foundation stone was laid on 8th November, 1915, and the new building was consecrated by Bishop J. J. Willis (Bishop Tucker's successor from 1912) on 13th September, 1919. The architect was Professor Berresford Pite. Sir Apolo Kagwa's leadership in local money-raising, Rowling's general oversight on the cost side, and F. H. White's skill as clerk of works combined to realize Pite's vision of a great cathedral, romanesque in its general design, but not as foreign-looking as Nairobi cathedral. The cost, at one time estimated at £36,000, was kept below £30,000 and £20,000 was contributed by the church in Uganda.

In 1911 Bishop Alfred Tucker retired after an episcopate of twenty-one years. He was, as Bishop Willis recalled, 'immensely strong physically'. As a young man Tucker and his three brothers had climbed the four highest peaks in the English Lake District in a day, involving sixty-four miles of rough walking in twenty-four hours. This physique was a valuable gift in his early days in Uganda when he covered great distances on foot. For the first nine years of his episcopate he was Bishop of Eastern Equatorial Africa which included not only Uganda but all the territory between Uganda and the Indian Ocean and the northern part of German East Africa. When the diocese was divided in 1899 Bishop Tucker elected to remain bishop of its western portion, which included western Kenya with Uganda until 1921. In this diminished but still enormous diocese he led the Uganda church in its expansion beyond Buganda and designed its constitutional framework. He was an accomplished artist and writer and his book *Eighteen Years in Uganda and East Africa* (1908), with his own illustrations, is a missionary classic. His belief in the potential indigenous leadership of the church was unwavering.

> The greatest service which Bishop Tucker rendered the Uganda Church was to believe in it; and this faith of his was often in conflict with the rest of the missionary body during the years when the leading strings were being woven.[46]

In its minute on his retirement the Uganda missionary committee recalled how he had found the mission, on his arrival in Uganda in 1891,

> with but a handful of converts, one Gospel in their own tongue, and a very slender band of missionaries. . . . He leaves it with over 100,000 adherents, including 70,000 baptized converts, and not only the whole Bible translated and circulated by tens of thousands but an extensive religious literature. There are now over one hundred missionaries (including wives) on the European staff and two thousand native agents.[47]

'It is strange to reflect,' Professor Roland Oliver wrote,

that Tucker, who walked 22,000 miles in the service of the African Church, never mastered an African language. Perhaps it was his intuition as an artist which enabled him as an administrator to guide so successfully the religious stirrings of a people among whom he can have formed fewer individual friendships than any other missionary of his time.[48]

Bishop Tucker's retirement raised another constitutional question. It was recognized by all concerned that the appointment of his successor would be made by the Archbishop of Canterbury after consultation with the local governing body of the mission and with the diocesan synod. On 17th October, 1911 the Archbishop discussed the procedure for appointment with C. C. B. Bardsley, the honorary clerical secretary of CMS. It was arranged that the Archbishop, on receiving legal notice of resignation from Bishop Tucker, would send an official letter to CMS asking for nominations. Names were informally discussed. The Archbishop in the end nominated the Rev. John Jamieson Willis, Archdeacon of Kavirondo. The nomination was not wholly welcome in Uganda. Walker wrote to Baylis (13th January, 1912) regretting that there had been no consultation with the 'constituted Church' in Uganda about the kind of man needed for bishop. Walker agreed that there was no one so capable as Archdeacon Willis in the Uganda mission itself, but they had hoped for a successor to Bishop Tucker of 'wide experience and commanding ability'.[49] At the diocesan council on 20th January, 1912 the protest at lack of consultation was formally expressed: The Church of Uganda was a fully constituted church with its own synod, and the synod felt that it had not received fair treatment from the CMS. It recognized that the Society paid the bishop's remuneration, but the Uganda church should have been asked whether it wished to nominate one of its own members or whether it wished to approve of any individual for nomination by the CMS to the Archbishop.[50] When the time came for the appointment of Bishop Willis's successor, happily not for another twenty years, care was taken to consult the synod of the Uganda church before the nomination was announced. Bishop Willis was consecrated on 25th January, 1912, and arrived at Namirembe on 12th March.

On 7th November, 1911 C. W. Hattersley, Headmaster of Mengo High School, wrote to CMS headquarters, complaining in vague terms, of the teaching given at King's School, Budo. He commented on the lack of ministerial candidates coming from the school. In his view the aim of the mission was to call out an educated clergy, but 'at present the mission has not one clergyman who can be called an educated man'. He felt the only way of protest was to resign from the mission.[51] Hattersley's motives were, to say the least, mixed. He was already thinking of taking up a secular appointment in Uganda; there was some, normally healthy, rivalry between Mengo High School and the Budo school for the sons of chiefs; and it was true that the educational level of candidates for the ministry was not high. But Hattersley's no doubt sincere conviction that this lack of candidates for the ministry was due to the 'unsound' teaching given by the Rev. H. W. Weatherhead and his brother, the Rev. H. T. C. Weather-head, was, and remained, unproven. However, the charge once made had to be investigated, and it appears that Archdeacon Walker was already worried about the teaching at Budo. He had no doubt that the teaching given had been com-pletely misunderstood – 'of this we are all quite satisfied'. Mr Weatherhead senior, he said, had promised him some time before to give no expression to opinions that he knew CMS would not agree with.[52] On 7th March, 1912 Walker wrote to Baylis regretting that no explicit advice had been given. 'I as your Secretary have no standard of limit by which I am to judge of the teaching given.'[53] It seems, at this distance in time, strangely arrogant that a mission secretary should suppose that he had any function as a theological assessor among his fellow-missionaries; but at the time Walker was, in effect, in charge of the diocese as well as the mission; his letters on other subjects show similar evidence of strain; and it was not out of character for a mission secretary in those days to see himself, the Society's representative on the spot, as guardian of its doctrinal position. Walker's scrupulous fairness to the Weatherheads is heartening. He personally distrusted liberalism as likely to undermine the gospel. He shared Hattersley's anxieties. But he was the Society's obedient servant in this as in other matters and he wanted clear instructions.

The parent committee wanted facts and found them hard to come by. Hattersley's complaint was discussed at two meetings of the general committee in London (13th August and 10th September, 1912). Unable to obtain from Hattersley any definite statement in support of 'the grave charges made by him', it could not accept them as reasons for his resignation from the Society. Between the two meetings a letter was received from Hattersley to say that he must resign because of an agreement he had already entered into with a business firm in Uganda. On 9th November, 1912 Walker wrote to say that he did not think the 'Higher Critical' teaching given at Budo school was the reason for Hattersley's resignation. He himself had heard from 'certain missionaries' that the teaching was of this character, but the chief source of information about it appeared to be some Africans whose 'moral character, on enquiry, proved to be not good'.[54] In December Bishop Willis reported the result of his own inquiries. There was obviously, he wrote, 'a distinct variety of views' among the missionaries, but he did not think that in any single case could the views be called extreme; and he was convinced that all the great essentials of the faith 'are in all the teaching jealously safeguarded'. H. T. C. Weatherhead wrote to say that the result of the inquiries made by the bishop had reassured his brother and himself. He was not prepared to make a new statement as it could be as easily misconstrued as an earlier one had been. He was ready to resign or to appeal to the 'full committee' of CMS if he could himself be present.[55] He con-sidered that this teaching was 'not against the CMS'.

The Group III committee made its report on 21st May, 1913. They had considered, it said, the statement made by Hattersley that the teaching at Budo school 'was unworthy of a clergyman of the Church of England and calculated to instil into the minds of the natives doubts about the Bible as the revealed Word of God'. They were thankful to be able to report that 'this strong statement cannot be borne out by the facts of the case'. They concluded that no action was called for beyond a reminder to those engaged in teaching in the Uganda mission of the dangers, mentioned by Bishop Willis, 'of raising and suggesting doubts prematurely and heedlessly'. The bishop had assured them that the Principal of Budo school would be on his guard against this danger. The committee also expressed the hope that 'community of spirit may prevail in the mission and all unfair criticism by missionaries of one another's teaching may be avoided'.

This hope was fulfilled. Hattersley remained in Uganda as manager of a business firm and Budo school had many years of peaceful development under H. T. C. Weatherhead until his retirement in 1924.

In the immediate pre-war period pioneer missionary work was still going on in the three western kingdoms of Bunyoro, Toro and Ankole, and was in the earliest stages in the north-east of the Uganda protectorate. A. B. Fisher gives a fascinating glimpse of the church at Hoima in Bunyoro in November 1910. He records 172 baptisms for the year 1909–10, including 44 children.[56] One morning each week the king and chiefs were attending classes in the church and 'three afternoons they came to my house. We are dividing the time between Scripture, Church History, the Articles and secular subjects.' Two years later Fisher was planning the evangelization of the Northern Province from Bunyoro. In December 1912 he reports that the Gulu people had already put up a little church. He hoped to locate twenty Bunyoro teachers in the neighbourhood of Gulu, supported by the Bunyoro church. By September 1913 the mission house at Gulu was complete and twenty out-stations had been started by Bunyoro evangelists assisted by 'Gang' (i.e. Acholi) teachers.

The full integration of missionaries within the diocesan structure for which Bishop Tucker had patiently laboured, was still proving difficult. In 1913 Ernest Millar, who had taken over from Walker as mission secretary, asked for advice about the instructions to be given to missionaries about their location and duties. Were they to be given by the bishop on advice from the missionary committee or by the committee on its own volition, as the CMS Regulation 31, Part II seems to imply? In reply (14th August, 1913) G. T. Manley gave the following pointers: (1) The Society's regulations must not be interpreted in such a way as to conflict with the constitution of the Church of Uganda; (2) each missionary should receive written instructions from the missionary committee when these had been settled in consultation with the bishop; (3) these instructions should not appear to interfere with matters under the exclusive control of the bishop; (4) no missionary should be expected by the bishop to undertake work outside the scope of his written instructions without further consultation with the missionary committee.

The issue was raised again in 1917. Rowling, who had become mission secretary after Millar's death, questioned certain actions of the bishop 'which in appearance at least show that he intends to act as director of the Mission'.[57] Bishop Willis made his own views clear to CMS headquarters in a letter of 4th April, 1917. He recognized that the missionary committee ought to deal with such matters as funds, houses, locations, etc., but it was not in a position to give any work under the constitution of the Uganda church which ruled that 'all licensed clergy shall be located in consultation with the body supporting or responsible for such licensed clergymen'. To say that the missionary committee agreed to consult with the bishop about location was in his view 'rather an invasion of the Constitution'. While remaining grateful for the missionary committee's help, and having no wish to consult them less than in the past, he felt that 'a system of dual control would be disastrous'.

The parent committee's reply was a comprehensive resolution approved on 14th August, 1917.[58] It welcomed the transfer of authority from the Europeans to the Africans, and desired, wherever possible, to avoid distinctions based solely on racial considerations. All missionaries, and especially the licensed clergy, owed canonical obedience in ecclesiastical matters to the bishop of the diocese. But a missionary before accepting any duties such as chaplaincies among Europeans, war service, etc., should receive the sanction of the parent committee through the missionary committee, who would be glad if the bishop could devise some procedure which would avoid any appearance of conflict in regard to appointments of CMS missionaries affecting missionary expenditure and the duties of missionaries as such.

This was a tall order. The laws and regulations of the Church of Uganda, approved by the diocesan synod in June 1917, declared the bishop to be 'the ultimate authority within the Diocese in all matters affecting ecclesiastical discipline'; but as long as missionaries' allowances, and other expenses of mission under 'All Other Heads' (AOH) were being paid by CMS from London, the Society could scarcely, in terms of its stewardship, renounce all interest in local expenditure; and the locations and duties of missionaries were inextricably related to such expenditure. There was not at that time a body of African opinion which could express itself effectively through the synod. The bishop properly regarded himself as the trustee for the African voice in the church, as well as having a special relationship with all clergy who held his licence, whether African or European. Short of detailed spelling-out of accountability in by-laws (which might have created a new range of problems) the management of locations had to be left in the end to the tact and good relationships of all the parties involved.

In Uganda, as elsewhere in British colonial territories, the outbreak of war in August 1914 was greeted with a patriotic fervour that took little account of the staffing problems of the mission. On 6th August the missionary committee resolved that a letter be sent to the provincial commissioners offering the services of all missionaries; that all itineration should cease and missionaries keep at their stations until further notice; and that all building construction should be halted.[59] On 10th August Millar reported that boys from Mengo High School, under the Rev. J. Britton, were being drilled at a military centre and some of them had enrolled as cyclist messengers under the direction of the Rev. W. B. Gill. Drs A. R. and J. H. Cook with the ladies of Kampala had started an ambulance service. The threat of invasion from German East Africa at first seemed imminent, but by the end of 1916 the German forces had been driven southwards far out of range of Uganda.

In April 1917 concern was caused by a Compulsory Service Ordinance, already in force in the East Africa protectorate and soon to be applied to the Uganda protectorate, which would make clergy on the mission staff liable for combatant service. The bishop sent a telegram to the Archbishop of Canterbury for his advice. The ordinance was amended excluding members of recognized missionary bodies from compulsory call-up but 'if the Bishop or other head of any such body is of the opinion that any member thereof can reasonably well be spared he shall submit his name to the War Council for selection'. The missionary committee through Rowling asked the parent committee to thank the archbishop for his help in obtaining this concession.[60] In 1917–18 seven members of the mission staff were on war service as chaplains or in other capacities. The statistics of the Uganda church reflect the effect of the war on church membership, though other factors (e.g. the losses sustained through the Malakite movement) make it difficult to be precise about this. A comparison of returns at five-year intervals shows that the rapid growth from 1909 to 1914 was not maintained in the next half-decade and two important indicators – 'adult baptisms for the year' and 'native teachers' – show a decline in numbers: but baptized membership rose between 1914 and 1919 from 98,477 to 109,725, and communicants from 25,833 to 30,498.

In an article in *The Church Missionary Review*, September 1918, Bishop Willis paid tribute to the resourcefulness and evangelistic zeal of Baganda teachers in initiating mission in three principal centres – Mbale, Ngora and Gulu. 'To see local congregations,' he wrote, 'springing up as if by magic in unexpected, distant parts of the country; everywhere signs of new life, as in a fresh moral and spiritual spring.' He wrote also of the grave anxieties that accompanied this sudden flowering; the 'hopelessly inadequate' staff to shepherd the vast numbers of converts and inquirers. A policy of restriction on teachers and on the administration of baptism was, he said, 'eminently sane advice, but as impracticable as it is sane! . . . As well plant a tree in fertile soil, and seek to limit the length of its roots or the size of its branches.' They must seek to follow Christ's own way – broadcast the message first, then train the chosen leaders of the future.

In the same article the bishop mentioned requests made to the Board of Missions of the Uganda church in January 1918, for help beyond the borders of the protectorate, in Kiziba or Buwaya west of Lake Victoria. Buwaya (or Buhaya) also had some links with the Uganda church, but from a much earlier period. In the days following the Pilkington 'revival' of 1893–4 small groups of evangelical Christians who had heard the gospel in Uganda had set up house churches; one of their leaders, Anderea Kajerero, had been appointed a junior lay reader by Bishop Tucker. Buhaya was, however, in German East African territory and in 1910 the Bethel mission established a mission station at Bukoba, an important trading post on the western shore of Lake Victoria and a district headquarters of the German colonial government. In June 1916 the retreating German forces evacuated Bukoba and it was occupied by a British army contingent under Major D. L. Baines. In December 1916 the German mission-ary in charge, Pastor E. Döring, was ordered to leave; but before he did so a request for help was forwarded to the Anglican Church in Uganda through Major Baines. In April 1917 R. H. Leakey visited Bukoba accompanied by six African teachers. He found a small Christian community who had held together in worship and mutual support, and on his return to Uganda he took Kajerero with him to put the needs of Bukoba before the Uganda church synod in June. In January 1918 the Uganda Diocesan Board of Missions accepted responsi-bility for work in Bukoba and Leakey was appointed leader of the mission. The number of adherents grew rapidly from about a hundred in 1918 to some fifteen hundred in 1924. In that year the Uganda Board decided to hand over their responsibility to the South African Wesleyan Methodist mission which had been looking for a 'field' in East Africa.

Carl Hellberg, in a well-informed account of the Bukoba mission, saw it as part of the spontaneous expansion southwards of the Baganda church. Although Leakey was there much of the time, in the six years of CMS oversight 'most of the actual evangelization was carried out by Baganda'.[61] Local churches were organized on the Uganda pattern. The African leaders had more authority and freedom of decision than had been thought desirable in the time of the Bethel mission. Such church organization was successful, in Hellberg's opinion, because it ran parallel to the *omuteko* (age-group) organization of the traditional Haya society. The CMS was involved once more in Bukoba when the Wesleyan mission retired from the area in 1928, but this time the initiative came from Bishop Chambers in the newly-formed Anglican diocese of Central Tanganyika. (See further in Tanganyika chapter.)

By the end of the first world war the CMS Uganda mission was feeling the loss of its leaders of the first generation. Archdeacon Walker retired in 1913. He had reached Uganda three years before Bishop Tucker and had become one of his most trusted lieutenants. His later letters as secretary of the mission are at times peremptory in the fashion of the time. 'The mission has no money,' he wrote to one of his colleagues who had asked for £15 to build a cook-house; 'can't you put up some sort of shelter till next year's money comes in?' But he cared greatly for the church in Uganda and regarded a sacrificial standard as necessary equipment for missionaries who were privileged to serve it.

Walker's successor as mission secretary, Ernest Millar, was a quiet man with a rare gift for friendship with Africans. He died at Mengo, where he had served for a quarter of a century, in January 1917.

A. B. Fisher, pioneer missionary in Bunyoro and northern Uganda, resigned for family reasons in July 1914, in spite of Bishop Willis's efforts to persuade him to stay. The mud-spattered pages of his journal, which he wrote up each night in his early days at Hoima, are among the treasures of CMS archives.

J. E. M. Hannington's resignation in 1920 severed another link with the past. He had served for fifteen years in Busoga where he had baptized a son of the chief on whose orders his father, Bishop James Hannington, had been speared to death in 1885.

Aspects of the 1920s

'The 1920s saw the withdrawal of nearly all the missionaries from any commitment to the life and struggles of the Buganda Church in its pastoral and evangelistic aspects'.[62] What was true of Buganda, the central kingdom, was true by and large of the rest of Uganda. The number of clerical missionaries began to decline and the majority of those who came out in this period were drafted into specialist, non-parochial jobs. Rowling wrote dispiritedly (24th January, 1920) of 'the constant committee meetings, supervision and routine work' making such demands that 'the reduced staff now available cannot find time for intimate, pastoral, spiritual work'. 'Lack of such contact,' he went on, 'gives the impression that the mission and the missionaries no longer care for the people and their affairs, and this fosters dissatisfaction and race feeling.'[63] The remedy, in the view of such men as Rowling and Ladbury, his successor as mission secretary, was for the parent committee to send out more pastoral missionaries as well as the specialists necessary for the new large institutions; but such recruits were in short supply and the money to underwrite their allowances was not being found by the home constituency. A 'short-service' scheme had been suggested in 1915 by the missionary committee. The hope was that such a scheme would supply the necessary replacements for 'ordinary station work' and set free experienced missionaries for evangelistic tours (for which the shorthand word was still 'itineration'). Short-service workers came out in considerable numbers in the 1920s and 1930s but nearly all of them were, or became, specialists. The more far-sighted missionaries were fully aware that this withdrawal upwards into administration, or sideways into specialism, was not the fulfilment of Venn's vision of the 'euthanasia' of a mission. But another solution, put forward by the parent committee, proved almost too painful to contemplate. In the early 1920s the Society asked the Uganda mission to face the possibility of complete withdrawal; or to make alternative suggestions for drastic reduction of the cost of missionary agency. Other CMS missionaries were asked the same question. The reply from Uganda was given in a joint letter of 10th January, 1922, signed by Bishop Willis, Archdeacon Kitching, and H. B. Ladbury, the mission secretary. The letter concluded:

> We would with all our strength oppose any suggestion, based on an imperfect understanding of a native's capabilities, to withdraw prematurely from a country whose future influence in Central Africa it is impossible to calculate. God has given into our hands a great strategic position. It would be folly to abandon it.[64]

In a supplementary letter two months later Bishop Willis developed more fully the reasons why he and his fellow missionaries were convinced that this was the wrong time for a complete handover to the Native Anglican Church. The African clergy, he said, were still of the first generation, trained before there were any schools in the country and left for the last ten or twenty years 'with almost no books and only an occasional gathering at Budo'. They were for the most part relatively uneducated and below the present educational standard of many boys and girls. The salaries of clergy were inadequate and many of them had to undertake private trading. A conference was being arranged with leading chiefs and representatives of the diocesan council to consider how the claims and needs of the clergy could be met.[65]

One result of this painful self-scrutiny was a new administrative structure for the local governing body of the mission. From 1924 the local governing body of the Uganda mission was the missionary conference, including all missionaries out of probation, and all wives who had completed one tour of service and who had passed one language examination. There was also a standing committee to act between meetings of the conference, consisting of the bishop, and the secretary (or acting-secretary) of the mission *ex officio*; up to eleven members of the conference elected by the conference, one at least of them to be a doctor and one at least engaged in education work. The parent committee retained the right to appoint not more than three others of whom not more than two were to be appointed from outside the missionary body. The bishop, if present, was chairman both of the conference and standing committee; otherwise each body elected its own chairman.[66] These new arrangements did not solve the problem of the dual authority of mission and church; but they helped to avoid for the future the possibility of a local governing body consisting of two or three senior missionaries ruling as a kind of *junta*. In 1929 the composition of the standing committee was revised to include the archdeacons and the education secretary as additional members. Of the three appointments in the hands of the parent committee, one was to be direct, and the other two were to be from outside the mission on nomination by the missionary conference.[67]

Division of the Diocese and Jubilee of the Mission

In 1921 that part of Uganda diocese which was in Kenya colony was transferred to the diocese of Mombasa. The area that remained, co-terminous with
the protectorate of Uganda, was still over-large for one bishop and plans were
already being considered for sharing its episcopal oversight. Early in 1920
Herbert Gresford Jones, archdeacon and vicar of Sheffield, offered to serve in
Uganda 'in any capacity'. The offer was not taken up at once and in March
1920 he accepted nomination by the Crown to the deanery of Salisbury. On
23rd March Archbishop Davidson wrote him a typically far-sighted letter.[68]
There would be no difficulty, he said, about his withdrawing from the deanery
if the way opened for him to go to Uganda. 'In the story of the growth of the
church of Christ on earth,' the Archbishop continued, 'there can be no question
at all that the opening in Uganda is a more important one than the Dean of
Salisbury, for which plenty of other people are available.' Several members of
the CMS secretariat in London were none too happy about Gresford Jones
going out to Uganda, not on personal grounds, but on the score of health, age
and climate. In reporting this to the Archbishop, Bardsley took the opportunity
of mentioning the 'considerable nerviness among the missionaries in Uganda'
about what seemed to them to be the unnecessarily authoritarian methods of
the bishop. It would be better, therefore, in spite of his open offer, if Gresford
Jones went out as suffragan bishop rather than as a general missionary to be
subsequently appointed suffragan.[69] The Archbishop concurred and he was
duly consecrated with the title of Bishop of Kampala.

The fears of the CMS secretaries unfortunately proved to be justified. Bishop
Willis evidently hoped that Gresford Jones would become his general assistant
in episcopal orders and did not at first link his appointment with discussions
he was having with Bishop Gwynne and others about a division of the diocese.
As not infrequently happens with suffragan bishops in England, the Bishop of
Kampala came to feel, in Willis's words, that 'the position of Suffragan Bishop
in the mission field was an intolerable one.' 'He would clearly work more
happily,' he wrote to Archbishop Davidson 'and so perhaps more effectively,
if he were given an independent charge. However this would be neither possible
nor wise without the entire concurrence of the CMS and at present the Secretary,
at any rate, is strongly opposed to the idea.'[70] The Uganda missionary committee
shared Bardsley's apprehension about the financial implications of a division
of the diocese. Bishop Willis, aware that the Bishop of Kampala felt he was
not being given enough work and responsibility, told the missionary committee
that he was to be regarded as bishop-in-charge of the mission and work east of the
Nile, though there was no definite agreement as yet about dividing the diocese.[71]
Bishop Willis thought it would be well to establish a local mission committee in
Busoga, but the Uganda missionary committee felt unable to accept this suggestion either for the area east of the Nile or for the three western kingdoms.[72]

By December 1921 it had been made clear to Bishop Willis that the CMS regarded a division of the diocese as impossible under the financial conditions of that time; but he continued to hope, 'not least for the sake of the Bishop of Kampala, that it may prove possible in the not far distant future'.[73] As an interim measure Bishop Willis put forward to the Archbishop and the Uganda missionary committee a suggestion for the 'internal' division of the diocese based, as he claimed, on the precedent of the diocese of Bombay. The diocese would remain one, but each bishop would administer his own area. The two bishops would be of the same status, 'though not the same seniority'. They would both sit in any episcopal synod that might be formed, and each, in the absence of the other, would administer the diocese as a whole. He hoped that after a few years of work on these lines 'the eastern half of the diocese should be in every way better fitted to stand alone than it can be today'.[74]

The larger aim was achieved in 1926, but the interim period did not work out as Bishop Willis had hoped. Bishop Gresford Jones went to live in Jinja in Busoga, but he found that the eastern section of the diocese, with only six mission stations, gave little scope for an episcopal ministry. He found himself out of sympathy with the way the mission was being led. Both he and his wife found the climate very taxing. In November 1923, having accepted the living of Pershore, he resigned from the Uganda mission. In his letter of resignation he suggested an age-limit 'of, say, thirty-five' for taking up work in the tropics.[75]

In September 1924 Bishop Willis and Bishop Gwynne (Bishop in Egypt and the Sudan) met at CMS headquarters to discuss the possibility of a Nile diocese. The plan now agreed between them was for a diocese that included all Muganda east of the Nile except Busoga, together with the two Sudan provinces bordering on Muganda. Bishop Willis was clear in his own mind that no Uganda clergyman was ready yet for episcopal orders, and that none of the younger missionaries would be ready for this responsibility for another ten years. But there was a senior missionary, Archdeacon A. L. Kitching, who had at least some of the qualities required. He had been a pioneer missionary in northern and eastern Uganda. He was an accomplished linguist – a necessary qualification in a mixed language area. The necessary consultation with the Archbishop of Canterbury and the CMS took place and in 1926 the diocese of the Upper Nile was formed, with Kitching as its first bishop. Growth of church membership was sufficient reason for this division. Compared with a static missionary force (the rapid increase of educationists supported by government grants had scarcely begun in 1925) this growth had been rapid in the post-war years; paid church-workers had increased two-and-a-half times; the total Christian community had almost trebled, and the number of adult baptisms a year, though showing a slight decline in the war years, had increased by almost five times.

The fiftieth birthday of the CMS mission in Uganda was celebrated in 1927 with great rejoicing. The main event was a Jubilee Thanksgiving service in Namirembe cathedral. The Bishops of Nyasaland, Zanzibar, Masasi and

Mombasa were present to represent their dioceses, and the Bishop of Nyasaland unveiled a memorial tablet to the Uganda martyrs. The Mugabe of Ankole, the Mukamas of Toro and Bunyoro brought greetings from their western kingdoms. CMS headquarters was represented by Wilson Cash, general secretary; Miss E. Thorpe, and Miss E. M. Baring-Gould. Among others who came for the celebrations were Miss Mabel Warburton, Prebendary E. N. Sharpe, and Bishop Taylor Smith. There was a schools thanksgiving service for which 5,000 boys and girls marched in procession from the Kabaka's *Lubiri* to the cathedral. Schoolgirls from Mt Elgon had walked two hundred miles to share in it and were no doubt glad of a lift back by lorry. There were also school parties from Busoga, Toro and Ankole.[76]

The Jubilee was marked by an evangelistic mission led by Archdeacon Blackledge, assisted by the Revs. A. Binaisa, A. K. Balya, E. Aliwali (Rural Dean of Kyagwe) and G. G. Garrett. They held evangelistic meetings in many places, gave lectures on the history of the Uganda church, and solicited support for a Jubilee Fund for the diocese with a target of Sh. 500,000. Special mission meetings were held for women, and for the Malakites.[77]

In an article written in preparation for the Jubilee in *The Church Missionary Review*, Canon H. T. C. Weatherhead singled out six major achievements of the Uganda mission in its first fifty years: (1) the existence of a fully-organized Anglican Church; (2) the check on the Muslim advance in East Africa; (3) the extension of the church largely through the efforts of African evangelists; (4) the self-supporting Native Anglican Church; (5) an organized system of national education; (6) the rapid translation of the Holy Scriptures into the vernacular. But a number of things caused him concern. He thought the diocese tended to be over-organized and cited the cathedral chapter 'as a superfluous body for the Bishop to consult'. Honorary canonries, he said, had been planned originally to represent different kinds of work in the diocese, but in a short time they had become 'as meaningless as they are in England'. He was worried about the future recruitment of African clergy. Being paid from church offertories, they had much smaller stipends than the schoolmasters who were paid from school fees. He noted the comment of the Phelps-Stokes Educational Commission of 1924 on the 'utter inadequacy of the bush-schools'. In the field of translation, he regretted that the whole Book of Common Prayer had been translated so early, because it had the effect of inhibiting the development of indigenous forms of worship. Attempts had been made to introduce African hymns and tunes, but so far they had not been very successful.[78]

Had Canon Weatherhead been writing a few years later he would no doubt have added an appreciative comment, on this last point, about the work of the Rev. J. M. Duncan. From 1925 until his death in 1936 Duncan was honorary organist at Namirembe cathedral. He had a real concern for indigenous worship and in 1930 published Luganda tunes for the church hymnbook. He also made valiant efforts through musical festivals to spread through the church better standards of church music. Like many creative musicians he met with a certain amount of resistance, although in the context of genuine appreciation. In 1931 the standing committee of the mission expressed a 'strong wish' to the bishop that the musical festival should consist of 'some well-known oratorio such as the Handel's *Messiah* or some other musical work of devotional value such as Stainer's *Crucifixion*'.[79]

Happily Uganda, with its proud tradition and the Jubilee coming when it did in 1927, escaped the kind of *malaise* which almost crippled the Palestine mission in this period. All the same, the evidences of strain cannot be overlooked. They are part of the history of the period. Retrenchment stands high on the list of depressive factors.

Retrenchment and Recruitment in the 1920s

In 1922 the missionary committee was asked to make a reduction in the 1923 budget of 25 per cent under 'AOH' (i.e. mission expenses other than missionaries' allowances, passages and personal equipment). The committee was also asked to inquire from missionaries whether they would be willing to accept a reduction of stipends, or allowances, by 20 per cent or 10 per cent. Most of the Uganda missionaries were ready to accept a cut at one or other level,[80] but a further reduction of AOH in the 1927 estimates was described by Ladbury as a 'deadly blow' to the mission. All its reserves had been used up in meeting previous cuts.[81]

Missionaries were for the most part ready to accept financial hardship for themselves, provided that 'the work did not suffer': but the work did suffer if the flow of missionary recruits was not maintained and a reduction in the number of new missionaries was the aspect of retrenchment which often weighed hardest. The authorities of the Uganda mission tried every means of persuasion and entreaty to get more recruits sent out. The plea varied almost from year to year. At one time it was the threat of closure of important work 'when we ought to be going forward'; at another the loss in general effectiveness when retired missionaries were not replaced. Sometimes there was a spontaneous invitation to the home church to share in the blessings of harvest – a telegram for example sent on the 2nd May, 1925: 'UGANDA CALLING. ANOTHER FIFTEEN THOUSAND BAPTISMS. WHAT ABOUT IT?'

Towards the end of the 1920s the appeal for recruits was often related to the rapid expansion of Roman Catholic missions. In January 1929 Ladbury wrote, in connection with government education grants: 'The Roman Catholics have put in more men and women than they have received grants for, while CMS is looked upon as having failed to do their part.'[82] A year later Daniell, acting secretary of the mission, put the point more graphically: 'At the present rate of progress Uganda bids to become the fairest jewel in the Papal crown. We *must* be re-inforced by men and women.'[83] Another report from the mission in

1930 supported Daniell's general warning with facts and figures. At the Mill Hill Sisters' training college in Yorkshire, Mother Kevin was training young nuns exclusively for service in Uganda and there were forty in residence at the college. CMS had no intermediate day-schools for girls. The Roman Catholics had seventy-nine; there were seventy-three Roman Catholic European missionaries in the field of elementary vernacular education whereas CMS had only five.

A further and poignant plea for recruits was related to overworked missionaries, especially in the 'vitality-sapping' climate of Busoga. There were frequent references in the later 1920s to the health of missionaries in Busoga. In 1926 the missionaries' conference suggested that women missionaries stationed there should have special privileges. 'Experience has shown,' Ladbury wrote, 'that it is very difficult to secure continuity owing to constant invaliding', and he asked the parent committee to consider granting extra holiday expenses for those working in Busoga. One missionary invalided home after her first tour was Florence Allshorn. She had worked with Archdeacon Gresford Jones in Sheffield and at the age of thirty-two had come out with him on his appointment as Bishop of Kampala. It appears from local records that the ladies' committee proposed that Miss Allshorn should be located to Mityana but that the missionary committee overruled this and sent her to Iganga in Busoga.[84] She was at once put in charge of a high school for chiefs' daughters under the general direction of a senior woman missionary whose temperament, as well as 'the debilitating and nerve-racking effect of the climate' had been responsible for the early departure of seven of Florence Allshorn's predecessors in as many years.

Typically, in her first letter, Florence was able to thank God 'for something absolutely impossible'. First there was the school-work: 'Can you imagine,' she wrote, 'forty-two girls, none of them *wanting* to learn anything?'; but she added, in a Pauline postscript: 'yes, two do.' Then there was Iganga itself 'a hopeless sort of place. . . . My colleague has stuck it: it just happens not to have affected her health, but it has absolutely rotted her nerves.'[85] In 1924 the Phelps-Stokes Commission described the boarding-school at Iganga as 'a particularly good piece of work', but in November 1924 Florence Allshorn was invalided home with tuberculosis. It was not diagnosed for many months, and then she was told she might not live for more than two years. In fact she lived for another twenty-five to give distinctive service to the CMS in the training of women missionaries.

One casualty of the financial pressures and staff-shortages of the 1920s was the mission in Bukoba. In January 1924 the Rev. M. J. White, of the South African Wesleyan Methodist Mission, told the Uganda missionary committee that his society was ready to take over Bukoba if CMS were unable to cope with it; and on the proposal of R. H. Leakey it was unanimously decided that, as CMS were unable adequately to staff the mission, the SAWMM be asked to take it over, subject to the approval of the Bishop of Mombasa.[86] The parent committee demurred, but Bishop Willis explained the situation to G. T. Manley in an interview at CMS headquarters in September 1924. The offer, he said, had come at a time when Leakey was on the point of leaving Africa. The SAWMM proposed to bring in three or four white workers at once. He agreed that the Uganda committee had acted beyond their powers in this matter, but thought the transfer should now be regarded as a *fait accompli*. If the Wesleyans were pressed to go elsewhere and CMS could only place one worker at Bukoba – and even this would be extremely difficult – the African Christians would feel they had been badly treated.[87] The bishop's arguments were accepted by the parent committee, but it proved to be an unfortunate decision. A considerable number of the African Christians refused to accept the leadership of the SAWMM and the return of the Bethel mission to Bukoba in 1926 created further dissension.

In the eastern and northern provinces of the Uganda protectorate the growth of the church was rapid. In Busoga, for instance, the number of baptized Anglicans doubled in the years 1921–6 (8,156 to 16,456). In the Ngora district W. S. Syson reported 5,423 baptisms in the year 1923. In 1927, the Jubilee year, Miss Warburton reported that a mass movement was in full swing in the eastern province.[88]

The 1930s : Retirements and Renewal

The two events which are accorded the fullest attention in the Uganda mission records in this decade are: (1) the carefully phased change of episcopal leadership as Bishop Willis approached retirement; and (2) the revival movement which swept through the diocese in the later 1930s and made exacting demands on Bishop Stuart's leadership.

The question of Bishop Willis's successor began to occupy the attention of senior missionaries as early as 1930. 'He must be a man in the prime of life,' Blackledge wrote in a memorandum to the parent committee, 'One who can learn the language; a scholar; a man with a heart of love, patience, and sympathy. Such a man will be able to follow him who has so nobly led the Mission and Church of Uganda for the last eighteen years. May God raise up such a man.'[89] Blackledge was clear in his own mind that a full combination of these qualities could not be found in any of those serving in East Africa at that time. He would have to come from outside. In September 1931, Bishop Willis wrote to H. D. Hooper, Africa secretary of CMS:

I have just been on safari in Ankole, Kigezi and Ruanda . . . accompanied by Stuart. I have now seen quite enough of him to be confident that he is the best possible man to take over from me when I retire.

Cyril Edgar Stuart was a former chaplain of Ridley Hall, Cambridge and for the previous six years chaplain of Achimota College in the Gold Coast. The only doubts Willis had were about Stuart's ability to learn the language and whether he would stand the physical and mental strain of a bishop's life in Uganda, but he felt that his positive qualities far outweighed such doubts. Wilson Cash saw the Archbishop on 16th October, 1931 and assured him that CMS thought Stuart to be 'very suitable'. The Archbishop agreed to the proposal that he should be consecrated as assistant bishop 'with a view, ultimately, to his becoming bishop of the diocese'; but he asked that Bishop Willis should consider some means by which the diocese could be consulted, in accordance with a Lambeth conference resolution of the previous year.[90] Bishop Willis wrote to the Archbishop (10th December, 1931) saying: 'We have a properly constituted Cathedral Chapter, clerical and lay, representative of the whole diocese.' He had already called a meeting of the chapter for 19th January, 1932, he asked the Archbishop also whether there was any chance of Stuart being consecrated 'out here'. The chapter gave unanimous approval for Stuart's nomination and the synod unanimously welcomed it; but the Archbishop made it clear that the consecration must take place in England as there was no Province of East Africa. He was consecrated in Lambeth Palace Chapel on 25th July, 1932.

Bishop Willis left Uganda in 1934. For the next fourteen years he worked as assistant bishop in the diocese of Leicester. In the Uganda standing committee's minute on his retirement[91] his fellow-missionaries recalled that he had been a pioneer missionary in Ankole in 1900; the first European chaplain at Entebbe (the seat of the protectorate government) in 1903; again a pioneer missionary in Kavirondo in 1906 where he remained until his consecration as Bishop of Uganda in 1912. Then

> for twenty-two years he had patiently built on the foundations laid by Bishop Tucker. . . . His indefatigable labour, his patient forbearance, and his alert leadership has been an inspiration to all, and this influence will outlast our generation.

The minute also recorded gratefully the 'loving care of the missionaries' by the Bishop and Mrs Willis, 'as shown by the gift of their house at Lweza as a place of rest for them in Uganda'. J. J. Willis was a diocesan bishop in the traditional English sense; austere, exacting, at times imperious, he was not afraid to rebuke royalty whether African or British. It was a proud moment when he was invested with the CBE by the governor at the last Kabaka's garden party he attended as bishop. But in his old age the title he wanted most for himself was that of a missionary.

> From early childhood [he wrote] my mind became set on missionary work, though to the best of my recollection, I had never met a missionary nor read a missionary book; nor had we ever had a missionary in the family. . . . It always seemed to be the obvious thing that, if one honestly desired that people that sat in darkness should see a great light, someone must go and tell them.[92]

'It looks,' Ladbury wrote in November 1931, 'as though there will be a new Bishop, a new Secretary, a new Senior Doctor, and a new Archdeacon all at the same time. This will make the new Bishop's task very difficult.' His forebodings were not justified as things turned out, but the years 1931 to 1934 saw sweeping changes in the leadership of the Uganda mission. Archdeacon G. R. Blackledge retired, as already noted, in 1931 and Archdeacon A. B. Lloyd, finally in 1934. They had come out to Uganda in the same year, 1894, and their wives also in the same year, 1899. They represented the tradition of the 'pastoral-evangelist' missionary which had been the glory of the Uganda mission in its formative years.

In 1933 the Rev. and Mrs H. B. Ladbury retired after thirty years' service. Ladbury had done the longest stint of any mission secretary during the war and inter-war years, and his fellow-missionaries recorded their appreciation of his 'patience, tact, firmness and calm judgment' in that exacting office. At times, as his diary shows,[93] he found the long hours of committee and office work very wearisome and the happiest hours of his later years were when he was able to get out on tour of the new areas of mission such as Ruanda and Bukoba. The Ladburys decided to remain in Africa and bought a house in the Kenya Rift Valley, where Mrs Ladbury lived to the age of 102.

In 1934 Sir Albert Cook retired from Mengo hospital, but he remained in Uganda, a vigorous senior statesman, until his death in 1951.

On 30th May, 1930 Apolo Kivebulaya died. Ordained deacon by Bishop Tucker in 1900, and priest in 1903 he had been for thirty years a symbolic figure of Uganda's growing response to Christ. His story has been told by A. B. Lloyd, and more recently retold by Anne Luck.[94] 'Big flat feet with spread-out toes enabled him to walk everywhere. He never wore shoes.' In later years he was persuaded to acquire a bicycle, and chose the ladies' model preferred by men who wore the long *kanzu*. His clothing and church robes were kept spotless. Beauty and reverence in church services were very important to him. 'He always placed a cross on the altar and grew flowers to decorate the sanctuary.' But it is as a teacher, evangelist and soul-winner that Apolo will always be remembered. When in 1922 he appointed him a Canon of the Church of Uganda, Bishop Willis wrote:

> I have chosen you on account of your great patience and perseverance in Toro and the Congo all these years, and your patience in suffering and persecution for the name of our Lord, and for taking that name to the heathen.

When on 30th June, 1927 Mackay's bones were brought up from Usambiro, south of the Lake, to be buried in Namirembe churchyard, he was chosen to read Heb. 11.32–12.2. Apolo's body was buried near the church he had built at Mboga. This great Baganda evangelist had in fact been a 'foreign' missionary for most of his ministry, because the Boundary Commission of 1907–8 included

Mboga in the Belgian Congo. But for the Uganda church and mission it was unthinkable that the church Apolo had called into being and had shepherded for so long should be left after his death without help from Uganda.

In March 1933, shortly before Apolo's death, the standing committee of the mission heard that the Belgian government had refused to register the Mboga church lands on the grounds that no European missionary was being sent there. Bishop Willis hoped that European staff would be available from the CMS Sudan mission to serve in the Mboga district. Failing that, he would appeal for recruits at the CMS annual meeting in London. 'It would be tragic,' he said, 'if we had to withdraw altogether.'[95] In June the CMS executive committee accepted Albert Lloyd's offer to return to Uganda for one year (from December 1933 to December 1934) in order to settle European missionaries at Mboga. The financial responsibility took some months to settle. The Uganda standing committee took the view that the establishment of a European mission station at Mboga should be paid for entirely out of an Apolo Memorial Fund which Wilson Cash was raising in England. The parent committee thought that the continuation of Apolo's work should be laid upon the Native Anglican Church. In the end, when it was clear that the Native Anglican Church could not under-write the cost, the parent committee agreed to a grant of £300 from the special fund for houses for European missionaries and a non-recurring grant from the same fund towards AOH expenses, 'in the hope and expectation that the Native Anglican Church of Uganda will be prepared to assume responsibility for such expenditure in the future'.[96]

Lloyd reached Mboga in February 1934. He found a flourishing church, with three hundred people preparing for baptism. In May he sent the standing committee a copy of his appeal for £1,000 for an Apolo Memorial School at Mboga. He was hopeful that the Belgian Congo government would make a grant to the school.

In 1935 Bishop Stuart, accompanied by W. S. R. Russell, Rural Dean of Toro, spent eleven days in the Mboga district. The two missionaries, R. C. Palin and A. C. Rendle, for whom Lloyd had prepared the way were now settled there. Palin in his annual letter paid tribute to 'the splendid way' in which Lloyd had carried on during 1934 in face of uncertain health. He was grateful especially for the 'comity' arrangements Lloyd had made with the AIM and other missions in the area. In a note marked 'not for publication' (the time for restriction is surely past) Palin wrote:

> The pygmy tribes of the forest have played a large part in the written accounts of work at Mboga and many (? most) people at home visualize Mboga as a sort of pygmy settlement. Actually the work done amongst the pygmies . . . is very little indeed, though perhaps in the future we may be able to con-centrate more on this phase of the work. But today our work lies primarily among the Banyam-Boga, and forest tribes such as the Balega, who are not pygmies.

Rendle reported that the school for which Lloyd had appealed was now built and hard-pressed to accommodate the increasing number of children attending daily.[97] Lloyd's books about Apolo, especially *Apolo of the Pygmy Forest* (1933), had a wide circulation and proved a strong incentive to missionary giving and service; but as Mrs Luck's more careful study made clear, there was a good deal of imaginative reconstruction in Lloyd's books which contributed to the misunderstanding to which Palin refers.

'The worldliness of the Church' had been a recurrent theme of missionary reports in the 1920s and the early 1930s. What is often called the 'third generation problem' had confronted the Anglican Church in Uganda much earlier than in Kenya and Tanganyika, because in many respects it was a generation ahead of its sister-churches in East Africa. In his book *Dayspring in Uganda* (1921), A. B. Lloyd wrote of 'the clouds in the sky' overshadowing the early sunlight of the Uganda church – drunkenness, immorality, concubinage, continuing belief in witchcraft and in the power of the spirits of the dead. In 1931 A. R. Cook made a similar diagnosis: 'The danger is that the Christian profession is emasculated by the practice of its adherents'; and he gave, as instances of this, the frequency among church members of the practice of 'marriage without a ring', the small number of marriages in church, and the low level of church support both in terms of money and in church attendance.[98] But by this time revival was on its way. It began, says Dr Stanley Smith, 'quietly and almost imperceptibly' among the African staff at Gahini hospital,[99] and in the deep brotherhood discovered in mutual confession by Dr Joe Church, a Ruanda missionary, with two African teachers Blazyo Kigozi and Yosiya Kindu. In 1933 'Bible teams' began to go out from Gahini led by these three and by Blazio's brother, Simeoni Nsibambi, whom Church had first met at Mukono in 1929. In December 1935 Bishop Stuart invited a team from Gahini to lead a convention at Mukono. The missionaries' annual conference and retreat, and the retreat for African clergy in January 1936 both had 'the general subject of life-changing'. They felt themselves called, the bishop wrote, to self-examination about faith, prayer, preaching, and about bringing souls to Christ by individual work, visiting and open-air witness.[100] To mark the Diamond Jubilee of the CMS mission (1937) a campaign of evangelism was planned throughout the diocese. 'Messengers' were chosen in every parish and Canon Herbert was released from most of his other work to go round to every deanery and hold missions for clergy and teachers. Dr Joe Church held a ten days mission at Mukono and three area missions for the chosen messengers. The staff and students of Bishop Tucker College, Mukono, took responsibility for the diocesan mission in two districts.

The executive committee of the Ruanda mission in June 1937 seconded Dr Church to organize and develop the revival movement. In a memorandum (5th August, 1937) he put forward a plan for training in evangelism and 'for the building up of a true holiness movement in Uganda based exclusively on the

Bible'. His vision was of a team of young missionaries – a 'Uganda seven' – to be recruited in England for evangelistic and pastoral work. They would be assigned to work with ordained African clergy. They would meet, perhaps quarterly, with Bishop Stuart for consultation, prayer, and possibly language study. It was assumed that because the need was urgent they would be given interpreters to start with.[101]

Bishop Stuart was in two minds about the wisdom of Dr Church's proposals. He wrote to Hooper (26th August, 1937): 'I am not willing to go with the scheme at the cost of additional schism in Uganda.' Even when modified, as he thought it would have to be,

> it is going to meet with very great opposition. All of us who have been viewing the revival with sympathetic eyes are constantly amazed at the depth of spiritual perception of these people; but unless they are taught systematically and sympathetically it may all turn to friction or worse.

The bishop had second thoughts, however. He had a postscript to the letter (marked 'same day') in which he said:

> I am not sure if I have been quite fair to the revival. It is a very real thing for which we wholeheartedly thank God . . . people have begged us to come again next year as they feel they are only starting. It may be just what God is calling us to do.[102]

Wilson Cash was in Kampala in September 1937 and wrote cautiously commending Church's scheme. 'They would be missionaries of the Society, under the direction of the Local Governing Body, but they would be sent out specifically for evangelistic work.'

Church, back in England, went ahead making contact with possible candidates. On 11th November, 1937, he sent Cash a list of six people 'who were more or less prepared for interviews'.

Difficulties of a not unfamiliar kind began to accumulate. One of the possible men felt under pressure to break an undertaking given to his diocesan bishop in England in respect of his curacy. Another had doubts about whether there was a place in CMS for his own point of view. Some of the interviews arranged by the CMS candidates committee did not suggest that the scheme was completely understood and approved by the Society as a matter of urgency. The money problem, never far in the background of any new initiatives in this period, had stalked into the foreground once again. By April 1938 an individual sponsor had been found for only one of the seven, and the CMS secretariat were having to work fairly strictly to an annual quota of new missionaries.

Meanwhile in Uganda the things that Bishop Willis and Church feared might happen, if wise guidance was lacking for the revival movement, had started to show themselves. Archdeacon Herbert wrote, in his annual letter of 1939, about 'bands of young Africans, influenced in the first instance by the Ruanda Revival' holding aloof from the local church where it did not conform to their mode of thought. They were claiming that each convert, on profession of faith in Christ 'is filled with the spirit and needs no other training to enable him to work for God'. The archdeacon hoped, nevertheless, that under wise and sympathetic guidance 'these enthusiasts may be won for full service in the Church in which they were brought up; that a split may be avoided; and that they may be used of God to stir up new spiritual life in the Uganda Church'. Inevitably, the main burden of shepherding this movement of renewal fell on Bishop Stuart, and his letters show that at times the burden was almost beyond endurance. 'I do not think I've ever had a more difficult time,' he wrote to Hooper in July 1941. One student at Mukono had written to the bishop to say that he was disliked and distrusted by everyone for taking a middle path, and that as the bishop would not lead the revival he, the student, must do it himself.

He found support for his difficult role as mediator in reflections on church history. 'I always remember,' he wrote, 'that St Francis must have been an awful nuisance to the Church authorities of his day, but they had the sense to keep him in the Church, to its great advantage; whereas we in England drove out the Wesleyans, to our great loss.'[103]

In a later letter, in September 1941, the bishop told Hooper that he would 'probably have requests for my resignation before long'. In fact, he had seriously thought of asking to be relieved of a post that was becoming intolerable; but he believed that God had called him to that office, and he must stick to it.[104]

It is pleasant to add J. V. Taylor's tribute to the bishop:

In the church of Uganda it was probably the unshakeable patience of Bishop Stuart, more than any other human factor, which prevented an external breaking of the revival from the church. More and more those who were in the movement, and those who were not, came to recognize and accept it as belonging to the church for the sake of the church.[105]

Translation, Writing and Bookselling, 1910–42

The rapid growth of the Anglican Church in Buganda owed much to the conviction of the pioneer missionaries that the translation of the bible was a necessary part of their proclamation of the gospel.

The Luganda Bible was the fruit of long experiment. By 1880 Mackay had translated the Ten Commandments and some Psalms; 350 copies of his translation of St Matthew's Gospel were circulating by November 1885. Henry Wright Duta, Sembera Mackay and Mika Sematimba worked with Mackay, Pilkington and Gordon to complete the Luganda New Testament by 1890. Pilkington revised all previous work, completing the whole Bible in 1896.[106] Translation into the other main languages of the Uganda protectorate followed quickly.[107] Between 1896 and 1905 Crabtree and Rowling produced three of the four gospels in Soga; Maddox first translated the gospels into Nyoro, and completed the whole bible in Nyoro by 1912; Crabtree reduced Gisu (Masaba) to writing and translated the gospels into that language; Kitching, with the help of Sira Dongo, reduced 'Gang' (Acholi) to writing and translated St Mark's Gospel in 1905. H. Clayton and Miss M. T. Baker were at work on Nkole in the same period. In 1930 W. J. W. Roome, the British and Foreign Bible Society representative in East Africa, recorded the following circulation of the Scriptures: 'Ganda, 457,257; Nyoro, 119,754; Teso, 91,674; Gang, 55,998; Nkole, 38,398.'[108]

In the first part of the period, until about 1925, the 'Translation Committee' of the diocese was a body of some importance. Revision of earlier work and questions of orthography created problems which the pioneer translators did not have to face; and mass circulation involved relationships with printers and publishers in England, unlike the early days when Mackay had his own primitive printing-press. Publishing projects were normally put forward by the translation committee, through the committee of the mission, to the parent committee in London, who then made arrangements with the appropriate publishers. The publishers chiefly involved were: the British and Foreign Bible Society – for Bibles, Testaments and individual Gospels and 'portions'; the Religious Tract Society – for books other than the bible or prayer book; and the Society for the Promotion of Christian Knowledge – for prayer books, hymn-books and, from about 1919 onwards, in the promotion of bookshops and book sales.

Inevitably, the process of publication was a slow one, and sometimes the mission secretary wrote to ask what had happened to this publication or that, apparently lost in the pipe-line; but on the whole it worked tolerably well, considering the number of stages there were between completion of a manuscript and delivery of copies in Uganda.

The great need of the 1920s, created by the earlier achievements of the translators, was an adequate system of book distribution in Uganda. SPCK rose to the occasion, and William Edward Hoyle proved himself to be the right man for the job. Hoyle first went to Uganda in 1903 to help start a general store in Kampala. From 1914–17 he was stores manager for Mengo Planters Ltd, working under C. W. Hattersley, the former headmaster of Mengo High School. When Hoyle resigned from this post in 1917 Bishop Willis invited him to take over the CMS bookstore at Namirembe Hill, Kampala. In 1919 the Rev. W. K. Lowther Clarke, secretary of the SPCK, wrote to Hoyle to say that his society wished to extend its work in East Africa and suggesting that they should confer about this when he was next in England. He and Bishop Willis went together to see Lowther Clarke, and SPCK promised liberal support by way of credits for a new bookshop and agency in Kampala, and offered to pay one-third of Hoyle's salary as manager. Bishop Willis undertook to find another third. On 2nd January, 1920 the bishop saw G. T. Manley at CMS headquarters. They agreed to invite Hoyle to become manager of the bookshop which would remain under diocesan control in co-operation with SPCK who would have the disposal of two-thirds of the ultimate profits while the bishop retained one-third for diocesan purposes.[109]

The bookshop was opened in Nakasero, Kampala, on 1st August, 1920 in a small room in the Bible Society's premises. It was an immediate success. In 1925 Lowther Clarke was able to report an estimated annual profit of £1,000 of which SPCK's share would be £600. The SPCK committee had approved a grant of £150 to missionary work in the eastern province of Uganda where the bulk of the profits were made.[110] In 1927 the bookshop was incorporated as a 'company not for profit' under the joint oversight of the dioceses of Uganda and of the Upper Nile. When Hoyle retired in 1929 the bookshop was employing six Europeans and fourteen Baganda assistants at Kampala, and small bookshops had been opened at a number of mission stations in the two dioceses. The whole Bible Society premises in Kampala had been purchased, taken over, and considerably enlarged. The Uganda bookshop, thanks largely to Hoyle's energy and vision, became a considerable financial asset to the diocese, making grants to the training college at Mukono and other diocesan institutions. The SPCK contribution (to the salary, allowances, and passages of the manager and his wife) 'was never called upon and its share of profits had been all put back into the business or given to the missionary work of the diocese. The Society's help being no longer needed, the diocese henceforward was solely responsible for the shop.'[111]

Missionaries in Education, 1910–42

In 1910 all general education in Uganda along European lines was undertaken, financed and administered by the missions and the African church. By 1942 central and local government was taking a large share of the responsibility for educational finance and administration. The practice of education, however, remained almost exclusively in mission hands right to the end of this period. A few government schools were started, but they did not survive. Only one government institution, Makerere University College,[112] began its distinguished career before 1942.

The change from independence to partnership with the government did not happen without considerable heart-searching and anxiety in missionary circles. It was feared that, as educational paymaster, the protectorate government would have an increasing voice in the character of the mission itself – in the flow of recruits for missionary service, in the qualifications required of them, and in their location when they arrived.[113] Such anxieties would have been less severe, if the financial position of CMS had been more buoyant. They were given substance by the fact that the government's offer of greatly increased educational grants-in-aid coincided with a period of decline in missionary giving in Britain, and with the world depression from 1929 onwards.

The educational committee of the diocese meeting on 29th November, 1916 was against setting up government schools, but was more favourably disposed to the possible appointment of a government inspector of schools. At this time, and for several years previously, government grants to Anglican schools were running at £800–£900 a year.[114] The mission wanted a lot more financial help. It hoped such help would be given in recognition of past services, and that it would not imply any substantial increase of governmental control.[115] John Britton in an article in *The Church Missionary Review* (April 1917) described six types of school for which the diocesan council was responsible:

(*a*) *village schools* – little thatched buildings, with a pupil-teacher in charge, 'very elementary';

(*b*) *junior day-schools* – under schoolmasters trained at the 'normal' school of the rural deanery;

(*c*) *senior day-schools* – sited in the central village of a pastorate under teachers more full trained at Mengo Normal School;

(*d*) *central schools* – one for each deanery, with teachers educated at King's School, Budo, and at which regular fees were paid;

(*e*) *boarding-schools* – for 'children of higher social grades'. (Mengo High School at Kampala; at Maseno, for Kavirondo; at Hoima, for Bunyoro; at Kamuli, for Busoga; at Ngora, for Bukedi; and at Mbarara, for Ankole.) In these boarding-schools the fees were expected to cover all expenses except the salary of the missionary in charge;

(*f*) *diocesan institutions* – King's School, Budo for boys and Gayaza High School for girls, both originally restricted to the sons and daughters of chiefs.

After the first world war the need for more government help became more urgent but the old fears of its consequences remained. A report of the educational sub-committee, received by the mission committee on 23rd April, 1919, linked an appeal for recruits with a request that the Society should press for larger government grants, 'though not to such an extent that pressure might lead to the appointment of an Educational Officer of their own'.[116] In January 1920 Bishop Willis sought help of the parent committee in obtaining greater assistance from the government, and Manley promised to visit the Colonial Office to inquire about their policy with regard to government grants.[117] In May 1920 Sir Robert Coryndon, Governor of Uganda, advised CMS to tell the Colonial Office that it could not carry on without larger grants. The matter would then be referred back to him in Uganda and he would advocate such grants.[118]

These negotiations had a substantial result. New grants, out of all proportion to those received previously, were reported at a special meeting of the Uganda missionary committee on 24th September, 1920: (*a*) £3,000 for 'normal school' work (i.e. teacher-training) and (*b*) £4,000 over four years for general education. It was clear to the parent committee that the government would expect liaison in educational matters to be with the Society rather than with NAC and so it decided that grants should therefore be distributed by the missionary committee.[119] The missionary committee did not think this was the right course. It thought that the board of education of the NAC – which included two government commissioners, the bishop, several senior missionaries and 'some twenty leading members of the Native Government' – should have been allowed more say in the allotment of grants. Ladbury feared that the result of the parent committee's decision would be that 'next year the matter (i.e. the distribution of grants) will be taken out of CMS hands altogether', and the assessments earmarked by the government.[120] His fears were not well-founded. Although the conditions attaching to grants became tighter as time went on, the protectorate government preferred, for administrative reasons, to make a block grant to the Society rather than to the NAC. The mission authorities continued to press for the recognition of the NAC by the government, but to no avail.

The Phelps-Stokes Commission visited Uganda in 1924, and in its report on *Education in East Africa* commended the Uganda missions warmly.

An educational system which branches out into the whole Protectorate has been brought into being in co-operation with the Native chiefs, but without any supervision from the Colonial Government, and until recently without any financial support. It is an educational achievement of which the missions can legitimately be proud.[121]

Dr Garfield Williams, the CMS headquarters secretary in charge of foreign educational work (1921–4), was a member of the Phelps-Stokes Commission, and he made a personal report to the parent committee. Its main points were: (1) the need for rapid expansion of educational work in the eastern province commensurate with the rapid evangelistic advance; (2) the recognition of Makerere College as 'the crown of the mission system' of education; (3) the need for a board of education in Uganda, 'predominantly missionary and presided over by the Director of Education, on which the missionary societies are properly represented by educationists who are actually responsible for the organization and working of mission education'; (4) boards of governors should be appointed for Budo and Gayaza schools.[122]

In 1925 Eric Hussey was appointed Director of Education under the protectorate government. He had been brought in two years earlier from government service in the Sudan to advise on the development of education, so he was already familiar with the Uganda situation. An advisory council for native education was appointed, at Hussey's suggestion, in which the missionary societies were associated with the government in the evolution of educational policy.[123] It met for the first time on 6th June, 1926. It opposed Hussey's tentative plan for non-denominational religious schools to replace the CMS 'central' schools and their Roman Catholic equivalents, and Hussey modified his plans. He agreed that intermediate education should remain entirely in the hands of the missions, and that there would only be one government school at this level – for Muslims. Hussey's plans for an inspectorate and for the decentralization of educational administration won the advisory council's approval.[124] His criticisms of the village schools produced an able rejoinder from G. T. Manley in *The Church Missionary Review*. If more care had been taken, he wrote, to distinguish the many different types of out-school or bush school, some which were regarded as inefficient 'might have been described as vigorous and efficient centres of evangelization.... To call this primitive insitution a "school" at all is half a misnomer; but to speak of it as an "inefficient elementary school" is to misunderstand or overlook its origin and function.' The mission would welcome government help in making its educational work more efficient. But the schools proper were connected so closely and organically with the whole spiritual work of which they formed a part and the differences were so great between different localities that 'advance can best be made by working as far as possible through the agency of the missions themselves rather than, at first, by direct government intervention'.[125]

Another of Hussey's proposals won the approval of Manley and the local missionary leadership. This was his plan to introduce 'Jeanes teachers', that is African teachers trained to travel round the village centres and to stay long enough in one place to share new methods and skills with the village teachers. 'This system,' Manley wrote, 'is full of hope for a country like Uganda with its multitude of scattered schools.' He also thought that a government inspectorate was compatible with the missionary system of school inspection and district supervision. The first government inspectors were appointed in 1925.

An education ordinance in 1927 required all schools to be registered with the government education department. Unqualified teachers were allowed to continue in 'sub-grade' schools provided they confined their teaching to religious instruction and other specified subjects. Grants were to be made on the recommendation of the advisory council and the director, and in relation to the budgets and annual accounts for each grant-aided school. Grants could be withheld on grounds of inefficiency. On the 1926 estimates approved by the advisory committee, the CMS and Roman Catholic missions each received £10,250 in government grants.[126] The Uganda education department report (31st December, 1925) gave the following statistics:—

	Schools	Boys	Girls	European Teachers	Native Teachers
Anglican	1,607	63,854	41,536	7	1,882
Roman Catholic	1,587	40,700	25,871	94	2,162
Non-Mission	12	608	33	—	24
Total	3,206	105,162	67,440	101	4,068

Bishop Willis, commenting on these figures, wrote:

> It will be seen that the Roman Catholics have roughly one European mission-
> ary to every 700 in their schools against one CMS missionary to 15,000. It
> would be worth making any effort to secure a better European supervision
> than has hitherto been possible.[127]

This effort was made, and the pace of recruitment for educational missionaries
increased under the stimulus of the larger government grants; though the
representation of European missionary teachers under CMS remained very
much smaller than under the Roman Catholic missions.

The problems relating to the allocation of grants were worked through
amicably in the next few years. In August, 1926, for example, Ladbury reported that the Director of Education had agreed that the surplus from grants
for European salaries could be spent on missionaries' houses 'so long as the
whole grant for a specified school is spent in connection with that school'.[128]
Where the parent committee failed to supply a teacher for any of the time
covered by the grant, the grant could still be claimed provided it was spent on
the school for buildings, repairs, equipment, etc.[129] This sounds, and was
intended to be, generous; but it obviously could not last. In August 1928
Hussey wrote to say that during the past two years this had been allowed to
give the Society time to collect staff, but 'we cannot in fact conscientiously pay
the salary of a man who does not exist'.[130]

In 1929 the Uganda standing committee appealed to the parent committee
'to change its policy with regard to the position and support of missionaries
sent out from England in connection with Educational Government Grants'.
The mission, it claimed, was worse off now than in the leaner years before 1925.
When the scale of grants was first discussed the parent committee did not want
the whole salary and expenses of educational missionaries to be paid by the
government, so £300 per annum for men and £210 per annum for women
had been the agreed rate. But this did not cover extras, or the outfit and passage
of wives, etc. Further, during the last three years the parent committee 'has
made it perfectly clear that their policy is not to pay any of the expenses of
workers sent out as *additional* recruits'. The result of this policy had been to
divide the NAC and the CMS into two totally distinct bodies with interests in
some instances *opposed* to each other, and with 'some of the workers (even
European) working against each other so as to maintain and develop the action
which especially appeals to them'. The standing committee therefore pleaded
that (1) all government grants received be credited to the parent committee (the
mission undertaking to obtain the utmost possible from the government);
(2) the parent committee to pay all the salaries, passages, and outfits for edu-
cationalists just as they did for other missionaries. The administrative work
involved was 'outside the capabilities of the ordinary missionary and accountant'.[131]

Ladbury had been asking for these arrangements for some time and he was now able to quote the Director of Education in support of them. 'He is very anxious,' he wrote, 'that the parent committee should undertake the pooling of funds and send out all missionaries on the same basis. He is strongly opposed to individual institutions running their own finances.'[132] Advised by its financial secretary, the parent committee agreed to try out the 'pool' system advocated by the Uganda mission and to recruit all missionaries, educational and pastoral, on the same basis, and standing in identical relationship with CMS.[133]

In the early 1930s the government education department, working through the district education boards, sought to encourage the use of Swahili. There was a plausible reason for this policy. The three East African territories (Uganda, Kenya, and Tanganyika) were considering the possibilities of some form of federation or 'closer union', and Swahili had some claim to be already the *lingua franca* of the other two territories. But in Uganda opposition was strong, both to the idea of 'closer union' and to the use of Swahili in schools. The Baganda chiefs opposed it. They claimed that Luganda was already the *lingua franca* of the greater part of the protectorate, and they feared that the use of Swahili would be a barrier to learning English. The Batoro chiefs wanted neither Luganda nor Swahili but English in their schools. The missionaries broadly speaking were against the use of Swahili on the grounds that it was not the language of any tribe in the protectorate: and it was also the language of Islam in East Africa. Eventually it was agreed that Swahili should be used as a medium of instruction only in the mixed language areas of the protectorate and there only in the elementary vernacular schools. The CMS mission standing committee continued to protest, but was prepared to co-operate in the teaching of Swahili, as a subject, in the upper classes of such schools where the people themselves desired it and where qualified teachers were available.[134]

As one would expect, the protectorate government began to require teaching qualifications for missionaries whose salaries it paid or to which it contributed by grants. In February 1932 the acting secretary of the mission (Daniell) wrote to say that in future the government would not pay salaries of men in grant-aided posts unless they had attended the London Day Training College or were otherwise satisfactorily qualified.[135]

In 1931 the Rev. James Dougall was appointed educational adviser to the non-Roman missions in Kenya and Uganda; and in 1932 the Rev. A. M. Williams was appointed education secretary of the CMS mission, and Miss Norah Ainley, Principal of Gayaza Normal School, as mission inspectress of schools. These appointments were timely, because, under Sir Philip Mitchell's governorship from 1935 a somewhat *laissez-faire* attitude to education was replaced by a more vigorous policy that required a more adaptable and flexible approach from the missionary bodies. 'I saw . . . that my duty lay,' the new governor wrote, 'in promoting to the utmost the development of University education including, of course, advanced teacher-training', and secondary schools would need to be developed to supply the university and training colleges with teachable pupils in sufficient numbers. 'If this meant that the education of the masses must remain for a while – a while that might be a generation, the muddle that it then was – I could not help that.'[136]

In 1935 Harold Jowitt (Director of Education, 1934–45) recognized that most of the subgrade schools were in fact mainly mission-outposts and 'could not be expected to do much more educationally until [their teachers] can be replaced by better qualified men'. Mitchell's policy was to concentrate on higher education as the best long-term hope for elementary education. This policy met with the approval of some of the leading missionary educationists. H. M. Grace, headmaster of King's School, Budo, regarded secondary education as appropriate for a small *élite* and co-operated with the government education department's policy in reorganizing his school to achieve higher academic standards.[137] Williams, on the other hand, saw need for training of Africans of 'general ability' as well as of an *élite*. He was not greatly worried about the low standard of academic education achieved in the 'middle' (formerly 'intermediate') schools.

In 1936 two schools, King's, Budo and the Roman Catholic secondary school at Kisubi, began courses in their senior departments leading to the Cambridge School Certificate. The annual report of the Uganda education department for 1936 presents, says G. P. McGregor:

a clear, and in some ways curious picture. The first thing one notices is how much of Hattersley's system remains. . . . Of the roughly 250,000 children at school, 228,000 attended unaided 'sub-grade' schools – clearly almost identical with Hattersley's 'bush schools' of nearly forty years before. From this 'foundation' an educational pyramid rose steeply.

At its apex there were five 'junior secondary schools' with 248 pupils between them, and all boys. Three were CMS – Budo (96); Nyakasura (30); Mwiri (11); and two were Roman Catholic.[138]

In 1937 the de la Warr Commission on Higher Education in East Africa (Col. No. 142, 1937) endorsed Sir Philip Mitchell's policy of concentration on higher education. It recommended that the government, while continuing to assist mission schools, should expand secondary education by setting up its own secondary schools.

In 1939 the governor appointed a committee under the chairmanship of H. B. Thomas, Director of Lands and Surveys, to draw up a plan for the development of African education 1941–5, and to review the principle of grants-in-aid. The committee recommended that the contribution through grants to primary education be increased on the basis of a five year plan, with the ironing out of disparities, together with the orderly planning of public education in each local authority area. It recommended the reorganization of district education boards, giving them fuller responsibilities for planning and financing primary education. The recommendation was accepted, and from 1942 the district boards began to be replaced by local education authorities, chaired by the district commissioner with the provincial education officer in attendance, three African members nominated by the Native Administration, three members nominated by each denomination, one of whom was to be an African and one a woman. The de la Warr commission (1937) had proposed native administration elementary schools as well as government secondary and normal schools, but one member of that commission, John Murray, in a minority report, suggested that denominational education was suited to the genius of the people and that education in Uganda should therefore remain in the control of the missions. The Thomas committee proposed native administration and government schools, but only in areas unserved by the missions.[139]

In 1940 the government, following recommendations of the Thomas committee, assured complete financial responsibility for the leading secondary schools, including the two major 'diocesan institutions', King's School, Budo, and Gayaza High School. These two schools began in the same year. Miss Alfreda Allen began teaching four girls at Gayaza in January 1905. H. W. Weatherhead began at Budo with six boys in October 1905, though King's School was not officially opened until 29th March, 1906. They served the same purpose – to give the sons and daughters of chiefs the best education that the missionaries knew, that of an English 'public school', modified to suit local needs and conditions. The two schools expanded at roughly the same rate. Gayaza had seventy-five pupils by 1910, Budo had seventy-six by 1912. By the end of this period they had an even closer connection. In 1942 three girls from Gayaza passed the entrance examination to Budo senior school to prepare for the Cambridge School Certificate.

A brief summary of their separate development is all that space allows. At Gayaza High School Miss Allen continued as headmistress for twenty-five years. She was succeeded in 1930 by Miss C. J. Smyth who had been with her on the staff since 1909. Miss Smythe was followed in turn by Miss Margaret Bolton (1934–8) and Miss Nancy Corby (1938–50). In 1932 the teacher-training department at Gayaza became a separate institution at Buloba.

King's School, Budo, like its sister-school, owed much to the enthusiastic and at times courageous patronage of the Katikiro of Buganda, Sir Apolo Kagwa. It was he who supported H. W. Weatherhead, against much Baganda opposition, in the choice of King's Hill, Budo, as the site for the school. H. W. Weatherhead, the first much-loved headmaster, retired because of ill-health in 1912. He was succeeded by his younger brother H. T. C. Weatherhead (1912–24); G. G. Garrett (1924–6); H. M. Grace (1926–34); L. J. Gaster (1934–9), and D. G. Herbert (Lord Hemingford) 1939–47. The first school chapel, now a library, was built as a gift of Bishop T. E. Williamson as a memorial to three boy-martyrs and was dedicated on 11th July, 1912. In 1924 it was noted that of those who had so far left the school, thirty-five were in native administration posts, five were county chiefs, thirty-two were district chiefs and seventy-one were schoolmasters. The Old Boys Association became an important social factor in Uganda.

In 1927 Mengo High School was transferred to Budo to become the nucleus of its 'middle' school, with a new junior department starting below it, and the senior school working to higher academic standards. Grace appealed to the Baganda for £27,000 for new buildings. £8,000 was contributed, mostly by the Kabaka himself. In 1927 Dr Julian Huxley visited King's School and described it as the best school he had seen in Africa.[140]

The Training of Clergy

In 1913 the small divinity class moved out from Kampala to Mukono about twelve miles to the east and the first theological college was built – mud walls and a thatched roof. During the first world war four hostels were built of sun-dried brick with thatched roofs. In 1924 a new block consisting of the chapel, assembly hall, library, classrooms and offices – 'one of the most attractive buildings in the country'[141] – was built to the design of Professor Berresford Pite. They were opened by the governor, and Bishop Willis consecrated the chapel, on St Mark's Day, 25th April, 1925. A bronze tablet, inscribed in memory of Bishop Tucker, records that 'This college was built by those who loved him, for the training of clergy and other workers in the Church of Christ of Uganda. Whose faith follow.' The college itself served the needs of ordinands and lay readers; and in 1929 a primary teachers' training department was added. The teacher-training at Mukono, as elsewhere, was financed, inspected and grant-aided by the government but the theological college remained the sole responsibility of the church.

In 1935 the suggestion was made that the total resources of training at Mukono and at Buwalasi in the Upper Nile diocese should be pooled, with a consolidation of theological training at one place and of teacher-training at the other. The missionaries' conference of the CMS Elgon mission was unanimously against this.[142] The development of a strong community life at Buwalasi College, still in its earliest stages, depended in their view on keeping ordinands and teachers-in-training together on the same site, and the travelling costs involved in the scheme would, they thought, be prohibitive.

In 1938 the Uganda mission standing committee decided to separate the primary teachers' training college at Mukono from the theological school as soon as it could be done conveniently, each institution to be conducted as an independent financial unit, though on the same site. A. M. Williams, the general secretary of the mission, explained that both J. C. Jones, the warden in charge of the ordinands, and A. V. P. Elliott, in charge of teacher-training, wanted this. The director of education also wanted it, and many of the missionaries favoured it. Williams himself was not so sure. He thought that by such separation the schoolmasters would lose much of their 'diocesan' spirit while the theological students would 'miss a little of the sharp edge of teachers' minds'.[143]

By the end of the 1930s there was a growing conviction that the often lonely and difficult work of the clergy required that their wives should be with them, and should share to some extent in their pre-ordination training. Buwalasi had started on the assumption that students' wives would come with them; and in 1940 six mud and thatch cottages were built in the grounds at Mukono for the ordinands and their wives. Other cottages were added later to make what came to be known as the 'Ordinands' Village'.

In October 1941 a disciplinary crisis occurred at Bishop Tucker College. A number of students who belonged to the 'Revival' movement had been holding corporate meetings for prayer from 4.0 to 6.0 a.m. At first the warden had allowed this, but as the claims for freedom to meet when they wished grew to the point of disrupting college discipline he put his foot down. On 22nd October he announced a new college timetable which precluded these early meetings, and other meetings in college could only be held with his permission. Twenty-five students refused to accept the warden's ruling and were told that they must go unless they did so. They were not 'expelled', and Bishop Stuart and J. C. Jones did everything they could to smooth the way for their return. Several of them, after an interview with the bishop, had what he described as 'a change of heart' about the whole matter and came back into training.[144]

It cannot be claimed that the training of clergy went well in Uganda during this period. Despite the excellent 'plant' at Mukono from 1925 onwards, it suffered from lack of continuity. The missionaries in charge of clergy-training either lacked the necessary gifts for it; or were removed to other work before they could create a good tradition; or were distracted by competing responsibilities while remaining in charge. At the end of the period J. C. Jones, later to become Bishop of Bangor, began a new and happier tradition in theological training in Uganda on which others, notably J. V. Taylor, were to build in the later 1940s. Clergy training was not a 'cinderella' in the sense of being neglected and excluded from among the priorities of the church and mission; a great deal of anxious thought was given to it by Bishop Willis and others. Twice (in 1924 and 1930) Bishop Willis planned to bring the ordinands from Mukono to Kampala in the hope that this might raise standards academically and spiritually. But the causes for the apparent lack of new initiatives and sense of direction in clergy training were deep-seated.

John Britton, in an article quoted above,[145] put his finger on one reason – the separation, under the 1909 constitution of the Uganda church, of its Board of Education and Board of Theological Studies. This separation, he believed, had the effect of drawing ordinands increasingly from the ranks of catechists and not, as earlier, from the sons of chiefs and others trained at King's School, Budo. Another reason, not suggested by Britton, was the doctrinaire insistence by Bishop Tucker on the complete self-support of the Native Anglican Church which in the long run meant a much lower salary scale for clergy compared with teachers. This difference was already making itself felt in 1917 when Britton wrote. Later, when government education grants increased to cover nearly all the cost of training apart from clergy-training, the difference in status was accentuated. It lay behind the standing committee's decision in 1938 to separate the two sections of Mukono. But the problem was not one for Uganda alone.

The cause of the apparent neglect of theological training lay not in the indifference of mission boards, but in the harsh economic fact that the ministry was the only modern profession in the developing countries which was not artificially subsidized by local governments and international aid.[146]

CMS Medical Mission, 1910-42

By 1910 Mengo hospital, with its red buildings clustered on the green slopes of Namirembe Hill,[147] was the best known hospital in East Africa; and Dr Albert Cook, who started it in 1897, was already a missionary doctor of international repute. Tropical medicine was in its infancy in 1900-2 when he and his brother, Dr J. H. Cook, helped to identify the cause of sleeping-sickness; and they also made substantial contributions to the treatment of ankylostomiasis (hookworm) and tick-fever (spirella).[148] Their partnership at Mengo lasted until 1919 when for family and health reasons J. H. Cook returned to England to become the secretary of the medical committee at CMS headquarters in London, a post which he held with distinction until 1940.

In 1910 the hospital received its first X-ray installation, brought out from England by Dr E. N. Cook, a nephew of the two brothers. In 1912 and 1915 two more buildings were added – the Annie Walker Hospital, with fourteen beds, for European patients, the gift of Mr Theodore Walker of Leicester; and a hospital with twenty-eight beds for Indians and Goans. On the outbreak of war in 1914 the hospital offered its services to the protectorate government, and new wards were built to accommodate 'the convoys of sick and wounded, mostly the former'. The years 1917-18 saw the start of two far-reaching enterprises in medical education – a medical school for male assistants and a maternity training school.

The medical school, the first in the Uganda protectorate, was opened in January 1917 with seventeen students. It was supervised at first by J. H. Cook, assisted by A. C. S. Smith and L. E. S. Sharp, and later by E. N. Cook and E. V. Hunter. When, in 1922, Hunter went to build up the medical mission at Ngora he took with him the students in training at the time, and in 1924 a government medical school was started at Mulago close by, but the Mengo medical school was re-opened in May 1924 and reorganized by R. Y. Stones.

The maternity training school was founded by Mrs A. R. Cook, who as Katherine Timpson reached Uganda in 1896 as the first trained nurse. In 1918, after twenty-one years as matron of Mengo hospital, she returned from furlough to begin her greatest work. She had long wanted to develop maternity training, and there was great need for it in Uganda. The infant mortality rate of Buganda was running at 500 to 800 per 1,000 births, and the Baganda were coming to be regarded as a dying race.[149] Mrs Cook started maternity training with thirteen students in January 1919 in temporary quarters and in 1920 six of them passed the government midwifery examination, among them a daughter of Sir Apolo Kagwa. Meanwhile an appeal for £5,000 had been made for the new buildings and equipment needed. When £4,000 had been raised locally the protectorate government added the last £1,000. The maternity training school was opened by Sir Robert Coryndon, the Governor, and Lady Coryndon (after whom it was named) in June, 1921. On 24th October, 1925 a maternity centre and practising school was opened at Nakifuma in Kyagwe about forty miles from Kampala. The land had been given by the Kabaka and the cost was largely met by Mr and Mrs Ernest Carr of Nairobi, benefactors of many missionary projects in Kenya and Uganda.

In the first seven years of the maternity training school fifty-two Baganda women gained the government diploma. By that time (1928) twenty-six welfare centres, each staffed by two certified midwives, had been opened. The effects were most heartening. The infant mortality rate in Buganda had been greatly reduced, but was still pathetically high in Toro, Ankole and Bunyoro. By 1942 the maternity training school had sent out into the villages of Uganda about two hundred qualified maternity nurses who had passed the equivalent of the English SCM. Most of them had charge of small hospital wards for confinements as well as dispensaries for ante-natal and post-natal treatment and advice. The death-rate among children under one year for all Uganda was reduced from 500 per 1,000 in 1922 to 158 per 1,000 in 1936; and in Buganda to 81 per 1,000. Although it remained closely connected with the CMS medical mission the maternity training school was a co-operative venture in which the government and Roman Catholic missions took a full share. Lady Cook retired in 1930. Her later years as matron at Mengo hospital had been stormy and difficult,[150] and she was never an easy person to work with: but she initiated a revolution in maternity and child-care in Uganda which saved countless thousands of lives and put the whole country in her debt.

By 1925 Mengo hospital was beginning to feel the effects of the large government hospital at Mulago built in the previous year. By September 1934 a sub-committee of the medical sub-conference of the mission reported an accumulated deficit of £10,000 and an annual deficit of £2,000. It recommended that the Ndeje nurses' training school be closed; that Dr R. Y. Stones, Sir Albert's successor at Mengo, should be asked to meet the recurrent deficit by economies; and that arrangements be made for the repayment of the accumulated deficit in ten years.[151] Sir Albert Cook wrote strongly opposing the suggestion that the training of nurses should be moved back from Ndeje to Kampala,[152] but Miss

E. M. Baring-Gould, of the CMS headquarters staff, gave an adverse report on Ndeje, and the standing committee of the mission, while expressing their sympathy for the distress it would cause to Sir Albert and Lady Cook, supported its closure. In June 1936 Sir Albert met the Africa secretary and general secretary at CMS headquarters to discuss the future of Mengo hospital. He said that it had suffered from government competition, and that the accumulated deficit now stood at £8,754. It was agreed that the hospital should continue on a reduced scale.[153]

In 1937, after several anxious years, the fortieth anniversary of Mengo hospital was celebrated with great thanksgiving for its past service and with renewed hope for the future. The Katikiro of Buganda spoke of the immense debt the country owed to Mengo in combating epidemic diseases and infant mortality. Lady Cook died in the following year (1938) but Sir Albert lived on in his house overlooking Lake Victoria for another thirteen years until his death in 1951. His relationship with the ruling family of Buganda was very close. The Kabaka, H. H. Edward Mutesa II, was born in his house, and he described Sir Albert as his father's 'great friend'. It was fitting that, when H. H. Daudi Chwa died in 1939, he should be invited to preach at his funeral service. The hospital Albert Cook founded and directed for so long set standards for missions and governments in other African territories; but he is remembered not only as a great doctor and medical administrator but as a pioneer missionary, one of that company who walked up from the coast to bring the gospel of Christ to Uganda.

There were two other CMS medical missions in Uganda during the period 1910–42: Toro hospital, near Kabarole which will always be associated with the name of Dr Ashton Bond; and the hospital at Ngora with the adjacent Ongino leprosy settlement which owed most, humanly speaking, to the vision and skill of Dr E. Villiers Hunter and Miss Margaret Laing. Dr Bond worked for over twenty years at Toro, from 1903 when he opened the hospital to 1924 when he left the CMS staff to become a district MO. By then it was a sizeable hospital with a hundred and twenty-five beds in the main block, and a sleeping-sickness unit and a venereal disease treatment centre close by. A brick-built dispensary had been added on his initiative in 1917, and an Indian ward was to be built at the expense of Indians.[154] By 1929 the number of beds had been reduced to a hundred, largely due to increasing government commitment in medical service; and in 1934 it was decided to close the hospital, largely as an economy measure in relation to the deficit at Mengo.

The hospital at Ngora, in the Teso district, a hundred and fifty miles north-east of Kampala, was started in 1922. It played a notable part in the evangelization of an area which, from 1926, was included in the diocese of the Upper Nile. The parent committee had been reluctant, on financial grounds, to commit itself to a medical mission at Ngora, but Mr Ernest Carr had generously promised to cover all expenses for the first three years. A suitable doctor was available in Uganda, Villiers Hunter, and local needs and the distance from Kampala made it a good site. Ladbury reinforced the case of his committee with further arguments. Dr Hunter was unlikely to remain much longer at Mengo in any case and was the obvious man for pioneer medical work. In April 1922 the parent committee, urged on by Dr A. R. Cook, agreed to appoint Hunter to Ngora provided that no permanent expenditure should be incurred beyond Mr Carr's gift.[155] In 1926 the CMS Africa committee, subject to the concurrence of the local governing body approved the commencement of leprosy work at Ngora in co-operation with the Mission to Lepers on the understanding that the parent committee would not be committed financially.

There were occasional difficulties during the period in the relationship of medical mission staff at the hospitals to the general body of missionaries and the local governing body. In February 1927, for instance, the standing committee of the mission took strong exception to the request, made direct to the parent committee, that a Mengo doctor should be an *ex officio* member of the committee.[156] Dr A. R. Cook argued the case for this at length in an interview at CMS headquarters. The issues involved are touched on in the report of a mission sub-committee on 'Medical Mission Policy in Uganda' (1931),[157] 'Instructions to all members of hospital staffs,' it proposed, 'were to be given by the Standing Committee of the Mission', in consultation with the medical superintendent of the hospital concerned. The medical superintendent would be responsible for all internal arrangements in the hospital. If any member of the hospital staff wished to refer any matter affecting the hospital to the local governing body or to the bishop he should do it in writing through the medical superintendent; and no official action should be taken without consulting the medical superintendent. Doubt about 'the chain of command' was always a potential source of friction in this as in other missions. The parent committee jealously guarded its function as a court of appeal for missionaries who felt themselves to be under local pressure; on the other hand the local governing body could reasonably claim that its task became impossible if some individual missionaries had greater ease of access to the headquarters secretariat than others. The task of the local governing body was also made difficult if individual institutions in the mission, whether hospitals or schools, were so run that the standing committee's relationship with missionaries working in those institutions was reduced to a formality once their appointment had been made. Some spelling-out, along the lines of this 1931 report, was necessary. For the most part the Uganda mission found its way through these administrative problems with a minimum of friction, aided by a generosity of spirit among the missionaries towards each other to which the records of the time bear a cumulative and impressive witness.

NOTES

1. W. S. Churchill, *My African Journey*, 1908, p. 86.
2. See Roland Oliver, *The Missionary Factor in East Africa*, Longmans, 1952, p. 162.
3. H. B. Thomas and Robert Scott, *Uganda*, Oxford, 1935, p. 44.
4. Nomenclature differs in minor details. The map followed here is in Harold Ingrams, *Uganda*, HMSO, 1960, facing p. 158.
5. Thomas and Scott, op. cit., pp. 86, 87.
6. See A. R. Dunbar, *A History of Bunyoro-Kitara*, OUP, Nairobi, 1965, pp. 69ff.
7. D. A. Low and R. C. Pratt, *Buganda and British Overrule, 1900–1955*, Oxford, 1960, p. 9.
8. Oliver, op. cit., p. 188.
9. Thomas and Scott, op. cit., p. 451.
10. G3/A7/P2, 1910/45.
11. P2, 1910/89.
12. Low and Pratt, op. cit., pp. 224ff.
13. P4, 1929/137.
14. Low and Pratt, op. cit., p. 240.
15. The Kabaka of Uganda, *The Desecration of My Kingdom*, Constable, 1967, pp. 63, 64.
16. P2, 1914/184.
17. P2, 1915/34.
18. P3, 1915/xxvi.
19. Low and Pratt, op. cit., p. 277.
20. John V. Taylor, *The Primal Vision*, SCM Press, 1963, p. 63.
21. F. B. Welbourn, 'God and the Gods' in *East Africa Past and Present*, Editions Présence Africaine, Paris, 1964, p. 170. He mentions E. E. Evans-Pritchard, E. B. Idowu, G. Lienhardt in studies respectively of the Nuer, Yoruba and Dinka peoples.
22. F. P. Faupel, *African Holocaust*, Geoffrey Chapman, 1962, p. 3.
23. Thomas and Scott, op. cit., p. 96.
24. J. K. Russell, *Men without God*, Highway Press, 1966, pp. 82, 83.
25. See Dunbar, op. cit., Ch. 3.
26. See J. Middleton, *Lugbara Religion*, OUP, 1960.
27. Taylor, op. cit., pp. 77, 78.
28. ibid., p. 29.
29. See e.g. W. J. W. Roome, *Through the Lands of Nyanza*, Marshall, Morgan and Scott, 1930.
30. Thomas and Scott, op. cit., pp. 336, 337.
31. F. B. Welbourn, *East African Rebels*, SCM Press, 1961, Chs. 3 and 5; see also J. V. Taylor *The Growth of the Church in Buganda*, SCM Press, 1953, pp. 97, 98.
32. C. P. Groves, *The Planting of Christianity in Africa*, Lutterworth Press, 1958, IV, pp. 124, 125.
33. Welbourn, op. cit., p. 81.
34. Stock, III, pp. 94–112, 402–54. IV, pp. 83–104. Also J. V. Taylor, op. cit. 1958, pp. 19–105; and Mary Stuart, *Land of Promise*, Highway Press, 1957.
19–105; and Mary Stuart, *Land of Promise*, Highway Press, 1957.
35. Faupel, op. cit., p. 217
36. Oliver, op. cit., pp. 182, 183.
37. Taylor, op. cit., 1958, p. 86.
38. P2, 1910/88.
39. P2, 1910/78.

40. P2, 1910/xviii.
41. P2, 1910/100.
42. P2, 1910/245.
43. P2, 1911/1.
44. P2, 1910/276.
45. Taylor, op. cit., 1958, p. 83.
46. Taylor, op. cit., 1958, p. 84.
47. P2, 1911/102.
48. Oliver, op. cit., p. 222.
49. P2, 1912/29.
50. P2, 1912/57.
51. P2, 1911/180.
52. P2, 1912/29.
53. P2, 1912/76.
54. P2, 1912/191.
55. P2, 1913/86.
56. See Fisher papers (CMS archives).
57. P3, 1917/66.
58. P2, 1917/xxv.
59. P2, 1914/157.
60. P3, 1917/69, 74.
61. Carl-J. Hellberg, *Missions on a Colonial Frontier West of Lake Victoria*, Gleerups, 1965, p. 133.
62. Taylor, op. cit., 1958, p. 92.
63. P3, 1920/55.
64. P3, 1922/following 29.
65. P3, 1922/42.
66. P3, 1924/viii.
67. P4, 1929/23.
68. G/Y/A7/2, loc. cit.
69. ibid., Bardsley to Archbishop of Canterbury, 12th April, 1920.
70. ibid., Willis to same, 15th August, 1921.
71. P3, 1921/28.
72. G/Y/A7/2, memo by G. T. Manley.
73. ibid., Willis to Archbishop of Canterbury, 22nd December, 1921.
74. ibid., same, 12th January, 1922 and P3, 1922/17.
75. ibid., Gresford Jones to Bardsley, 30th January, 1922; P3, 1923/103.
76. *CMR*, 1927, pp. 220ff.
77. *AR*, (MS), 1927–28, pp. 72–74.
78. *CMR* 1926, 'Some Achievements and Lessons of Fifty Years', pp. 306ff.
79. P4, 1931/18.
80. P3, 1922/63, 79.
81. P3, 1927/2.
82. P4, 1929/8.
83. P4, 1930/16.
84. P3, 1921/2.
85. J. H. Oldham, *Florence Allshorn*, SCM Press, 1951, pp. 24–27.
86. P3, 1924/29.
87. P3, 1924/83.
88. *CMR*, 1927, p. 225.
89. G/Y/A7/3, Blackledge, memo, 30th April, 1930.
90. ibid., memo of interview with Archbishop of Canterbury, 16th October, 1931.

91. P4, 1934/21.

92. Willis MS, p. 2.

93. Ladbury Diaries (Makerere College Library).

94. A. Luck, *African Saint. The Story of Apolo Kivebulaya*, SCM Press, 1963.

95. P4, 1933/17.

96. Africa committee minute, 26th June, 1934 (see also P4, 1934/63).

97. *AR* (MS), 1935–6, pp. 97–99.

98. Grovcs, op. cit., IV, pp. 222, 223.

99. A. C. S. Smith, *Road to Revival*, Church Missionary Society, 1947, p. 54.

100. G/Y/A7/2, MS report on Uganda Diamond Jubilee Mission 1937.

101. ibid., 'Uganda Seven'.

102. ibid.

103. Uganda diocese file (577).

104. ibid.

105. Taylor, op. cit., 1958, p. 104.

106. ibid., pp. 238, 239.

107. R. Kilgour, *The Bible Throughout the World*, World Dominion Press, 1939, pp. 43ff.

108. Roome, op. cit., p. 172.

109. P3, 1920/14. See also H. B. Thomas article on W. E. Hoyle, *Uganda Church Review*, 1959, p. 4.

110. P3, 1922/28; 1925/70.

111. W. K. Lowther Clarke, *A History of the SPCK*, SPCK, 1959, p. 202.

112. See Margaret Macpherson, *They Built for the Future: A Chronicle of Makerere University College, 1922–62*, Cambridge, 1964.

113. Letter from Walker to Treasurer (Uganda), 24th July, 1911, listing grants expected in April 1912, total £917 6s 8d (Walker MSS, Namirembe).

114. P3, 1916/131.

115. Walker to Baylis, 25th July, 1912, on rising education costs (Walker MSS, Namirembe).

116. P3, 1919/48.

117. P3, 1920/15.

118. P3, 1920/97.

119. P3, 1923/xvi.

120. P3, 1924/35.

121. Phelps-Stokes Fund, *Education in East Africa*, Edinburgh House Press, 1925, p. 151.

122. G/Y/A7/2.

123. Felice Carter, 'Education in Uganda 1894–1945' (unpublished thesis), Chapter IV.

124. ibid., p. 173.

125. *CMR*, 1925, pp. 222, 223.

126. P3, 1925/77.

127. P3, 1926/64.

128. P3, 1926/86.

129. P4, 1927/110.

130. P4, 1928/76.

131. P4, 1929/20.

132. P4, 1929/38.

133. P4, 1929/xxiv.

134. P4, 1931/96.

135. P4, 1932/14.

136. Quoted Ingrams, op. cit., p. 119.

137. Carter, op. cit., p. 245.

138. G. P. McGregor, *King's College, Budo: The First Sixty Years*, Oxford, 1967, p. 88.

139. Carter, op. cit., p. 415.

140. Julian Huxley, *Africa View*, Chatto, 1931, p. 282.

141. J. V. Taylor, *Mukono*, CMS, 1950, p. 1. (pamphlet).

142. Mukono file (131) minutes, Elgon Missionaries' Conference, August 1935.

143. ibid., Williams to Hooper, 10th October, 1938.

144. ibid., Stuart to Hooper, 6th November, 1941.

145. *CMR*, 1917, pp. 184ff.

146. *CMS News-Letter*, No. 314, March 1968.

147. *Jubilee Report of the CMS Mengo Medical Mission*, CMS, Kampala, Uganda, 1927, opposite p. 9.

148. op. cit., pp. 14, 15. See also P. L. Garlick, *The Wholeness of Man*, Highway Press, 1943, pp. 44, 45.

149. Garlick, op. cit., p. 156.

150. P3, 1917/136.

151. P4, 1934/105.

152. P4, 1934/36.

153. G/Y/A7/2, memo by Cash, 30th June 1936.

154. P3, 1917/29.

155. P3, 1922/xxvi.

156. P4, 1927/21.

157. P4, 1931/17.

Ruanda

Ruanda and Urundi[1] were coveted before the first world war by several of the European colonial powers.

The aura of romanticism – the picturesque mountainous countries inhabited by the Tutsi, the Hutu and the Twa – explains in large part the importance which the imperial powers attached to them.[2]

There were also practical considerations which intensified interest in this region. Britain had plans for a Cape-to-Cairo railway linking her dependencies to the north and south. Belgium wanted an outlet from the Congo Free State to Lake Victoria, and so to the Indian Ocean. Germany coveted it as part of her Central African Empire. German oversight of the two kingdoms was recognized by the Anglo-German agreement of 1st July, 1890, by which the 1° south parallel of latitude was extended as a colonial boundary across Lake Victoria to the Belgian Congo. 'Mount Mufumbiro' was, however, excluded from the German sphere, and this caused difficulty later.

German occupation before the first world war was not intensive. Four military posts were established in Ruanda-Urundi, but Germany appears to have been chiefly interested in the dual kingdom as a reservoir of plantation labour for the future development of her territories further east. After Germany's defeat, Belgium claimed Ruanda-Urundi as her share of the spoils of victory. Her troops had overrun the country in their advance from the Congo to Tanganyika and 'she was anxious to add it to the uplands of the eastern Congo to which, geographically and ethnologically, it belongs'.[3] In 1922 'the dual Kingdom of Ruanda-Urundi' was placed under a League of Nations mandate to be administered by Belgium, and the mandate was formally ratified on 20th October, 1924. In the discussions about East Africa at the Peace Conference in 1919 Lord Milner explained that the Cape-to-Cairo railway would need to run through the Kagera valley. For this reason a strip of eastern Ruanda was excluded from the Belgian mandate at first; but the railway project was abandoned, and in 1923 British Ruanda was handed over to Belgium.

'Belgium's acquisition of Ruanda-Urundi', Louis suggests, 'is surely one of the great ironies in the history of Africa. For her statesmen did not want it. They intended to use it as a pawn to gain the southern bank and mouth of the Congo river';[4] but Patrick Balfour, writing in 1937, gives a happier picture of the Belgian use of the mandate:

> To-day Ruanda-Urundi is the Benjamin of Belgium's Colonial empire. . . .
> On its present showing the Belgian is probably the most altruistic of the
> mandated administrations. Ruanda-Urundi bids fair to become a thoroughly
> successful essay in native development on a basis of disinterested trusteeship.[5]

The Belgian mandated territory, roughly the size of England, was one of the most densely populated areas of tropical Africa with an estimated population by 1939 of 3,385,000. 85 per cent of the population belonged to the Hutu people, but the fifteenth century Hamite invasion from the north established the Tutsi as a ruling caste. The Twa people were a small aboriginal group. There was very little fusion of the Bantu and Hamite cultures. The Hutu remained agriculturalists and the Tutsi maintained their dominance as breeders of long horned cattle. There was, however, some difference in political development between the two kingdoms. The kings, or *Mwamis*, of Ruanda tended to be autocrats like the Kabakas of Buganda; the king of Urundi was never more than the most powerful of the chiefs. In the German colonial period Urundi was much less stable than Ruanda. In 1912 the Germans sent a punitive expedition to one district, at the request of the *Mwami* whose authority was being threatened.

European missionaries, both Roman Catholic and Protestant, entered the country in the period of German rule. They both found the Hutu more open to the Christian proclamation than the Tutsi, who tended to keep aloof from Christianity and Western education. As in Uganda, the White Fathers were the first Roman Catholic missionaries, and in 1912 Ruanda and Urundi were organized as a separate province under Bishop Hirth. The German Lutheran Bethel mission began work in Ruanda in 1907 and the Neukirchen mission in Urundi in 1911. By the outbreak of war in 1914 the overall number of white missionaries had risen to eighty, mostly Roman Catholic.

First Approaches to Ruanda, 1916–24

In December 1916 two young doctors from Mengo hospital, Leonard Sharp and A. C. Stanley Smith, spent their local leave in Ruanda. Their interest in the country had been aroused through reading *In the Heart of Africa* by the Duke of Mecklenburg; and for some time they had been convinced that God was calling them to pioneer missionary work there. Their visit had the blessing of Bishop Willis and the Uganda missionary committee, which, at the bishop's request, gave a senior missionary, the Rev. H. B. Lewin, 'permission to visit the

Ruanda country with Drs Sharp and Stanley Smith with a view to finding openings for future work there'.[6] By this time Ruanda was occupied by Belgian troops, the German forces having withdrawn eastwards into Tanganyika in April and May 1916. The Uganda government gave the three missionaries a permit to enter the country. Apparently there was some confusion, and the Belgian occupying forces were not informed. However nothing untoward happened, and the two doctors spied out the promised land. But the next steps towards occupation were painfully slow. They will be recorded at some length as an example of the difficulties encountered in starting a pioneer mission from a settled base which had its own list of priorities.

At a special meeting of the Uganda missionary committee on 8th January, 1917, it was noted that Dr Sharp wished to volunteer for medical work in Ruanda, but that Dr A. R. Cook said he could not be spared from Mengo hospital at that time, as a new project for training medical assistants was about to begin. At a meeting of the missionary committee on 18th January the bishop read an appeal he had received 'from the natives in Ruanda and Kigezi', and it was agreed to locate Archdeacon Kitching and the Rev. H. M. Grace to Ruanda, accompanied by an African medical assistant from Mengo so that medical work could begin at once. It was hoped that Sharp might be able to join the party in January 1918. The Uganda missionary committee begged the parent committee to send reinforcements 'so that these stations in Ruanda and Kigezi may be properly manned, and the great gaps in the ranks of the Uganda workers may be filled up'. Further, it appealed to the CMS parent committee to allow a medical mission to be opened as soon as possible in Ruanda 'as the natives there had proved very unresponsive to the preaching of the Gospel and a way to their hearts might be found through their bodily needs'. The two doctors, who were not yet full missionaries of the CMS, began to wonder whether their call to Ruanda might not have to be followed up independently. Stanley Smith wrote in April 1917 to CMS headquarters reaffirming his conviction of God's call to pioneer work and pastoral work in Ruanda. He could only stay in the Uganda mission if there was some prospect of the fulfilment of his desire.[7] The Uganda missionary committee, on 29th March, pleaded with the parent committee to allow such terms of agreement as would retain Sharp and Stanley Smith in the Uganda mission, and to promise them location to pioneer medical missionary work in Ruanda 'should it be propitious to open work in Ruanda'.

For the next two and a half years there is scarcely any mention of the Ruanda project in the Uganda mission records. Sharp was located to Kabarole hospital, Toro, and Stanley Smith remained at Mengo for some of the time. In 1919 they were both on leave in England, and took the opportunity of developing their plan for Ruanda in more detail. G. T. Manley, the Group III (Africa) secretary at CMS headquarters, was sympathetic, but felt bound to point out the apparently intractable difficulties that faced the Society in financing the venture. The doctors therefore decided to start raising funds for a medical mission in Ruanda from sources outside the Society.[8] On 7th November, 1919 the Ruanda sub-committee of the Uganda missionary committee had before it a 'personal state-ment' in which Sharp and Stanley Smith guaranteed the expenses of non-medical missionary work in Ruanda for four years, money for a hospital having been already promised. But the sub-committee was still hampered by the difficulty of 'adequately staffing and maintaining existing work'.[9] Kigezi was suggested as an alternative area for a pioneer mission. Being within the Uganda protect-orate, it had some obvious advantage over Ruanda. On 24th December, 1919 Sharp wrote from Wimbledon to say that, after consultation with Stanley Smith, he was prepared to work in Kigezi – but only as a stepping-stone to Ruanda, and on condition that activities not limited to Kigezi and Ruanda should be ended as soon as possible; and that 'they be not deflected to Mengo or Toro Hospitals except in acute emergency and quite temporarily'. He felt that Mengo was becoming 'more and more philanthropic in contradistinction to missionary in character'. Neither he nor Smith viewed such work as essential to the evangelization of Africa, 'nor could they spend their lives at it'.[10]

In January 1920 Bishop Willis was in London and on 2nd January he had a long talk with G. T. Manley and followed it up with a letter.[11] The Bishop thought it would be preferable to start right away in Ruanda if political con-ditions allowed. Kigezi would be much easier to evangelize from Ruanda than vice versa. He would not advocate opening there at the cost of closing down existing work, but Ruanda was a most important country because of the intel-ligence and numbers of its people and because of 'the place they are certain to occupy in the future government of the country'. A great opportunity should not be allowed to pass.

On 10th February, 1920 the parent committee thankfully accepted the offer of the two doctors with the following provisos: (1) they would be located to the Uganda mission for pioneer work (in Ruanda if possible) under the instructions of the Uganda missionary committee, and subject to their not being required to work in one of the existing hospitals; (2) the Uganda missionary committee was empowered to negotiate with the Belgian government about opening medical mission work in Ruanda, in terms of a single mission station under its direction; (3) the parent committee saw no prospect in the immediate future of further reinforcing the mission staff, and all plans must be carried out on the basis of existing resources.[12] This was all very cautious, but gifts from the 'Friends of Ruanda' were flowing in, and the doctors were strengthened in their resolution to go forward by the parent committee's acceptance of their personal offer of service.

More testing was to come, however, in the next few months. Rowling, the Uganda mission secretary, pressed the claims of Ngora, in eastern Uganda, as a better siting than Ruanda for a pioneer medical mission.[13] The Uganda medical sub-committee urged the consideration of Bukoba, as it was in British, and not Belgian, territory.[14] The parent committee stood firmly behind Sharp against these alternative proposals. It saw no reason to go back from the position of its earlier resolution locating Drs Sharp and Stanley Smith to Ruanda; and it regarded the strengthening of the staff of doctors at Mengo as of prior importance to the opening of new work at Ngora or Bukoba.[15]

On 8th April, 1920 the Uganda missionary committee minuted its unanimous opinion that it would not be right to undertake fresh responsibilities unless the parent committee was prepared to equip and maintain an adequate staff. If a Ruanda mission was established, a missionary of trained experience should be sent as its leader; it would not be possible for the Uganda committee or its secretary to control and direct it 'in any sense efficiently'. Sharp (Wimbledon, 21st June, 1920) took up the point about oversight and suggested that Ruanda should have its own missionary committee. Clearly the Uganda committee did not want this responsibility, and at that distance reference of day to day matters would be impossible.[16] On this point the parent committee remained firm – Ruanda must come under the Uganda committee as its local governing body; but it would approve 'any arrangements which avoid delay in the financing and management of this work subject to the approval of the Uganda Missionary Committee'. The parent committee pointed out that Ruanda was at present in Mombasa diocese, but expected some arrangement to be made about this between Bishop Willis and Bishop Heywood.[17]

Meanwhile, friendly contact had been made with the Rev. Henri Anet, secretary of the Protestant Missionary Society of Belgium. In conversations at CMS House (January 1920) Anet gave assurance that, if the Belgian society started work in Ruanda-Urundi, it would be in a different language area and some distance from the proposed CMS mission, possibly in Urundi;[18] and his society would welcome help from the CMS. Bishop Willis, Sharp, and Anet met in G. T. Manley's office and together with him decided that it would be mutually advantageous for both societies to be represented in Ruanda. The question of siting of stations could be left open for the present, but CMS was ready to settle in former German stations. On 16th April Anet wrote again to say that his mission would welcome co-operation with CMS in Ruanda and would back the CMS application to the Belgian authorities.[19]

Unhappily for these plans, now well-advanced, the Belgian government refused permission for a CMS mission in Ruanda. Anet still persevered in the hope that a favourable answer might be given about Urundi. In November the two doctors visited Brussels and met the Belgian Resident (Urundi). He offered them a warm welcome to his territory, and in December they left England only to receive news at Marseilles that permission for Urundi had also been withdrawn. It seemed that it would have to be Kigezi after all, as a stepping-stone to Ruanda later. On 6th January, 1921 the Uganda medical sub-committee approved the choice of Kigezi as suitable for a pioneer medical mission and unanimously decided that Dr Sharp and Dr Stanley Smith should work there together.[20] But the latter, still patient and resourceful, had to combat yet another proposal for an alternative location – this time Kavirondo instead of Kigezi. He wrote from Mengo (21st January, 1921) to uphold Kigezi against the counter-claim. It was, he said, densely populated. There was the barest trace of missionary work there. The need in Kigezi was far greater than in Kavirondo, which was not a pioneer area.[21]

On 24th February, 1921 Algernon Stanley Smith and his wife, Leonard Sharp's sister, reached Kabale, in Kigezi. The site was chosen by H. B. Lewin. It was only a mile away from the headquarters of district government. It stood 'on a fine bluff of a hill which juts like a buttress into a wide valley some twenty miles long, running about north and south, 6,000 ft. up'. The Sharps soon joined the Stanley Smiths. Sharp was appointed MO at a government dispensary. In May 1921, Sister Constance Watney from Mengo joined them as the first nurse, and soon Kabale hospital was being built. The remarkably rapid growth of the mission in Kigezi will be described later.

The efforts to open the way into Ruanda could now be continued from a base quite close to its border. In the short period from January 1922 to the end of 1923, while a strip of eastern Ruanda was under British control, Sharp was able to explore it and prepare for the future. Later he claimed that in this short interval the gospel had been planted in its strategic centres.

Constitutional Development, 1924–40

On 5th February, 1924 the CMS Africa committee held a special meeting to consider a letter from Sharp, with an accompanying memorandum on the growth of the Ruanda mission. The committee recorded their intention to maintain this work and gladly gave its sanction to Sharp to approach individuals to obtain financial support for it. Certain questions of administration raised by him were referred to the Uganda missionary committee for their opinion and advice. Should there be some form of separate organization, under the Uganda missionary committee, for Ruanda and Bukoba? Other questions were about the allocation of AOH grants; the problem of staffing Kigezi and Ruanda in relation to the staffing needs of the rest of the Uganda mission; and the relative responsibility of the CMS as compared with other societies working in the new field.

Sharp's progress report was impressive. At Kabale building had gone at a great pace. Three missionaries' houses had been built at a cost of £500; a hospital with 125 beds (£1,500); boys' and girls' boarding-schools; two other boys' schools for sons of chiefs; and scores of churches and village day schools. Over a hundred African evangelists and teachers were at work. Thirty thousand people were under daily instruction. Two hundred had been baptized. In five years £5,000 had been raised for the mission from subscriptions, the earnings of the doctors, and from other sources. The memorandum ended with an appeal to CMS to send out a band of missionaries for the evangelization of tribes who had already proved themselves 'so ready to receive the Gospel'. If the Society could not do this itself, might it not be done in co-operation with another society which would work on 'similar church lines'?[22] The Uganda missionary committee was cautious about rapid development, and suggested that the staff needed for the next two years was one doctor, one nurse, and one clergyman, preferably with long experience.[23] Bishop Willis was also inclined towards caution. Ruanda proper was 'a very much larger affair' than British Ruanda. It should not be attempted unless the parent committee saw the way clear to carry it through. 'In Uganda itself,' he wrote, 'so much has been undertaken which cannot be carried through; and a further effort, however heroic, with anything like the present staff, would be disastrous.'[24]

At last in 1925 the way was opened into Belgian Ruanda. On 26th July, Leonard Sharp and W. J. W. Roome of the BFBS approved the site which Geoffrey Holmes had selected at Gahini. By the end of 1925 twelve missionaries had been accepted for service in the Ruanda mission and, with such numbers, the case for some form of separate organization was much stronger. In a letter (19th March, 1926) Stanley Smith proposed the formation of a 'Ruanda Committee' with a view to arousing interest and raising funds; and a 'committee of reference', sympathetic with the conservative doctrinal views of the Ruanda staff and acceptable to the parent committee of CMS. The purpose of these bodies would be 'to obtain support for the work and, as opportunity offers, to win back CMS supporters now alienated from the Society'. One member of the committee of reference would be responsible for interviewing prospective candidates before passing them on to the parent committee. Money could be sent, earmarked for Ruanda, to CMS; or direct to the Ruanda account at Barclay's Bank. Such arrangements, Stanley Smith suggested, would bring relief to CMS general funds, and would attract money which would otherwise be lost to CMS. He recognized the danger that the proposed preliminary testing of candidates might insinuate a doubt of the 'soundness' of the rest of CMS, but steps would be taken to guard against this. He also recognized the possible danger that money might be alienated to Ruanda which would otherwise have come to CMS general funds, but care would be taken to emphasize 'funds not otherwise available to CMS'.[25]

Stanley Smith's proposals were received sympathetically and details were worked out with the CMS secretariat in London. At one stage the title favoured for the home base committee was 'The Ruanda Association', on the analogy of a number of diocesan associations which raised funds for the support of a particular area of mission;[26] but a separate diocese for Ruanda was judged to be premature, and the title 'The Ruanda Council' was finally agreed. It was formed in 1927 with the Rev. E. L. Langston as its first chairman and the Rev. H. Earnshaw Smith as its secretary. The Rev. A. St John Thorpe succeeded as chairman in December 1933. The council was from the start self-elective. The intention was that it should be 'composed of members of CMS in whole-hearted sympathy with the Protestant and Evangelical principles of the Society'.[27] Administratively, the Ruanda mission would come under the CMS Africa committee. It was agreed that the Ruanda council would not undertake new work elsewhere, and that CMS would be under no obligation to engage in work in Ruanda unless funds raised through the council were either in hand, or were guaranteed, to cover its cost. The Ruanda mission had been largely self-supporting from the start, but it achieved full self-support for the first time in the year 1928–9.

The formation of the Ruanda council in England did not imply immediate self-government in the field and the standing committee of the Uganda mission felt unable to accept a suggestion from the Ruanda sub-conference of missionaries that Sharp and Stanley Smith should represent it as occasion required at meetings of the standing committee. This apparent rebuff should be read in a wider context. The standing committee was under pressure at this time from other directions, to extend its *ex officio* membership (e.g. the senior doctor of Mengo hospital) and it was concerned that its selective character should not be impaired. Nevertheless, this blocking of direct representation of the Ruanda mission on the standing committee strengthened the case for a separate local governing body for Ruanda. In June 1928 the Ruanda council in London decided that in future the Ruanda sub-committee in Uganda should administer the block-grants from England, making 'adequate provision for all departments of the work'.[28] On 6th October, 1931 Bishop Willis and Ladbury (secretary of the Uganda mission) met three representatives of the Ruanda mission sub-conference, Dr Leonard Sharp, the Rev. H. E. Guillebaud and Dr J. E. Church. Together they worked out a new scheme for local administration. Its main features were as follows: (1) 'Ruanda' would be a separate mission with its own local governing body, missionaries' conference, and financial arrangements – except that the financial secretary of the Uganda mission would continue to act for Ruanda missionaries in matters of freight, passages etc.; (2) the Ruanda mission would continue to depend for the present on the more advanced Church of Uganda for the training of clergy and senior teachers; (3) the ultimate objective of a separate diocese would be kept in view, but Ruanda would remain for the present under the bishop and diocesan organization of Uganda. Search would be made meanwhile for an 'ecclesiastical leader' who could be appointed as archdeacon or suffragan bishop as the first step to a separate diocese; (4) the annual conference of Ruanda missionaries would in future take place at Kabale in Kigezi, or in Ruanda, not at Kampala.[29]

The Ruanda council considered these proposals on 20th November, 1931, and appointed a sub-committee to draw up a constitution.[30] The draft constitution was approved by the Ruanda council on 24th October, 1932, and by the parent committee of CMS on 9th November, 1932, on the understanding that the 'native church' in Ruanda would remain part of the diocese of Uganda until a new diocese was formed.[31]

The main provisions of the constitution were as follows:

1. The local governing body of the Ruanda mission to be the *Annual Conference* of all missionaries in full connection. Wives of missionaries to be allowed to attend, and to vote after passing the language examination; probationers and others, by invitation, to be allowed to attend without voting powers. The conference to deal with all major matters of policy. The Bishop of Uganda to be its chairman *ex officio*, and its secretary to be appointed by the general committee of CMS after consultation with the Ruanda council.

2. The transaction of ordinary business to be in the hands of an *executive committee* under delegation from the annual conference; to meet not less than twice a year; and to have a total membership of eleven, eight of whom were to be elected by the conference, and in such a way that all departments of work and all missionaries had representation.

3. *The location of missionaries* to be channelled through the secretary of the Ruanda council, who would also act as the main link with the CMS general committee.

This constitution was the happy outcome of discussions from February 1924 onwards between the parent committee of the CMS, the committee of the Uganda mission, and the Ruanda council.[32] The first secretary of the Ruanda mission was Dr Leonard Sharp (1932–5). He was followed by the Rev. W. A. Pitt-Pitts (1935–9) who was also appointed Archdeacon of Ruanda in 1935. The archdeacon was succeeded as secretary by Dr Stanley Smith (1939–42).

Stanley Smith made this comment on the doctrinal preamble to the constitution. It enshrined, he said, three principles: (1) the complete inspiration of the bible, as being, and not merely containing the Word of God; (2) the commission to preach 'full and free salvation through simple faith in Christ's atoning death on the cross'; (3) full guarantees, received from the CMS, for the Ruanda General and Medical Mission to operate on 'Bible, Protestant, and Keswick lines'.[33]

The last step towards self-government – a separate diocese – was prepared for, though it was not taken in the period up to 1942. In December 1934 the Ruanda council suggested that, in view of the development of the work in Ruanda and the probability of advance into Urundi, the time had come for the appointment of a bishop of Ruanda-Urundi as an assistant bishop of Uganda.[34] Bishop Stuart, however, advised the appointment of an archdeacon as preferable at this stage rather than an assistant bishop.[35] Arthur Pitt-Pitts was appointed Archdeacon of Ruanda in 1935. Three years later he told the Ruanda council (3rd October, 1938) that he was willing to withdraw from the archdeaconry if this would help forward the formation of the diocese. The Bishop of Uganda thought that a 'further short space' was needed before a separate diocese was formed. Cash, general secretary of CMS supported him. It was, he said, premature to suggest a separate diocese when there were as yet only two ordained African clergy. The council, after a full discussion, decided not to pursue the proposal in the immediate future, but to continue to work towards it.[36] In 1939 a diocesan council was formed to act as the standing committee or executive committee of 'the Church in the Archdeaconry of Ruanda and Urundi together with the district of Kigezi in Uganda'. It met for the first time in January 1940.

The Ruanda Mission at Work

1. Kigezi

From 1921 until the late 1930s Kabale was the headquarters of the Ruanda mission and its chief mission station. The hospital buildings were completed in 1924, on an impressive scale. Five main blocks, each 95 ft by 35 ft, were joined together by a front corridor 500 ft long. In 1925 the two men's wards were destroyed by fire caused by lightning, but they were soon rebuilt. By 1927 the hospital had in its care three branch dispensaries, and in 1930 a new block was built for Asian patients. By the end of the 1930s a government hospital had started work nearby, and in 1939 Kabale mission hospital was closed. Its primary purpose, evangelization through medicine, had been fully achieved in the rapid growth of the church. Hospital contacts played a large part in winning the confidence of the Bakiga.

In 1924 the Rev. Jack Warren joined the Ruanda mission as pastor and schoolmaster for Kigezi. Kabale boys' school for the sons of chiefs was soon flourishing and two other boys' schools were opened, one at Kisoro in Bufumbira district and one at Rukira. In 1927 the large church at Kabale was consecrated by Bishop Willis. It had been built (of brick, with a corrugated-iron roof) in eleven months, and was paid for largely through the efforts of Jack Warren's friends in England.[37] The total cost of the church was £800 of which local Christians contributed £100. In 1927 Kabale was described as 'one of the finest mission-stations in Uganda, with six missionaries' houses, three boarding-schools, a hospital, and a new church to hold 2,000 people, the largest in the diocese apart from Namirembe cathedral'. In the Kigezi mission there were 170 churches, 200 teachers, 10,000 'readers', 1,200 baptized Christians and 250 confirmed.[38] Jack Warren's death from tuberculosis shortly after reaching England early in 1929 was a sore loss to the mission. His achievement in five years at Kabale would have been ample for a much longer life. The energy of his love remained an inspiration to those who worked with him, and after him. In 1930 the Ruanda sub-conference applied to the director of education, Uganda for a grant from 1931 for qualified schoolteachers at Kigezi Boys' High School.[39] In 1934 Miss Constance Hornby started the Girls' Normal School at Kabale.

When Dr Theodore Goodchild was at Kabale hospital in the early 1930s it was still very full and busy; and the opening of a leprosy centre on an island in Lake Bunyoni, six miles from Kabale, for a time at least increased Kabale's importance as a medical centre. The CMS medical committee had, in 1928, agreed to the opening of a leprosy treatment centre on Bwama Island provided that no capital and maintenance expenses were involved for the Society. Building started in 1929 and a hospital of forty beds was provided by the joint efforts of the Uganda government, BELRA and the Ruanda mission (which received gifts for it as a memorial to Canon Stather Hunt). Lake Bunyoni leper colony was opened in January 1931. By 1934 over six hundred patients were being cared for in the colony, and the number continued to grow as new houses were built for them.

2. Ruanda

On 20th July, 1925 Gahini, east of Lake Mohasi, was chosen as the site for the first mission station in Belgian Ruanda. Capt. Geoffrey Holmes settled there with Kosiya Shalita, a Mututsi who had been born near Gahini but whose parents had moved to Ankole when he was a child. He had been educated at Mbarara High School and King's School, Budo. He was later to become diocesan Bishop of Ankole. By 1928 a hospital with seventy-five beds was completed at Gahini. In 1932 the missionary in charge, Dr J. E. Church, was joined by his brother, Dr W. F. Church, the first of the Ruanda missionaries to take the Belgian diploma in tropical medicine. By 1933 the number of outpatient attendances at Gahini hospital had risen to twenty-two thousand a year, and four out-stations had been recognized by the Belgian mandatory government as first-aid posts.

Medical missionary work was well-received in Ruanda from the start, but educational work was more difficult to establish. The Roman Catholic Church was responsible for virtually all education in the Belgian Congo at this time and the Ruanda missionaries had reason to fear that the Roman Catholic missions aimed at a complete monopoly in the mandated territories.[40] They had had early experience of Roman Catholic opposition when they started opening schools, and the matter had been referred to J. H. Oldham, secretary of the International Missionary Council. He made representations to the Colonial Office and the governor-general. The Roman Catholic schools were receiving government educational grants; but the Ruanda council (July 1933) warned its missionaries that no attempt should be made to obtain government educational grants. Tension continued, and in January 1934 cases of 'violent aggression' by Roman Catholic priests were reported from the missionaries at Gahini. Such hostility from other missionaries was naturally unpleasant and disturbing, but in Belgian mandated territory it was not wholly unexpected.

Gahini is remembered not only as the first mission station in Ruanda, but as the birth-place of the 'Revival'. It began among the African staff at Gahini hospital.[41] In 1933 a convention was held at Gahini, and 'a great increase of zeal' resulted from it. How the Revival movement spread from there to Uganda has already been described. It is probably unwise to single out one place or individual as the origin, humanly speaking, of the movement that was to spread widely over East Africa in the later 1930s. Yet wherever the story of the Revival is told, Gahini will have an assured place in it. It was true there, as elsewhere, that although it was primarily a movement of the Spirit among African Christians, the willingness of missionaries like Joe Church to submit themselves to a searching discipline in love and fellowship with Africans was a vital part of it. Earlier CMS missionaries in East Africa, such as Baskerville and Douglas Hooper, had found such open fellowship. It was now being recovered.

The next two stations to be occupied in Ruanda were Kigeme and Shyira. In November 1930 a party of missionaries, the Sharps, the Guillebauds and the Churches, set out together to find new sites. Kigeme, in southern Ruanda, about twenty-five miles from Astrida, had already been selected; and the missionaries, moving further west, chose Shyira, on a hill-top south-west of Kigeme. Government permission to occupy Kigeme was reported to the Ruanda sub-conference in February 1932. Geoffrey Holmes, now both ordained and married, went to Kigeme with his wife early in 1932. Stanley Smith followed in 1933 to start full medical work, and a fourteen-bed hospital was opened there. The Rev. and Mrs Jim Brazier came to Kigeme in 1934. H. D. Hooper visited the station in 1937 and was present at a great open-air service of confirmation attended by some 2,600 people. Brazier was also the first resident missionary at Shyira, working there for a few months until H. S. Jackson returned from leave. In 1934 Dr Norman James started the hospital at Shyira.

The Ruanda council had two important items on the agenda when it met on 2nd July, 1934. Mr Ernest Carr, present by invitation, spoke of the need for a secretary or leader in the field who was free of the responsibilities of running a station. He offered generous financial help for a suitable appointment. The leader was found in Arthur Pitt-Pitts and, as already mentioned, he was appointed secretary of the Ruanda mission and archdeacon in 1935. He had been a missionary in Uganda and in Kenya, chaplain to Bishop Heywood of Mombasa, and secretary of the Kenya CMS mission. From 1935 until his death in 1940 he gave himself unstintingly to the work of the Ruanda mission. A true evangelist, he found the duties of archdeacon burdensome, especially when it was necessary to represent ecclesiastical policies which some of his fellow-missionaries found irrelevant to their primary task.

The second item of important business at the July 1934 meeting of the Ruanda council was the advance into Urundi. The council approved the report of a sub-committee which recommended that the first stage of advance, as resources became available, should be the full establishment of the two recently opened stations in Ruanda – Kigeme and Shyira – providing each of them with a hospital, a church, a school and missionaries' houses; next, the existing stations in Ruanda, Gahini included, should make fuller provision for the training of African teachers, 'paying regard to quality as well as to quantity'.

Subject to the foregoing conditions, the sub-committee recommended advance into Urundi, one station at a time, as the funds and workers became available. Additional expenditure was not to be undertaken unless funds were guaranteed to meet the cost of them.[42]

3. Urundi

On 1st October, 1934 the council agreed to accept Sharp's proposal for three new stations – Buhiga, in eastern Urundi; Matana, in southern Urundi, and a third in northern Urundi; but as 'ultimate objectives', to be occupied as soon as the necessary funds were provided.[43] Buhiga was a site on a gently sloping hill on the main road running north-east from Kitega, in a thickly-populated area. It was occupied in 1935 when W. F. Church began work there. Matana, also occupied early in 1935, was ninety miles south-west of Buhiga in grazing country. Mwambutsa, king of Urundi, helped in the choice of this second site and government permission was quickly obtained for both stations. Matana hospital was opened by the Belgian governor on 14th July, 1937. Kosiya Shalita was working there alone for a time, living in a tent; then Leonard and Esther Sharp joined him; a boys' school was started, and three out-stations opened. H. D. Hooper, the CMS Africa secretary, noted that sites for sixty out-stations in the district had already been selected when he visited Ruanda in 1937. The third Urundi station finally chosen was Ibuye, on the high plateau separating Ruanda and Urundi. In 1937 Geoffrey Holmes went there. It was not an easy start. In April 1938 the local administrator accused the mission of anti-government propaganda, but the difficulties eased after Holmes had talked things over with him. The Ruanda mission was the only CMS mission in East Africa between the wars working in non-British territory, and the mandatory government was one with a strong Roman Catholic tradition. Misunderstandings were bound to arise from time to time; but the service rendered to the peoples of Ruanda-Urundi by the Ruanda mission, especially in the field of medicine, was recognized by the government; and the mission, for its part, was scrupulous in the attention it gave to the requirements of the Belgian authorities.

Co-operation and Translation

Ecumenical relations were established at an early date with M. Anet's society, and with other missions as opportunity was given. In 1932 the Danish Baptist mission made a direct appeal to the Ruanda mission for help in Urundi. In 1935 the Alliance of Protestant Missions in Ruanda-Urundi was formed. The Protestant Missionary Society of Belgium, the Danish Baptist mission, the Society of Friends, the Methodists and the Anglican CMS mission took part in the alliance. In 1942 the first of a series of alliance conventions for Europeans and Africans was held at Muyebe.

Translation work was a useful field for inter-mission co-operation. The CMS

Ruanda mission translators worked in close association with other Protestant missions in the area. Pride of place among translators must go to Harold Guillebaud. A scholar of Pembroke College, Cambridge, he came to Ruanda in 1925 with his wife and three of their children. Seven years later he had translated the New Testament and the Psalms, Job and some of the prophetical books into the Ruanda language. In 1932 he returned to England, but he was back in Ruanda for a short tour of one year in 1936, hoping to start at once on translating the New Testament into Kirundi; but his fellow missionaries felt the need for the Pentateuch in Lunyaruanda to be more urgent, and two of the gospels had already been translated by Danish Baptist missionaries into Kirundi. So Guillebaud worked most of that year on the Pentateuch, and in the few remaining weeks of his tour translated two of the gospels and some of the shorter epistles into Kirundi – his daughter, Rosemary, completed a translation of the bible in Kirundi, 1941–67. Stanley Smith completed the Lunyaruanda Old Testament after Guillebaud's death.

After the death of Arthur Pitt-Pitts in May 1940, Bishop Stuart invited Guillebaud to return once again to Ruanda as archdeacon. He was taken ill during his preliminary tour of stations and on 22nd April, 1941 he died at Matana. Mrs Margaret Guillebaud continued to serve for some years as a Ruanda missionary as did their son Peter (the first trained educationist of the mission) and their daughters Lindesay and Rosemary. Family tradition was strong in the Ruanda mission. Two sons of Dr J. E. Church, John and Robin (both doctors), served in the mission at Gahini and Kabarole respectively; Geoffrey Stanley-Smith (doctor), Nora Stanley-Smith (wife of Richard Lyth, Bishop of Kigezi from 1967), John Sharp (doctor) at Kisiizi and Pat Hindley are among the second generation missionaries who followed their parents.

It was the policy of the Ruanda mission in its formative period to plant stations strategically at widely separated points in Ruanda and Urundi. By 1939 schools had been opened at all stations, and there were girls' boarding-schools at Kabale, Gahini, Kigeme, Shyira and Matana. The European staff of the mission at the outbreak of the second world war was forty-seven – nine clergy, ten doctors (one of them a woman), seven nurses, seventeen missionary wives, and four other women missionaries. There were two African clergy and 1,807 other African church workers. The world depression of 1929–33 slowed up the progress of recruitment for a time. In 1935 a friend of the mission had promised a sum of £6,000 per annum for five years. This gift helped the mission to start work in Urundi and to put up a large number of permanent buildings; but as Stanley Smith remarked, so large a gift 'carried with it an element of precariousness', especially as it was withdrawn temporarily more than once owing to a difference of view between the donor and the committee. In 1939 the mission found it necessary to cut expenditure by £3,000 a year. 'To meet this situation missionaries at home were unable to return and some due for furlough had to be asked to find other jobs in England until the situation was righted.'[44] For all that, the mission was in good heart for the next phase of advance, and the vision of the two doctors, Leonard Sharp and Algernon Stanley Smith, still with many years of service ahead of them, had been marvellously realized in the rapidly growing church in Ruanda and Urundi.

NOTES

1. See Roger Louis, *Ruanda-Urundi, 1884-1919*, Oxford, 1963, Preface, for this spelling, rather than 'Rwanda' and 'Burundi'.

2. op. cit., p. xvii.

3. Patrick Balfour, *Lords of the Equator*, Hutchinson, 1937, p. 231.

4. Louis, op. cit., p. 255.

5. Balfour, op. cit., pp. 231, 232.

6. G3/A7/P3, 1917/6.

7. P3, 1917/67B.

8. Lindesay Guillebaud, *A Grain of Mustard Seed: The Growth of the Ruanda Mission of CMS*, Ruanda Mission CMS, 1960, p. 15.

9. P3, 1919/130.

10. P3, 1919/166.

11. P3, 1920/12.

12. P3, 1920/ii.

13. P3, 1920/33, 55.

14. P3, 1920/53.

15. P3, 1920/xv.

16. P3, 1920/129.

17. P3, 1920/xxxviii.

18. P3, 1920/41.

19. P3, 1920/91.

20. P3, 1921/24.

21. P3, 1921/29.

22. P3, 1924/9.

23. P3, 1924/47.

24. P3, 1924/70.

25. P3, 1926/31.

26. P3, 1926/40.

27. CMS *Annual Report* 1932-33, p. xxxiv. This is the first report in which Ruanda is listed as a separate mission.

28. P4, 1928/77.

29. P4, 1931/76.

30. P4, 1931/84.

31. P4, 1932/65, 71.

32. G3/A11/P1, 1933/2.

33. A. C. Stanley Smith, *Road to Revival: The Story of the Ruanda Mission*, CMS, 1946, p. 24.

34. A11/P1, 1934/23.

35. A11/P1, 1934/24.

36. Uganda diocese file (577).

37. W. J. W. Roome, *Through the Lands of Nyanza*, Marshall, Morgan & Scott, 1930, p. 138.

38. *AR* (MS), 1926–7, p. 81.
39. G3/A7/P4, 1930/47.
40. A7/P4, 1932/73.
41. Stanley Smith, op. cit., p. 57.
42. A11/P1, 1934/15.
43. A11/P1, 1934/16.
44. Stanley Smith, op. cit., p. 83.

Diocese of the Upper Nile

In 1926, after the long preparation already described,[1] this new diocese was inaugurated. It included all the Uganda protectorate east of the Victoria Nile except Busoga; it also included the southern Sudan south of the Bahr-el-Arab and Sobat rivers, an area equal in size to France and England combined, with a population estimated at four and a half million.[2] In March 1926 Bishop Willis wrote to the parent committee. He enclosed a letter from the Archbishop of Canterbury in which the Archbishop agreed to the boundaries, expressed his contentment that the new bishop would be a diocesan, not a suffragan of Uganda, and approved the choice of Archdeacon A. L. Kitching. Bishop Willis, in his covering letter, suggested that for the present there should be two local governing bodies of the CMS in the new diocese. The two areas were divided, he said, by a wide belt where sleeping-sickness regulations were in force, and the problems of the Sudan area were widely different from those of the Uganda area. He suggested a combined conference of the two missions, to be held every two or three years.[3]

The parent committee set its seal to the new arrangements. It made separate provision in the 1926 estimates for the Uganda section of the new diocese as a separate mission of the Society, to be known as the Upper Nile mission; and it appointed the Rev. W. S. Syson to be mission secretary. The CMS work in the southern Sudan would be carried on as a separate entity.

Lord Lloyd, High Commissioner for Egypt and the Sudan, sought to interdict Kitching's consecration. He felt aggrieved at not being consulted about the inclusion of part of the Sudan in a Uganda diocese and he feared that the delicate balance between CMS and Roman Catholic missions in the southern Sudan would be upset. His protest was not effective. Kitching was consecrated Bishop of the Upper Nile in Southwark cathedral on 29th June, 1926. He faced a formidable task. The division of the diocese of Uganda was an unpopular move among some CMS people both in East Africa and in Britain. The two parts of the new diocese were felt to be too distant from each other in more than a geographical sense. 'The two sections', one missionary wrote, 'differ in climate, races, and conditions and methods of work, and as in addition communication is difficult and the distances great, it is doubtful whether they can for long remain one diocese.'[4] A conference of missionaries in the southern Sudan felt that some difficulty and confusion might arise from the title 'Upper Nile Mission' being applied to the Uganda part of the diocese. The title was already in use for one of the provinces of the Sudan. Bishop Kitching reported this difficulty to the standing committee of the mission, and they asked the parent committee to approve the title 'Elgon Mission' for the Uganda part of the diocese.[5] This was approved and remained in use until 1937 when, following the severance of the Sudan section, the title 'Upper Nile Mission' was re-adopted.

Bishop Kitching wrote an effective apologia for the new diocese in *The Church Missionary Review*.[6] He justified it on two grounds: first, 'the immense expansion of the Uganda Church'. In the previous year (1925) 15,000 adults had been baptized, giving a baptized membership of 165,000 with 20,000 catechumens. 5,500 had been confirmed; and an African staff of 5,200 ministered in 2,600 churches: second, 'the vast size of the Sudan'. It was, he said, impossible for the Bishop in Egypt and the Sudan to supervise an area which involved a journey of 3,000 miles from his headquarters. The new diocese was a logical extension of the arrangement which had held for three years previously, by which the Bishop of Uganda undertook pastoral oversight of the southern Sudan. Bishop Kitching did not, however, minimize the contrast between the two sections of the diocese. In the Uganda portion, an area of 50,000 square miles, inhabited by one and a quarter of a million people, were to be found two of the most densely populated regions of the Uganda protectorate. The church, numbering thirty thousand members, was served by ten African clergy and eighteen hundred African church workers. Fifty thousand men, women and children were under daily instruction in a thousand churches and bush schools. (Only one of the ten African clergy, however, was indigenous to the area.) By contrast, in the southern Sudan, there were still less than a thousand Christians, no African clergy and not a single African woman worker. Of ten mission stations occupied since 1909 some had been abandoned for lack of staff.

Bishop Kitching outlined 'six lines of policy' by which he hoped this almost unworkable unit of the church could be made viable.

1. *To evangelize the sleeping-sickness area* that divided the main centres of mission, so that the mass movement towards Christianity in the south might exert a more powerful influence in the southern Sudan. The same languages were spoken on both sides of the quarantine belt. He hoped to re-occupy the deserted mission station of Opari near the Sudan-Uganda border and to set up a chain of out-stations manned by Christian workers from Gulu and Kitgum;

2. *To develop Christian schools in co-operation with the government*. Both governments followed a similar policy of working through the missions in the

educational field. He hoped for a growing number of 'Jeanes teachers' who would help to raise standards in the bush schools; and for boarding-schools for boys and girls for every large tribe;

3. *To train African staff* for pastoral and school work;

4. *To provide vernacular literature* in line with the Le Zoute conference (1926) stress on the importance of the vernacular in the early stages of education and for public worship;

5. *To work for a Christian home life.* In the Gulu district women converts formed only two per cent of the congregation. Husbands fell away through the influence of pagan wives; and fathers disliked school for their daughters as it made them too independent;

6. *To encourage self-expression in African worship.* The bishop quoted the report of the Le Zoute conference on the Christian mission to Africa, 1926 – 'Everything that is good in the African's heritage should be conserved, enriched and ennobled by contact with the Spirit of Christ.'[7]

In the next decade both sections of the diocese grew considerably in church membership, and in each the policy under Bishop Kitching's six heads was implemented in respect of (2), (3) and (4). There was some advance, mixed with disappointment, in relation to (5). Little was done about (6); and the first point, 'aggressive evangelism' across the no-man's land – never got going. In those items of the bishop's policy statement where real progress was made, his personal leadership counted for much; but there was little co-operative development between the two parts of the diocese, and scarcely any emergence of a diocesan structure. It is therefore not surprising that on Bishop Kitching's retirement in 1936, the ten-year experiment was brought to an end. The Sudan portion returned to the diocese of Egypt and the Sudan but with a suffragan bishop who was given territorial responsibility for the rapidly growing church of the south. The Uganda portion continued as the diocese of the Upper Nile with the West Nile district added as an additional responsibility.

The remarkable growth of the Anglican Church in the southern Sudan in the years 1926–42 has been described in another chapter.[8] Developments in the Elgon mission were no less remarkable and now demand attention. The area consisted of five districts of the Eastern Province – Budama, Bugwere, and Bugishu (known collectively by the derogatory title of Bukedi long after 1923 when the Bukedi district was divided); Teso to the north-west; the sparsely-populated Karamoja district to the north; and four districts in the Northern Province – Lango, straddling the northern arm of Lake Kyoga with Gulu to the north-west and (from 1936) West Nile further to the west and Chua to the north.

Church membership figures for the Upper Nile diocese taken from CMS annual reports at five yearly intervals (1927, 1932, 1937, 1942) give a broad indication of the growth-rates of the Christian church.

The baptized membership of the Anglican Church in the Upper Nile diocese,

Uganda section, increased by four times in fifteen years from 39,000 to 170,000; the number of missionaries and African clergy increased, but at nothing like a comparable rate; the number of African church workers was almost static. The figures confirm the point frequently made in letters from missionaries that during these fifteen years the 'mass movement' in eastern Uganda was losing its momentum through the lack of trained leadership, European and African.

The areas of most rapid growth were in Bugishu, in Acholi to the mid-1930s and in Lango thereafter. Bishop J. K. Russell prefaces a note on the comparative rates of growth in Lango and Acholi with this comment:

> The continent of Africa is perhaps the most difficult place in the world in which to collect statistics and, in particular, those dealing with church membership figures are liable to enormous errors – as much as 40 per cent or even 50 per cent. Probably the most reliable figure is that which shows the amount of money collected voluntarily for the work of the Church.

On this basis he gives figures for Lango and Acholi from 1915 to 1963.[9] Those relevant to the period 1910–42 are:

	Lango	*Acholi*
1915	192s	1,418s
1919	298s	812s
1925	6,400s	9,383s
1935	10,060s	8,060s
1050	38,583s	25,003s

Bishop Russell thinks that the falling away of the Acholi church, compared with the continuing rapid growth in Lango was due to serious misconceptions in the preaching of the Christian gospel in Acholi. (See above, p. 212.)

> In Lango the traditional pattern of evangelism may have operated: 'You know of a High God who has left you: we tell you that he has come back and visited his people.' But in Acholi the proclamation misfired from the start. It was neither one thing nor the other. There was no High God for the Acholi with whom the new teaching could be linked: but on the other hand most of the early missionaries seem to have thought there was, even to the extent of forcing the word *Lubanga* into the mould of their preconceptions.

This thesis, as Bishop Russell admits, leaves unexplained the 'astonishing speed' with which the proclamation travelled in Acholi; 'right through the 1920s and early 1930s the Acholi Church led the way'.[10] He suggests a partial explanation – the high value set by the Acholi on the by-products of the Christian proclamation.

> In Acholi, perhaps more than in any other part of Uganda, dini was welcomed for what it could give: entry to the new world. That part of dini which was connected with arithmetic and learning to speak English was of obvious and immediate practical value. That part of it connected with saying your

prayers and singing hymns – and not marrying more than one wife – was of doubtful value but accepted as part of the whole. But if you can have the one part without the other – then you'd be a fool not to. And for the most part, that is what the Acholi have done.[11]

Comparable published studies of the nature of the response in other tribal areas of the Upper Nile diocese – in Lango and Teso for example – are so far lacking; but it is a reasonable assumption that similar motivation operated elsewhere, and it provides an explanation, alongside the lack of trained teachers, for the widespread 'falling away' that often troubled the missionaries towards the end of the 1930s.[12] Even so, the progress and growth of the church in these eastern and northern parts was remarkable, and its leadership, both African and European, was dedicated.

In 1926 twenty-four European missionaries were grouped together at five stations, three of which, Gulu (1913), Mbale (1900) and Lira (1925), were also district administration headquarters. This had obvious advantages as co-operation in education with the protectorate government developed. Mbale in the 1930s was the fourth largest town in Uganda and an important centre of communications. As to the other two CMS stations, Nabumali (1900), high on the slopes of Mount Elgon, proved a good centre for mission among the Bagishu; and Ngora, selected by Bishop Kitching in 1908 as the centre for the Teso area, became the mission headquarters and the bishop's place of residence. It was already, before the new diocese was formed, the chief CMS medical centre east of the Nile. By 1942 there were four more centres with a resident European missionary. The most important of them for our story was Buwalasi, on a flat-topped outlying hill of Mount Elgon, thirteen miles from Mbale. In addition to CMS stations there were, by 1942, AIM stations at Aura and Kulura in the West Nile district and BCMS missionaries in Karamoja near Lake Rudolf.

In their *History of the Upper Nile Diocese*,[13] Mrs Bishop and Miss D. Ruffel stress the vital part played in the growth of the church by Baganda and Basoga teachers, among them two members of the group of young men known as the 'Budo Advertisers' whom G. G. Garrett had encouraged at King's School to offer themselves in missionary service – Samonsoni Kiobe in Lango; and S. Tomusange, who came to Nabumali High School in 1925 and later was the first Anglican Bishop of Soroti. The contribution made by Bunyoro teachers, especially in Acholi, was also noteworthy. The first Mugishu to be ordained was Erisa K. Masaba (1933) and the first Mugwere, D. Daka (1939).[14]

In education the Upper Nile diocese shared in the arrangements for government grants which operated in Uganda diocese; but H. D. Hooper, Africa secretary of CMS, visiting in 1937, noted that the mission was expected to attain the same educational standards as the more central parts of the protectorate, though it had meagre resources. By then there were boys' and girls' secondary or primary schools in all the main mission centres, and standards were rising rapidly. In 1934, the Rev. H. T. Wright, secretary of the CMS

Elgon mission, welcomed the challenge of government grants and supervision. Numbers of first grade catechists and teachers were being provided. Another missionary, the Rev. P. A. Unwin, who was training bush-school teachers for the Grade C certificate at Nabumali High School, was disturbed by their lack of concern for evangelism. He thought that not many of the abler men in training were likely to remain in village school work on a wage of 10s a month. In 1932 Miss D. M. Foster Smith moved the Elgon girls' training school from Mbale to Kabwangasi eight miles away, where there was more room for development. By the end of the first year on the new site there were seventy girls in training from nine tribes, and the language problem was 'very acute'. Most of the work was done in Luganda, but Swahili was taken as a subject. In 1933 when the government was pressing hard for the use of Swahili as the medium of instruction in mixed language areas, Miss Foster Smith thought this was too high a price to pay for a government grant. She decided in 1935 to hand over the principalship to Miss G. M. Langley who could do all the work in Swahili.[15]

An educational landmark in the 1930s was the opening of Buwalasi Training College on 2nd March, 1934. It was planned as a dual purpose institution – for the training of ordinands and catechists and also for the training of teachers. There were some twelve hundred sub-grade village schools in the diocese and a great effort was made from 1930 onwards to raise the £10,000 thought to be necessary for a new training-college for them. The chapel at Buwalasi was the gift of Ridley Hall, Cambridge, whose principal, Paul Gibson, was himself a former head of Peradeniya Training Colony, Ceylon, and largely through his enthusiasm £1,100 was raised for the building of the chapel and towards the endowment of the principal's salary at Buwalasi. Three bishops who were former students of Ridley Hall – A. L. Kitching, C. E. Stuart, and E. S. Woods – were present at the opening. The first principal, S. J. Berry, in charge of the theological department and W. H. Macartney, in charge of teacher-training, were also old Ridleians. By 1939 there were eight ordination candidates in training, with their wives, and they came from six different tribes.

The chief centre of medical work in the diocese was the Freda Carr Memorial Hospital at Ngora. (See Uganda chapter). In 1927 Dr C. A. Wiggins retired from the post of Director of Medical Services, Uganda, to work, under CMS, in the development of leprosy treatment in the Teso area. The British Empire Leprosy Relief Association gave a grant of £2,000 for initial expenses. In 1928–9 nearly four thousand lepers were treated in six centres. A hospital for lepers was built at Kumi, ten miles from Ngora, and an adult leper settlement at Kapiri. In 1935 the adult settlement moved to Ongino, four miles from Kumi. Dr Wiggins, who gave not only his skill and experience but generous financial help, retired in 1931. Miss Margaret Laing developed the Kumi hospital with vision and skill. Dr Muir, secretary of BELRA, described it in 1938 as 'the best leper work I have seen anywhere'.

In 1936 Bishop Kitching retired. He had served in Uganda since 1901. Appointed archdeacon in 1915, he had, in the last ten years of missionary service, put the new diocese on its feet. His book, *From Darkness to Light*[16] is sub-titled 'A study of pioneer missionary work in the Diocese of the Upper Nile'. No-one could write on this subject with more authority. The bishop from the earliest days, and Mrs Kitching from their marriage in 1916, had given themselves generously to the proclamation of the gospel and the nurture of an infant church. He was succeeded as Bishop of the Upper Nile, shorn of its respon- sibilities for the southern Sudan, by Lucian Usher-Wilson who had taught at King's School, Budo, and who at the time of his nomination was rural dean of Busoga. He was consecrated in St Paul's Cathedral on 28th October, 1936 and enthroned in Ngora pro-cathedral on 9th April, 1937.

One passage in Bishop Kitching's book[17] gives some insight into the kind of problems and heartaches he experienced as chief pastor.

A sadly large part of the time of the Church Councils [he wrote] is taken up with questions of discipline. Teacher A has left the work and gone off to trade; he had accumulated debts which he could never pay out of a teacher's wages. Church B is found unmanned; what has become of the evangelist? He got tired. What is he doing? Just 'sitting-down' – i.e. unemployed. It turns out afterwards that he has been dabbling in witchcraft. A pastor has to be dismissed; his church is nearly empty, he is at loggerheads with the chief, and the Council discover that he has been exacting fees from the candidates for baptism and confirmation and putting them in his own pocket. Chief C. has been dismissed by Government for embezzling public moneys, or Chief D is frequently drunk and encourages night dances. Teacher E has quarrelled with his wife, sent her off and taken another woman in pagan marriage.

The bishop was clear about the remedies – a larger staff engaged in pastoral work and 'a widening of the circle of prayer'.

Happily such disappointments were only one side of the coin. Bishop Kitching must often have rejoiced in the gifts and faithfulness of some of his African colleagues in the diocese, Musa Ali, for example. Kitching had himself baptized him, the first Acholi to receive Christian baptism, on 26th November, 1905. Musa Ali after his conversion is said to have destroyed a clan-ritual shrine in the manner of Gideon. Once, in the pagan reaction that followed the first preaching, he was almost beaten to death. When the missionaries retired for a time, Musa Ali and a few others kept up their 'reading', with occasional visits of encouragement from H. W. Tegart in Bunyoro. He became a lay reader, and his signature appears more frequently than any other in the Gulu church register in the 1910s and 1920s. He died suddenly on 9th February, 1930. He was preparing for ordination to the diaconate.

Another name that interweaves with Musa Ali's in the Gulu service register is that of Sira Dongo. An Alur by race, he was brought to Bunyoro as a slave but was released when the British occupied the country. He was baptized in 1903 and was one of the Bunyoro teachers Lloyd and Kitching took with them to Acholiland in 1904. He did more than anyone to keep the small group of Christians together between 1908 and 1913 when missionaries returned. Sira Dongo was made deacon in 1917 and later he was appointed a Canon of the Upper Nile diocese. He died at Lira in 1938.

High on the list of 'church-builders' in the diocese is Harry Mathers, Archdeacon of Eastern Uganda (later of Elgon) from 1923 until his retirement in 1947. He put a hand to most things in his long service, from pioneer missionary to prison chaplain at Mbale. One of his ideas, a highly successful one as it proved, was an annual village school festival at Nabumale. Hundreds of village schools took part in these festivals and exhibited whatever the people of the village could make best – woodwork, ironwork, basketry, pottery, ropes, hats, etc.[18] The Nabumale gathering received impetus from the Phelps-Stokes Commission in 1924, with its stress on vocational rather than literary education.

Miss E. L. Pilgrim (1895–1930), who was one of the first party of women missionaries to reach Uganda, served mostly in Bugishu. Coming first to Nabumale in 1907 she was long remembered for her work among women and girls. Three secretaries of the Elgon-Upper Nile mission, W. S. Syson (1909–30), H. T. Wright (1905–36) and H. F. Davies, were also teachers who made their mark on the development of education in eastern or northern Uganda (1911–49). Syson had the distinction of introducing the plough to the Teso and the boys' school at Ngora owed much to him. Dr Wright and Canon Davies set high standards at Gulu. Mr and Mrs H. G. Dillistone were beloved missionaries at Ngora where he started the boys' school. Mrs Dillistone had been a sister at Mengo before their marriage in 1911 and her nursing skills were valued in an area where medical care was at first in short supply. The chief of church-builders in a literal sense was an Australian, Canon T. L. Lawrence (1923–41). He built churches at Boroboro and Kitgum and he and Mrs Lawrence were the first resident missionaries at Lira. She started the girls' school there. A fellow missionary wrote of him: 'The Australian Church gave a great gift to Africa in Tom Lawrence . . . none of his work was lop-sided.' The tribute was a nice allusion to his building operations but, of course, it had a wider reference. It could be well applied to the whole achievement of the Upper Nile mission in this period.

NOTES

1. See Uganda chapter.
2. *CMR*, A. L. Upper Nile, 'A New African Diocese', December 1926, pp. 319ff.
3. G3/A7/P3, 1926/36, 37.
4. *AR* (MS) 1927–8, p. 91.

5. G3/A10/P1, 1927/29.

6. *CMR*, 1926, ibid.

7. E. W. Smith, *The Christian Mission in Africa*, IMC, 1926, p. 108.

8. See Sudan chapter.

9. J. K. Russell, *Men without God*, Highway Press, 1966, p. 18.

10. ibid., p. 17.

11. ibid., p. 37.

12. *AR* (MS), 1938–9, p. 110.

13. MS read in the Department of Religious Studies, Makerere University College.

14. L. Pirouet, 'The Coming of Christianity to Acoli' (MS).

15. *AR* (MS), 1934–5, p. 115.

16. SPCK, 1935.

17. op. cit., pp. 46, 47.

18. *CMR*, Bishop H. Gresford Jones, 'Technical Education in Uganda: the Bukedi Experiment', 1925, pp. 212ff.

PART THREE

The Middle East

The Middle East: Introduction

The designation 'Middle East' for the Arabic-speaking countries plus Turkey and Iran is now generally accepted in the Western world. So used, it is of recent origin, 'Middle' replacing 'Near' as an area of military command in this region in the second world war. 'Near East' continued to hold a place in the affections of missionaries of this period, but CMS followed the change in usage in its official documents, and by the late 1940s 'Middle East' was well established. A CMS pamphlet, quoting a definition of 1943, applied it to Turkey, Syria, Palestine and Transjordan, Egypt, the Arabian Peninsula, Iraq, Iran and the states of the Persian Gulf: an area with a total population at that time of sixty-five million.[1] 'Middle' may be thought more courteous than 'Near' to the inhabitants of this region since it no longer implies that the centre of the world lies beyond its western border. It also is in line with the Q'uran's description of the Muslim community as 'a people in the Middle'.[2] The greatest unifying factor for this region is that the heartlands of Islam lie within it still, and Islamic culture remains dominant, or very influential, in almost every country in it. There are, of course, other unifying factors: a common political background of four centuries or more of Turkish rule (except for Iran); a common heritage in Arabic language and literature (again excepting Iran); the immense importance of oil in the economic and political development of the region (Iran included); but its common inheritance in Islam is, of all these, the most potent still.

Throughout the period 1910–42 the CMS sustained missions in the Middle East – in Egypt; the Sudan; Palestine and Transjordan (later Israel and Jordan); Persia (later Iran); and, until 1920, in Turkish Arabia (later Iraq). The chapters that follow will set the development of these missions in the context of more local political, social and cultural changes. This chapter is concerned with those changes as they affect the region as a whole, and with the wider Christian movement in which CMS played its part.

The End of the Ottoman Empire

At its zenith in the sixteenth century the Turkish (Ottoman) empire could stand comparison with the Roman empire. 'It stretched from the Persian Gulf to the gates of Vienna, and from the Caspian to Algeria.'[3] But it lacked the administrative integrity of Rome. It was a vast area of taxation rather than of effectively unified government. Local administration in its outlying territories was far below Roman standards. In the nineteenth century the long decline of the Ottoman empire became more rapid: first European territories (Greece, Bulgaria, Roumania, Montenegro) broke away, then Egypt. By the beginning of the present century it was dependent, both politically and economically, on Western European powers. From 1906 onwards the nationalist movement in Turkey itself began to break the unifying strands of Islamic culture. In the first world war the Arab countries rose in revolt, stimulated by promises from the allies of self-determination; and Turkey, having entered the war on Germany's side, emerged from it shorn of two-thirds of her imperial territory, and half her population. In the immediate post-war years, Britain and France extended and intensified their interest in the Middle East, and established, chiefly through the League of Nations system of mandates, a suzerainty over the whole of the fertile crescent. The Western nations involved cannot look back on these mandates with much pride. They were not so much allotted, as submitted to, by the League: and the Permanent Mandates Commission, though Lugard gave much time and experience to it, had insufficient teeth to be effective.[4] Egypt, virtually a British dependency from 1882, remained so until the Anglo-Egyptian Treaty of 1936, and the Sudan was a British colony in all but name until the end of 'Condominium' rule in 1956. But the Western powers made little headway in other parts of the Middle East. Three vigorous new national states arose from the ruins of the Ottoman empire. Mustapha Kemal Ataturk (1880–1938), in a remarkably short time and against huge political odds, transformed Turkey into a compact modern nation, brushing aside the legal and cultural heritage of Islam; Persia, under the leadership of Reza Khan Pahlavi, denounced in 1921 the Anglo-Persian Treaty of 1919, and followed an independent path parallel to that of Turkey, but with a less radical attack on past culture and social norms of behaviour. In Arabia Ibn Sa'ud emerged as the greatest Arab politician of recent times; he showed that the desert could be reclaimed; and, much helped by the discovery of oil, he made Saudi-Arabia a significant centre of several treaty-related Arab states determined to break free of Western interference and pursue their own destinies. So, apart from a brief period of resumed military control by British and Free French armies in the second world war, the Middle East was transformed in thirty years from a dying empire into a number of self-conscious nation-states, most of which intensified their loyalty to Islam, while modifying some of its traditional features.

Islam in Transition

Marshal Lyautey once compared the world of Islam to a resonant box: 'the faintest sound in one corner of the box reverberates through the whole of it'.[5] Since its heartlands are to be found in the Middle East, and the rapid changes in that region affected the whole community of Islam, it is convenient to use this chapter as an observation-post for a brief general survey of Islam during the period. The population of Islam was estimated in 1924 as 235 million. Nearly half of this population was in countries under British rule (106 million if the kingdom of Egypt is included, 94 million if Egypt is excepted): of this 70 million were in British India, 7 million in the rest of Asia, 17 million in Africa. Something like 85 per cent (or 200 million) of all Muslims were at this time under Western rule or 'protection' – 39 million under Dutch rule in the East Indies, 32 million under French rule, and 15 million under Russian; leaving only some 35 million in independent Muslim states.[6] The largest language-group spoke Arabic (45 million); over 11 million spoke Persian, 24 million Bengali, 17 million Urdu.

In most countries of the Middle East, the dominance of Islam remained unquestioned, and even in Turkey the tide of secularization had begun to turn by the 1940s. In the mid-twenties the population of Iraq was 95 per cent Muslim, and a similar figure would hold for Iran, Transjordan and the northern Sudan. Egypt, with its Coptic Christian minority of a million steadily losing ground to Islam, could claim to be about 90 per cent Muslim. Syria was 80 per cent Muslim; but in Lebanon the population of one and half million was about equally divided between Muslims and adherents of the ancient Christian churches.

Four-fifths of the total world population of Muslims were orthodox Sunnites, but the Middle East had a higher than average proportion of Shiites who outnumbered Sunnites by eight to five in Iraq; and this ancient deviation from orthodoxy was completely dominant in Persia. Shia Muslims were fairly numerous also in the Yemen. The militant Wahhabi sect conquered Mecca in 1924 and remained a vital element in those parts of Arabia which found unity under Ibn Sa'ud. The Ahmadiyya sect, founded by Mirza Ghulam Ahmad in the Punjab, was still only about 50,000 strong at the time of Ahmad's death in 1908, but it played a vital part in the expansion of Islam in Africa. Alike among orthodox and unorthodox, however, Islam was under exceptional pressure in the first four decades of the present century. The range of apprehension and commitment among believers was wide, ranging from a superficial veneer over animism in its remoter areas to formalism and nominal membership in regions more accessible to Western secularism. Though, as with the Christian church, plotting 'levels of faith' on a regional or a cultural basis may falsify the situation of Islam as much as it clarifies it. In some primitive areas, notably in its penetration into central Africa, Islam was gaining in depth; and in its westernized fringes, an anti-secularist reaction into militant orthodoxy was always possible and frequently took place. This is one reason why the abolition of the characteristic institutions of Islam by the Turkish revolutionary government under Mustapha Kemal did not lead to the widespread collapse which many Western observers anticipated.

The ending of the Caliphate by the Turkish National Assembly on March 3rd, 1924, led to confident prophecies of a rapid disintegration of the world-community of Islam. Lord Cromer's oft-quoted dictum: 'Islam reformed is Islam no longer' doubtless led to a good deal of wishful thinking, not least in missionary circles; but, as Dr Kenneth Cragg has pointed out, Cromer's conclusion

> for all its obtuseness, would have been echoed by numerous shaykhs and mosque preachers of the time . . . the institution [Caliphate] had endured, after all, from the immediate hours of the Prophet's death and through all its fortunes had been taken as a *sine qua non* of Islamic life and order. . . . The religious efficacy of the duties and ritual of Islam were understood to depend upon the existence of the Caliphate who was head of the faithful.[7]

Some Western students of Islam at the time, notably Professor D. S. Margouliouth, warned Christian churchmen not to build their hopes too high either on the ending of the Caliphate or the conquest of Mecca by the Wahhabis which was thought at the time to be another sign of imminent collapse. 'In our time,' he wrote in *The Church Missionary Review*, '. . . the Moslem world sends far more pilgrims to Paris than it does to Mecca', and 'for some centuries a dead Caliph was as well able to fulfil his functions as a living one'.[8] A missionary report in 1926 sounded a like note of caution, suggesting that 'hatred of the West may bind together the sundered forces of Islam'.[9] The resilience of Islam in face of these pressures, particularly its reaction to the loss of the Caliphate, is an object-lesson in the capacity for survival and regeneration latent in a variegated cultural-religious community with more than a thousand years of development behind it. If Islam had been truly a monolithic structure (as some of its popular apologists claimed) the loss of its fountain-head of authority would have been devastating. As things turned out, recovery was remarkably rapid. The passing in and out of Western colonial rule, which was the lot of many countries in the Middle East at the end of the first world war, appears to have brought about a new self-consciousness of Islam. The break-up of the former Ottoman empire into independent national states brought new vigour to the sundered parts: and the theological realignments which accompanied or followed the crisis were far from being counsels of despair.

One of the first outspoken *post facto* comments on the demise of the Caliphate was made by Ali Abd-ar-Raziq (b. 1888). 'The Caliphate,' he wrote in 1925, 'was and continues to be a discredit to Islam and to Muslims.'[10] He argued that Muhammad never intended it, and that what mattered was 'the non-recurring authority of the prophetic speech'. Raziq's position was far from traditional Muslim orthodoxy and provoked angry comment. But the crisis found more orthodox champions ready with arguments to show that the loss was not critical. Mawlana Azad (1886–1958) in his commentary on the Qu'ran sought to recover the *fitra*, or true religion, of the first generation of Muslims. Like the champions of New Testament Christianity in the same period (such as Roland Allen) he was concerned with the original setting of the words and deeds of the Prophet. Another Indian Muslim, Mawlana al-Mawdudi (b. 1904) took up a 'fundamentalist' position, which also had its familiar Christian counterparts. He claimed that the Qu'ran revealed the whole order of life and society, and appealed for a renewal of sound faith and pure discipline in terms of unquestioned acceptance of 'scripture'. At the other extreme Muhammad Iqbal (1876–1938) was little concerned for original meanings: as the 'poet trumpeter of a renewed Islam. . . . He turned his fire on Western materialism and mullah-ignorance with equal zeal'.[11] The Qu'ran emerges from his hands as a kind of 'Space, Time and Deity' treatise of a twentieth century philosopher. Islam found its counterpart to Schleiermacher in the work of Taha Husayn (b. 1889), an Egyptian scholar-layman for whom religion was essentially feeling: and the 'Jesus of History' school had a counterpart in the writings of Muhammad Husayn Haykal (1888–1956) who in 1935 wrote a life of the prophet which stressed his humanity.

It is clear from these few examples that there was no united theological front in face of the crisis caused by the ending of the Caliphate and the new phase of confrontation with the West which had temporarily placed the majority of Muslims under Western political rule. But the theological ferment had its counterpart in a political struggle, in which 'leaderless' Islam sought to recover its unity. In this connection the most significant figure was Hasan al-Banna (1906–49), the founder of the Muslim Brotherhood in Egypt. He saw the Brotherhood as a means of spiritual re-awakening, through dedicated groups of people, centred upon the local mosque. 'The mosque, as Hasan al-Banna used it, became a vital centre of social conscience and moral antiseptic'.[12] In 1933 he moved to Cairo and from that time until his assassination in 1949 he developed the Brotherhood into a political instrument; but his aims were never narrowly nationalistic. He strove for a unified Islam, with the renewal of the Caliphate as a necessary goal.

The Caliphate was not revived, but there was no failure of nerve through its demise; although the life of converts to Christianity was made a little easier in some of the new independent Muslim states between the wars, missionaries in these countries were not accorded the adventitious help from political change which at one time seemed likely. Where national unity replaced the ideal of Pan-Islam, pressure against Christian communities as an alien influence was intensified. Missions were regarded as denationalizing converts and were in Turkey and elsewhere accused of exploiting poverty, illness and youth as a means of perverting the helpless to another faith.[13]

The Christian Presence in the Near East

'It is my belief, O Christ! that the conquest of the Holy Land should be attempted in no other way than as Thou and Thy Apostles undertook to accomplish it – by love and prayer, by the shedding of tears and blood.'[14] There is no doubt that missionaries working in the Middle East – the homeland of Christianity and later of Islam – shared Ramon Lull's conviction about the motives and methods appropriate to their task. In his Preface, written in 1920, to the fifth edition of his book, *The Reproach of Islam*, Temple Gairdner explained that he had changed this title, because of its *double entendre*, to *The Rebuke of Islam*. But, he went on to say: 'nothing more was intended than that Islam is a perpetual reminder to Christendom of the latter's failure to represent her Lord'. The extent to which Christian missionary witness in the Middle East in the last century and a half was a conscious act of penitence and reparation for the crusades deserves to be the subject of a special inquiry. A more prominent and frequently reiterated motive was that of a mission of help to the ancient Christian churches which had survived the onset of Islam.

The total membership of these churches was estimated in 1926 as $7\frac{1}{2}$ million.[15] Four-fifths of this membership was to be found in the Ethiopic Church of Abyssinia ($5\frac{1}{2}$ million) and in its sister Coptic Church in Egypt (855,000). Much smaller communities represented the ancient patriarchates of the Eastern Orthodox Church – of Constantinople, Antioch, Alexandria and Jerusalem. There were small groups of Assyrian (Nestorian) Christians in Iran, Iraq and Syria; of Syrian (Jacobite) Christians in Lebanon, Syria, southern Turkey and Iraq; and of Armenian (Georgian) Christians chiefly in Iraq. There were also small groups of Maronites, remnants of the Syrian national church which submitted to Rome in 1181; and of Uniate churches, in communion with the papacy but keeping some autonomy in liturgy, language, and church government. Most of these churches were numerically static or declining; and two groups in particular, the Assyrians and Armenians, suffered grievously by massacres or communal ejections during the period under review. Most of the adherents of other ancient Christian communities, without suffering overt persecution, lived in a depressed state as second class citizens in predominantly Muslim states.

When William Jowett was sent by CMS to Malta in 1815 to establish a 'listening post' there, he was instructed to make contact with the leaders of the Eastern churches, and stress was laid on the necessity to work with and through these churches. The American Board of Commissioners for Foreign Missions (Congregational) gave similar instructions to its missionaries in Persia in 1834: The 'main object will be to enable the Nestorian Church, through the grace of God, to exert a commanding influence in the spiritual regeneration of Asia'.[16]

It proved increasingly difficult for missionaries from the West to remain loyal to this aim. The authorities in the Eastern churches found the activities of Protestant missionaries disturbing and unwelcome; and many who responded to the gospel as preached by the missionaries felt constrained to separate themselves from churches which now appeared to them to be less than fully Christian. In the middle decades of the nineteenth century, largely through the agency of American Protestant missionaries, small Evangelical (*Injili*) churches sprang up in Syria, Lebanon, Turkey, Iran and Egypt. When CMS resumed work in Egypt after an interval of twenty years in 1882, its mission was directed no longer specifically to the renewal of the Coptic Church but to the direct evangelization of Muslims.

Between 1882 and 1899 the number of CMS missionaries in the Middle East increased rapidly from eleven to eighty-four. The growth of missionary concern for the conversion of Muslims was maintained in face of formidable difficulties and of frequent disappointment at the small response. Throughout the period the number of CMS missionaries serving in this region was steadily in excess of a hundred and fifty and rose above the hundred and eighty mark in the late 1920s. The small churches born of and nurtured in these missions are now included in the Anglican Archbishopric of Jerusalem. The Anglican Church in Persia had its own bishop from 1912; the Church in Egypt and the Sudan was under the jurisdiction of the Bishop in Jerusalem until 1920, when a separate diocese of Egypt and the Sudan was inaugurated. A separate diocese for the Sudan was not formed until 1945.

As the number of Anglican and Protestant missionaries increased in the Middle East the authorities of the ancient Eastern churches felt the need to express their concern about the effects of this witness on their own church members. In 1920 the Ecumenical Patriarch of Constantinople issued an encyclical in which he appealed to the churches of the West not to engage in proselytism. An eirenic response, in which Temple Gairdner and other CMS missionaries played their part, was made in a statement: 'Working Principles of the Anglican Church in Egypt', approved by the Archbishop of Canterbury in 1923 (see Egypt chapter).

The lack of response to the gospel by Muslims, and the apparent lack of evangelistic concern in the ancient Christian churches was frequently a matter for heart-searching by the missionaries of the period.

Missionaries Confer about their Task

The presentation of the Christian gospel to Muslims was one of the subjects before Commission IV of the World Missionary Conference at Edinburgh in 1910. Its report noted a widespread dissatisfaction with Islam, especially in Turkey, but discouraged facile hopes of greater openness to the missionary message because of it. 'We may expect,' it says, 'a neo-Islam, as there is a neo-Hinduism. The awakening of the national consciousness in Moslem lands, and the beginnings of constitutional government in Turkey and Persia, may probably prove a hindrance to Christian missions.' Some of the missionaries quoted in the report appealed for a greater willingness to listen to what Islam is saying to the church:

> Contact with unitarian, deistic Islam forces the Christian Church to work out again her theology experientially. And so the 'Mohammedan question' may possibly be as life from the dead for the Christian Church itself. . . . Christians who preach the Trinity must know the secret of the Trinitarian life.[17]

The 1910 report lays stress on the need for special training for missionaries going to Muslim lands, and on the need for kindly sympathy, candour, and prudence in the presentation of their message.

In 1911, as part of the general follow-up of the Edinburgh conference, a 'Conference for Workers in Moslem Lands' was held in Lucknow. It made preparations for a further meeting in 1915, but war intervened and it was not until 1924 that this meeting was held on the Mount of Olives in Jerusalem, 3rd–7th April. Following the new style of conferences developed at Edinburgh, the way had been prepared by the circulation of surveys and specialized papers and by three regional meetings earlier in the same year for missionaries at Constantine (for North West Africa); at Heluan (for Egypt, the Sudan and Abyssinia) and at Brumana (for Syria and Palestine). It was thus made possible for most of the time at the Jerusalem conference to be given to open forum and group discussions. The conference took a more optimistic view of the political and social developments in Muslim lands than had been taken at Edinburgh. It saw promise of greater religious freedom in the new mandates for Middle East territories and in the new constitution (1922) for Egypt. It deplored the fact that so little was being done to use these new opportunities of mission effectively: 'missions to Moslems have received vastly less attention, fewer missionaries, and less adequate financial support than those to any other great non-Christian religion'.[18] In spite of the infectious optimism of Dr John R. Mott's opening address as chairman, not all of the eighty-four delegates could see their task as more than marginally eased by new developments. As one of them put it: 'Our task is to induce the proudest man on earth to accept the message he detests from a people he despises'.[19]

The Jerusalem conference recommended that in each region there should be an inter-mission education committee to cover the whole subject of Christian education in the light of the special conditions of the region and of the total resources at the command of the Christian forces. As 'Edinburgh' had done, it stressed the importance of specialized training, 'in linguistics and Islamics'. Medical and social work were commended not merely as a means of obtaining a hearing for the Christian message where other means fail, but as fulfilling 'the work of our Lord who came as well for the body as the soul'. It suggested that missionaries should work for reform of law and custom in the fields of (a) infant welfare, (*b*) child marriage, (*c*) child labour, (*d*) industrial conditions, (*e*) temperance, (*f*) traffic in women and children, (*g*) cruelty to animals.

Perhaps the most significant outcome of the Jerusalem conference was in the co-ordination of the production and distribution of Christian literature. Each delegate received a three-hundred page report, 'Christian Literature in Moslem Lands' which advocated the setting up of a central literature bureau and co-ordinating committee on literature. The conference endorsed these proposals, and CMS released two of its missionaries, Temple Gairdner and Constance Padwick, to give specialized service in this field. The conference also prepared the way for the formation in 1927 of the Near East Christian Council. Membership was open to any church body, missionary society, or other Christian agency. It was a purely advisory body whose decisions would have no greater weight than their intrinsic merit. The council set up committees on evangelism, education, and medical work.

The last major missionary conference held during the period was the meeting of the International Missionary Council held at Tambaram, Madras, 12th–19th December, 1938. The delegates had among their papers the report of an inquiry compiled by the secretary of the Near East Christian Council, the Rev. H. H. Riggs, based on a questionnaire addressed to about three hundred missionaries and local workers in the area, about the presentation of the Christian message to Muslims. The replies showed a consensus of opinion of a great majority on a number of points in presentation.[20] It was agreed that far-reaching efforts were needed to eliminate from the Christian approach those elements, not essential to the presentation of Christ, which make acceptance particularly difficult for Muslims. Public criticism of what Muslims hold sacred should always be avoided.

> Our aim should be to make Christ known to men who need Him; not *primarily* to win them away from Islam. . . . We should start on the assumption that the Muslim knows and reverences Jesus enough to listen to Him: and proceed to enrich that knowledge of His personality and power that will win loyalty to Him. . . . Our primary effort should be to get people to follow Jesus and find the new life in Him, avoiding anything that diverts attention to controversial subjects.

Literature not in harmony with these principles should be revised, or else its use absolutely discontinued.

Among questions raised by the Christian Council enquiry yet to be answered, the report includes these:

> How can the Message of Christ be so presented that it shall mean the same to the hearer that it does to the speaker? How can the acceptance of the Jesus-way of life, and of Jesus as Saviour, be separated, in the mind of the Muslim, from the idea of a transfer of loyalty from the Muslim to the nominally Christian social-political-religious group?

This was the crucial question for a new generation of scholar-missionaries beginning to emerge at the end of the period. One of them, J. Spencer Trimingham, commenting on the lack of response to previous missionary approaches to Muslims, suggests that a modern or 'leavening approach' arising out of the liberal attempt to find common values between Islam and Christianity, is not likely to prove any more effective if it continues to think of Christianity as a purely personal experience and Islam simply as a communal environment.

> The vast developments in popular religious experience within the Islamic system [he wrote in 1948] show that Islam must of necessity cater for certain human needs, but it is not realized that only that can be accepted within the system which is at harmony with its own inner spirit. The dynamic of Christ's working in the Christian environment does inevitably become the wraith of a *nabi Isa* within the Muslim environment. Our preaching to Muslims therefore falls upon deaf ears because it seems to them irrelevant to life as they know it. Our preaching is directed to needs which the Muslim does not recognize as his needs.[21]

A missionary message allied to an individualistic conception of religion could not but fail to penetrate the group solidarity of an Islam which had been consolidated defensively by Western penetration, so that

> Christianity is entangled in the Muslim mind with Westernism and European Imperialism, and the Muslim feels with an unconscious antagonism that the missionary, too, belongs to that world; so *tabshir* (evangelization) is identified in his mind with *isti'mar* (colonization and foreign rule), and therefore distrusted and feared.[22]

The institutional emphasis of so much missionary effort in Muslim countries; the difficulty of maintaining such institutions under war conditions; and the increasing involvement of governments in social welfare and education, were, by the end of the period, leading to a realization that the whole of missionary policy in the Middle East and elsewhere 'must be re-orientated in the light of the primary aim of Christian missions – the establishment of the visible church'.[23]

NOTES

1. *Focus Middle East*, CMS, 1950, p. 8.
2. Kenneth Cragg, *Counsels in Contemporary Islam*, Edinburgh University Press, 1965, p. xi.
3. Jan Romein, *The Asian Century*, Allen & Unwin, 1962, p. 45.
4. George E. Kirk, *A Short History of the Middle East*, Methuen, 6th ed., 1961, p. 130.
5. A. J. Arberry and Rom Landau, *Islam Today*, Faber, 1943, p. 1.
6. *AR* (MS), 1923–4, p. 83 (quoting S. M. Zwemer): cf. *The Call from the Moslem World*, Press and Publications Board, Church Assembly, 1926, p. 75.

7. Cragg, op. cit., pp. 67, 68.

8. *CMR*, 1925, D. S. Margoliouth, 'The Present State of Islam', p. 7.

9. *The Call from the Moslem World*, op. cit., p. 9.

10. Cragg, op. cit., pp. 69, 70.

11. ibid., pp. 59, 60.

12. ibid., p. 114.

13. International Missionary Council, *Tambaram Series*, Vol. VI, OUP, 1939, S. A. Morrison, 'Muslim Lands', pp. 64–161.

14. J. Spencer Trimingham, *The Christian Approach to Islam in the Sudan*, OUP, 1948, p. 43.

15. *The Call from the Moslem World*, op. cit., p. 77 (cf. a later estimate by R. Park Johnson, *Middle East Pilgrimage*, Friendship Press, New York, 1958, p. 75).

16. Johnson, op. cit., p. 92.

17. *World Missionary Conference, 1910*, Vol. IV, Oliphant, Anderson & Ferrier, pp. 132, 135.

18. International Missionary Council, *Conference of Christian Workers among Moslems, 1924*, IMC, 1924, p. 13.

19. *CMR*, 1924, W. Wilson Cash, 'The Jerusalem Conference', p. 130.

20. International Missionary Council, *Tambaram Series*, op. cit., Vol. III, pp. 226–54.

21. Trimingham, op. cit., pp. 46, 47.

22. ibid., p. 45.

23. ibid., p. 49.

Egypt

The Country and its People

About the time that Abraham set out from Ur of the Chaldees, a pharaoh of the twelfth dynasty is said to have built a wall across the Sinai peninsula to prevent 'Asian plunderers' coming to water their flocks in the Nile.[1] No trace of this wall remains, but the story underlines one recurring factor in Egypt's history. From the time of the Persian invasion under Cambyses until the day in June 1956 when the last British soldiers boarded ship at Port Said, she was almost continuously under the control of a foreign power. Egypt's conquerors quickly found in the Nile a key to a continuing light-handed control. No tributary joins it within seventeen hundred miles of the sea and until the delta is reached north of Cairo the Nile valley is a narrow cut about six miles wide. West of the river for much of its course is a wilderness of burnt rock; east of it jagged uplands fall steeply to the Red Sea. With a negligible rainfall, Egypt's dependence on the river has been almost absolute. Throughout all her most recent history it has been true that 'a handful of men in Cairo have the life of Egypt in their hands'.[2]

Topography and climate also explain the high concentration of population in a relatively small area of the country. Only about one thirtieth of Egypt's 400,000 square miles is inhabited and under cultivation; and although the area of cultivation increased rapidly through new irrigation schemes during the first half of the present century – from five to six million acres – population rose more rapidly to make Egypt one of the most densely populated areas in the world with, in places, 1,300 people to the square mile.

The Suez Canal (1869) underlined Egypt's ambivalent character among the nations. Already a hinge between two continents, the Canal accorded to Egypt a no less uncomfortable role as 'the gateway to India'. Britain's protective interest in Egypt, many times declared to be temporary, had a look of permanency as long as the Canal could save 3,500 miles for British shipping. The declaration of a British protectorate over Egypt in December 1914, and the

British ultimatum to King Farouk for a change of government in February 1942 are an indication of the enhanced importance of Egypt, with Suez, in two world wars.

From 1883 to 1914 Egypt was a semi-colonial territory under the eye of a British Resident and Consul General. On 18th December, 1914 Egypt was declared a British protectorate; on 28th February, 1922 – again by a unilateral declaration – the protectorate was abolished and Egypt was recognized as a national state under King Fuad I (1922–36). Since Britain, however, retained control of the Canal Zone, with direct responsibility for defence, for the protection of foreigners, and for the Sudan, Egyptian sovereignty was not substantial. On 26th August, 1936 an Anglo-Egyptian Treaty gave some substance to it. The treaty provided for the withdrawal of British troops except for a ground force of 10,000 troops and air force bases in the Canal Zone. Britain was to retain the naval bases at Alexandria and Port Said for eight years only. The 'capitulations' were abolished. In 1936 Egypt entered the League of Nations as a sovereign state.

At the end of the first world war an indigenous political leadership began to emerge under Sa'd Zaghlul. He was the son of a well-to-do *fellah* of Upper Egypt, with a natural eloquence and gift for enjoying life, and he proved himself an able statesman. On 13th November, 1918, he appeared before the British High Commissioner, Sir Reginald Wingate, demanding Egypt's independence; and from that time until his death in 1927, as the leader of the *Wafd* he worked hard and skilfully towards its achievement. *Wafd*, meaning 'delegation', had for a time an almost mystical significance in relation to Egypt's independence. Zaghlul's subsequent career seems like a preview of the chequered career of nationalist leaders in many parts of Africa a generation after him. His deportation to Malta in March 1919 together with three other Wafdists, was the signal for riots, strikes, and acts of sabotage all over the country, and for student marches in Cairo. There was a further outbreak of disorder in 1921 following Zaghlul's deportation to the Seychelles. But the framing of a constitution in 1923 gave the *Wafd* a chance of proving itself at the polls. It gained an overwhelming victory and Zaghlul became Prime Minister in January 1924.

For the next twenty years the *Wafd*, with full independence and the unity of the Nile valley as its political platform, enjoyed spells of power interrupted from time to time by the suspension of the constitution or rigged elections when the court faction under Fuad (1922–36) or Farouk (1936–52) came out on top. The British found they could work with the *Wafd*, and the old ruling-classes saw in it a safety-valve for revolutionary aspirations. But after 1942, when Zaghlul's successor, Nahas Pasha, was recalled as Premier under strong British pressure, the *Wafd* no longer held the initiative. Its genuine nationalist fervour had become domesticated, and to some extent corrupted, in a predominantly middle-class and Westernized political party. The initiative was already passing to more revolutionary groups, notably the Moslem Brotherhood. Founded in

Ismailia in 1928 by Sheikh Hasan al-Banna, in part as a counter-weight to the
YMCA, it sought through groups of dedicated young men to make a revivified
and purified Islam a force of renewal for the Egyptian nation. In one aspect the
Moslem Brotherhood represented an anti-Western Islamic fundamentalism,
concerned with the clarification of the meaning of the Qu'ran; in another aspect,
it represented a more radical nationalism than the *Wafd*. Organized in cells
along semi-military lines, it gave to many patriotic Egyptians a sense of purpose
in the later 1930s when the older nationalist movement had failed to represent
the demands of the *fellahin* for thorough-going land reform. As a pressure-
group which could give credence to its claim to stand for the people of Egypt,
in a way that the *Wafd* had never done, the Brotherhood had a bright political
future in 1942.

Islam in Egypt

The conversion of Egypt to Islam came early, in the first wave of Muslim
expansion in the seventh century, and it was no superficial conquest but a
conversion in depth. It was not long before Egypt could begin to claim intellectual leadership in Islam. Al Azhar University, 'the Sorbonne and Cathedral
of Moslems all over the world', was founded in AD 970. After Turkey's collapse
as a political power during the first world war and the abolition of the Caliphate
in 1919, Egypt's role in Islam was enhanced. Like Iran, it remained unmistakably a Muslim state. For example, Article 12 of the 1923 constitution
guaranteed liberty of conscience, but elsewhere the constitution made it clear
that the religion of the country was Islam. Conversion from Islam to another
religion was not regarded as legal,[3] and Christians would continue to be regarded as inferior citizens, appropriate to their inferior revelation. This inferior
status of even so large and long-established a minority as the million-strong
Coptic Church, goes some way to explain the high annual loss of Coptic
Christians to Islam, a frequent subject of comment by CMS missionaries. One
of them wrote in 1927 'Even today it is estimated that not fewer than five
hundred members of the Coptic Church become Moslems each year'.[4] In the
next decade it was frequently reckoned as a thousand or more.

All the same, the Islamic culture of Egypt was considerably modified in the
first half of this century. Mustapha Kemal's progressive leadership in Turkey
had a considerable influence particularly in relation to education, to the status
of women, and to the overriding concern for national self-determination. As
early as 1908 an independent Egyptian university was founded with leanings
towards Western culture, and in 1926 Al Azhar added a course in modern
subjects to its traditional Islamic courses of study. In the nationalist rising of
1919 some Coptic Christians made common cause with Muslims and flags were
carried bearing the crescent and the cross. There was a further break with
tradition when women addressed public meetings during the outbreak. Such

things can happen, in moments of general excitement, without indicating any social trend; but the feminist movement in Egypt did in fact gain strength in the 1920s. Many women ceased to wear the veil or reduced its size to mere decoration. By 1925 the seclusion of women was less rigid. Girls were being allowed free access to the higher schools, and were being trained in midwifery and nursing. New legislation made sixteen the minimum marriageable age for girls and eighteen for boys. Divorce remained very easy for men, but polygamy was less frequent. Women's magazines were numerous and had a wide readership.[5]

This loosening of traditional Islamic social structure did not mean, however, a greatly enlarged opportunity for Christian evangelism or church-building. The 'millet' system was still in operation, requiring registration of members of different denominations according to their differing customs, rules on marriage and divorce, etc. This system bore hardly on small Christian minorities such as the Anglican Egyptian Church, which was not prepared to identify itself with the Protestant *Maglis Milli*. 'We haven't joined,' wrote E. G. Parry in 1940, 'because the Maglis allows divorce and is identified with Protestantism.'[6] As in Iran, the official attitude towards Christian evangelism tended to become more, not less, restrictive. In 1940, for example, a bill confining evangelism to places of worship was introduced into the Egyptian parliament. The bill was shelved, but in 1942 increasing pressure on non-government schools to provide Islamic teaching was a further cause for anxiety. (See below, pp. 313–15)

The Christian Churches

The 1917 census gave the Christian community in Egypt as just over one million in a total population of 12¾ million. Of this million, four-fifths was claimed by the Coptic Orthodox Church. This substantial remnant of the ancient Christian church in Egypt became separated from the Catholic Church in the fifth century, partly through the Monophysite controversy and partly through the slow break-up of the Roman empire. The Arab-Islam invasion of the seventh century greatly increased this isolation. Fortress-like monasteries with inner secret rooms as a last place of retreat can still be seen as a witness to the strain imposed by centuries of isolation. Liturgical conservatism, a largely hereditary clergy, a rigidly defined community are also best taken as part of the price paid for survival. From the time of William Jowett's first visit to Egypt in 1818, the CMS set its face against proselytizing among the Copts and sought rather through its missions to strengthen the life and witness of the ancient church. This policy, already modified in the 1880s when the CMS mission in Egypt was renewed, became for many missionaries an almost intolerable strain in the 1920s. (See below, p. 309)

The Coptic Church is not the only branch of Eastern Christendom represented in Egypt. In the late 1930s there was a Greek Orthodox community of nearly 70,000 members, a slightly larger Syrian and Lebanese community (partly Orthodox and partly Roman Catholic and Maronite) and 30,000 Armenian Christians, mostly Orthodox. For the most part the adherents of these Christian groupings were ethnic minorities not indigenous to the country. The one real exception was the Evangelical (Injili) Church in Egypt, built up chiefly by American Presbyterian missionaries. Its membership was largely drawn from Orthodox Copts, not, during the period under review, by active proselytizing, but by steady enrolment, without re-baptism, of those who wished to join. Several presbyteries were entirely self-supporting by 1922. By 1937 its governing body, the Synod of the Nile, represented a membership of 21,000 in 150 organized congregations and 200 'unorganized' groups of evangelical Christians in Egypt and the northern Sudan.

The Anglican Church

Until 1920, Egypt was included under the jurisdiction of the Anglican Bishop in Jerusalem, although from 1908 Llewellyn H. Gwynne assisted, with the title of Bishop of Khartoum. In 1920 Egypt and the Sudan were constituted a separate diocese under Bishop Gwynne. Himself a former CMS missionary pioneer, alike in Khartoum and in the southern Sudan, Bishop Gwynne had two CMS missionaries from West Africa as assistant bishops, Guy Bullen (1935–7) and A. M. Gelsthorpe (1937–45). In 1945 the Sudan was made a separate diocese under Bishop Gelsthorpe, a division of oversight which had been contemplated for a number of years. Bishop Gelsthorpe had been invited to transfer from Nigeria with the definite intention that he should succeed Bishop Gwynne, and in the hope that, if there was a division of the diocese when Bishop Gwynne retired, he would accept the Sudan.[7]

No-one could have done more than Llewellyn Gwynne to make the Anglican Church in Egypt a reality. It had grown up in part from the activities of the CMS, in part by the initiative of British expatriates – 'godly laymen, who felt that they could not live their lives and carry on their business without the spiritual inspiration of their church'. Such laymen built churches and drew together small congregations in Cairo, Alexandria, Port Said and Suez. There was not much episcopal oversight until 1905, when the Bishop in Jerusalem built St Mary's Church in Cairo and also schools in the same compound. The building of All Saints' Cathedral, Cairo was largely the personal achievement of Bishop Gwynne although it was Bishop MacInnes who opened a cathedral fund in 1915 and who secured the services of Adrian Gilbert Scott, brother of the architect of the Anglican cathedral in Liverpool. The first plans received in 1933 pleased Gwynne greatly. 'The graceful, dignified and beautiful tower grows on me every time I see it.' He wrote to Scott: 'We are recommending the committee to accept your design for the whole group of buildings. I am very anxious to begin this autumn.' The building complex included a bishop's house and provost's house, set opposite across a courtyard, with diocesan offices adjoining the cathedral. The work was finished in 1938 and the cathedral was consecrated by William Temple, then Archbishop of York. For twenty-five years it was a dominant feature of the Nile sky-line until the tower-blocks of the late 1950s overshadowed it.

Cheerful, prayerful, golf-playing, a much respected Assistant Chaplain-General in the first world war, Llewellyn Gwynne was *persona grata* with the British community in Egypt in the inter-war years; and he was thrilled, during the second world war, to see his new cathedral thronged several times a Sunday with British troops. In some ways he was a typical British establishment figure of his time. When in 1933 his friend Harry Blackburne, Canon of St George's, Windsor, wrote inviting him to preach before HM King George V, he wrote:

> I am a loyal subject of His Majesty the King, though it always sends a shiver up my spine when I have to preach to royalty as I did in France. But I am not coming home this year. . . . I regret not being able to take you on at golf on the King's links. I should feel happier there than in the King's pulpit.

For all that he remained a missionary at heart. He described a meeting of the Near East Christian Council in the Lebanon as like being on the Mount of Transfiguration:

> Quite ordinary, matter-of-fact, courageous folk from Persia, Arabia, Iraq and Turkey were transfigured when they spoke of Christ meeting with them in all sorts and kinds of experiences in their sacrificial lives of service as missionaries. It seemed to me so marvellous that what God was doing in our small part of the world He was doing to multitudes of His servants all over the world.

In the early 1930s the Oxford Group Movement made a considerable impression on him. 'I think,' he wrote to Wilson Cash, 'the best thing for me to do personally is to get inside by attending one of the house-parties, and then to play full back as it were, letting the young people do all they can on their own.' The great aim, in which he thought this new movement might help, was to 'make our congregation real soul-winners'. Gwynne was always outspoken about what seemed to him the faults and failings of Egyptian politics and social order, and this caused difficulties when assumptions of British over-rule, in any guise, had become quite unacceptable. But he gave much to Egypt in genuine friendship and had communicated to the little Anglican Church in Egypt some portion of his buoyant faith.[8]

Guy Bullen was a colleague after Gwynne's own heart, and he looked forward to his coming as assistant bishop in 1937; but Bullen's service in Egypt and the Sudan was tragically cut short in an air accident not many months after his arrival. Maurice Gelsthorpe's service as assistant bishop during this period was mostly in the Sudan.

The CMS in Egypt

In brief recapitulation, the 'Mediterranean Mission' of the Society started in Malta in 1815 and extended from there, in the middle decades of the nineteenth century, to Egypt, Abyssinia, Greece, Turkey, Asia Minor and Palestine. At first in Egypt the CMS aimed primarily at reforming the Coptic Church, seeking to reach the Muslims through the Copts. A seminary was opened in Cairo in which a number of Coptic clergy, one of whom became a bishop, received training. The visible results of this mission were small and it was discontinued in 1862. A quarter of a century later in 1887, following the British occupation of Egypt, the Society sent the Rev. F. A. Klein to Cairo. He had formerly been a missionary in Palestine, and his instructions were to direct his efforts towards the conversion of Muslims, while maintaining a friendly attitude towards the Coptic community. Klein appealed for the help of a doctor and in March 1889 Dr Frank J. Harpur arrived to found the medical mission which was later to be known by his name. He chose Old Cairo, the Nile port three miles from Cairo itself, as preferable to Suez on the grounds that 'for medical missionary work there should be a large population both at the centre and in the country around'. The hospital began in a private house, but moved to new buildings on its present site eight years later. It soon became the strong centre of the CMS mission in Egypt, and Harpur's name, corrupted to 'Harmul', 'became a generic name for all and sundry who had any connection with the Old Cairo Hospital'.[9]

By the turn of the century other missionaries had begun to arrive in Cairo and by 1910 the range of work undertaken by CMS missionaries had expanded considerably – a teacher-training class, a small boarding-school and two day-schools for girls in Cairo: the hospital and a boys' day-school with a small boarding hostel attached, in Old Cairo, and a school for the daughters of well-to-do Egyptians in Helouan. Also in Cairo was the book depot from which an illustrated magazine in Arabic, *Orient and Occident*, was published. The missionary strength at this time was thirty–five clergy, four laymen, seven wives, and fourteen other women. Among them in 1910 were the Rev. W. H. T. Gairdner who had been entrusted with the writing of the popular report of the Edinburgh World Missionary Conference in June 1910;[10] Canon Rennie MacInnes, secretary of the mission 1902–14; Drs F. O. Lasbrey and E. Maynard Pain working happily together at Old Cairo hospital, 'both of us in the prime of life, both of us perfectly at home with every section of the work';[11] Dr Frank Harpur itinerating in a house-boat along the canals of the Nile delta, setting up a temporary dispensary at its moorings for a few months at a time, and drawing people from many towns and villages around; the Rev. Wilson Cash who, in January 1910, started CMS work in Menouf; and Miss Mary Cay and Miss Janet Lewis who in November 1910 settled at Shubra Zanga, fifty miles north-west of Cairo and six miles from Menouf, where they were to live 'an isolated, self-sacrificing life for many years' dealing out simple remedies, and teaching and evangelizing as opportunity offered.

1911–29

Gairdner returned to Egypt after a year's absence in 1911 to find the YMCA in Cairo nearly moribund. 'I threw myself into it as a matter of course,' he wrote, 'and speedily became pretty much involved.'[12] This, and the day-to-day personal contact with converts and catechumens meant less and less time for the Arabic scholarship which part of him longed to put first; but R. F. McNeile, a former Student of Christ Church, Oxford, was understudying Gairdner in his literary work, and assisted him in the Cairo Study Centre which he had started in 1912. It was intended to be something more than a language school for missionaries in their first tour of service, but owing to repeated shortages of staff its more ambitious projects in Islamic and Arabic studies were not fully developed.

In October 1911, a new out-station dispensary was started at Ashmoun; and the following year Harpur abandoned his house-boat and settled at Ashmoun. In 1913 a further branch dispensary was started at Hamoul, and Harpur ran both dispensaries till 1915 with the help of a Syrian doctor. On 12th February, 1913, Maynard Pain died after a very short illness. He had contracted cerebral meningitis from a patient at Old Cairo hospital. Son of a former Bishop of Gippsland, Australia, and the first missionary doctor to be sent out by the New South Wales Church Missionary Association, he had worked at Old Cairo hospital since 1902. He had helped it to grow from small beginnings to one of the great mission hospitals with over 14,000 out-patients a year. His friends in Australia raised over £2,000 for the hospital as a thanksgiving for his work.

On the outbreak of the first world war two of the CMS doctors, A. R. Hargreaves and R. Y. Stones, and two of the clergy, Cash and McNeile, volunteered for service with the forces, but the last two were able to stay in Egypt for a time. McNeile did not return. He wrote in 1917 saying that his eight years in the Egypt mission had shown him that he was not temperamentally fitted for missionary work. This left Gairdner alone once more in the field of study and scholarship, with added and far from welcome duties as secretary of the mission in succession to MacInnes. In 1914 MacInnes was consecrated Bishop in Jerusalem, but until the end of the war he spent a good deal of time in Cairo. Egypt at that time was still within his diocese. (See also Palestine chapter.)

The war brought certain inevitable hardships, but it caused less disruption of normal life than in most other countries where the CMS was at work. The most grievous hardship was a diminished staff in face of expanding opportunities. In April 1915 a new hospital was opened, by Bishop MacInnes, at Menouf, chiefly for victims of ankylostomiasis (Egyptian anaemia) with Dr Harpur in charge. He continued to superintend the Ashmoun dispensary from Menouf but the Hamoul dispensary was closed.

On 13th December, 1915, Mrs E. B. Bywater died. She and her daughter were the first women missionaries, apart from 'wives', to serve in Egypt. She had done notable work since 1890, chiefly at the Cairo girls' boarding school. Shubra Zanga was left without European missionaries for some months in 1915 following an attempt to poison Miss Cay and Miss Lewis, but by October they were both back, and the dispensary open again.

The disturbances in Cairo during March and April 1919 caused very little disruption of missionary work, though the involvement of Coptic Christians was saddening for some CMS missionaries. Two Copts found places as ministers in the first Wafdist government following an overwhelming victory at the polls in January 1924. In 1919 Cash had returned to become secretary of the CMS mission in succession to Gairdner. S. A. Morrison, a lay missionary who arrived in 1920, had some success with Bible-study circles for students, following a mission conducted by Dr Sherwood Eddy, an American evangelist. In January 1925 a student discussion group began meeting regularly in his flat in Sharia al Falaki, Cairo. Here, in the atmosphere of a home rather than a lecture hall, other activities developed, including a course in classical Arabic, meeting twice a week. Its members included Muslims, Bahais and Jews. In 1926 the experiment was made of student lectures in the assembly hall of the American University in Cairo to which the public were admitted. Things went well at first, with several hundred students attending, but at the third lecture, on a given signal, all the Muslim students walked out and thereafter picketed the meetings. The meetings at S. A. Morrison's flat continued however, moving later to the YMCA.[13]

In 1921, partly in response to the Lambeth Conference 'Appeal to All Christian People' of the previous year, Bishop Gwynne, Temple Gairdner and others founded the Fellowship of Unity in Cairo. Annual unity services were held in the Coptic, Armenian and Greek Orthodox cathedrals, and regular conferences under Bishop Gwynne's leadership made possible a breadth of understanding and fellowship amid diverse Christian groups which was rare at that time. An inter-mission council was also started in 1921, largely due to Cash's efforts, and its standing committee on the relations of missions to government became an increasingly important organ for negotiation and exchange of opinion a decade later.

The post-war financial crisis affected all missions of the CMS, and the Egypt missionaries' conference was faced with the dispiriting task of recommending retrenchment to meet a five per cent reduction in parent committee grants from June 1922. Fortunately Bishop Gwynne was able to offer help from the diocesan missionary fund, and Old Cairo hospital not only took over the salaries of the colporteurs and bible-women connected with it, but guaranteed £300 per annum for the general work of the mission.

A CMS headquarters delegation had visited Egypt in 1921, and one result was the appointment of a sub-committee within the mission. It reported to the missionaries' conference in May 1922. The secretary (Wilson Cash) recalled how in 1906 the conference had agreed that the object of the Egypt mission was the building up of a native church, chiefly from Muslim converts; and that its attitude towards the Copts should be one of friendly co-operation. Since the war, however, and as a result of the nationalist movement the relation of the Copts to the mission was 'in many cases hostile'. The sub-committee believed that a change of policy was necessary. 'It could not be right to refuse church membership to those who failed to find in a Coptic Church, or in any other church, the spiritual life they needed.'[14] The sub-committee's memorandum containing fourteen points of policy was adopted by the conference. Bishop Gwynne consulted the Archbishop of Canterbury, who in turn asked Bishop Gore to act as an assessor, and in 1923 a policy statement, drafted by Gairdner, was issued with their approval in the following terms:

> The primary aim of the Anglican Church in Egypt is the evangelization of the non-Christian population, and . . . it does not desire to draw adherents from either the Coptic or the Evangelical Churches. Those who, in sincerity, find the Anglican Church their spiritual home are welcome to join it . . . but the Church does not set out to gain their allegiance. Instead, it seeks to extend the right hand of fellowship to the Coptic Church so as to render it every possible form of service, and, at the same time, it strives for closer co-operation and greater unity between all the Churches in Egypt.[15]

Adherence to this purpose was not easy. Missionaries longed to share with other Christians of an unreformed tradition their full liberty in Christ; and they found the explicit ban on proselytism irksome, though they welcomed the equally explicit invitation to young Copts who were genuinely out of touch with the church of their baptism. Members of the Egyptian Anglican Church, conscious of their small numbers, could not fail to notice that inter-denominational proselytizing continued to be practised by other Christian bodies. But the intention was for the most part well kept, and the slow growth of the Anglican Church in Egypt can only be understood in the light of this policy.

The Egyptian membership of the Anglican Church remained small – 219 communicants, and 429 baptized members in 1922; 431 communicants and 745 baptized members in 1942 – but Gairdner could write early in 1923 of 'great Egyptian fellow-workers'. One of these, Girghis Bishai, was made deacon on Whitsunday 1924 and ordained priest in the following Advent. Five years later, in 1929, Khalil Tadros Boula, a vigorous evangelist in Giza, west of the Nile, was made deacon; and a group of lay readers was trained by Gairdner, who held before them the vision of a 'truly militant, evangelical, and therefore evangelistic Church, however small, a truly Catholic Church with power to absorb and unify the most diverse elements, and gifted with historical order and reverent, inspiring and liturgical services'.[16]

In October 1924 the CMS mission moved its headquarters from 35 Sharia al Falaki to more ample quarters in Boulac, the most thickly populated area of Cairo, in the neighbourhood of the railway station. A group of buildings there, belonging to a German Lutheran mission, had been entrusted to the CMS under the Peace Treaty and these were now taken over. They provided a more settled home for the girls' school, and flats for women missionaries. The buildings taken over included the Church of the Saviour, Boulac. Gairdner found it rather formidable at first but felt more reconciled when he had removed from the church walls 'flat plaster cherubs and plaques of opulent fruit'. By 1928 it had a congregation drawn from forty families which was 'beginning to realize it had a mission and a message'.

1924 saw also the beginning of the Boulac Community Centre. In the autumn of that year Morrison, with funds promised or in hand from the YMCA and the Old Cairo hospital, was searching 'for land for the development of a slum evangelistic centre'.[17] A year later he opened a club for youths and boys in a former coffee house in Boulac. On the first evening one hundred and twenty of them crowded into a room intended to hold half that number. The programme included games, gymnastics, and a weekly cinema. Morrison did not expect an easy start. For the first two weeks there were stones and brick-bats every night. The police threatened to withdraw permission and the landlord talked of eviction. But soon the club settled down with sixty regular members, four-fifths of them Muslims. Gradually other activities of an evening institute type were added to the programme. Accommodation in the Lutheran mission buildings made further development possible, including clubs and classes for girls of different ages.

It was in the Lutheran mission compound in Boulac that Temple Gairdner made his last home. In February 1927 he returned to Egypt from furlough 'singularly unrefreshed'. He recovered some of his old zest, finishing a colloquial Arabic translation of Galatians, with commentary, shepherding his Arabic congregation, and greatly enjoying silver wedding celebrations with Mrs Gairdner and his children. But in November came the first sign of septic complications following a tooth extraction, and he died in the Anglo-American hospital in Cairo on 22nd May, 1928. Bishop Gwynne wrote of him: '[He] used to magnify my office for the sake of discipline. He was cleverer, abler, knew more than I, yet he served me.' Canon Oliver Quick, who visited him in hospital, spoke of his intellectual unselfishness: 'I am sure he was absolutely interested in God's world rather than in his own or in any particular set of views about it.' One of his 'children in the Lord', Yusef Effendi Tadros, said: 'Other teachers taught us how to refute Islam: he taught us how to love Muslims.'[18]

1929–42

In the late 1920s the drop in world cotton prices had an immediate effect on the hospitals at Old Cairo and Menouf as their income was almost wholly derived from patients' fees. At the same time the world depression began to affect the amount of money available from Britain for general mission purposes. The annual report of the mission for 1929–30 noted a reduction of five per cent in the stipend of some Egyptian catechists and colporteurs and the dismissal of others. In June 1931 Ashmoun girls' school was closed as a measure of re-trenchment and the Cairo bookshop premises were sold. The literature bureau was by this time housed in the basement of the German buildings in Boulac. No home grant was received for literature work for the year 1931. In 1934 Cairo girls' school was closed as a result of the decision to return the former German properties in Boulac to the Lutheran Church. The school had suffered through-out its life from insecure housing and unsatisfactory buildings, but for short periods under Miss Coate and Miss Liesching it had a high repute.

Anti-missionary propaganda, always an occupational hazard for missionaries in Egypt during the long struggle for independence, flared up again in 1932 and lasted for several months. It was followed by a marked stiffening of the examination for doctors qualified abroad who wished to practise in Egypt, and entry permits limited to missionary replacements. For a time, too, permits to build new churches were held up and new legislation in 1934 was designed to give the Ministry of Education control over non-government schools.

In 1930 the native church councils took over from the CMS the administration of the social and evangelistic activities which the Society had initiated, with the large exception of those which were directly associated with the hospitals and schools. In 1932 new buildings were acquired for the club and welfare work of the Boulac Community Centre, and in the same year part of the land be-longing to the Old Cairo hospital was sold to the native church council for the erection of the Temple Gairdner Memorial Church.

This beautiful small church, opened in 1934 and named in consecration 'The Church of Jesus the Light of the World', became, as Gairdner would have wished, a true home for the Egyptian Episcopal Church. A memorial tablet on the south wall reads:

> This church was built to the glory of God and in memory of Temple Gairdner who for twenty-eight years served Christ in this land. For Egypt he gladly spent himself, offering her his life as a disciple; his gifts as linguist, thinker and writer; his far-seeing leadership and joy in the holiness of worship; his delight in music and beauty; his enriching friendship; and his tender care for little children and for those newly entering the household of Christ. He died, as he had desired, among his friends in Egypt, on May 22nd, 1928.

It was fitting that Adeeb Shammas, the first young Egyptian to receive orders in the Anglican Church, and trained like Gairdner himself at Wycliffe Hall, Oxford, should be instituted to the charge of this church in 1937. Shammas, later to become Archdeacon of the Egyptian Church, also ministered to the staff of Old Cairo hospital for some years, and superintended the work of voluntary evangelists in the hospital. Also in 1934 a new church was built in Giza, across the Nile from Old Cairo.

Old Cairo hospital continued to expand in the 1920s. In 1925 a new wing was added to the men's hospital, and in 1929 the operating theatre of the women's hospital was enlarged. A familiar figure in the hospital wards was an ageing man with a white topee and fly whisk, distributing gifts of oranges and cucumbers, and religious tracts in colloquial Arabic. He was Sir William Willcocks the distinguished constructional engineer, by then retired. It was estimated that he gave away to hospital patients some 14,000 copies of Christian tracts of his own compilation, such as *The Sayings and Doings of Christ*, *The Sayings of Sadhu Sundar Singh*. Dr Harpur returned to Old Cairo in the 1920s and was also a familiar and beloved daily visitor in the wards until he finally retired in 1932.

In 1929 Dr Lasbrey resigned to become general secretary of the Edinburgh Medical Missionary Society. An able administrator, he was also a deeply committed missionary. In 1923 he had written home to the medical committee saying that he wished to retire from missionary work and would value help in finding a job in Britain. It was typical of the man, that when Cash was recalled to London, and knowing how much Gairdner dreaded becoming secretary of the mission again, he volunteered to succeed Cash in that office; and for six years he combined its duties with those of medical superintendent at the hospital. It was largely due to Lasbrey that the excellence of the hospital's work in medicine and surgery went a long way in making up for equipment inferior to government hospitals of comparable size. Its reputation owed much also to the integrity of the nursing staff, both Egyptian and European. A Cairo taxi-driver told a visitor on one occasion that people liked the CMS hospital best because 'although you have to pay fees it works out less than the baksheesh you have to give in other hospitals'.

At the time of Lasbrey's withdrawal in 1929, Old Cairo hospital was allocating £1,000 a year for evangelistic agencies connected with the hospital and substantially underwriting the running-costs of Menouf hospital as well. But income fell steeply from £16,990 in 1929 to £10,994 in 1931, and the Society reluctantly decided to close Menouf hospital. Happily the Egyptian doctor, Abd el Malik Saad, was prepared to take over the hospital and run it at his own expense; and as the Old Cairo accounts for 1932 showed a surplus of £1,000, the closure of Menouf proved unnecessary.

'Medical camps' were a feature of the medical mission in the 1930s. In the cooler months – December to March – doctors with orderlies visited several districts each year. Usually they rented a small house and visited villages in the neighbourhood, combining Christian teaching with medical services. Infant welfare work was developed at Old Cairo by Miss D. Sands and Miss E. Johnson, and Dr Charlotte Stuart ran an ante-natal clinic. Dr Cutting reported 27,000 new out-patients for the year 1935, with in-patients coming from as far afield as Mecca. In 1940, its Jubilee Year, Old Cairo hospital was re-planning its work, in the light of a CMS medical committee report, with increased emphasis on preventive medicine. The new plans included evangelism by voluntary church workers in the hospital wards and hookworm pavilions. Rural reconstruction units were started in a number of villages of Giza and Menoufia provinces, providing dispensary and welfare work, and a school at each village centre.[19] With the onset of the second world war these plans proved as difficult to implement as the rebuilding of the hospital at Old Cairo.

Work among the blind had an important place in a country which in 1931 was said to have no less than half a million blind or partially blind people. Miss Adeney and Miss Liesching did notable work among blind women and girls, and Gindi Effendi Ibrahim, himself blind, worked among students. In March 1925 he opened a blind school in a rented house in Sharia al Falaki, near Al Azhar university. There for a time he taught Braille reading and writing and also handcraft. By 1929 a hundred and fifty or so students were attending his classes.

In the 1930s, and particularly after the 1936 Treaty, the mission schools were under considerable pressure from the government, and from public opinion, to conform to the requirements of the new Egypt.

A road-widening scheme in 1933 made it necessary for Old Cairo girls' school to move to a new site on Rodah Island. It was not an easy time for promoting special appeals for missionary institutions, but fortunately the proceeds of the sale of mission property in the Sharia el Falaki were available to help in rebuilding the school. The new buildings were completed by the end of 1937 at a total cost of £E6264.976, covered by earmarked funds, local gifts, and a small loan.

The figures for pupils attending CMS schools 1938–40 indicate the scale of the CMS mission's commitment at the end of our period. Figures for Muslim pupils are given in brackets.[20]

	Old Cairo Girls	Old Cairo Boys	Menouf Boys	Menouf Girls
1938	273(166)	260(99)	123(61)	143(69)
1939	280(184)	304(117)	125(66)	152(76)
1940	274(177)	272(106)	150(96)	179(91)

These figures do not suggest any loss of confidence in spite of mounting pressure of Egyptian nationalism during these years. In January 1938, for example, it was reported to the standing committee of the CMS mission that the Minister of Education had agreed to the inspection of teaching in foreign schools. The inter-mission council was asked to investigate. By May the fears of government 'interference' in mission schools were largely dispelled when it was made clear that general inspection was not intended. The request for government inspection had come from a group of Egyptian teachers in mission schools who sought parity with teachers in government schools. The standing committee found no reasonable grounds for objecting to the inspection of the work of individual teachers at their own request.

Another issue that caused anxiety among the missionaries was the provision of a 'conscience clause' in relation to Christian teaching and school prayers. In 1933, when this issue was first raised, the mission standing committee agreed that each institution should exercise discretion about accepting a conscience clause 'with due regard to the interests of every other mission school in the neighbourhood'. The CMS and the American Presbyterian mission kept in close touch, and made joint representations through the inter-mission council. On 15th May, 1940 the standing committee of the CMS mission accepted for its schools a conscience clause of the 'contracting-in' type. Christian teaching and prayers would be maintained as part of the schools' provision for moral training. Children could be exempted from both on written application from a parent or guardian, to be renewed annually. 'Christian teaching' was held to include the Old as well as the New Testament. The educational sub-committee of the mission was asked to recommend arrangements for exempted pupils. In the autumn of 1940 the following applications for exemption were recorded: Old Cairo boys' school, 67; Old Cairo girls' school, 1 only; Menouf boys' school, 12; Menouf girls' school, 15.[21]

On 3rd August, 1940, a conference of 'heads of certain foreign schools' met at the American university in Cairo, to consider a letter sent to them by the Egyptian Under-Secretary of State for Education.

> The Ministry [it read] is well aware of the services rendered to this country by the foreign schools where education has reached a high standard. For this reason it intends to offer these schools the greatest possible assistance so as to facilitate their task in giving a good education to the large number of Egyptian students admitted therein, and providing them with necessary amount of national culture, which any educated Egyptian ought to acquire. . . . The Ministry intends to examine, together with the headmasters and principals of the schools in question, the syllabus to be given to their Egyptian students, viz. Arabic language, National History, Geography of Egypt, Civics and if necessary the Muhammedan Religion.

The tenor of this letter was only too clear. There had been a press campaign urging that the curriculum in foreign schools should conform to that of government schools of equivalent range, and demanding Qu'ranic teaching for Muslim pupils in Christian schools. A Ministry of Education circular had already required Muslim pupils in primary schools to pass an examination in the Qu'ran before moving up at the end of the school year. The conference unanimously agreed to the requirements in other subjects, but the majority opinion was that mission schools ought not to be expected to give Qu'ranic teaching to their Muslim pupils. The standing committee of the CMS mission had already (15th May, 1940) urged CMS schools to refuse to teach or examine in this subject, advising instead that their Muslim pupils should make their own arrangements for it outside school hours. On 6th February, 1941 it was reported at the standing committee that the Ministry of Education was itself holding examinations in Qu'ranic teaching. The committee was unanimous in rejecting a proposal made by a government inspector that Menouf boys' school should provide a Muslim place of prayer in its premises. Government pressure on mission schools continued in 1942 but it was less severe than in Iran. There was nothing comparable to the enforced sale of Stuart Memorial College, Isfahan in 1940.

The fact that the CMS mission in Egypt remained steadily and effectively at work under the pressures of the 1930s owes much to the calm competence of S. A. Morrison. A classical scholar at Oxford, he served for a time on the staff of the Children's Special Service Mission before joining Temple Gairdner in Cairo in 1920 to work among students at Al Azhar University. In 1929 he succeeded Lasbrey as mission secretary and for the next twenty years his exceptional mastery of Arabic and intimate knowledge of Egyptian affairs helped the missionary bodies and churches to find their way through many a hazard in public relations. One of his greatest achievements was the committee of liaison, in which all the churches were represented, which established a common Christian front in relation to the Egyptian government on educational and other matters. Morrison was a formidable person in some ways, especially to those who were doubtful of their own efficiency and self-discipline. 'He worked every minute of his waking life,' a colleague wrote of him, 'and organized his time to the second.' The hundred-page report on Church and State in Muslim Lands which he drafted for the Madras Conference 1938 is a masterpiece of compressed information; and in his book *The Way of Partnership* (1936) his description of the call to the Anglican Church in Egypt reveals his own personal commitment during thirty years of missionary service within it, 'to evangelize the Moslems and to work for Church union'. In 1951 he was appointed executive secretary of a committee of the Near East Christian Council which sought to bring relief to Palestine refugees: and, three years later, he was engaged, as secretary of the Christian Council of Kenya, in equally arduous relief work following the Mau Mau troubles. He died in 1956.

Translators and Writers

H. D. Hooper, Africa secretary of CMS, visited Egypt in 1938, and wrote afterwards of the 'remarkable ventures in the field of literature which owe so much to the genius of Temple Gairdner and Constance Padwick'. Miss Padwick volunteered for this work in 1923 and for the last five years of Gairdner's life she was his valued collaborator and assistant. After his death she wrote a life of Gairdner, as he had written the life of his friend Douglas Thornton twenty years before.[22] It is remarkable that two such good missionary biographies should come from the same small mission. Constance Padwick shared with

Thornton and Gairdner the conviction that Christian literature, in Egypt at all events, should be something more than a dispensable handmaid of the church and mission. They all three regarded literature work as integral to any Christian advance in a country with an ancient culture, a growing literacy, and a wide range of newspapers and magazines.

All three were critical of the Christian literature for Muslims which they found in circulation, filled 'with the spirit of disputation rather than of worship and of love, and apt to hammer rather than to woo and win'.[23] Thornton had been a great believer in tracts, widely disseminated, and Gairdner wrote a number of them in Arabic and English for students (e.g. *The Secret of Life*, and *The Divinity of Christ*, SPCK, Cairo, 1942). The magazine *Orient and Occident*, started by Thornton and Gairdner in 1905, was published without a break throughout the period 1910–42 though it changed from a fortnightly to a monthly. 'It was,' wrote Miss Padwick quoting Gairdner, 'a regular magazine designed to reach more than the student class only, with articles for young and old, sheikh and effendi, on religious and on general subjects'.[24] It circulated far beyond Egypt and had regular subscribers in Palestine, Syria, India, Ceylon and Java. It was not a CMS publication but the Society's Missionary Service League saw it through a financial crisis in 1926 by covering a considerable deficit and adding a donation of £200. CMS evangelists, Syrian and Egyptian, at that time made fortnightly journeys to collect subscriptions in Alexandria and other towns and villages, selling other items of Arabic Christian literature as they went. In 1939 *Orient and Occident* had a monthly circulation of 2,400 copies. It was still being issued twenty years later by Mr Habib Said who had begun working with Miss Padwick in 1917.

From 1925 the CMS Arabic literature department was merged in the SPCK Near East Council, and after Gairdner's death Constance Padwick continued as a specialist worker in the field of Christian literature. Her outstanding work with the Central Literature Committee for Moslems carried forward the tradition of a sensitive and wide-ranging programme of publications. The 1939 catalogue of Arabic publications contained nearly ninety items.[25] Production and circulation was stepped up considerably by H. E. J. Biggs, a CMS missionary seconded to work with SPCK in Cairo in 1937.

The Tambaram Conference in 1938 received a report from the Muslim Lands Group urging 'wider-based support for . . . the Central Literature Committee for Muslims'.[26] In 1938 a start was made on newspaper evangelism, but it did not develop as successfully as it had done in Japan.

The production of Christian literature in Egyptian Arabic was not confined to a small group of specialists, either associated with SPCK or the Nile Mission Press. S. A. Morrison wrote a number of tracts, and Sir William Willcocks persevered with translating and retranslating the gospels colloquially. Nor did the specialists confine their undertakings to literature. For example, Miss Elsie Anna Wood, whose New Testament wall pictures proved as popular in their generation in Western countries as in the Near East, started an embroidery industry in the Boulac centre to help women whose husbands were out of work. There can have been few, if any, other places where in the first half of this century, Christian literature work was so well integrated into the general work of mission and church-building.

Conclusion

It is always tempting, but usually unwise, to compare one area of mission with another in terms of achievement. The Egypt mission, during the period here reviewed, continued to draw into service an unusual number of gifted missionaries; but the development of work in the southern Sudan and the Nuba mountains made 'the Sudanese half of the diocese . . . very much more important than Cairo'.[27] A discerning visitor in 1938 felt that 'the tall buildings and cosmopolitan character of Cairo itself with more than one million inhabitants, reduced the perspective of missionary activity to negligible proportions'; and that the effect of working in so large a centre was 'to departmentalize our work and militate against a closer integration of hospital, schools and social clubs'.[28] 'The small Episcopal Church in Egypt,' wrote Bishop Gwynne in 1943, 'has not yet found its feet . . . (its) members to a large extent are drawn from other Christian Churches, and are largely families of CMS workers at the hospitals or schools'; but he ended the letter with the kind of conviction which had kept many a missionary going in times of disappointed hopes and restricted opportunities:

Those who are called to be missionaries to Moslems, let them prepare their souls for a heart-breaking job. God gave us a Douglas Thornton, Temple Gairdner, Rennie MacInnes, Drs Harpur, Hall, Bateman. He will send us more men like these from His exhaustless resources, if only we believe.[29]

NOTES

1. Jean and Simonne Lacouture, *Egypt in Transition*, Methuen, 1958, pp. 11–19.
2. Lacouture, op. cit., p. 79.
3. S. A. Morrison, *The Way of Partnership*, CMS, 1936, pp. 74, 75.
4. *CMR*, June 1927, pp. 134ff., S. A. Morrison, 'The Church in Egypt'.
5. *CMR*, March 1925, pp. 54ff., Daisy G. Phillips, 'Women and Present Day Social Conditions in Egypt'.
6. G/Y/E 2, Parry to Cash, 18th May, 1940.
7. G/Y/E 2, Cash to Gelsthorpe, 4th February, 1941.
8. Gwynne to McLeod Campbell, 13th October, 1938, Gwynne, Private and Personal Letters 1924–33 (Cairo archives).
9. *These Fifty Years: Old Cairo Medical Mission 1889–1939*, Old Cairo, CMS, 1939, p. 25.

10. W. H. T. Gairdner, *Edinburgh 1910. An Account and Interpretation of the World Missionary Conference*, Oliphant, Anderson and Ferrier, 1910.

11. *These Fifty Years*, op. cit., p. 43.

12. Constance E. Padwick, *Temple Gairdner of Cairo*, SPCK, 1929, p. 217.

13. *CMO*, August 1927, pp. 156ff., S. A. Morrison, 'The House of Free Speech'.

14. G3/E/P3, 1922/34.

15. S. A. Morrison, *Near East*, Highway Press, 1955, p. 10.

16. Padwick, op. cit., p. 264.

17. C. E. Padwick, *Home-Building in Egypt*, No. 10, 1922-1923-1924, p. 23.

18. Padwick, *Temple Gairdner of Cairo*, pp. 286, 302, 316.

19. G/Y/E 2, Morrison to Cash, 26th May, 1941; S. A. Morrison, memorandum to CMS Egypt Mission Medical Sub-Committee, 20th November, 1939 (Cairo archives).

20. Egypt Standing Committee file (591), 4th November, 1938, 31st October, 1939, 28th November, 1940.

21. ibid., 28th November, 1940.

22. W. H. T. Gairdner, *D. M. Thornton*, Hodder & Stoughton, 1908.

23. Padwick, op. cit., p. 148.

24. *CMO*, December 1926, pp. 246ff., C. E. Padwick, ' "O & O", Cairo'.

25. *CMO*, June 1939, pp. 121ff., H. E. J. Biggs, 'Christian Literature in Egypt and Beyond'.

26. International Missionary Council, *Tambaram Series*, Vol. III, OUP, 1939, p. 444.

27. G/Y/E 2, Cash to Gelsthorpe, 4th February, 1941.

28. H. D. Hooper, *Report of a Visit to CMS Missions in East Africa, the Sudan, Egypt and Palestine, 1937-38*, CMS, 1938, p. 59.

29. G/Y/E 2, Gwynne to Warren, 9th November, 1943.

The Sudan

The Country and its Peoples

Belad el-Sudan, 'the country of the blacks', was the name the Arabs gave to Africa south of the Sahara. The Sudanese Republic, although only an eastern section of this vast area, covers a million square miles of territory, ranging from desert and semi-desert to savanna, papyrus swamp and tropical forest, stretching thirteen hundred miles from the Egyptian border at Wadi Halfa to the Uganda border south of Juba, and almost as broad as it is long; a country as large as Western Europe without Germany. Its population at the 1937 census was 5,900,000, but it was increasing rapidly, and doubled in the next ten years.

In the northern and central provinces of the Sudan (from the 22nd to the 10th parallel of latitude north) Arabic is the *lingua franca*, and its people largely Islamic in culture and outlook. North of latitude 17° north there is very little rain, and the sparse population is mostly to be found in small villages along the Nile, as in Upper Egypt, or among nomads, such as the *Beja* tribes of the Red Sea littoral. The larger towns are to be found in the central region – Khartoum, 450 miles from the Egyptian border, named the 'elephant trunk' from the spit of land on which it is built directly south of the junction of the Blue Nile and the White Nile; Omdurman, truly Sudanese and not 'foreign' like Khartoum, lying a few miles north of it on the west bank of the main Nile after the junction, and joined to Khartoum by a road bridge from 1928; Atbara, 190 miles north of Khartoum, the principal railway centre, with a mixed population; Wad Medani, capital of the Blue Nile Province, 120 miles south from Khartoum, and Port Sudan on the Red Sea, a mere village at the beginning of the century, which developed rapidly into a substantial port and railhead, with a fine harbour. South of Khartoum lies the fertile Gezira plain, formerly the chief granary of the Sudan but developed extensively for cotton-growing after the completion of the Sennar Dam in 1925. In the period immediately before independence cotton provided fifty per cent of the revenue of the Sudan. In the grasslands of the southernmost part of the central Sudan, there is still a large cattle-breeding region.

The southern provinces of the Sudan (south of the tenth parallel of latitude) show a bewildering variety of ethnic groups and languages – particularly so in and beyond the *Sudd*, a swampy, papyrus-growing region extending over 35,000 square miles east and west of the White Nile. A navigation channel was cut in 1898, but the Nile steamer still took a fortnight from Khartoum or ten days from the railhead at Kosti to reach Juba, which became the administrative centre of Equatoria Province in 1929.

Geography and history have combined to make the unification of the Sudan a difficult problem. The African tribes of the south have had no racial or cultural relations with Egypt, and developed a deep distrust of the Arabs, based on some eighty years of slave-trading. The fact that in the southern provinces English was the language selected by the Condominium government, and was also the language recommended by the Protestant missions and accepted by the Roman Catholic missions, 'was to give a later generation of Northern Sudanese the impression, wholly unfounded in fact, that the missions were in some way partners in a British colonial domination'. The south certainly grew up in cultural separation from the rest of the country.[1]

Turco-Egyptian rule over the Sudan (1820–84) was on the whole a failure because its main aim was exploitation rather than the development of the country. Constant attempts to produce surplus revenue for Cairo led to increasingly rapacious methods of tax-collection. Conditions under the Mahdists (1885–98) were little better; but the Mahdi himself, Muhammad Ahmed ibn 'Abdullah, is honoured by many Sudanese as the 'Father' of their nation's independence, and as a great religious reformer who brought unity to the tribes of the Sudan. The Mahdi died in June 1885, only six months after the capture of Khartoum and the death of the last Khedival Governor-General, C. G. Gordon. Fourteen years later in January 1899, following upon the British-Egyptian conquest, Anglo-Egyptian conventions were drawn up for the government and pacification of 'certain provinces in the Sudan which were in rebellion against the authority of His Highness the Khedive'. The *Condominium Agreement*, as it came to be called, provided an instrument of government for the Sudan which lasted, on paper at any rate, until 31st December, 1955. It provided for a governor-general appointed by the decree of the Khedive (from 1922 to 1952, by the King) of Egypt on the recommendation of the British government. Although the British and Egyptian flags were flown side by side, Britain in fact claimed a predominant voice in all matters relating to the Sudan. All the governors-general were British,[2] and were officially responsible to the British high commissioners in Egypt; and the Sudan was at first (up to 1912) dependent on Egypt for an annual financial grant. Lord Kitchener (1899) and Sir Reginald Wingate (1899–1916) set high standards for British administration, and the higher administrative posts under Condominium were entirely staffed by British officers and civilians.

A nationalist movement called the Sudan United Tribes Society started in the north in 1921, led by an army officer of Dinka origin, Ali Abd al-Latif. Its aim was national independence. After a term of imprisonment, al-Latif was involved in a new organization, the White Flag League, which sought to free the Sudan from British rule with the help of Egypt. He was again imprisoned in June 1924. On 19th November of the same year, Sir Lee Stack, the Governor-General and Sirdar of the Egyptian army, was mortally wounded in a Cairo street. Allenby, the British High Commissioner in Egypt, presented King Fuad with an ultimatum requiring the immediate withdrawal of Egyptian troops from the Sudan; an end to Egyptian immigration into the Sudan; the right to draw off Nile water for the Gezira irrigation scheme 'to an unlimited extent'; and an indemnity of £500,000. The mutiny of the 11th Sudanese Battalion, following the withdrawal of Egyptian troops, cannot be taken as evidence of a widespread nationalist movement at this time, but the result of Lee Stack's murder was to reduce Egyptian participation in the Condominium 'to vanishing point'.[3] A Sudan defence force was organized in entire separation from Egyptian military forces and it was not until the Anglo-Egyptian Treaty of 1936 that Egyptian troops were allowed back in the Sudan, and immigration again permitted without restriction, 'except for reasons of public order or health'. These events encouraged the British administration in the introduction of 'Indirect Rule' through tribal and then territorial institutions, a system which later provided the basis of conciliar local government.

In the 1936 Anglo-Egyptian Treaty, the two governments affirmed that 'the primary aim of their administration in the Sudan must be the welfare of the Sudanese', but the Sudanese had not been consulted when the treaty was drawn up; and resentment, already aroused by similar treatment over the Nile Waters Agreement of 1929, was accentuated.

In 1938 a Graduates' General Congress was formed, for membership of which 'graduates' of intermediate schools, as well as of Gordon College in Khartoum, were eligible. The Congress was a kind of civil servants' trades union, with an increasingly nationalist colour. On 3rd April, 1942, a letter from the congress was addressed to the civil secretary, Sir Douglas Newbold, claiming Sudan's right to self-determination immediately after the war.[4] The government's rejection of these demands strengthened the more uncompromising elements in the congress who began to look to Egypt for help against the independence party supported by Abd al Rahman al-Mahdi (the posthumous son of the Mahdi).

Condominium brought the Sudan some of the ablest and most dedicated British administrators that were to be found anywhere in the world during the colonial period. One of them, writing shortly before the end of Condominium rule, found a clue to their achievement

in an attitude of mind on the part of the British who have lived uncomfortably in that hot, harsh land and have loved its people. . . . The British administrator is no martyr. He stays there because he is happy: because in some strange manner and almost in spite of himself he finds, in the service of the Sudanese, fulfilment of life.[5]

Islam in the Sudan

The northern Sudan was once a Christian land, but from the Funj period in the sixteen century until the mid-nineteenth century virtually all contact with Christianity was lost. During the period 1910–42 the country north of the 10th parallel was Arabic-Islamic in culture, apart from the pagan non-Arab tribes of the Nuba mountains; and south of the 10th parallel predominantly pagan, with Christian missionary penetration at least keeping pace with Islamization.

The 'favouritism' shown by the Condominium government to Islam, which irked and sometimes exasperated the missionaries throughout the period, requires explanation. Administrative regulations for the early days of the Condominium laid down that 'no mission station may be formed north of the tenth parallel of North Latitude in any part of the Sudan which is recognized by the Government as Moslem'. The policy behind this regulation was due to the fear of fanatical reaction, and this remained an element in it; but as time went on it was guided by the conviction that Christian missions would be no more successful here than elsewhere in the Islamic world in producing extensive individual conversions, and that it was in the best interests of the community not to introduce a disturbing factor.

This policy was congenial to the leaders of the Muslim religious 'orders' who had assisted considerably in the reconquest of the country. These religious brotherhoods were the growing points of Islam in the Sudan. Many *zawias*, or religious houses, were connected with one or other of the orders. In many villages mosque, school, sacred grove and holy burial ground could be found on the same site.[6] Islam in the Sudan showed a vitality and intensity which was seldom found in Egypt in the same period.

The Condominium government gave the Sudan a legal system independent of that of Egypt, and the directives of the local grand *Qadis* (Jurists) carried a legal weight unknown further north. A legal circular of 1912 made the Sudan the first Muslim country to provide for the registration of religious conversion.[7]

It was in the sphere of education that the missionaries found the government attitude most puzzling and disturbing; but a discerning missionary, himself secretary of CMS northern Sudan mission at the end of the period, would not allow lack of missionary success to be attributed to the government's favourable policy towards Islam; it was due, he maintained, rather to 'the foreignness of the Christianity with which he seeks to assault the fortress of the religio-social solidarity of Islam'.[8]

The dispute over the freedom to preach and teach Christianity and Islam in the southern Sudan was inevitable in the presence of two mutually exclusive religious faiths.

In practice, however, intolerance has not been an abiding feature of Sudanese history. . . . Both the Anglo-Egyptian Condominium of 1899–1955 and the Sudanese Republic established in 1956 relegated the operation of Islamic Law to the jurisprudence of Muslim private status and adhered to the Western principle of the one-tier secular state under which citizenship is equal for the adherents of all religions or none.[9]

Christian Missions

The first modern missionaries to the Sudan were sent out by the Roman Catholic Church, following the creation of the apostolic vicariate of Central Africa in 1846. They persevered with great courage and faithfulness in the most adverse circumstances.

The principal centres of Roman missions in the 1920s were at Lul and Tonga among the Shilluks, and at Dilling in the Nuba Mountains. Lord Cromer had laid down 'spheres' for missionary development in the southern Sudan before the CMS began work there in 1905, but as early as 1915 these territorial lines were ceasing to be observed, and the Roman mission contended repeatedly for the abandonment of the sphere arrangements. The CMS wished them to continue. The boundaries were re-drawn in 1932 but the problem of infiltration into the CMS areas remained. (See below pp. 342–3)

The American United Presbyterian mission, led by Dr Kelly Griffen and others, began work in Khartoum about the same time as the CMS (1899–1900), and among the Shilluks, at the junction of the Sobat with the Nile, in 1902. *Injili* (evangelical) congregations grew up in a number of towns, and the Presbyterian mission worked chiefly among expatriate Egyptians. They opened a boys' school in Khartoum in 1905, and a general understanding was arrived at by which the Americans would concentrate on educating boys and the CMS on educating girls. The Sudan United Mission (an interdenominational mission manned in this area by Australian and New Zealand missionaries) began work in the Nuba Mountains in 1920, encouraged by an unwritten agreement with the government that they should be free to develop education on non-Muslim lines among the pagan Nuba.[10]

The Anglican Church

The first Anglican missionary to the Sudan was Llewellyn G. Gwynne, a Nottingham vicar who had answered the CMS centenary appeal for a pioneer party to the pagan areas of the Sudan. He arrived in Cairo in November 1899. He was not allowed to enter the Sudan until after the Khalifa's death; but then, as the year ended, Gwynne and Dr F. J. Harpur were permitted to go forward to Omdurman, but not to speak to Muslims about Christianity. Soon the embargo was lifted sufficiently to allow Harpur to open a dispensary from a mud hut in Omdurman and Gwynne to open a school; and, at long last in 1905 under Gwynne's leadership, the first party of six left for the southern Sudan. On the eve of their departure Wingate wished Gwynne success on the journey; 'but please do not forget that you are an archdeacon of the Sudan and not a director of missionary enterprise in the Aliab country'.[11]

Gwynne was one of the great pioneer missionaries of the CMS. Forty-eight years after his first missionary journey, he was still the moving spirit of all the mission's activities. The Anglican Church in the Sudan, a living and growing church at the end of our period, was still being led by the man who started it.

In the northern Sudan missionary activity was restricted; and throughout the period the Anglican Church remained small, largely identified with a few missionary institutions and chaplaincies for expatriates. In 1942 the CMS had schools for girls and infants at Omdurman, Atbara, and Wad Medani; a large medical mission at Omdurman, and two stations in the Nuba Mountains, in Kordofan Province, some 450 miles south-west of Khartoum. There were also diocesan chaplaincies and churches at Wad Medani (St Paul's), Atbara (Philip the Deacon), Wadi Halfa (St Mary's) and Port Sudan (Christ Church); and a fine cathedral at Khartoum, consecrated in 1912.

Built of local red and yellow sandstone, with a ground plan in the form of a Latin cross, Khartoum cathedral attempted with fair success to combine Gothic and Byzantine features. The architect was Mr Weir Schultz Weir. An appeal fund initiated by Bishop Gwynne received strong support in Britain as a memorial to Charles George Gordon, Governor-General, 1877-9. It was consecrated on the anniversary of Gordon's death, 26th January, 1912, by A. F. Winnington-Ingram, Bishop of London. A tower and bells were added in 1931 in memory of Sir Lee Stack.

Bishop Gwynne was ambitious that the cathedral should be used as a meeting place for all Christian traditions, and from 1924 a unity service was held each year in which representatives of Orthodox and other Eastern Christian Churches regularly took part as well as Presbyterian and Free Church representatives. Archdeacon B. J. Harper did much to make the cathedral the spiritual home of all Christians in Khartoum.

In the southern Sudan, where the Anglican Church was virtually coterminous with the CMS area of mission, opportunities of growth were much greater. By 1942 the church was growing rapidly and claimed 16,000 adherents, half of whom were baptized, and 3,454 communicants. There were three stations in the Upper Nile province, at Malek among the Dinka, and at Ler and on Zeraf Island among the Nuer tribes; seven stations in the Equatorial Province – at Yambio and Maridi among the Azande; at Yei, Loka and Kajokaji among the Bari-speaking tribes; at Lui, among the Moru, and at Akot among the Dinka.

There were boarding-schools at all these mission centres; an intermediate school at Loka, attended by boys of many different tribes; a well-developed medical mission based on Lui, and small medical missions at Ler and at Juaibor on Zeraf Island.

Until 1920 the Anglican Church in the Sudan was within the jurisdiction of the Bishop in Jerusalem, with Bishop Gwynne (assistant bishop from 1908) normally resident at Khartoum. During Gwynne's absence as Assistant Chaplain-General on the Western Front during the 1914–18 war, the remoteness of episcopal oversight was keenly felt in the southern Sudan. Bishop Rennie MacInnes (consecrated Bishop in Jerusalem in 1914) was fully occupied in Cairo confirming troops and raising money for a Palestine relief fund. Understandably he could ill afford the time for a journey to the south, which Shaw estimated would take two months from Khartoum and back.[12]

In 1920 Egypt and the Sudan became a separate diocese under Bishop Gwynne who took the first confirmations in the south in the same year. For the purposes of CMS administration the new diocese was divided into two missions, on the grounds that the work in Egypt and the northern Sudan was 'mainly among Mohammedans, and in the Southern Sudan among pagans'. The 1924–5 report added this significant note:[13]

> In regard to the character of its work, the Southern Sudan has closer affinities with Uganda than with the rest of the Egypt Mission. The proposed railway developments will, if carried out, form a further link. Accordingly the episcopal oversight has been handed over to the Bishop of Uganda for the next two years.

In 1926 the formation of a diocese of the Upper Nile was approved by the Archbishop of Canterbury, consisting of the northern and eastern sections of the Uganda diocese (the CMS Elgon mission) and the southern Sudan CMS mission. The first bishop of this new diocese was A. L. Kitching (1926–36). In 1935 the southern Sudan was returned to the diocese of Egypt and the Sudan, and first H. G. Bullen (1935–7) and then A. M. Gelsthorpe (1938–45) were appointed assistant bishops. In 1945 the Sudan was made an Anglican diocese under Bishop Gelsthorpe.

In a complex political-ecclesiastical situation, a good case can be made out both for the temporary withdrawal of the CMS in the southern Sudan into association with the strong Anglican Church in Uganda, and also for its subsequent return. By 1942 it was becoming clear that if there was ever to be a Sudanese church in the north of the country, the contribution of Christians from the south would be indispensable. But in the growth of the Anglican Church in the Sudan, as in its cultural development, the division between north and south was clearly marked. It will be convenient to tell the stories of the two regions separately in turn.

CMS in the North

In the Sudan and in Egypt . . . substantial buildings do not delude a visitor into imagining that the tenure of Christian missions is anything more than a very precarious leasehold. Adherents of the Christian faith must face the formidable disabilities of an outcast minority.

So H. D. Hooper wrote in his report on a visit to the northern Sudan in 1938.[14] This restricted opportunity was the subject of frequent comment and explanation by missionaries. Dr Edmund Lloyd, for twenty years superintendent of the CMS hospital in Omdurman, wrote in 1915:

I realize more and more how passionately devoted even the most ignorant of the people are to all that Islam means to them, and how any reference to Christ as the crucified Son of God jars every fibre in a man's being. Ethics and morals they will discuss all night, but there lies the obstacle. What we have to do, I believe, is quietly to keep these new ideas before their minds that they may get so far used to them as to be willing to look at them carefully and with lessening prejudice, until finally they can bring themselves to weigh up all that is good in Islam with the truth as it is in Jesus.[15]

It would be wrong to give the impression that the missionaries accepted continuing restriction as inevitable. Gairdner, as secretary of the Egypt-Sudan CMS mission from 1914 to 1919, and Lloyd from the standpoint of his special responsibilities, did not cease to batter their respective committees of reference at home with requests for more recruits and more grants-in-aid to make the northern Sudan missionary enterprise even minimally efficient. When Gairdner described the Sudan mission as 'the smallest and the feeblest' of all the missions of the CMS no criticism was intended of the missionaries.[16] It was a broadside fired in a ten-year struggle for the survival and upbuilding of Omdurman hospital.

In 1910 the CMS medical committee in London, hard-pressed by annual deficits, ordered the Omdurman hospital to be closed and Dr Lloyd to return to the southern Sudan. The decision was reviewed and then reversed on the plea of the governor-general, Sir Reginald Wingate, and Bishop Gwynne. The parent committee finally agreed that a small hospital should be built, with a grant to increase the money in hand to £2,000, provided that the government refrained from building another hospital in Omdurman which would restrict its usefulness. By mid-1914 the new CMS hospital was being built on land given by the government, 'almost in the centre of the long city'. The possibility of a government hospital in Omdurman was not, however, ruled out; and the completion of the CMS hospital, and the development in resources and personnel of the mission in general, came too slowly to give Lloyd and his missionary colleagues any confidence of an effective move forward. They began to inquire about the possibility of closing down the CMS northern Sudan mission or alternatively, handing it over to another society, and two of them, Lloyd and Miss Lilian Jackson, offered their provisional resignation unless the Society found itself able to make an immediate advance in the development of the mission. At the Egypt and Sudan missionaries' conference in August 1917 Lloyd said that he felt the Society's work in the northern Sudan was badly organized and inefficient in staff and plant and 'unlikely to lead to permanent results, i.e. the gathering out of a native church'.[17]

In 1918 the parent committee gave its considered reply. The hospital at Omdurman was to be completed with wards for both men and women as planned in 1912. The northern Sudan should be recognized as an integral part of the Egypt mission, which should not extend its sphere to Alexandria until the work already undertaken was thoroughly efficient.

In November 1919 Lloyd was back in Omdurman after some months of relief work among wounded civilians; and he was instructed by the missionaries' conference to draw up plans for the new hospital buildings on the basis of a £4,000 tender. Wilson Cash, the mission secretary, gave every possible help, and found the money for it from various sources. It is pleasant to record that when, twenty years later, the possible closure of the hospital was again threatened, due to local criticism of one of Lloyd's successors as medical superintendent, Cash, as general secretary of the CMS, was able to bring the full weight of his local experience to bear against closing the hospital.

There are frequent references to the hospital in the records of the 1920s and 1930s. The number of out-patients increased from 13,444 in 1920 to 96,171 in 1937, and in-patients from 219 to 1,318. Lloyd himself proudly described it, shortly after his retirement in 1928, as 'a well-equipped hospital, with forty beds and a large out-patient department, besides welfare work in another part of the town. The hospital staff also have charge of a leper colony for forty lepers, and of a home for twenty-four bedridden destitute old people', both these last being financed by the government. The hospital chapel, dedicated by Bishop Gwynne in 1924, delighted Gairdner who had a keen eye for such things. 'It is floored with clean, cool, Sudanese tilings. The chairs and furniture are Sudanese.' He was equally delighted with the work Dr A. N. Worsley (Lloyd's colleague from 1919 to 1925) was doing on Sudanese Arabic so that missionaries could start learning it straight away.[18]

The dispensary 'in another part of the town', of which Lloyd wrote, was at Abu Rof in the north of the straggling city of Omdurman. It was started in 1926 and a decade later, with its baby welfare clinic, children's home, and girls' elementary school, impressed H. D. Hooper as the kind of missionary complex that ought to be imitated elsewhere. If the northern Sudan mission was forced by circumstances to be predominantly institutional, it was good to have places where medicine and education at a simple level were combined, giving natural access to the homes from which mothers came with their babies to the clinic, and from which small children went to school.

In its educational work in the northern Sudan the CMS concentrated on schools for girls, leaving the American Presbyterian mission to develop boys' schools. Bishop Gwynne used to speak of himself as the first 'headmistress' of the first of these schools, opened on the simplest lines at Khartoum in 1902. Moved later to a new site in Victoria Avenue, the school provided education for the daughters of Egyptian expatriates rather than Sudanese children. In the early 1920s it was threatened with closure as an economy measure, but the reaction from the field was prompt. The missionary conference talked about the serious effect on the government if the school was closed. The governor-general asked Gwynne to convey to the Society his opinion that it would be a bad move to hand over the school to the American mission, and offered part of the proceeds of a sale of work in his garden for its support.[19] A few years later Miss Mabel Warburton, during a visit to the Sudan, suggested that the diocese should open a school for the higher education of girls. An appeal for £3,000 was made and in 1928 the Khartoum CMS girls' school was handed over to the diocese and renamed the Unity High School for Girls.

Mrs A. C. Hall, who returned to the Sudan after her husband had died in 1903, and her sister, Miss Lilian Jackson, who joined her as a CMS missionary in 1909, together made the greatest contribution to girls' education in the Sudan during the period. They were jointly responsible, with Bishop Gwynne, for opening schools in Omdurman and Atbara in 1908, and in 1912 Mrs Hall opened a girls' school at Wad Medani on the Blue Nile. Eva Hall continued 'in frail health, visiting and teaching, universally known, universally beloved' until her death in 1925.[20] Lilian Jackson, for many years headmistress at Atbara, retired in 1947. Several able teachers joined them later, notably Mary Myers, who came from Palestine to Wad Medani in 1917 to help out during Mrs Hall's illness and retired in 1940 with an MBE after twenty-three years in the school there.

Each of the three girls' schools (Omdurman, Wad Medani, and Atbara) suffered at time from illness, shortage of staff, and lack of money. Wad Medani school, for example, was nearly closed in 1928 through lack of money for a new roof. Each of them developed a full range of teaching from kindergarten to secondary school, including a teacher-training class; in 1941 over twelve hundred girls were being taught in the three schools, and there were a number of small village schools dependent on them and run by teachers they had trained, many of them Copts. The majority of the children taught were Muslims. The proportion of Sudanese girls was low at first. It was realized that the level of fees was more appropriate to Egyptian and Greek families of the merchant class but less so to Sudanese parents. Attempts to deal with this problem were partially successful. Wad Medani school grew rapidly with the development of the Gezira cotton-growing area after the opening of the Sennar Dam in 1925. Miss Myers described the school shortly before her retirement in 1940 as having sixty per cent Muslim pupils, but also Coptic Syrians and Greek

Orthodox Christians; with 260 girls from kindergarten to 'second' secondary standard. Most of the lessons were in Arabic but a little English was used. There were daily Scripture lessons, from which withdrawals at the request of non-Christian parents were rare; and school prayers were attended by all children. It comes as a shock to read at the end of this account, which might in many other respects be a description of the curriculum of a church-aided school in England, 'most of the girls marry at the age of twelve or thirteen'.

The Nuba Mountains

In the early part of 1933 it fell my lot to travel up the Nile to Khartoum and from there to trek 500 miles south to the Nuba Mountains in order to examine the openings for missionary work . . . . In one half of the mountains the Sudan United Mission is doing most excellent work, but in the other half there is no missionary work of any description. It was here that the Government invited the CMS to open schools for the education of the people.[21]

So Wilson Cash described the beginnings of a venture in which, as the Society's general secretary, he was to continue to play a decisive role. It was a bold move forward into a new field at a time of financial stringency. The early 1930s were not friendly to new enterprises, but in terms of missionary strategy this project had much to commend it. Although the Nuba Mountains were geographically in the northern Sudan, in the otherwise purely 'Arab' province of Kordofan, the Nuba themselves were a negroid people of mixed tribal origin, having more affinities with the tribes among whom the Society was already working in the south.

The opening of a new mission among them would put new heart into the northern Sudan mission by demonstrating that the needs of the north were not to be permanently disregarded in favour of more promising openings in the south; although not on a direct line, such a mission would form a natural and vital link between Cairo, Omdurman and Juba; and it would go far to justify the re-integration of the southern Sudan mission with the northern mission (since 1926 it had formed part of the Upper Nile diocese) with the ultimate aim of a separate Anglican diocese in the Sudan. A further strong incentive was the government's intention to foster a distinct Nuba culture under Christian influence, so different from its long-standing 'Northern' policy of not offending Islam;[22] and its readiness to allocate a missionary 'sphere of influence' to CMS alongside but not overlapping the Sudan United Mission's sphere in the eastern hills.

The outcome of Cash's visit was an agreement with the government which allowed for government subsidies for education work in the Nuba Mountains, provided that qualified teachers were employed. The CMS was asked if possible to train Nuba clerks; to provide social services, including infant welfare work; to relate education to the practical needs of the people; and to undertake linguistic and anthropological studies.[23] Salara was agreed as the site for the first CMS school.

In February 1935 a CMS pioneer party of four left Omdurman for the Nuba Mountains. They travelled 430 miles south-west by train to El Obeid, and then, for the last hundred miles to Dilling, in the governor's car. The four were: a woman doctor, Elfrida Whidborne (later Mrs Gelsthorpe); a nurse, Frances Quinlan; a chaplain, Dermot Kerr; and a teacher, Reginald Evan Hopkins. For the first six weeks they trekked out to the surrounding villages, with three mules for porterage (later they were presented with a Ford 'V.8' lorry by the bishop and the British community in Khartoum) and found a ready welcome in the villages of the Nyamang language group. Kerr visited Salara, the village fourteen miles west of Dilling which had been chosen for the first school and mission station, but it was not until the end of the year that building began there.

Three years later a visitor, General E. M. P. Stewart, wrote with enthusiasm about the venture:

> (1) the confidence and goodwill of the Nubas at Salara and immediate district have been gained. (2) A genuine sense of gratitude and appreciation for the care and solicitude shown by the Mission staffs for their welfare is slowly but steadily permeating the district. (3) The Nubas, who for many years have firmly resisted Islamic influence and rejected the Moslem faith and cult, are more inclined to follow the example and precepts impressed on them by contact with the members of the Mission who proclaim the doctrine of love and self-sacrifice.[24]

Kerr, however, was less sanguine. 'It seems,' he wrote in 1936, 'that we are almost too late in coming to help the Nubas to face civilization in the right way and to give their contributions as Christians to it';[25] and a year later C. F. L. Bertram, the secretary of the northern Sudan mission, wrote of a growing lack of confidence on the part of 'certain government officials', in the ability of the Society to undertake the work agreed upon.

> The continued failure to find further recruits, coupled with the speeding up of civilization in the Nuba Mountains, is forcing Government to develop education without much reference to CMS. . . . We have already lost the battle for English, rather than Arabic, as the medium of education in post-vernacular schools.[26]

A word of explanation about this linguistic battle is necessary. Sir Douglas Newbold, appointed Governor of Kordofan province in 1932, had lost no time in addressing his mind to the peculiar problems of education in the Nuba Mountains. He had become convinced that Arabic rather than English was the proper medium of instruction above the elementary vernacular level. Between 1936 and 1939, on his initiative, four new government elementary schools were opened, near the mission stations of the SUM and the CMS. They were to be staffed by Egyptian Coptic teachers and the missionaries were encouraged to provide Christian religious instruction in them. Perhaps without injustice, the administration was dissatisfied with the progress made in the field of education in accordance with the 1933 agreement.

In 1939, in response to government pressure, the Society transferred the Rev. R. S. Macdonald and his wife, Dr Catharine Macdonald, to the Nuba Mountains. They opened another CMS station at Katcha, near Kadugli, a hundred miles south of Salara; and the Katcha school, opened in 1940, made a promising start.

The Nuba Mountains venture was a race against time, and came too late to be really effective. By 1942 Arab and Muslim influence in the Nuba Mountains had grown apace; and in 1959 the new Sudanese government took over the Nuba mission schools and all missionary staff were replaced,[27] though church congregations remained active.

The hopes held out for the Nuba Mountains mission as a link between the thriving Anglican Church in the south and the struggling little 'institution-centred' church in the north were not to be realized, but by 1942 young men, many of whom had had contact with the southern Sudan church, were coming north in a steady stream looking for work. Clubs for them were started in Khartoum in 1941 and in Omdurman in 1942. General Christian instruction was given in both clubs and there were special classes for catechumens. Three Morus and one Nuba were baptized in September 1943 and more baptisms quickly followed. The secretary of the northern Sudan mission could write of the growing together of a Sudanese Anglican Church. 'It is our task in the north . . . to establish Christian centres in the lands of entrenched Islam so that the Christianity of the south will have points of contact when it flows northwards.'[28]

Southern Sudan, 1910-25

'There is no possible reason against a mission station,' General Gordon wrote in 1887, 'but it is a most deadly country, and very few could possibly stand the climate – it is only fit for a man who is sick of life, has no ties, and longs and yearns for death. Now these men are not common.' The early history of the Gordon Memorial Mission in the southern Sudan appears to confirm at least one phrase in Gordon's sardonic and oft-quoted comment: 'a most deadly country'. Of the six members of the pioneer party of 1906 only one was at work there two years later – Archibald Shaw. Shaw returned from furlough in October 1908 to Malek, on the right bank of the Nile about five miles south of the government post at Bor. He brought with him a missionary recruit, W. H. Scamell. The mission station consisted of a large corrugated iron bungalow with four rooms on iron girders, and some African huts. 'It was by no means mosquito proof, and to go to bed under a net was the only thing to do after sunset. The school and services were held on the verandah of the bungalow.'[29]

January 1910 found Shaw visiting Bor Dinka villages around Malek, at that time the only CMS station in the south. He noted that the villagers had never seen a cart before and regretted having to leave Scamell alone at Malek where there was so much to be done. The station was then employing weekly labourers together with 'some half-dozen young men who are serving us for three years, at the end of which they will receive a young cow as wages'. There was a small dispensary at which the two missionaries treated burns, abscesses and eye-complaints.[30]

Neither then, nor at any period in the next forty-five years, would anyone who knew him have described Shaw in Gordon's other phrase as 'a man sick of life'; but some might have said, without injustice to this ebullient and devoted missionary, that a good strong argument was one of the things that kept him going. He found one such argument in the Society's estimates of expenditure for 1910, with a reduction notified for the southern Sudan. Did the parent committee, he asked, intend to give up the mission? If so, what would happen to the appropriated monies given specifically for work among the pagan tribes of the south? 'Unless P. C. can grant the sums asked for,' he wrote in his journal, 'it will mean giving up school classes and itineration, and will reduce work to such proportions as only to need one European.'[31] Suiting action to word, he dismissed all the workers except just enough to keep the place going, and he advised Bishop Gwynne that 'Mr Scamell will fold his hands until we hear again'.[32]

Shaw won his point. The figures he asked for were restored to the estimates. Yet anxiety remained. In June 1910 he wrote pleading for a separate fund for the southern Sudan:

> The Khartoum Mission is medical and educational, and in such work the greatest outlay is incurred at the beginning, in buildings and plant. On the other hand, the work among pagans is pioneering, and amongst a population scattered over a large area, partially closed to the Mission by Government. .... Large sums have been given by those interested in the pagan tribes, with no intention of the money being spent on work among Mohammedans and Christians 1,000 miles away.[33]

The 'fund' was not divided between north and south, but the next annual report provided a separate heading for the southern Sudan. From 1920 it was listed separately from the Egypt and Sudan mission, and a closer relationship with the Uganda mission of the CMS was gradually built up until 1935.

Early in 1910 Bishop Gwynne became interested in the possibility of extending the area of Anglican mission to a stretch of country known as the Lado Enclave. It was an area lying between the Nile-Congo watershed and the White Nile south of latitude north 5° 30'. By an agreement signed by Great Britain on behalf of Egypt in 1894 it had been leased to the Congo Free State on condition that it would revert to the Anglo-Egyptian Sudan on the death of King Leopold II of Belgium. Leopold died in December 1909 and the Enclave was due for incorporation into the Mongalla province of the Anglo-Egyptian Sudan in the autumn of 1910. Both the Roman Catholics and CMS were anxious to enter this area and the Sudan government made arrangements to apportion it between them as areas of mission. Shaw was not altogether happy at this prospect. The response of the Bor Dinkas in the Malek area had been disappointing, certainly, but the logical next step in missionary extension was to open new stations within the large 'sphere' already allocated to CMS by Lord Cromer; and the threat of reduced financial support, and slow progress in recruiting new missionaries for the south, made him reluctant to take on new responsibilities. But the bishop's enthusiasm for the project, coupled with the prospect of the Rev. C. A. Lea-Wilson's arrival in September 1910, encouraged him to make plans to visit the area. Perhaps the strongest incentive for Shaw was the news, received in August, that five hundred Muslim soldiers and junior officials from the northern Sudan had been drafted into the Enclave and that Friday had become the official day of rest. 'At present,' he wrote, 'the natives can only conclude that Mohammedanism is the religion of England.'[34]

Meanwhile C. T. Studd, whose Heart of Africa Mission was working across the adjacent Belgian Congo border, became interested in the prospect of extension into the Sudan; and it was agreed that they should together tour the southern part of Bahr-el-Ghazal Province and the Lado Enclave. They met at Rumbek on 3rd May, 1911 and travelled south to Meridi, where Shaw noted the cool climate and comparative freedom from mosquitoes, and then to Yei in the Enclave. There were no government posts on this last stretch of the journey and the missionary prospectors were given a police escort, which 'hampered one in learning the attitude of the people towards unofficial strangers'.[35] The villages of the Lado Enclave were found to be small and scattered; and the custom of moving a village to a fresh site every few years would make the selection of a permanent mission station difficult.

Yei, from 1917, and Meridi, from 1922, were to become significant church and mission centres in the southern Sudan but, for the present, sleeping-sickness regulations were to have the last word. Shaw wrote from Malek on 9th February, 1912: 'The Sleeping Sickness Commission has decided that it is undesirable and dangerous at present to start a mission station in the Lado district.'

The arrival of more missionaries, though the work of several of them was quickly interrupted by illness, made possible a move westwards from Malek. Lea-Wilson arrived in the autumn of 1910; in 1911 three more clergy – H. F. Davies, A. G. King and K. E. Hamilton; and in November 1912, Mr G. P. Thomas, an 'industrial agent', and the Rev. E. C. Gore. Gore and Hamilton both came from Australia.

Lea-Wilson describes the next step:

Permission to open a station in the Lado Enclave . . . was suddenly withdrawn. . . . We therefore turned to the north-west instead of to the south-west, and after crossing the river (White Nile), Mr Shaw and I travelled inland 110 miles to Rumbek. It was however decided to return to Lau.[36]

Lau was a clearing about forty miles from Shambe on the White Nile to the north-west of Malek. It appeared to be the headquarters of the Cic (or 'Cheech') Dinkas, and there was a small government post there. Lea-Wilson arrived there in February 1912, and Hamilton soon joined him. Lea-Wilson described the people as 'the usual Jieng type, very tall and thin'. A dispensary was opened, and before the end of 1912 they had given '4,000 treatments for yaws, ulcers and accidents'. The language proved to be close enough to Bor Dinka to allow simple evangelistic instruction in the language to be understood. Two reading-classes were started and after only a few months Lea-Wilson wrote: 'All have learned the Lord's Prayer and the Ten Commandments and a few prayers in their own language.' Progress in evangelism was slow. The missionaries gained a temporary, and not wholly welcome, reputation as rain-makers during a drought in 1914. Prayers for rain were followed by a heavy rain-storm; then eight days passed without further rain, and as 'they have sown a good deal of corn, they were coming to us again'.[37] An attempt was made in the eight years 1912–20 to test the possibilities of Lau as an effective centre of mission; but it showed little promise, and occupation by European missionaries ceased after 1920.

The third station to be opened, Yambio, had a much happier history. 250 miles west of Gondokoro, and forty miles north of the Belgian Congo frontier, it became an effective centre of mission among the Azandi in the southern part of Bahr-el-Ghazal Province. Though entirely forest the Yambio district was healthy, forming a watershed between the Nile and Congo at between 3,000 and 4,000 feet above sea-level.[38] From the start the Azandi people of the region proved more responsive to the Christian gospel than the Dinka.

In the early months of 1912 it appeared probable that a missionary society other than the CMS would take responsibility for this area, the newly-formed Eastern Sudan Evangelical Mission, but negotiations proved difficult. Bishop Gwynne was unable to subscribe to the constitution of this new society, and its chief sponsor, Mr W. G. Bradshaw, while recognizing the necessity of co-operation with the bishop, was doubtful whether it could be achieved. At a conference at Church Missionary House, London, on 8th May, 1912, he offered substantial monetary help to CMS if they would start work among the 'Nyam-Nyam' (Azandi), and showed himself willing to abandon the project of a separate society. This offer was further defined in a letter of 25th September, 1912 from Mr Bradshaw. He offered £500 towards the initial expenses, and £200 maintenance for five years: 'it being understood that CMS will not send Missionaries to those stations who hold what are called Higher Critical views of the Scriptures'.[39]

Meridi was the first choice for the new CMS Azandi station, but current sleeping-sickness regulations put it out of bounds and Yambio, ninety miles further west, was chosen. On leave in England during the summer of 1912 Shaw was already busy planning its 'occupation'. This military term, already familiar in missionary use, kept much of its original force when used in Shaw's letters. 'If a start is to be made in Yambio this year,' he wrote from Edgbaston on 12th July, 'mules and carts for transport must be ordered at once.' Slightly late on schedule, he and Hamilton with a party of young Dinkas left Malek for Lau on 12th January, 1913, reached Meridi on 3rd February, and Yambio on 13th February, taking the full month he had foreseen as necessary for the journey.[40] Dense tropical forest had to be cut away to form a clearing for the mission station which was a quarter of a mile south of the present buildings. Gore reached Yambio in March, and Shaw stayed to see them in until mid-April. By then the basic buildings were up and a school had been started. Bishop Gwynne, though delighted by this start among the Azandi, was concerned that neither Hamilton nor Gore 'had even the elementary knowledge of medicine which Livingstone College gives', and suggested to CMS London that a Syrian doctor should be sent to Yambio until such time as an English doctor became available. No such doctor was sent, but Dr R. Y. Stones wrote from Old Cairo in January 1914 offering to make a medical survey in the southern Sudan instead of taking his furlough. He stayed several months in the Yambio area in the summer of 1914.[41] By then Hamilton had left the mission at his own request, but Gore quickly identified himself with the work among the Azandi and served devotedly for twenty-five years.

The new station did not have an easy start. Shaw wrote, in August 1913, pleading for 'a technical man at once' for Yambio, to comply with the government requirement that some useful trade should be taught in every mission station. He complained that the officials of the Bahr-el-Ghazal Province 'openly and cynically prefer RC's to the CMS'. But news of the appointment in October 1913 of S. L. Ewell as an industrial agent on short service brought some comfort. Shaw arrived at Yambio with Ewell in March 1914, and during the summer he accompanied Stones on an extensive tour of the forest clearings in the large Yambio district. Stones was unable to recommend a full-scale medical mission in the area, but on a return visit in April 1917 Shaw wrote: 'Yambio station has developed wonderfully in the two years since I was here last.' He admired the 'beautiful little church' which had been built since his last visit, and reported a 'congregation of 550 on Easter Sunday, and over 200 last Sunday'. In a two-year report of the mission in 1918 thirty catechumens and nineteen inquirers were recorded, and twenty-five of the sixty boys regularly attending the school at Yambio were said to be sons of chiefs.[42] On Easter Day 1919 the first three members of the Azandi tribe were baptized; and three years later the first twenty-two were confirmed by Bishop Gwynne.

The Azandi baptisms were not quite the first in the Anglican Church in the southern Sudan. The Dinka country and people remained Shaw's first love, and it was a great moment for him after long years of waiting when, on Sunday, 17th September, 1917, he baptized Aruor, the first man of the Dinka tribe, who took the Christian name of Jon. Two of his children were baptized a fortnight later.

Shaw's involvement in the pioneer stages of the mission among the Azandi and Bari peoples meant that Scamell and King were left for long stretches at Malek, which tended to become a reception centre for missionary recruits who would soon go off elsewhere. This placed them both under considerable strain, since the visible results of their work were few. In June 1918 Shaw noted in a letter that both King and Scamell considered Dinka work at times not worth while. King had already written a letter of resignation in February 1918 stating, as grounds for his decision, his inability to work harmoniously with Shaw. Shaw, for his part, thought that a contributory cause was that King 'took to heart very much the appointment of another to Yei'.[43] Scamell resigned a year later, 'because of various family considerations and in view of having completed ten years of service in the Sudan'.[44] In April 1920 he joined the CMS headquarters staff and gave valuable service for many years in charge of the exhibitions department.

Converts among the Dinka remained discouragingly few. 'Alier e Kut and Anyang have decided for Christ,' Shaw wrote in August 1917. 'They did so two years ago but went back on account of polygamy and the native night dances which they would not give up. Alier has been my chief language helper for many years. Together we translated St John's Gospel. Anyang has been a house-boy with me since he was an infant.' He was baptized in 1918 with the name Luke.

The Baganda teachers, of whom Shaw expected much, were unable for the most part to settle in the Sudan and all returned home after a few years.[45] They found the food and the language difficult and, as early as 1917 two years after the first arrived, Shaw was doubtful whether the succession would be kept going. One teacher at Malek, Paulo Buguru, and his wife, were a great help in the dispensary.[46] But the slow progress among the Bor Dinka at Malek and among the Cic Dinka at Lui, together with the resignations of King and Scamell, drove Shaw to make a suggestion that must have come hard to him, namely, that CMS should invite the Sudan United Mission to take over its work among the Dinkas. A conference of missionaries held at Juba in June 1920 resolved that if the SUM were unable to take over, European missionaries should be withdrawn from Malek and Lau 'unless more effective occupation becomes possible'. An increase of European missionary staff from nine to sixteen people was held to be necessary in order to man present undertakings, including the Dinka areas.

The SUM were unable to accept the responsibility for the Dinka areas, and in December 1922 Shaw (by then Archdeacon of the southern Sudan) wrote, perhaps with a sense of relief, 'Lau is now abandoned to the white ants'.[47]

The early 1920s were a difficult period, with a missionary staff inadequate for newly accepted responsibilities. Davies moved from Lau, in 1920, to Opari in the territory of the Acholi tribe north-east of Kajokaji. He did not settle happily. Finding the post too isolated he applied for a transfer to the Uganda mission. Shaw, convinced that Davies' problem of isolation could be solved 'within his own mission',[48] persuaded him to stay in the Sudan for a time at least, and it was agreed that he should join the Rev. William Haddow at the newly opened station at Meridi.

Meridi, ninety miles or so to the north-east of Yambio, was roughly on a line from Malek, and only sleeping-sickness regulations had prevented it from being the first Azande station ten years earlier. It was hard when, after a promising start at Meridi, Haddow died there of blackwater fever on 28th January, 1924.

Cash, the CMS secretary in Cairo, wrote to headquarters raising the question 'whether it is right for the Sudan work to be so spread out and missionaries left so isolated'.[49] Davies, now alone at Meridi, put the same question at a mission conference at Juba in March 1924. He was back in England in the autumn and was granted extended leave. Bishop Gwynne advised a year later that it was unwise for this 'promising missionary' to return to the Sudan and suggested his transfer to northern Uganda. It was one of the fruits of the formation of the new diocese of the Upper Nile under Bishop Kitching (1926) that Davies was able later to supervise the Opari district in the Sudan from Gulu in Uganda.

For several years after Haddow's death there was no European missionary at Meridi, but the Lavericks and later the Rileys nursed a vigorous church life there. In 1933 All Saints Church, Meridi, was consecrated in memory of William Haddow.

At an informal mission conference at Malek in March 1916, Shaw, Wilson, King, Haddow and Scamell being present, the need for extension of the mission was discussed as a matter of urgency. They agreed that postponement of advance even for a few years must mean that the effort to convert the pagan before he became Muslim would have failed. Extension either into the country of the Moru tribe in the centre of the CMS sphere or of the Bari[50] to the south would provide direct contact with Uganda, but new resources of men and money were needed.[51] The Bari development in fact came first; to be followed, a few years later, by the Moru station at Lui.

Shaw had been watching the Lado Enclave hopefully since 1915. He made no secret of his opinion that sleeping-sickness regulations set up artificial and unnecessary barriers to missionary advance within the southern provinces.[52] In June 1917 the Rev. P. O'B. Gibson opened a new CMS station at Yei, a hundred miles south-west of Juba, as a centre for evangelization of the Bari tribe. A boys' school was opened at once; and the Bangala language which the Belgians had helped to become the *lingua franca* of the region, was used in teaching. Five years later Bishop Gwynne wrote with approval of this school for chiefs' sons, recognizing its promise, but pleading with CMS to send out men and women on short service to assist Gibson at Yei. He saw that the education of girls, for which he had done so much in the northern Sudan, was in danger of slipping behind that of boys in the south, and he knew the problems inherent in such a lop-sided development.

In 1924 there were forty boys in Yei boarding-school, and already two old boys had opened 'bush' schools in their own villages. The government policy of moving villages to the roads (villages were traditionally mobile) was proving helpful to evangelism. With the modification of sleeping-sickness regulations, travel in the Yei district became easier, and Gibson did a good deal of visiting of villages in 1925 on a light motor-cycle.

In 1920, a second Bari station had been opened at Juba, at that time only a small village on the west bank of the White Nile nine miles north of Rejaf. A school was opened in July, and Lea-Wilson wrote in November to say that the school was now well-established. There were forty-one boys on the role, all boarders except two. They came from many tribes but one or other of the Bari, Acholi or Dinka languages was understood by all.[53] Ever since a bout of enteric fever in 1911, Lea-Wilson's health had been precarious, and he returned to England with reluctance in 1924 after thirteen years of notable service to become a CMS organizing secretary in the dioceses of Gloucester and Hereford.

Of all the CMS centres in the southern Sudan the next to be mentioned, Lui, was the most successful in combining specialized service of the community with effective evangelism and church-building.

To the north and west of the Bari area, in a territory of some 15,000 square miles, the predominant tribe is the Moru. A language barrier had to be crossed once again when an attempt was made to evangelize this central part of the area allotted to CMS by Lord Cromer in 1904. Shaw had been advocating a move into this area since 1914, and he was able to quote the provincial governor's 'strong wish that CMS would start one if not two stations there'.[54] A mission station in the Moru district would provide a better line of communication with remote Yambio than the somewhat roundabout route through Lau. It was not, however, until January 1921, after a few weeks getting acclimatized at Malek, that Dr Kenneth and Mrs Eileen Fraser arrived at Lui in the heart of the Moru territory, fifteen miles south of the government post at Amadi.[55]

For the first few months they lived in a mud and wattle rest house, but by the end of 1921 there was a small mud building for the boys' school and another mud building for the first hospital. In 1922 the first European nurse, Miss M. Law, arrived at Lui. She described the one ward of that time as 'a square room with mud floors and walls and a ceiling of matting'. Fires were lit by each bed to keep the mosquitoes away. Each patient provided his own food and at night the patient's friends would sit beside him on the verandah.

Fraser was the first missionary doctor to serve with the CMS mission in the southern Sudan, and his medical skill and attractive personality made an immediate impact on some sympathetic Moru chiefs: 'They assured us,' he wrote in 1924, 'that when we had cured all the sick in the Moru tribe we should have nothing to do but lie in our hammocks all day, and perhaps take an occasional stroll in the forest to shoot game.' His description of a typical hospital day could be matched in many parts of the world at some time or another, but was becoming less common in the 1920s:

> In the morning we just have a hymn and prayers and then set to work. The babies are yelling, the ulcers are smelling, and every one is wildly speculating as to who will be last and who first to be attended to; and so I take our opportunity in the evening when their minds are receptive.[56]

That same year, 1924, twenty-four men and youths were admitted cate-chumens and Mrs Fraser began a class for women and girls. The first church was built, and work began on permanent hospital buildings. They were in large part a gift from Mrs Fraser and her sister Miss Galbraith in memory of their brother, Norman Galbraith, who had died on war service in 1915. The new hospital was opened on 8th August, 1926; Dr Fraser noting with some satisfaction that it took only twelve hours of voluntary labour to demolish the old hospital.

1926–42

By 1926 the southern Sudan mission was well-established. Some at least of the early strains and anxieties could now be forgotten, and a period of fairly rapid expansion began. In the decade 1926 to 1935 the number of missionaries more than doubled; and in the areas around Yambio, Yei and Lui, in particular, church membership was growing rapidly.

One of the new missionaries, Arthur Riley, arrived at Yambio on 6th December, 1926. The Lavericks were temporarily in charge during the absence of the Gores on furlough. Some years later Riley wrote down his first impressions:

> There was a flourishing Elementary Vernacular Boys' School housed in a fine new brick building. There was also a girls' boarding school and a women's school attended by enthusiastic scholars. I was also very interested to see the dispensary to which numbers of people came every morning with every conceivable ailment. There was a camp in which people lived in temporary shelter and were treated for tropical ulcers which were very numerous in those days. Evangelistic activity was apparent in the keenness of the Christians to go out during the weekends to the villages nearby for open-air meetings. The local leper-camp and the prison at the Government post were also visited.[57]

Riley was soon busy supervising the completion of a second mission-house which was about three feet high at the time of his arrival. 'It was a beautiful situation, surrounded with the flowering Golden Mohur trees, yellow cassias and mauve jacarandas.' After about eight weeks the Lavericks moved to Maridi. 'I was then left alone on the mission-station at Yambio and there being no English-speaking Zande, I simply had to learn the language.' Supervising the building of a large brick church was another of his tasks. It was finished, apart from the tower, early in 1929.

By 1929 there were a hundred baptized church-members in the Yambio district, and about two hundred others preparing for baptism. The church was supporting Christian teachers in the surrounding villages and twelve village schools had been started. The dispensary, with about fifty patients daily, was in charge of a Zande Christian, Yosepa.

1929 was also an important year for the boys' school at Juba. Since Lea-Wilson's retirement through ill-health it had been carried on by the Rev. Gordon Selwyn and others; but by 1927 Juba had become a main up-river port, and it was thought wise to find a new site for the school. Loka was chosen, sixty miles west by south of Juba, some three thousand feet above sea level, and comparatively free of mosquitoes; and the move took place in January 1929. The Nugent school was soon to establish itself as an intermediate school to which the more promising boys went from all the CMS mission centres. Juba continued to be a mission centre with a boys' elementary vernacular boarding-school, and a school for women and girls from 1931. The first church was built there in 1932, and the mission headquarters was established there.

1929 also saw the opening of a further station at Kajokaji among the Kuku tribe, a hundred miles south-east of Yei. A boys' elementary vernacular school with boarders was started in 1929, followed by a school for women and girls in 1931.

Lui continued to expand in the later 1920s. In 1926 Dr Fraser opened a camp for sixty lepers, with the support of a government grant. By 1929 leprosy patients were numbering 158–180 a year. The Frasers returned from furlough in that year with the medical committee's approval for eight new district dispensaries and with the promise that a medical colleague would be found for Dr Fraser. In 1930 the Simpson ward for women was opened at the main hospital. In 1934 Fraser wrote an article in *The Mission Hospital* describing the purposes which the Lui station sought to serve. It provided training for men dressers; treatment of the more serious illnesses; training for teachers and evangelists; and a general education for those who passed from bush school to central school. The ten out-stations (the number was to grow to nineteen by 1939) were strategically placed at regular distances from Lui. Each was a centre of evangelism, healing and teaching, in regular communication with Lui hospital by means of cyclist messengers. Fraser was able to claim that yaws had been almost eliminated among the Moru – but cerebro-spinal meningitis, dysentery, and sleeping-sickness took their toll of life, and the leprosy rate was high.

On 10th January, 1935 Kenneth Fraser died at Lui. Handley Hooper, Africa secretary of the CMS, wrote after a visit in 1937: 'The work at Lui bore the impress of singular imagination and genius, and spoke volumes for the vision and devotion of the Frasers in planning its scope and execution.' Bishop Gwynne paid a characteristic tribute to Fraser himself: 'Woe betide the man who bullied the weak or tried to bully him. . . . [he] was a trained gymnast and very handy with the gloves; yet he was gentle and tender as a woman when hundreds of the poor broken things crowded round him for sympathy, treatment and healing'.[58] A plaque in the south chapel of Khartoum cathedral gives thanks to God 'for Kenneth Fraser, M.D., physician and evangelist, by whose skill and healing and goodness of living Christ's light has shone upon the darkness of the Moru people'.

Lui continued to develop after Kenneth Fraser's death. In 1936 more than twenty-seven thousand different patients received treatment at the hospital or at one or other of its village dispensaries. In April of that year Bishop Guy Bullen, on his first visit to Lui, confirmed twenty-five boys and two women. One of the first two deacons in the Anglican Church in the southern Sudan, Andarea Apaya, ordained in 1941, was a convert through the ministry of the Frasers. He had been put in charge of the first Moru out-station in 1927, returning in 1934 to become headmaster of Lui elementary school.

In December 1929 a boys' school was started among the Agar Dinkas at Akot, eighty miles west of the Nile and a few miles east of Rumbek, by the Rev. R. S. Macdonald. In him the mission found an educationalist of out-standing quality and, with his doctor wife Catharine, he was to leave his mark on the southern Sudan before going to the Nuba Mountains. The Agar Dinkas proved to be more approachable and less conservative in their outlook than the Bor Dinkas around Malek, and the school flourished. After the Macdonalds left, Edward Arnold gave devoted service at Akot for twelve years from 1933–45.

The last extension of mission to another tribal area in the period was in the southern part of the Upper Nile Province. Shaw, prospecting in February 1930, left Akot by lorry, 'sloshing through water and mud'. He saw possibilities of a station among the Nuers, and early in 1932 Dr H. H. W. Bennett and S. L. Ewell arrived at Ler, among the Nuer people. Bennett described the journey and arrival in his diary:

We crossed two or three swampy patches before getting there and one very sluggish river crossed by a causeway with a few culverts in it. Ler is a low ridge taking its name from the trees in an almost treeless region. The Nuers are an entirely naked race except for married women who wear skins and one or two men who have some European garment. We lived in tents at first and built three small round-ended houses and a dozen huts. Mud brick was the only possible material as there is no stone or timber.[59]

A small fourteen-bed hospital was built, but before it was completed Bennett moved in May 1935 to Uganda where he did notable work for many years as superintendent of Ngora hospital. Dr Casson took charge of Ler in January 1937 and, when he moved south to join Mrs Fraser at Lui, Dr William Manwell took over. He proved himself a born pioneer, and intervened successfully to stop a local war between the northern (Rill) Nuers and the local Dok Nuers. Canon S. L. Ewell spent many years in effective service at Ler.

In January 1936 a second Nuer station was opened by the Macdonalds at Juaibor on Zeraf Island. It was heavy going for the missionaries in a literal as well as in a figurative sense: 'the country is virtually a swamp for half the year,' Macdonald wrote in 1938, 'during the rains we only get about by wading . . . . Injections for yaws are highly popular, but only once a year.'[60] Two Dinka assistants, trained at Akot, left after six weeks, and for part of 1938 the only dispensary assistant was a cripple. However, Dr Catharine Macdonald performed a hundred operations in 1936, and the dispensary was well used. A boys' school was started, with fifteen boys, in 1937. The Macdonalds had to leave Zeraf Island in 1939 as he had been seriously ill. The Rev. C. F. L. Bertram and his wife, Dr May Bertram, took over and worked with similar devotion in trying conditions.

In December 1941 a new station was opened on the Gel river. 'The start owed much to Malek,' wrote L. W. C. Sharland, 'as all but one of the African Christians who went with us were members of Malek Church. Nikanwa Aciengkue, a young convert of Daniel Deng's, has turned out to be a fine leader himself.'

A Problem of 'Spheres'

A perennial problem for the CMS in the 1920s and 1930s was how to expand its area of occupation in such a way as to justify the Sudan government in continuing to support the delimitation of missionary spheres laid down by Lord Cromer. The Roman Catholic missions had developed their allotted area more effectively, from the government point of view, than the CMS. Shaw, as CMS mission secretary, was conscious of increasing government pressure to expand educational and medical operations. 'Unless the staff of the mission is increased,' he wrote in January 1924, 'the Government are not likely to remain content to see CMS neglecting the opportunities and responsibilities hitherto entrusted to them.'[61] Cash, newly appointed general secretary of the CMS, made the same point in a memorandum in 1926: 'Either we must go ahead in the Sudan or relinquish the northern part of our area to the RC mission.'

Cash's reaction to government pressure was to play for time, hoping to build up the CMS missionary force, with promised educational and medical grants from the government. In this policy he was supported by Bishop Gwynne. In October 1925 we find the bishop urging the CMS parent committee 'expressly to declare its willingness to accept Government grants on the same conditions as in Uganda'. He argued that 'the opinion of any individual missionary must not be allowed to endanger Government support for the work in the southern Sudan'.[62] This was clearly a reference to Shaw, who was against accepting government grants and whose reaction to criticism of CMS was to take the war into the enemy's camp and to accuse the Roman Catholics of 'invading' the CMS sphere.

In 1932 the dispute about spheres came to a head. Archbishop Hinsley, head of Roman Catholic missionary work in Africa, complained that both the government and the CMS upheld the sphere system, which no longer made sense in a situation very different from that of 1904.

On 13th October, 1933, the governor-general, Sir John Maffey, after an interview with the Africa secretary of CMS, in which he had spoken of the strained relations in Hiriwo's country between Protestants and Roman Catholics, wrote asking that CMS would send orders to their Sudan representatives for the immediate withdrawal of CMS schools from this area, in accordance with the government instructions of November 1932. Gibson telegraphed from Juba on 24th October saying that no tension was visible or reported and that pressure on these grounds was considered to be unwarranted. But capitulation became inevitable, and on 11th November, 1933 Gibson wrote to Gore giving instructions for the withdrawal of the teachers. In an interview on 6th June, 1934, a new governor-general, Sir Stewart Simes, told Shaw that the sphere system could not be defended morally or legally, and on 30th October in the same year the Under-Secretary of State for Foreign Affairs reported confidentially to the CMS that the governor-general's proposals, for the abrogation of mission boundaries and the promotion of local agreements between heads of the mission bodies concerned, had received the approval of the Foreign Office.

There was a grim inevitability about the course of this dispute. The Sudan government felt unable to withdraw a definite instruction. The CMS committee in London trusted the government's declared intention to continue the observance of spheres, and regarded a readjustment of boundaries as best calculated to strengthen that intention. A majority at least of the missionaries on the spot felt that the parent committee was insufficiently informed and had expressed its mind on a complicated matter too hastily and without proper consultation.

Missionary Education in the South

The sphere system could not have survived so long, as an opportunity for the planting and nurture of Christian churches in the southern Sudan, had it not been for the fairly consistent application of a 'southern policy' by the Sudan government. This policy distinguished the southern provinces from the provinces of the Muslim north. It was defined by the Civil Secretary in 1921 as 'the encouragement of native chiefs to administer their own tribes in accordance with native customs in so far as these customs are not entirely repugnant to the ideas of justice and humanity. And to aim at non-interference except where necessary.' English rather than Arabic was made the language of government and higher education, and until the late 1920s, all education was left in the hands of Christian missionaries. Thereafter, for another twenty years, government activity in the field of education was confined to grants-in-aid for missionary elementary vernacular schools (EVSS) and intermediate schools, together with inspection and supervision which extended to missionary bush-schools.

Grants-in-aid became a subject of discussion between the Sudan government and the CMS in 1926, and the first grants were received in March 1929, in respect of seven EVSS at Yei, Lui, Maridi, Yambio and Malek (already operating) and at Kajokaji and Loka (in process of foundation). The accepted basis was £150 per annum for the European missionary in charge, plus initial building grants. Shaw was not happy about the acceptance of these grants. He feared that they would mean that the government would increasingly decide the line and pace of missionary advance; and they would inevitably involve the Society in additional expenditure. 'It is quite certain,' he wrote in June 1929, 'that these stations with their schools will not be run on the £150 per annum from the Government alone, and they will entail increases in secretarial expenditure.'[63] He came increasingly to regard the acceptance of these education grants as a 'sell-out' by CMS,[64] but he must have known that in the 1930s the requisite money and manpower for educational development was not at the Society's disposal except in co-operation with the government.

Government grants were accepted for the intermediate school and for an increasing number of EVSS. The government remained sympathetic, and indeed at times long-suffering, about the efforts of the missionaries to provide education for Sudanese boys and girls which would pass muster as 'genuine' education and not simple Christian evangelism and nurture. The Society, for its part, was continually hindered in effective co-operation by financial stringency which made any new commitment in any mission a matter of anxiety. When the Africa secretary, H. D. Hooper, discussed educational matters in Khartoum in November 1937, he was faced with a government proposal for three new middle schools with grants for three more men to open these schools. 'This was not,' he wrote in his report, 'a suggestion which the Society could entertain.' As an alternative he and Bishop Gwynne proposed a longer period at the elementary vernacular schools, but this 'alternative proposal had to be subjected to considerable modification'. The government education department was beginning to see that 'financing "station" missionaries without any special equipment in educational method to pay half-time attention to schools in addition to their other multifarious duties . . . was not a success'. It was prepared to offer double grants (£300 instead of £150 per annum) to missionaries with educational qualifications who would make the care of the schools their main task. Hooper had to point out that an ending of the present system would mean throwing back upon the CMS the full support of ten men who were receiving a staff grant of £150. Unless the plan could be modified the Society would inevitably have to close stations, transfer missionaries, and abandon work.[65]

A compromise was reached, which owed much to the diplomacy of Bishop Guy Bullen. It was on his way back to Juba, after a successful conference in Khartoum early in December 1937, that Bishop Bullen was killed in an air crash. In two short years he had endeared himself to everyone, and had established excellent relations between the Anglican missions and the government.[66] Missionaries of a new generation, such as G. F. Earl and R. S. Macdonald, proved themselves able advocates of the relevance of educational work to the total missionary task. Thus Macdonald, writing in 1940, recognized the uneasiness caused in the minds of some CMS supporters that acceptance of government subsidies to, and some measure of government control over, CMS schools in unevangelized areas 'is to put the cart before the horse and to direct the energies of the Societies from their proper end'. But this argument, he went on to suggest, was based on an outworn definition of education.

Bring up the children as the family of God and train them for citizenship of the Kingdom of Heaven. That is the policy of the CMS in the Southern Sudan, and the policy endorsed and supported by the Government. . . . There is no better way of influencing a people than by gathering the children into a boarding-school; there is no better way of learning a language than by trying to teach in it; there is no better way of understanding the mind of a people than by studying their attempts at self-expression; there is no better way of understanding the Scriptures than by trying prayerfully to translate them; in short there is no better way of evangelization than through elementary education.[67]

Earl described the feeding-system for the Nugent school at Loka as it was working in 1937. Each of the eleven CMS stations at that time had an elementary school in which teaching was given in the group language. Each year the cream of these schools was sent to Loka, two boys to the Nugent school and one to the technical department. The Nugent school aimed to provide teachers for elementary schools, clerks, dispensers, interpreters, stenographers, agricultural and sanitary supervisors, also some heirs to chiefdoms. He described Loka as a 'Tower of Babel' with 112 boys speaking about twenty-five languages, 'as different as Greeks and Icelanders . . . as lacking in mutual respect as Germans and Jews'.[68]

Loka remained a solitary educational peak within the CMS area of mission. The church in the southern Sudan would have been better prepared for its ordeal in the 1960s if it had not remained so, and if secondary education had been developed more effectively within the protecting walls of 'Southern Policy'. The language barriers, and the absence of a *lingua franca* among the tribes apart from English, help to explain this lack of secondary educational development. All the senior missionaries, including Bishop Gwynne, thought there was plenty of time for the south to catch up with the north; but northern pressure to create one nation in the Sudan was increasing rapidly in 1942; and the effective continuation of southern policy depended on the production

of a greatly increased supply of English-speaking teachers. The Governor of
Equatoria Province described this as a 'colossal task'. Machinery for producing
600 of these teachers had been put in motion in the CMS sphere by 1939, but
training them was a slow process.

Translation Work

Whatever their commitment as school-teachers, the work of translation
remained an absorbing task for the missionaries. Shaw set an example of
diligence in this, continuing on his Dinka translation work from his retirement
in 1940 until his death in Kenya in 1956. By 1916 Lea-Wilson had translated
St Mark's Gospel into Bor Dinka, and Gore the same gospel into Zande. Mrs
Fraser continued work on the translation of the New Testament into the Moru
language after her husband's death in 1935, and Gordon Selwyn, among
others, worked in the Bari language. Canon and Mrs Gore worked on Azandi
translation, as later did Archdeacon Riley.

From Mission to Church

In his 1938 report, H. D. Hooper described the work of the CMS in the
southern Sudan in terms of five mission areas, Bari, Moru, Zande, Dinka and
Nuer, each with one or more districts, each in charge of a European missionary
who was responsible for oversight of an elementary vernacular school. The
mission sub-structure of the church in the southern Sudan was very much in
evidence. The younger missionaries arriving at that time still felt themselves, with
some justice, to be in a pioneer situation. 'One is likely,' Earl wrote in 1937, 'to
be of necessity one's own secretary, clerk, and accountant, builder (and re-
builder, when the erections begin to totter), head gardener, tailor, matron, house-
keeper and the school "sergeant-major".'[69] The government was still able to
regard missionaries as potentially useful allies in a disturbed political situation.
But the church which the missionaries had come to prepare, and in which they
must find their place, was growing. It might almost be said that the Revival,
which spread in 1938 and 1939 to all parts of the southern Sudan, was not so
much a revival as an initial 'baptism of the Spirit' for the church there. The
revival movement began at Lui in 1938, and during 1940 over a hundred men
and boys were baptized there. 'Among the Zandes,' Bishop Gelsthorpe wrote,
'one has seen the movement of the Spirit spreading like a bush fire. . . . I had
over four hundred for confirmation.' Even the more conservative Dinka and
Nuer tribes were brought under its influence.[70] For the most part the movement,
as in Uganda, was kept within the church and used effectively for its upbuilding,
especially by Arthur and Grace Riley.

In 1941 there were 3,000 baptisms and 1,000 confirmations in the Anglican
Church in the southern Sudan, and the total Christian community was estimated
as 18,600. In that year, 1941, the first ordinations took place. Daniel Deng Atong

and Andarea Apaya were made deacons. Both were aged thirty. Andarea was a Moru who had been brought up in the church at Lui; Daniel, by birth a Mandari, had been placed in Archdeacon Shaw's care as a small child and was brought up as a Dinka. Baptized in 1926, he was to become the first Sudanese bishop in the Anglican Church in 1955. 'Daniel Deng was a strong influence upon many after the blessing he himself received at Loka.'[71] The first Zande deacon, Amosa Rakpi, was ordained three years later in 1944.

There were a number of changes in the leadership of the mission in the late 1930s. In 1937 Canon E. C. Gore left the Sudan in poor health and he died the next year. Paul Gibson succeeded Archibald Shaw as archdeacon in 1940; and following Bishop Guy Bullen's all too brief period of service in 1936 and 1937, Bishop Morris Gelsthorpe quickly won the affection and trust of both Africans and Europeans. One missionary wrote in May 1941 that, largely owing to his leadership, 'the South has come through its years of stress and storm (from the staff point of view) into calm and sunny waters'.

In the same month Gelsthorpe was looking ahead, with prescience, to the future leadership of the church: 'Others as well as myself begin to realize that you have a possible Bishop in Oliver Allison.'[72] Twenty years later, in the early 1960s, it was this young missionary who was to bear, as bishop, the main burden of leadership at a time when the policy of integration by the northern-dominated Sudan government brought great suffering to the Christians in the south.

NOTES

1. Richard Hill, 'Government and Christian Missions in the Anglo-Egyptian Sudan 1889–1914', *Middle Eastern Studies*, Vol. 1, No. 2, January, 1965, pp. 131–2.

2. P. M. Holt, *A Modern History of the Sudan*, Weidenfeld and Nicolson, 1961, p. 111.

3. op. cit., p. 130.

4. J. S. R. Duncan, *The Sudan*, Blackwood, 1952, pp. 190–2.

5. op. cit., p. 275.

6. *CMR*, June 1926, S. M. Zwemer, 'The Anglo-Egyptian Sudan', p. 140.

7. Holt, op. cit., p. 119; International Missionary Council, *Tambaram Series*, Vol. VI, OUP, 1939, p. 321.

8. Trimingham, *The Christian Approach to Islam in the Sudan*, OUP, 1948, p. 29.

9. Hill, op. cit., p. 114.

10. Lilian Sanderson, *Journal of African History*, IV 2 (1963), p. 237.

11. Hill, op. cit., p. 119.

12. Gibson MSS. See exchange of letters, Shaw and MacInnes, 27th December, 1915 and 17th April, 1917.

13. CMS *Annual Report*, 1924–5, p. 29.

14. H. D. Hooper, *Report of a Visit to CMS Missions in East Africa, the Sudan, Egypt and Palestine, 1937–38*, CMS, 1938, p. 53.

15. *Mercy and Truth*, July 1915, p. 204; see also *CMR*, June 1919, W. H. T. Gairdner, 'The C.M.S. in the Anglo-Egyptian Sudan', pp. 114ff; *CMO*, March 1926, 'The Sudan Faces Westward', p. 60.

16. *CMR*, June 1919, Gairdner, op. cit., p. 118.
17. G3/E/P3, 1917/51.
18. *CMO*, February 1929, E. Lloyd, 'Gum and Cotton in the Sudan', pp. 26–8; *CMR*, September 1924, W. H. T. Gairdner, 'Omdurman Revisited', pp. 237–43.
19. P3, 1922/48.
20. Gelsthorpe (ed.), *Introducing the Diocese of the Sudan*, 1946, p. 20.
21. ibid., p. 26.
22. Sanderson, op. cit., pp. 239–40.
23. ibid., p. 240.
24. *Introducing the Diocese of the Sudan*, op. cit., p. 27.
25. *AR* (MS), 1935–6, p. 135.
26. *AR* (MS), 1936–7, p. 130.
27. Sanderson, op. cit., pp. 241ff.
28. Trimingham, op. cit., p. 49.
29. Gibson MSS.
30. Annual letters, CMS 1910, p. 15, W. H. Scamell.
31. G3/S/P1, 1910/4.
32. P1, 1910/5.
33. P1, 1910/12.
34. Shaw MSS, 'Journal', Vol. II, 14th August, 1910.
35. P1, 1911/35.
36. *Letters from the Front*, CMS 1912, p. 16.
37. CMS *Gazette*, August 1914, p. 242.
38. *CMR*, March 1915, R. Y. Stones, 'The Azandi of the Bar-el-Ghazal', pp. 166ff.
39. P1, 1912/61. This offer was accepted (see CMS *Annual Report*, 1912–13, Finance Section, p. 279).
40. Shaw MSS, 'Journal', Vol. III, 1913–15.
41. P1, 1913/25; 1914/5.
42. *Report of the Gordon Memorial Sudan Mission, March 1916 – February 1918*.
43. P1, Letter of 29th June, 1918.
44. P1, 1919/7.
45. P1, 1924/3, 'The one remaining Luganda schoolmaster is now due to return home and Uganda authorities hold out no hope of sending more'.
46. Gibson MSS.
47. P1, 1922/25, memo of 5th December, 1922.
48. P1, 1921/13.
49. P1, 1924/8.
50. 'Bari' was used in CMS records of this period to include such tribes as the Fajelu and Kuku whose language was akin to Bari.
51. P1, 1916/5.
52. Shaw's opinion in this matter was irresponsible. One who knew him well writes: 'The [Sleeping Sickness] regulations were desperately important, and Yei, Maridi and Yambio were flourishing under them'.
53. Shaw MSS, letter from Lea-Wilson, 18th November, 1920.
54. Gibson MSS.
55. Eileen Fraser, *The Doctor Comes to Lui*, CMS, 1938, p. 7. She explains why Lui appears in CMS records for about four years as 'Yilu'. Yilu was the name of the sub-chief who lived in the village and who became an enthusiastic helper of the Frasers.
56. *The Mission Hospital*, April 1924, p. 85.
57. Gibson MSS.
58. H. C. Jackson, *Pastor on the Nile*, SPCK, 1960, p. 211.
59. Gibson MSS.

60. Gibson MSS.

61. P1, 1924/3.

62. P1, 1925/28.

63. P1, 1929/20.

64. Southern Sudan mission file (160/13), Gelsthorpe to Hooper, 14th November, 1940.

65. Hooper, op. cit., pp. 47–9.

66. Martin W. Parr in *Guy Bullen*, Highway Press, 1938, pp. 101–29.

67. *CMO*, June 1940, R. S. MacDonald, 'Christian Education in the Southern Sudan', pp. 84–5.

68. *CMO*, July 1937, G. F. Earl, 'A Schools Opportunity in the Southern Sudan', pp. 152ff.

69. ibid.

70. *CMO*, October 1940, A. M. Gelsthorpe, 'The Southern Sudan in War Time'.

71. Gibson MSS, C. O. Allison, writing in 1945.

72. Southern Sudan mission file (160/13), W. H. Carey to Hooper, 27th May, 1941; Gelsthorpe to Hooper, 15th May, 1941.

Palestine

The Country and its Peoples

Palestine was the name used in the later Roman empire to describe three provinces in the 'diocese' of Oriens. Palaestina Prima and Secunda correspond roughly to the biblical Israel and Judah, the strip of cultivable land between the eastern Mediterranean seaboard and the Syrian desert. From the reign of Suliman the Magnificent (1520–66) to Allenby's entry into Jerusalem on 9th December, 1917 it was a divided country, a portion of several provinces of the Ottoman empire. During the period of the British mandate (1922–48) Palestine comprised two areas of administration under differing forms of government; the country west of the river Jordan being directly under British rule; and Transjordan, ruled by an Arab emir with a handful of British military advisers, under the protection of British forces. Palestine is used here, as it was used consistently in the CMS records for the period 1910–42, to signify broadly the present whole territories of Israel and Jordan.

Before the first world war, and throughout this period, the great majority of Palestinians were Muslim Arabs. A great many of them lived in hill villages with an average population of six hundred people. 'The Arab villages in the hills spring from the rock as though they were part of the hillside, built of the white limestone of which the country has an unending supply.'[1] By the mid-1930s the pattern of human habitation had become more variegated. Modern Jewish villages, with red-roofed houses built of concrete and stucco, were beginning to dot the coastal plain. Haifa and Tel Aviv were growing rapidly into large towns. The population of western Palestine doubled between the world wars, from 800,000 in 1922 to 1,650,000 in 1942. The 1931 census gave a total figure of 1,050,000 of whom 800,000 were Muslims, 90,000 Christians, and 100,000 Jews, representing a growth of 36 per cent in nine years. All three communities had grown, but the Jewish population had increased by 108 per cent and in the next decade it would double again. Of the many factors that made Palestine a troubled country throughout this period the growth of the

Jewish population was the most significant. It affected every aspect of life, including the kind of missionary opportunity discerned over a period of nearly a century by the CMS Palestine mission. For this reason, if for no other, the story of the Jewish 'exodus' must be briefly retold here.

European interest in Palestine was stimulated by the opening of the Suez Canal in 1869; and by 1880 France, Britain, Germany and Russia were involved politically and economically in the region. Restrictive edicts aimed at the Jews by Tsar Alexander III in 1881 led to a massive Jewish exodus from Russia in the next three decades, estimated at two and a half million people. Few of them came to Palestine but about three thousand settled in and around Jaffa; and between 1881 and 1914 Jewish immigration averaged two thousand a year. Many of them acquired land on the malaria-infested Plain of Sharon and the names they gave to their settlements reflected their apocalyptic hopes – *Rishon le Zion* (the first step in Zion), *Rosh Pinah* (the corner-stone). From 1897, when Theodor Herzl founded the Zionist organization, the dream of a Jewish National Home in Palestine began to take political shape; and it won some weighty support in Britain, especially among the leaders of the Liberal Party. When Zionist plans to purchase the country from the Turks foundered, Britain in 1903 offered an alternative site in the Kavirondo (Nyanza) area of western Kenya. Herzl was disposed to accept this offer, but his Zionist colleague, Chaim Weizmann, would be content with nothing less than Israel's ancient homeland.

In the 1914–18 war Britain had a complicated diplomatic problem on her hands in the Middle East. She needed, and bargained for, Arab military assistance against the Turks; she also needed Jewish wealth and sympathy in the struggle against Germany. By 1916, looking beyond the collapse of the Ottoman empire, she was negotiating with France for control of Turkish territory in Asia. In the course of these complex diplomatic exchanges, promises were made, and agreements entered into, which were mutually incompatible. By the Sykes-Picot Agreement of May 1916, Britain was to have control of a narrow strip of the coastline of Palestine between Haifa and Acca as a Mediterranean outlet for southern Mesopotamia; France was to have control of the Lebanon and north Palestine; Russia, France and England were to make a further agreement on a special regime for Central Palestine, including the Holy Places. An Arab state, or federation of states, was to be formed to the east of these regions. In the same year Sir Henry McMahon, High Commissioner for Egypt, in correspondence with Sharif Hussein of Mecca, promised British support for Arab independence over a wide area in return for aid against the Turks. An ill-defined area of western Syria was excluded from the region in which Britain would recognize Arab independence. McMahon later declared that the intention was to make Palestine part of this excluded area: but as Arab nationalism grew in strength, it was inevitable that uncertainty of definition should itself become a cause of conflict.

A year later, on 2nd November, 1917, came the famous Balfour Declaration. Mr Balfour, British Foreign Secretary, wrote to Lord Rothschild, the President of the Zionist Federation in England, stating that

> His Majesty's Government view with favour the establishment in Palestine of a National Home for the Jewish people, and will use their best endeavours to facilitate the achievement of this object, it being clearly understood that nothing will be done to prejudice the civil and religious rights of existing non-Jewish communities in Palestine or the rights and political status enjoyed by Jews in any other country.

The declaration was designed as a counter-move to German overtures to the Zionists, inspired by exaggerated hopes for the role of Russian Jewry in relation to the Kerensky government.[2] It incensed the Arab community of Palestine: Muslim-Christian associations organized meetings throughout the country to denounce it, and Arab-Jewish riots broke out in Jerusalem on Easter Day, 1920.

A conference of the Allied Powers at San Remo in April 1920 allotted League of Nations mandates to Britain for Palestine and to France for Syria; and although the Palestine mandate was not ratified until 1922 Britain brought the wartime military administration to an end. On the 20th July, 1920 Sir Herbert Samuel took office in Jerusalem as high commissioner. The King's Message, which served as his introduction to the country, mentioned the decision of the Allied Powers to secure the gradual establishment of a National Home for the Jewish people, but added: 'these measures will not, in any way, affect the civil or religious rights, or diminish the prosperity of the general population of Palestine'. This double pledge to Jews and Arabs set the mandatory government an impossible administrative task. There were further Arab riots on Labour Day 1921; and the Churchill White Paper of 1922, which sought to reassure the Arabs of Britain's modest intentions for Jewish settlement, left the politically powerful Zionist organization suspicious and dissatisfied.

There was little trouble during the remainder of Samuel's term of office as high commissioner. In a gesture of impartiality he appointed the Grand Mufti of the Holy City (Haj Amin al Hussaini) controller of the *wakfs* and gained him recognition as President of the Supreme Muslim Council. Samuel's successor as high commissioner, Lord Plumer (1925–8), also had a fairly quiet term of office although the Arab uprising against the French in Syria encouraged the Palestinian Arabs to hope for national self-determination. Economic depression greatly reduced the rate of Jewish immigration: in 1927 more Jews in fact left the country than entered it. But peace was short-lived. After more riots in 1929, the Permanent Mandates Commission, ignoring the realities of the situation, commented on the Mandatory's lack of a constructive policy of integration such as 'would have enabled them to convince the fellahin more easily of the *undeniable material advantages* that Palestine has derived from the efforts of the Zionists'.[3] After 1930 the British mandate was little more than a ring-holding operation; and Britain reported to the Mandates Commission that self-government for Palestine was impossible.

Following an Arab general strike in 1936, in which trains were wrecked and many Jewish settlements raided, the Peel Commission proposed partition as the only viable solution: a small Jewish state in a coastal strip from Haifa to Jaffa; and a larger Arab state, and a considerable wedge of territory from Jaffa to Jerusalem to continue under mandate. At first Zionists appeared ready to accept partition, but the Arabs rejected it from the first and in 1937 the Zionist Congress followed suit. The Africa secretary of CMS, the Rev. H. D. Hooper, visited Palestine at this time and reported: 'For the Christian, partition spells loss of security whether power passes into the hands of Jews or Moslem Arabs'. He went on to say that the rank and file of the church had strong incentives to make common cause with their Muslim fellow-countrymen.[4] A further commission in 1938 reported against partition as unworkable.

The persecution of Jews in Nazi Germany, long before the 'final solution' of the Jewish problem was put into action, gave a new urgency to the demand for open-door immigration. The immigrant ship *Patria*, blown up by Jewish extremists in Haifa harbour with the loss of 268 lives and later beached beneath Mount Carmel, bears poignant witness to the agonized decisions of that time. The Palestine White Paper of 17th May, 1939 made a last desperate effort to hold together the two halves of the Balfour Declaration by fixing the annual total of Jewish immigration for five years, after which further increases were to depend on Arab acquiescence; but long before this Chaim Weizmann's habitual talk of 'stretching out hands to the Arabs in friendship' had lost all substance. Throughout the period Jewish immigration seemed to the Palestinian Arabs a threat to their homeland; and most CMS missionaries sent, as they believed, to bring the Christian gospel to Muslim Arabs, showed sympathy with the Arabs' distrust of Western policies. They had to endure the pain and bewilderment of seeing Christians (converts of their own mission as well as the far more numerous adherents of the Greek Orthodox Church) making common cause with Muslims against the race to which, according to the flesh, their Lord and Master belonged, and in the land which they called 'Holy' for his sake. But they were aware, too, that such missionary opportunity as remained owed much to the British mandate. No other country in the Middle East during this period was so 'open', though it is impossible to use that word in such a grim human situation without irony.

Religion in Palestine

It was of little benefit to the purpose for which CMS entered Palestine as a mission field that holy places of the three great monotheistic religions are found within its borders. If these shrines had been confined to Jerusalem, the problems they presented for evangelism might have been more tractable; but Hebron,

Tiberias and Safed were numbered among the holy towns of Judaisim; and Muslim places of veneration also spread well beyond Jerusalem. There were, in addition, centres of deviationary movements from the ancient faiths. The Samaritans, numbering only a few hundred people, kept their shrine and law-scrolls on Mount Gerizim. The Druses, an eclectic sect with roots in Islam, were a considerable community in Galilee and in the Hauran east of the Jordan. Bahaism, a rapidly growing sect, had its headquarters at Acca and Haifa.

The guardianship of shrines and holy places does not generate a spirit of tolerance towards other faiths or to divergent forms of one's own faith; and Palestine had more than its share of religious fanaticism. Article 15 of the British mandate provided for freedom of conscience and for the free exercise of all forms of worship, subject only to the maintenance of public order and morality. Article 16 made the mandatory power responsible for the supervision of religious and charitable bodies of all faiths. Under Transjordan's separate mandate there was also a guarantee of freedom of worship, and evangelism was permitted; but there the *Sharia* law still operated in relation to Muslim converts to Christianity. In western Palestine conditions were made easier for converts. For example, the Succession Ordinance of 1923 allowed a convert to inherit from Muslim relations; and the Change of Religious Community Ordinance of 1927 allowed women as well as men to change their religion by notification.[5] The spirit of intolerance cannot be exorcised by legislation alone, and conversion from Islam still carried penalties of ostracism, and the subtler forms of perse-cution continued. But these steps towards religious liberty were not valueless. In the period of Ottoman rule up to 1917 missionaries frequently quoted cases of direct threats to the life of a convert, and it was often thought wise to help baptized Christians out of the country. Such extreme measures were no longer necessary after 1917.

The Christian Churches

In spite of its greater religious freedom under the mandate, and the high rate of Jewish immigration, Palestine remained a predominantly Muslim country, and Transjordan almost exclusively so. The Christian minority groups in communion with ancient churches were much smaller than the Coptic com-munity in Egypt but somewhat larger than the Armenian community in Iran. The 1931 census gave 97,000 as the total Christian population. Most of them were Greek Orthodox. The Roman Catholic Church, though strongly rep-resented in the guardianship of the Holy Places and in numerous monasteries, had not developed an indigenous community of any size. The Anglican Church of some 3,000 members (1931) consisted of three groups: Palestinian Arabs, largely the product of the CMS mission; Hebrew Christians, in association with the Church Missions to Jews (formerly the London Jews' Society); and British officials and residents.

Although it was not the policy of the CMS to proselytize among Eastern Christians, the Anglican Church had been built up in the past mainly from members of these Churches[6] and the 'community conception' of Christianity remained a problem for missionaries. 'They cannot believe in a Moslem ever becoming a Christian. How could a Turk become a Greek?'[7] But their children attended CMS schools in many parts of the country.

Other non-Anglican missionary societies at work in Palestine included the American Alliance Mission in Jerusalem and Beersheba; the American Friends principally at Ramallah; and the United Free Church of Scotland at Hebron, Tiberias and Safed. No other Protestant societies had more than a single centre.[8] There were, however, numerous single-station missions and free-lance missionaries, whose zeal, not always matched by wisdom, caused considerable embarrassment to the more responsible missionary bodies.

The Anglican Church and Bishopric

The Anglican bishopric in Jerusalem and the East celebrated its centenary in 1941. It had been set up by the joint efforts of England and Prussia to serve the Anglicans and Protestants of Syria, Chaldea, Egypt and Abyssinia. During the first forty years of the bishopric German pastors and congregations were placed under the bishop's 'protection', the United Evangelical Church of Prussia shared in the endowment of the bishopric, and the King of Prussia nominated alternately with the British Crown. Having lapsed for five years after Bishop Barclay's death in 1881, the bishopric was revived in 1886 on more normal Anglican lines, without Prussian involvement, and with the CMS and LJS both promising financial support. The new bishop, George Francis Popham Blyth, formerly Archdeacon of Rangoon, held office from 1887 to 1914. During his long episcopate and especially in its earlier years, his forthright criticisms of CMS policy led to prolonged controversy, but missionaries came to appreciate his personal kindness. The nomination of his successor, Rennie MacInnes (1914–1931), though accepted by Randall Davidson, caused the Archbishop temporary disquiet on the grounds that MacInnes had been a CMS missionary, and he was being urged 'from all quarters . . . to appoint the best man and to let the Societies adapt themselves to new conditions'.[9] The third Bishop in Jerusalem to serve during the period was George Francis Graham Brown (1932–42). He was no stranger to Palestine; as Principal of Wycliffe Hall, Oxford, he had taken his students there on three long vacation terms. Like his predecessor, he worked hard, amidst many frustrations, to prepare for and plan diocesan development.

There were two other Anglican missionary societies working in Palestine throughout the period. The Jerusalem and the East Mission, founded by Bishop Blyth in support of missionary enterprises that he initiated, and the Church Missions to Jews, which in addition to joint undertakings had sole responsibility for the large English mission hospital; a boarding school, day school and industrial mission classes in Jerusalem; also a hospital and school at Safed in Galilee and work at Jaffa. Christ Church, near the Jaffa Gate in the Old City of Jerusalem, was the CMJ centre of worship for Christian Jews. Christ Church served as the Anglican cathedral until 1898 when the Cathedral Church of St George the Martyr was consecrated. The cathedral was extended in 1912.[10]

The aims of the CMS Palestine mission, started at Bishop Gobat's request in 1851, were defined in 1879 as being 'the spiritual enlightenment of the Mohammedans. The means judged most suitable for that purpose are the preaching of the Word and the establishment of schools for children among the native Christian population.' At that time, and for long afterwards, no public preaching among Muslims was allowed, and there was a rigid press censorship.[11] A medical mission was started at Gaza in 1886 and at Nablus in 1891. Unmarried women missionaries, first sent by the CMS in 1887, greatly increased in numbers after 1899 when the Society took over the work of the Female Education Society at Nazareth, Bethlehem and Shef Amr. Many of these former FES missionaries were still serving in 1910.

In 1905 the Palestine Native Church Council was re-formed to bring together in conference the Arab pastors and full-time church workers with representatives of the constituent pastorate committees. The intention was that the council should hold property, administer funds raised in the pastorates, and should take over responsibility gradually for the schools. Three 'visitors' were appointed by the missionary conference with the right to attend meetings of the council. A CMS grant-in-aid (initially of £1,320 per annum and representing the sum the Society was spending in 1905 in work taken over by the council) was to be steadily reduced over a period of fifty years.

Everything seemed to conspire against the successful working of this genuine attempt at devolution. The control of property, accorded in principle to the council by the CMS, was not recognized by Turkish law; and Bishop Blyth and his successors were not prepared to treat the council as a diocesan body. This somewhat ambiguous status was a frequent cause of tension in the period 1910–42, particularly as retrenchment had the effect of requiring the pastorates to increase the pace of self-support without any tangible increase of self-government.

In 1910 the CMS was at work in four main centres: three west of Jordan – Jerusalem, Nablus and Gaza; and one in Transjordan – Es Salt. There were medical missions at all these places, except Jerusalem. The chief educational institutions maintained by CMS were the Preparandi Institution and Bishop Gobat School in Jerusalem; a girls' boarding-school, with teacher training, at Bethlehem; the orphanage at Nazareth; and some forty-eight elementary schools, of which the largest was at Gaza. There were eleven Arab pastors in association with the Palestine Native Church Council, and the European staff of the mission consisted of five clergy, seven laymen, eleven wives and twenty-

eight other women missionaries. The Christian community associated with the
CMS and the PNCC consisted in 1910 of 2,400 baptized members, of whom 938
were communicants. Comparable figures for 1942 were 3,352 and 1,838 respectively. This was a small but significant growth in church membership in a
predominantly Muslim country. Greater freedom for evangelism under the
British mandate from 1922 onwards was counterbalanced by the effects of Arab
nationalism in reaction to Jewish immigration; and the CMS mission was subject
to internal stresses of unusual intensity and persistence.

Mission and Church, 1910–26

The year 1910 began sadly with the death at Jaffa, on the 4th January, of
Canon T. F. Wolters. He had begun work as a lay agent of the Society in
Smyrna in 1857. In 1874 he married a daughter of Bishop Gobat, and had been
in Palestine since 1876. He was an accomplished linguist, speaking seven
languages with equal fluency, and an untiring evangelist. A fellow-missionary
wrote of him: 'I have never known anyone who lived out the command "Be
ye holy" as he did.'[12]

The last weeks of his life had been clouded by a dispute about the right of the
Palestine Native Church Council to hold property.[13] The British consul in Jerusalem and the German consul in Jaffa had given their opinion that since the
PNCC had no legal status with the Turkish government, it had no mandate
for holding property. Miss F. E. Newton, a missionary who wished to build a
church at Jaffa in memory of her sister, was aware of this situation, and wanted
the church to remain in charge of the CMS Palestine conference until the
parent committee and the church council agreed that the latter should take over
the responsibility and trust.[14]

In December 1911 Bishop Blyth agreed to a *firman* being applied for in the
name of the president of the CMS, but objected to any formal affiliation of the
church at Jaffa to the PNCC since that body was not recognized either 'by the
Turkish Government or himself'. In June 1914 the transfer of the Jaffa site
from Miss Newton's name to that of Sir John Kennaway, President of CMS,
was at last accomplished. Then the war came, and it was not until 1923 that
the new church, St Peter's, Jaffa, was consecrated.

Another dispute which disrupted the harmony of the Palestinian church
concerned the pastor and congregation at Es Salt in Transjordan. The Es
Salt congregation was the largest in the Arab church, numbering over four
hundred members, and it had won fame as the nursery of most of the Arab
pastors serving elsewhere. In June 1910, the Rev. Nicola abu Hattum wrote to
CMS London, protesting against the action of the PNCC in transferring him
from Es Salt to the smaller charge of El Husn, and asking for reinstatement.
The bishop's reading of the situation was that the people of Es Salt were
'warm-hearted but hot-headed' and the congregation was 'split down the

middle' into two parties, each numbering about two hundred. The PNCC and the CMS mission secretary had, in his view, lost authority. He suggested that CMS should deal with the congregation direct from London; that a large church should be built at once; that Pastor Musa, who had been appointed by the PNCC to Es Salt, should be allowed to continue there quietly and that Pastor Hattum should be re-offered the post at El Husn. In March 1911 CMS headquarters received a petition from the 'heads of families' in the Es Salt congregation alleging that a hospital dispenser was the cause of the trouble, and appealing for the removal of the dispenser and the reinstatement of Pastor Hattum. Eventually the advice of the bishop was followed.[15]

It was not only Arab pastors and congregations who appealed to London headquarters against what they felt to be the unsatisfactory local organization of the church and mission. In February 1914 Miss F. E. Newton wrote to say that she would have to resign unless the parent committee intended to make conditions in the mission such 'that a self-respecting woman can work there'. In May 1914 Miss K. M. Strong, another missionary at Haifa, wrote to say that she had decided, with Miss Newton, not to attend the missionary conference; and she resigned in 1915 'on account of the policy pursued in Palestine'. Bishop MacInnes reported that he thought it useless to ask her to reconsider it. The proportion of resignations of missionaries on the grounds of dissatisfaction with the mission policy was unusually high in Palestine in the period before and after the first world war. One reason for this was the large number of single women who were serving as 'honorary' missionaries at their own charges. Having bought their own house and land in Palestine, and having developed their own distinctive line of missionary service, they were unwilling to accept directives from the mission secretary in Jerusalem or the standing committee of the missionary conference.[16] Another less explicit reason was impatience on the part of many women missionaries of male direction in the mission at a time when women of their own class and calibre were fighting for their rights in England. It seems clear, however, that the most pervasive reason for anxiety among missionaries was financial retrenchment, and a suspicion that the CMS might give up its Palestine mission altogether. 'P.C. seem to have dealt with Palestine differently from other Missions,' Mr Sykes, the mission secretary, wrote in June 1910: 'has [it] been realized that since 1907 the Estimates have already been reduced by more than £2,500, and now comes a demand for a further reduction of £700. It seems that the Mission is being hardly and unfairly dealt with.' Others, without Mr Sykes' access to comparative figures, felt this cloud hanging over them. 'As one looks back over the past year,' Miss E. A. Lawford wrote in November 1910, 'one word stands out all through – Retrench. At our conferences, at our work, the one thought has been, How can we reduce things? What must be kept? What must go? How can we economize? What is really our Master's will in this call of retreat?'[17]

By the outbreak of war in 1914 retrenchment and other causes had reduced the CMS missionary force in Palestine within a decade from sixty-eight to fifty-two. The reduction in staff had fallen most heavily on village evangelism and elementary education. Apart from English College, which was under threat of closure, the larger educational and medical institutions were in good heart and extending their influence. Bishop Gobat School, Bethlehem girls' boarding school, and the Nazareth orphanage under Miss Newey from 1910, were sending out a steady stream of teachers and civil servants. The CMS hospitals at Gaza under Canon R. Sterling, and at Nablus under Dr Gaskoin Wright were extending their scope in new buildings dating respectively from 1908 and 1904. The hospital at Jaffa, made over to CMS in the will of Miss C. A. Newton in 1908, earned special mention from Bishop Gwynne after his visit in 1912 as having 'done more to impress Moslems' than any other agency.[18] Dr Brigstocke and Dr Charlotte Purnell at Es Salt were building for the future in Transjordan. The PNCC, under the chairmanship of the Rev. Asad Mansur, was gaining new confidence by the autumn of 1914; but the war years were to test the Arab church severely, and missionaries were forced to leave the country for three and a half years.

Most of them left unwillingly. A telegram from CMS headquarters in August 1914 authorizing missionaries to leave Palestine, was suspected of ulterior motives. Turkey had not yet entered the war, and the acting British consul in Jerusalem had assured the mission secretary that it was not usual for the subjects of belligerents to leave Turkish territory in such circumstances. The standing committee of the mission judged that in sending this telegram 'the finance difficulty probably weighed largely with the Parent Committee'.[19] It decided, nevertheless, that eight women missionaries should leave 'for home or Egypt' at once; though two others, Miss Morris and Miss Smithies, should be allowed to return with Dr Sterling to Gaza.

By the end of October 1914 the parent committee's concern for the missionaries in Palestine was justified. Five of the six missionaries remaining in the country were interned – Dr and Mrs Sterling for a short time at Gaza, and later with Mr and Mrs Webb and Mr Sykes at Jerusalem. It was thought at the time that they were being held as hostages against the bombardment of open ports by the allies; but they were not badly treated and, through the efforts of Dr Glazebrook, the American consul in Jerusalem, they were allowed to leave for Egypt, reaching Alexandria on 28th December, 1914.[20] Miss Lawford refused to leave the Nazareth orphanage at first, and when required to do so she was allowed to remain in the town for about two years before being taken to Damascus.

The Palestine missionaries were a welcome accession of strength to the Egypt mission. Dr Brigstocke took charge of Old Cairo hospital for a time in Dr Lasbrey's absence, and Dr Purnell also helped there. Other women missionaries worked in the girls' schools, or undertook military nursing.

In October 1917 Robert Sterling died in England. He had worked as a doctor at Gaza since 1893 and had built up the hospital almost single-handed, 'the beloved *hakim* who seemed to be everywhere at once'. After his internment and deportation in 1914 he served with the RAMC in the Middle East, returning to Palestine with Allenby's force; but he was invalided home in the summer of 1917. In 1915 he wrote, in retrospect, of the daily routine in Gaza hospital:

> Bible-reading and prayer for all the workers, scholastic as well as medical, at 8.0 a.m. Then come ward visits, prayers and an address with the in-patients, and an address to the out-patients. Next the varied needs of the out-patients are attended to. These number from 150 to 200 daily, and in the busiest season even more come, from far and near. In the afternoon there may be operations to be performed, ward visits to be paid, and again prayers and Bible teaching for the in-patients. In the evenings a well-attended class is held for Mohammedan inquirers.

Somehow, in the midst of his hospital routine, he had found time to build a large girls' elementary school and a boys' school and maintain the oversight of them: 'Hospital and school act and react upon one another. . . . The language of the medical mission is one that is universally understood.'[21]

The war meant hardship for some Palestinian Christians. The pastor at Jaffa, the Rev. Butrus Nasir, and leading church workers, were imprisoned and later exiled, as agents of a British society; and, as the war went on, church services elsewhere were suspended or only held in private. In Jerusalem all the buildings of the mission were taken over; but the efficient, and at times heroic, leadership of Ibrahim Baz inspired confidence in church members. He managed to sustain his claim that St Paul's Church was the property of a national organization and carried on throughout the war with uninterrupted services.[22] He ministered to British prisoners wounded in the battle of Gaza in 1917 with courageous devotion. He was twice courtmartialled as a spy, and was about to be sent into exile when Allenby entered Jerusalem on the 9th December, 1917. He was later made a canon of St George's Cathedral.

Although advance into Galilee only began in September 1918, the war in southern Palestine virtually ended with the capture of Jericho in February. Missionaries began to return in that month, although at first they were only allowed to do so as agents of the Syria and Palestine Relief Fund. This fund had been started by Bishop Rennie MacInnes in Cairo. He had been consecrated as Bishop in Jerusalem, in succession to Bishop Blyth, in 1914 but it was not until the 17th March, 1918 that his enthronement could take place in St George's, Jerusalem.

Although a CMS missionary of long standing, Bishop MacInnes was to find relationships far from easy with some senior missionaries now returning to Palestine, and no easier with the PNCC. Mr Sykes was reluctant to return to Jerusalem without a clear mandate to continue as mission secretary; and for all his long and devoted service, his return was probably a mistake. New leadership and new policies were necessary if there was to be a recovery of harmony and confidence in the Palestine mission. Some re-alignment of policy was attempted in a parent committee statement early in 1918.[23] It re-affirmed the primary aim of the mission as the evangelization of Muslims. It gave priority to restarting the medical work at Gaza and Jaffa, then at Nablus and Salt. It advocated consultation, before a general resumption of pre-war commitments, with the other Anglican societies working in Palestine; and the re-opening of the English College and Bishop Gobat school on a new site, with such increase of staff as would make possible an effective outreach to the educated classes. Mr J. H. Oldham, secretary of the IMC, lent his weight in support of such co-operation, and a sub-committee was appointed at CMS headquarters to look into it.

By 1919 it had become clear, to some informed observers at least, that the war had done nothing to solve the problems of the mission. Temple Gairdner wrote from England on the 18th February, 1919 calling for an immediate inquiry by a qualified deputation into the highly unsatisfactory state of affairs in Palestine.[24] The problem was not wholly one of personal relationships. All mission property had suffered damage, in greater or lesser degree, as the tide of war flowed back and forth over Palestine. Gaza hospital was almost completely destroyed, largely by the bombardment of British forces, in the battle of 1917. To re-establish Arab village schools on anything like the pre-war scale was clearly beyond the capacity of the Society; but those missionaries who had devoted themselves to village evangelism were, understandably, reluctant to abandon this front line. To develop higher education effectively seemed likely also to be beyond the financial capacity of the Society in the immediate post-war years. As hopes of the recovery of the pre-war spread of work dwindled, Mr Sykes resigned in April 1920. Evidently he hoped that his resignation would enforce attention to the distresses of the mission, and he was troubled and hurt when the Society appointed the Rev. Wilson Cash in his place, especially as Mr Cash was to continue to serve also as secretary of the Egypt mission. The appointment of Bishop MacInnes as chairman of the missionary conference was also interpreted as a change of policy. Mr Sykes was not alone in his criticisms. The Rev. S. C. Webb wrote from Jaffa in November 1920 saying that Cash's dual role was taken by many of his fellow-missionaries as evidence that the parent committee regarded the doctrinal differences between the Egypt and Palestine missions as unimportant. 'It is also feared,' he wrote, 'that the doctrinal position of the Mission is threatened by the Bishop.' The Rev. F. Carpenter wrote from Nazareth in December 1920 saying that he would rather resign, with his evangelical views, than attend a conference where there could be no unity. The distress evident in these letters[25] can only be understood in the light of the wider doctrinal controversy in which the Society was involved at this time (see pp. 462–73): but the necessity of a headquarters delegation could hardly be denied, and arrangements were put in hand for the spring of 1921.

The delegation had three members: Major-General E. R. Kenyon, one of the Society's vice-presidents; the Rev. G. T. Manley, headquarters secretary for 'Group III' missions, in which the Palestine mission was included; and Miss E. Baring-Gould. They spent a month in the country, March 17th to April 19th, and Cash was with them for most of their visit. Manley was able to assure the missionary conference that the parent committee had no desire whatever to change the policy of the mission except as naturally demanded by the new conditions arising as a result of the war.[26] Partly because of his known sympathy with theological conservatism, he was able to reassure those who were troubled on doctrinal issues. The delegation also brought some encouragement to the mission by a strong recommendation in its report that, in view of the heavy material losses through the war (estimated at £25,000), any funds raised by the sale of properties in Palestine should not be applied to the general deficit of the Society, but should be utilized in Palestine.

The delegation's report suggested the development of four strategic centres for mission west of the Jordan and it made a special point of the opportunity east of Jordan, 'peopled by roaming Bedouin . . . who constitute a great untouched field of missionary labour'. Though the American Alliance Mission might be ready to increase its responsibilities around the Dead Sea, no other mission was willing or able to enter Transjordan between the rivers Arnon and Yarmuk. The outstanding need in Transjordan, as the delegation saw it, was the recruitment and training of pastors and catechists. More generally, a strengthened relationship between the mission and the PNCC was desirable, and the delegation suggested the appointment of two members of the PNCC to the recently formed United Missionary Council for Palestine.

The delegation's report was received by Group III committee on the 5th July and by the general committee on the 13th July, 1921. It did much to clear the air and to give missionaries confidence that the Palestine mission was not going to be starved of financial support, or taken over. Webb, after a full and free discussion with Cash, had agreed that he could work happily with him, though he still disagreed about the joint secretariat for Egypt and Palestine. Another missionary who had offered her resignation, Miss A. Cooper, withdrew it, and was located to Gaza. The suggestion about strategic centres and areas was implemented, and the mission was divided into five districts, each with a missionary supervisor as follows: Jerusalem, including Gaza (Rev. W. W. Cash); Jaffa (Rev. S. C. Webb); Nazareth (Rev. F. Carpenter); Nablus (Rev. A. J. Mortimore); and Transjordan (Rev. J. L. Macintyre). The supervisors would be entitled to sit in as visitors at all meetings of local pastorate committees, but only three (Cash, Carpenter and Webb) at the PNCC itself.[27]

In November 1921 one of the leading Arab Christians, Dr Habeeb Salim, died at Nablus at the early age of forty-five. The son of a CMS catechist, he had been trained at Bishop Gobat school and the Syrian Protestant College at Beirut. After a period as a teacher at Nazareth and Haifa and as a doctor at Es

Salt hospital, he settled with his family at Nablus. As a leading member of the PNCC he collected £800 in a few weeks to replace a proportion of the support from CMS funds for the work of the council. Dr Salim was a noted preacher and evangelist and at the time of his death he was planning a missionary campaign in Nablus. 'He was the arbiter in many a dispute, the peacemaker in many a quarrel.'[28]

The Arab church was growing in strength and numbers at this time. Communicant figures for 1923 were given as 1,164 compared with 1,005 for 1922, and comparable figures for baptized church members were 2,620 (1923) and 2,507 (1922).

Much of the increased stability and confidence in church and mission was due to Wilson Cash, and it was hard for him as for many others when a medical report on his wife's health in November 1923 made it clear that he must resign from missionary work overseas. But he was soon serving in the Society with much wider responsibilities, first as home secretary, and then from 1926-41 as general secretary.

The educational policy of the mission was not easy to clarify without raising disturbing questions of closure. In December 1923 the CMS headquarters education secretary, Dr Garfield Williams, met three representatives of the mission. There was general agreement that there should be a policy of concentration on two 'higher-class' boarding-schools, the British High School for Girls (soon renamed the Jerusalem Girls' College), and Bishop Gobat school plus two boarding-schools with lower fees – Bethlehem girls' boarding-school and another 'possibly at Nazareth'. English College, which the 1921 delegation had commended for development, was seen in this discussion as the summit of the educational pyramid. Nazareth orphanage, after several years of uncertainty, was kept open; but the threat to a major institution inevitably increased tension between the local governing body of the mission and the parent committee.

In the autumn of 1924 the PNCC, still anxious to get its position clarified as a property-holding body, was asked by the mandatory government to make a declaration about its status. The draft presented for the council's approval included the words 'under the jurisdiction of the Bishop in Jerusalem'. The PNCC was loath to make any declaration which defined its ecclesiastical position in these terms, and it was supported in its reluctance to do so by the three missionary 'visitors' to the council, Carpenter, Webb and Hardman. In September 1924 they wrote a joint letter to CMS headquarters explaining their position. First they outlined the historical background. The training given to the Arab clergy and lay church workers in past days at Bishop Gobat school and elsewhere was 'of a strong, constructive *Protestant* nature'; and before the war, as the basis of this training, there had grown up 'an unrecognized indigenous Protestant Episcopal *Church of Palestine* for which episcopal functions were performed by the Anglican Bishop in Jerusalem'. Since the war, however, the bishop had made it his object to undertake all the duties of a bishop of the diocese, and to co-ordinate its work, including that of the congregations connected with the CMS. The church council had been glad to receive Bishop MacInnes personally at its meetings and at other times, and his advice and co-operation had been welcomed; but the council desired to maintain relations with the bishopric similar to those of pre-war days.

The letter went on to summarize what, in the opinion of the three visitors, were the present aims and aspirations of 'the members of the Church connected with the CMS in Palestine'. These were: (*a*) to remain strict evangelicals, conforming to the *present* Prayer Book and the sacraments of the church; (*b*) to remain independent of the bishop, apart from such legal, ecclesiastical and ceremonial relations as the administering of confirmation and ordination, and representing them in case of need in approaching the government and other authorities; (*c*) to obtain recognition by the government as a legal entity, capable of administering property, trusts, etc.; (*d*) to be quite independent and self-controlled with regard to the holding and free administration of all property connected with the church; (*e*) to be assured that no bishop has the right to call upon them to make any alterations in the form of their services; no right to impose upon them, as of necessity, any revised edition of the Prayer Book, or to demand any change in the ritual in any church, in its furniture, in the robes of the clergy, in times of services (e.g. Evening Communion) or to insist on the appointment of one of his nominees as pastor of one of their churches; (*f*) to be assured of the right of inter-communion and of interchange of pulpits without reference to the bishop.

The questions raised by this letter were at once delicate and critical. Its writers were convinced that a declaration without such safeguards as these written into it would, if persevered with, lead to a break-away Protestant church in Palestine. They pressed for a recognition by the parent committee of the fact that 'the Church of England form of Government (as distinct from the form of Service) is unacceptable to the Protestant Christians of this country'.[29] The CMS was not, of course, committed to a policy of diocesanization irrespective of local conditions; but as a society within the Anglican Communion it could hardly encourage the kind of *imperium in imperio* which the PNCC proposed, and which its missionary 'visitors' formulated.

The Africa committee (formerly Group III committee) of CMS meeting on the 12th November, 1924 requested the bishop and the local governing body 'to use the whole of their influence' to induce the Palestine Native Church Council to approve the draft declaration at the time of the first council meeting in 1925, or before. It also recommended that the local governing body be authorized to point out that the church properties now held by the Society are held in trust for congregations of the Church of England, and 'that they cannot recognize as such any which do not acknowledge the ecclesiastical authority of the Bishop'. Further, and in amelioration, it affirmed the committee's agreement with the 'Fundamental Provision', recently adopted in the constitution of the diocese of Mombasa concerning the primacy of Holy Scripture, and disclaiming any intention to alter any of the existing standards of faith and doctrine of the Church of England, and with the expressed desire for such larger church unity as was consistent with these conditions.[30]

The PNCC was not in a frame of mind to accept directions from London as to what they should do in the vital matter of their church development, and Hardman continued to act as interpreter of the case with the conviction of one who was wholly in sympathy with it. 'Up to 1924,' he wrote, 'the Council had been taught to look forward to . . . independence; now they are told they must consent to an Autocracy . . . which has never existed before.'[31] On the 19th February, 1925 Bishop MacInnes met a delegation from the council and the whole question of their relationship was discussed, but 'without much positive result'; but two months later the council, after lengthy discussion, and with a letter from the visitors before it pointing out the serious results that would follow from a refusal to acknowledge the jurisdiction of the bishop, at last approved a draft letter which brought the dispute to an end.[32]

A headquarters delegation which visited Palestine in 1926 was not primarily concerned with this diocesan issue, but a comment from its report is relevant: 'Ultimately we think complete diocesanization of the work must come. For the present we should like to see a common diocesan policy in which CMS work would form an essential part.'[33] Some progress along these lines was made during the four remaining years of Bishop MacInnes' episcopate and his successor, Bishop Graham Brown, sought to carry further the development of normal diocesan structures in spite of opposition from the PNCC.

By 1942 the CMS grant to the PNCC had been reduced in twenty-five years from £1,500 per annum to £100; evidence, as Cash observed, of the church's growth in responsible self-support. In 1945 the Archbishop of Canterbury approved 'Regulations for the Palestinian Arab Evangelical Episcopal Community' which fell short of the council's highest hopes but at last assured the identity for which it had so long contended.

The immediate grounds for the appointment of the 1926 headquarters delegation was another crisis of confidence between the local governing body and the parent committee. Dr R. G. Sterling had followed his father at Gaza hospital, after war service, in 1919. He had built a new hospital amid the ruins of the old one almost single-handed.[34] Complaints had been laid against him in connection with his work at the hospital which the local governing body took very seriously. In March 1926 the CMS Africa committee decided, on the strength of Dr Sterling's answers to these charges, that he should return to Gaza. Hardman and Carpenter, as appointed representatives of the LGB, sought to alter the mind of the Africa committee but were unable to do so. In July 1926 the missionary conference, with Bishop MacInnes in the chair, resolved that the retirement of Dr Sterling would be to the best interest of the work and that the other missionary chiefly concerned, Miss A. Cooper, should be retained in the mission. Mr Hardman telegraphed to London on the 17th July, 1926 that eleven missionaries out of probation and six in probation seriously contemplated resignation unless this resolution was accepted. It is doubtful, on the evidence obtained from missionaries later, whether anything like that number would have resigned,[35] but there was clearly a great deal of misunderstanding to be cleared up, and the general secretary (Mr Cash) and the medical secretary (Dr J. H. Cook) were appointed by the parent committee as a delegation to visit Palestine. They spent most of October seeing missionaries individually, and visiting every station. They recommended a reduction in the number of committees appointed by the missionary conference, annual retirement of a proportion of the members of such committees as remained, and voting powers on them for missionaries still in probation. The existing probation committee should be abolished and instead the secretary of the mission should form a small *ad hoc* group, to report on each probationer, consisting of those who knew him or her best. They reaffirmed the right of any missionary with a grievance to appeal to the parent committee. They proposed that Dr Sterling should spend a year in Jerusalem studying Arabic and Islamics before returning to Gaza, and that Miss Cooper should be located to Gaza; and that Mr Hardman, who had been offered work in Uganda, should remain as secretary for two months in order to hand over to the Rev. F. S. Cragg, who had been appointed from the headquarters staff as secretary in his place.

On more general questions, the delegation recommended closer co-operation with other societies working in the same region, both Anglican and non-Anglican, more particularly with the Egypt mission of the CMS and especially so in the field of literature for Muslims. They welcomed a scheme to set up a School of Languages and Islamics in Jerusalem, and strongly recommended that if Mr E. F. F. Bishop of English College were to be invited to be its director, the parent committee should agree to his appointment. In the educational field the delegation was clear that the society could no longer finance a widespread system of primary schools, and the Society should abandon any attempt to compete or keep pace with the government programme at this level. In Transjordan, however, where government provision of primary education had developed little, there was still an opening for mission primary schools. In the field of secondary education Bishop Gobat school had a major role, and English College and the girls' high school should be retained as co-operative institutions with a strong CMS representation. Nazareth orphanage had a new importance since the closing of Bethlehem girls' school in 1925, and it should be retained.

Turning to medical mission, the delegation raised the question whether CMS was justified in maintaining so many hospitals and a large medical missionary staff in so small a country. Two Syrian doctors had run the hospital at Jaffa and Gaza for many months most competently; and Es Salt hospital might well be run by a non-European doctor with supervision from Amman.

The delegation recommended that the present work at Ramallah, Lydd, Ramleh, Shefr Amr and Haifa should cease to be a charge on the Society's funds. In general an effort should be made to reduce considerably the heavy expenditure incurred by the Palestine mission. The delegation's report concluded with this comment: 'We believe that the future of the Palestine Mission lies very largely in the hands of the new Secretary.'

Few mission secretaries can have had so heavy a responsibility laid upon them as F. S. Cragg when he arrived in Jerusalem in the autumn of 1926. His health broke down after two-and-a-half years, and he was forced to return to England. But he did much in that time to implement the policies prepared in the delegation's report, and he prepared the way for a period of constructive and harmonious development under his successor, Mrs MacInnes.

In an appendix to the joint delegation report, Dr Cook commented in turn on all the CMS hospitals he had visited in Palestine. He described the hospital at Es Salt (26 beds) as 'an oasis of cleanliness and order' and Gaza hospital as the best-equipped of the CMS group, but he thought it was larger than was necessary for present needs, as a government hospital had been built in Gaza. Hebron hospital with 18 beds, had recently been over-crowded. The work of Dr A. G. Alexander was greatly appreciated in the Hebron district.[36]

A memorandum of 1925[37] gave the current cost of the mission to the Society as £17,449. This figure has some significance for the history of the mission in the remainder of the period since repeated efforts were made to bring the total cost down to £10,000.

New Ventures and Reconstruction, 1926-32

The later 1920s saw a number of new initiatives. The Rev. Eric Bishop started a Brotherhood for converts from Islam in the Jerusalem diocese in 1926; Miss B. I. Hassall opened the Palestine Enquirers Home at Kefr Yasif, a village five miles from Acca.[38] Its purpose was to give employment to Muslim inquirers, 'chiefly men and lads', on a small poultry farm and in industrial work such as glass-polishing. Missionaries provided £400 from their own pockets for the initial cost of this venture. In 1928 the most significant of these new enterprises, the Newman School of Missions, began its valuable service under Eric Bishop's direction as 'a co-operative venture in the education of missionaries'.

In October 1927, at Shefr Amr, a considerable group of Muslim inquirers – members of some forty families – began to join the Christians in worship. A catechist from Nablus and two women missionaries helped some of the group to prepare for baptism. Nothing on a comparable scale happened elsewhere, but the Shefr Amr incident put new heart into missionaries in many other parts of the country.

In 1929 pressure of retrenchment was once again causing anxiety. The

missionary conference in April viewed 'with the gravest concern' the unwilling-
ness of the parent committee to sanction the 'essential extension' of Bishop
Gobat school.[39] In July 1929, S. C. Webb, acting secretary of the mission, and
Eric Bishop wrote to the Africa secretary protesting that the closing of Bishop
Gobat school and the discontinuance of primary education work was not the
best way of saving £1,270 per annum. They suggested that for the year 1930,
instead of a reduction in the grants made annually to the Palestine Native
Church Council, the council should be asked to take over financial responsibility
for pastoral work in Amman and El Husn. Bishop MacInnes joined with the
director of education in support of Bishop Gobat school, and in November
1929 the parent committee decided that the school should remain open, but
that Jerusalem Men's College (English College) should close after the summer of
1930. The Rev. A. C. MacInnes, son of the bishop and a CMS missionary in
Transjordan, was appointed principal of Bishop Gobat school.

Inevitably, with the world slump at its worst, the Palestine mission was asked
to take its share of further general cuts in grants. Mr Bishop, writing in September 1931, pointed out how near to the bone these repeated cuts were getting.
Since 1925 the total grants to the mission had been reduced by something like
£6,000 roughly £1,000 in each year. 'Even if we are to become a medical mission
chiefly,' he wrote, 'we must do something more than just carry on.'

In the autumn of 1931 a mission policy sub-committee made an interim
report in favour of greater concentration, in view of reduced missionary personnel, on definite centres of work and influence. It suggested concentration on the
districts of Samaria, Transjordan, and the Maritime Plain with Nablus, Es Salt
and Gaza (or Jaffa) as centres for Muslim contacts. Jaffa would probably have
to be abandoned. The work in Jerusalem would concentrate more and more on
leadership-training, with Bishop Gobat school as the centre for ordinands,
teachers and other posts requiring higher education – possibly serving a wider
area than Palestine.[40]

On Christmas Eve 1931 Bishop Rennie MacInnes died. It was in his rooms
at Trinity, Cambridge that the Student Volunteer Missionary Union started
in 1892, and he was one of the seventy undergraduates in Cambridge who
offered to CMS in that year. He was CMS mission secretary in Cairo for twelve
years before his consecration in 1914; he had brought to his difficult task as
Bishop in Jerusalem a wide knowledge of the Middle East and the Muslim
world, and a sympathetic understanding of the ancient Christian churches. 'He
was neat and dapper and adored railway time-tables and all sorts of small
calculations and averages. . . . He became master of a very simple rather limited
but quite practical and effective Arabic style.'[41] He inherited some almost
intractable problems in group relationships in the mission and Arabic church,
but he worked hard for better understanding, and added much to the dignity
and effectiveness of his office in an increasingly troubled area of the Middle
East. It was a happy thing that within a year of his death his widow, Mrs J.

MacInnes, was established in office as secretary of the Palestine mission with their son giving valuable service as principal of Bishop Gobat school. Mrs MacInnes was not able to take over at once and, to the great relief of Mr Bishop and others, Canon S. C. Webb returned for a spell as temporary secretary during the summer of 1932: but his health broke down, and he finally retired after thirty years of able and faithful service in Palestine.

Years of Peaceful Re-assessment, 1932–42

Bishop MacInnes' successor, Francis Graham Brown, arrived in Jerusalem in the autumn of 1932. He had been a member of the commission which opened the way to 'full communion' between the Church of England and the Old Catholic Church, and an Old Catholic bishop took part in his consecration. In the ten years of his episcopate he gave much of his time and energy to the improvement of education in Palestine, especially in building up St Luke's School, Haifa, and in founding Bishop's School, Amman. Shortly after Bishop MacInnes' death, and in relation to the appointment of his successor, Dr Cash wrote to the Archbishop of Canterbury, outlining the policy and commitment of the Society in Palestine.

> There is in being [he wrote] a Native Church that is spiritual, evangelical and conservative. It has seven ordained clergymen, all Palestinians, 2,715 adherents and 1,220 communicants. During the last ten years . . . there have been practically no transfers from the Greek Church to the Anglican Native Church of the country. This little Church is probably the best educated church in the country. Its members are in many senior Government departments.

He mentioned 'some quite outstanding instances of conversion from Islam, notably in the application for baptism of almost all the Moslem men of one village in Galilee' and emphasized 'the great opportunity for Moslem evangelism under the British Mandate and with liberty of conscience now a reality'. There were, he said, forty CMS missionaries in the country, in occupation of sixteen centres. The Society was responsible for thirteen schools and four hospitals. The cost of the mission for the year 1930–31 was £13,272. Cash concluded his letter: 'Our policy still remains as in Dr MacInnes' time, and we wish our Mission to be a Mission of the Diocese, in no way separated from Diocesan policy.'[42]

In the decade before the second world war the Palestine mission, with a much reduced staff, discovered a new purpose and effectiveness and the unhappiness and dissensions of earlier years were largely forgotten. With Mrs MacInnes as secretary of the mission, with the Rev. Eric Bishop now among the senior missionaries, and the Rev. Donald Blackburn (from 1934) taking hold of the situation in Transjordan, there was a greater readiness to treat retrenchment not as an affront but as a challenge to new initiatives and good planning. Bishop

Graham Brown made clear his conviction that the CMS was still needed in Palestine, especially in the provision of good secondary education.[43] In 1933 he appointed the Rev. Asad Mansur to the canonry of St George's, Jerusalem, left vacant by the departure of Canon Webb. Dr Charlotte Purnell received an OBE in the New Year Honours in the same year for her outstanding services to medicine.

In 1934 extensions to Bishop Gobat school were put in hand without cost to CMS. When Es Salt hospital was faced with the likelihood of closing down in 1934 the bishop stayed execution by offering to administer it for a year as a diocesan responsibility. In November 1934 the medical committee in London approved its continuance as a CMS institution with local support and not as a charge on MMA funds.[44]

Voluntary night-schools for the illiterate were being organized by members of Jaffa church. The congregations associated with the PNCC at Jaffa, Jerusalem and Haifa were not only self-supporting, but helping the poorer pastorates. The Jerusalem girls' college, under Miss Winifred Coate, was undertaking teacher-training at a high level of efficiency, and the training of village evangelists was being developed in connection with Nazareth orphanage.

In spite of greater freedom and resourcefulness in the evangelization of Muslims, and a fuller share in evangelism on the part of the Palestinian Arab church, the response was almost as cautious as in the days before religious liberty. 'It still requires a brave man,' said Dr Gaskoin Wright, 'to turn his back on Islam and become a Christian.' Converts still faced the probability of expulsion from the family circle, loss of employment and friends. The problems of mixed motives in accepting baptism, and lapses after baptism, remained.[45]

On a visit in 1937 the CMS Africa secretary, the Rev. H. D. Hooper, was glad to note the close unity of administration between the diocese and the CMS mission in Transjordan, but he noted with regret the effect of withdrawal of CMS grants for elementary schools ('it was difficult to keep even Salt going') and the lack of teaching opportunity for many pupils coming out of Nazareth orphanage. Mr Hooper paid tribute to the determination and initiative of women missionaries who 'with trifling encouragement have built up communities and institutions which are playing an active and important part in the destinies of the country'.[46]

By 1936 the Arab-Jewish political conflict was being transposed into guerilla warfare. The village clinics of Nablus hospital had to be closed for a time. Bishop Gobat school, still growing, was the only school in Jerusalem which did not close in the summer term. Only Transjordan, which had remained a wholly Arab state, remained comparatively peaceful. Amman was growing rapidly as the seat of government and centre of commerce, and under the leadership of the Rev. Donald Blackburn, the CMS mission was finding new opportunities of witness and service. The Transjordan government, which had begun to concern itself more actively with education, welcomed the contribution the CMS was able to make in this field.

Blackburn, writing early in 1942,[47] noted the need for 'special training and experience in knowledge of Arabic and of Moslem thought and belief' if direct evangelism was to be maintained. 'Very few missionaries of any society,' he said, 'are yet qualified for this work, and this is one of the main reasons for lack of outward success in the Moslem world.' The Newman School of Missions was making a brave attempt to meet this need, and the Society in 1942, after decades of adversity and difficulty, was still in service in Palestine 'as the agent of the Anglican Church for the express purpose of Moslem evangelization'.[48]

NOTES

1. Norman Bentwich, *Palestine*, Benn, 1934, p. 24.

2. Elizabeth Monroe, *Britain's Moment in the Middle East, 1914–1956*, Chatto & Windus, 1963, p. 43.

3. G. E. Kirk, *A Short History of the Middle East*, Methuen, 6th ed., 1961, p. 131n.

4. H. D. Hooper, *Report of a Visit to CMS Missions in East Africa, the Sudan, Egypt and Palestine, 1937–8*, CMS, 1938, pp. 65, 66.

5. International Missionary Council, *Tambaram Series*, Vol. VI, OUP, 1939, pp. 138–143.

6. G/Y/P2, Cash to Archbishop of Canterbury, 14th January, 1932.

7. *CMR*, March 1918, G. T. Manley, 'Palestine, Past, Present and Future', p. 122.

8. Report of Delegation to Palestine, 1921 (CMS Archives).

9. G/AM6, notes of interview with the Archbishop of Canterbury, 13th July, 1914.

10. *Handbook of the Anglican Bishopric in Jerusalem and the East*, Jerusalem, 1941, p. 28.

11. H. G. Harding, *Land of Promise*, CMS, 1919, pp. 84, 85.

12. *CMR*, April 1910, p. 232.

13. G3/P/P6, 1901/155.

14. P6, 1910/71; 1911/88, 200; 1914/18, 93.

15. P6, 1910/83; 1911/32.

16. P6, 1910/90 (Miss E. E. Watney); 1912/85 (Miss I. J. Morphew).

17. Annual Letters 1910, CMS, p. 259.

18. P6, 1913/64.

19. P6, 1914/135.

20. P6, 1914/184.

21. *C M Gleaner*, 1915, pp. 69ff. R. Sterling, 'Locked Doors and a Golden Key'.

22. Harding, op. cit., p. 78.

23. P6, 1918/5.

24. P6, 1919/19.

25. P7, 1920/89, 123.

26. P7, 1921/35.

27. P7, 1921/62, 63; 1921/113; 1921/123.

28. *CMR*, March 1922, pp. 64–6.

29. P7, 1924/131.

30. P7, 1924/xliv.

31. P7, 1924/179.

32. P7, 1925/21, 45.

33. P7, 1926/97, Report of the Palestine Delegation 1926.

34. *CMO*, October 1923, pp. 199ff., R. G. Sterling, 'The Light of Gaza'.
35. P7, 1926/97, Delegation Report.
36. ibid., Appendix.
37. P7, 1925, Hardman, 'Memo on CMS Work in Palestine'.
38. *CMO*, February 1928, pp. 30, 31, B. I. Hassall, 'The Palestine Inquirers' Home'.
39. P8, 1929/34.
40. P8, 1931/128.
41. 'In Memoriam', Bible Lands, April 1932.
42. G/Y/P7, Cash to Archbishop of Canterbury, 14th January, 1932.
43. P8, 1933/19.
44. P8, 1934/56.
45. S. A. Morrison, *The Way of Partnership*, CMS, 1936, pp. 23, 24.
46. Hooper, op. cit., p. 69.
47. *CMO*, February 1942, D. Blackburn, 'A Quiet Spot in the Near East'.
48. G/Y/P/7, Warren to Archbishop of Canterbury, 7th January, 1943.

Turkish Arabia

The CMS Turkish Arabia mission began in 1883 and was constituted a separate mission of the Society in 1898. It was directed initially towards Muslims of the Shi'a sect who made pilgrimage in large numbers to the shrine of Hosein at Kerbela, eighty miles south-west of Baghdad, and to other holy places in the neighbourhood. A hospital was started in a private house in Baghdad in 1896 and a second centre was opened at Mosul, 220 miles north of Baghdad, in 1901. Communication between the two CMS stations was difficult. Mosul was a three days' boat-journey on the Euphrates from Baghdad.

In spite of faithful work by a small company of missionaries – twelve in the last full year of operation, 1913–14 – the Turkish Arabia mission was unable to achieve the strength and stability needed to justify its permanent resumption after the first world war. The expectation that members of the Shi'a sect would prove more open to the Christian gospel than Sunnite Muslims proved to have little foundation. There was some readiness to receive Christian literature, but converts were few. The small hospital at Mosul was not welcomed by the leaders of the ancient Christian churches, and the building of a larger hospital at Baghdad was halted by the outbreak of the war in 1914. Two CMS missionary doctors, F. Johnson and G. W. Stanley, were interned for several weeks in the British Residency in Baghdad. Most of the missionaries from Turkish Arabia worked in the CMS Egypt mission during the war years. Three of them, Dr E. E. Lavy, Miss E. E. Martin, and Dr Stanley, returned to Baghdad for a short time on relief work after the war; but a sub-committee at the Society's headquarters, appointed in 1919 to consider the future of the Turkish Arabia mission, reported in favour of withdrawal. The home and foreign committee accepted this recommendation on the 11th November, 1919. It named among the causes for this decision: the dislocation caused by the war; the reduction of the staff of the mission to five, all of whom were willing to accept work elsewhere in the Arabic speaking area; the Society's financial position; and the widespread existence of the opinion that a policy of concentration was called for in the interests of efficiency. The resolution gave thanks to God 'for the zeal and high courage of all who had faithfully laboured' in the Turkish Arabia mission. Among them Dr Frederick Johnson deserves special mention. After thirteen years in the CMS Palestine mission, mostly at Kerak, he went to Baghdad in 1908. As secretary of the mission for most of its remaining years he made strenuous efforts to build up its staff and institutions to a level of efficiency. He pleaded for the appointment by the parent committee of 'a senior Missionary to Baghdad of the type of the late Bishop Valpy French, Bishop Stuart, or Rev. H. McNeile', who would serve for a limited term and give effective direction to the mission.[1] After the first world war he recognized the force of the arguments for withdrawal of the CMS, but hoped that the Wesleyan Methodist Missionary Society would take over its plant and pastoral responsibilities.

An approach was made both to the WMMS and the Church Mission to Jews to take over from CMS, but neither society felt able to do so. In December 1921 Johnson wrote urging the early disposal of the properties at Baghdad and Mosul in view of falling prices.[2] In June 1924 the parent committee approved the sale of the Baghdad property to an interdenominational body, the Joint Committee for the United Mission in Mesopotamia; but negotiations broke down and it was sold in 1925 to the YMCA for £4,000. It was not until 1934 that the Mosul property was sold for a nominal sum of £100.[3]

NOTES

1. G2/TA/P, 1910/38.
2. TA/P, 1922/12.
3. Information supplied by the Financial and Administrative Secretary of CMS, 1st February, 1966.

Iran

The Country

The country was commonly known outside its borders as *Persia*, a name linguistically related to the present southern province of Fars. In March 1935 its government requested foreign missions (religious and otherwise) to use in future the indigenous name of *Iran* – a usage which the Anglican Church in Persia and the CMS Persia mission adopted at once.[1] This usage is followed here except that the adjective 'Persian' is usually preferred to 'Iranian'.[2]

Geography and climate have never been regarded by the CMS as decisive factors in the choice of an area of mission – witness the heroic early days in West Africa and elsewhere – but the forbidding geography of Iran has inevitably affected to some extent the character and development of CMS work. Equal in area to Spain, France and Germany combined, Iran had a population of approximately ten millions in 1910 rising to fifteen millions by 1940. With a rainfall of only five inches a year in Isfahan and Kerman, the country can be fairly described as arid and is still sparsely populated. Apart from the narrow Caspian littoral in the north, Iran is, as one missionary said, 'as dry as a chip' – seventy per cent desert and steppe, with only seven per cent of its area fit for agriculture. It consists in the main of a vast plateau, 4,000 to 5,000 feet high, strewn with mountains, some of them eroded or exploded into startling shapes. Two more continuous mountain ranges provide a higher rim to the plateau – the Elburz to north and north-east of Tehran and the Zagros along the country's western border; while two huge, scarcely differentiated deserts, the Dasht-i-Kavir and the Dasht-i-Lut stretch out south-east and south of Tehran for many hundreds of miles, with here and there great salt plugs reminiscent of a lunar landscape.

By an inter-mission agreement of 1895 CMS activity was restricted to the south of the country, which Anglo-Russian agreements of 1907 and 1942 marked out as an area of British 'influence'. The south of Iran is even more sparsely populated than the north, apart from the oil-fields of Khuzistan near the Persian Gulf which, from the 1920s onwards, became a magnet for the young from all parts of Iran. Elsewhere in the south life changed little, at least for the peasantry. They continued to live in sparsely scattered villages, usually on the slopes of mountain valleys, at scarcely above subsistence level. Social change came more rapidly to urban areas, but even so the larger inland towns of the south – Isfahan (the ancient capital); Kerman (420 miles south-east of Isfahan); Yezd (roughly half-way between them), and Shiraz (about 300 miles due south of Isfahan) – remained isolated from each other.

These four towns of the south are important for our story since each of them had become the centre of a CMS mission by 1900. The distance of these towns from each other is also significant for the story. Caravanning in the ancient manner, with panniered camels and donkeys, Yezd was reckoned as ten days out, and Kerman as three weeks out from Isfahan, the mission headquarters. Motor transport and somewhat better roads did something to reduce this isolation from the mid-1920s, but communication was still slow and difficult, and missionaries in Yezd, Kerman and Shiraz were apt to feel that decisions were being made over their heads at the headquarters of the diocese and mission in Isfahan.

Its Peoples

This inhospitable land houses a people who are for the most part hospitable, lively, intelligent, conscious heirs of a national tradition far older than the Islamic-Arab culture which swept across Iran in the first wave of Arab advance in the seventh century AD. Geography, which made centralized government difficult to maintain over the centuries, has also hindered the assimilation of other races – Turkic, Arab, Mongol, Kurd, Pathan, Baluch – with the basic Indo-European stock.[3] Resilient and self-sufficient nomadic tribes continued to roam the country during the period 1910–42. Notable among these are the Bakhtiari, ranging close to Isfahan in the summer and moving south to Khuzistan in the winter; the Kurds in the Zagros mountain area; and the Qashqais (Kashgais) in the province of Fars. Strenuous efforts to settle these nomads in agriculture in the 1920s and 1930s met with little success. The attractions of the oil industry show signs of succeeding where the government failed. Apart from the nomads, Iran has a number of ethnic-religious minority groups – Armenians, Jews, and Assyrians – each numbering tens of thousands.

Islam and Bahaism

Throughout the period 1910–42, in spite of considerable social and cultural change, Iran remained an Islamic state with ninety per cent of its people nominally Muslim. The dominant form of Islam is the 'heretical' Shi'a rather than the orthodox Sunni, and Islamic mysticism (Sufism) has developed more fully in Iran than elsewhere in the Muslim world. The Shi'a maintain that Muhammad's cousin and son-in-law was the true successor of the prophet and that the first three Sunnite caliphs were usurpers. Ali's sons, Hassan and Hussain, are commemorated as martyrs, and Shi'a Islam has its own places of pilgrimage in Iraq. The CMS Turkish Arabia mission was started in 1883 to bring the gospel to Shi'ite pilgrims there. There are good grounds for relating this Persian independence within Islam to its pre-Arabic national culture and religious traditions.

For example Zoroastrianism, the ancient dualistic religion of Iran dating from the sixth century BC, is more than a quaint survival from the past. It is true that the Zoroastrians, or Parsees, form only a tiny religious minority in present-day Iran: but the ancient religion still lives on beneath the surface, and its cultus still provides some of the elements of popular religion among nominal Muslims. Again, many of the great poets of Iran, notably Hafiz, pay no more than lip-service to Islam. When they hymn the beauties of their own land and its cities, and when they lament with scarcely-veiled scepticism the meaninglessness of life and the transience of all things mortal, they provide a powerful counter-weight to the passionate simplicity of Muslim faith. It is also true, though their value in relation to Christian evangelism was sometimes over-estimated, that the martyr-cults in Shi'ite Islam provide for Iran something akin to the religious patriotism which arose in Judaism after the Maccabean revolt. It would be wrong to infer, however, that a Shi'a-Islamic state is by nature more tolerant towards religious minorities and more susceptible to the proclamation of the Christian gospel than a Sunni-Islamic state. 'In its normal form it is just as oppressive towards non-Muslims. There are the same doctrines of the subordination of *Dhimmis* ("protected peoples" of other religions) and of the right to slay an apostate out of hand'; and while Iran, during the reign of Reza Khan Pahlavi (1925–41), moved a long way towards freedom of religion, 'the forces of Islam retain more of their inherited influence' than in Turkey.[4] It is true that in his reign Christianity, Judaism and Zoroastrianism received official recognition, and new legal codes virtually replaced the Islamic *Sharia* law; but Islamic sentiment was still conveniently at hand in support of government measures against foreign influence; and while the Christian convert might retain property and civil rights, he was still marked out as an apostate and liable to persecution in one form or another.

A missionary observer in 1938 summed up the situation as 'hopeful, at least for the indigenous church. The law against religious propaganda places serious restrictions upon evangelism and curtails the activities of foreign missions. A turn in the political wheel may at any time change the situation for better or for worse.'[5] At the end of Shah Reza's reign, in the years immediately before his abdication in 1941, it was changing for the worse; but by then, in the area of CMS mission, an indigenous, mainly convert church was beginning to grow, and it continues to give courageous witness under Persian leadership.

Bahaism appeared to some missionaries in the 1920s as a revolt against the exclusiveness of Islam which might produce more favourable conditions for the proclamation of the Christian gospel in Iran.[6] It began in the mid-nineteenth century when Mirza Ali Muhammed, a native of Shiraz, won many followers by proclaiming a form of syncretism which sought to draw together the best qualities from the great world religions and which laid stress on universal peace and tolerance. He proclaimed himself the *Bab* (i.e. the 'Door') between flesh and spirit, and his followers were known as Babists. He was executed at Tabriz in 1850, and shortly afterwards, following a plot against the Shah's life, thousands of his followers were massacred. Persecution led, as so often, to further development; but it also provoked divisions in the movement. The leader of one section, Mirza Hussein Ali, took the title of ullah Baha' ('Divine Splendour') from which the name Bahaism is derived. Mysticism, combined with current liberal ideas, provided the ingredients of a universal religion untrammelled by liturgical rites or any form of priesthood, and Bahais were encouraged to 'practise deceit' and to take cover in other religious groups.

Against the background of centuries of Islamic rigidity, it is not surprising that a new teaching emphasizing the brotherhood of men and high moral standards should be looked at hopefully by missionaries as a potential ally. By the early 1930s, however, the disruptive effect of Bahaism on tiny Christian congregations of former Muslims was more evident. One missionary, G. J. Rogers, described the movement as 'the wolf in sheep's clothing'.[7] Another, J. R. Richards, made himself a master of the Bahai doctrines and proved so successful in refuting them that Bahai teachers were forbidden any converse with him. Bahaism has spread widely beyond the borders of Iran but its effective use of literature[8] and its pioneer work in the education of girls remained a challenge to the Christian church in the country of its origin. Bahai infiltration was felt to be so serious a danger locally that the church pastorate committee at Yezd in 1936 specifically excluded Bahais from joining enquirers' classes.

In the age of Western imperialism Iran retained independence as a buffer state between Russia and British India. Twice in the present century, however, in 1907 and 1942, Anglo-Russian agreements divided the country, north and south, into 'spheres of influence' and although respect for its territorial integrity, sovereignty and political independence was written into these treaties, in both world wars there was virtual occupation of Iran as a counter measure to German influence and infiltration.

In 1905 a revolution, organized by mullahs and merchants with pan-Islamic aspirations, led to the granting of a constitution. In 1909 Shah Mohammed Ali was expelled and succeeded by Sultan Ahmad (1909–25), a child at the time of his succession. Shortly afterwards, in 1911, Russia invaded the country from the north in support of the exiled Shah; but, after a brief period of German ascendancy in 1915–16, Britain became the dominant influence in Iran at the end of the first world war. Lord Curzon, then British Foreign Secretary, concluding that the country was 'incurably feeble and unable to stand by herself', sponsored in 1919 an Anglo-Persian Agreement which placed the country firmly under British tutelage, with British civil and military advisers and a £2,000,000 loan. The treaty was never ratified by the Persian parliament (Majlis) and a nationalist reaction swept a new ruler into power who succeeded, where others had failed, in bringing dignity, unity and a large measure of social reform to the nation.

Reza Khan Pahlavi deserves to be remembered as one of the great men of his times, and as 'one of the great figures of all Persian history'.[9] From the day, 21st February, 1921, when, an almost unknown army major, he led three thousand Persian Cossacks into Tehran to overthrow an already toppling government, until the last clouded year or so of his reign, he showed a fine sense of political timing, a deeply-based patriotism, and a sensitivity to constitutional procedures. But he was certainly ruthless. His father and grandfather were officers in the old Persian army, and Reza Khan rose through the ranks of the Persian Cossack Brigade to a position of leadership at a critical time for his country. The new Russia was beginning to recover initiative in international affairs and was showing a particular and unwelcome interest in Persia's future. £130,000 of the £2,000,000 British loan had been paid over and had disappeared into the pockets of the old ruling caste.

One of Reza Khan's first acts after investing Tehran was to denounce the Curzon Agreement, and his dealings with communist Russia were to prove equally firm. By building up an efficient army and gendarmerie he put an end to internal strife and brigandage, and gave his country a taste of unity and tranquillity such as it had not known since the golden age of Shah Abbas (1586–1628). By a series of astute economic moves he provided within this framework a financial stability which made possible a vast programme of road and rail construction, elementary and higher education, and social reform which transformed Iran into a modern state. Reza Shah could be ruthless, particularly towards the mullahs* who had exercised an almost druidical control of the mores of the people; but for the most part he acted through parliament, with moderation, and without those engineered crises which were the familiar stock-in-trade of Western dictators in the same period. Missionaries were quick to appreciate his qualities, although some at least of the new legislation bore heavily upon their work, as will be seen. 'I am full of admiration,' the bishop wrote, 'at the way in which these great social reforms have been introduced . . . [the Shah] has been able to carry the vast majority of his people with him.'[10]

Miss V. Sackville-West was present at his coronation in 1926, and she found Reza Shah's appearance alarming – 'six foot three in height, with a sullen

---

* The term *mullah* or *mulla* usually describes the 'parochial clergy', so to speak, of Islam in Iran – men who had not carried their studies to the highest grade, but who wore large distinctive turbans, and had an obtrusive influence in local and, at times, national affairs.

manner, a huge nose, grizzled hair and a brutal jowl . . . but there is no denying
that he had a kingly presence'. She went on to describe how at the coronation
the mullahs, 'dirty, bearded old men in long robes and huge turbans' crowded
the steps of the throne; but 'with his own hands Reza Khan raised and assumed
the crown'.[11] The scene described, though traditional, was prophetic of the
political setting of the Christian church and mission for the rest of the Shah's
reign. The political power of the mullahs was eclipsed by that alliance of the
army and the emergent bourgeoisie under a strong leader which had its counterparts in many Asian countries between the wars. But those who hoped for the
disappearance of Islam's influence in politics were to face disappointment.
The power of Islam was still there. It would be invoked as one aspect of the
new national consciousness when political expediency demanded it. For all its
considerable achievement in opening up and uniting the country, in the emancipation of women, in a stable economy, in education and national culture,
Reza Shah's Iran remained an uneasy place for missionaries to work in and a
cold climate for the growth of an indigenous church.

The Christian Churches

Christianity was introduced into Iran in the third century AD, and it has
been claimed that Nestorian Christians formed about a third of the population
before the Arab invasions of the seventh century. Their descendants remained
as a small indigenous Christian group, chiefly in western Iran, throughout the
period of Islam's ascendancy.

The earliest and largest of the modern Christian missions was the American
Presbyterian mission. In 1835 the Rev. Justin Perkins and Dr Asahel Grant
began work at Urumia under the American Board of Commissioners for Foreign
Missions (Congregational). The declared objective of the mission was 'to enable
the Nestorian Church through the grace of God to exert a commanding influence on the spiritual regeneration of Asia'. In 1870 the mission was transferred to the Presbyterian Board of Foreign Missions, USA, and at the same
time its aim was broadened to include the people of Persia rather than just the
Nestorians. Further mission stations were opened at Tehran in 1872, and at
five other towns in the north between 1873 and 1911. Schools and hospitals
were started at each of these stations. The mission had two centres of higher
education in Tehran: Alborz College, developed from a boys' school in 1898 and
for the next forty years under the distinguished leadership of Dr S. M. Jordan;
and Sage College, separated from the Iran Bethel girls' school in 1933 with
Miss Jane Doolittle as principal.[12]

In 1935, following the first general synod of the Evangelical Church in
Iran in the previous year, the church became virtually independent of the
Presbyterian mission. It took over responsibility for the care of churches,
evangelism, education, and the production of literature. The mission remained

directly responsible for the centres of higher education. In 1939 all foreign schools for Iranians were closed, and the major school properties owned by the mission were made over to the government. The Iran Bethel Foundation, under Miss Doolittle, and the Alborz Foundation, were endowed from the compensation paid when the property was transferred; and they continued to serve educational and social purposes as opportunity allowed.

There were also a number of smaller missions during this period. German Lutherans worked among the Kurds and in Tabriz; the General Assemblies of God among Assyrians in Tabriz; and Seventh Day Adventists among Eastern Christians in Tabriz and Urumia. The Lutheran Orient mission of the USA began work among the Kurds in 1910, but had only three missionaries by 1935. At that time the Christian and Missionary Alliance of the USA had five missionaries at Ahwaz in the Persian Gulf. Both the American, and the British and Foreign, Bible Societies employed colporteurs in Iran for many years but the American Society withdrew in 1914. From the BFBS headquarters in Isfahan colporteurs covered a wide area of the country, and by 1938 some 50,000 copies of the scriptures in Persian were being circulated annually. Roman Catholic missionaries, chiefly French Lazarites and Sisters of St Vincent de Paul, worked in Tehran, Julfa and Isfahan.

The CMS was not the only Anglican missionary society at work in Iran. The London Society for Promoting Christianity among the Jews (later the Church Missions to Jews) had continuous work from 1888, centred upon the Church of the Illumination of the Holy Spirit in Tehran. By the 1930s it had two flourishing primary schools in Tehran under the guidance of the Rev. Jolynoos Hakim and Miss Gertrude Narullah. The Rev. J. L. Garland gave devoted service under the society in Isfahan from 1897. The Bible Churchmen's Missionary Society began work in Seistan on the eastern border of the country in the early 1920s. It was hoped to make this a jumping-off ground for missionary work in Afghanistan and by 1928 there were eight BCMS missionaries in Zahedan; but ill-health in this most isolated station took its toll, and by 1929 BCMS was represented by one Indian doctor with a small hospital. This was taken over by the government during the second world war.

For the first thirty-six years of Anglican missionary work in Iran no diocese was constituted in the country. In 1883 Bishop Thomas Valpy French of Lahore, with commission from the Bishop of London, had performed episcopal functions on his way back to England. In 1894 Bishop Edward Craig Stuart, who had sailed with French forty-four years earlier as a CMS missionary to India, resigned his see of Waiapu in New Zealand, and came to Iran as a missionary, and in that capacity, for sixteen years, exercised an episcopal ministry. Bishop Stuart's resignation in 1910 raised the question of a permanent and properly constituted bishopric in Iran. 'The office of Bishop,' wrote Dr Robert Bruce in 1912, 'is now no longer a luxury to be enjoyed occasionally by the Persian Mission, but a necessity for its healthy growth and progress.'

The name of Charles Harvey Stileman was put forward, supported by W. A. Rice, the secretary of the CMS Persia mission, as well as by Dr Bruce. Stileman himself had been mission secretary for a time before ill-health had compelled him to return to Britain in 1906. He had by then served eleven years in Iran and before that for two years in Baghdad. He was consecrated with the title Bishop in Persia on the 26th July, 1912, but after scarcely more than two years in office he resigned. The exacting demands of travel, particularly in war-time, proved too great a strain. He was remembered as a man of much grace and charm. 'His knowledge of things Persian, his grip of the language, and his acquaintance with Moslem religious thought enabled him to do a valuable work even in that short time.'[13]

No attempt was made during the first world war to replace Bishop Stileman, and there was some discussion during the interregnum about the desirability of separating the bishopric from the office of secretary of the CMS Persia mission. 'I strongly agree with Rice,' Dr D. W. Carr wrote in 1917, 'that it would be far better to have a Bishop who is quite free from the CMS secretariat . . . and who would be free to take a wider view of the whole situation in Persia.' The separation was not achieved easily or at once. G. J. Rogers became secretary for a few years (1935-38), but on his return to England the secretaryship reverted to the bishop.

On the 18th October, 1919, James Henry Linton was consecrated the second Bishop in Persia. He was among the CMS missionaries who in 1915-16 were forced to leave Persia for several months. Looking back he wrote: 'Most of us felt that if ever God in His Providence brought us back to Persia we would work more definitely for the building up of a Persian Church.'[14] The steps taken during his episcopate to translate this vision into reality, and the obstacles encountered, will be recorded later. When he retired from Iran in 1935 to become Rector of Handsworth and assistant bishop in the diocese of Birmingham, his place was taken by William Jameson Thompson who carried further forward, in face of many hazards and difficulties, the work of building up the church. He was consecrated third Bishop in Iran in St Paul's Cathedral on St Luke's Day, 1935. He retired in 1960.

The CMS mission in Iran dates from 1869. In that year the Rev. Robert Bruce, a CMS missionary returning to India by way of Iran, settled down to work in Julfa, an Armenian settlement dating from the time of Shah Abbas, across the river from Isfahan. What was intended merely as an exploratory visit lengthened into a stay of several years; and in 1876, largely owing to Bruce's persuasion, Iran was accepted by the Society as one of its fields of mission. In 1879 he was joined by the Rev E F. Hoernle, MB – the first of many missionary doctors who were to serve in this country. Robert Bruce described his own pioneer work in memorable words: 'I am not reaping the harvest; I scarcely claim to be sowing the seed; I am hardly ploughing the soil; *but I am gathering out the stones.*'[15] Slowly the ploughmen appeared. One of them, who arrived in 1894, was Dr Donald Carr who had heard Bruce speak when an undergraduate in Cambridge in 1888.[16] Five women missionaries had arrived by then, among them Mary Bird who succeeded in opening a dispensary in Isfahan itself. It was soon closed after a hostile demonstration. Miss Bird, the Rev. W. St Clair Tisdall and Dr Carr made repeated efforts to get a permanent footing for a medical mission in the city, for the aim of the mission had become clear – [to] 'devote our efforts in the main to direct work amongst Persians, rather than to seek to influence them indirectly through the Armenian congregation'.[17] It was not until 1898 that a dispensary was fully established in Isfahan, soon to be followed by the building of a hospital on a new site. By the time of the CMS centenary in 1899 there were twenty missionaries in Iran and new centres had been opened. Work began in Kerman in 1897; in Yezd in 1898; in Shiraz in 1900.

A decision of the Baghdad missionary conference in 1895, confirmed by the CMS committee in London in the same year, had defined the CMS sphere as lying south of a line from Khorramabad (Luristan) to Kashan, then along latitude 34° north to the Afghan frontier. The four sizeable inland towns of the south – Isfahan, Kerman, Yezd and Shiraz – remained the chief centres of mission up to the second world war, apart from a period of fourteen years (1910–23) when there were no missionaries in Shiraz.

During most of the period 1910–42 the work of the mission and the life of the growing church centred around the men's and women's hospitals and girls' schools in each of the four towns, the Stuart Memorial College at Isfahan, and a boys' school at Kerman. There were also boys' schools at Yezd and Shiraz for part of the time.

In 1910 there were forty-five missionaries of the Society working in Persia – eight clergy, seven laymen, eleven wives and twenty-seven other women. This number increased to fifty-five in the early 1930s, but was back to forty-four in 1940. In a country where medical missionary work developed early and fully, the number of women doctors serving was notable.

Missionaries at Work, 1910–25

In 1910 Bishop Edward Stuart retired, with the phenomenal record of fifty-nine years of missionary service, and died in England in the following year. The CMS boys' high school in Isfahan, soon to develop senior classes, and in new buildings to be renamed Bishop Stuart Memorial College, was a fitting memorial to him; and two daughters and two nieces were to keep his name alive in Iran for many years to come. On the 26th March, 1909, shortly before his retirement, Bishop Stuart dedicated the first Christian church to be built in Isfahan in modern times. It was built on a site in the hospital grounds between the men's and women's hospitals and was the gift of the family of Archdeacon Williams of New Zealand. This Commonwealth link was strengthened in the

1920s when the New Zealand CM Association undertook the support of one ward in Kerman men's hospital.

In October 1909 J. H. Linton had had to leave Shiraz for Isfahan because of ill-health; and a year later the boys' school in Shiraz was closed, and all work there ceased until 1923; but the years immediately before the first world war saw the mission developing in the remaining three centres at Isfahan, Yezd and Kerman, profiting by an atmosphere of comparative religious toleration, but hampered at the same time by increasing brigandage and lawlessness. Near famine conditions were not unusual. 'Everywhere,' wrote one missionary in 1912, 'there is the same misery; silent deserted roads, underfed horses, and in the post-houses no food to be had as the people are starving.'[18]

In such conditions, the CMS hospitals were meeting the needs of wide areas of Iran. Dr Carr's reputation was such that patients would be brought to Isfahan hospital on journeys of fourteen to sixteen days, and Dr Henry White reported that 1911 was the busiest year up to that time of the Yezd medical mission. Fame had its drawbacks and medical feats were sometimes expected beyond the normal range of doctoring. Describing a visit to the small dispensary at Mohammedabad, Dr White wrote:

> Last Sunday I saw 150 patients, including two donkeys. We frequently get animals to treat. I have had camels, horses, mules, donkeys, dogs and a turkey being among them. (The latter had had its leg severed by a stone thrown at it, and they wanted me to stick it on again!)[19]

Evangelism in the immediate pre-war years was less harassed by opposition than at any previous time. Mr H. W. Allinson, returning to Iran in November 1912 after six years absence, noted the 'evident effect of greater religious freedom'. Bishop Stileman held confirmations in Isfahan, Julfa, Yezd and Kerman, always with a few Muslim converts, and in April 1914 reported from Isfahan: '350 Persians in church on Good Friday morning and 628 on Easter Day.'[20]

Shortly after the outbreak of war, on the 16th August, 1914, Mary Bird died at Kerman from typhoid fever. 'Intrepid' is an adjective to be used sparingly, but its use is apt for this pioneer missionary who served so long in Julfa and elsewhere in the Persia mission, bringing fame both for her medical skill, in which she had little formal training, and for her fearless Christian preaching. 'She has alarmed the opponents of the Gospel,' Dr Dodson wrote of her, 'far more than all the rest of us put together.'

The following year on the 12th April, 1915, Stuart Memorial College in Isfahan occupied its new buildings. Hostile demonstrations, stirred up by the mullahs, gave it an uneasy start with only about thirty boys attending at one period in May; but opposition declined thereafter and its educational achievement in the next twenty-five years was on the highest level of the great missionary schools.

Contact with the nomadic tribes of southern Iran, particularly the Bakhtiari and Qashqai, was often possible and always welcomed as an opportunity of evangelizing coherent and independent groups outside the towns; and when in August 1915 a Qashqai chief invited Dr Carr to visit them, he and Mr Linton responded eagerly and spent a fortnight among the tribespeople, teaching and healing.

Because of the great distances and poor communications between the CMS mission stations it proved peculiarly difficult to devise a local governing body for the mission that was both efficient and representative. A meeting of the missionaries at Kerman on the 14th March, 1910 expressed 'strong dissatisfaction' with the CMS committee in Isfahan. 'Only too frequently [it] requests . . . opinions on business when it is too late for the meeting at which Isfahan discusses it and draws up resolutions about it.' The solution suggested by the Kerman missionaries later that year (13th December) was that agenda papers should be telegraphed to other stations. In 1913 the constitution of the local governing body of the CMS mission was revised to provide for the election of three members by ballot, one of whom was to be elected by women missionaries only. The new constitution also set up 'sub-conferences' at Yezd and Kerman, to consist of all resident missionaries.[21]

The 1914-18 war at first seemed unlikely to cause any crisis for the mission. Dr White, Mr and Mrs Linton and Mr Thompson had left London on the 10th October, 1914, on their way back from furlough and reached Yezd from Bushire on the 14th December. Less than a year later CMS headquarters in London received a telegram from Dr Carr, dated 9th September, with disturbing news: 'Community ordered evacuate Isfahan go Ahwaz wire money direct Yezd and Kerman.' It was followed by another wire dated 4th October from Ahwaz saying, 'All arrived safely.' Between these brief messages lay what must have been a nightmare journey. There were as yet no railway lines and no metalled roads in southern Iran, and the British community which left Isfahan consisted of fourteen families, including six children, two of them babies under a year old. They travelled often by night as well as by day crossing twenty mountain passes in nineteen days, arriving in Ahwaz at 1 a.m. on the 26th September.

The cause of this withdrawal was, as Dr Carr explained in a letter, purely political. The representatives of the allied powers had decided to withdraw expatriates as a protest against the pandering to Germany of the central and local government.[22] The assumption that missionaries should withdraw under consular orders was not in those days questioned in Iran or elsewhere and on 12th December W. A. Rice telegraphed from Kerman to say that the missionaries there were obliged to leave. By the end of 1915 there were no CMS missionaries left in the normal centres of the Iran mission. Dr Carr stayed for a time in the oilfields before going to Shikarpur. Mr Thompson entered the army as an engineer until 1920; most of the party from Isfahan sailed for Bombay on the 12th October, 1915, some returning to England and others staying in India.

Nearly all returned within eighteen months. Following the occupation of Isfahan by Russian forces in March 1916, Miss Braine-Hartnell, Dr Emmeline Stuart and Miss Jessie Biggs were back in the city by 16th May, soon to be followed by the Carrs and the Schaffters, and the Isfahan hospitals were re-opened in August. Stuart Memorial College was found to be in a sorry state, but the damage was 'mainly superficial'. It was re-opened in 1921.

The missionaries, grateful to God for being able to return so soon, were fired with a new resolve to build, within the scaffolding erected in past years, a truly indigenous church. They realized that the hospitals and schools built up with so much love and labour would be precarious assets, and show diminishing returns, unless alongside and within them the church itself grew stronger, and came to share more fully in evangelism. It was typical of Bishop Linton's leader-ship to suggest at the missionaries' conference at Isfahan in June 1921 that a recent cut in parent committee grants might prove to be 'a call to increase our work by drawing more fully on the resources of the Persian Church'.

Proposals made in 1918 for strengthening the Isfahan CMS mission as a train-ing centre for indigenous church workers produced predictable reactions from Yezd and Kerman. The Yezd sub-conference (6th February, 1919) accepted the need for this provided that an 'irreducible minimum' of missionary staff was maintained at the other stations. The Kerman sub-conference (10th July, 1919) thought it was a mistake to continue to concentrate missionaries at Isfahan and asked for the other two stations to be staffed 'as Isfahan has been for the last fifteen years'. The Kerman missionaries were also unenthusiastic about a proposal to make greater use of trained Armenian church-workers. 'We believe,' they wrote, 'that the Armenian is almost as much a foreigner as the European of ten years' standing.'

Preaching tours among outlying villages and towns and healing missions among the nomadic tribes are frequently the subjects of missionaries' letters towards the end of the 1914–18 war and in the post-war years. In 1918, for example, Dr C. M. Schaffter spent his annual leave in the mountains. Through-out nearly forty years of missionary service in Iran he made it his rule to read for two hours each day, usually stiff works of theology. His immensely busy life as a doctor was never allowed to interfere with this. At the request of the Bakhtiari, he opened dispensaries for the tribe. Itinerancy in villages or towns within reach of the town mission centres became an annual undertaking. Usually missionaries went out with Persian and Armenian lay workers.

Miss Winifred Kingdon visited villages near Yedz in May 1921 and described one such visit to Taft in her diary for 29th May. 'Sekineh and Nazanin came for reading. Then I went to Sekineh's house, where we had a nice little meeting, about 25 or so. They listened well.' Sekineh was the mother of a future Bishop in Iran, who was then about one year old.[23]

Miss A. I. Stuart reported a large number of inquirers in Kashan in 1923, and Miss Kingdon stayed several days in each of the thirty-two villages, and visited others in the neighbourhood of Kerman. In 1924 Miss Alice Verinder spent some days travelling among the Qashqai tribe. In 1924 Dr Westlake was reported as 'doing excellent work in villages over a wide area' around Shiraz.

Soon after his consecration as Bishop in Iran on the 18th October, 1919, Bishop Linton began to provide the diocese with the means of self-expression. In September 1920 the Persia diocesan association was started, and the Persia Mission Letter changed its name to Persia Diocesan Letter in 1923. Seeing an indigenous ministry as a necessary first step to an indigenous church, he ordained a Persian, Mirza Abol Gasem Khan, as deacon in St Luke's Church, Isfahan, in October 1921, and another deacon Mirza Akbar on 30th November, 1922.

In the same month, November 1922, the first diocesan conference was held in Isfahan and a constitution was proposed and accepted for the diocese. Based on an African model, the ninety-three articles of this constitution were later judged too elaborate for the needs of the Church in Iran, and it was simplified considerably in 1942.

The changed political situation after the first world war, and the limited sphere of operation of the American Presbyterian mission, encouraged CMS to explore the possibilities of extending operations to northern Iran. Although this did not prove acceptable, growing contact with the Christians in the north form a significant part of the story in the later 1920s and 1930s.

The demand for education was growing all over Iran and one missionary reported that the Muslim governor of a large town had offered to meet the expense of a Christian school by levying a tax on the district; and others had offered to build schools 'if only we will send teachers'.[24] A new girls' school was opened in Kerman in December 1921, and a school for Muslim girls at Yezd in November 1922. A school for Parsi girls had been open there for some years.

In 1923 Miss Jessie Biggs took over a large house in Isfahan to develop the 'industrial school' for women and girls which had been started in 1916. It provided regular employment (mostly in fine needlework) for some of the poorer Christian women, and it continued to grow. On the 23rd November, 1928, new buildings were dedicated, including a large work-room and a missionaries' house. Later known as 'The Garden of Arts' it was officially approved as assisting the revival of indigenous Persian crafts, and several items produced by the school were shown in the Persian Art Exhibition in London in 1932. By 1935 it was providing maintenance for an orphanage for ten girls and was making a regular grant to Isfahan hospital in return for medical care of the workers.

From May 1923 there were CMS missionaries again in Shiraz. Dr Carr, Dr Emmeline Stuart and Miss A. Verinder began to build up medical work there particularly among the indigenous employees of the Indo-European Telegraph Company. In the same month in Kerman, on 20th May 1923, Bishop Linton baptized thirteen men, all but one being converts from Islam. A grant from the Anglo-Persian Oil Company in 1923 allowed the Stuart Memorial College to strengthen its staff and to add to its buildings.

There were many such signs in the early 1920s of the mission moving out confidently into new fields and, if converts were still few, the number of baptisms was significantly larger than those of any other CMS mission in Muslim lands. Such a demonstration of affection as was given by great crowds at the funeral of Dr Catherine Ironside in November 1921 must have strengthened the hope of a Christian church being accepted within the common life of Iran. But the way ahead was not going to be easy. Reza Khan's rise to power brought new problems. Since 1894, when the first tentative moves were made outside Julfa, the chief difficulties in the way of Christian evangelism had been of a tangible, expected kind – the aggressive reactions of the mullahs against any new move by the missionaries; the persuasive effect of thirteen hundred years of Islamic culture with its fatalism, its low estimate of womanhood, its tough measures against apostasy; the isolation of one group of missionaries from another because of the great distances involved and the poverty of inter-city communication. Thus there were many adversaries before 1925, but they were known, and wisdom in dealing with them could be handed down from one generation of missionaries to the next. As one missionary put it: 'You know where you are with the mullahs.' But now a new age was beginning in Iran in which many familiar landmarks would be obliterated and the growth from mission to church was to encounter difficulties of an unfamilar kind.

Restricted Opportunity, 1925–42

The changes implicit in the new regime did not show themselves immediately. In 1925 Bishop Linton felt able to enumerate a number of signs of a growing Anglican Church in Iran. There were new Persian clergy at work. The diocese had its constitution. Each year Lent self-denial offerings were being sent to assist the missionary work of another church. Voluntary evangelistic bands were going out into the countryside. Over twenty-thousand copies of the scriptures were being sold every year.[25] The hospitals and schools were still expanding. One of four surveys of Anglican missionary work published in 1926, *The Call from the Moslem World* claimed, with some justice, that no Anglican sphere in Islamic lands was so promising. Certainly an Anglican Church of over four hundred members in a Muslim country was something to write home about; and for those at home, a cause for humble thanksgiving and growing hope.

Better communications and safer roads (the first obvious effect of Reza Shah's reforms) made inter-mission conferences more feasible, and in the summer of 1925 forty delegates, including representatives of the Persian church, met in conference at Hamadan.

Another conference in 1926 was planned to coincide with the visit to Iran of Dr S. M. Zwemer, whose wide knowledge and experience of Christian

missions in Muslim lands gave authority to any advice he offered. The burden
of Dr Zwemer's message to the conference was the paucity of Christian literature, and the need for resolute action both to increase the output and to improve
its quality. He pointed out that all existing Christian literature in the language
of Iran made a pile fifteen inches high and could be bought for twenty-seven
shillings. There was no Persian Christian newspaper except a small monthly
magazine published in Tehran; but he and Mrs Zwemer had collected over
eighty different Muslim newspapers in current circulation. 'In the preparation
and the distribution of Christian literature (except the Bible . . .) the missions
are not keeping pace with the Moslem, or Behai, or Bolshevist presses.'[26] The
conference took his challenge to heart; made plans for a new Christian magazine;
and appointed two representatives for Christian literature, one for the north
and another, the Rev. H. E. J. Biggs, for the south. The conference also proposed the setting-up of an inter-mission training institution for itinerant
evangelists.

The question of church unity was also raised as a matter of urgency, and the
1926 conference included in its findings the affirmation:

> We believe that there should be one undivided Church of Christ in Persia
> and that it is the privilege and duty of all to work for the founding and
> growth of such a Persian Church.

The case for a united church in Iran appeared strong and, at first approach,
not too difficult to implement. The Presbyterians in the north and the Anglicans
in the south were virtually the only representatives of non-Roman Catholic
communions in the country; and the comity agreement of 1895, aided by
geographical isolation, had been well kept. Now that the former isolation was
breaking down, contact between these two small Christian groups was likely
to be more frequent; and Bishop Linton could write of 'a great responsibility
to give the right lead to the Persian Church in its desire for organic unity'.[27]
In a longer perspective, it is fair to assume that this desire for unity on the part
of Persian Christians was at best partly induced by missionaries, under the
inspiration of the 1920 Lambeth Conference 'Appeal to all Christian People',
and partly, and understandably, by a feeling that Western divisions were of
small importance in Iran, and should not stand in the way of a natural desire
of Christians to become one in Christ. The deep-going differences of ecclesiology between Anglicanism and American Presbyterianism, and the reluctance
of Assyrian and Armenian converts of the 'Evangelical Church' of the north
to accept again the yoke of episcopacy, slowly emerged as factors which would
make the path of organic unity long and difficult. Bishop Linton put forward
for discussion at the 1930 Lambeth Conference a proposal that at future ordinations in Iran two ordained ministers from the Northern (Presbyterian) Church
should join in the laying-on of hands at Anglican ordinations, and that the
bishop should do likewise at Presbyterian ordinations. The conference saw

'inherent difficulties' in this proposal, and recommended further exploration along the lines of the South India scheme.[28]

In 1933 the Archbishop of Canterbury wrote to Bishop Linton advising delay, and enclosing the report of an advisory committee under the chairmanship of Bishop E. J. Palmer. The committee found the scheme for dual ordination defective; and suggested that three thousand Presbyterians, mostly of Armenian and Assyrian origin, would swamp eight hundred Anglicans.

Co-operation between the two churches developed considerably in the 1930s. In 1931 an inter-church conference at Tehran brought together ninety-five delegates from twenty-six local churches. Joint summer-schools at Hamadan in 1937, at Isfahan in 1939, and at Tehran in 1941 did much to foster spiritual unity and fellowship, but they were not directly concerned with plans for church union.

In 1942 an inter-church union committee, appointed with elected representatives from both churches two years earlier, presented a draft constitution for a united 'Church of Christ' in Iran. It had much in common with the South India scheme, but had one unique feature among reunion schemes of that period in its suggestion that bishops should be elected for a limited period of five to eight years, with the possibility of re-appointment by a 75 per cent majority vote of the election by each congregation of a body of ruling elders on the Presbyterian model or alternatively of a pastorate committee following Anglican practice in Iran. It was made clear that the inaugural laying-on of hands, by the newly-consecrated bishops, on all ministers did not imply re-ordination and that there would be no loss of existing intercommunion with other churches. The full autonomy of the church was underlined: 'No foreign ecclesiastical authority shall have jurisdiction or control, direct or indirect, in or over the united church.' This draft constitution was submitted to both churches and a modified draft was printed in 1945. The 1948 Lambeth Conference expressed 'deep sympathy with the Bishop and Church in Iran in the difficulties arising largely from the relative isolation and from the small scale of the Church in that country, by which they are confronted'; it encouraged the continuance of negotiations; and it recommended to the bishop and the other negotiators that they should ask the assistance of theologians.[29]

From the late 1920s legislation and governmental pressures of various kinds began to bear heavily upon the missionary institutions in Iran. In 1927 a new regulation of the Department of Education required the teaching of the Qur'an and the Shariat (Muslim Law) as the condition for government recognition of a school, and forbade the teaching of Christianity in the curriculum. This ordinance was not fully enforced. One CMS missionary reported that in classes I, II, and III the Shariat was dealt with on the last three or four pages of a text book, and that this teaching could be effectively given outside school hours. Bishop Linton had the support of most CMS missionaries when he told the mission standing committee in February 1927 that he was against taking up the question of religious freedom with the League of Nations or the International Missionary Council. A parent committee minute gave him strong support in deprecating any such appeal 'to concede religious liberty before public opinion in Persia is ready and ripe to welcome it'.

Freedom for the teaching of Christianity was further eroded by a regulation of 1930 forbidding the use of Christian hymns in school prayers; and local regulations bore heavily on individual schools and teachers. In 1931 Miss Ella Gerrard was told by the education officer in Shiraz that she was not entitled to be principal of the girls' school as she had no educational diploma; and that she must not give Christian teaching either inside or outside school hours. Boys at the mission school in Kerman were forbidden to use the library of Christian books. In 1932 Persian subjects were prohibited from attending primary schools under the control of foreigners. This was a severe blow as it affected six CMS schools, and a larger number of the American Presbyterian mission schools. After protracted negotiations Stuart Memorial College was allowed to continue its 5th class for another year and its 6th class for another two years, meanwhile building up its secondary section. The girls' schools in Isfahan, Yezd and Shiraz won freedom for a time by changing their status to *melli* (national, privately-owned) schools. This was possible because their respective principals, Misses Nevarth and Armenouhie Aidin, and Miss Ella Gerrard, had Persian nationality. The American Presbyterian mission annual meeting adopted a similar proposal for saving at least some of its elementary schools by putting them 'under Persian Christian auspices'.[30]

Though distracting and time-consuming, the educational restrictions of the 1930s were accepted, by some missionaries at least, as the inevitable outcome of intense government activity in the field of education. By the end of 1935 the education department's budget was second only to that of the army, and compulsory primary education for all children was planned for 1938.[31] But when in 1939 the government gave notice that all remaining foreign schools must close in 1940, the order seems to have been dictated less by the development of a coherent educational policy than by the international pressures that had been building up towards the end of Reza Shah's reign, especially from Russia. The Presbyterian mission again suffered more severely than the CMS by this order for closure. The work of thirty-one of their missionaries was directly affected by it; and their two fine colleges in Tehran were made over to the government by compulsory purchase. For CMS it meant the closure of Stuart Memorial College and Kerman boys' school. They were sold to the government for £17,500.

The three girls' schools, with their 'national' principals, remained open, but their future was put in jeopardy by a circular from the Minister of Education making Friday the only weekly holiday for all schools. The joint standing committee of the mission and diocese, 13th to 14th February, 1941, welcomed an assurance from Miss Gerrard that if she was forced to open school on Sundays she would close altogether and open a girls' hostel in its place. As Miss Gerrard owned the Mehr-Ayin School at Shiraz and it was registered in her name, the joint standing committee had no control over her decisions; but it suggested that she should resign and appoint another principal; absent herself on Sundays; and open a hostel in part of the school buildings. Miss Gerrard resigned temporarily, but her appointment as principal was approved after a year or so and she remained in charge until the 1951 oil crisis, when she sold the school to the government. Miss E. N. Aidin, principal of the Behesht-Ayin School, Isfahan, stood down for a time while a government representative was put in charge; but in the autumn of 1941 she received a letter from the education department appointing her as principal. Her sister, Miss A. A. Aidin, was similarly appointed to Yezd girls' school. Both of them resigned temporarily from CMS in order to be acceptable to the government for these posts. It was reported to the diocesan executive committee on the 25th October, 1941, that Miss E. N. Aidin 'had an understanding' with the local education officer in Isfahan that Christian teachers and children might absent themselves from school on Sundays. A few months later (8th August, 1943) she wrote saying that there was still a morning assembly with Bible readings; ethics lessons gave an opportunity for Christian teaching: there was a Christian Union in the school, and a half-day on Sunday instead of Thursday.[32]

By the autumn of 1941, after Reza Shah's abdication, Bishop Thompson was quite hopeful that at least some boys' schools might be restarted as Christian national schools. On 9th September he wrote to Mr C. H. Allen, American Presbyterian missionary at Hamadan, suggesting co-operation in opening such schools. He thought it unwise to make a direct request for the return of foreign schools.

> The Iran Government might not be able to comply because they might have to grant the same privileges to the Russians, and this they might not want to do. But if Persian Christians are granted recognition and are given the right to have *Melli* schools this difficulty is overcome.

Allen wrote in October saying that he was unable to secure the opinion of churches of the north and advised the south to go ahead with the Christian national schools project.[33] Exploration continued for a time. Permission was sought to re-open Julfa girls' schools in August 1942; but the boys' schools remained closed, and the loss of Stuart Memorial College was keenly felt, by non-Christians as well as Christians. One of the last students to take his diploma from the college, in June 1940, was Hassan Dehqani-Tafti, later to become the first indigenous Bishop in Iran.

The new national self-consciousness and impatience of foreign influence affected the CMS hospitals as well as the schools, though not with the same intensity of impact. Dr Dodson wrote wryly from Kerman hospital in 1934 of the time consumed in applying for leave to practise, by the ever-changing directives from Tehran and by the conditions for registration of property: 'It will be advisable to send out Jobs, and not men of like passions as we are, in the future to Persia.' The import of drugs and other hospital necessities became increasingly difficult owing to import restrictions and new tariffs. One doctor, V. St G. Vaughan, resigned after four years at Shiraz hospital as a result of government regulations for doctors. Law-suits against Dr Stuart and Dr Vaughan for alleged negligence appear to have been inspired by the hostility of Persian doctors towards mission hospitals. All foreign doctors were required to have five years' experience before being allowed to practise in Iran, though they might work under other doctors, and were not allowed to move from one town to another without permission. Dr R. H. Carpenter was not allowed to act as doctor-in-charge at Shiraz hospital during the furlough of Dr Theodora Mess in 1935. 'I think,' Dr Mess wrote about this time, 'the day of the medical mission is passing. There is still work for us to do, but we must watch for the point at which we are more hindrance than help.' This remark was typical of the reaction of many missionaries to conditions of work in the new Iran. They appreciated much that was being done, particularly for education and medicine by a forward-looking and efficient government; they realized that if the church in Iran was to grow, it would not be on the basis of a privileged position for missionary institutions. 'The many new regulations and restrictions,' wrote another missionary, J. R. Richards, 'may be irksome to the foreigner, but we should not forget how irksome foreign control must have been to the Persian with progressive ideas.'[34] How the mission fared, and the church grew, in the years of Reza Shah's reign, must now be the subject of more direct inquiry.

The Extension of the Church, 1926–42

A number of senior missionaries retired or returned to England for health reasons in 1926 – Archdeacon S. H. Biddlecombe (1904), Miss A. P. S. Braine-Hartnell (1896), Miss Annie Stuart (1894). Understaffing became an anxiety at this time to those who remained. Dr H. T. Marrable, reporting annual attendances of 40,000 out-patients at Isfahan hospitals, said that two men and two women doctors was their normal staffing requirement – 'but never in all the twenty years . . . have we had them'.[35] Dr Edward Molony used the word 'Minimax' to sum up the situation at Isfahan men's hospital: 'minimum equipment and staff; maximum work both in amount and quality: and maximum evangelistic enterprise by native assistants'. Dr Lucy Molony was the only medical missionary at Yezd in 1926 and there was no European nurse in either of the Yezd hospitals. But the new men's hospital at Yezd was completed, with seventy to eighty beds in regular occupation; and the welfare and maternity centre at the women's hospital was being increasingly used as it won the confidence of the people. Town officials at Shiraz asked Dr Stuart to train mid-wives; and pressure on existing staff of the hospitals was not allowed to stand in the way of continuing itineration. Dr Winifred Westlake visited sixty-four villages in the neighbourhood of Isfahan in 1926. She reported crowded, and noisy, evangelistic meetings, and a good response to 'lantern' services.

Among the new recruits of 1926 was one who, in the brief time allowed him, left an indelible mark on the life of the church in Iran. Clifford Harris joined the staff of Stuart Memorial College on short service. Four years later, on the 4th March, 1930, he died. 'His was a wonderful life of witness,' a colleague wrote of him, 'It is amazing to think how many lives he touched and influenced in that short time.'[36]

Two happenings of 1927 promised well for the growth of the Persian church. First the new church in Yezd was finished. This was an important event because hitherto the church buildings in the CMS mission centres had been either unobtrusively erected within hospitals precincts, as in Isfahan; or, as in Kerman, unmistakably English in design. The new church in Yezd broke away from all this. Designed by R. N. Sharp, it incorporated traditional Persian features (such as the ten-centred arch) and Persian glass and tile-work; and it was openly a church, built for no other purpose than for Christian worship.[37] It was the first of several churches which Sharp was to build in eastern style, including the Church of St Simon the Zealot in Shiraz, finished in 1938, cruciform in shape and with a dome surmounted by a glass cross, and with a font made from one huge block of stone.[38] The church bell is inscribed: 'To the Church of St Simon the Zealot Shiraz from the Church of the Holy Trinity Cambridge in memory of Henry Martyn who also came to you from us, 1811–1939.'

The second new development in 1927 was that Bishop Linton entrusted Biggs with the task of gathering into book form the Persian hymns that were beginning to be written, notably by Jalil Aqa Qazzaq. Some of these hymns were already circulating in manuscript and being used in regular worship, but the decision to produce a book of them was of particular significance for the Church in Iran – a country, like Wales, where poetry and song matter greatly, and where quite ordinary people would play the quotation game with lines from their great poets. In 1928 the first hymnbook was printed in Cairo. It was so popular that larger collections of hymns were soon called for, and the first inter-church hymn book (Anglican and Presbyterian) was published in 1936. Older translations of hymns were revised; some were eliminated. Miss Vera Eardley made hymn-collecting a preoccupation of many years; she and others, especially R. N. Sharp, wrote many of the tunes. Bishop Hassan Dehqani-Tafti wrote thirty or more fine hymns.[39]

A glance at another year, 1930–1, shows longer lists of inquirers, signs of spiritual revival in the church in Yezd, and in Shiraz an indigenous Christian congregation growing – with fifty communicants on the roll. Miss Brighty changed the day of her evangelistic meetings for women in Isfahan from Sunday morning to Friday afternoon and reported some increase in numbers.

'Joy centres' organized in Isfahan by Miss Eardley for children during the summer holidays spread to other mission stations.

In November 1930 Bishop Linton and J. R. Richards visited Qalat, a mountain village thirty miles north-west of Shiraz, and the bishop confirmed three men and one woman.

The story of this little Christian community, 'the first village church in Iran', is a heroic one. An Armenian colporteur of the Bible Society had some response to the proclamation of the Christian gospel and in 1929 reported that there were inquirers there. The mullahs tried to get people to give up their Christian books, and the converts and inquirers had a great deal of opposition to face. In 1929 the Christian 'dervish', Mansur Sang, visited the village for the first time. He was an illiterate Christian preacher, known all over Iran as 'the slave of Christ', was converted through a Bible Society colporteur and baptized in the Presbyterian church. In March Richards and Mansur Sang went out from Shiraz and two men were baptized;[40] in the following year Miss Moore made contact with a number of women in the village. Persecution was for a time so bitter that police protection had to be sought for the Christians, but a church was built and consecrated by Bishop Thompson in September 1936. By this time Mansur Sang and the first two men baptized had died, and the Christian community still lacked an obvious leader, but there were twenty-four baptized Christians and a beginning had been made. The story of Qalat gave point to the plea of J. R. Richards and others for fellow-workers who could be set apart for village work alone. 'Our hospital,' he wrote from Shiraz in 1933, 'is visited regularly by crowds from outlying villages; they hear the Gospel, and are very often attracted to Christ. They return to their villages and nothing more is heard of them. Occasional visits to villages do very little good.'[41]

'A landmark in the history of the Christian Church in Persia' was one missionary's description of the first summer school for Christians held in Isfahan in 1933. One hundred men and women attended it, from the north as well as the south, and they had to work hard – thirty-six weekdays with four or five hours of lectures each day, and 'field-work' on many afternoons, visiting and teaching in surrounding villages. Summer schools became a feature of inter-church co-operation in the next few years. At the third school in August, 1936 numbers were deliberately restricted but fifty-four people attended and were given practical training in evangelism as well as formal instruction. Evening prayers were held in the Gregorian (Armenian) Church in Julfa.

The first synod of clergy of the Anglican Church met in Yezd in December 1933, and all clergy working in Iran who held the bishop's licence were present. The synod worked chiefly on the revision of the Persian Prayer Book. Two translations were then in use; that of Dr Bruce in Shiraz, and Bishop Stileman's in Isfahan. A revised translation of the Holy Communion service and the collects was completed from drafts prepared chiefly by the Rev. R. N. Sharp, whose literary and artistic gifts were to be at the disposal of the Persian church for many years to come. Special collects for the Epiphany and Pentecost made reference to the presence of Persians in the beginning of the Christian story. The synod also discussed matters of church discipline and conditions for the catechumenate, and it was a Persian clergyman rather than missionaries who urged stricter conditions for baptism. 'One obvious weakness' of the synod, wrote one of the missionary clergy, 'was that all but one of us were foreigners'. It was a recognized weakness. There had been no further ordinations in the indigenous ministry since 1922. But in 1935 Jolynoos Hakim, an Iranian Jew, and representative of the Church Missions to Jews in Tehran, was ordained priest and Ali Khan Nakhosteen, the Bible Society agent in Isfahan, was made deacon. Two others, converts from Islam, were ordained in the period under review – the Rev. Nasrullah Sulh-i-kul, and the Rev. Sayyed Mahmoud Rezavi.

The inevitable 'foreignness' of the synod of clergy meant that greater weight was given in the representative assemblies of the diocese to the diocesan council which met once a year. The five established churches of the diocese elected their representatives to the council on a proportional basis.[42]

In 1933 Archdeacon Garland, who had served with CMJ in Iran since 1897, died, and was succeeded by W. J. Thompson, who remained Principal of Stuart Memorial College until 1936. In the Persian Diocesan Letter of February 1934, Bishop Linton reported two undertakings which showed that 'diocese' meant something wider than the far inland towns of the south. One was the consecration of a church in Abadan, the oil island in the Persian Gulf, 'the first in that area'; the other was a mission he was planning in Tehran for the summer of that year: 'We hope to work somewhat on the lines of the Oxford Group, similar to the mission I had at home.' The mission was carefully prepared and the Bishop and G. J. Rogers trained a team of forty workers to preach and testify.

The same letter paid tribute to Dr Emmeline Stuart, one of the pioneer women doctors of the mission field, who had gone out to Iran in 1897.

Two other pioneers were soon to be lost to the church and mission in Iran. In 1937 Miss M. E. Brighty retired after thirty-eight years' service, first in the Parsee girls' school in Yezd and, since 1920, in evangelistic work among women and girls in Isfahan and Julfa. 'Auntie Brighty' was something of a character, with a will and way of her own; but she was also a devoted evangelist who near the end of her time in Iran could write happily of Persian Christians becoming 'spiritual leaders at whose feet we are glad to sit for teaching'. On the 9th May, 1937, Dr G. E. Dodson died of typhus in Kerman. He sailed for Iran in 1903. He was a gifted surgeon and a pioneer in bringing surgical aid to the carpet weavers. He initiated welfare and preventive medical work that led to legislative reform of the carpet industry in Kerman and elsewhere. A Persian wrote of Dodson many years after his death:

As I was trying to find information about his origin and family and homeland, it came to me that these sorts of people belong to no government or nation in particular, but belong to everybody. All places are their homeland. . . . Perhaps he would only have a flap of bread with a little yoghourt or milk in the whole of one day. . . . What about his rough coat and baggy trousers? You can tell he was a hard worker with no thought of his own position. What else? Clearly he was a man who lived on another plane. He is standing waiting for the next needy person and eager to serve him. He doesn't bother about whether they are Muslim or Christian, Iranian, English or foreign. He is looking far away to a region most of us never see.[43]

Kerman had been noted in the past as the most difficult centre of mission of Iran. It had the characteristics of a frontier town. 'The Kermani is an independent thinker and doer,' one missionary wrote, 'but we have great hopes for the church here.' He noted that inquirers were themselves becoming evangelists and bringing others to instruction classes.[44]

It is possible to detect a note of strain in some missionaries' letters in the mid-thirties. The combined effects of understaffing and government regulations made heavy demands on their patience. 'We need two men and one woman doctor urgently, also a qualified dispenser.' 'It is all very well to have six women missionaries in Yezd, but it is ridiculous to have only one man. Naturally the women converts out-number the men, leading to marriage problems.' But Dr Donald Carr, revisiting Iran from retirement in 1938, was cheered by what he saw and heard:

The impression left in my mind was this: that the Spirit of God is moving in the face of Iran more manifestly than ever before. Very many are groping for the light, and many are finding it.[45]

The second world war was soon to bring new troubles and restrictions. As already recorded, all CMS schools were bought out or taken over by the government in the summer of 1940. A draft law of April 1940 threatened to restrict evangelistic preaching to churches and buildings licensed for purposes of worship. But a political revolution was imminent.

By 1941 there was a strong German fifth column in Iran, and a German victory was confidently expected. Reza Shah was negotiating a treaty with Germany. Britain and Russia, for whose allied undertakings Iran was considered as an essential life-line, threatened to occupy the country unless these negotiations were broken off and German agents expelled. Dissatisfied with the response made by the Persian government, the Allies invaded the country simultaneously from north and south on the 25th August, 1941. Reza Shah abdicated and took ship with some of his family to Bombay. He was not allowed to land but was taken to Mauritius, and then, at his own request, to South Africa, where he died in Johannesburg in 1944.

The Allied occupation, though strictly limited to the period of war by the Tripartite Treaty of January 1942, was not popular; and it made things harder for the Christian church, which was still too readily thought of as a foreign institution.

There were other troubles to be faced, unconnected with the war. On the 6th April, 1941, a large part of the town of Yezd was engulfed in a disastrous flood. It wrecked many buildings, including the hospital and the church which had been built only thirteen years before. The old prayer-room in the hospital was brought back into use as a temporary church and the pastor went to live in the out-patients' block of the hospital, which was still habitable. In 1942 the effects of the Shah's abdication were being felt in a return to the kind of brigand-age and lawlessness which had been endemic before his accession; and on the 3rd August Dr Leslie Griffiths of Isfahan hospital and his eleven year old son Ian were murdered by tribesmen. Less than a year later Sister Hilda Night-ingale, who had worked with Dr Griffiths in the reorganization of Isfahan women's hospital, died of typhus. Neither of them could be easily spared.

The winter of 1942–3 was a time of widespread suffering in Iran. A return to lower standards in local government, combined with war shortages of food, brought all but the very rich to the verge of starvation, and the mission centres had additional burdens thrust upon them of relief work for the starving and the care of refugees. But these were not unfamiliar burdens. The missionaries were back in the situation of Robert Bruce seventy years earlier in Julfa, demon-strating the compassion of Christ for direct human need; but they were no longer mere foreigners. By 1942 the roll of those who had lived and died in Iran, close to her people and beloved by them, was already long – Mary Bird, Cath-erine Ironside, Ruth Salisbury, Clifford Harris, G. E. Dodson, and others with them. Fallow ground had been broken, and the seed sown. The Persian hymns of Jalil Aqa Qazzaq and Hassan Dehqani-Tafti were already being sung in churches built in Persian tyle. Occasionally among ordinands and readers, more often among church members and inquirers, there were lapses and losses to be grieved for, but the church was there, and it was growing, and Persian leadership was strengthening within it.

A revised constitution of the Episcopal Church in Iran was accepted in 1942. Its fundamental bases are worth quoting as a symbol of the hopes and aspira-tions for the church and the CMS mission at the end of this period.

> The Constitution of the Church shall be in accordance with the Principles of the Anglican Communion throughout the world and so maintain its Catholic nature.
> The Constitution shall contain no privileges or disabilities on national or racial grounds, for we are all one in Christ Jesus. Foreigners – missionaries and others – shall take their place in the church alongside nationals. Foreign missionaries shall be missionaries of the church and not of a foreign society.

NOTES

1. *Iran Diocesan Letter*, No. 30, April 1935.
2. See Roger Stevens, *The Land of the Great Sophy*, Methuen, 1962, p. 4.
3. Clarmont Skrine, *World War in Iran*, Constable, 1962, p. xiii.
4. International Missionary Council, *Tambaram Series*, Vol. VI, OUP, 1939, p. 120.
5. ibid., p. 125.
6. *The Call from the Muslim World*, Press and Publications Board, Church Assembly, 1926, pp. 40, 41.
7. *AR* (MS), 1930–31, p. 211.
8. *CMR*, S. M. Zwemer, 'Persia Faces the Future', March 1927, pp. 42ff.
9. Donald L. Wilber, *Iran: Past and Present*, Princeton University Press, 1948, p. 103. See also Richard N. Frye, *Iran*, Allen & Unwin, 1954, p. 75.
10. *Iran Diocesan Letter*, No. 33, June 1936, p. 5.
11. V. Sackville-West, *Passenger to Teheran*, Hogarth Press, 1926, pp. 142, 147, 149.
12. John Elder, *A Century of Mission Work in Iran (Persia) 1834-1934*, American Press, Beirut, 1936.
13. W. Wilson Cash, *Persia, Old and New*, CMS, 1929, p. 69.
14. *CMO*, J. H. Linton, 'Persia: a Church Coming into Being', February 1925, p. 24.
15. Stock, Vol. III, p. 125.
16. Dr Carr MS, 'The Birth of a Church', lent by Bishop W. J. Thompson.
17. Resolution passed by the Persia Mission in 1894 (see *Tambaram Series*, op. cit., Vol. II, p. 66).
18. *CMS Gazette*, 1912, p. 48.
19. Quoted H. Anderson, MS 'History of CMS Medical Missions', p. 206.
20. *CMS Gazette* 1914, p. 183.
21. G2/PE/P3, 1913/96.
22. *CMS Gazette* 1915, p. 337.
23. Hassan Dehqani-Tafti, *Design of My World*, Lutterworth Press and USCL, 1959, p. 13.
24. *CM Gleaner*, W. J. Thompson, 'The Leavening of Persia' 1920, pp. 223ff.
25. *CMO*, February 1925, p. 26.
26. *CMR*, March 1927, p. 47.
27. *CMO*, Bishop in Persia, 'Steps Towards a United Church in Persia', July 1927, p. 146.
28. *The Lambeth Conferences 1867–1948*, SPCK, 1948, pp. 224, 171–172.
29. *The Lambeth Conference*, SPCK, 1948, Part I, p. 42; Part II, pp. 60, 61.
30. Annual Meeting Actions of the Persia Mission, Presbyterian Church, USA 1932, VIII.
31. *CMO*, W. J. Thompson, Bishop in Iran, 'A New Name for a New Country', January 1936, p. 1.
32. Letter of Miss E. N. Aidin lent by Miss Mary Isaac, Isfahan.
33. Diocesan Executive Committee Minutes, 14th October, 1941.
34. J. R. Richards, *The Open Road in Persia*, CMS, 1933, p. 8.
35. *CMO*, H. T. Marrable, 'The Influence of a Mission Hospital in Persia', September 1926, p. 177.
36. *AR* (MS), 1930–31, p. 209.
37. H. E. J. Biggs, *The Four Gardens*, Iran Diocesan Association, 1962, p. 8.
38. *CMO*, A. Verinder, 'The House of God in Shiraz', April 1939, p. 80.
39. Biggs, op. cit., p. 9, conflated with a note from Miss Eardley, May 1968.

40. J. N. Hoare, *Something New in Iran*, CMS, 1937, p. 39.

41. Richards, op. cit., p. 27.

42. *Tambaram Series*, Vol. II., Rt. Rev. W. J. Thompson, p. 66.

43. Translated from M. Sanatizadoh, *Things Past*, Tehran 1968, lent by Miss M. Isaac.

44. *AR* (MS), 1935–6, p. 167.

45. Carr MS.

PART FOUR

The CMS at Home

The CMS at Home 1910-42

A missionary society is no less subject than the church itself, to political, social and economic forces. These forces limit its freedom of action, set their imprint upon many of its plans and policies, and from time to time they declare a bonus in the shape of new opportunities for effective service. In the period 1910 to 1942 profound changes were taking place in the way of life of the British people, and in the relationship of Britain to its overseas dependencies; and a recollection of some of the more important changes is necessary for understanding the Society's activities in Great Britain, both at its London headquarters and in the country at large.

A Nation in Trouble

(a) 1910–14: Years of Apprehension and Hysteria

Giving names to blocks of years sometimes puts the truth in hazard, but it may also serve the truth by dissolving earlier myths – the myth, for example, of a nation in August 1914 'more or less dancing its way into war, to a sound of lawn-mowers and ragtime, to the hum of bees and the popping of champagne corks'.[1] There was an element of truth in this picture. The vulgar affluence of the English leisured classes in the Edwardian era lingered on until the outbreak of the first world war. But from 1910 onwards the country was far from placid. The years 1910–14 'were marked by a rising passion of hysterical excitement in every sphere of public life, and by August 1914 the growth of this spirit had brought the nation to the very edge of civil war. Had it not been for the German invasion of Belgium in that month, civil war in Ireland and violent social revolution in England and Scotland could hardly have been prevented.'[2] A number of historians have come to think of the year 1910 as a critical one. In that year, says Halévy, the strike movement first seriously alarmed the wealthy classes. Cole and Postgate find it hard to explain 'why simultaneously so many groups, whose grievances and aspirations were not after all new, began about

1910 to demand what they wanted in a violent fashion that had been well-nigh
forgotten in British political life'. The output of social legislation suddenly
stopped after 1910. The strikes became more frequent and, when war broke
out in 1914, the new trade union 'triple alliance' of miners, railwaymen and
transport workers was 'just setting about its preparations for the biggest strike
of all'.[3]

The suffragettes, already active for several years before 1910, alienated
public opinion further by a new policy of aggression in the immediate pre-war
years. They slashed famous pictures, maimed racehorses, set fire to cathedrals;
they even staged 'sit-ins' at Lambeth Palace and Fulham Palace to the embarrassment of the Archbishop of Canterbury and the Bishop of London. The
government's counter-measures against both strikers and suffragettes were
harsh, and indicated a fear of social disintegration. In relation to the Irish
problem both Liberal and Unionist party policies showed a preference for
direct action, and a contempt of the rule of law, which lacked precedent in
British politics. It was thus a troubled, apprehensive and divided nation which
heard the call to arms in August 1914.

(b) 1914–18 : 'Carnage Incomparable and Human Squander'

These words of Wilfred Owen, the war-poet who was killed on the Western
Front in 1918, sum up the devastation of these years, in which some seven
million men died in arms and in which, if the influenza epidemic of 1918–19
is included as a side-effect of war, about twenty-five million people died. Trench-
warfare in France and the Low Countries was, from the standpoint of a later
time, an almost unbelievable holocaust of young male lives. At Passchendaele
in 1917 a British advance of five miles through the mud cost 400,000 men.
About a million men from Britain and the Commonwealth died in arms, and
three times that number were maimed. The fact that Britain was slower than
France and Germany to accept a war of unlimited liability and did not introduce compulsory military service until 1916, meant that the flower of its youth
was destroyed. The casualties among 'schoolboy' officers, whether in the
trenches or in the air battles above them, were disproportionately high. The
loss of a whole generation, as it seemed, was keenly felt thoughout the next
three decades.

The first world war had a number of lasting social effects. Class privilege was
drastically reduced, though class barriers remained. It became unthinkable in
post-war Britain that a great landowner should spend £50,000 a year on
house-keeping alone, as Lord Derby was reputed to be doing before 1914. In
the war years the number of men and women in domestic service was halved,
from 800,000 to 400,000, and in the 'twenties modest middle-class households,
including many vicarages, said goodbye to their maid, or maids, for the last
time. The war proved decisive for the enfranchisement of women. The wartime
employment of a million women in munitions and clerical work was far more

persuasive than the militant suffragette movement in securing the parliamentary vote, first in 1918 for women over thirty with a property qualification, and ten years later for all women over twenty-one.

More generally, the 1914–18 war brought the ordinary citizen into the orbit of the state in a quite new way.

> Until August 1914 a sensible, law-abiding Englishman could pass through life and hardly notice the existence of the state beyond the post-office and the policeman. . . . Still, broadly speaking, the state acted only to help those who could not help themselves. It left the adult citizen alone.[4]

Although some war-time controls, on trade and shipping for instance, were withdrawn in 1919, the war brought an end to *laissez-faire* capitalism. The Unemployment Insurance Acts of 1920–22 extended the range of Lloyd George's legislation of 1911 and removed the strict actuarial basis by introducing the 'dole' from government funds. From now on, successive governments recognized some responsibility for the unemployed.

The most far-reaching effect of the first world war was that, through the Russian revolution of 1917, Marxism ceased to be the dream of a few intellectuals and became embodied in a European state.

(c) 1919–39 : Years of Disillusionment

More colourful names have been given to these two decades or parts of them, such as 'the hapless years', 'the years of the locust'. Roger Lloyd described them as 'the twenty shabbiest and most disastrous' years in English history. This harsh judgment was no doubt coloured by his own experiences as a curate and vicar in Lancashire towns during that time; but for many ex-soldiers, and for a new generation of manual workers and their families, there was much unrelieved misery. In any large town 'seedy men wearing scraps of uniform . . . their worried-looking women and underfed children' became an all too familiar sight. Unemployment throughout the 1920s never dropped below a million and was often hovering around the two million mark. In September 1932 it reached three and three-quarter million. After that a slow economic recovery began, but manual workers continued to bear the brunt of the nation's economic ills, and the 'hunger-marchers' from Jarrow and the Welsh mining valleys sought to make this clear. Post-war strikes included, alarmingly, one by policemen as well as the almost perennial strikes of railwaymen and miners. The general strike of May 1926 was a short-lived demonstration in sympathy with the miners; but the miners stayed out for another six months with nothing to show for it at the end. The Trade Disputes and Trades Union Act of 1927 made 'sympathetic' strikes illegal.

The flippancy and frivolity of the well-to-do, as portrayed in the novels of P. G. Wodehouse and the plays of Noel Coward, had their counterpart in a low standard of public morality. Lloyd George's sale of honours for party funds reached scandalous proportions in 1922; and ten years later Winston Churchill wrote: 'I cannot recall any time when the gap between the kind of words which statesmen used and what was actually happening was so great as it is now.' More generally there was a revolt against authority in most of its traditional forms and a distrust of existing institutions. There was a sharp decline in the habit of churchgoing, and an open repudiation of Christian faith and Christian standards for which many found encouragement in the writings of H. G. Wells, Bernard Shaw, and Bertrand Russell.

Abroad, as at home, the 1920s and 1930s were an unhappy period for Britain. The attempt to solve the Irish problem by excluding the 'six counties' from home rule in the Government of Ireland Act in 1920 was the prelude to civil war in Ireland in 1922. The Government of India Act of 1919 attempted to allay unrest in the sub-continent by establishing a central legislature with seventy per cent elected members on an extended franchise. But after General Dwyer on the 13th April, 1919 ordered his troops to fire on an unruly crowd in Amritsar and 379 Indians were killed, Gandhi's campaign of boycott and civil disobedience intensified.

Collective security in Europe on the basis of the Peace Treaties, the League of Nations, and of the Locarno treaties of 1925, was soon in jeopardy. Germany was admitted to the League in 1926 but seven years later, with Hitler established as Chancellor of the Third Reich, she repudiated all that the peace treaties stood for. In 1931 Japan invaded Manchuria. In 1932 the World Disarmament Conference broke down, and year by year after that the threat of a second world war became more menacing. When in October 1935 Italian armies invaded Abyssinia, sanctions were called for under the covenant of the League of Nations, but their application was timorously ineffective. They succeeded only in angering Mussolini and so prepared the way for the Rome-Berlin axis (which Japan soon joined), for the deployment of large numbers of German and Italian forces in the Spanish civil war, and for Hitler's further moves into Austria, Czechoslovakia and Poland which precipitated the outbreak of general war in September 1939.

The British government's part in all this is remembered with little pride, and scapegoats are not difficult to find. Stanley Baldwin's bland insularity and his boredom with foreign affairs is now recognized to be a caricature of a Prime Minister who worked hard for disarmament and, later, for a balance of power based on mutual deterrents; and Neville Chamberlain's words in a broadcast at the time of the Munich crisis, on the 28th September, 1938, reflect an agonized loyalty to a nation's hope of peace as well as a crass indifference to the plight of Czechoslovakia in face of German aggression. 'How horrible, fantastic, incredible it is that we should be digging trenches and trying on gas-masks here because of a quarrel in a faraway country between people of whom we know nothing.' Strictures on Baldwin and Chamberlain need balancing by Ernest Bevin's comment: 'If anyone asks me who was responsible for the

British policy leading up to the war, I will, as a Labour man myself, make a confession and say "All of us". We refused absolutely to face the facts.'[5]

All this, and more, could be written on the debit side for these twenty years of British history. But they were not years of impenetrable darkness and disgrace. Many who grew up to manhood and womanhood during these years did not find them wholly unhappy. An honest attempt was made to deal with the seemingly intractable problems of the country's economy, and to ameliorate the lot of the unemployed; and towards the end of the period the new Keynesian economics were pointing the way past economic fatalism towards a policy of comprehensive welfare legislation and full employment. The two Labour governments of 1924 and 1929, though short-lived, provided for the Labour movement at least a sampling of political power which was to prove valuable after 1945.

King George V during his long reign exercised a steadying influence on the middle and working-classes, and he acted with dignity and courage in a number of exceptionally difficult constitutional crises, notably the question of the House of Lords reform at the very beginning of his reign in 1910–11 and the economic crises of 1931–32. Towards the end of his life wireless telegraphy, which had been put on the map by its use in Crippen's arrest in 1910, brought King George into intimate social contact with his people in Christmas day broadcasts from 1932 onwards. The celebrations which marked the jubilee of his accession in May 1935 surrounded him and Queen Mary with evidences of affection which touched him deeply. 'I'd no idea,' he said, 'they felt like that about me.'[6] And there was sufficient depth in this feeling to carry past the shock caused by the abdication of his eldest son in 1936, and to support King George VI as a true successor to his father.

During the reign of King George V the sovereignty of the British crown and parliament over the whole empire was exchanged for an equal partnership of 'freely associated members of the British Commonwealth of Nations'. The formation of an Imperial War Cabinet in the first world war; the independent status, accorded somewhat grudgingly, to Canada, Australia, New Zealand, South Africa, and India at the peace conference in 1919, and their individual membership thereafter of the League of Nations, prepared the ground for the Statute of Westminster of 1931 and the India Act of 1935. The development of the doctrine of 'trusteeship' in relation to African dependencies, though still mixed with a cautious paternalism until the second world war, was directed towards their eventual partnership in the Commonwealth. From the standpoint of the 1960s it became possible to regard the whole period of British history since the beginning of the century '. . . as one long complex development of the British people from being the industrial and commercial heart of a world-wide overseas empire into an economically very vulnerable member of a Commonwealth of free states'; and this development had its domestic counterpart in a transformation of the United Kingdom from 'the most powerful and successful example of a liberal capitalist economy . . . into a prototype of the social-democratic Welfare State'.[7]

The missionaries who served with the Church Missionary Society between 1910 and 1942 did not have the advantage of this long perspective. The economic vulnerability of their home base, already becoming apparent in 1910, spelled, too often for their comfort, recurrent deficits on the Society's annual accounts, with consequent reduction in grants to missions, restriction on recruitment, and loss of opportunities. But they were patriots, proud of their country and commonwealth, grieving and rejoicing in its changing fortunes, and yet steadfast in their faith that God's good purpose, through their country and for it, would not fail.

A Church in Decline and Renewal

Missionaries in their letters home during this period tended to take a rosier view of the state of the church than the facts warranted. One sometimes gets the impression from these letters that they felt it was only the niggardliness and defeatism of CMS headquarters staff which prevented successful appeals for more recruits and a substantial increase in monetary support. The reason for this over-optimistic view was partly, no doubt, that distance lends enchantment; and memories of the affluence of the 'home' church were starkly contrasted with the poverty of the churches in which they were serving overseas. But a major reason for it was that the great parish churches in Britain, whether in the north or the south, were still well-attended with flourishing organizations; and it was precisely the churches which were most resistant to the tide of secularism which were foremost in missionary support and in which the strongest personal contacts were made with missionaries. Thus an 'own missionary' from St Helens, or Bradford, or Islington, or Hampstead would receive an enthusiastic welcome when he was on furlough and would see little to disturb him about the state of the church at home. But the progress of secularization in English society, thus hidden from the eyes of many missionaries, was something that the secretariat at headquarters could not ignore. A good many of the misunderstandings that arose from time to time between local governing bodies of missions and the Society's headquarters need no explanation beyond this different angle of vision.

At one time it was common practice to blame the first world war for a steep decline in religious observance, but in a longer perspective it would appear that the war only hastened a process which had been discernible in the 1890s and was carried further in the immediate post-war years. The prophets of scientific humanism, such as Goldsworthy Lowes Dickinson, had a large following among those with a university education; and the publications of the Rationalist Press found a ready market among the self-educated. As early as 1909 Neville Figgis could startle a Cambridge audience by stating that 'in the last generation men were unable to take Jesus as Lord, and were sad. Now they are choosing other masters, and are glad.'[8]

In the 1920s three-quarters of the population continued to be baptized in the Church of England, and four-fifths of all marriages were solemnized in its parish churches, but regular church-going and Sunday-school attendance were falling away, and the view that a man's religion was his own affair was gaining wide acceptance. The National Mission during the first world war and the 'Religion and Life' weeks of the early 1940s made little impact outside the churches. The evangelical free churches were the first to show a serious decline in membership. 'The nonconformist conscience ceased to count in politics, as Lloyd George discovered when he attempted to mobilize it.' England remained Christian in morality though not in faith. 'Only one Prime Minister between 1916 and 1945 (Baldwin) was a Christian in any strict sense.'[9]

The anger and dismay felt by committed Christians at the radical views of biblical scholars is more easily understood in this context of advancing secularism. It seemed to many that an enemy within the gates was joining forces with the enemy without to undermine the foundations of Christian faith; and in this situation it was not always easy to distinguish between friends and enemies. Albert Schweitzer, for example, in his book *The Quest of the Historical Jesus*, did good service in re-affirming the eschatological element in the gospels which a century of liberal protestant scholarship had ignored; but when this book was translated into English in 1910 what stayed in people's minds was his picture of Jesus dying in absolute despair, and his theory that New Testament ethics were not universally valid. J. M. Thompson's radical book, *Miracles of the New Testament* in 1911, was followed by a collection of essays entitled *Foundations*, edited by B. H. Streeter (1912); and by Hastings Rashdall's *Conscience and Christ* (1916) with its assertion that the value of the Christian ethic did not depend on the certain knowledge that it was taught by Jesus himself. The riot of speculative scholarship, much of it intended as a Christian apologetic confronting scientific humanism, reached a climax at the Modern Churchmen's Conference at Girton College, Cambridge in 1921. The conference papers were published with a provocative preface by Dr H. D. A. Major in a special issue of *The Modern Churchman* in which he asked 'our traditionalist fellow-Churchmen and the whole Anglican Communion' whether they would 'concede to modern Churchmen the right to modify the use of the Creeds . . . for use in parishes where they are desired by the parishioners . . . with the authority of the Bishop'. In May 1922 the House of Bishops declared its conviction that 'adhesion to the teaching of the Catholic Church, as set forth in the Nicene Creed – and in particular concerning the eternal pre-existence of the Son of God, his true Godhead and his Incarnation – is essential to the life of the Church', and called attention to the fact that 'the Church commissions as its ministers those who have solemnly expressed such adhesion'.[10] This reply seemed inadequate to many clergy, both Anglo-Catholic and Evangelical, and the doctrinal controversy which came to a head in the CMS general committee in July and November 1922 was in part a reflection of the wider debate about the adequacy of credal re-affirmation to deal with the challenge of modernism.

The Church of England was deeply divided during this period on the question of Prayer Book revision. In 1906 a Royal Commission on Church Discipline had concluded that 'the law of public worship is too narrow for the religious life of the present generation'; and the work of drafting a new prayer book began soon afterwards and culminated in debates in the Convocations and the two Houses of Parliament in 1927 and 1928. The 'deposited book' was twice accepted in the House of Lords and twice rejected by the House of Commons where Joynson-Hicks and Inskip, both members of the government of the time and both noted evangelicals, voted against it. The chief grounds for their concern, shared in varying degrees by most evangelicals, were that the proposed order of Holy Communion, and the rubrics authorizing the use of vestments and reservation of the sacrament for the use of the sick, departed from the principles of the Reformation. Some evangelicals were averse to any change in the Book of Common Prayer; others, including many CMS committee members, felt that a revision of the language and a simplification of the forms of service was desirable. The controversy among evangelicals which came to a head in the CMS committee in 1922 was, in its earlier phases, centred upon standards of public worship rather than on doctrine, and reflected the wider contemporary debate about the revision of the Prayer Book (see below, pp. 462–73).

For the Church of England, as for the nation in general, this was not a period of unrelieved gloom and disenchantment. If the revival for which many hoped and prayed failed to come in its fullness, there were many signs of vigorous life; and a number of projects were carried through which helped the Church of England to regain confidence in its mission and message and to strengthen the commitment of its members. Seven such enterprises can be briefly noticed. (1) *The Life and Liberty Movement* founded by William Temple, H. R. L. Sheppard and others in 1917 prepared the way for the Enabling Act of 1919 and the National Assembly of the Church of England (later known as the Church Assembly), and ensured fuller participation of the laity in church government both centrally and locally. (2) *The Industrial Christian Fellowship*, started by P. T. R. Kirk in 1918, sought to combine personal evangelism with research into the application of Christian principles to industrial relations. (3) *The Bible Reading Fellowship*, begun as a parochial project by L. G. Mannering, vicar of St Matthew, Brixton in 1922, provided aids to personal and group bible-study which were widely appreciated. By 1947 the BRF had a membership of over 350,000. (4) *The Way of Renewal* was a more official project. It was launched by a pastoral letter from the Archbishops of Canterbury and York in 1929. It sought to find an answer to 'dullness of spirit, languor of worship, and reluctance to make fresh adventures for the cause of God's Kingdom at home and overseas'. In some dioceses, such as Chichester, it was organized with great thoroughness, and many clergy and laity all over the country found inspiration in the schools of prayer and fellowship initiated by it. Some 'Way of Renewal' Groups were still meeting regularly at the outbreak of the second world war. (5) *Men, Money and the Ministry*, was one of several pioneer projects thought up and set in motion by Leslie Hunter, Archdeacon of Northumberland at the time (1935) and later Bishop of Sheffield. Its purpose was to find a way through the tangle of anomalies and injustices which had attached themselves over the years to the income of benefices and to work towards a rational pay structure for the clergy. Using familiar methods of study, conference, and explanatory literature, MMM gave the more radical younger clergy grounds for hope that the Church of England was not completely moribund. (6) *The Parish Communion Movement*, in its earlier days, had no central organization and cannot be dated in the same way as the movements previously mentioned; but it was stimulated by a book of essays with that title, edited by Father Gabriel Hebert of Kelham, in 1937. In the course of the next few decades it completely altered the pattern of Sunday morning worship in a great many parishes, and the watchword often used, 'Let the Church be the Church', showed a new generation how to steer clear of both Erastianism and Sectarianism and to build up a strong sense of family life round the central act of worship on Sunday morning. (7) *Worship and the Arts*. It is even more difficult to provide foundation dates for this movement. It owed much of its inspiration to George Bell, Dean of Canterbury (1924–29) and Bishop of Chichester (1929–45). One landmark was Bell's invitation to E. Martin Browne in 1930 to be director of religious drama in his diocese. Another was the commission to T. S. Eliot to write a play for the Canterbury Whitsuntide Festival in 1935. The play, *Murder in the Cathedral*, produced by Martin Browne, set new standards in religious drama, and it was followed by Charles Williams' *Thomas Cranmer* and Dorothy Sayers' *The Zeal of Thine House*.[11] Bishop Bell's quiet persistence and his sharp eye for talent, not only in drama but in music, painting and sculpture, provided the way for the church to become, once again, a patron of the arts, and to use its large buildings imaginatively.

There was thus no shortage of new ideas, and no shortage, either, of able leadership in the Church of England between 1910 and 1942. All three Archbishops of Canterbury during this period possessed a vision which ranged beyond domestic concerns and anxieties. Randall Davidson (1903–28) is now generally recognized as among the greatest of the successors of St Augustine of Canterbury. He was a tremendous worker, in spite of lifelong ill-health. He maintained the comprehensiveness of the Church of England against formidable odds. To hold such men as Charles Gore and Hensley Henson as brotherbishops within the same church made great demands on his patience, wisdom and charity; and it was due in large measure to Davidson's own spiritual and moral stature that the Church of England retained some power of leadership in the life of the British people. Davidson was also, and most effectively, the 'managing director' of the whole Anglican Communion. He came to be trusted and revered as one who skimped no duty of his office, and who for all his worldly wisdom, remained 'a quiet, simple, religious man'. It was no mere rhetoric appropriate to a great occasion when he said in his opening address at the World Missionary Conference at Edinburgh in 1910: 'The place of mission in the life of the Church must be the first place and none other.' The skill with which he brought together the three bishops concerned in the Kikuyu controversy (see pp. 142–51); the care he expended on episcopal appointments in the many African dioceses under his direct oversight; and the leadership he exerted in the National Mission of 1916–17 are but three evidences of the profound conviction which lay behind his words at Edinburgh.

Cosmo Gordon Lang, Davidson's successor at Canterbury from 1928 to 1942, and for twenty years before that Archbishop of York, was a more complex, and, in some ways, a less sympathetic character. No-one ever doubted his ability, but some, including Lang himself, feared that he might enjoy power more than a Christian leader ought to do. His range was not the equal of Davidson's. It can be said without injustice that he was less at ease than his predecessor in his dealings with the evangelical wing of the Church of England. But his chairmanship of the committee of the 1920 Lambeth Conference which produced 'The Appeal to All Christian People' was superb, and his stand against vindictiveness in the first world war was an act of courage which cost him a great deal.

William Temple was Archbishop of Canterbury for only two and a half years (1942–44), but he had followed Lang to York in 1929 and his leadership in thought and action had been conspicuous for three decades. His larger theological treatises *Mens Creatrix* (1917), *Christus Veritas* (1924), *Nature, Man and God* (1934) are not much read now, but they fed the minds of clergy for a generation; and his *Readings from St John's Gospel* (1939–40) has become a devotional classic. There was scarcely any forward movement in the Church of England during this period which did not profit from the stimulus of Temple's rare combination of theoretical and practical wisdom. The ecumenical movement, especially in the field of Faith and Order, owed him much as chairman of the Conference on Church, Community and State at Oxford in 1937 and as chairman from 1938 of the provisional committee of the World Council of Churches.

Temple's facility for producing order out of chaos by brilliant drafting of resolutions was seen at its best in the Oxford Conference on Church, Community and State in 1937, when differences on the question of intercommunion seemed totally irreconcilable. At the Malvern Conference in 1941 this facility was felt by some delegates to have imposed rather than exposed a consensus, but his 'Penguin Special' on *Christianity and Social Order* was read and studied by a great number of people and did much to range Christian opinion behind the social and economic reforms proposed in the Beveridge Report (1943) and in the welfare-state legislation which followed.

Temple played a conspicuous part in the leadership of the International Missionary Conference at Jerusalem in 1928 and the 'missionary perspective' of the church's work was as clear to him as to Davidson. 'The plain fact,' he wrote, 'is that in the missionary enterprise we are ministering to the heart of the world's need, and satisfying the world's age-long quest. Nothing else in the same way touches all contemporary problems alike of practical life and theoretical enquiry.'[12]

Missionary Co-operation

'Edinburgh 1910', and Its Outcome

For William Temple, and for many other young men and women who were to become the church leaders of the next generation, the World Missionary Conference held in Edinburgh in June 1910 was a mountain-top of vision. They were apt to say, in later years, of many of their major undertakings: 'It started at Edinburgh.' Roger Lloyd in his history of The Church of England, 1900–1965 called 1910 'the significant year' because of this conference. The policy of the CMS, as of all other missionary societies, was consciously shaped by it and by the new organizations and aspirations which grew out of it. It appears, sixty years later, to have been one of those moments in which Christ took hold of his church and said: 'This is the way you must go now: these are the things you must attempt together.'

In one sense there was nothing obviously new about the Edinburgh conference. Decennial conferences of missionaries had become standard practice in India, China, and the Muslim lands in the previous thirty years. There had been over a thousand missionaries at an 'all-China' conference in 1907, and an 'all-India' conference at Madras in 1902 had used the 'commission' method, dividing the membership into subject-groups with carefully prepared material to work on. There had been three earlier international gatherings of missionaries on a comparable scale – at Liverpool in 1860, London in 1885, and New York in 1900. The vision of 'Edinburgh 1910' was also in certain respects a limited one. As M. A. C. Warren has pointed out, it had nothing prophetic to say about the ambivalence of Western imperialism; it greatly underestimated the degree to which the tide of faith was on the ebb in the Western world; and it paid curiously little attention to Africa, where great things had been happening for many years past.[13] In one sense, and not unworthily, the Edinburgh conference was backward-looking, a gathering up of a century's achievement in sharing the Christian gospel with the peoples of Asia. What saved it from a possibly ruinous triumphalism were certain factors in its organization and methods of working which pointed forward rather than backward, and which suggested a humble yet confident claiming of the future in Christ's name.

This positive and creative aspect of the Edinburgh conference owed most to its chairman, John R. Mott, and its secretary J. H. Oldham. Mott, aged forty, an American Methodist layman, was already an ecumenical figure of towering influence through his work in the World Student Christian Federation and the World Alliance of YMCAs. He was 'born to lead, with a presence, an utterance, a will and a mind all beautifully tempered for the tasks to which he gave himself'. Woodrow Wilson once described him as 'the world's most useful man'.[14] Mott was for the most part a silent chairman, but in complete command of the business, and when he did speak he would accurately assess and harness the corporate mind of the delegates, as in his statement: 'the end of the conference is the beginning of the conquest; the end of the planning is the beginning of the doing.'

Oldham, small of stature with a small donnish voice, had gifts which complemented Mott's. It was typical of him that when invited to act as secretary he agreed to do so only if two conditions were fulfilled: first, that it should be truly a 'world' conference in which the younger churches, and all shades of Anglican churchmanship were represented; second, that it should be a working conference, amply prepared for in terms of years rather than months. Oldham's conditions were accepted. An international preparatory committee began meeting in July 1908, and an intercession sheet began circulating in October of the same year; the question-papers for the eight 'commissions' on special subjects were ready in February 1909. It was largely through Oldham's persistence, and his contacts through the Student Christian Movement, that high church Anglican leaders were persuaded to attend. Bishop Gore agreed to come on the assurance that no terms of church union would be formulated; Archbishop Davidson hesitated about attending until March 1910. Of the 1,200 delegates CMS provided the largest contingent of 93; SPG, hampered by its constitution, eventually provided 34 unofficial delegates. There were 17 representatives of the younger churches, 14 of whom were appointed by missionary societies or mission boards. Bishop V. S. Azariah of Dornakal, lonely among so many Americans and Englishmen, made his famous appeal: 'You have given your goods to feed the poor: you have given your bodies to be burned: we also ask for love. Give us friends.'

The conference itself was responsible for some valuable forward thinking about the autonomy of the indigenous church, about the study of other great religions, and about the needs for missionary education at the home base and for more adequate training of missionaries. But its greatest achievement was the provision of structures for future development. The conference was at first apprehensive at the thought of any permanent organization, but voted unanimously for the appointment of a continuation committee of thirty-five members on an international basis. Twenty of the members of the continuation committee were British and American (ten of each) but there were also ten representatives of continental European missions and one each from Australia, China, Japan, India and Africa. At the first meeting of the continuation committee at Auckland Castle in 1911 plans were made for a journal of constructive missionary thinking. Oldham was appointed editor, and Miss G. A. Gollock, a former member of the CMS home staff as assistant editor. *The International Review of Missions* began publication as a quarterly in January 1912.

In 1912 also the Conference of Missionary Societies of Great Britain and Ireland was formed, with Dr Ritson of the British and Foreign Bible Society as chairman, and Oldham and Kenneth Maclennan as secretaries. From its inception CMS played a large part in the development of the CBMS and was strongly represented on its standing committee. At its annual conference at The Hayes, Swanwick, in June 1916 questions arose which affected directly the policy and administration of the constituent societies. Oldham indicated these questions in an article in *The Church Missionary Review* on 'Principles and Practice of Co-operation', January 1917. If co-operation was to have any future, Oldham wrote, two fundamental principles would need to be recognized: first it must be carried out by and through the committees of missionary societies, and not apart from them; second, the societies must recognize it as a regular and normal part of their own work. If, as he expected, an increasing proportion of the funds of a society were to be expended on work undertaken in conjunction with other societies, intelligent assent and whole-hearted approval must be secured; but such joint action was necessary in order to 'accomplish the large things to which we are called by the present situation in the mission field'. Oldham went on to give examples of 'large things' that could not be accomplished in isolation but were becoming possible co-operatively. The Women's Christian College in Madras, opened in 1915 and for which six British, five American, and one Canadian society were each contributing £200 per annum would raise the whole level of women's education in India; medical schools in China, adequately staffed and equipped, were sorely needed and could not be achieved by missions in isolation. Surveys of needs in the field of literacy and literature could only be undertaken co-operatively. The problem of German missions which before the first world war had served a total Christian community of not less than 400,000 people concerned all societies, and would require an immense effort of rehabilitation after the war.

When Oldham shared these thoughts with the CMS constituency early in 1917 he was still having to push hard to get missionary co-operation moving in Britain, but eighteen months later Stock was able to describe a whole range of activities that were already being undertaken by the Conference of British Missionary Societies and its constituent committees, such as the United Council for Missionary Education, the Board of Study for the Preparation of Missionaries, the Advisory Board on Medical Missions, and further committees on education, literature, work among Muslims, and missionary survey.[15]

In 1920, 2 Eaton Gate, London, SW1, was purchased as a centre for these co-operative ventures, and was named Edinburgh House. It soon became also the British headquarters of the International Missionary Council, founded at Lake Mohonk, New York State, in October 1921, with Mott as chairman and

Oldham and A. L. Warnshuis as secretaries. The CMS continued to contribute to the income of the CBMS on a basis proportionate to its own income which worked out as more than that of any other Anglican society, and CMS normally sent the largest number of delegates to the annual CBMS conference at Swanwick.

Fellowship with non-Anglican societies in the evangelical tradition was congenial to most CMS supporters. Missionary co-operation within the Church of England was also accepted as necessary by most of them, though with rather more misgiving.

The Missionary Council of the National Assembly of the Church of England

This council was started in 1921 with St Clair Donaldson, Bishop of Salisbury, and previously Archbishop of Brisbane, as chairman. It was not a wholly new venture. There had been provincial boards of missions for Canterbury and York since 1884 and a Central Board of Missions for the Church of England since 1908. The Pan-Anglican Congress of 1908, inspired by Bishop Montgomery, Secretary of the SPG, brought five thousand delegates to London, raised £350,000 for Anglican missions, and did much to strengthen corporate missionary effort in the Anglican Communion. The formation of the National (Church) Assembly in 1919, however, gave the opportunity for a new, officially constituted council, 'to cement the relationship of the Missionary Societies to each other and to the Church at large and to foster the growth of missionary education at home'. Bishop Donaldson was perturbed that a great many church people apparently took no interest in overseas missions. 'There is not one English missionary society,' he wrote, in 1924, 'whose resources are not strained to the uttermost . . . if we are to grip the great mass of our Church we must act together as a Church.' He was ambitious for the missionary council to become the power house of missionary propaganda at home and the foreign office of the Church of England. Its objective was to get the church to function through its normal machinery in bringing the missionary obligation home to every churchman. 'The society method,' he wrote, 'is at all events at present essential to our work,' but a common policy was needed so that 'sporadic and individualist efforts we have been making may be made vastly more efficient'.[16] There were phrases in the Bishop of Salisbury's article, and in other statements about the aims of the missionary council, which made some CMS officers and members reluctant to commit themselves to its rapid development. They believed that the 'society principle' was something more than an *ad hoc* arrangement to be kept going for the time being; and they did not regard their present undertakings as 'sporadic and individualist'. But in C. C. B. Bardsley CMS provided the first whole-time secretary of the council and all his successors for the next three decades were former CMS missionaries.

In January 1924 the missionary council began a missionary education scheme for the whole Church of England which was borrowed from CMS. The organizer of the scheme, C. M. Blagden, writing in 1926, made full and generous acknowledgement of this borrowing: 'CMS, which was the pioneer in this work, and has put all its material and all its experience at the disposal of the Missionary Council.' Local training schools were organized on a parochial basis with a syllabus of seven or eight lectures; and central residential courses were organized for dioceses or archdeaconries to provide leadership for the local schools.[17]

Another of the early undertakings of the missionary council was a thorough survey of the overseas commitment and needs of the Anglican Communion. Four of these 'World Call' reports were published early in 1926 – on Africa, India, the Far East, and the Muslim World. They were based on information and suggestions from bishops of all the dioceses in these areas. The reports were inevitably somewhat uneven documents, packing a great deal of information into some two hundred pages in each report. The Africa survey broke new ground and underlined the dire need for new recruits and new financial support in almost every diocese if present opportunities were to be seized. At St Paul's-tide in 1925 a World Call Convention at Westminster brought together three thousand delegates from all over the country. The four reports together asked for £250,000 per annum of new money and at least seven hundred new missionary recruits. The societies could not be other than grateful for this practical help in their problems of finance and recruitment, but caution about the missionary council's undertakings remained.

IMC Conferences, 1928–38

The CMS became increasingly conscious, as the 1920s advanced, of the existence and effectiveness of the International Missionary Council. Its constituent members were either associations of missionary boards or societies (in the Western countries) or national Christian councils in Asia, Africa and Latin America. By 1938 twenty-seven national organizations were associated in IMC, fourteen of them groups of missions in the 'sending' countries and thirteen councils of churches in the 'receiving' countries. One of the most effective national Christian councils was in India from 1921. Its development owed much to William Paton, a Presbyterian minister who, with J. H. Oldham and William Temple, ranks among the British founders of the modern ecumenical movement. He left India in 1927 to become secretary of the IMC and editor of the *International Review of Missions*, and was quickly involved in the preparation for the first of the international missionary conferences arranged by the IMC in Jerusalem in 1928. Mott was chairman as he had been at Edinburgh eighteen years before, and he was still far from being a spent force. He rejoiced that, compared with Edinburgh, a third of the delegates at Jerusalem were from non-Western churches. His own indefatigable touring of the world in the years between the two conferences was largely responsible for the change.

The Jerusalem conference made a number of notable advances. The scope of its discussions was widened to include religious education, racial conflict, industrial and rural problems. It was much more aware than Edinburgh had been of the erosion of faith by the rising tide of secularism, and clearer also about the vocation of the church in contemporary society. 'On all sides doubt is expressed whether there is any absolute truth or goodness. A new relativism struggles to enthrone itself in human thinking': but its message was one of confidence in Jesus Christ. 'He is the revelation of what God is and of what man through him may become.' The end of the Christian mission 'is nothing less than the production of a Christlike character in individuals and societies and nations through faith and fellowship with Christ the living Saviour, and through corporate sharing of life in a divine society.' The conference attempted a definition of an indigenous church in the following terms: '(1) When its interpretation of Christ and its expression in worship and service, in custom, art, and architecture incorporate the worthy characteristics of the people, while conserving at the same time the heritage of the Church in all lands and in all ages; (2) When through it the Spirit of Jesus Christ influences all phases of life, bringing to His service the potentialities of both men and women; (3) When it actively shares its life with the nation in which it finds itself; (4) When it is alert to the problems of the times and as a spiritual force in the community it courageously and sympathetically makes its contribution to their solution; (5) When it is kindled with missionary ardour and a pioneering spirit.' Two years earlier Mott had proposed a definition of an indigenous church which included the words 'it must be self-supporting, self-governing and self-propagating': but the Jerusalem conference was not prepared to apply that test, 'as there is not today in any mission field in the world a national church which is either completely self-supporting or adequately self-propagating'.[18]

Ten years later in December 1938 the IMC met at the Madras Christian College, Tambaram. It brought together 471 people from 69 different countries or territories. It aimed at, and achieved, a roughly equal representation of East and West, of 'older' and 'younger' churches, and half the delegates were under thirty-five years of age. The chosen theme was 'the Church', dealt with under five main divisions of the church's faith, witness, life and work, environment, and unity. The choice of theme purposefully related the Tambaram conference to the two great ecumenical conferences of the previous year, on 'Faith and Order' at Edinburgh and on 'Church, Community and State' at Oxford. Preparatory material included a large treatise, specially commissioned by the committee, Dr Hendrick Kraemer's *The Christian Message in a Non-Christian World*, which reflected the insights of the theological revival associated with the name of Karl Barth. J. Merle Davis, director of the Council's Department of Social and Industrial Research and Counsel, which had been formed as an outcome of the Jerusalem conference, provided a series of preparatory studies on the economic basis of the church; and two preparatory volumes on evangelism were edited by Mott and Paton. Mott was once again chairman, and Paton and Warnshuis were the conference secretaries.

The conference 'Message to All People', adopted at the closing session at Tambaram, looked out on a world in which 'the ancient pestilences which destroy mankind are abroad with a virulence unparalleled'. The man-made consuming evils of war, race hatred, greed and hunger filled the horizon.

We do not know the man wise enough to have saved the world from its present sufferings – and we do not know the man wise enough to deliver us now. But it is just at this point that we are forced back upon our Faith and rescued from pessimism to a glorious hope. We know that there is One who, unlike ourselves, is not defeated and who cannot know defeat . . . [and] even in this present time evidences multiply that men and women still go forth as faithful and untiring ambassadors of Christ.

With insight clarified by the prospect of imminent catastrophe, the conference findings saw nationality as 'not only a divine gift but also a power corrupted by sin and used as an instrument for sin'; and the emergence of communism for all its defects as 'a rebuke to the Church for entanglement in the evils of an unjust society and acquiescence in the *status quo*'. The Tambaram picture of the indigenous church was freed from the residual paternalism of the Jerusalem conference: 'An indigenous church, young or old, in the East or in the West, is a church which, rooted in obedience to Christ, spontaneously uses forms of thought and modes of action natural and familiar in its own environment', but 'it is not a church which makes conditions easier for its members by releasing them from a brave and dangerous confession. . . . Woe unto us if we try to remove or conceal the rock of offence which consists in the absolute claim of Christ to be Lord of all.'[19]

The conference was sharply divided by Kraemer's 'biblical realism', his assertion of the fundamental discontinuity between the revelation in Christ and the whole range of human religion, and his challenge that the conference should make a simple choice between the theology of Karl Barth and Clement of Alexandria. The findings of Section V on 'the witness of the Church in Relation to the Non-Christian Religions' recognized that Christians were not agreed about the sense or degree in which such religions manifested God's revelation: but they pleaded for 'a deep and sincere interest' in the religious life of those to whom the church carried its message; a fuller and more adequate understanding of other religious faiths as total systems of life; and a recognition that, although 'the Gospel is not necessarily bound up with forms and methods brought in from the older churches', the scriptures of other religions could not take the place of the Old Testament as introductions to the Christian gospel.[20]

Perhaps the most valuable forward-thinking at Tambaram, which other IMC conferences were to carry further, was on the indigenous ministry both ordained and lay, and its insight that ministry is a function of the whole body of Christ and cannot be claimed by, or attached exclusively to, one order in the church. Much ground had been covered and appropriated since questions of faith and church order were deliberately excluded from the agenda at Edinburgh in 1910; and meeting at that time, in that place, with its large and influential Asian and African delegation, the Tambaram conference had a value far beyond its published findings. Its 'treasures of darkness' sustained the faith and hope of many Christians cut off from physical communion with each other during the second world war.

The Policy of the Society

Venn's Formula Reviewed

The most influential CMS statement of policy was one formulated by Henry Venn in 1854 and reproduced for many decades in the Society's official paper on Native Church Organization:

> The object of the Church Missionary Society's Missions, viewed in their Ecclesiastical aspect, is the development of Native Churches, with a view to their ultimate settlement upon a self-supporting, self-governing, and self-extending system. When this settlement has been effected, the Mission will have attained its *euthanasia*, and the Missionary and all Missionary agency can be transferred to the regions beyond.[21]

This definition of aim had lost little of its force in the period now under review. Many of the Society's missions had reached a stage of development at which Venn's vision of an 'ultimate settlement' seemed capable of fulfilment in the immediate future, and the three hyphened words – self-supporting, self-governing, self-extending – were frequently used by local governing bodies of missions as they sought to justify to the parent committee some item of expenditure not provided for in the mission's budget or some project for advance which had been queried in London. Any one of the three words, taken out of its full context and used as a slogan, was open to grave objection. 'Self-support,' wrote Dr Basil Mathews, 'as an end in itself is vicious.' Dr Merle Davis listed under five heads the results of an unimaginative application of the principle of self-support on the Indian church. (1) It meant a reduction in the quality of the indigenous ministry; (2) clergy became absorbed in supporting their family and collecting their assessment; (3) divisions and party-government were encouraged by it as 'the power of the purse' took on increasing importance; (4) the moral integrity and authority of the pastor was subjected to severe strain; (5) alarm was caused by having to shoulder unaccustomed financial burdens. Bishop Azariah of Dornakal voiced similar anxieties. Self-support was only too often understood as 'the support of the individual pastor by the individual congregation, leading to a narrow, selfish, parochial outlook, and an unworthy conception of self-government.'[22] Bishop Stephen Neill, in his *History of Christian Missions*, notes that

> later experience has placed many question-marks against Henry Venn's formulation. Any such sharp separation between Church and mission as is

implied in Venn's solution seems to lack theological foundation in the New Testament. And the first attempts to carry out the principles of Venn's dictum proved almost wholly disastrous. . . . Bishop A. R. Tucker of Uganda (1890–1908) drew very much nearer to the true solution of the problem. He envisaged a Church in which African and foreigner would work together in true brotherhood, and on a basis of genuine equality. For the most part missionaries of almost all the Churches were blind to this kind of possibility.[23]

Roland Allen, a prophet who was listened to in his generation if not understood, put his finger on the main problem of self-support. It was the underlying Western assumption about ministerial livelihood, structures of authority, and 'learned' clergy, that made its application harmful. 'There is not in the Pastoral Epistles one word about means of livelihood,' he told a CMS missionaries' conference in 1927, 'no suggestion at all that ordination will make any difference in respect of livelihood. . . . I venture to suggest to you that if we ordained local elders as [St Paul] ordained them, several in each place, and did not attempt to teach them their duty by defining duties precisely, they would teach us what the duty of presiding elders in a church is; they would know extremely well, before we taught them.'[24] Too much stress, he thought, was laid on the intellectual and literary qualifications of pastors. Instead of worrying about qualifications in Western terms, missionaries should search out for men of generosity and dignity, men whose words carry weight, men of good repute among the Christians and among their heathen neighbours, and then leave them to get on with it.

Allen's views were too radical to gain ready acceptance at that time. It was a full generation later before they began to be taken seriously. But they provided a necessary qualifying footnote to the criticisms of Venn's formulation quoted above. It could be argued that it was not the ideas themselves, but their wholehearted application, that was lacking in the 1920s and 1930s; and it would certainly be wrong to suggest that there was no new thinking during this period about the relationship of the foreign missionary to the indigenous church.

Instructions to Missionaries

A good place to look for evidence of new thinking is the annual 'instructions' to outgoing missionaries. These instructions were prepared with great care by the CMS chief secretary or one of his colleagues, agreed by the secretaries' meeting, and then submitted to the general committee for approval. Few subjects received more careful and repeated attention in these instructions than the fostering of an orderly growth in the indigenous church; and in no other connection is the changing role of the missionary more frequently underlined.

The instructions of 1911 doubt whether the Society has yet 'learnt to reckon, as it ought, with the organized and corporate life of the Church. . . . the Church in the mission field, as it now is, and as it makes further progress, demands from all missionaries a new degree of thought, of sympathy, and of honour.' Outgoing missionaries are asked to face squarely the question whether they are yet adequately recognizing the body of Christians at their side:

> Have they yet become something more than your children, pupils and dependents? Have you and they learnt to consider their Church's future as of far more account than the future of your Missions as such? Are their influence, devotion, knowledge and sacrifice being called forth at their best by being made the life and energy, not of a foreign Mission, but of an indigenous Christian Church?

The tendency to keep 'the most prominent positions and honours for and in the Mission at the cost of the Church' is deprecated in 1911, and again in 1916:

> In a most real sense the best missions are home missions, the foreign missionary is but a temporary makeshift. Further, he is likely to do the least permanent good while it is he that controls the situation. So long as the native workers are *his* agents, *his* helpers, *his* nominees, the whole venture takes on a foreign aspect; Christianity itself appears as a foreign faith, and suffers under all the prejudice and suspicion which things foreign usually evoke.

Reading such instructions as these in the 1960s it is easy to see in them the influence of a *zeitgeist* that was to pass, yielding later to a reassessment of the 'foreignness' of the foreign missionary, seeing it not as a matter for shame but as an ineradicable element in his function *within* the indigenous church. But perhaps this stage of acute self-consciousness was necessary before the further stage could be reached when 'foreignness' would no longer imply missionary dominance. By 1939 the assumption of over-rule by missionaries had almost completely disappeared.

> Our policy is to undergird these younger Churches, to give them our fellowship, and to share with them the rich heritage of our Christian experience. The missionary is a member of the Church in the area where he works. His loyalty and service belong actually to this Church.

This aim and policy implied a process of *diocesanization*. The use of this inelegant but indispensable term appears to date from the Report of the CMS Delegation to India, 1921–22, which advocated it as a matter of urgency. The subject is given prominence in the 1932 instructions. It is approached somewhat cautiously as though the committee is aware that diocesanization is unlikely to be greeted with spontaneous enthusiasm by missionaries going out for the first time. The Pastoral Epistles are first brought into play as providing authority for a three-stage model for mission: first, evangelism; next, the church; then the forming of dioceses with the necessary labour of drawing up constitutions and of appointing synods.

> In this way [say the 1932 instructions] the work slowly becomes Church-centric and the mission out of which the Church sprang becomes a mission

of that Church rather than a mission of the CMS. The missionary finds a new loyalty forced upon him by the work he has built up. He becomes in fact a humble member of a Church he may have helped to found. . . . While the CMS may decrease, the Church must increase. It is because of this essential principle in New Testament Church building that the CMS has adopted the policy of diocesanization.

This policy is frankly recognized as unacceptable to some missionaries.

It is feared, partly because it means a loss of missionary authority, partly because the Church takes the place once occupied by the CMS, and partly through fear lest by handing over the power to the native Church the pure Gospel will not be preached as formerly.

There was nothing illusory about these fears, as the committee had good reason to know: many missionaries shared them for reasons other than mere conservatism of outlook. But the instructions, having stated the policy unambiguously, are prepared to reason with the fears to which it gives rise; they go on to justify the process of making dioceses as being integral to the real growth of the church.

The one essential element in Church life is spiritual growth, and we believe this can be best accomplished by missionaries becoming partners and co-operators in the Church. They will secure all the power they need by a voluntary leadership conceded to them by the young Church because of their Christian character and worth. No amount of authority over a Church imposed from without will keep it either doctrinally sound or spiritually pure.

Diocesanization did not, however, imply a repudiation of former loyalties or of the 'Society principle'. 'All of you,' outgoing missionaries were told in 1926, 'will be called upon to make some contribution to the diocese in which you work, but you need be none the less loyal to CMS ideals; you will make your best contribution only as you continue thus loyal.' The Society was under considerable pressure during the controversies of 1917 and 1922 to express them in doctrinal formulae to which outgoing missionaries would be required to give assent. It did not do so, but the 1923 instructions include this affirmation:

The Society of which you and we are members unites those who differ in opinion on many matters, but the task of all is to preach Jesus Christ as the only Name by which the world can be saved, His miraculous Birth, the Atonement He has provided, His resurrection from the dead, His coming again and the gift of the Holy Spirit. You go to preach Jesus Christ as the very Son of God; if it were not so, you would not go.

The CMS Commission, 1932–34

The fuller implications of this policy for CMS missions were set out in the recommendations of a special commission, appointed in 1932 under the chairmanship of Martin Linton-Smith, Bishop of Rochester. Its report, entitled

Looking Forward, was published in 1934. The commission re-affirmed the policy of diocesanization. It suggested four essentials for securing devolution on sound lines: (*a*) a relationship as close as possible between the evangelistic activities of the mission and of the local church; (*b*) integration of higher educational institutions for which the Society was still responsible with the growing life and witness of the young churches so as to 'become the source of the needed manpower for the ministry and other services of the church'; (*c*) fresh emphasis, in every mission, on the training of a true native leadership and on providing increasing opportunities for its exercise; (*d*) provision of continued training and help for indigenous clergy during their ministry as they assumed increasing responsibilities.

The commission was not in favour of making 'block grants' to a diocese to be used at its discretion. The Society should retain ultimate control of grants, and should satisfy itself that such grants were calculated in each case to stimulate, and not weaken, the life and witness of the church; and it should remain free to survey the whole field of need, giving help when it considered help to be most needed. Mission-built churches should in due course be transferred to the diocese, but CMS should retain the ownership of much of its other property, and reserve the right to receive the proceeds of sale of such property. It ought to be made clear both to the dioceses and to its missions that the Society's power to maintain the regularity of grants depended on the free disposal of all its resources.

The commission recommended, as a necessary counterpart to these financial arrangements, that CMS should continue to have its own field secretary, or representative, in each diocese to watch over its affairs, sign cheques on the Society's bankers, and deal with personal matters affecting its missionaries. In certain areas the secretary should be assisted by a small committee, though care must be taken to avoid the dangers of creating a dual authority within the diocese. Individual missionaries should be encouraged to preserve existing links, through correspondence, with the Society's representatives in the diocese and with the Society at home; and to strengthen fellowship among themselves by the continuance of periodical conferences and by other means.[25]

These proposals of the CMS commission of 1932 to some extent endorsed current practice but they also set a pattern which by and large was adhered to for many years in dioceses where CMS missionaries were at work. Taken together, the proposals provide a powerful braking-system on devolution from mission to diocese, and seem strangely at odds with some passages in the instructions to missionaries quoted earlier; at odds also with the following statement from the Report of the Committee on Recruiting, Selection and Training of Candidates published in 1937:

The day for foreign missionary domination has gone, and the old classifications of missionary and native must go with it. The missionary will be as much a member of the young Church as the national of the country himself, and will be expected to fit into the whole scheme of the Church's activities.[26]

The apparent inconsistency is reduced, if not wholly resolved, if it is seen as a difference between the aspirations thought to be appropriate to the individual missionary recruit, and the need felt by the Society both to husband its resources in a time of financial restriction and to reassure its supporting constituency in the home church that missionaries would not cease to be agents of the Society. It also needs to be understood that at the stage of development reached in the 1930s CMS was no longer 'paymaster' in a significant sense. The upkeep of the indigenous church was largely in its own hands. But CMS was providing support for a number of living agents, who were recruited on the basis of clearly understood evangelical principles, and whose deployment and function was judged to be a continuing responsibility of the Society as well as of the bishop and synod of the diocese. The nearest approach to complete integration of mission and diocese was achieved in the newly-formed diocese of Central Tanganyika, under a constitution approved in 1931. The monochrome evangelical character of that diocese, the fact that no other Anglican society was working in its territory, and the administrative talents of its first bishop, G. A. Chambers, combined to create the most favourable climate for rapid integration.

The proposals of the CMS commission's report (1934) on self-support and self-extension were in line with its recommendation on self-government. No grants for pastoral work should be permanent and they should be on a diminishing scale; but the rate of reduction should be regulated so as to stimulate local financial effort rather than discourage it. Grants on a diminishing scale for a limited period were also appropriate for specifically defined objects, such as high schools, teacher-training colleges and theological colleges where they could not yet be fully carried by the diocese, and to assist the local church in primary evangelism in less developed areas. The general educational work still under missionary leadership ought to be planned specifically 'for the raising up and training of men and women who shall be active and witnessing Christians'. Social work in rural and industrial areas 'should always be encouraged, not only as the natural expression of Christian discipleship, but also as a means of strengthening the Church and of giving a direct witness to the power of the Gospel over all life'.[27]

Medical Mission Policy

At the beginning of the period 1910–42, medical missionary work was still suffering from what Dr Harold Balme called 'a too rigid application of the "wedge" theory'. In other words, it was valued only as a means of opening the door for direct evangelism and not as an integral, co-ordinated and permanent part of the missionary work of the church. In 1885, for example, a report of the CMS medical sub-committee pronounced as a matter of policy that 'medical work should always be subordinated to the spiritual'. This attitude was part of a long tradition. Dr Harold Anderson notes that in the first seventy-five years of CMS 'more than half of the doctors sent out were ordained before they sailed, and that of those sent out without ordination not one achieved ten years service – hardly surprising since the lay and auxiliary nature of their work had been in most cases made very plain to them, and few had been given any missionary training'.[28]

Changes of attitude are notoriously difficult to date in such matters, but certainly in the early 1890s missionary doctors such as Arthur Neve (India) and Duncan Main (China) felt able to press their claims for more substantial support for medical missions. A centenary conference of missionaries at Shanghai in 1907 accepted the view that 'high professional standards in medicine are a stimulus to high standards in evangelism'. By the time the CMS commission reported in 1934 the change of attitude was virtually complete. There was nothing apologetic about its proposal that, where possible, medical, educational and pastoral work should be integrated, as church, school and hospital 'help and are helped by each other'. The commission did not regard the emergence of government medical services as a reason for running-down medical missions, but rather as a challenge to make them more mobile, with greater stress on village welfare by means of travelling dispensaries. The care of the body, and interest in social conditions, should be the concern not only of European missionary specialists, but of the indigenous church; and both clerical and lay missionaries should be encouraged to do elementary courses in medicine to take their full share in this movement.[29]

In 1935 a CMS medical commission was appointed with thirty members, 'to review in detail the policy of Medical Mission, especially with reference to village needs and mobile medicine'. Its report was printed in 1939. It reinforced the plea for a more mobile medical service. Healing must be taken to the sufferer, not simply wait for him in an institution. But base mission hospitals were still needed for training, for maintaining standards, and for skilled treatment. It suggested that the future development of medical mission should be in the field of preventive medicine, promoting standards of hygiene and checking the beginnings of disease. The fields requiring special development were: (1) *Rural medicine.* Church teachers should be trained as medical lay evangelists, under a supervising doctor. (2) *Maternity and child welfare.* This could be extended either by means of mobile medical teams or by a system of village welfare centres with resident trained midwives, etc. (3) *Leprosy relief.* Established leprosy treatment centres should be expanded in conjunction with other agencies, and new experimental work undertaken. The 1939 report made a confident claim that 'the ministry of healing has now come to be recognized as an integral part of the Christian message. . . . No presentation of the Gospel is complete unless it includes the care of the body and the enlightening of the mind, for only thus will that new value to human life be given to humanity which came into the world through the Incarnation.'[30]

The Society's Policy in Education

The conviction that the Christian ministry of health and healing belongs to the essence of the gospel was comparatively recent in 1910; a similar conviction about the ministry of teaching goes back to the very beginning of the modern missionary movement; but by the late 1920s its proper exercise had become for most Christian missions, especially in tropical Africa, a vexing problem. Nearly all primary education was still in mission hands. To take one example: in Uganda in 1929 there were 183 pupils in three government schools; there were over 228,000 pupils on the roll of 5,529 mission schools, 5,300 of which were classified as sub-grade schools. But in Uganda and elsewhere government education departments were making substantial grants-in-aid to mission schools and naturally matching these grants with regulations and a demand for higher standards. This new situation meant that missionaries primarily engaged in school teaching were often so burdened by administrative and routine duties that the specific missionary purpose receded into the background; and their missionary colleagues felt with some reason, that the educational missionaries were increasingly imprisoned in their institutions and less available for other necessary tasks in the life of the church. The question how far missions should engage in education thus became an urgent one. Was it possible 'so to control conditions that the spiritual as well as the technical purposes of a school can be effectively realized'?[31] The educational policy developed by the Society in the 1930s might be summarized as: 'quality rather than quantity' – a concentration on a few good schools rather than trying to hold on to the whole system. As the chapters on individual missions have shown, the desire to retain control of the schools system, in order to have freedom to realize the spiritual purposes of education, wilted under sheer pressure of numbers; and the administrative burden imposed by government regulations on mission secretaries prepared the way for a more ready acceptance of a policy of concentration. As a corollary, the Society aimed at supplying the need of the indigenous church for an educated leadership, rather than attempting to meet the more comprehensive need of the whole community for an educated *élite*.

The CMS commission's report (1934) re-affirmed 'the importance of Christian education as an integral part of the work of evangelization, for the development of Christian character, and the building of the Church of Christ'. It welcomed the support given by the government of India and in British territories in Africa to Christian education wherever an adequate standard was reached; and desired to secure and maintain opportunities for Christian education under systems dominated by other principles. In either case, the need of the day was for the Society to maintain a limited amount of educational work of high quality rather than to attempt to extend the quantity of its undertakings; and it should be specially concerned (*a*) to equip the churches with well-trained leaders, (*b*) to give through a limited number of schools and colleges an expression of the meaning, content, standard, and methods of Christian education.

The commission supported the view of the Lindsay Commission on Higher Education in India that Christian colleges at present under mission control should be transferred to local boards of directors. It recommended that senior educational posts should increasingly be held by nationals; but missionaries of the Society should continue to have a substantial share in educational work, and should be encouraged to take further specialized training during furlough. Facilities should be available at CMS headquarters for helping missionary teachers solve the technical problems of their profession.

The 1937 report on recruiting laid similar emphasis on professional competence. Educational recruits should have had teaching experience before going overseas, possess the best qualifications available for their particular type of work, and must be prepared to accept the regulations imposed by the competent authority in the country in which they went to work.[32]

The Society's Policy about Co-operation

Law XXIII of the current CMS Laws and Regulations reads: 'A friendly intercourse shall be maintained with other Protestant Societies engaged in the same benevolent design of propagating the Gospel of Jesus Christ.' This injunction reflects a long-standing practice in relation to non-Anglican societies, and co-operation was developed further after the formation of the Conference of British Missionary Societies in 1912 and the International Missionary Council in 1921. The five largest British missionary societies had, in 1913, 3,360 missionaries (excluding wives); by 1931 this figure had risen to 4,533 – a rise of thirty-six per cent despite a static or declining income after 1922. The CMS commission's report (1934) recommended increasing consultation between the Society and other Christian agencies, especially those working in the same areas, and it favoured the development of a co-ordinated policy, including the joint running of some institutions. Co-operation was not to be regarded as an end in itself, and the Society must do all in its power 'to foster such a spirit among the Churches as will ultimately lead to the unity of the Body of Christ'. Missionaries should encourage the young churches in their desire for a united church and, where the stage of active planning for union had been reached, the South India Scheme, commended by Resolution 40 of the 1930 Lambeth Conference, should be used as a basis of discussion. On the much debated question of intercommunion, the commission recommended that the Society should state that, in its opinion, acts of intercommunion, in special circumstances, would be found to be of real service in the promotion of Christian unity.

Relations between the CMS and the Missionary Council of the Church Assembly required careful definition; and the CMS commission's report set out its understanding of the relationship in some detail. The official bodies of the church would not initiate any policy which was likely to hamper the Society's work; the Society would be given the fullest opportunity to share in any general plans for missionary advance in the home dioceses, and would look for support from diocesan organizations in carrying out its share of these plans. The Society should re-affirm its view that recognized status as an 'agency' of the church 'does not involve any obligation on its part to compromise its doctrinal and ecclesiastical outlook, or to admit the right of the Missionary Council to control the affairs of the Society, or to be the only link between the home Church and the provinces and dioceses overseas'. The Society must maintain its freedom to initiate fresh work or new missions overseas and to make its own appeals and statements of needs to the church in Britain. As far as possible all funds coming to the missionary council for work abroad ought to be paid through the societies and not direct to the dioceses overseas.

This rather tough attitude towards the missionary council reflected the commission's conviction that the 'society principle' was the right one. 'Missionary support,' it affirmed, 'owes much of its inspiration to direct links between the donor in England and the work abroad. Anything that breaks this personal link will involve a serious loss not only in income but in individual prayer, fellowship and interest.' For its part, the CMS would continue to supply the missionary council with all necessary material and help, recognize its advisory functions, and accept it as a platform for discussion of common problems, and for planning joint activity. It would also encourage its staff and its individual supporters to co-operate locally with diocesan missionary councils in their projects, expecting in return a recognition of the continuing place and function of missionary societies within the church.[33] The effects of this policy could still be seen long after 1942 in the restricted opportunities of the missionary council and the diocesan missionary councils.

The Finances of the Society

Had the Society at home, like a gangly schoolboy, overgrown its strength; or perhaps outgrown the measure of enthusiasm in the Home Church which was so apparent in those wonderful last ten years of the nineteenth century?[34]

The answer 'yes' can be given to both these questions. In a sense they are two sides of the same coin. The financial difficulties which oppressed the CMS during this period were in large measure due to the very rapid expansion in the number of missionaries in the last thirteen years of the nineteenth century, and the evident unreadiness of the Society's constituency in Britain to provide for the continued support of such numbers. In 1887, at the beginning of the period of most rapid expansion, the estimates committee gave warning that candidates for missionary service were increasing faster than were the funds to support them, but the general committee made it clear that it would not refuse any suitable candidate merely on financial grounds. In the next twelve years the yearly average of new missionaries sent out by the Society was 70.5 compared with 19 in the previous forty years. The financial effects of this sudden expansion were to some extent cloaked by the large number of recruits who were able to go abroad at their own charges or supported by friends, without coming on the Society's budget. But by 1909 the gap between financial provision and overseas expenditure was such that the estimates committee felt bound to reduce by £33,000 the budget figures received from the missions for the year 1910–11.

In November 1909 a conference was held at Church House, Westminster, of the officials and members of CMS associations. It was resolved that, if the finances of the current year 1909–10 proved seriously inadequate to meet the needs of the year, 'it could not encourage the Committee to maintain the existing work or add to the necessary increase of equipment'. But it also proposed an appeal for a £50,000 Sufficiency and Efficiency Fund to be raised by 31st March, 1910. At the Society's annual meeting in May 1910 the president, Sir John Kennaway, had to report that nothing like this sum had been received in response to the special appeal, and it would therefore be necessary to consider making some restrictions on the sending out of missionaries. In April 1911 the general committee reluctantly decided to withdraw from the Society's missions, either temporarily or permanently, many missionaries on furlough at the time; to send out no fresh recruits save in exceptional cases or as honorary missionaries, and to discontinue as far as practicable the further training of candidates not yet accepted as missionaries. A year later the financial position had improved considerably and in May 1912 the committee decided that missionaries detained in Britain could rejoin their mission not later than the autumn: but some restriction on the sailings of recruits continued. A Legacy Equalization Fund was started in 1911. Any sum in excess of £50,000 received from legacies in a single financial year was transferred to the fund. This proved a useful stabilizer in subsequent years, but it had no more than a marginal influence on the immediate problem of an accumulating deficit.

In May 1913 a conference was held at The Hayes, Swanwick, which proved that the Society had the will and the spirit to tackle this problem. Some three hundred leading supporters of the Society, members of committees and representatives of the larger associations, met for four days to consider three related questions: (1) self-support in the indigenous churches connected with CMS; (2) retirement from any field in which CMS was then working; (3) the possibilities of advance. At the end of the conference, being convinced 'that God is now calling the Society to a strong move forward', those present pledged themselves 'to do their utmost by their personal gifts and efforts to secure a strong permanent advance'; and they recommended an immediate appeal for one thousand gifts of not less than £100 each. The members of the conference gave a splendid lead by pledging £12,500 before dispersing. By 8th July the Swanwick fund had reached £74,000 and the full target of £100,000 was reached within the financial year in £100 gifts, with a further £13,685 in smaller sums. This was more than enough to wipe out the accumulated deficits, and helped to sustain a confident purpose during the four years of war.

Post-war inflation, with steeply-rising prices and heavy losses on exchange rates for sterling, was the chief cause of another financial crisis. In November 1919 congresses of CMS workers met in Sheffield and London to consider what sort of commitment was appropriate to the post-war situation.

Is there too much dissipation of forces? Are we not over-slow in handing over control to native Christians? Are we persistent enough in our efforts to establish strong indigenous churches? Are we sufficiently alive to the importance of making the social life of tribes and nations Christian in its fullness?

These questions were referred back to the associations and their reports were considered at another congress, this time in Birmingham, in 1920. This congress, at which seventy of the larger CMS associations were represented, called on the committee to go forward in a spirit of faith, 'to keep no missionaries back, to increase allowances to native workers who had been badly underpaid, and to expect an income for the year of £700,000'. The 'miracle' of Swanwick 1913 was not repeated. The response fell short of expectation, leaving a net deficit of over £145,000, and this evoked the somewhat rueful comment in the Annual Report, 1920-21: 'the heavy deficit makes it clear that the ideal relationships between such a congress and the General Committee have yet to be worked out'. Instead of making a further special appeal to the constituency so soon after the tremendous effort put into the Thank-offering Appeal of 1918-19, the Society decided to meet the deficit by selling some of its overseas property; and to reduce its total expenditure to £500,000 for the year 1922-23, chiefly by cuts in expenditure abroad and by reducing the budget for training of missionaries and for headquarters staff.

In 1924-25 a 'Tax Free Scheme' of covenanted subscriptions was introduced for the first time, and, like the Legacy Equalization Fund started in 1911, it had a healthy long-term effect on the Society's income. A debenture issue in 1924 by the Church Missionary Trust Association, the holding body for CMS properties, helped the Society through the world depression, and repayment of the debentures in 1936 was a useful counterweight to the perennial deficit. It was not until 1941, with postponement of furloughs, fewer recruits and reductions in the headquarters staff, that it became possible at last to record no deficit in the year's operations, and the upward trend in the Society's finances continued in the remaining years of the second world war. From January 1st, 1942, cuts in missionaries' salaries, made necessary in previous years, were restored.

From this brief survey it can be seen that at no time in this period was the Society able to balance its budget until the second world war; though it came near to doing so in the 1914-18 war. In each case the same reasons applied: a wartime reduction in missionary staff, furlough travel, and training. The sense of moral obligation to subscribers to balance the budget annually led to what Stock called disparagingly, 'the appeal by deficit'. The SPG and CIM, he wrote in 1919, never say a word about deficit and surplus at meetings. 'The CMS may claim to be more frank, in a sense; but then we can never even roughly estimate the value of our properties in the mission field. "Debt?" The Society has not really been "in debt" since 1842! If we wound up, we should have a great surplus!'[35] Certainly, these annual and accumulated deficits were written large in the annual reports of the period, but it is difficult to see what else could have been done. As we have seen, the Society, in the 1920s, realized some of its assets in property both in Britain and abroad, but it would have been irresponsible to carry this process too far. Perhaps the recurrent deficits can be seen, in perspective, as the underside of a healthy financial development. CMS was becoming more and more firmly rooted in the supporting parishes and in the regular giving of small subscribers. The special appeals, such as that initiated at Swanwick in 1913 and in the Thank-offering Scheme at the end of the first world war, could not be repeated at too frequent intervals. Middle-class wealth no longer existed on the scale of the Edwardian period.

There was a danger, certainly, that the appeal by deficit ministered to failure, and at times during this period the Society seems to have committed itself to a kind of negative propaganda: 'We are doing badly; so come and help us.' On the other hand 'a policy of faith', which continued to be advocated by some at least of the Society's most wholehearted supporters, also had its dangers. It tended to encourage the continuance of missionary overlordship and to make the missionary's sense of an inward call decisive at the expense of the long-term needs and opportunities of the growing indigenous church. The most significant change in the Society's finances during these years was due to the great increase, especially from the late 1920s onwards, of government grants which provided all or most of the salaries of missionary educationists in tropical Africa. These grants not only made it possible to maintain a total missionary force comparable in numbers with the pre-war period; they were a chief factor in a massive redistribution of missionary forces between Asia and Africa. (See p. xiv.)

It is not suggested that the relief provided by government education grants in tropical Africa was the sole reason for this remarkable change in the distribution of missionaries; but it was undoubtedly true that recruits were sent out in largest numbers to missions where such government grants were available; and because of the continuing financial pressure on the general funds of the Society, replacement of missionaries was considerably restricted in areas where such grants were not available.

No picture of the finances of the Society would be complete without mention of two new sources of missionary support which provided relief to the general funds. In the 1920s the Ruanda Council and the Hausa Band brought into being self-supporting groups within CMS; and the Australian Federal CMS and the New Zealand CMS recruited, equipped and maintained rapidly expanding teams of missionaries, especially in Tanganyika and North India.

Had it not been for these, the commonwealth associates of CMS and the special groups with their own sources of finance, withdrawal from some major mission areas in the inter-war years would have been unavoidable. As it turned out, only two very small CMS missions, in Turkish Arabia (Iraq) and Mauritius, were discontinued during the period.

By the late 1930s the note of financial anxiety, in the annual 'Review of the Year', began to give way to an acceptance of the situation. This change of outlook was more positive than a mere resignation to a day of small things. It could be described as financial realism, and it owed a good deal to Wilson Cash, the Society's general secretary from 1926 to 1941. The 1934 instructions to outgoing missionaries, after recording a reduction of expenditure of £60,000 in the previous seven years, went on to say that every mission was being asked for a programme of work 'based on the actual financial situation, and not upon the expectation of extra support from the home base'. In his signed instructions of 1940 Cash developed this financial doctrine more fully.

In the past [he said] missions have developed often in proportion to the increase of funds from the home base. Methods of work were determined by finance. Projects were started with the wealth of the West behind them. Fortunately during the past fifteen years God has been preparing us for a new approach to His work. No longer can we count on increasing or even stabilized grants from home. No longer can we expand our work as in the good old days of the nineteenth century. But in this seeming frustration of much that we cherish we see how God is working to a plan. The emergence of the Church is the significant fact for these days. God's purpose in calling out missions was that His Church might be founded in all the world. This is being fulfilled before our eyes.

The Society's Home Organization

Church Missionary House

Throughout the period 1910–42, as for nearly a century before, the headquarters of the Society were in Salisbury Square, off Fleet Street, London EC4. This western area of the City of London had a traditional association with church 'orders', and memories of the Knights Templar, the Dominican 'Black Friars' and Carmelite 'White Friars' are still kept in street and place names. Salisbury Square itself derives its name from long associations with the Bishops of Salisbury who had their town house on the site until Bishop Jewel (1560–71) exchanged it for land in Wiltshire. CMS first rented a house in Salisbury Square in 1813, and gradually acquired the whole property on the west side of the square, though the last house in the block, No. 17, was not purchased until 1911. The first unification and enlargement was completed in 1885, in a northerly direction. By 1913 the headquarters had again become too cramped for the contemporary needs of the various departments. A move to Westminster, or to some other more central position, was considered and five possible sites were examined; but it was finally decided to rebuild part of the Salisbury Square property, this time in a southerly direction downhill towards the Thames. Four of the old houses were pulled down and the foundations of the new wing were put in. On 5th September, 1913, the young Kabaka of Uganda, H. H. Daudi Chwa, laid a foundation stone of Cornish granite.

The new extension and renovation of 'the old House' was completed two years later and dedicated by Archbishop Randall Davidson on the 1st February, 1915. The chief features of the new building were a 'noble proportioned hall and book saloon', 40 feet by 20 feet, to the left of the main entrance; an electric lift; a wide first floor corridor giving access to the large committee room, 68 feet by 30 feet which could seat 250 people comfortably, or could be divided by folding partitions into two or three small committee rooms. Central heating by water-pipes replaced coal-fire grates throughout the house. Departments which had been inconveniently dispersed in different parts of the old building were now brought together. Provision was also made for a missionaries' room, pleasantly furnished, on the right of the main entrance; and for a prayer room, immediately adjacent to the committee room. By 1926 this prayer room was proving inadequate for the needs of the house. Some of the headquarters staff had wanted a chapel for years and C. C. B. Bardsley had been promised £500 for this purpose in 1910. But the secretariat decided to move cautiously. Sixteen years later the idea of having a chapel in the house was more readily accepted. The pre-1915 committee room in the older part of the building was adapted and furnished for this purpose and it was dedicated by Bardsley, by then Bishop of Peterborough, on All Saints' Day, 1926.

Church Missionary House suffered slight damage in the air raids which devastated much of the City of London in 1940. On the nights of 27th and 29th December incendiary bombs lit a number of fires on the roof. Most of them were dealt with, but on the second night one came through the roof of the candidates' department, burning it out, destroying its records, and causing considerable damage to the floors below. St Bride's, Fleet Street, the 'parish church' of CMS, was completely gutted on 29th December and committee room 'A' was placed at the disposal of the Vicar for Sunday services. Hospitality was also given for a time to the staff of the Church Pastoral Aid Society, whose headquarters had been destroyed on the same night as St Bride's.

Headquarters Administration

Unlike the SPG, which left the administration of funds raised in Britain largely in the hands of overseas dioceses, and the CIM, which had an administrative director in China, CMS from the first administered its mission from London. This meant that its headquarters housed the 'foreign' departments of the Society as well as its 'home' organization, and many of the committees that met at Salisbury Square were directly concerned with day-to-day operations overseas. There was a considerable amount of reorganization of departments and committees during the period, as new needs made themselves felt.

On 8th February, 1916 a special general meeting of the CMS approved a number of changes in the 'Laws and Regulations' of the Society. Law I was changed to allow its officers to be drawn from 'churches in communion with' the Church of England. Of the five standing committees appointed by the general committee in May each year one, the patronage committee, had its duties extended to cover the nomination of secretaries, departmental secretaries (see below p. 440) and heads of CMS institutions in Britain. At the same time two time-honoured but cumbersome names were changed. The committee of correspondence became the foreign committee and the funds and home organization committee was renamed simply the home committee.

On 10th April, 1917 a general meeting of members of the CMS ratified an amendment to Law XI. By this amendment twelve women members of the Society, and 'twelve Honorary Members for Life being women' were to be elected to the general committee at the annual meeting, in addition to twenty-four laymen. It is not easy, half a century later, to realize how bold and revolutionary this change seemed at the time. In 1910 Bishop E. G. Ingham, home secretary of CMS, on his way back from a visit to Ceylon, described the proceedings of a missionaries' conference at Trinity College, Kandy. 'The Conference was divided . . . into an upper house and a lower house. I sat for a short time in the lower house (the Women's Conference) . . . Their resolutions, when passed, came up as recommendations to the Men's Conference and were either approved, amended or rejected.'[36] Two years later, in 1912, a women's (foreign) committee had been formed at Salisbury Square to consider general matters affecting women on foreign service and on furlough but its status was still that of a lower house. Its chairman and secretary were entitled to attend meetings of any of the (foreign) group committees but without voting powers. In the next year or two women were give a few voting places on the home and foreign committees but Stock, who had long been a chief advocate of voting membership for women on all the Society's committees, evidently thought that any progress beyond this point could not be expected for a long time. In 1915 he wrote: 'Whether the further step of putting women on the General Committee will ever be taken lies in the womb of the future.'[37] It is worth noting that election of women to the governing body of CMS in 1917 ante-dated by a year the parliamentary vote for women.

In November 1917 a sub-committee was appointed 'to consider the possibility of a more democratic method of administration, giving greater influence in the Society's Councils to the various sections of the home constituency.' A year later on the 19th November, 1918, the general committee approved the sub-committee's scheme for merging the home and foreign committees, and for making it at the same time more representative of CMS support in the country. Apart from the officers and 104 members appointed by the general committee there were to be additional members (at that date 81) nominated as follows: (1) one from each archdeaconry contributing £1,000, provided that each diocese in England and Wales shall have at least one representative; (2) one from each of the universities of Oxford and Cambridge; (3) in lieu of archdeaconry representation, one from each deanery in the diocese of London sending £2,000 (there were three such at the time); (4) one from the deanery of Croydon (an isolated portion of the diocese of Canterbury contributing over £1,000); (5) four from the Hibernian CMS; (6) one from Scotland. In order to assist those travelling from a distance, it was decided that the home and foreign committee and the general committee should meet on consecutive days each month, the general committee normally dealing with the business of the previous month; and third class travelling expenses were to be offered to all members of the home and foreign committee living twenty miles or more from Salisbury Square. The sub-committee which formulated these proposals declared its preference for a more thorough-going democratic structure for CMS committees based directly on membership; but it recognized that this would take time to work out, and 'it was not desirable to delay too long the bringing of the country generally into a fuller share of the administration of the Society'.[38]

Further steps in reorganization were taken in March 1923 when the general committee adopted proposals, on a year's experimental basis, for an executive committee to replace the home and foreign committee. Instead of two hundred members it was to have fifty members – twenty elected by representatives on the general committee of the major associations outside the London area, and twenty elected by other members of the general committee; two representatives of the Hibernian CMS, and eight co-opted members. The new committee, though still on the large side for conducting executive business, was far less unwieldy than the combined home and foreign committee. It met twice a month until the second world war, but from that time onwards one monthly meeting proved sufficient and exacted less travelling time from its northern membership. The method of election was changed to give fuller representation of the associations outside the London area.

Officers of the Society

The Vice-Patron

From the earliest days of the Society until 1963 the office of Patron was 'reserved for the royal family', and that of Vice-Patron for 'The Primate of All England if, being a member of the Society, he shall accept the office.' From 1841 onwards all Archbishops of Canterbury were willing and from 1963 the 'reserve' was withdrawn, and the Archbishop became Patron. In the period 1910–42, successive archbishops (Davidson, Lang and Temple) treated their title of Vice-Patron as something more than honorific. Almost invariably they took the chair at the annual meeting and kept in close touch with the Society through its chief secretary, particularly in the matter of episcopal appointments in overseas dioceses in which the Society was at work. In the case of Archbishop Randall Davidson the relationship was wide-ranging and affectionate. In his speech at the opening of the extension to CMS headquarters in 1915 he said:

> For many long years past there has been no sort of question as to the close association between Lambeth and Salisbury Square . . . no Archbishop of Canterbury would regard the Church's work as other than crippled and hampered in what is vital to its life if it lacked that element which has been, and is, contributed by the Society.[39]

He continued to show by his actions, interest, and wise counsel generously given, that these were not empty words.

The President

The Society's 'working-head' was given this title from the first. By Law II he had to be a layman of the Church of England, and, by tradition, a man eminent enough in the affairs of state to help the Society in its public relations. The presidents chosen had a remarkable record of longevity. With the exception of Hon. Francis Maude who was already eighty-seven on his appointment in 1886 and who only survived for a few months, the average term of office between 1812 and 1969 was thirty-one years.

The president at the start of our period was Sir John Kennaway, Bart. He was appointed in 1887 and he retired in 1917 at the age of eighty. He was an MP for a Devonshire constituency and a Privy Councillor. In 1871 he had been appointed as a member of a parliamentary committee to inquire into the African slave-trade, and his special interest in African affairs was reinforced when Lieut. George Shergold Smith, son of the agent for his Devonshire estates, became one of the Society's first two missionaries in Uganda. In laudatory notices on his retirement Stock and Bardsley both recalled the hospitality and piety of his home at Escot and his personal concern for the Society's officers and missionaries. It was a natural choice that the women's training college, purchased in the year of his retirement, was called Kennaway Hall.

The next president, Sir Robert Williams (1917-43) had been long involved in the service of the Society, as a member of the committee since 1874 and its treasurer for twenty years. He continued his habit, until near the end of his life, of visiting Church Missionary House at least once a week.

In 1943 the committee decided to appoint future presidents for a term of five years, subject to renewal at not more than five years in each term, but, happily for the Society the next president, Sir Kenneth Grubb, served for five terms from 1944 to 1969, and gave the fullest possible value to the concept of 'working head' of the Society.

The Treasurer

When Sir Robert Williams became president in 1917 he was succeeded as treasurer by Sir T. F. Victor Buxton, whose father had held the same office from 1886 to 1895. Two years later he was killed in a car accident. His loss was felt keenly. He had been for many years chairman of the Group III (Africa) committee, and had represented the Society at the Jubilee of the Sierra Leone Church in 1913, opened the Buxton High School, Mombasa, in 1904; and through the East Africa Industries Company and the Uganda company, formed by him between 1903 and 1906, he had sought to further that alliance between the gospel and legitimate commerce to which his forebear, Sir Thomas Fowell Buxton, had given his life. His successor, Mr S. H. Gladstone, described by Stock in 1915 as 'distinctly one of the leaders' of the CMS committee, had been chairman of the finance committee. He resigned in 1922, becoming treasurer of the BCMS from its inception in that year. The next treasurer was Mr Robert L. Barclay, whose wide knowledge of the banking world, especially the field of investments, proved of great benefit to the Society. He was also a generous personal benefactor, always ready to help in the rather frequent financial crises of the period. Mr Barclay died in 1939 and was succeeded by Mr S. Kingsley Tubbs, who was still serving in the office thirty years later.

The Vice-Presidents

According to the Law II as it stood in 1910 the vice-presidents 'shall consist of all Archbishops and Bishops of the Churches of England and Ireland who, being members of the Society, shall accept the office: and of such other persons, as being also members, shall be appointed thereto'. The list at the beginning of the period included 138 archbishops and bishops, nine deans, the Master of Trinity College, Cambridge, the Regius Professor of Divinity at Oxford, and three other clergy (Canon A. M. W. Christopher, Preb. H. E. Fox, and Preb. H. W. Webb-Peploe); and twenty titled and twelve other laymen. In the course of the next thirty years the tally of vice-presidents became slightly more democratic and international. By 1930 although the number of bishops had grown to 180, there were ten ordinary clergy, five women, an African and an Indian. By 1942 there were forty-seven non-episcopal clergy, twenty-eight women, eight Africans, three Chinese, and one Indian.

The Honorary Governors for Life

Under Law VI as it stood in 1910 the committee could appoint 'such persons as have rendered essential service to the Society' as either honorary members for life or honorary governors for life. In 1910 the number of governors for life was a hundred (this upper limit had been made in 1882), and there were seventy-two members for life, all women. In 1922 women as well as men became eligible for appointment as honorary governors for life, and the list continued to grow until a limit of 150 was set for each sex. An increasing number of former missionaries were appointed, and people of other races who had assisted the Society in various ways. The 1940 list included Canon Aberi Balya (Uganda), the Rev. K. H. Chang (Foochow), Canon S. B. Kuri (Kenya) and the Mukama of Bunyoro, Tito Winyi II.

The Members of the Society

Throughout the period, and until 1949, membership consisted of annual subscribers of one guinea and upwards (and if clergymen, half a guinea) with collectors of one guinea and upwards, during the continuance of such subscriptions and collections. Benefactors of ten guineas and upwards in one sum were made members for life. Proposals were made at various times to revise this basis of membership. Stock advocated 'the SPG system or something like it', by which all incorporated members of the Society would be admitted by individual election and would then have the right to vote for diocesan representatives on the committee. But there was a residual reluctance to identify CMS local organization too closely with diocesan structures, on the ground that the voluntary principle required freedom for local associations to develop in their own way. It was not until the Third Jubilee of CMS in 1949 that the advocates of a more meaningful scheme of membership won support for their point of view and the laws were changed. Anyone 'who supports, recruits, or works for the Society in certain specified offices and functions', and others in sympathy with the Society's aims and policies, could thereafter become registered members on a simple undertaking to further the Society's work. The monetary basis was abolished.

The Secretaries

The day to day leadership of the Society throughout the period was in the hands of a body of eight or more full-time secretaries, clerical and lay, with the honorary clerical secretary acting as *primus inter pares*. The title 'honorary' gave a false impression of the whole-time commitment of this extremely busy executive officer; and by the 1920s the number of evangelical clergy with sufficent private means and the requisite gifts to sustain this office was much smaller than in the past. When Dr Cyril Bardsley resigned in 1922 to become secretary of the Missionary Council of the National Church Assembly he was succeeded by Dr Herbert Lankester with the title of general secretary, and this title continued to be used for his clerical successors from 1926 onwards.

The other full secretaries were either heads of departments – home organization, editorial, 'lay' (i.e. finance) – or responsible, with a 'group' committee, for one mission area. Under this group system, introduced in 1881, Group I consisted of China, Japan, North-West Canada (discontinued in 1920) and Ceylon (later transferred to Group II); Group II covered India, Persia, and Mauritius (discontinued in 1919); and Group III Africa and Palestine. Each group had its own committee which in 1910 was still meeting for a full day each month, with frequent extra meetings to get through its vast agenda. The three foreign secretaries were accustomed to give much of their time to personal contact with missionaries on furlough and with candidates for service overseas as well as to detailed oversight of the missions in their group, largely through extensive correspondence with the mission secretaries. During this period overseas travel became a normal commitment of the group secretary. By this means they acquired an intimate knowledge of the situation in each of the missions for which they were responsible.

In 1914 a sub-committee was appointed by the general committee with Sir Richard Pennefather as chairman, to examine the organization of work at the Society's headquarters. It proposed a reduction in the number of full secretaries from seven or eight to 'four, or at the most five', with 'five or possibly six' departmental secretaries, two of whom should be women. In making this proposal, the sub-committee had taken note of the report on the home base of the 1910 Edinburgh conference, and was persuaded that 'a small number of responsible heads tends to produce more unity in counsel and to define responsibility' and also 'has the advantage of leaving open more posts to younger men, whose energy and powers are more needed than their counsels'. The sub-committee also proposed that the office of honorary secretary should be retained. He should remain as the chief representative of the Society before the church and the world. He should be given a travel allowance and other expenses, and be provided with a private secretary. For the foreign department they proposed that the Rev. F. Baylis should be given the title of 'Chief Foreign Secretary' and that the successors of the other two group secretaries (G. T. Manley and E. H. M. Waller) should be departmental secretaries. Their supporting argument for this change of structure was that devolution in recent years had transferred considerable responsibility from headquarters to the local governing bodies of missions, thus reducing the load on the 'foreign' secretariat at Salisbury Square. The unification of the foreign department would make it easier for the candidates department to be regarded as a section of it under the general oversight of the chief foreign secretary. The three group committees would still be necessary but their membership should each be limited to twenty-four members, three of whom should be chosen with regard to their qualifications in medicine, another three for their educational, and one for industrial, expertise.

Most of the proposals of the sub-committee were approved and implemented, but not those relating to the secretariat. The three group secretaries and their successors remained full secretaries of the Society and for a short period, 1921–23, a fourth secretary, Dr Garfield Williams, was added to the foreign department. The editorial secretary remained a full secretary alongside the home and financial secretaries and by the end of the period the secretary of the medical committee was given like status. The 'small cabinet' proposal was perhaps unrealistic. Eight full secretaries has not proved too large a number for effective sharing of counsel and leadership. The suggestion of departmental secretaries, later to be called under-secretaries, proved a valuable innovation.

The CMS commission appointed in 1932, with Bishop Martin Linton-Smith of Rochester as chairman, surveyed the Society's home organization thoroughly. It did not suggest any major changes in the secretariat, but it recommended a statement defining the responsibilities and relationships of the secretaries in the following terms. The secretaries are appointed by the general committee subject to confirmation at the next annual meeting of the Society, and are responsible to the general committee, normally through the executive committee. This responsibility is corporate but the general secretary is *primus inter pares*. He is secretary both of the general committee and the executive committee, and the channel of communications with the primates and episcopate at home and overseas. All published statements of the Society's general policy are over his signature. He is the chief foreign secretary and should be kept aware of all the work and problems of the missions. All drafts submitted to committees should, so far as is practicable, be seen by him before the committee meets, and his judgment should be consulted by his colleagues. This 'primacy' does not, however, imply a purely dependent role for the other full secretaries. Each of them has a direct individual responsibility to the Society and to the general committee for the department specially committed to him. Collective responsibility requires that each secretary takes a full part in the secretaries' meeting and that 'no matter should be considered as the sole concern of a single secretary'. If real divergencies of opinion emerge among the secretariat that fact should be disclosed to the executive committee. The commission recommended the continuance of three 'group' secretaries each with his distinct sphere. These were defined as: *Far East Group* – China and Japan; *India Group* – Persia, India and Ceylon; *Africa Group* – Africa and Palestine. A woman with full secretary status, with duties to be defined later, was to be appointed in the foreign department, as soon as plans for reorganization recommended by the commission had been carried out.

For the Society's home department the commission recommended an organization that was flexible and adaptable to changing conditions. The home secretary should be kept as free as possible 'for inspirational leadership throughout the country'. He should have the assistance of a deputy home secretary dealing primarily with parochial contacts and a home education secretary whose duties would include liaison with the Missionary Council of the Church Assembly in educational work and contact with public schools, universities, and the teaching profession. Women's work in the home department should be more fully integrated and to this end the commission recommended the appointment of a woman on the staffs of the deputy home secretary and the home education secretary.[40]

Most of the recommendations of the commission relating to the secretariat were implemented in the course of the next few years but eight years elapsed before an appointment was made of a 'Woman Secretary' of the Society. Miss Ena Price, previously women candidates secretary, was appointed to this office in 1942.

The Chief Secretaries of the Society, 1910–42

In May 1910 Prebendary Henry Elliot Fox resigned after fifteen years in office as honorary clerical secretary.

> [He] had full experience of the task of vindicating the Society from charges of going too far in different and quite opposite directions. No Secretary has more truly represented its clear and yet broad and inclusive lines without compromise and without prejudice. As an effective pleader for the cause of Missions he had no equal among his predecessors. And two sons and three daughters were his gift to the foreign field.[41]

Fox was by temperament and conviction a conservative. After his retirement from the secretariat he used his considerable influence to combat a policy of comprehensiveness which seemed to him disruptive of the Society's traditional position.

His successor as honorary clerical secretary in 1910 was Cyril C. B. Bardsley, vicar of St Helens, Lancashire. He lost no time in making personal contact with members of the headquarters staff in Salisbury Square. On the very afternoon of his appointment he and Mrs Bardsley toured the house. 'Most of the clerks had never even spoken to, much less shaken hands with, an Honorary Secretary before.' He did much in his twelve years of office to encourage a family atmosphere in the house by an annual staff party, and a children's party. Unlike Fox, Bardsley believed that the future of CMS lay in a broadening of relationship both within the Church of England and in the ecumenical contacts that developed rapidly after the Edinburgh conference.

> He was from the first [wrote J. H. Oldham] a warm supporter of missionary co-operation and in view of his position as Secretary of the largest missionary society in Great Britain the warmth of his support counted for a great deal. His generous action in persuading CMS to vote a very substantial grant for Edinburgh House, which alone made its establishment possible, was perhaps his outstanding contribution.[42]

In March 1916 he was given leave of absence for the rest of that year to become one of the secretaries of the National Mission, and, at the specific request of the Archbishop of Canterbury, this leave was extended until February 1917. Purely in terms of his leadership within the Society, this long absence was unwise. There was growing tension at that time between liberal and conservative viewpoints, especially in the committee rooms, and Bardsley never really regained control of the situation. When he left early in 1923 to become the first secretary of the Missionary Council of the Church Assembly, the president referred to his 'boundless energy, wide outlook and clear vision'. In 1924 he became Bishop of Peterborough and when the diocese was divided in 1927 by his own choice Bishop of Leicester. He retired in 1939 and died a year later.

On Bardsley's resignation, largely because of the controversy that came to a head in the autumn of 1922, the Society decided to depart from precedent and appoint a layman, Dr Herbert Lankester, as chief secretary. He had been a familiar and trusted member of the headquarters staff for over thirty years, first as secretary of the Medical Mission Auxiliary from its inception in 1891, then as physician and secretary of the medical committee (1894-1903), head of the home department (1903-10) and thereafter 'lay' secretary in charge of the Society's finances. He had started a number of new ventures, all of them highly successful, such as the Million Shillings Fund, and summer schools, and he had done much in his earlier days to bring the CMS associations into line with the diocesan and archdeaconry structures of the Church of England. The appointment of a layman made a change of title necessary, and the committee took the opportunity of attaching a salary to the post of 'General Secretary'.

Lankester's appointment was by intention short-term, and when he retired in 1926 he was succeeded as general secretary by the Rev. William Wilson Cash, formerly secretary of the CMS mission in Egypt and for the previous three years home secretary at headquarters. He served in this office until October 1941 when he resigned after being nominated to the bishopric of Worcester. Looking back over his fifteen years, he spoke to the executive committee, with a frankness that would have been impolitic earlier, about the troubled situation of 1926.

> The conservatives and liberals [he said] had made the CMS the cockpit for their party strife. I had to feel my way to a policy that would interpret the essential principles for which the CMS stands and that would keep the Society in the main stream of the Church's life. . . . Efforts were made to capture the CMS by both the liberal and conservative parties.[43]

Steadily throughout his time as general secretary, Cash took his stand on the intention of the founders to form, not an 'Evangelical Party' missionary society, but rather a church society whose special emphasis and message should be evangelical. He possessed two valuable assets for the role of peacemaker – courage and patience. As a frequent and acceptable speaker at the Keswick Convention he was able to reassure many of the conservative evangelicals that they still had a place in the CMS under his leadership, and the development of the Ruanda mission as an association within CMS owed much to his encouragement.

The committee minute of his resignation in 1941 spoke of 'the fire of spiritual devotion [which] illuminated and energized the intellectual and administrative powers which have marked Dr Cash's guidance of the Society's affairs. . . . He shares the buoyancy and enthusiasm of the founders, their strong perseverance and refusal to be daunted by difficult or adverse circumstances.' Cash was not a scholar in the sense that his two immediate successors were scholars but he was a diligent student of the bible and his 'helps' to the study of Philippians, Colossians, and Ephesians were widely appreciated for their depth of insight. He never lost his love for Egypt or his conviction that the Society was committed to proclaiming the gospel in the Muslim world and was called to stand beside the Christian communities in Muslim countries with all possible help and encouragement. He led the Society with conviction and discretion in the field of co-operation with other missionary agencies which Bardsley had opened. 'When CMS accepted from the Church Assembly the position of an "agency" of the Church of England,' he said in the speech already quoted, 'it committed itself to work as a responsible agent, relating its activities to the Church's work as a whole. . . . The Missionary Council has been largely what societies made it, and the CMS owes more to it than it is always prepared to admit.' Not surprisingly, in one of the most difficult periods that the Society had so far faced, the strain of leadership told upon him and a note of exasperation sometimes found its way into his letters, but it was his achievement to nurse CMS through its convalescence and to leave it in good heart for the future.

After Cash's consecration as Bishop of Worcester, Mr J. Gurney Barclay, 'Far East' secretary, held the fort until March 1942 when the general committee appointed the Rev. Max Warren as general secretary.

Space will not allow more than passing mention of the other headquarters secretaries of this period. F. Baylis and G. T. Manley were outstanding among the 'foreign' secretaries. Archbishop Davidson had a high regard for Baylis and would have liked to appoint him an overseas bishop. He had charge of the Africa group of missions from 1893 to 1912 and then succeeded B. Baring-Gould as 'Far East' secretary until 1921. Manley who had been Senior Wrangler and Smith's Prizeman at Cambridge and a fellow of Christ's College (1895–1910) became an assistant in the home division of CMS in 1906, and followed Baylis as Africa group secretary from 1912 to 1925.

Always a formidable personality and capable on occasion of being intimidating through the sheer brilliance of his acutely logical mind, a man for whom principles were always of major importance, George Manley was yet deeply concerned with the individual. . . . A deeply convinced Evangelical and conservative in his leaning, he could respect the convictions of others, remaining in unbroken Christian fellowship with those with whom he might violently disagree.[44]

Two home secretaries, C. R. Duppuy (1911–20) and H. St B. Holland (1920–23) gave distinguished leadership at a comparatively early age. Both had a gift for friendship as well as organizing ability and inventiveness. Duppuy left to become Bishop of Victoria, Hong Kong and Holland was later Bishop of Wellington, New Zealand and Dean of Norwich. Length of service was one among many gifts to the Society of Miss E. M. Baring-Gould (54 years) S. W. W. Witty (52 years) and A. H. Elgie (46 years). Miss Baring-Gould was one of the CMS delegates to the Edinburgh conference in 1910. She was also one of the first women members of the general committee and the first woman to take the chair at one of its meetings, in April 1941. She visited all the Society's mission areas overseas except West Africa, and it was natural in her later years at Salisbury Square that she should be asked to stand in for group secretaries who were ill or visiting overseas. Witty, after helping Lankester to organize the medical department in its early days from 1894, became the Society's chief clerk in 1913 and later assistant financial secretary. Elgie was an assistant in the finance department (1911–28) and assistant foreign secretary (1928–38). He became the friend and confidant of hundreds of missionaries through his duties in connection with the personal grants committee.

The first woman to be appointed a full secretary of the Society was Mrs Elaine Thornton, in 1927. She had had a long apprenticeship. After the death of her husband, Douglas Thornton, in Egypt in 1906 she was given charge of the Highbury hostel where some women candidates were trained, and in 1910 she was appointed women candidates' secretary at headquarters. From 1915 she had varied responsibilities in the foreign department deputizing for group secretaries as need arose. She retired in 1934. Miss Elsie Thorpe, women candidates secretary (1921–36) and assistant foreign secretary (1936–41) had a remarkable personal ministry among women missionaries, and her help and friendship was as readily given to those who were not accepted for missionary service.

The Associations

The life of the Society as a fellowship within the Church of England was most fully expressed through its local associations of members and supporters. These associations were first introduced as early as 1812 to bind together collectors of penny-a-week subscriptions. By 1849 five-sixths of the Society's income was received through them. These associations differed greatly in size, from whole counties like Lincolnshire and major cities such as Sheffield to single parishes. Dr Herbert Lankester, as joint home secretary from 1903 to 1910, set himself the task of producing a more standardized pattern of diocesan and archdeaconry associations. This plan was never arbitrarily imposed but, after patient discussion and explanation locally, it came to be accepted over the greater part of the country. A number of smaller associations remained in being where there was a strong local demand for their continuance; but the development of 'major' associations made devolution possible not only in fund-raising but in missionary education. After the first world war H. St B. Holland, seeing the danger of associations becoming so large that local initiative could be inhibited rather than stimulated, encouraged the formation of several area committees within diocesan and archdeaconry associations. He also devised means of strengthening the links between the associations and the general committee in London. From 1922 a major association was defined geographically as comprising twenty-five or more supporting parishes and financially as contributing £2,000 or more each year. All such associations were from that time entitled to supply one representative on the general committee for each £2,000 contributed annually. By the end of the period, in the early 1940s, there were ninety major associations and well over half the society's annual income was contributed through them.

Many of the largest and most effective associations were in the north of England, which had its own ways of doing things and a healthy spirit of resistance against regimentation from London. In 1918 a commission of enquiry under the chairmanship of Guy Warman, vicar of Bradford, recommended the formation of a northern council, with its own full-time secretary, to be responsible for CMS activities in the Province of York. The proposal for a northern council was endorsed at a CMS congress in Sheffield in November 1919 and received the general committee's approval at its December meeting. The council's function was 'to correlate and develop the work of the CMS in the Northern Province under the Home and Foreign Committee (after 1923 under the Executive Committee) with a view to the deepening and widening of interest, the promotion of prayer, the calling forth of candidates, and the raising of funds'. The members of the council, initially eighty-four in number, were chosen from the northern dioceses on a basis proportionate to the financial contributions of the diocese, with ten co-opted members and as *ex officio* members, a northern secretary, a travelling secretary for women's work, and the organizing secretaries serving in the northern province. The first northern secretary to be appointed was the Rev. J. M. Cunningham, vicar of Littleover, Derby (1919–22). He was an efficient administrator who had firm convictions about filling the unforgiving minute. He left a demanding pattern of work to his successor, the Rev. G. F. Trench (1922–27).

The Organizing Secretaries

The associations were kept in touch with headquarters and were stimulated in their activities by a team of full-time salaried organizing secretaries, normally twenty-five in number. Their maintenance and travelling expenses made up the largest item in the Society's home expenditure. As a rule each organizing secretary had the oversight of CMS concerns in two or more dioceses in England and Wales, and three served the Hibernian CMS in Ireland. For much of the period the field staff included a 'missionary missioner' whose task was to correlate evangelism at home and overseas. The Rev. Hubert Brooke (1910–16) and the Rev. Colin Cutler (1919–28) served many parishes most helpfully in this ministry, as did Bishop J. H. Linton of Persia during a year's extended leave, 1932–33. Missionary missions were resumed in 1940 under the leadership of Bishop G. W. Wright with support from the Rev. G. J. Rogers, the Rev. R. M. Scantlebury and Miss Elsie Thorpe.

The organizing secretaries provided a two-way link with headquarters throughout the country. They supplied up-to-date information about the plans and activities of the home department to the CMS supporting parishes directly or through the associations; and were expected to be knowledgeable about the news from overseas. They also passed back to London the wishes, needs and new ideas of supporters in their areas. Towards the end of the period each organizing secretary was provided with a car, a film-projector and other visual aids, and a wide selection of books and pamphlets. Many of them were former missionaries who had had to return to Britain for health reasons, but a larger number came out of the parochial ministry for a stint of five years or so, and were apt to look back on them as the toughest and most rewarding years of their ministry. By 1941 there were women assistant organizing secretaries in five of the larger areas. The first woman to be given full charge of a district – Chester diocese – was Miss L. D. Bowlby (1940–43).

The CMS commission's report (1934) suggested a regional grouping of organizing secretaries in four or five major areas with some specialization in each team – one specialist in youth, another in education and so on. This proposal was not followed up and the organizing secretaries continued to cover much the same areas as fifty years ago, spending much of the time on the road with more reliable cars but also far greater traffic problems.

Deputations

The organizing secretaries were expected to do a good amount of preaching and talking themselves on behalf of the Society, but they were also involved in the local arrangements for 'deputation'. Missionaries on leave were expected to give an agreed proportion of their time, usually a month or six weeks, speaking at meetings and, if clergy, preaching on Sundays. By the end of the period it was usual for most associations to have an annual CMS Sunday, frequently followed by an open meeting in the largest local hall on the Monday night. As the number of ordained missionaries declined and the number of women missionaries increased this pattern had to be modified. Few bishops would allow women missionaries to preach from the pulpit; Bishop Barnes of Birmingham did so if they were graduates, but he was a rare exception. A further difficulty about deputation, which caused heart-searching at Salisbury Square, was how to obtain a balance between the natural desire of supporting parishes to have a missionary speaker at least once a year and the need, increasingly recognized, for missionaries to use some of their leave in taking refresher courses and for those on first furlough to be freed from other commitments in order to continue their training. A further difficulty was that some of the most effective missionaries were not persuasive preachers or speakers in this country. Fortunately there were many missionaries who had returned to Britain in middle age, on health grounds or because of the needs of their growing children, who enjoyed deputation work and were very good at it; and others who retired from missionary service at the normal age but who kept their health and vigour for many years and welcomed calls for this service. Among the most used during this period were Bishop J. J. Willis (Uganda), Bishop R. S. Heywood (Mombasa), W. E. S. Holland (India), A. B. Lloyd (Uganda) and W. H. Murray Walton (Japan).

The headquarters secretaries were almost by definition able, and well-informed on the Society's message, and many of them had served overseas for a considerable time. It was customary for them to spend many weekends each year travelling round the country and the larger city-hall type of meeting tended to rely on the presence of one of them, usually accompanied by a missionary on furlough.

Anniversaries, Congresses, Summer Schools

In the period 1910 to 1942 the impact of the 'great meeting' was at first still considerable, but it soon began to lessen as a result of the cinema, radio, and other cultural and social changes. Missionary meetings were not immune from the effects of these changes, but those who supported them tended to be drawn from one of the most conservative social groups, and 'May Meetings' still had a favoured place in the calendar of an evangelical family in the 1920s. These meetings, spread over a week or so in London, were arranged by a number of evangelical societies; the British and Foreign Bible Society and CMS meetings usually commanded the largest attendances. By tradition on the Monday before the first Wednesday in May the CMS annual service was held, and the annual sermon preached, at St Bride's Church, Fleet Street. The first annual sermon was preached there in 1817 and between 1834 and 1940, when St Bride's was gutted in an air raid, there was no break in this tradition, which was resumed as soon as St Bride's was rebuilt. Until the end of the nineteenth century a full hour's sermon was expected and 'Mr Handley Moule's sudden close at about forty minutes in 1898 was almost resented'.[45] It was also part of tradition that a bishop and a presbyter preached in alternate years. Among the longest remembered sermons of the period were two from Bishop Azariah of Dornakal, in 1920 and 1927, by Archbishop Randall Davidson in 1925 and Archbishop William Temple in 1934. From 1928 to 1940 the singing at the annual service was led by the choir of Croydon parish church; and the lessons were always read by lay members of CMS committees.

The official annual meeting of CMS was held from 1908 to 1933 at the Queen's Hall, and after 1933 at the Central Hall, Westminster or the Kingsway Hall. In the early days the annual meeting lasted from 10 a.m. to 4 p.m., but later customs dictated a three-hour limit. The president normally took the chair, though occasionally the Archbishop of Canterbury was invited to do so as vice-patron of the Society. A diocesan bishop from one of the English dioceses was by custom the first speaker.

On the same day as the annual meeting there was a large open meeting in the evening, at the Albert Hall from 1905 onwards. It was intended 'rather as a demonstration of sympathy than as a channel of information' but as the zest for attending many meetings declined, it tended to deplete the official meeting earlier in the day. A more intimate occasion of the anniversary was the honorary secretary's (later the general secretary's) breakfast on the morning following the annual meeting, at which he could share his thoughts and concerns with members of the committees and other invited friends. There was also a largely-attended children's service, held in duplicate until 1940 at St Paul's for children from parishes north of the Thames and at Southwark cathedral for those from the south of the river. Sectional meetings filled in the anniversary programme, for the Gleaners' Union (later the Missionary Service League), the Medical Mission Auxiliary on the Wednesday or Friday, and the clergy breakfast, later changed to a tea-time meeting, on the Tuesday.

Special anniversaries sometimes called for an Albert Hall meeting. One of the most notable of these was the Uganda Jubilee meeting on the 27th January, 1927 when the Archbishop of Canterbury, Bishop Willis and Mrs A. B. Fisher were the main speakers. The Uganda Jubilee celebrations included an exhibition at Salisbury Square in which Mackay's printing-press, Bishop Hannington's diary, and early letters and maps were on view. Meetings were also held all over the country in the first three months of 1927.

As the anniversary declined in importance, congresses and residential summer schools were introduced. The first congress was held in Sheffield on the 25th to 27th November, 1919, at the inauguration of the CMS northern council. Its programme included a public meeting, with an audience of 2,000 people, with addresses by the Archbishop of York (Dr Lang) and the Rt Hon. W. Adamson, the leader of the Labour Party in the House of Commons. Most of the time of the congress was taken up with working sessions for delegates only. The second congress was in Birmingham in 1920 and thereafter two were normally held each year, one in the north and one in the south of England. An attempt was made to relate the work of the congress to that of the associations on the one hand and the general committee on the other. For example, the Cheltenham congress considered a number of questions prepared by the general committee and the congress recommendations were passed to the associations who reported back to the general committee.

The first CMS summer school was held at Keswick in 1904. Dr Lankester had seen the value of these on a visit to the USA and it was on his initiative that they became an annual feature of CMS activity in Britain. Until 1921 they were held at some holiday resort in June or July, before the August rush. Inevitably at such a time of year their membership was overweighted with the leisured and the elderly, and so in 1921 the experiment was made of holding a holiday school in August at Llandudno. Five hundred people registered for it, at least a hundred of whom were professional teachers. From 1923 until 1940, except for one year at Oxford, the summer school was held at Malvern Girls' College for a week in August. It served excellently for the purpose. A men's camp in the grounds accommodated up to a hundred, mostly students. On more than one occasion Wycliffe Hall, Oxford took in the Malvern summer school as part of its long vacation term. Each morning began with a session of bible-study, and for the rest of the morning and in the evening there were either lectures or study groups. Average attendance was about 700, but more than once the membership topped the 1,000 mark. These Malvern summer schools were vital to the life of the CMS in the inter-war years. Through them many young men and women were challenged to a deeper commitment to Christ which in many cases led on to an offer for missionary service.

There were many faithful supporters of the Society whose circumstances did not allow them to attend summer school, and their need was met by a week-end CMS laymen's conference at Swanwick or High Leigh, Hoddesdon or by regional conferences which provided opportunities of informal discussion of the world mission of the church, and of CMS responsibilities and opportunities.

The Missionary Service League and other Unions

At the peak of CMS influence in the 1880s and 1890s there was a considerable number of CMS unions, some catering for different age groups and vocations, and one, the Gleaners' Union, founded by Eugene Stock in 1886, which was of a general character for all members of CMS who valued a direct link with head-quarters.[46] Its membership grew rapidly to reach 80,000 about the time of the CMS centenary in 1899, and it provided support for twelve 'Own Missionaries'. In 1921 the Gleaners' Union changed its name to the Missionary Service League and sought to adapt its methods to the conditions of the post-war years. The MSL took as its badge the Celtic cross of St Cuthbert, signifying the unity of missionary service at home or overseas. In 1936 it had 1,025 branches with a total membership of 24,000. A typical branch in the north of England had a membership of forty people, mostly about 25 years old. It met on the first Monday evening of each month, supported a hospital bed in India and pledged itself to see that the support of its parish for CMS would never be reduced. Membership of the MSL was open to all over sixteen and a number of young people's leagues and communicant guilds registered for group membership. Its aim was 'a church filled with the missionary spirit, constrained by the love of Christ, with a passion for the salvation of men, revealing to the world the healing, renewing, uplifting power of the Christian gospel, witnessing with fearless courage for righteousness and brotherhood'.

For those under the age for the MSL the Young People's Union provided opportunities of learning in fellowship. 'Its object,' wrote Miss Monica Sharpe in 1921, 'is to train; not to rouse a spasmodic interest, but to cultivate a way of thinking; not to impose our views and ideas on children, but to help boys and girls with matters which are their vital concern as Christians, and to arrive at their own conclusions.' Miss Sharpe was joint secretary of the YPU from 1919 to 1928 and her clerical colleague for part of this time (1924–27) was Clifford Martin, later Bishop of Liverpool. The YPU adopted as its 'own missionary' in 1921 W. J. Thompson, headmaster of Stuart Memorial College in Isfahan, and later Bishop in Iran, and two other missionaries in Iran and one in the Sudan were later supported by the English and Irish YPU.

The Companions of the Way was started in 1928 particularly for girls and young men who were prepared to face the call to foreign service. A junior branch of the Companions, the Knights of the Round World, had close links with the Scout and Guide movements.

A Sunday-school affiliation scheme provided graded lessons on missionary themes from 1921 and over 1,000 Sunday schools made this link during the inter-war period. Many of them took up one or more £5 'shares' for regular support of a mission station.

The Medical Mission Auxiliary

The MMA differed from the other subsidiary groups in CMS mentioned above in having a specific financial commitment. From 1904 to 1943 it made itself responsible for the support of all the Society's medical work and in its last five years as an auxiliary its average budget was £70,000, and many parishes raised money for it in addition to supporting CMS general funds. By 1924 as many as 2,270 parishes were supporting MMA and under the dynamic leadership of the Rev. Stuart Cox, secretary of MMA from 1925 to 1940, it played a significant part in missionary education in the home church. The medical court became a feature both of CMS and united missionary exhibitions, and from 1929 Cox put on regular child welfare exhibitions at Salisbury Square. There had been a Boys' Brigade section of MMA almost from its inception in 1893, but Cox strengthened this link, especially in Boys' Brigade and Life Boy support of medical dispensaries in Northern Nigeria. By 1942 the Boys' Brigade movement was contributing over £1,000 annually through MMA.

A chief method of fund-raising in the early days of MMA was the supported beds scheme by which the name of a parish, or Sunday-school or YPU branch could be associated with a bed in a CMS mission hospital. With a change of medical policy in which mobile medical teams and preventive medicine became more important, this method of support became anachronistic and in the late 1930s it began to be replaced by the £5 share scheme. This provided a more fluid income not tied to institutions but available for village dispensaries, maternity centres and so forth. Over 1,000 of these shares had been taken up by 1942.

The Medical Mission Auxiliary held its jubilee between May 1942 and May 1943. Receipts rose by £25,000 during this period in spite of war conditions. Statistics often quoted at jubilee meetings were impressive. For example the claim was made that half the patients in Anglican mission hospitals and one tenth of all the patients in all medical missionary institutions were being cared for by the CMS with MMA support. It was however pointed out that two-thirds of the expenditure on CMS medical missions was raised in the mission field. The jubilee appeal was helped by two books specially written for it: *Where There's a Will* (1942), a popular introduction to CMS medical missionary work written by Mrs Eleanor Anderson and *The Wholeness of Man* (1943) by Phyllis

Garlick, which was one of the most influential books ever published by CMS because it allowed thoughtful readers to share in a reappraisal of medical mission policy at an early stage.

For several years before the jubilee the 'auxiliary' character of MMA had been under scrutiny, and on the 16th February, 1943 the general committee of CMS approved recommendations of its medical committee for a closer integration of MMA funds with the CMS general fund. The initials MMA were retained but 'A' now stood for 'Appropriations' not 'Auxiliary'. The existing arrangements for bed-support, medical shares, and 'our own missionary' schemes were not affected by the change, but the annual accounts, hitherto published separately, were amalgamated. The approved recommendations included fuller medical representation on the executive committee, and the addition of medical representatives on local governing bodies of CMS missions. Medical group advisers were appointed overseas and the secretary of the medical committee of London headquarters was given the status and responsibilities of a full secretary of the Society.

CMS Literature, 1910–42

1. *Periodicals.* The centenary of 1899 was the high-water mark of the Society's influence on the church in Britain, and after it the circulation of its periodicals began to decline. This was not due to a lack of imaginative effort or of efficient service by the editorial staff at Salisbury Square, and there was plenty of consumer-research going on all the time through the organizing secretaries around the country. The decline in circulation was due in the main to the contraction of the CMS constituency which has already been noticed in other fields.

In 1910 the main monthly publications of CMS were: *The Church Missionary Gleaner*, a magazine of a 'popular' character aimed at the membership of the Gleaners' Union; *The CMS Gazette*, essentially a workers' bulletin started by Lankester in 1905; *Mercy and Truth*, the organ of the Medical Mission Auxiliary which began publication in 1897; *The Church Missionary Review*, started in 1907 as a successor to *The Church Missionary Intelligencer*, which was an intellectual counterpart to *The Gleaner*; and a children's paper, the *Round World*. In 1914–15 a sub-committee on the Society's publications collated evidence from the organizing secretaries and others about their effectiveness as channels of information and for missionary propaganda. The replies were on the whole reassuring without being complacent. There was considerable support for the view that the Society was publishing too many periodicals and that they were in fact competing with each other. The sub-committee recommended the amalgamation of the *Gazette* with the *Gleaner*. This was done from 1919 to 1926. Then for eight years the *Gazette* was again published separately as a workers' bulletin until 1934, when it was discontinued. The only periodical that had a rising circulation in 1915 was the *Round World*, but that too began to feel the effects of wide-circulation newspapers and magazines which made any periodical with a comparatively small circulation appear poor value for money. The CMS periodicals were not expected to be entirely self-supporting, still less profitable, but in a period of retrenchment they could not be heavily subsidized, and some casualties were inevitable.

The first casualty was *The Church Missionary Review*. In 1918 it was changed from a monthly to a quarterly. Stock generously acknowledged at the time when this change took place that it had 'reached a higher level in recent years than it occurred to me even to aim at',[47] but a forty-eight page monthly consisting of four or more fairly heavy articles, with book reviews and editorial comment, was not easily sustained either in quality or circulation. The change to a ninety-six page quarterly gave *Review* a further lease of life for nine years and during that time it achieved a new level of creative writing in articles by such missionary statesmen and prophets as J. H. Oldham, William Paton and Roland Allen: but the frequency of such outside contribution made its future questionable. *International Review of Missions* and the excellent *The East and the West* published by SPG were occupying the same limited field with a growing confidence, and it became increasingly doubtful whether a single missionary society could or should maintain its own periodical at this level. In 1927 both *The Church Missionary Review* and *The East and the West* ceased publication, and from 1928 their place was taken by *The Church Overseas*, sponsored by the Missionary Council of the Church Assembly, and jointly edited by G. S. Gillett of SPG and G. H. Harris, the editorial secretary of CMS. In 1935 it was in turn replaced by *East and West Review*, a joint responsibility of SPG and CMS and published by SPCK.

In 1922 *The Church Missionary Gleaner* changed its name to *Church Missionary Outlook*, a title which was still proving acceptable, after considerable changes of format, nearly fifty years later. In the same year *Mercy and Truth*, the organ of the MMA, became *The Mission Hospital* and changed again in 1940 to *The Way of Healing*. These changes of title were both symptomatic of a change of policy in medical missions. 1922 was the heyday of institutionalized medicine and great efforts were being made to increase the number of hospital beds. By 1940, following the report of the CMS medical commission, it gave a false impression of the strategy of medical mission and so the further change was made.

In the 1930s the sales of both *Outlook* and *Round World* were declining, and shortage of paper and other publishing restrictions following the outbreak of the second world war led to a drastic curtailment of CMS periodicals. The quarterly bulletin for clergy, started in 1917, was dropped altogether. The *Outlook* was reduced to four large pages each month. *The Way of Healing* was incorporated with it, and did not resume publication after the war. The *Round World* was reduced from sixteen to eight pages in some months and the monthly

CMS Intercessions Paper became a bi-monthly publication. The general secretary's *News-Letter*, a valued innovation by Wilson Cash, maintained by his successors, continued to be issued in eleven months of each year.

2. *Books.* CMS continued and expanded its output of books during the period. From 1926 a special imprint, *The Highway Press*, was used for books which might be expected to have a circulation outside the Society's normal constituency and which might be hampered by its initials on the cover. The Highway books at first carried a colophon on the title page representing a road winding over rounded hills towards a rising sun. They included biographies of missionaries and, occasionally, weightier statements of policy but there was no distinctive format which separated them from books carrying the CMS imprint.

Among the best-selling books published by the Society during this period, pride of place goes to A. B. Lloyd's romantic account of the life and witness of Canon Apolo Kivebulaya, *Apolo of the Pygmy Forest*; R. W. Howard's life of Clifford Harris, entitled *The Merry Mountaineer*; Mrs Donald Fraser's *The Doctor Comes to Lui*; and F. D. Walker's *The Romance of the Black River*, an account of the CMS Niger mission.

3. *Annual Reports.* The Society's annual reports at this time were substantial bound volumes giving detailed accounts of the work of each mission and a complete list of contributions with subscribers' names. The need for a more popular account of the year's work which could be circulated separately from the official report was recognized after the first world war and the veteran ex-editor, Eugene Stock, was called in to compile the first of these, *The Ever-Growing Church*, in 1923. Later Miss Phyllis Garlick and Miss Ethel Doggett became adept at writing these popular reports.

In general it appears that in its publishing policy CMS kept in line with current standards and trends, adapting itself as need arose to new conditions, and supplying for its supporters a well-presented array of books and journals which fostered the sense of partnership in a great enterprise.

The Training of Missionaries

It is surprising, from the different standpoint of the 1960s, to see how vulnerable any policy of training was to the Society's immediate financial position. Cutting back on the supply of missionary recruits was almost invariably an ingredient of a retrenchment programme; the able and devoted men and women who ran the candidates' department at Salisbury Square, and the heads of the training institutions, must often have despaired of working out a coherent policy and programme of training. The havoc caused by the first world war touched the Society at this point more than any other, but even as late as 1934 it was decided 'largely on financial grounds' to reduce the number of women in training, although the proportion of the CMS income expended on the whole process of selecting and training all candidates was only 3¼d in the £. The turning point was the report of a special committee on recruiting, selection and training of candidates, published in 1937. Until then, judging by the standards of a generation later, although the process of individual selection was meticulous, the provision of training for those selected was in many cases uncertain and was far from being treated as a priority in the Society's budget. There was a noticeable difference in policy between the training of men and of women for most of the period, so it will be convenient to look at each in turn.

The Training of Men Candidates

In 1910 there were two centres of residential training for men, the CMS college at Islington and the preparatory institution at Blackheath. Islington college, with almost a century of glorious history, had declined somewhat in numbers and effectiveness after the Rev. F. Drury left to become Principal of Ridley Hall, Cambridge, in 1900. It was not the fault of his successor, the Rev. J. A. Lightfoot, that retrenchment was added to other problems inhibiting a vigorous life for the college. Until 1908 it had been customary for some missionaries trained at Islington to come into residence again during their first furlough to take the Durham BA, but in that year the senate of Durham University made it a condition that degree candidates should first have taken the Licentiate of Theology. In 1912 the CMS committee decided that in future accepted candidates should do a three years' theological course at Islington followed by one year at Durham. The outbreak of the first world war postponed these plans and before the war was over Islington college was no more.

The preparatory institution, 'for young men of promise but not of superior education', served as a feeder to Islington college, although not all candidates went on there. It provided a three-year course, 'probably leading to Holy Orders', a shorter course of four terms for others, and a year's course in theology for university graduates or doctors. The CMS committee had begun to question whether the Society ought to be faced with the expense of preparing men for Islington and in 1912 the preparatory institution at Blackheath was closed, and the few remaining students were accommodated at Islington for a year's preliminary training. The severe retrenchment ordered by the committee in 1911 had already reduced the number of men candidates accepted for training and the outbreak of war in 1914 reduced the numbers in the college to a handful. In 1915 it was closed temporarily and two years later the whole property was sold, though the proceeds of sale were kept in reserve for purchase of other buildings when needed.

In 1920 two adjacent houses, 173 and 175 Green Lanes, Stoke Newington, were bought by the Society for the residential training of men candidates and were given the name of St Andrew's. In December 1922, following further retrenchment measures, St Andrew's was handed over for the training of women candidates, and for the next four years the Society had no place of training for men. In 1927 however, the Henry Venn Hostel was bought with a fund specially raised to re-establish men's training. As its name implies it was not a training college in the full sense but a hostel for graduates doing special courses elsewhere, for missionaries on furlough taking similar courses, and for members of overseas churches connected with CMS who were studying in Britain. In 1934 the Venn hostel was closed and men candidates returned to St Andrew's.

Full consideration was given by the 1936–37 committee on recruitment, selection, and training to possible alternative sites for training, and sub-committees were appointed to investigate the possibilities at Selly Oak, Birmingham, where there were already a number of missionary training colleges, and at Oxford. The conclusion of the special committee was that London provided the best facilities for special lecturers, greater opportunities than elsewhere of training in pastoral skills, and preparation courses of a range and quality not to be found elsewhere. The committee put forward a further reason for keeping the training centres in or near London. It regarded as of 'the utmost importance' a close and easy contact between the candidates and the secretaries at Salisbury Square. After a period of *ad hoc* arrangements during the war years Liskeard Lodge, Blackheath, was purchased by the Society for men's training and was opened in May 1946, and the name continued to be used after a move to Chislehurst in 1952.

The 1937 report on recruitment, etc., noted that in the five years 1932–36 no less than sixty men had sailed without any special preparation 'due largely to the urgency of the demands from Missions as a result of the quota system'. This system related the number of recruits sailing each year to the Society's general budget for that year. It inhibited general appeals for missionary service and had the effect, disastrous to any coherent plan of training, of requiring recruits to go out at short notice as replacements. The 1937 report asked the Society to reconsider the quota system and it recommended that every male recruit should have a period of training at St Andrew's, normally not less than six months. This training should be planned to cover the needs of three types of recruits – clergy, doctors and educationists, the curriculum for all groups to include language study at the School of Oriental Studies in London; courses on the bible, doctrine, general church history, the science and history of Christian missions, and the development of indigenous churches with special reference to the religious and cultural background of peoples. It further recommended that men as well as women candidates should make use of their first furlough for further training.[48]

The Training of Women Candidates

It was not until 1917 that CMS undertook full responsibility for the training of its women candidates. Before that three training homes were used: 'The Willows', in Church Street, Stoke Newington, one of the Mildmay Institutions where candidates of the Church of England Zenana Missionary Society also trained; 'The Olives', at Hampstead, run privately by Mrs Bannister from 1891 to 1911, when it was closed on account of her failing health; and the Highbury Training Hostel, run by two sisters, the Misses Cates, for those who through 'lack of means or of adequate educational advantages, or from other causes are ineligible for admission to The Willows or other institutions'. In 1917 CMS purchased The Willows from the Mildmay Trustees and renamed it Kennaway Hall after Sir John Kennaway.

Kennaway Hall had room for twenty-five students and a certain number of places were reserved for CEZMS candidates. In 1923, as already recorded, the pressure on accommodation for accepted women candidates, combined with a continuing uncertainty about the scope and character of men's training, led to the annexation of St Andrew's as an additional centre for women's training.

In 1928 Florence Allshorn, who had been invalided home from Uganda four years earlier, was invited to fill a temporary gap as warden of St Andrew's Hostel. She had never been to a missionary college herself, nor had she the normal academic qualifications expected in such a post, but she felt that 'if God was calling her to pass on to others what she had learned in the hard school of experience, it was her duty to obey'.[49] In 1934 when St Andrew's Hostel was returned for use in men's training, and women's training was concentrated on Kennaway Hall, Miss Allshorn was appointed principal. Apart from a house-mother and visiting lecturers she was for most of the time single-handed. Her approach to training was intuitive rather than theoretical. She once claimed that the only things she knew anything about were domestic science and personal relations, and it was in the field of personal relations that she made a distinctive and enduring contribution to the training of missionaries. 'Her conception of what was essential,' wrote J. H. Oldham, 'was original and profound. . . . Her ideas go to the roots of the problem of training for the Christian ministry and for all forms of Christian work.'

In 1934 Florence Allshorn wrote an article in the *International Review of Missions* on 'Corporate Life on a Mission Station'. It is quoted by Oldham as perhaps the best introduction to the ideas which governed her approach to her task. She was determined to get at the root cause why there are so many defeated women at forty. 'The failures amongst missionaries are those who have lost the forward impulse, the life of the Spirit, because they have never got through their own spiritual, personal and social problems.' She believed that one great mistake in the current training of missionaries was that 'we have spent much time in educating the girl in her spiritual life and preparing her for her work, but her . . . emotional life – this queer hinterland which is in all of us'– had been left largely to take care of itself. She believed that this emotional life must be tackled with a loving ruthlessness. She could not believe that mediocrity was inevitable for anyone and she held that shallow undisturbedness was something that had to be fought with all the weapons of love's armoury. 'For most women candidates the training should be long enough to give time for self-understanding and for stabilizing emotional life on some kind of conquering basis.'[50]

Florence Allshorn was never completely satisfied that Kennaway Hall was a suitable site for the kind of training needed and in 1938 she initiated a move to Foxbury, Chislehurst, 'a charming house with accommodation for forty students in eight acres of lovely grounds'. On the outbreak of war in 1939, Foxbury was taken over for a time by the Society as its temporary headquarters and Miss Allshorn was asked to take a reduced number of students to Carey Hall, the Baptist Missionary College at Selly Oak. They returned to Foxbury for a few weeks but in October 1940, when serious bombing had begun in the London area, there was a second evacuation to Ridley Hall, Cambridge.

The principal had already decided that the time had come for her to resign and after one term in Cambridge she did so. It was her conviction that preliminary training of missionaries was only the initiation of a much longer process of learning and it was with this in mind that she started looking for a place where young missionaries whom she had trained could find quiet, and grow, a search which led her to found at Oakenrough, in 1941, what later became known as the St Julian's Community. She was succeeded as principal of CMS Women's Training College by Miss Margaret Potts, formerly headmistress of Lagos girls' school, who shared much of her insight about missionary training and who had the trained mind which could continue to work out its implications.

The Candidates Department

At the beginning of the period the candidates department reflected the man-woman two-tier system of the committee structure generally. The department was controlled by the men candidates' secretary, and the women candidates' secretary worked under him. But in 1920 the two secretaries and their respective committees were given equal status and after the formation of the executive committee in 1923 each secretary was made directly responsible to it. A manuscript notebook kept by the men candidates' secretary in the 1920s reveals a fairly flexible, although thorough, method of selection. Reports are received on each candidate from three referees. He is interviewed separately by five members of the candidates' committee, including the candidates' secretary and usually one of the foreign 'Group' secretaries. A note is made of the kind of offer made by the candidate. Sometimes it is an open offer, but quite often it is for a a specific post – J. L. C. Horstead for Fourah Bay College, C. S. Milford for St Paul's College, Calcutta; or for a particular mission – J. W. Welch for Nigeria. Sometimes recommendations are made about the place and length of training but quite often no such recommendations are made. A fair number of the offers noted were for short service posts, and in the decade 1927–36, sixty-six men and fifty-three women went overseas as short service candidates, many of them later to become full missionaries of the Society.

The 1937 report on recruiting recommended an extension of the short service scheme to older women educationists who had reached pensionable age for relief-duties in under-staffed mission schools or for pastoral and evangelistic work. The report also made general recommendations about the qualifications necessary for acceptance as CMS candidates. These qualifications included – a 'full agreement with the Evangelical principles which the Society holds as an integral part of the heritage of the Church of England'; an awareness of the need for co-operative work with other branches of the Christian church, and a readiness to work in full partnership and harmony with members of other races; a clear understanding of the relation of the mission to the church and an ability to help in the church's growth towards self-support, self-government, and self-extension. The report recommended that for men candidates a university degree was usually desirable and that doctors and educationists should have the best qualifications for their particular type of work.

The section of the 1937 report which dealt with the training of missionaries reflects the help given to the special committee by two consultants, Bishop R. O. Hall of Hong Kong and Dr J. H. Oldham. An address which Oldham gave to the committee on the 30th June, 1936 was printed as an appendix to the report. In it he shared his convictions that the right selection and training of missionaries 'is beyond all comparison the major consideration in the whole missionary enterprise'. The task of the missionary is, he said, to communicate a life, and his training must be related to his capacity to grow, to learn and to live in fellowship with others.

> In the last resort the important thing about missionaries is not how much they know, but what they are themselves. . . . The really critical period in a missionary's career is his first term of service, because it is only then that he learns what he really wants. A great deal of the instruction given before he sails is lost to him because he cannot relate it to anything in his life.

It was in line with this last point that the committee recommended the appointment, as furlough advisers, of one man and one woman who were in touch with the thinking and need of each younger missionary.

A major recommendation of the 1937 report was the replacement of the existing training colleges committee by a governing body for Kennaway Hall and St Andrews, to consist of the president of CMS, the general secretary, and the two candidates' secretaries *ex officio*; two members nominated by each of the candidates committees, preferably with missionary experience; six members elected by the executive committee, at least two of whom, one man and one woman, should have special knowledge of religious education; and two members annually co-opted by the governing body.

The functions proposed for the governing body included the determination of the subjects of instruction, including practical and extra-mural work and additional courses at other institutions where suitable; the fixing of an upper limit of accommodation for CMS candidates in training, and for candidates accepted in the CMS colleges from CEZMS and other societies; to recommend to the appointments committee, for nomination to the executive committee, the college principals as vacancies occurred, and to appoint, on the nomination of the principals, the other members of the teaching staff. These, and other recommendations of the 1937 report, noted earlier, were substantially adopted in the next few years.

The Care of Missionaries' Children

One of the most severe deprivations of the missionary's calling during the period was the separation of parents from children, sometimes when they were little more than toddlers, frequently at the age of seven or eight. For missionaries in China during the 1920s the separation could still be as long as eight years at a time, rather less for those in India and Africa. Air travel had hardly begun to affect missionaries before 1942, though it was used occasionally in emergency. Everything possible was done to ease this burden of family separations. Missionary families were often quite large ones, and brothers and sisters could support each other in their parents' absence; some relatives in Britain counted it a privilege to share in the work of overseas missions by caring for the children; and the necessary sense of security was greatly helped by a confident recourse to prayer through which parents and children felt themselves to be firmly held together by God's unfailing care and love. Nevertheless, the deprivation was real, particularly when a parent died or when a child had no regular place to go when school term ended. For all, the reunions and partings were almost equally hard to bear.

The CMS, like other societies, gave much thought and care to providing for the children of its missionaries. Its first children's home was opened in Milner Square, Islington, in 1850 and, after several moves and extensions in that part of London, a new site of twenty acres was purchased at Limpsfield on the Surrey heights, and a new purpose-built boarding-school was opened in October 1887.[51] There were separate wings for boys and girls, each with accommodation for about fifty children, and also a junior house for those under eight years.

During the years 1910–42 there were four directors of the CMS children's home (renamed St Michael's in 1915). Three were clergymen – W. B. Tracy (1904–13); H. Summerhayes (1913–28); B. C. Corfield (1928–29); and from 1929 the first layman to be appointed, E. C. H. Moule. Tracy was a keen naturalist, and he did much to improve the grounds. He introduced the prefectorial system, and the house system was started by his successor, bringing the school into line with the English boarding-schools of the period. Most of the boys left at the age of thirteen or fourteen to go on to public schools, St. Lawrence, Trent, Weymouth, and Merchant Taylor's being the most favoured. The girls usually stayed for the whole of their school career and some went on to university.

In the 1920s the grown-up children of the Summerhayes were a great asset, 'benevolent, energetic young adults, teaching us, and doing interesting things around the world, they gave the adolescents some feelings for and hope about life outside the school'. The Corfields, who came to St Michael's for a year from missionary service in the Punjab, did a great deal for St Michael's in a short time. Their friendliness and enjoyment of life, and their young children, meant a great deal to the family life of the school. Mr and Mrs Moule reverted to the grandparental pattern: but his scholarliness and her gracious charm were welcome gifts to the lives of children who had, it is true, Surrey heaths and woodlands around them, but strict economy indoors. As time went on the Moules gave the older girls more contact with the everyday life of England.

Old Michaelians when questioned about their memories of the school tend to be puzzled when asked about the psychological effects of the long separation from their parents. Nearly all of those who were at St Michael's during this period seem to have been happy there. A high proportion became CMS missionaries themselves.

A Decade of Controversy, 1912–22

Few matters of CMS history are better known, and less happily remembered, than the controversy which came to a head in three meetings of the general committee in March, July and November 1922. What is less well-known is the process by which this controversy was nurtured, the range of disagreements involved in it, or the spirit in which the authorities of CMS sought to control its debilitating effects.

At the time when the controversy was at its height in June 1922 Eugene Stock wrote an article in *The Church Missionary Review* entitled 'Some Lessons from Past Times'. His purpose was to show that division of opinion among evangelicals in the Church of England was no new thing. He recalled that after the Predestinarian Controversy had abated at the beginning of the nineteenth century there had been the Trinitarian-Socinian debate of the 1830s which led to the formation of the Trinitarian Bible Society. Then, in the 1840s, there had been heated arguments about the wearing of the surplice in the pulpit. J. C. Ryle had been dubbed a 'neo-Evangelical' because, although he made a point of wearing a black Geneva gown when preaching in his own church, he would not refuse to wear a surplice if desired when preaching elsewhere. Stock drew on his own direct experience for memories of five occasions of 'painful controversy' in the 1880s. One of them concerned the holding of a CMS service in St Paul's Cathedral shortly after a new reredos had been installed. 'At this time,' he wrote of the 1880s, 'we were constantly told that the Society was going downhill, that it had lost the confidence of the country, that wealthy friends were altering their wills and leaving it no legacies, in fact that its days were numbered.' He recalled that plans were 'actually in progress' at that time for superseding the CMS by a new society 'more decided and exclusive in views and principles', but that nothing more was heard of the project after Sir Lewis Dibdin had drawn attention to it in a leading article in the *Record*.[52]

Stock made his point that what was taking place in 1922 was no sudden darkening of the sky, but, like many historians of his generation, he perhaps built too much on the cathartic value of remembrance from past days. In the decade before 1922 there had been a steady hardening of differences, ecclesiological as well as biblical, and sweet reasonableness was in short supply.

In January 1912 a group of clergy presented a memorial to the CMS committee deprecating, among other things, the invitations to speak at meetings of the Society being given to 'those who have encouraged the development of the Tractarian Movement'. The Bishop of London, A. F. Winnington-Ingram, had been the speaker at the valedictory meeting for outgoing missionaries at the Albert Hall in the previous October. In an open letter replying to the memorial the CMS committee recalled that from the early years of the Society it had been customary to invite bishops and others, not identified with its views, to speak at its meetings, particularly the Archbishop of Canterbury with whom the Society was necessarily in frequent communication, and the Bishop of London 'who ordains the Society's candidates'. The committee was not unmindful of the growth of sacerdotal principles, and of their duty to maintain the purity of the Society's message; but it called the attention of the memorialists to the new missionary situation which had arisen since the Edinburgh conference of 1910, and the recognition given by the Church of England in its official capacity in a new degree to 'the duty of carrying the Gospel to the non-Christian world'. The committee believed that the founders of the Society would have rejoiced in such a development, and they felt bound 'thankfully to co-operate in such general movements so far as they are able without sacrificing . . . those great Protestant, Evangelical and Scriptural principles (which are the true principles of the Church of England) on which our Society has been based.'[53]

The memorialists, however, clearly felt that the new era of comprehensiveness and co-operation following the Edinburgh conference was already tending to obscure or play down basic doctrinal differences, and Cyril Bardsley, the chief secretary of CMS, was under increasing pressure because of his share in the development of missionary co-operation. By February 1914 Theodore Woods, vicar of Bradford, and several other vicars of large towns in the north, felt that the attacks on Bardsley were serious enough to warrant a joint letter to the president of CMS expressing their 'complete confidence in the leadership of our present Honorary Secretary' and asking that 'before any important decisions affecting either the principles or the management of the Society are reached, there should be a duly convened meeting of the Society's representatives in all parts of the country.' Some, though not all, of the signatories of this letter were members of a fellowship known at that time as the 'Group Brotherhood' and later (from 1923) more widely known as the Anglican Evangelical Group Movement. This group, which began meeting informally on Merseyside in 1906, had by 1914 drawn together a number of like-minded clergy mostly in the north of England. They were perturbed at what seemed to them to be an introverted and defensive attitude within the evangelical party. Taking 'the mind of Christ' as the supreme authority for thought and life, they welcomed what they called 'the positive results' of biblical criticism, trusting the Holy Spirit to sort out the gold from the dross. They also coveted greater freedom in worship and ceremonial than was customary at the time in evangelical parishes, and thought that 'the beauty of holiness' required a less defensive attitude to matters of ceremonial and better standards in church music and furnishings.

One of the early members of the Group Brotherhood in the south of England was J. E. Watts-Ditchfield, vicar of St James-the-Less, Bethnal Green, and from 1914 first Bishop of Chelmsford; another was Guy Rogers, who became vicar of West Ham in Chelmsford diocese in 1917; and it was out of a series of conferences at West Ham vicarage in the autumn of 1917 that a memorial was drawn up representing views very different in tone and purpose from the memorial of 1912. As it was Watts-Ditchfield who presented it to the CMS general committee on the 13th November, 1917, it became known as the Chelmsford memorial. Three-quarters of its eighty or so signatories were thought to be members of, or closely associated with, the Group Brotherhood.[54]

The Chelmsford memorial requested the CMS to make three affirmations which its signatories believed to be in the spirit of the founders of the Society. First, that 'it gladly accepts the services of all who are attracted by its tradition and who [are] striving to interpret evangelical truth in accordance with the Holy Spirit's guidance in each succeeding age'; second, that 'the Society, while adhering firmly to its own principles, works in co-operation with other communions, and welcomes fellowship with societies representing other schools of thought within the Anglican Communion'; third, 'the Society's position with regard to revelation and inspiration is defined for it simply by the formularies of the Church of England; and that no further restriction or definition of belief on these subjects is sought for from its candidates, agents or supporters'. The memorial added to these three points a plea that the CMS should advance further and speedily along the lines of administrative reform and secure a constant supply of younger men and women upon its committees.

After a lengthy discussion at its meeting on the 13th November, 1917, the committee appointed a representative sub-committee to consider the Chelmsford memorial, to suggest what action should be taken in the light of its proposals, and to take account of 'other questions raised among the Society's members and friends about the position of the Society.' A second memorial, largely the work of the Rev. D. H. C. Bartlett, a Liverpool incumbent, was circulated with the agenda for the December meeting of the committee. It was signed by some 500 clergy and almost the same number of laity. A third memorial, deprecating the first and signed by 63 laymen, was also submitted and passed on for the consideration of the sub-committee.[55]

The Bartlett memorial countered the plea for greater comprehensiveness in the CMS. The Society's founders, it claimed, built exclusively on evangelical principles such as 'the absolute authority of Holy Scripture; the perfected sacrifice and finished work of our Redeemer; the Divinely-appointed Way of Salvation through faith in the Personal Christ, and the Atonement wrought by him once and for all; the necessity of the work of the Holy Spirit in the regeneration and sanctification of the sinner'. It claimed further that there had been a number of recent departures from these principles, notably in the placing of native students at Tokyo and Calcutta under influences alien to them, and in the ever-increasing readiness for co-operation, rather than simply the maintenance of friendly relations, with societies not holding these views. The result had been to obscure 'before the Church and the Nation . . . the essential difference between their position and ours'. The memorial also commented on the readiness of CMS missionaries to adopt the 'eastward position' in the Holy Communion service which 'in the eyes of a large number of Churchmen of all Schools of Thought is the expression of a sacerdotal act and office'. In conclusion it asked for a definite assurance by the Society that it would not deflect or depart from its principles.

The memorials sub-committee met for several days in January 1918 under the chairmanship of Bishop F. J. Chavasse of Liverpool. Its twenty-two members included the Bishop of Chelmsford, Bishop Ingham, a former home secretary of CMS; Dean Wace of Canterbury; Preb. H. E. Fox, formerly honorary secretary; Mr S. H. Gladstone, the treasurer; L. G. Buchanan, Guy Rogers, Martin Linton-Smith, and Guy Warman. Its report was presented to and adopted by the general committee on the 12th February, 1918. The report noted five chief subjects in the three memorials which it had been asked to consider and commented on each in turn. (1) *The General Spirit of the Society*. In facing the ever-changing circumstances of missionary work in the world, the Society, while maintaining 'its historic resistance to erroneous tendencies . . . should always uphold and express its own principles with the breadth of sympathy which has been its characteristic from the first'. (2) *Ceremonial*. The north end position of the celebrant at Holy Communion was the normal practice of the officers of CMS, but the eastward position had been declared not illegal, and parochial clergy had a right to adopt it. If a CMS representative agreed to celebrate Holy Communion when visiting a church, considerations of Christian courtesy arose, and the decision must be left to the individual conscience. (3) *The Authority of Holy Scripture*. The sub-committee, 'having regard to the special difficulties of students and young people', recommended that every candidate be interviewed by some 'who know and understand the life of students to-day' and that, as 'personal devotion to Christ as Lord and Saviour should be a primary condition for acceptance', doctrinal definitions more appropriate to maturer years should not be required. The candidates committee should have attached to it an officer of the Society who possessed a personality attractive to students as well as to other candidates, so that the Society could 'carry on a work in the student world calculated to show that the Society is neither out of date nor impervious to new ideas or new methods of working.' The sub-committee deprecated any attempt to lay down a formal definition of the inspiration of the Bible. Articles VI and XX made it clear that inspiration is attributed to Scripture as a whole. The use and treatment of Holy Scripture should be in harmony with that of Christ. 'It is the duty of the student of Holy Scripture . . . to take into the fullest consideration every light that scholarship and saintliness can furnish.' (4) *Relations with Other Societies*. Apart from the CEZMS, the Society had not thought of union with another missionary society. CMS had played a large part in the Conference of British Missionary Societies and was specially called upon to show brotherly fellowship towards the mission-ary agencies of its own church, provided that in all such intercourse the ad-herence of the Society to great evangelical principles be maintained. Each new call, such as co-operation with central and diocesan boards of missions, 'must be considered . . . in the light of our responsibility to our own tradition and to the needs of the Church as a whole'. (5) *The Administration of the Society*. The Society should give attention to this matter without delay, not waiting until after the war as decided in the general committee minute of the 20th March, 1917.[56]

When Bardsley saw an advance copy of the report, he was delighted. 'Mercies beyond words!' he wrote to the president, '. . . The Report is unanimous and signed by the 22 members. . . . Big new possibilities open up before us. I can hardly realize at present how much it is going to mean to me. It immediately puts me in my right place in the centre, and I feel that a long struggle, with many mistakes, for more freedom in CMS, is over.'[57] Unhappily Bardsley's hope that a lasting concordat had been achieved was not justified. *The English Churchman*, 21st February, 1918, took up again the questions of the eastward position in unambiguous terms. 'Without quibbling, the man who takes the eastward position claims to be a sacrificing priest. He ostentatiously attributes a sacerdotal character to the Christian ministry. He goes behind the Reforma-tion in a vital matter.' The same paper a fortnight later protested that CMS students were being taught by a Mirfield monk. A statement by some liberal leaders in *The Challenge*, 22nd February, did not help matters. 'The Younger generation,' it said, 'is asking for liberty and the Report gives them what they need. It is a great declaration of freedom – freedom in respect of Biblical criticism, cere-monial and co-operation with other societies.' In a letter in the same issue of *The Challenge*, E. S. Woods, a chaplain at Sandhurst (later Bishop of Croydon and of Lichfield), regretted the critical attitude of the paper towards the CMS and its memorials report.

> Many of us [he wrote] had good reason to fear that the CMS had no room for the services of Christians who are unable to dress their Christianity in the clothes of past generations. The CMS have now assured us, definitely and publicly, that this is not the case; and I, for one, thankfully accept their assurance, and mean to do my utmost, such as it is, for the work of the Society. [He felt certain] that the new CMS is marked by progress and liberty, and is dominated by the vision of the Kingdom of God.[58]

Meeting on the 14th March, 1918 the council of the Church Association took note of 'the unsatisfactory nature of the CMS Memorials Sub-Committee Report' but did not deem it advisable to take any public action at present. In a situation from which magnanimity had departed it was perhaps inevitable that the happy acceptance of the report by one group should reinforce the doubts of the other.

With heavy heart Bardsley renewed his attempts to draw the two sides together. He explained to one correspondent that it had always been his custom, before he accepted the call to CMS, to take the eastward position where it was the normal practice of the church; and that he accepted the findings of the report *ex animo*. To another correspondent he explained that the 'Mirfield Monk' who was teaching CMS students was in fact the Rev. H. Kelly of Kelham; that he was a temporary member of the United Theological College of the Nippon Sei Ko Kwai in Tokyo; that only four students were involved, and that they were under special and constant charge of CMS missionaries. One could wish that Bardsley's reference to Herbert Kelly had not been so bald and defensive. Kelly was the founder of the Society of the Sacred Mission, Kelham and had gone to teach in Tokyo so as to give elbow-room to his successor as director of the SSM. He was long remembered in Japan as a beloved missionary and a teacher of quite exceptional gifts. What Kelly wrote later in a wider context might well have appealed to Bardsley and his colleagues who were trying desperately to hold the Society together.

> Look where we will, on the Continent, in the mission field, at home, is it not the cause of all our weakness that what God meant as complementary, men have treated as antithetical? And the righteousness of God has been fulfilled in judgment. The forms, reft of the spirit, have stiffened into death: the spirit, unstayed by form, continually dissolves into states of our own feeling. But Thou, O Lord, have mercy upon us. Wilt Thou not turn again and quicken us, that Thy people may rejoice in Thee?[59]

Bardsley still clung to his hope of a comprehensive society.

> The CMS [he wrote] has always been the channel of service and sacrifice for the whole Evangelical School for the time being. For it to become repre-

sentative of only a part of the Evangelical School would be to go back on tradition. In other words, the CMS must be comprehensive if it is to fulfil its vocation and be true to its history. There have always been Conservatives and Liberals amongst us. Again and again the Conservatives have attacked the position of the Liberals and tried to limit the Society in accordance with their own views, but such attempts have caused heartburnings. . . . Unless the principle of comprehension is accepted there cannot be peace, and the deepest life and best service in the CMS.[60]

Four years later this principle was accepted but only after further bitter controversy and at heavy cost.

The Committee Meetings of 1922

At a meeting of the CMS general committee on the 15th March, 1922 Bartlett moved a resolution which, he urged, should be adopted as a declaration of the committee's views. In putting the resolution he made special mention of a series of sermons preached by a CMS missionary (the Rev. E. W. L. Martin) to the British congregation in Hong Kong cathedral which put forward 'higher critical' views of the Old Testament. As the sermons had been preached *extempore* he and others had to rely on press reports of them. There had also been widespread concern at an address at the CMS summer school at Llandudno in the previous year by the Rev. Hume Campbell. Bartlett's motion read as follows:

Whereas the authority of Holy Scripture as the Word of God necessarily involves the trustworthiness of its historical records and the validity of its teachings; and whereas Holy Scripture claims this authority for itself, and our Lord, Whose utterances are true, endorses that claim; we, the Committee of the CMS, because we believe that the acceptance of this authority, so endorsed, is necessary to the fulfilment of the missionary ideal hitherto associated with CMS, hereby undertake neither to send out as missionaries nor to appoint as teachers or responsible officials any who do not thus wholeheartedly believe and teach.

The March meeting, at which this resolution was put forward, was held in the library of the Memorial Hall, Farringdon Street, as many more members than usual had signified their intention to be present. 425 signed the attendance register compared with the usual 60 or so. Most of those who spoke against the motion said that they personally accepted it as a statement, but they were unwilling to tie CMS to any particular formula other than the formularies of the Church of England interpreted on well understood evangelical lines. Eventually the Dean of Canterbury proposed the postponement of the whole question until after a private conference which the Bishop of Chelmsford proposed to hold in June to promote unity among evangelical churchmen. This motion was carried by a large majority.[61]

The Bishop of Chelmsford's conference was held at Coleshill, near Birming-

ham, from 12th to 17th June, 1922. In the printed invitation to the conference
the bishop made it clear that it was not intended to draw up any creed for
evangelicals in general nor for the CMS in particular, but that its members
should 'speak together in the presence of God, seeking together for the Spirit
Himself.' Among those who agreed to speak or to lead sessions were Bishop
Ingham, Canon H. W. Hinde, Dean Wace, the Rev. D. H. C. Bartlett and the
Rev. E. L. Langston. First reports on the meeting suggested that reconciliation
had been largely achieved and the general committee meeting on 12th July
started hopefully. The attendance was even larger than at the March meeting.
It is generally given as about 1,000, though only 614 names were entered in the
attendance register. Bartlett moved his resolution again in a slightly amended
form and with the additional words 'On this basis we are prepared to appoint a
sub-committee to devise plans for the promotion of unity and brotherly co-
operation in the work of the Society.'

The main issue was still whether the limits of legitimate comprehensiveness
could be defined to the satisfaction of all parties without a doctrinal formula that
was more explicit than the Book of Common Prayer and the Thirty-Nine
Articles. Guy Warman, by that time Bishop of Truro, moved an amendment
seeking to make unwavering acceptance of the Nicene Creed 'in its historical
interpretation down the ages', and of Article VI, the basis for service on the
staff of CMS at home or abroad. After lunch Bishop E. A. Knox put forward a
further amendment which he and the Bishops of Chelmsford, Liverpool and
Truro had been working on during the lunch hour. It asserted the supreme
authority of Holy Scripture and its trustworthiness in 'all matters of faith and
doctrine', but did not include a statement about the truth of our Lord's utterances as the endorsement of the authority and trustworthiness of the Scriptures.
As the debate continued Bishop Chavasse made a personal appeal to Bartlett,
who had worked in his diocese for eighteen years, to accept the Bishop's
amendment; but Bartlett said it left out the vital part of his resolution and that
he must vote against it. The debate went on until after 4 p.m. and Bishop
Knox had to leave before his amendment was put. Stock, looking back on this
meeting, thought that with another half hour and a small alteration in phrasing
about 'legitimate differences' almost if not quite the whole assembly would
have voted for Bishop Knox's amendment. But there was a natural reluctance
to alter it in his absence; and when the vote was taken a minority voted against
it including Dean Wace, Prebendary Fox, Bishop Ingham, Bartlett, and
Gladstone.[62]

At the August meeting of the general committee there was no general confrontation on the basic issue but three things happened which showed how
tenuous were the hopes of reconciliation. First, a letter from Bartlett was read,
dated 8th August, saying that he did not see his way to withhold his resignation
from the home and foreign committee but that he would still support the
medical mission auxiliary, thereby retaining membership of the general com-

mittee. Second, anxious consideration was given to the case of a candidate who when interviewed by the candidates committee stated that at present he had an open mind about the virgin birth of our Lord; he did not disbelieve it, and affirmed his strong belief in the deity of Christ and his desire to present Christ as a Saviour from sin to the students he was hoping to teach in India. His acceptance as a missionary on 'special agreement' for a term of five years at St Paul's College, Calcutta was confirmed. Third, in pursuance of the committee's resolution of 12th July, the nominating committee put forward names for a special sub-committee 'to secure harmonious co-operation by adequate representation of all such differences of opinion both in administration at home and in service abroad'. Twenty-one of those nominated accepted service on the sub-committee, but three found themselves unable to do so – Bishop Ingham, the Rev. W. Bardin and the Rev. D. H. C. Bartlett.[63]

The sub-committee met for three days at the Queen's Hotel, Norwood, and published its report early in November 1922. It reaffirmed the resolution approved in July (see Appendix) pointing out that the first two paragraphs governed the third in defining what constituted legitimate differences. It also commented on the unsatisfactory nature of the Society's general committee and proposed the formation of an executive committee to be appointed in the first instance by the home and foreign committee from any of its members. As a matter of urgency, and not later than the annual meeting of 1923, this provisional executive committee should bring forward a scheme for its own election in future and for the reorganization of the general committee and all other committees of the Society. The sub-committee in making proposals for administrative reform a matter of urgency laid its finger on a problem which lay beneath the whole doctrinal debate. A society which placed its ultimate authority in the hands of a committee which had an average attendance of sixty but which could swell to many hundreds at short notice, was not well-equipped to formulate doctrinal standards, and the normal committee procedures of resolutions and amendments to resolutions became chaotic under pressure of deeply held convictions in what was virtually a large public meeting: but it is very doubtful whether at this stage the formation of a new, smaller, less comprehensive society could have been avoided by administrative reforms.

On the 27th October, 1922, before the sub-committee report was published, a group of about thirty clergy and laity met at the headquarters of the Christian Alliance of Women and Girls, 24 Bedford Square, London, and they decided, after prayer and heart-searching, to found the Bible Churchmen's Missionary Society. In the weeks following the July meeting of the CMS general committee those who had voted against the resolution, and others who thought with them, had considered the various alternatives – such as withholding their contributions from CMS in hope of a change or joining other societies – but in the end the decision was made to start a new organization which stood by the principles set out in Bartlett's resolution. At the meeting on the 27th October

Bartlett was appointed secretary of the new society and Gladstone was appointed treasurer; but it was decided not to implement the decision immediately in the hope that an acceptable compromise might still be forthcoming at the meeting of the CMS general committee on the 22nd November.[64]

The meeting was held once again at the Memorial Hall and about 350 members were present. The Norwood sub-committee's report was tabled and its adoption moved by Bishop Chavasse and seconded by Rev. H. W. Hinde, vicar of Islington. Its first paragraph declared the Society's 'unwavering acceptance of the supreme authority of the Holy Scriptures, and its full belief in their trustworthiness in all matters of faith and doctrine'. Amendments were quickly proposed. One such amendment was that the statement should stop after the word 'trustworthiness' thus avoiding the qualifying phrase about 'matters of faith and doctrine'; another amendment proposed stopping after the word 'Scriptures', with the same intention. The first amendment was defeated, 210 voting against it and 130 for it. This led to the strange assertion, put out in more than one pamphlet and repeatedly thrown back to CMS in letters from anxious inquirers, that the Society had rejected the historical trustworthiness of the Bible by 210 votes to 130.[65] As Stock pointed out, the adoption of either amendment would without doubt have resulted in the Society being charged with questioning the trustworthiness of the Scriptures even in matters of faith and doctrine. The second paragraph of the sub-committee's statement began, unwisely in the tense circumstances, by referring to the difficulty of formulating a statement 'on so profound a subject as the degree in which the union of the Godhead and Manhood in our Lord Jesus Christ may have led Him to forgo the full exercise of His omniscience in matters which were intended in the Divine Providence to be left to our reason'. (See Appendix.) Bishop Ingham had no lack of support when he moved the omission of this passage so that with the addition of a few words the second paragraph would read:

> We fervently acknowledge the Lord Jesus Christ to be our Lord and our God, the Way, the Truth, and the Life, Who spake as never Man spake, and Who made upon the Cross (by His one oblation of Himself once offered) a full, perfect and sufficient sacrifice, oblation, and satisfaction for the sins of the whole world; and we believe that His teaching, as recorded in the New Testament, is free from all error, and that His authority is final.

Further debate followed on the last sentence. The Bishop of Chelmsford suggested that four or five leaders should retire for half an hour and the Bishop of Liverpool, Bishop Knox, Bishop Ingham, Dean Wace and Mr Gladstone agreed to do so while the committee gave itself to prayer. The five referees returned with the proposal that Bishop Ingham's wording of the second paragraph be retained but concluding with the words 'and we believe in the absolute truth of His teaching and utterances, and that His authority is final'. Some objections were made, by the Bishop of Truro and others, to the inclusion of the words 'and utterances' and Canon Guy Rogers moved and the Bishop of Hereford seconded their omission, but this amendment was not put. Then Bardsley appealed for the withdrawal of these two words for the sake of unity and the president spoke in a similar sense. G. T. Manley recalled:

I then ventured to appeal to Bishop Ingham and Archdeacon Joynt (his seconder) to withdraw the words, stating that I did so, partly in the spirit of conciliation, but also because I regarded the remaining words 'we believe in the absolute truth of His teaching' as fully safeguarding the doctrine of our Lord's infallibility as a teacher. Bishop Ingham and his seconder accepted my suggestion, and withdrew the two words 'and utterances', so that the amendment was put to the Committee without them, and accepted.[66]

The sober and carefully weighed account of this incident in the History of the BCMS recalls that leading representatives of the liberal school protested against the inclusion of the two words on the grounds that they 'would rule out modern critical views as to the 110th Psalm and the Book of Jonah – one of them saying that this mode of expression would put him out of the Church Missionary Society; it was also declared that it would split the Society and lead to the resignation of missionaries in Asia'. But the withdrawal of the words, integral as they had been from the start to Bartlett's concept of an effective doctrinal safeguard, proved decisive for the formation of the BCMS. 'All hope of reconciliation had now disappeared, and preparations for the organization of the Bible Churchmen's Missionary Society went steadily forward.'[67]

The formation of another missionary society, so close in name, and in most of its aims and purposes to the CMS, was a heavy blow. Three vice-presidents resigned (Dean Wace, Preb. H. E. Fox, and Mr S. H. Gladstone) and four honorary governors for life (Mr T. H. Bailey, Mr C. E. Caesar, Lt Col. Seton Churchill, and the Rev. G. Denyer). Only two serving missionaries were recorded as resigning specifically on this issue – the Rev. Dr and Mrs F. E. Keay of Meerut, though the resignation of a few others about this time was directly connected with doubts about the CMS position as a result of the vote on the 22nd November, 1922. The loss of CMS supporters and subscribers in Britain was considerable. Organizing secretaries were asked to send in lists of their names. By March 1923 thirty-five Missionary Service League branches had withdrawn support because of the controversy and two more at least did so later, out of a total of some 1,300 branches. The collated lists of the organizing secretaries showed that, by March 1923, seventy-eight clergy had resigned their membership of CMS and thirty were still uncertain. Thirty-eight honorary lay officers of associations were listed as 'definitely resigning'. The largest number of clerical resignations in one area was eleven. This was in the Midland area comprising the dioceses of Birmingham, Worcester, Lichfield and Coventry. The whole executive committee of one Lancashire association, Bolton, including two clergy, resigned. In Scotland, two churches, St Silas, Glasgow and St Thomas, Edinburgh withdrew their support.[68]

The headquarters secretariat and the organizing secretaries in their districts had a very difficult year or two. A good deal of publicity was given to the 'rejection' by CMS committee of the trustworthiness of the historical records of the bible by 210 votes to 130,[69] and to the 'modernism' of educational missionaries in India. On the 4th December, 1922 the home secretary of CMS H. St B. Holland, wrote to all the organizing secretaries to say that after many hours' deliberation the secretaries of the Society had decided not to publish the charges with refutations attached as it would only lead to 'another game of theological tennis'.

> One of the problems [his letter went on to say] is that mis-statements are few but misrepresentations are many and however cleverly the latter are answered, the very answer to them will always challenge further counter statements. . . . Experience of other Societies seems to prove that it will be infinitely better to allow the propaganda directed against us to wear itself out, for any attempt to meet it by denial only means so much additional fuel to the fire. The truest way to deal with such propaganda is by the strongest presentation of our case on the spiritual and constructive and positive side and that is what we hope to do in the months to come.

This policy was maintained not only for months but for years. On the 23rd January, 1928 another home secretary wrote to the organizing secretaries: 'Our policy all the way through has been to ignore the charges so far as possible and get on with our work as hard as we can go. . . . It is very easy to become so busy rebutting the charges made against us that there is no time left for really constructive work.'

On the 22nd November, 1926 Wilson Cash, general secretary of CMS, wrote to E. L. Langston about the Society's policy in this matter of controversy.

> We adhere to the Committee's Minute of November 1922, and we shall not attempt to modify it in any way, partly because we are persuaded that it is not through credal statements that confidence is secured, and partly because we are convinced that rightly interpreted this Minute absolutely establishes the integrity of the Society's faithfulness to God's truth. . . . Perhaps it will assist you and others who are doing so much to help the CMS if I put down a few statements as to what I believe with all my heart to be the true facts about the position of the Society.
>   1. The CMS stands to-day, as it always has stood, for the unique Inspiration of the whole Bible.
>   2. The CMS believes in the true and essential Godhead of our Lord Jesus Christ, and only accepts candidates who believe in this truth.
>   3. The CMS believes that Jesus Christ on the Cross made a full, perfect, and sufficient sacrifice for the sins of the whole world, and requires this faith in all its missionaries.
>   4. The CMS accepts, and has never denied, the absolute truth of all our Lord's words and teachings.

5. The CMS never has denied nor does it send abroad missionaries who do deny the Virgin Birth of Our Lord.

6. The CMS aims in all its work at the individual and personal conversion of men to God through the saving grace of our Lord Jesus Christ. . . .

The real test of a missionary society must be the blessing which God graciously gives to the work undertaken in His Name, and anyone who reads the records of CMS work in recent years will at once see how abundantly God has blessed and is blessing it.[70]

NOTES

1. George Dangerfield, *The Strange Death of Liberal England 1910–14*, Capricorn Books ed., 1969, p. vii.

2. Roger Lloyd, *The Church of England, 1900–1965*, SCM Press, 1966, p. 65.

3. E. Halévy, *A History of the English People*, Vol. VI: *The Rule of Democracy: 1905–14*, Ernest Benn, 1934, p. 453; G. D. H. Cole and Raymond Postgate, *The Common People, 1746–1946*, Methuen, 1962, p. 473; Dangerfield, op. cit., p. viii.

4. A. J. P. Taylor, *English History, 1914–1945*, OUP, 1965, p. 1.

5. Quoted Ronald Blythe, *The Age of Illusion: England in the Twenties and Thirties*, Hamish Hamilton, 1963, p. 235; see also Keith Middlemas and John Barnes, *Baldwin*, Weidenfeld & Nicolson, 1969, pp. 751–9; and David Thomson, *England in the Twentieth Century*, Penguin, 1965, p. 178,

6. Harold Nicolson, *King George the Fifth: His Life and Reign*, Constable, 1952, p. 525.

7. David Thomson, op. cit., p. 18.

8. Lloyd, op. cit., p. 62.

9. Taylor, op. cit., pp. 169, 317.

10. Lloyd, op. cit., p. 268.

11. R. C. D. Jasper, *George Bell, Bishop of Chichester*, OUP, 1967, pp. 121–6.

12. F. A. Iremonger, *William Temple*, OUP, 1948, p. 601.

13. M. A. C. Warren, 'The Non-Christian World 1910 and 1960', CBMS Report 1959–60, pp. 46, 50.

14. Norman Goodall, *The Ecumenical Movement*, OUP, 1961, pp. 9–10.

15. *CMR*, 'E.S.', 'Partners in Other Ships', 1918, pp. 336–46.

16. *CMR*, St Clair Sarum, 'The Missionary Council of the National Assembly', 1924, pp. 295–304.

17. *CMR*, Claude M. Blagden, 'The Missionary Education Scheme for the Home Church', 1926, pp. 17–25.

18. Lloyd, op. cit., p. 442.

19. *The World Mission of the Church: Tambaram, 1938*, IMC, London and New York, pp. 184–5; pp. 22, 31.

20. International Missionary Council, *Tambaram Series*, Vol. I, OUP, 1939, pp. 203–16; and *World Mission*, op. cit., pp. 25–6.

21. Stock, II, p. 83.

22. Carol Graham, *Azariah of Dornakal*, SCM Press, 1946, pp. 83–4.

23. Stephen Neill, *A History of Christian Missions*, Pelican Books, 1964, p. 260.

24. *CMR*, Roland Allen, 'Indigenous Churches: the Way of St Paul', 1927, pp. 147–59.

25. *Looking Forward*, CMS, 1934, pp. 20, 21.

26. *Report of the Committee on Recruiting, Selection and Training of Candidates*, CMS, 1937, p. 6.

27. *Looking Foward*, pp. 22–8.

28. H. G. Anderson, MS 'History of CMS Medical Missions', p. 21.

29. *Looking Forward*, pp. 47–51.

30. *Medical Commission Report*, CMS, 1939, p. 10.

31. J. H. Oldham and B. D. Gibson, *The Remaking of Man in Africa*, OUP, 1931, pp. 161, 23.

32. *Looking Forward*, pp. 35–46; *Report of the Committee on Recruiting, etc.*, p. 17.

33. *Looking Forward*, pp. 52–6, 81–90.

34. H. G. Anderson, op. cit., p. 302.

35. *CMR*, E. Stock, 'The Anniversary Past and Present', 1919, p. 159.

36. CMS Gazette, April, 1910, p. 104.

37. G. A. Gollock, *Eugene Stock*, CMS, 1929, p. 173.

38. *CMR*, 1918, pp. 476, 477.

39. *CMR*, 1915, p. 175.

40. *Looking Foward*, pp. 91–6.

41. Stock, IV, p. 442.

42. J. H. Oldham to the author, 15th January, 1959.

43. G/C1/100, p. 325.

44. ibid., p. 336.

45. *CMR*, 1919, E. Stock, ibid., p. 153.

46. Phyllis L. Garlick, *And then? Gleaners' Union – Missionary Service League 1886 to 1936.*, CMS, 1936.

47. *CMR*, 1918, E. Stock, 'The Book of the Wars of the Lord', p. 13.

48. *Report of the Committee on Recruiting, etc.*, pp. 39, 40.

49. J. H. Oldham, *Florence Allshorn*, SCM Press, 1951, p. 46.

50. ibid., pp. 56–60.

51. Edith E. Wright, *The Children of Thy Servants*, St Michael's, Limpsfield, 1937.

52. *CMR*, 1922, p. 110 n.

53. *CMR*, 1912, pp. 176–7.

54. G/C13, H. E. Fox to Bardsley, 28th January, 1918.

55. W. S. Hooton and J. Stafford Wright, *The First Twenty-Five Years of the Bible Churchmen's Missionary Society*, BCMS, 1947, p. 5.

56. *CMR*, 1918, pp. 103–11.

57. G/C13, Bardsley to President of CMS, 24th January, 1918.

58. H/H1, AX1.

59. Herbert Kelly, SSM, *No Pious Person*, Faith Press, 1960, p. 117.

60. G/C13, Bardsley to A. C. Rice, 15th November, 1918.

61. *CMR*, E. Stock, 'The Recent Controversy in CMS', 1923, p. 32.

62. ibid., p. 34.

63. G/C1/86, pp. 163, 214.

64. Hooton and Wright, op. cit., pp. 10–12.

65. For example, D. H. C. Bartlett, *Why a New Society?*, Bible Churchmen's Missionary Society, 1923, p. 11.

66. G. T. Manley in the *Record*, 8th February, 1923.

67. Hooton and Wright, op. cit., pp. 13, 14.

68. H/H1, AX2.

69. D. H. C. Bartlett and S. H. Gladstone in the *Guardian*, 15th March, 1923.

70. H/H1, AX1.

Appendices

APPENDIX I

Resolution of the General Committee, 12th July, 1922

That, in accordance with the tradition of the Church Missionary Society which, while faithful to the Protestant and Evangelical principles and teaching of its founders, has always rested content with the formularies of the Church as its standard of doctrine, the Committee, for the allaying of widespread unrest as regards the faithfulness of the Society to fundamental doctrine, places on record its unwavering acceptance of the Nicene Creed and of the teaching of the Thirty-Nine Articles, especially in their references to Holy Scripture; and it assures the supporters of the Society everywhere of its determination to appoint only those men and women who can subscribe to the aforesaid formularies and hold with conviction the Evangelical interpretation of them to serve on the staff of the Society either at home or abroad.

Further, the Committee, realizing once again with gratitude to Almighty God its sense of fellowship through Him Who is the Spirit of unity, in loyalty to Our Lord Jesus Christ, the Divine Saviour, the Way, the Truth and the Life, and in faith in Him as the One and only sufficient Sacrifice for the sins of the whole world, and also in humble reliance upon the supreme authority of Holy Scripture and its trustworthiness in all matters of faith and doctrine as God's Word written, calls all friends of the Society to an immediate forward movement, both in missionary effort overseas and spiritual enterprise at home, through the agency of converted and spiritually-minded men and women whom God has called to the work.

And in view of the fact that within the above-named limitations there are certain legitimate differences of opinion amongst us, we hereby resolve that a special Sub-Committee shall be appointed to secure harmonious co-operation by adequate representation of all such differences of opinion, both in administration at home and in service abroad.

APPENDIX II

Statement Adopted by the General Committee, 22nd November, 1922

(After the presentation of the Report of the Special Sub-Committee appointed in accordance with the Resolution of 12 July 1922.)

Inasmuch as there has been misunderstanding in regard to the Resolution of July 12, 1922, we whole-heartedly reaffirm that resolution in its entirety, pointing out that the first two paragraphs govern the third, and we undertake to regulate the operations of the Society in accordance with the principles therein laid down, and declare once more our unwavering acceptance of the supreme authority of the Holy Scriptures and our full belief in their trustworthiness in all matters of faith and doctrine.

We fervently acknowledge the Lord Jesus Christ to be our Lord and our God, the Way, the Truth, and the Life, Who spake as never Man spake, and Who made upon the Cross (by His one oblation of Himself once offered) a full, perfect, and sufficient sacrifice, oblation, and satisfaction for the sins of the whole world, and we believe in the absolute truth of His teaching, and that His authority is final.

In the interpretation which we, as Evangelical Churchmen, place upon the Creeds and Thirty-Nine Articles of Religion, we humbly believe that we have been and are being guided by the ever-present power of the Holy Spirit and by the teaching of the Holy Scriptures.

We rejoice to believe that in the foregoing statement we have the concurrence of the body of our CMS brethren in the Mission-field, with whom we are in closest fellowship.

We earnestly call upon all at home and in the field to unit in the faithful proclamation of this essential and glorious Gospel to the whole world which needs it, that all may share with us in the blessings of that wonderful Redemption.

APPENDIX III

Summary of Income, Expenditure and Revenue Accounts 1910–1942

Notes

^a Pan-Anglican Thank Offering
^b Peace Thank-offering
^c Sale of Mission Properties
^d Part of proceeds of Special Appeal
^e Missionaries (Active and retired) Special Appeal
^f American Benefaction
^g Working Capital Replacement
^h Working Capital Replacement and CM House Debt Liquidation
ⁱ CM House Debt Liquidation
^j Sinking Fund for Redemption of Loan
^k

	1938	1939	1940
Emergency Fund	5,000	5,000	5,000
Pension Provision	10,073	9,629	3,767

Missionary Society of Canadian Church £25,000 and CBMS £3,000
^m For Restoration of Missionaries Allowances   £10,000
    Hospital Endowment Fund   5,700
    Medical Missions Building Account   1,400
ⁿ Transfer from Working Capital Fund
^o War Damage Awards
^p War Damage Award (balance) £116 and transfer from a reserve amount £600
^q Transfer from Property Reserve
^r Transfer from Capital Reserve £91,703 less Mengo Hospital deficit £6,473
^s Transfer from Emergency Fund
^t Transfer from Capital Reserve £34,171 and Legacies £20,172

CHURCH MISSIONARY SOCIETY
Summary of Income, Expenditure and Revenue Accounts 1910–1942

		1910	1911	1912
Total Contributions received through				
Associations	1	227,542	226,765	230,043
Income available for general purposes				
Contributions through Associations	2	169,636	157,331	168,263
Direct Contributions	3	50,561	39,554	55,975
Legacies	4	53,221	49,073	50,000
Income from Investments	5	4,699	5,129	4,396
	6	278,117	251,087	278,634
Appropriated and Auxiliary income	7	103,305	106,129	105,719
Other (special) receipts	8	8,913[a]	2,654[a]	
Gain (or loss) on investments and other items (net)	9	448	2,230	362
Total Income	10	390,783	362,100	384,715
Expenditure				
Missionaries' Allowances, etc.	11	323,648	318,881	312,175
Missionaries' Pensions, etc.	12	10,720	11,144	11,200
Miscellaneous Mission Expenses	13	265	333	750
Training of Missionaries	14	7,175	6,557	5,146
Supplementary expenditure financed from Appropriated or auxiliary income	15		6,930	10,779
Home Organization and collection of funds	16	24,301	24,117	24,374
H.Q . Administration	17	17,861	18,487	17,624
Interest of Loans	18	2,088	2,763	2,381
Special provisions	19	10,002[g]	8,983[g]	8,832[g]
Grants	20			
Total Expenditure	21	396,060	398,195	393,261
(Deficit) or surplus for year	22	(5,280)	(36,095)	(8,546)
(Deficit) or surplus at beginning of year	23	(30,642)	(35,922)	(46,398)
Proceeds of special appeals	24		23,904	
Medical Missions Auxiliary Refunds	25		1,715	
Sales of Mission properties	26			
Gain (or loss) on investments and other items (net)	27			
Other credits	28			
Accumulated (deficit) or surplus at year	29	(35,922)	(46,398)	(54,944)
Medical Mission Auxiliary transactions included above				
Contributions	30	36,302	35,768	37,292
Expenditure	31	39,113	42,620	42,206

1913	1914	1915	1916	1917	1918	1919	1920	
226,655	322,362	236,747	247,539	239,909	259,830	290,619	460,297	I
159,199	189,016	169,216	183,035	150,067	183,765	180,514	270,033	2
47,649	47,683	46,292	56,987	44,313	43,998	39,117	93,442	3
36,156	33,462	38,068	43,110	28,885	35,807	40,465	45,310	4
4,503	4,250	4,200	4,325	4,074	6,115	6,852	5,499	5
247,507	274,411	257,776	287,457	227,339	269,685	266,948	414,284	6
114,302	130,818	106,046	85,839	97,926	89,783	104,944	119,295	7
							120,000[k]	8
(593)	(143)	369					(1,969)	9
361,216	405,086	364,191	373,296	325,265	359,468	371,892	651,610	10
307,377	303,368	297,773	276,064	278,100	273,742	331,380	458,303	11
10,730	11,456	11,118	10,484	10,811	11,875	12,135	13,675	12
779	1,480	1,222	1,138	1,249	1,319	1,890	3,086	13
3,831	4,484	4,737	4,851	2,739	2,408	2,587	5,795	14
15,097	30,482	19,653	12,781	8,972	11,689	18,143	24,877	15
24,094	25,037	24,448	25,218	22,881	22,933	26,189	38,898	16
18,584	18,955	19,320	19,104	20,199	19,472	22,016	27,231	17
3,287	2,258	2,879	1,864	2,242	1,675	2,978	2,691	18
5,753[g]	5,495[g]	8,779[h]	9,831[h]	7,417[h]	12,824[h]	13,673[h]	9,043[h]	19
								20
389,532	403,015	389,929	361,335	354,610	357,937	430,991	583,599	21
(28,316)	2,071	(25,738)	11,961	(29,345)	1,531	(59,099)	68,011	22
(54,944)	(74,421)	2,071	(23,667)	(11,569)	(23,966)	(22,349)	(81,544)	23
8,839	74,421							24
			2,444	17,984			19,404	25
								26
			(2,307)	(1,036)	86	(96)		27
								28
(74,421)	2,071	(23,667)	(11,569)	(23,966)	(22,349)	(81,544)	5,871	29
41,996	41,648	38,737	41,724	49,645	45,739	43,644	50,900	30
43,099	45,102	42,342	31,545	31,059	35,981	41,717	71,172	31

		1921	1922	1923
Total Contributions received through Associations	1	384,041	349,887	316,149
Income available for general purposes				
Contributions through Associations	2	256,263	233,666	198,092
Direct Contributions	3	46,819	36,002	36,868
Legacies	4	47,993	48,526	65,915
Income from Investments	5	9,851	7,776	7,144
	6	360,926	325,970	308,019
Appropriated and Auxiliary income	7	148,305	168,659	153,670
Other (special) receipts	8	41,630[b]		
Gain (or loss) on investments and other items (net)	9		1,015	729
Total Income	10	550,861	495,644	462,418
Expenditure				
Missionaries' Allowances, etc.	11	486,971	388,420	347,678
Missionaries' Pensions, etc.	12	13,880	17,372	19,938
Miscellaneous Mission Expenses	13	2,932	9,339	4,883
Training of Missionaries	14	9,237	7,330	4,132
Supplementary expenditure financed from Appropriated or auxiliary income	15	55,033	47,859	51,733
Home Organization and collection of funds	16	50,968	44,821	38,215
H.Q. Administration	17	32,412	33,059	29,099
Interest of Loans	18	3,501	4,807	3,865
Special provisions	19	1,983[i]		
Grants	20	28,000[l]		
Total Expenditure	21	684,917	553,007	499,543
(Deficit) or surplus for year	22	(134,056)	(57,363)	(37,125)
(Deficit) or surplus at beginning of year	23	5,871	(112,022)	(138,676)
Proceeds of special appeals	24			
Medical Missions Auxiliary Refunds	25	(19,404)	12,194	20,531
Sales of Mission properties	26	33,813	18,515	37,324
Gain (or loss) on investments and other items (net)	27	1,754		
Other credits	28			
Accumulated (deficit) or surplus at year	29	(112,022)	(138,676)	(117,946)
Medical Mission Auxiliary transactions included above				
Contributions	30	49,658	59,948	76,449
Expenditure	31	95,690	67,069	65,981

1924	1925	1926	1927	1928	1929	1930	1931	
312,154	307,937	313,746	341,637	311,881	347,850	304,796	291,619	1
203,369	196,518	195,477	211,404	189,083	178,393	179,005	171,886	2
48,266	60,433	56,207	54,266	45,566	36,939	63,593	48,425	3
53,290	50,756	47,213	46,789	54,071	52,266	50,721	53,443	4
7,395	6,024	4,384	4,094	5,061	4,746	5,179	5,123	5
312,320	313,731	303,281	316,553	293,781	272,344	298,498	278,877	6
142,617	146,876	148,089	156,963	157,470	151,974	175,426	162,655	7
	2,000[c]		12,618[d]					8
850		(14)		(76)		(109)		9
455,787	462,607	451,356	486,134	451,175	424,318	473,815	441,532	10
330,658	355,382	338,146	315,715	309,905	306,121	301,376	281,003	11
26,937	31,201	34,578	37,498	38,148	39,027	39,959	40,000	12
5,585	3,592	4,104	3,030	3,389	3,312	3,348	3,356	13
4,600	5,819	4,434	5,031	5,530	6,644	7,017	7,226	14
42,405	47,040	40,641	40,391	42,554	39,099	61,101	47,216	15
39,526	41,996	41,905	40,825	41,513	40,087	37,725	38,582	16
31,501	31,766	29,464	30,568	31,190	30,770	31,120	31,377	17
4,359	5,266	8,151	8,505	7,561	7,096	7,178	8,873	18
	2,000[g]	4,256[g]	4,571[g]	4,576[g]	4,576[g]	4,576[g]	4,576[g]	19
								20
485,571	524,062	505,679	486,134	484,366	476,732	493,400	462,209	21
(29,784)	(61,455)	(54,323)		(33,191)	(52,414)	(19,585)	(20,677)	22
(117,946)	(161,114)	(46,444)	(98,434)	(77,532)	(88,365)	(27,692)	(41,175)	23
			20,902	11,338	40,654	939	339	24
14,666	2,654	547		1,000	1,000	1,000	1,000	25
		1,786						26
1,282								27
	173,471[n]			10,020[o]	71,433[q]	4,163[o]	832[o]	28
(161,114)	(46,444)	(98,434)	(77,532)	(88,365)	(27,692)	(41,175)	(59,681)	29
58,261	63,231	62,939	78,053	67,485	64,557	64,639	63,118	30
60,255	59,713	61,101	64,694	61,642	62,897	71,538	66,910	31

		1932	1933	1934
Total Contributions received through Associations	1	274,167	255,034	249,347
Income available for general purposes				
Contributions through Associations	2	155,696	144,685	144,178
Direct Contributions	3	45,318	38,908	34,036
Legacies	4	52,770	49,793	53,643
Income from Investments	5	4,724	4,908	4,981
	6	258,508	238,294	236,838
Appropriated and Auxiliary income	7	163,749	167,210	154,838
Other (special) receipts	8			
Gain (or loss) on investments and other items (net)	9			
Total Income	10	422,257	405,504	391,676
Expenditure				
Missionaries' Allowances, etc.	11	274,898	255,335	250,383
Missionaries' Pensions, etc.	12	40,000	40,000	40,000
Miscellaneous Mission Expenses	13	3,203	3,790	3,826
Training of Missionaries	14	5,608	5,717	5,144
Supplementary expenditure financed from Appropriated or auxiliary income	15	43,464	38,962	37,725
Home Organization and collection of funds	16	38,020	35,157	35,327
H.Q. Administration	17	30,973	28,265	29,734
Interest of Loans	18	10,429	8,924	9,154
Special provisions	19	2,288[g]		
Grants	20			
Total Expenditure	21	448,888	416,150	411,293
(Deficit) or surplus for year	22	(26,631)	(10,646)	(19,617)
(Deficit) or surplus at beginning of year	23	(59,681)	(84,917)	(74,166)
Proceeds of special appeals	24	395	357	659
Medical Missions Auxiliary Refunds	25	1,000	4,059	(10,238)
Sales of Mission properties	26			2,273
Gain (or loss) on investments and other items (net)	27			
Other credits	28		16,981[n]	
Accumulated (deficit) or surplus at year	29	(84,917)	(74,166)	(101,089)
Medical Mission Auxiliary transactions included above				
Contributions	30	60,960	57,431	56,566
Expenditure	31	65,409	65,579	69,963

*basis not strictly comparable with earlier years – on availability basis, not actual receipts in year.

1935	1936	1937	1938	1939	1940	1941	1942	
276,573	250,551	245,541	234,557	230,629	205,687	197,605	207,241	I
151,990	141,175	130,657	121,575	121,436	99,926	113,095	119,530	2
40,603	35,450	32,839	33,557	38,281	32,185	28,782	29,394	3
60,226	63,088	65,686	79,435	80,948	76,754	65,080	45,171	4
4,477	4,817	5,083	5,629	5,704	6,758	7,178	6,502	5
257,296	244,530	234,265	240,196	246,369	215,623	214,135	200,597	6
140,129	149,782	144,492	169,524	160,948	170,518	130,140	123,079	7
6,621[e]	3,340[e]						33,195[f]	8
								9
404,046	397,652	378,757	409,720	407,317	386,141	344,275	356,871	10
250,410	248,112	241,652	248,763	250,348	229,707	196,489	200,837	11
40,000	40,000	40,000	40,000	40,000	40,000	46,766	47,132	12
4,389	4,550	3,005	3,604	3,642	3,188	2,700	2,053	13
5,588	5,185	6,262	6,895	6,982	5,421	4,267	3,486	14
37,005	37,593	36,485	48,809	46,450	55,351	31,672	25,461	15
35,928	36,855	35,037	36,392	38,491	33,574	24,396	27,620	16
28,320	28,834	28,192	29,725	29,776	30,742	30,383	31,524	17
5,255	4,457	3,584	1,445	1,722	2,172	2,644	677	18
2,500[j]			15,073[k]	14,629[k]	8,767[k]			19
							17,100[m]	20
409,395	405,586	394,217	430,706	432,040	408,922	339,317	355,890	21
(5,349)	(7,934)	(15,460)	(20,986)	(24,723)	(22,781)	4,958	981	22
(101,089)	(78,929)	(80,686)	(10,000)	(30,986)	(55,670)	(58,476)	958	23
33,297	6,198	286		39	95	133		24
(11,707)	(21)	630						25
5,203								26
								27
716[p]		85,230[r]			19,880[s]	54,343[t]		28
(78,929)	(80,686)	(10,000)	(30,986)	(55,670)	(58,476)	958	1,939	29
60,596	76,299	72,687	66,015	66,455	62,437	50,567*	49,538*	30
66,194	66,425	68,914	77,002	81,462	77,973	55,817	58,347	31

Indices

SELECT INDEX OF PLACES, TRIBES AND CMS INSTITUTIONS

INDEX OF PEOPLE